COMPARATIVE STUDIES BY HAROLD E. DRIVER
and
ESSAYS IN HIS HONOR

edited by
JOSEPH G. JORGENSEN

with contributions by

David F. Aberle; Richard P. Chaney; Joseph G. Jorgensen;
Raoul Naroll, Gary L. Michik, and Frada Naroll

HRAF PRESS
New Haven
1974

International Standard Book Number: 0-87536-111-0
Library of Congress Catalog Card Number: LC 73-94184
© Human Relations Area Files, Inc.

Contents

Part One

Biographical Sketch and Bibliography
of
Harold E. Driver

1. A Short Biographical Sketch of Harold E. Driver

Joseph G. Jorgensen

Harold E. Driver has spent all but about four years of his relatively short yet extremely productive anthropological career teaching at Indiana University. Harold joined the Bloomington staff as an assistant professor in 1949 and has chosen to retire as a full professor in 1973. Between 1966 and 1968 he served as visiting professor, University of Hawaii, and visiting Distinguished Professor, University of California, Davis. Harold served as a member of the Board of Directors of the Human Relations Area Files from 1952-63, 1966, and 1968-72. During those long stints —interrupted by sabbatical leaves and visiting professorships—Harold served on the HRAF executive committee twice (1957-61, 1970-72), and once served as HRAF secretary (1962-63). He was also Associate Editor of the *American Anthropologist*, 1966-70.

During his twenty-two years at Indiana University, Harold Driver created many lasting friendships with his undergraduate and graduate students, and when any of us former students of his, no matter what our vintage, get together we slip into easy and pleasant reminiscences. Harold has always been willing to serve on dissertation committees, to open new courses that were requested by graduate students, and to listen to student grievances beyond the call of duty.

I suppose that Harold often wished that he had not volunteered to open new courses to accommodate student requests. A few years ago his students felt deprived that Indiana University, with its enormous linguistics staff, did not offer a course in componential analysis and structural semantics. Harold agreed to offer a course on the topic, but after spending a few weeks scouring the literature and directing class discussions he decided that except for "learning more and more about less and less," the topic was both boring and pretentious. He completed the course, but came out with no profound respect for the subject.

Harold Driver's anthropology reflects his willingness to explore new methodologies and modes of explanation, but it also reflects his hard-nosed empiricism and knowledge of inductive methods. Ultimately any methodology and "theory"—in the garden variety, ethnological sense of that term—must measure up to Harold's standard for validity, which requires formally explicit comparisons and controls in order to establish the empirical adequacy of an hypothesis. When his own work does not measure up, he is critical of it and even publishes his criticisms (see, for example, Chapters 2 and 3 in Part III). This is not a life-and-death matter to him,—indeed, he can laugh at himself and has entertained his students and colleagues for years doing so,—but it was not always that way for Harold.

Harold Edson Driver was born November 17,1907, in Berkeley, California, three years after his father, John Rush Driver, and mother, Florence Maine Flook, moved to California from Missouri. John Rush Driver was a sixth-generation Mennonite from a group of eighteenth-century German Mennonite immigrants. When he began teaching school in Missouri after finishing the ninth grade, John Rush Driver was the first Mennonite Driver to branch out from farming.

Harold's mother, Florence, was the daughter of a farmer turned banker, so Harold's matriline was first in his genealogy in exchanging red necks for white collars. Soon after John and Florence moved to Berkeley, Harold's family took up the white-collar business life. John began a transportation business, which, among other things, hauled all of the granite that went into University of California buildings at Berkeley until about 1920. John was president of the Berkeley Chamber of Commerce during this period, while John's elder brother, who also moved to Berkeley, served first as mayor of the city and later as sheriff of Alameda County. John declined to run for mayor, feeling that his brother, a poor businessman, was better suited for the job.

Harold, his older brother John Calvin, and his older sister Florence LaVerne, all attended the University of California, Berkeley. Harold and LaVerne did graduate work there, whereas John did graduate work in economics at Columbia. John Calvin spent his professional career as an economist-statistician for the Department of Defense. LaVerne has spent her professional life in nursing, social work, and psychological testing.

The Driver home life was dominated by John Rush's stern Mennonite disposition. The children were forced to be independent, and at twelve years of age Harold and John Calvin secured their first summer jobs. They moved away from home, camped out, and worked in the northern California fruit orchards. From that time on, they bought their own clothes and all incidentals, and paid their own ways through school. At fifteen, Harold lied about his age and got a summer job in a cannery. At seventeen, upon graduating from high school, he worked six months for Montgomery Ward rather than going directly to college, and later joined the teamster's union and worked summers on trucks.

Harold's father regarded universities as professional schools to train people for law, medicine, engineering, business, and the like, rather than a place to get a general education. Whereas he did not encourage his children to attend the University of California, John Rush was a sufficiently important local figure to be noticed, and he was embarrassed that his children were not attending so prestigious a university in his own community. John Rush Driver finally consented to provide room and board for his children while they attended school.

At the University of California Harold studied anthropology, but he had no intention of pursuing anthropology for a career. When he completed his bachelor's degree in 1930, however, the Great Depression had hit California, and Harold could not find a permanent job. So he enrolled in graduate school. When he had completed his master's degree and qualifying exams for the Ph.D. he again sought permanent employment, but when he secured none he returned to graduate school and began writing his Ph.D. thesis. In his words, "every time I failed to get a job I would go back to school. This happened several times and eventually I got a Ph.D. degree by default." That was in 1936.

Harold's major professor at California was Alfred Kroeber, but he also worked with Robert Lowie and,

to a lesser extent, Carl Sauer and Ronald Olson. Like so many of Kroeber's most brilliant students, Harold was ambivalent toward Kroeber. Whereas he respected Kroeber's intelligence, he felt that Kroeber was too much concerned with the fads that swept the profession and that as a consequence, he did not fully develop some of the most promising methodologies with which he tinkered and did not encourage some of his best students to develop interests that veered markedly from his own.

Harold's first publication, reprinted in abridged form as the first essay in this book, was written jointly with Kroeber during the first graduate seminar in which Harold participated. From time to time, Kroeber had dabbled with the use of statistics to infer historical relationships in archeology, linguistics, physical anthropology, and ethnology.[*] Harold suggested that as a seminar project he would invent a statistic that would control for shared trait absences among tribes by eliminating such nontraits from statistical consideration. Then he would compare and analyze the internal relationships among tribes, *sans* their common absences. Harold got the go-ahead from Kroeber and invented the statistic G, a function of Pearson's linear r, calculated the Q-mode relations (intertribal) among tribes that performed the Sun dance, among other topics, and analyzed the results. Kroeber, working from Driver's conceptualization, wrote the first draft of the paper. Whereas Harold disagreed with some of the interpretation, he was a first-year graduate student and did not challenge Kroeber,—at least he did not challenge him for several years. About the time he was finishing his dissertation, however, he responded to some of Kroeber's interpretations in their joint paper of 1932. We will read about these disagreements in the Introduction to "Culture Element Distributions: X," which is also reproduced here (Part III, Chapter 3).

A major issue of disagreement between Harold and Alfred Kroeber was the meaning of similarities among cultures. Whereas Kroeber throughout his professional life always emphasized historical relationships in explaining similarities among cultures, Harold developed a methodology that assumed that similarities could emerge from borrowing, inheritance, or independent inventions. Because he and Kroeber both used essentially synchronic data, Harold was skeptical of the historical inferences that Kroeber made. Harold's now classic paper "An Interpretation of Functional, Historical, and Evolutionary Theory by Means of Correlations" and his "Geographical-His-

---

[*]See item number 30 in the following bibliography for a complete discussion of Kroeber's contributions to formal methods in the various anthropological subfields.

torical *versus* Psycho-Functional Explanations of Kin Avoidances" (reproduced here, Part II, Chapter 3) are examples of his attempts to integrate historical and evolutionary explanations through the use of statistics on synchronic data. His work shows debts to the cross-cultural research school associated with George P. Murdock, the continuous area research school associated with Kroeber, and the European continuous area school associated with Jan Czekanowski and Stanislaw Klimek.

Harold's first ethnographic field work was conducted among the Wappo Indians in Napa Valley, California, following his first graduate year. Kroeber believed that a professional ethnologist did not train people to do field work, but that a student proved his worth by the kind of field work he did. Kroeber's assumptions that a person could not be taught how to do field work and that there was no accumulation of experience that the teacher of ethnology could impart to the novice prior to going into the field bothered Harold. On the other hand, direct questions to Kroeber received direct and succinct replies, and this took some of the fear out of preparing for field work. Harold's *Wappo Ethnography*, based on that first field experience, was published with practically no changes, although Kroeber made Harold write the manuscript in "telegraphic style" to conform with the other ethnographies in the University of California series.

For his doctoral dissertation, Harold made a study of the reliability of culture element data, part of which was published later and is reprinted as Part III, Chapter 2, in this volume. During the year after he received his Ph.D., Harold made a comparative analysis of girls' puberty rites in western North America. Harold veered from Kroeber-type explanations and accounted for puberty rites in terms of evolution, history, function, and psychology. It marked a major break from Kroeber's own work, even though it was based heavily on field work conducted under Kroeber's aegis by Kroeber's students in the Culture Element Survey. In fact, Harold spent all of 1935 conducting field investigations among California Indians for this project (see items 3, 5, and 7 in the bibliography).

After completion of the Ph.D., Harold tried to enlist Kroeber's support to obtain a postdoctoral fellowship to study mathematics and logic. Harold felt that he had barely begun to understand how mathematics, especially statistics, could be used in ethnology. Kroeber would not support him in this plan, but he awarded Harold a postdoctoral grant for 1936-37, and suggested that he make the comparative study of girls' puberty rites mentioned above. In 1937-38, Harold was further supported in his application of statistics to comparative problems by the Social Science Research Council, which gave him a grant to go to the University of Chicago and study factor analysis with L. L. Thurstone and then apply it to a comparative study of North American Indian kin terms. It was at this time, in late 1937, following an unusually productive and innovative period, that Harold became first exhausted,—rushing to finish the Girls' Puberty study, —then disillusioned with anthropology, its methodological looseness, its pretensions, and the resistance of Kroeber and others to his desires to go further with formal methods in ethnological analysis. Harold suffered from nervous exhaustion and left anthropology, selling his books and cutting his ties.

When Harolds' health improved, some three months later, he began working as a tree surgeon, picking up jobs whenever he could. In 1941, he went back to the trucking business and got on as a driver muscling around city deliveries. He loved the honest labor and appreciated going home tired each night, knowing that his employment would not terminate at the end of the academic year or at the whim of a boss who knew less than he did. He kept driving until 1946, when he became a traffic manager in the office of a Bay Area trucking firm.

It was not until 1948 that he returned to anthropology, as an unpaid research associate at the University of California. Toward the end of that year, he received a Wenner-Gren grant. His eight years of hard, manual work had given him an understanding of life and people which he did not possess previously and which helped to simmer down his nervous temperament. He returned to anthropology with a desire to work and with an ability to laugh at himself and his colleagues. He could criticize and accept criticism. He could enjoy anthropology without identifying too closely with the products of his own labor, or flinching at the rebuffs of the "humanists" in the discipline, or getting upset about the more fatuous claims of his colleagues.

In 1948 he began work on his monumental *Comparative Studies of North American Indians*. His partner in that enterprise, William Massey, planned to handle the Meso-American section of the study, but because of personal problems was able to complete only a portion of that section. Harold and his wife of a few years, Wilhelmine, completed the study, and it was published in 1957. Wilhelmine was a brilliant polyglot, an accomplished pianist, a graduate historian, and a former Professor of Music at the University of Washington, where she also taught Japanese language during the Second World War. After their marriage, she became an important partner in most of Harold's research and writing projects.

In 1956 and 1957, Harold and Wilhelmine conducted field work for six months among the Chichimeca-Jonaz of northeastern Mexico and produced a monograph on the subject. This was Harold's last primary field work, but by no means the last of his research. Between 1950 and 1973, Harold, sometimes jointly with Wilhelmine, published fifty-two books, monographs, and articles, and forty-three reviews, comments, reports, and short notes.

Harold's bibliography follows. A few of his most choice and least available items on comparative methodology, explanations, comparative empirical studies, culture area relations, and North American Indians are reprinted here. Harold's long-term skepticism of historical explanations made from continous area studies and functional-evolutionary explanations made from cross-cultural studies based on worldwide samples receives treatment in the second section. His important, but generally unnoticed (except by aficionados,) contributions to methodology —especially statistical theory, reliability, and statistical sampling—receive treatment in Part III. (It is worthwhile to note that Harold has been invited to deliver papers to a score of national and international conferences and university groups on comparative methodology.)

Part III also contains a fascinating paper which formalizes Wissler's hypothesis of culture trait diffusion and demonstrates via true mathematical theory (interpreted and tested axioms) that Wissler was not very far off in his formulations. The fourth section draws on Harold's career-long interest in the interplay among historical, ecological, and evolutionary factors in studies of both areal and worldwide scope. The final section provides three examples of Harold's most recent contributions to culture area systematics and to the importance of language and culture relations in comparative studies.

2. The Publications of Harold E. Driver

Books, Monographs, and Articles

1. (With Alfred L. Kroeber) "Quantitative expression of cultural relationships," *University of California Publications in American Archaeology and Ethnology 31*: 211-56, 1932 (reprinted in this volume).

2. "*Wappo ethnography*," *University of California Publications in American Archaeology and Ethnology 36*: 179-220, 1936.

3. "Culture element distributions: VI: Southern Sierra Nevada," *University of California Anthropological Records 1*: 53-154, 1937.

4. "Culture element distributions: VIII: The reliability of culture element data," *University of California Anthropological Records 1*: 205-18, 1938 (reprinted in this volume).

5. "Culture element distributions: X: Northwest California," *University of California Anthropological Records 1*: 297-433, 1939 ("Introduction" reprinted in this volume).

6. "The measurement of geographical distribution form," *American Anthropologist 41*: 583-88, 1939 (reprinted in this volume).

7. (With Walter Goldschmidt) "The Hupa white deerskin dance," *University of California Publications in American Archaeology and Ethnology 35*: 103-42, 1940.

8. "Culture element distributions: XVI: Girls' puberty rites in western North America," *University of California Anthropological Records 6*: 21-90, 1941 (reprinted in this volume).

9. (With Saul H. Riesenberg) "Hoof rattles and girls' puberty rites in North and South America," *Indiana University Publications in Anthropology and Linguistics, Memoir 4*, 1950.

10. "A method of investigating individual differences in folkloristic beliefs and practices," *Midwest Folklore 1*: 99-105, 1951.

11. (With Cooper, Kirchoff, Libby, Massey, and Spier) "Indian tribes of North America," *Indiana University Publications in Anthropology and Linguistics, Memoir 9*, 1953. (This is a map, with discussion, bibliography, and index.)

12. "Acorn eating in aboriginal North America," *Proceedings of the Indiana Academy of Science 62*: 56-64, 1953.

13. "The spatial and temporal distribution of the musical rasp in the New World," *Anthropos 48*: 578-92, 1953.

14. "Statistics in anthropology," *American Anthropologist 55*: 42-59, 1953.

15. "An integration of functional, evolutionary, and historical theory by means of correlations," *Indiana University Publications in Anthropology and Linguistics 12*: 1-36, with 8 maps, 1956 (see No. 41).

16. (With Karl F. Schuessler) "A factor analysis of 16 primitive societies," *American Sociological Review 21*: 493-99, 1956.

17. (With William C. Massey) "Comparative studies of North American Indians," *Transactions of the American Philosophical Society n.s. 47*: 165-456, 1957. 163 maps.

18. "Estimation of intensity of land use from ethnobiology: applied to the Yuma Indians," *Ethnohistory 4*: 174-97, 1957.

19. (With Karl F. Schuessler) "Factor analysis of ethnographic data," *American Anthropologist 59*: 655-63, 1957.

20. (With Dell Hymes) "Concerning the Proto-Athapaskan kinship system," *American Anthropologist 60*: 152-55, 1958.

21. "Shoshone," *Encyclopaedia Britannica, 20*: 582-83, 1959.

22. *Indians of North America*, Chicago, University of Chicago Press, 1961. 668 pp., 38 maps, 44 figures, 25 plates.

23. "Levirate," *Encyclopaedia Britannica 13*: 978, 1961.

24. "Introduction to statistics for comparative research," in Frank W. Moore, ed., *Readings in Cross-Cultural Methodology*: 303-31, New Haven; HRAF Press 1961 (second printing, reset: 310-38, 1966).

25. "The contribution of A. L. Kroeber to culture area theory and practice," *Indiana University Publications in Anthropology and Linguistics, Memoir 18*: 1-28, 1962.

26. "Bullroarer," *Encyclopaedia Britannica, 4*: 405, 1963.

27. "Couvade," *Encyclopaedia Britannica, 6*: 674, 1963.

28. (With Wilhelmine Driver) "Ethnography and acculturation of the Chichimeca-Jonaz of Northeast Mexico, " *Indiana University Research Center in Anthropoligy, Folklore, and Linguistics, Publication 26*: 1-265, 1963. 40 tables, 32 photographs.

29. *The Americas on the eve of discovery*, Englewood Cliffs, N. J., Prentice-Hall, 1964. (An anthology, with two articles and an introduction by Driver.)

30. "Survey of numerical classification in anthropology," in Dell H. Hymes, ed., *The Use of Computers in Anthropology*, The Hague, Mouton: 302-44, 1965.

31. "Geographical-historical *versus* psycho-functional explanations of kin avoidances," *Current Anthropology 7*: 131-60, 176-82, 1966 (reprinted in this volume).

32. (With Peggy R. Sanday) "Factors and clusters of kin avoidances and related variables," *Current Anthropology 7*: 169-76, 1966.

33. No. 32, reprinted in Paul Kay, ed., *Explorations in Mathematical Anthropology*, Cambridge MIT Press: 269-79, 1971.

34. (With Wilhelmine Driver) *Indian farmers of North America*, Chicago; Rand McNally, 1967.

35. "Indians, American," *Crowell-Collier's Young People's Encyclopaedia 9*: 353-91, 1966.

36. "Statistical studies of continuous geographical distributions," in Raoul Naroll and Ronald Cohen, eds., *A Handbook of Method in Cultural Anthropology*, Garden City, Natural History Press: 620-39, 1970.

37. No. 24, reprinted in Bobbs-Merrill *Reprint Series in Anthropology*, No. A53, 1965.

38. "Ethnology," *International Encyclopaedia of the Social Sciences 5*: 178-86, 1968.

39. (With Karl F. Schuessler) "Correlational analysis of Murdock's 1957 ethnographic sample," *American Anthropologist 69*: 332-52, 1967 (reprinted in this volume).

40. "Robert H. Lowie," *International Encyclopaedia of the Social Sciences 9*: 480-83, 1968.

41. No. 15, slightly revised and reprinted in Clellan S. Ford ed., *Cross-Cultural Approaches*, New Haven, HRAF Press: 258-89, 1967.

42. "Ethnological interpretations," in Earl H. Swanson, Jr., ed., *Languages and Cultures of Western North America Essays to Sven Liljeablad*, Pocatello, Idaho State University Press: 263-76, 1971.

43. *Indians of North America*, Chicago, University of Chicago Press, 2d ed., rev., 1969.

44. (With Richard P. Chaney) "Cross-cultural sampling and Galton's problem," in Raoul Naroll and Ronald Cohen, eds., *A Handbook of Method in Cultural Anthropology*, Garden City, Natural History Press: 990-1003, 1970 (reprinted in this volume).

45. "Horticulture" and "Other Subsistence Techniques," reprinted from *Indians of North America*, Chicago, University of Chicago Press, 1961, Chapters 4 and 5, Bobbs-Merrill Reprint Series in Geography, No. G57, 1968.

46. "Huron Indians," *Encyclopedia Americana, 14*: 612, 1969.

47. "Incest," *Encyclopedia Americana, 14:* 840, 1969.

48. "Indians American," *Encyclopedia Americana, 15:* 1-27, 1969.

49. "Indians today," *Encyclopedia International,* 1969.

50. "Girls puberty rites and matrilocal residence," *American Anthropologist 71:* 905-08, 1969.

51. "Statistical refutation of comparative functional-causal models," *Southwestern Journal of Anthropology 26:* 25-31, 1970(reprinted in Paul Kay, ed., *Explorations in Mathematical Anthropology,* Cambridge, MIT Press, 1971: 269-79).

52. "Indian wealth—Is it only a myth?" *The American Way* (American Airlines): 22-29, October 1971.

53. No. 52, reprinted in *Look to the Mountain Top,* San Jose, Gousha Publications: 67-74, 1972.

54. "Reply to Opler on Apachean subsistence, residence, and girls' puberty rites," *American Anthropologist 74:* 1147-51, 1972.

55. (With James A. Kenny, Herschel C. Hudson, and Ora May Engel) "Statistical classification of North American Indian ethnic units," *Ethnology 11:* 311-39, 1972. (reprinted in this volume).

56. "Cross-cultural studies," in John J. Honigmann, ed., *Handbook of Social and Cultural Anthropology,* Chicago, Rand McNally, exp. 1973.

57. "Culture groups and language groups in native North America" in Oswald Werner, Kenneth Hale, and Dale Kinkaid, eds., *Essays in Honor of Carl Voegelin,* The Hague, Mouton, in press (reprinted in this volume).

58. "Cultural diffusion," Raoul Naroll, ed., *Main Currents of Anthropological Theory,* New York, Appleton-Century-Crofts, in press.

59. "The culture area concept" in William Sturtevant, ed., *Volume I: Introduction, Handbook of North American Indians,* Washington, D.C., Center for the Study of Man, Smithsonian Institution, in press.

60. "Diffusion and evolution," in this volume.

61. (With James L. Coffin) "Statistical classification of North American Indian ethnic units from the Driver-Massey sample," in this volume.

Reviews, Comments, Reports, and Short Notes

R1. "Kulturkreise and statistics," *American Anthropologist 39:* 174-75, 1937.

R2. Review of "World renewal, a cult system of native Northwest California," by A. L. Kroeber and E. W. Gifford, *University of California Anthropological Reocrds 13:* 1-156. Reviewed in the *U. S. Quarterly Book List* for September 1950.

R3. "Anthropology at Indiana University," *Boletín Bibliográfico de Antropologiá Americana 13:* 93-98, 1951.

R4. "Report to the American Anthropological Association on the activities of the National Committee on the Mathematical Training of Social Scientists," *American Anthropologist 54:* 303-05, 1952.

R5. Review of "Material aspects of Pomo culture," by S. A. Barrett, *Bulletin of the Public Museum of the City of Milwaukee 20:* 1-507, 1952. Reviewed in the *American Anthropologist 55:* 715-16, 1953.

R6. Review of *Chateau-Gerard,* by H. H. Turney-High, Columbia, University of South Carolina Press, 1953. Reviewed in *U.S. Quarterly Book Review 10:* 73-74, 1954.

R7. "Anthropology at Indiana University," *Boletín Bibliográfico de Antropologiá Americana 15:* 145-49, 1954.

R8. "Indiana University," *Boletín Bibliográfico de Antropologiá Americana 17:* 121-25, 1955.

R9. Review of "Archeological investigations in the Oahe Dam area, South Dakota, 1950-51," by Donald J. Lehmer, *Bureau of American Ethnology, Bulletin 158. U.S. Quarterly Book List,* 1956.

R10. "Ethnographic maps," *American Anthropologist 58:* 184-85, 1956.

R11. "Anthropological activities at Indiana University," *Boletín Bibliográfico de Antropologiá Americana 18:* 114-17, 1956.

R12. Review of *An ethno-atlas,* by Robert F. Spencer, Dubuque, Iowa; William C. Brown Co., 1956, *Ethnohistory 4:* 226-29, 1957.

R13. Review of *An ethno-atlas,* Robert F. Spencer, Dubuque, Iowa; William C. Brown Co., 1956. *American Anthropologist 59:* 1111-12, 1957.

R14. Review of "Ethnographic interpretations" by A. L. Kroeber, *University of California Publications in American Archaeology and Ethnology 47, American Anthropologist 60:* 766-67, 1958.

R15. Review of *Status terminology and the social structure of North American Indians,* by Munro S. Edmonson, Seattle, American Ethnological Society and University of Washington Press, 1958. *American Anthropologist 61*: 330, 1959.

R16. Review of "North American Indian languages: Classification and maps," by George L. Trager and Felicia E. Harben, *University of Buffalo Studies in Linguistics, Occasional Papers 5*, 1958. *International Journal of American Linguistics 25*: 201-02, 1959.

R17. Review of "Migrations in New World culture history," by Raymond H. Thompson, ed., *Social Science Bulletin 27, University of Arizona Bulletin, 29*, 1958. *American Anthropologist 61*: 1107-08, 1959.

R18. Comment on "Lexicostatistics so far," by D. H. Hymes, *Current Anthropology 1*: 3-34, 1960. *Current Anthropology 1*: 34, 1960.

R19. Review of *Fishing among the Indians of Northwestern California*, by A. L. Kroeber and S. A. Barrett, *University of California Anthropological Records 21*: 1-210, 1960. *American Anthropologist 62*: 1078-79, 1960.

R20. Review of *Five Indian tribes of the Upper Missouri*, by Edwin Thompson Denig, Edited with Introduction by John C. Ewers, Norman, University of Oklahoma Press, 1961. Review in *Journal of Geography 61*: 230, 1962.

R21. Comment on "Forms and problems of validation in social anthropology," by William J. McEwen, *Current Anthropology 4*: 169-70, 1963.

R22. Comment on "On ethnic unit classification," by Raoul Naroll, *Current Anthropology 5*: 295-96, 1964.

R23. Review of *Indian and Eskimo artifacts of North America*, by Charles Miles, Chicago, Regnery, 1963. *American Anthropologist 66*: 1407-08, 1964.

R24. Review of *Aboriginal California: three studies in culture history*, by James T. Davis, A. L. Kroeber, Robert F. Heizer, and Albert B. Elsasser, Berkeley, University of California. *Ethnohistory 11*: 72-73, 1964.

R25. Comment on "A measurement of relative racial difference," by Munro S. Edmonson, *Current Anthropology 6*: 194-95, 1965.

R26. Review of *The native Americans*, by Robert F. Spencer, Jesse D. Jennings, et al., New York, Harper and Row. *Science 159*: 1364, 1965.

R27. Review of *Acorns: the staple food of the California Indians* (1962, 28 minutes, rental $12.50, purchase $245.00); *The beautiful tree—Chish-kale* (1965, 20 minutes, rental $10.00, purchase $190.00); *Buckeyes: a food of the California Indians* (1961, 13 minutes, rental $7.00, purchase $125.00); *Pine nuts: a food of the Paiute and Washo Indians of California and Nevada* (1961, 13 minutes, rental $7.00, purchase $125.00). All filmed and produced by the University of California Extension Media Center, with Samuel A. Barrett as consultant. All in color, 24 frames per second, with optical sound. Available from University of California Extension Media Center, Film Distribution, 2223 Fulton St., Berkeley, California. *American Anthropologist 68*: 596-97, 1966.

R28. Comment on "New mathematics for glottochronology," by Nikolas J. van der Merwe. *Current Anthropology 7*: 491, 1966.

R29. Review of *American Indian tomahawks*, by Harold L. Peterson. New York, Museum of the American Indian, Heye Foundation, *Ethnohistory 14*: 89-90, 1967.

R30. Comment on "Estimating aboriginal American population: (1) An appraisal of techniques with a new hemispheric estimate; (2) A technique using anthropological and biological data," by Henry F. Dobyns and H. Paul Thompson. *Current Anthropology 7*: 430, 1966.

R31. Review of *Red man's religion* by Ruth M. Underhill. Chicago, University of Chicago 1965. *Indiana Magazine of History 62*: 358-59, 1966.

R32. Comment on "Why exceptions? The logic of cross-cultural analysis," by A. J. F. Köbben. *Current Anthropology 8*: 21, 1967

R33. Comment on "Some implications of the theory of the particularity, or 'atomism', of Northern Algonkians," by Harold Hickerson. *Current Anthropology 8*: 331, 1967.

R34. Review of *Reference encyclopedia of the American Indian*, B. Klein and D. Icolari, eds., *Pacific Northwest Quarterly 59*: 51, 1968.

R35. Review of *American historical anthropology: essays in honor of Leslie Spier*, Carroll L. Riley and Walter W. Taylor, eds. Carbondale and Edwardsville; Southern Illinois University Press; London and Amsterdam; Feffer and Simons, 1967. *American Anthropologist 70*: 773-74, 1968.

R36. "On the population nadir of Indians in the United States." *Current Anthropology 9*: 330, 1968.

R37. Review of *Folk song style and culture,* by Alan Lomax, Washington, D.C., American Association for the Advancement of Science, 1968. Reviewed in *Ethnomusicology* 14: 57-62. 1970.

R38. "Innovations in cross-cultural method from Ethnomusicology," *Behavior Science Notes* 5: 117-24, 1970.

R39. Review of *Parker on the Iroquois,* by William N. Fenton, ed., Syracuse, Syracuse University Press, 1968. Reviewed in *Pacific Historical Quarterly* 38: 474-75, 1970.

R40. "Girls puberty rites and matrilocal residence," *Abstracts in Anthropology* 1: 25-26, 1970.

R41. Review of *Alfred Kroeber: a personal configuration,* by Theodora Kroeber, Berkeley, University of California Press, 1970. *Science* 170: 1391, 1970.

R42. Review of *The logic of comparative social inquiry,* by Adam Przeworski and Henry Teune, New York, John Wiley & Sons, 1970. *American Anthropologist* 73: 311-12, 1971.

R43. Comment on "Evaluation of a stratified versus an unstratified universe of cultures in comparative research," by Lenora Greenbaum. *Behavior Science Notes* 4: 284-86, 1970.

R44. "Brown and Driver on Girls' puberty rites again." *American Anthropologist* 73: 1261-62, 1971.

Part Two

On Functional, Historical, and Evolutionary Explanations in Comparative Ethnology

1. Introduction

Joseph G. Jorgensen

The following three essays by Driver explore explanations in the comparative anthropology of synchronic, or timeless-state relations among cultural phenomena. The first item, written jointly with Kroeber, asserts that history can be reconstructed from synchronic comparisons. Driver was skeptical of the assertions made by Kroeber, but did not challenge them for several years (see Part III). Then, as now, Driver did not think that "history" was being postdicted—rather, that the history was impressionistic at best.

In subsequent papers, Driver attempted to distinguish among several factors that influence cultural similarities and differences. He did not jettison the use of "history" in accounting for phenomena shared by two or more groups, but he did not let that hypothesis dominate his accounts, either.

In the essay on kin avoidances, we see how Driver attempts to separate history, evolution, and function explanations in a synchronic study. The treatments of correlations and partial correlations, language family and culture area relations, and the hypotheses about donor and recipient societies are important contributions to comparative inquiry. Yet, when Driver gets to the point where he must evaluate the historical relationships of borrowing and inheritance on kinship organization—especially kin avoidances—the only measures that he has of history are inferential, to wit: language and culture area relationships. Whereas language family membership is generally considered a valid measure of historical relatedness, culture area membership, as he points out, does not entail historical relatedness among societies to so unchallengable a degree. Because culture areas are impressionistic, it is not tautologous to use these areas to test for relatedness, but to cover his bets, Driver also cuts North America into grids and demonstrates that correlations within grids are greater than correlations among grids. Nevertheless, Driver has long criticized Kroeber and others (see item 25 in the bibliography) for treating culture areas as historical areas, arguing that cultures classified as belonging in the same area share some items because of common adaptations to a relatively similar environment and that these items need not be borrowed or inherited. He reasons that other items might be shared by cultures that help them adjust to an environment, but that, even among linguistically-related members of the same culture area, these items can be borrowed or inherited. Still other phenomena shared by cultures are shared, not because of common adjustments or strains toward integration, but for reasons such as nonpredictable ideologies about disease, curing, proper dress, and the like. These, too, can be borrowed and inherited.

The impressionistic measures of history used in the correlational analysis prove to be very powerful in accounting for hypothetical relations among kinship organization phenomena. So Driver ventures from his correlational analysis in an attempt to explain the historical relations that have influenced the correlations. At this point he does not lay bare the temporal factors that explain the synchronic correlations, but his speculations about historical relatedness—conditioned by his hypotheses about the development of kinship organization—provide us with some useful concluding hypotheses.

The third paper spells out some basic disagreements among evolutionists who attempt to account for history and those who do not and argues the necessity of analyzing borrowing and inheritance.

David Aberle's contribution to the volume is methodological and conceptual. In the spirit of a comparative, synchronic inquiry, which argues for delineation and specification of the interplay among borrowing, inheritance, and innovation in culture, Aberle, referring to Harold Driver's paper of 1956 (see item 15 in the bibliography), points out that his explanations of kinship organization for North American Indians suffer from too much dependence on evolutionary hypotheses which do not appropriately distinguish those things that are borrowed from those that are inherited, from those that are innovated, or from those things whose presence cannot be inferred with any surety at all.

Aberle refers the reader to his recent work with Isidore Dyen on proto-Athapaskan language and kinship, wherein rules for protoanalyses are presented. These rules should prove extremely helpful in reconstructing parts of protoculture—particularly parts of kinship organization—and should be a boon to comparative, synchronic inquiry. Here, in parsimonious fashion, Aberle outlines a reconstruction of aboriginal North American Indian social organization that varies from Driver's reconstruction. The interpretation of peripheral distributions is especially interesting and analogous to the interpretations of distributions of *märchen* made by Warren Roberts* (Fabula 1961) on a huge corpus of synchronic folklore materials over a decade ago. The point is that peripheral distributions of correlated phenomena are often more important than central distributions in inferring antiquity.

---

*Specifically, Roberts analyzed Tale Type 480, as classified in Stith Thompson's (revised) "The Types of the Folktale," *Folklore Fellows Communications 184*, Helskinki, 1961.

2. Quantitative Expression of Cultural Relationships

Harold E. Driver and Alfred L. Kroeber[1]

Aims

This essay differs from its predecessors in the same field in one or all of several ways.

First, it is concerned with the similarities of culture-wholes, or considerable blocks of cultures like the Sun dance. The factors treated numerically are therefore culture elements or "traits," or in some cases small clusters or "complexes" of these; the relationships inquired into are those between whole tribal cultures. The aim of the investigation is therefore the reverse of Tylor's and Hobhouse's.[2] Tylor investigated whether traits like matrilinear descent and avoidance of relatives-in-law were or tended to be inherently connected, causally interdependent, on the basis of their occurrence among all ethnic groups (tribes, nations) on whom data were available. We inquire whether the cultures carried or possessed by such ethnic groups are more or less similar to one another, on the basis of their containing or not containing traits such as matrilineate, avoidance, self-torture vows, the fire drill, sinew-backed bow, twined weaving, ridged houses, etc.

Second, we limit each inquiry to a series of geographically contiguous peoples or cultures; in other words, to a group of peoples accepted as having a certain historic unity, or as it is customarily called, constituting a culture area; or a part thereof. Tylor's and Hobhouse's investigations were on a world-wide basis, without consideration of geography. They sought to establish permanences which transcended the "accidents" of history and geography. We look for the precise historic relationships within a temporally and spatially delimited frame. They aimed at "laws," we at "natural" classifications. Such classifications carry genetic significance, in other words, permit of inferential historical reconstructions analogous to those of natural history.

Consequently a criticism does not apply to us which is generally made of Tylor's and Hobhouse's work, namely, that its results are invalid because it is not established that the elements dealt with (tribal cultures) are independent of each other.[3] It is true that the problem is shifted rather than done away with. Are our elements or factors, the culture traits, independent of each other? While we are not prepared to answer this question categorically, we believe that culture traits are in the main if not in absolutely all cases independent.[4] This is because so many of them have been shown over and over again, in all domains of culture and in all parts of the world, to occur at times dissociated even if at other times or places they are frequently or even preponderantly associated,[5] that it becomes a fair inference, until contrary cases are demonstrated, that all traits can occur independently of each other. That, at any rate, appears to be the implicit assumption of all anthropologists of the last generation, with the exception of the few survivors of the Tylor-Morgan-Frazer "evolutionistic" school, and possibly the group of functionalists.[6] If then we are in error on this point, we believe that nine-tenths of the anthropology and culture history practiced today is also in error in a fundamental if generally unexpressed assumption; and in that case a general inquiry on this point is in order.

Finally, we have utilized for our own purposes only quantitative measures so simple as to be intelligible with a knowledge of nothing more than arithmetic, and so humble as to have been generally overlooked by inquiries into statistical theory and little used by biological, psychological, and economic statisticians. These measures are all proportions: the proportion which traits shared by one tribe with another tribe form of all its traits; of all the traits of the second; of the traits occurring in both tribes; and the arithmetic and geometric means of the first two proportions. The values obtained by these measures have been treated by equally simple procedures: ranking the values found for all the similarities of each tribe; grouping the high and the low values to see if they segregate of themselves into series of tribes, or classes; testing these classes or groups for the simplicity and regularity or the complex irregularity of the total resultant scheme of classification; and testing this scheme again for fit with the known facts of geography and history, such as position, communications, etc.

Our procedure is to examine first the means of measurement used in the few previous analogous studies; second, several other measures; then to apply these, or some of them, to concrete cases chosen, on account of available data, from Polynesia, the Plains and Pacific coast areas of what is now the United States, and Peru; and to compare the results both among themselves and as regards the fit into wider knowledge.

Measures Previously Used

In 1926 Clements, Schenck, and Brown,[7] analyzed statistically Linton's comparative list of the forms taken by certain culture traits in six Polynesian island groups.[8] Their findings as to the relative strength of the 15 interrelationships involved did not differ profoundly from Linton's, nor did their genetic or historical interpretation of the relationships, except for being free of considerations of race and migration which Linton had injected. They were however of course able to express their findings both more sharply and more "objectively." Their significant figures for each relationship were two. The first gave the positive or negative excess of culture trait agreements over disagreements, common lacks of a trait being counted as agreements the same as common presences. The second figure was a value P, derived by a Pearsonian table from X^2, the "cell square contingency,"[9] and expressing the probability that the first figure was not attributable to real relationship but to chance. Thus Samoa and Tonga, in 238 Samoan-Tongan (out of a total of 282 Polynesian) traits considered, show an excess of +155 agreements, and a P of .000000, indicative not only of a high degree of similarity but of certainty that this similarity is actual, not the result of chance. For New Zealand and Tonga the excess of agreements is − 55, the P .000625: the relationship is remote, but the reality of the remoteness practically certain. New Zealand and Tahiti, on the other hand, show − 5 and .992051: the

relationship is neither close nor remote, but the probability is enormously high that the particular figure of − 5 is not expressive of actual relationship but rather of chance, in the data assembled.

Several general and particular observations can be made on the Clements treatment.

First of all, while P is not a function of E (the excess of trait agreements), it tends strongly, in most cases, to stand in inverse relation to it. What P expresses is the expectability of a similar distribution of presences and absences occurring through random chance. The directly significant values remain the relative E's, which for Tonga-Samoa are 193 − 45 = + 148, for Tonga-New Zealand 82 − 137 = − 55, for Tahiti-New Zealand 124 − 129 = − 5. Historical relationships are referable wholly from these counted E's. They allow the conclusion that Tongan and Samoan cultures are closely related; Tongan and Maori relatively unrelated within Polynesia; and Tahitian and Maori related to an intermediate degree. All that the P's add is that we can be sure that the extreme values express a real degree of relationship.

It is a part of Clements' method that common absences of traits are given equal weight with common presences. This touches a fundamental problem of theory in the interpretation of historical growths or culture developments, which is as troublesome in non-statistical as in statistical treatments. We are not ready to express ourselves on the theory of this problem. Obviously if Tonga and Samoa alone in Polynesia do not build rectangular houses, this is presumably as indicative of similarity and probable genetic relationship for the trait as the positive fact that they alone use lateen sails; especially in view of the fact that Tonga and Samoa are adjacent island groups. As regards the Plains Indians, who also do not build rectangular houses, the Tongan-Samoan common absence is unlikely to mean anything as regards relationship, that is, common cultural origin or common specific influences; just as it is unlikely that the recurrence of the lateen sail in Italy means anything of this sort. Clements saw this point and made clear that he was dealing only with *special* relationships *within* a specified, limited area. An impugnment of his method by Wallis on this score is therefore wide of the mark;[10] and Clements has sufficiently refuted it.[11] Nevertheless, it would be desirable to understand more clearly the theoretical principles involved, so that we might define better the circumstances under which the consideration of absent traits is respectively legitimate and necessary, or invalid and misleading.

Clements works over Linton's original Polynesian data by splitting many of these, until he can operate with the presence and absence of minimal unit elements. This plan is common to all statistical approaches to culture material yet attempted, including our own below; indeed is made necessary by the fact that no other relative or quantitative measure of culture phenomena has yet been devised. It is obvious that the units dealt with are not really commensurable. Some are broader in scope, or more important in the life of the culturebearers, than others. There is however no biased selection. The phenomena are broken up into the smallest units recognizable or definable. The data are assembled and listed by an ethnological expert conversant with the field, in this case Linton; the final splitting into units is done by another ethnologist. The presumption therefore is that the splitting will at least be more or less evenly irregular in all parts or aspects of the cultures considered.

Polynesia being a well studied area, Linton's tribal data are unusually even in fullness. Of his 282 traits, as systematized by Clements, information is lacking on 41 for Tonga, 22 for New Zealand, 6 for Tahiti, 4 for Samoa, 2 for Hawaii, 0 for Marquesas. This means that a positive presence or absence could be reckoned in 85 to 99 per cent of the cases, according to group. This is a higher proportion of known occurrences or lacks than is usually available.[12]

Clements leaves out of account all present or absent traits common to his six ethnic groups. This is legitimate and advisable, because what he is really concerned with is the relative degree of similarity and dissimilarity between groups within his circle of six, and the inclusion of common traits would have swelled his totals while reducing the sharpness of his differentiations. Had his study been concerned with the proportion of general Polynesian to locally specialized elements of culture, the common traits would of course have had to be included; in a comparison between Polynesia and other parts of the world, the universal or general Polynesian traits would obviously be far more significant than their locally diversified variants of detail.

In a later paper[13] dealing with the Sun Dance of the Plains Indian tribes on the basis of data assembled by Spier,[14] Clements used two other statistical measures, r and Q, respectively the well-known coefficient of correlation and coefficient of association.

Clements, in subsequent discussion with us, doubted whether these coefficients were properly applicable to data of the Sun Dance order, for reasons of statistical theory. We had already found fault with his culture-historical inferences from these Sun Dance coefficients, on the ground that they were out of fit with the known geographical, historical, and general cultural relations of the Plains tribes, and

therefore necessitated involved and seemingly improbable reconstructive hypotheses. This matter will be touched upon below.

Measures Used

The measures of relationship which we propose to test all deal with the traits shared or not shared by two tribes, each such pair being considered separately. The respectively greater and lesser relationships of the various pairs of tribes are then determined by ranking. In proportion as the rankings follow some consistent plan, on the basis of known geographical or historical facts, or simply according to an internal scheme of their own, the results give a "fit" and presumably possess reliability and significance.

Only three values enter into these measures. The first is the number of identical positive traits in the cultures of the two tribes or ethnic groups that are being compared. As these traits are shared or *common*, we shall call this value c. Next there is the total number of traits possessed by or known for the first tribe of the pair; and the same for the second tribe. We may call these two values a and b.

It would be desirable if one knew in all cases that the values of a and b were strictly comparable, that is, had been obtained by exactly the same method of inquiry. Unfortunately, this rarely is wholly so, and sometimes far from it. The data for tribe A may be much the fuller, not necessarily because the culture is richer, but because field studies have been more intensive. In that case we may not know whether a given trait occurring in A is present but not reported on in culture B, or is really lacking there. We can only trust—and reasonably so with data secured by ethnologists of experience—that a fair sample has been got of the total culture, so that the proportion of traits shared and not shared by tribe B with tribe A—its c and $b\text{-}c$ components—bear about the same proportion to each other as they would if the complete value which b has in nature had been obtained.

Sometimes the record will be clear as to a trait being lacking in one culture, but deficient as to its being present or absent in another. Thus a trait may be present in tribe A, known to be lacking in tribe B, uninquired into in tribe D. In that event, this trait goes into the value a for comparison with value b, but not with value d. In other words, the values a and b are likely to vary somewhat with each comparison made, when established trait-absences are distinguished in the data from gaps in knowledge. It is only when the condition of the data is such as to forbid this distinction being made generally, that a, and b, have constant values throughout all comparisons.

The simplest measure is c_{ab}/a, that is, the proportions which tribe A traits shared with tribe B bear to the total number of traits possessed by tribe A. The measure is however awkward because the corresponding value c_{ab}/b is normally different. For instance, Hidatsa and Blackfeet have 9 Sun Dance traits in common. But as the total of reported Hidatsa Sun Dance traits is 22, and of Blackfoot 38, the value of c/a is 9/22 or 41 per cent; of c/b, 9/38 or 24 per cent. This means that as soon as comparisons between different pairs of tribes are made, say of Hidatsa-Blackfoot with Assiniboin-Ponca, there are two values in each case. Wallis[15] solved this difficulty by arbitrarily choosing the lower one for each pair; but this procedure obviously may misrepresent the situation. If for instance, as is wholly possible, it should prove that the full Hidatsa dance consisted of only 22 traits, $c/a = .41$ would be a true value, and the substitution for it of $c/b = .24$ quite unwarranted.

The only valid procedure is to use some mean of the c/a and c/b values, in which case the means from all the pairs of tribes can be compared at once; or to retain both the c/a and c/b values and forego a general comparison. In the latter event it is still possible to rank the tribes B, D, E, F . . . . as to their degree of similarity to A; and the same for every tribe in turn. It will be seen below that this plan yields empirical results corresponding rather well, so far as they are comparable, with the results from other measures. But the piecemeal, cumbersome nature of the results renders it difficult for the figures to make a decisive impression on the mind.

We shall call this measure P, for simple proportion. More accurately, it is P_a and P_b, because there is almost always a two-way value. This P of course is not to be confused with the Pearsonian P discussed above in connection with E.

The difficulties just discussed are overcome by taking the arithmetical mean of the two values of P; that is, $(c/a + c/b)/2$. We designate this value as A. It allows the A's for all pairs of tribes to be compared at once.

Another measure is the geometrical mean, G, of the two P's; namely $\sqrt{(c/a) \cdot (c/b)} = c/\sqrt{(a \cdot b)}$. This is nearly as easily computed as the arithmetical A. Its value coincides with this when a and b are equal, but runs somewhat lower when a and b differ in value.

The measure $c/\sqrt{(a \cdot b)}$ is recognized in statistical theory as a form of r or correlation coefficient.[16] As such a coefficient, however, its validity depends on the sigmas of the values dealt with, and these cannot be ascertained for data of the kind we are dealing with. We therefore refrain from using this measure as one of correlation, and employ it merely as a mean of two proportions.[16a]

Another simple measure is the proportion which common or shared traits constitute of the *total* number of different traits possessed by the two tribes, and which we designate by T. The numerator, as in all our formulas is c; the denominator, a plus b, less however c, to prevent the c traits which are already included in a being counted again for their occurrence in b. Hence, $T = c/(a + b - c)$.[17]

To recapitulate, with an example:

A, Hidatsa tribe, total known Sun Dance traits, a, 22; B, Blackfoot, b, 38; traits shared by Hidatsa and Blackfoot, c, 9.

$P = c/a, c/b; c/a = 9/22 = .409; c/b = 9/38 = .237$.
$A = (c/a + c/b)/2 = (.409 + .237)/2 = .323$.
$G = \sqrt{(c/a) \cdot (c/b)} = c/\sqrt{(ab)} = 9/\sqrt{(22 \cdot 38)} = 9/\sqrt{836} = .311$.
$T = c/(a + b - c) = 9/(22 + 38 - 9) = 9/51 = .176$.

We shall now apply one or more of these measures successively to the tabulations of Polynesian trait distributions by Linton, of the Plains Indian Sun Dance by Spier, of Northwest Coast Indians by Kroeber,[17a] and of Northeast Peruvian Indians by Tessmann, in order to compare the results of the several measures both among one another and against the generally accepted ethnological, geographic, and historical situations to which the tabulated data refer and of which they form part.

Polynesia

The actual relationships in Polynesia are fairly clear without technical statistical treatment, in fact were approximately formulated by Linton in his original memoir,[18] although his treatment differs from Clements' and ours in considering migrations and racial factors jointly with culture trait distributions. This case, therefore, furnishes a specially good opportunity to match in detail the results of several measures. It is plain from Linton's data, and still more so from Clements' E:P expression of them, that the six Polynesian cultures considered fall into three groups. The most segregated comprises Samoa and Tonga. Next most distinctive is the pair Marquesas and New Zealand. The group of feeblest internal coherence is composed of Tahiti (Society) and Hawaii. Within this group, it is Tahiti that has much the closer relationships with both Samoa-Tonga and Marquesas-New Zealand. Hawaii, in other words, is related to the remainder of Polynesia largely through Tahiti. In the same way, the two other groups are related to each other mainly through Tahiti. They share few traits which they do not also share with Tahiti. On the other hand, they frequently share with Tahiti but not with each other. Tahiti thus is central in relationship, the five other populations peripheral to it. The situation might accordingly be depicted by a recognition of four groups, namely Tahiti, Hawaii, Marquesas-New Zealand, Samoa-Tonga, with the degree of relationship in this order. Within the last two groups, Marquesas is somewhat closer to Tahiti and the rest than is New Zealand, and Samoa is similarly closer than Tonga.

In general, the degrees of cultural affinity accord fairly with geographical position, but there is one important exception: Marquesas and New Zealand are almost on opposite sides of Tahiti. Either, therefore, the connections between them traveled around Tahiti; or the connection between them was later interrupted while Tahitian relations with Marquesas continued. This is an alternative that cannot be resolved by statistical method applied to a trait count, but requires a culture-historical evaluation and interpretation which is best given by Polynesian specialists, though they might conceivably be aided by statistics in the definition and analysis of their problem.

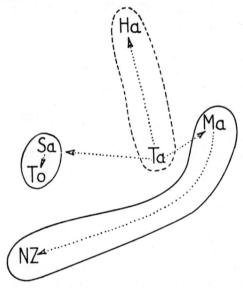

Fig. 1. Polynesian relationships. The distances are those on the map. Cultural similarities are indicated by enclosures of different strength; probable courses of cultural relationship, by arrows.

Both Linton and Clements have given such historical interpretations or reconstructions.[19] We wish only to point out that the one of Clements is an ethnological addendum to his statistical treatment, not an inherent consequence of it. As a matter of fact he assumes two or probably three former types of Polynesian culture, plus a later overlay which culminated in Tahiti but failed to reach New Zealand. However, it might just as well be assumed, granting the later overlay, that the older culture was originally one, an "old generalized Polynesian," and that this became differentiated in the three groups before the overlay began; or again, that Tahiti was the continuous center

of Polynesian influence early as well as late, but that the elements which reached relatively self-sufficient districts like Samoa-Tonga at once began to be specialized away from their original forms, while the Tahitian influence on New Zealand was later interrupted by a cessation of communications. As between alternative hypotheses like these, the opinion of a student saturated in the facts and feel of Polynesian culture will always be worth more, assuming that he is unbiased, than that of the statistician, whose technique after all is only ancillary to such problems.

Both the cultural and spatial relationships of the six cultures are illustrated in the diagram (fig. 1). It will be seen that even apart from the Marquesas-New Zealand relation, culture similarity is not a mere function of distance, since Samoa and Tonga are geographically about as near to Hawaii as is Tahiti, although culturally they are much more dissimilar.

Of course, the whole Polynesian problem can be solved only with consideration of the other cultures—Tuamotu, Easter, Rapa, Tubuai, Mangaia, etc.;[20] and even after the internal relations have become defined, there remains the larger problem of the relations of Polynesia as a whole to the remainder of Oceania. Still, we have now a quantitative and presumably reliable expression of 15 interrelationships of six major types of Polynesian culture; in other words, a definite and authentic classification, irrespective of its genetic interpretations. Against this, the results of the several statistical treatments can be matched, as in the adjoining table 1.[21]

In this table, the 15 known Polynesian interrelationships are ranked in the order which follows logically from the way in which the cultures group themselves, in other words *from the scheme of relationships viewed as a whole*. Now when the rankings according to the several formulas are matched against this ranking, it is seen that,

G: the ranking is perfect.
T: the ranking is nearly perfect, only 8 and 9 and again 11 and 12, marked in the table by asterisks, exchanging places by small intervals.
A: the ranking is the same, plus 10 and 11 interchanged.
E—P: the ranking is very irregular, the order 1, 2, 3, 4 .... 15 being replaced by: 1, 3, 2, 5, 7, 9, 10, 6, 4, 11, 8, 14, 12, 13, 15 for the E's, and similarly for the P's.

From this it can be concluded that the A, G, and T formulas are likely to yield results much more in accord in detail with the general trend of the facts than the E: P formula. In other words, A, G, and T results fit the general ethnological picture better, point for point, than E: P. They express the presumably actual scheme of classification, or relationships, regularly; E:P, irregularly.

Whether the slight edge of greater regularity of G over A and T is because it is a truer measure, or an accident of this set of figures, we cannot say. It will be noted that the irregularities all involve the degree of superiority of similarity of Samoa versus Tonga in relation to the remaining groups, or of Hawaii versus Marquesas in relation to Samoa-Tonga. These are all definitely small differences. In other words, the rankings from 8 to 14 obviously differ by small steps, and have not the significance of those elsewhere in the table or of the difference between themselves as a unit and the remainder.

The method followed in this case, namely of testing the fit of all parts of the situation, against a scheme expressing the set or trend of the whole situation, may be somewhat rough and ready, and may not have much statistical justification; but it does seem to rest on common sense and may engage the confidence of anthropologists who distrust or know little of statistical procedure.

Of course, the fewer the cultures compared, the easier it is to recognize the trend of their totality. The fit-test is therefore well adapted to cases like this Polynesian one, where the data refer to only 6 cultures and the total number of relationships is 15. For instance, the 19 tribes on whom there are Sun Dance data possess 171 inter-relationships; and unless these were unusuallly orderly, that is distributed according to some simple factor such as distance from a geographical center, or a unilinear successive historical transmission, there would expectably be enough irregularities in the set of the Sun Dance picture as a whole to make its scheme less easily apprehended.

TABLE 1

POLYNESIAN RELATIONSHIPS

		Rank	E†	P	c‡	A	G	T
Main Group II [	S-To	1	148	.000000	46	.68	.67	.51
Main Group IB [	M-NZ	2	64	.001011	90	.65	.64	.48
Main Group IA [	Ta-H	3	69	.000697	78	.60	.60	.43
	Ta-M	4	40	.065944	81	.59	.58	.41
Relations be-	H-M	5	3	.956276	79	.53	.54	.36
tween IA and IB	Ta-NZ	6	−5	.992051	60	.49	.48	.32
	H-NZ	7	−20	.677677	59	.46	.45	.30
	Ta-S	8	37	.321339	43	.45	.43	.27
	Ta-To	9	58	.049119	32	*.46	.41	*.28
	H-S	10	−24	.335656	32	.32	.31	.18
Relations be-	H-To	11	1	.930439	25	*.33	.31	.173
tween IA-IB	M-S	12	−51	.128463	35	*.33	.30	*.174
and II	M-To	13	−43	.216631	25	.31	.28	.15
	NZ-S	14	−46	.022856	24	.27	.24	.14
	NZ-T	15	−55	.000625	14	.20	.18	.09
Means for:								
Tahiti						.52	.50	.34
Marquesas						.48	.47	.31
Hawaii						.45	.44	.29
New Zealand						.41	.40	.27
Samoa						.41	.39	.25
Tonga						.40	.37	.24

† E = excess of positive *and negative* agreements over disagreements.

‡ "c" = common presences of traits.

Plains Indian Sun Dance

As already stated, this is a complex ceremony on which data sufficient for statistical treatment have been collected among 19 tribes or subtribes of the central United States. We have followed the basic list of Spier[22] as given on his pages 464, 466, 473 and summarized under "Number of Common Traits" on page 478.[23] It should be noted that Spier does not formally list any traits, such as the center pole, which are absolutely universal; nor, on the other hand, any which are wholly peculiar to a single tribe.

The Plains tribes do not segregate as much among themselves in their Sun dance as the Polynesians of various archipelagos differ in their whole culture. The Sun Dance is not only merely a fraction of a culture, but it is of less antiquity. There may be other reasons also. At any rate the groupings are much less incisive. The Cheyenne and Arapaho form a fairly clear unit in their Sun Dance, it is true; but this unit is not so well set off from other tribes as are Samoa-Tonga from the other Polynesians. The Arapaho dance is nearly as similar to Gros Ventre as to Cheyenne; this in turn is nearly as similar to Blackfoot as to Arapaho; whereas Cheyenne has a greater similarity to Ponca than Arapaho has; and so on. In other words, the interrelationships are thoroughly ramified. As there are 171 such interrelationships among 19 tribes—or 153 among 18 that we have dealt with[24] —the picture is too complex for an obvious, offhand organization of results. Some measure or mechanism of classifying the interrelations is desirable. Clements found this in consideration of the number of high and low Q's and r's shown by each tribe. We have followed the procedure of simple serial ranking of all other tribes with reference to each one in turn. This is more lengthy, but it preserves the particular facts as to each special relationship. At least, nothing of special or local significance is smeared out by premature generalization.

For comparative uses the chief defect of the Spier data is that they show only presences of traits, so that known absences of traits and absence of knowledge as to traits are not differentiated. For this condition, which is almost as unfortunate for ethnological as for statistical purposes, Spier is largely not to blame, the original sources being defective in that essentially they are descriptions made without sense of a wider problem. But the defect is doubly serious in measures like $E{:}P$, or r and Q if they are applicable, because these treat common absences, which may not be real, as common agreements. From this "doubleweighting" of possible error our P, A, G, T are free.

The error is likely to become particularly large in proportion as the original descriptive accounts are incomplete and the entered figures in the basic list correspondingly low. For instance, the Gros Ventre ceremony with 37 recorded traits, and the Blackfoot with 38, share 26 traits. They therefore possess respectively 11 and 12 not found in the other; or, there are 26 traits in which they are known to agree, 23 in which they are known to disagree. Our values P, A, G, and T are all derived from the distribution of these $26 + 11 + 12 = 49$ traits. We make no assumption in regard to the ($82 - 49 = 33$ traits on which there is no report for the Blackfoot and Gros Ventre, other than to assume that such of them as may exist but have not been reported are likely to be distributed in more or less the same way as the 49 which have been reported for one or both tribes. The $E{:}P$ measure, however, if it is applied at all to data like Spier's, must reckon the 33 wholly unreported traits as jointly absent from the Gros Ventre and Blackfoot dances. Hence: common, 26, plus common lacking (*sic*), 33, make 59 agreements; Gros Ventre only, 11, plus Blackfoot only, 12, make 23 disagreements; excess of "agreements" over disagreements, E, $59 - 23 = 36$. But with smaller number, Ute 14, Plains Ojibwa 8, common 2, therefore 62 traits not reported for either tribe. Hence, agreements $2 + 62 = 64$, disagreements, $12 + 6 = 18$, E, $64 - 18 = 46$, or 10 greater than the Gros Ventre-Blackfoot E. This in spite of the fact that Gros Ventre and Blackfoot share more than half, but Ute and Plains Ojibwa only one-eleventh, of the traits reported for one or both members of each pair of tribes. In the Polynesian basic list, absent traits were distinguished from traits not reported on, and the total data for each island group were much more nearly equal, so that the E values are undoubtedly significant. But for the Sun Dance, any comparison of pairs of tribes for which the data are deficient is bound to produce a high E.

The same thing holds for r and Q. Hence Clements' Q value for Gros Ventre-Blackfoot is .49, but for Ute-Plains Ojibwa, .65.[25] Even if r and Q are admissible in this case on grounds of pure theory of statistics, as Clements now himself doubts, it is evident that a classification or historical reconstruction based on them would tend to be erroneous because the inclusion of all gaps in knowledge among agreements would introduce a positive element of fallaciousness, as serious in proportion as the gaps were numerous. We had actually written an argument to show that Clements' Q findings yielded a complicated and unlikely internal picture and a bad fit to the generally known facts of Plains ethnology. This argument need not be given; but the circumstance indicates that wrong statistical method is likely to show in the ethnological results.

Table 3[25a] gives the various tribal rankings from the point of view of each tribe, for A, G, T, and P

16

in turn. To simplify typography, we have omitted decimal points, so that the figures are all percentages. It is evident that the A, G, and T rankings agree very closely. Where there is a difference in rank, it is usually on account of a difference of only a very few per cent, so that it is more conspicuous than intrinsic. The P value rankings agree rather well with the others, but not so closely as these with one another.

Our descriptive and inferentially historical scheme, as based on these rankings, is given in figure 2. We will merely say that the tribes are shown in their geographical positions,[26] connected by arrows according to the leading intertribal influences indicated by the numerical values. Particularly strong relationship is shown by double arrows; relationship which presumably was about equally reciprocal, by double-pointed ones. Broken-line arrows mark relations of

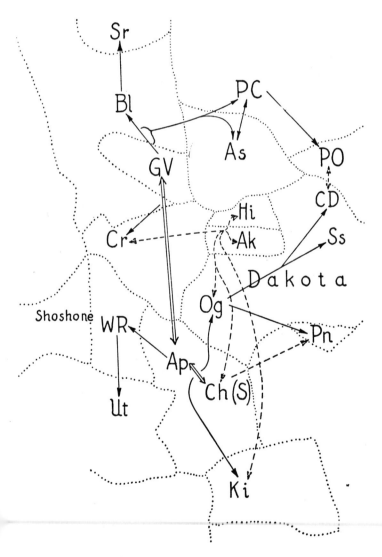

Fig. 2. Principal Sun Dance influences as reconstructed from values in table 3.[25 a]—Geography after Mooney.

secondary strength; in some cases, like the Kiowa, presumably older and overlaid ones. The direction of one-way arrows is determined by ethnological as much as statistical considerations. The Arapaho-Wind River A and G of 65 and 62 rank third for the Arapaho, but first for Wind River. Arapaho has six other G values above 50 (that is, numerous other close relations), Wind River has only one. Wind River's Arapaho value is therefore more significant to it than the same Wind River value is to Arapaho. The Arapaho are more centrally situated, the Wind River wholly marginal. Arapaho culture has a far richer ceremonial development, apart from the Sun Dance, than Wind River. And finally, twice as many traits are known for the Arapaho (54) as for the Wind River (28) Sun Dance. While this last is an isolated fact might be the result of inequality of observation, in the light of the foregoing considerations it is not likely to be wholly such. The outcome is that the arrow has been drawn from Arapaho to Wind River. This does not imply that the influence was entirely in this direction; only that the prevailing trend was such. This trend may have been overwhelming or far from it; but in the words of the legend of the diagram, it was at least the "principal influence."

Similarly for the other arrows. Not every ethnologist may agree with every one of them; but every student knowing the Plains tribes will see at least some obvious and more or less convincing reason for their directions.

We have avoided unnecessary arrows, as between Blackfoot and Arapaho, where the connection is obviously through Gros Ventre; or between Sarsi and Arapaho and Assiniboin, where the avenues are evidently Sarsi-Blackfoot-Gros Ventre-Arapaho and Sarsi-(Blackfoot-Gros Ventre)-(Assiniboin-Cree). We hold it as a merit and validation of our diagrammatic reconstruction that most of the connections of secondary strength are thus automatically expressed by being embodied in the primary connections.

In several cases influences more or less equally emanating from or impinging upon a pair of tribes have been indicated by forking arrows. Thus the Plains Cree and Assiniboin ceremonies are evidently related about equally to those of the Blackfoot and Gros Ventre; hence the connecting arrow is forked at both ends. It is not unlikely that the two more easterly dances were derived from the Gros Ventre-Blackfoot one before this was as fully differentiated into two as now. It is also possible that the Cree were the chief recipients from this source; but the high relationship of the Cree and Assiniboin ceremonies indicates strong influences between them, probably reciprocal. The Crow, Oglala, and Kiowa,

17

though not specially interconnected among themselves, all show fairly strong and about equal similarity to both the Arikara and Hidatsa, who however are not very closely connected between themselves. Here broken, forked, and double-ended arrows express the inference that a former relation of the three nomadic with the two sedentary tribes was overlaid by a later and stronger dependent relation upon Cheyenne-Arapaho-Gros Ventre, whereas the Arikara and Hidatsa perhaps drifted apart, or at any rate did not assimilate further. This case, by the way, contains the one instance, other than the known split of the Gros Ventre from the Arapaho, of a major relation running counter to geographical position of the tribes in the middle nineteenth century. The Kiowa, according to Mooney's account[27] of their traditions, were originally farther north, and until nearly 1800 in the Black Hills and in relations with the Crow and with the village tribes. One might expect this transient association, however, to have left less impress upon them than the later and perhaps longer one with the Cheyenne and Arapaho; which is precisely what our figures show and the diagram tries to express.

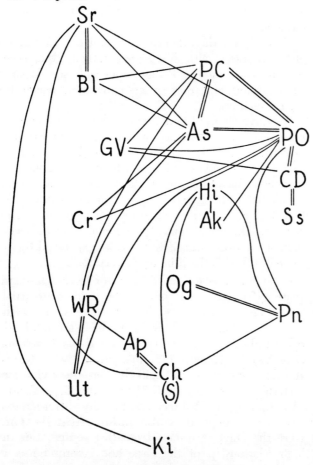

Fig. 3. Principal Sun Dance influences, diagrammed from the invalid (?) Q coefficients.

In short, we believe our diagram representing similarities and presumable historical derivations to be simple, self-consistent, and in excellent agreement with what is known of the recent geographical situation, movements, speech affiliations, and general cultural relations of the Plains tribes.[28]

For comparison we have drawn a similar diagram (fig. 3) expressing Clements' computed Q values, doubling the lines whenever the value exceeded .80. We submit that this is a far more crisscrossed and less coherent diagram than our figure 2. It is also full of anomalies on the side of the general ethnology and tribal history of the plains. The principal point of radiation is constituted by the peripheral and late intrusive Plains Ojibwa! The Kiowa connect not with the village tribes and Cheyenne-Arapaho with whom they had earlier and recent contact, but with the Sarsi; and again, not with the Blackfeet on whom the Sarsi are culturally dependent. The Gros Ventre link with eastern tribes instead of the Arapaho of whom they are an offshoot or the Blackfeet with whom they have lived a century. The prime Canadian and Sisseton Dakota relationship is not with the Oglala Dakota but with the non-Siouan Ojibwa. And so on.

Finally, we have ventured to diagram Spier's conclusions as to the historical development of the dance (fig. 4), in order to compare a non-statistical with a statistical culture-historical approach. Spier does not present a clear-cut historical reconstruction,[29] but rather discusses derivations as between particular tribes, or of special features like the "torture complex." He also quite properly uses documentary alongside inferential historical evidence. The diagram is therefore perhaps not quite as he would have drawn it; but it is at least an attempt to condense his opinions fairly.

It is obvious that the Spier diagram approximates our own much more closely than the one based on the Q association coefficients. The most important difference is that the Arikara-Hidatsa form of dance, although according to him more likely than not derived from the Arapaho-Cheyenne, is by Spier made the basis of an important secondary diffusion to the Crow, Blackfeet, and Assiniboin. The Crow and Blackfeet in turn have influenced the Kiowa; the Assiniboin, the Plains Cree. Our Assiniboin-Cree association as a secondary or tertiary center derived from Gros Ventre-Blackfoot is therefore broken up, to compensate, as it were, for the elevation into an important place of the Arikara-Hidatsa, whose historical status our scheme fails to define well. Other divergences are minor; such as the derivation of Wind River from Gros Ventre rather than Arapaho, and its passing on to the Ute via the Fort Hall Shoshone, plus some late influences from wandering bands of Cree.

We suspect the reason for the main discrepancy between Spier's conclusions and our own to be the fact that by the mid-nineteenth century the Arikara and Hidatsa village tribes were in heavy populational decrease and loss of intertribal influence, that the Sun Dance continued to luxuriate or grow elsewhere for another half century, and that nearly all data were recorded only after 1900. The two village tribes probably did have an important hand in shaping an earlier Sun dance, but then dropped out of activity while the Arapaho and other nomadic tribes kept developing the ceremony. The data being from a later period, the early village influences have been so heavily overlaid as to be unobtrusive in a numerical approach to the totality of phenomena, while the clues they have left may still be significant to historical insight.

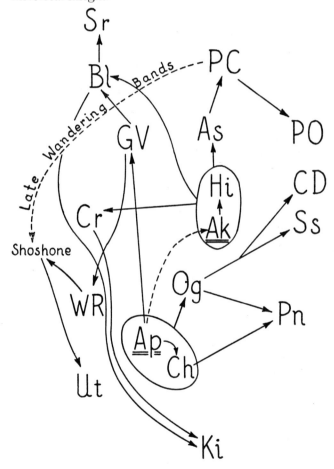

Fig. 4. Principal Sun Dance influences, diagrammed from Spier's conclusions.

Inasmuch as Spier knows more about the Sun Dance than anyone else, we find welcome corroboration in his interpretation. At the same time we are pleased to be able to reject a recent repudiation by

him[30] of his own Sun Dance history reconstruction, as being "misleading and unnecessary." If "unnecessary" means of no interest, that it is a matter of taste and therefore of choice which cannot be argued. But as to the Spier reconstruction being fundamentally unsound, our arriving by a different method at so nearly the same results makes this very unlikely. We prefer to believe that Spier is a better culture historian than he wants to admit. . . .

Northeast Peru

In 1930 G. Tessmann published a large and important volume on the Indians of the tropical forest of northeastern Peru.[31] In this he has included a tabular listing of the tribal occurrence of 212 culture traits assigned to six Kulturfamilien and Kulturgruppen, that is, to four cultures and two subcultures. The lists show the traits in which each of 34 tribes participates in each of these six postulated cultures. A series of colored cartograms visualizes the findings.

Obviously, all of Tessmann's results depend on the validity of the six cultures of which he regards traits as characteristic. Unfortunately, he does not make clear any empirical basis on which his cultures are founded. His argument as to their valid coherence probably rests in good part on intuitive reactions to the experience of gathering and arranging the data, but is presented somewhat dogmatically as the product of a philosophy concerned with the inner significance of culture aspects. This procedure is hardly one to inspire confidence: the six original cultures may be as essentially hypothetical as the Graebner-Schmidt ones. With the use of such assumptions, the classification of data can come out only in terms of the assumptions. The reader's sole check is the degree of coherence or order in the ultimate results. And here Tessmann fails to help out because he includes no one compact tabulation or map showing the degree to which his numerous tribes participate in the six assumed primary cultural units. There are six tabulations in as many parts of the book, and four cartograms with different symbols for the material, social, and spiritual parts of each of the cultures.[32]

However, there is valuable material in the distribution of 1,500 trait occurrences among 34 contiguous tribes, and we resolved to work over these data.[33] Tessmann generally distinguishes between absence of traits and absence of information,[34] but his lists are marked by several peculiarities, such as frequent negative wording of traits ("kein Hund"),[35] and some counting of traits as of double or half weight. For this reason we have compiled from his lists a new one, in which each trait is a positive and equivalent unit. Inasmuch as all our subsequent find-

TABLE 8

INTERTRIBAL G'S, PERCENTAGED, FOR TESSMAN'S 34 NORTHEAST PERUVIAN TRIBES, ON BASIS OF TRAIT LIST IN TABLE 7[36]

(Blackface, G's 70 or over; Italics, G's 50–69)

		1	2	3	4	5	6	7	8	9	10	11	12	13	14	15	16	17	18	19	20	21	22	23	24	25	26	27	28	29	30	31	32	33	34	Mean
A	1 Uitoto		87	86	86	50	44	40	48	49	48	28	44	44	32	30	29	38	35	42	37	30	33	28	26	29	31	38	30	31	31	37	31	29	36	40
A	2 Okaina	87		86	90	41	38	33	42	48	48	24	33	42	27	29	29	32	33	33	37	30	28	25	22	28	32	38	30	36	31	30	30	30	39	38
A	3 Muinane	86	86		83	36	37	35	41	48	48	26	44	42	35	30	37	36	38	46	40	34	28	28	33	34	29	35	35	35	32	33	30	37	37	39
A	4 Bora	86	90	83		41	30	35	43	39	38	24	36	42	30	26	37	33	33	40	31	27	23	23	26	27	31	29	33	29	33	27	25	27	35	36
Ba	5 Pioché	50	41	36	41		57	60	59	52	55	54	52	56	40	46	42	48	47	54	55	44	45	50	50	47	54	48	43	48	43					48
Ba	6 Seabela	44	38	37	30	57		57	60	50	60	60	42	60	53	63	43	48	45	43	49	42	35	41	48	47	33	37	43	38	38	40				43
Ba	7 Záparo	40	33	35	35	60	57		61	50	51	42	44	44	53	60	40	46	45	56	52	39	48	41	45	46	42	43	48	43	40	43				45
Bb	8 Tikuna	48	42	41	43	59	48	61		61	51	61	34	39	47	48	42	38	37	42	47	57	67	51	49	42	63	42	45	40	41	44			46	46
Bb	9 Yagua	49	48	48	39	52	50	50	61		57	49	47	41	31	37	36	39	41	51	51	51	39	43	41	46	33									45
Bb	10 Koto	48	48	48	38	55	60	51	51	57		38	48	48	49	30	32	46	45	47	49	50	53	53	43	47	51	54	52	40						47
Bb1	11 Iquitos	28	24	26	24	53	44	42	45	49	38		53	44	45	43	36	44	43	38	38	35	40	47	35	39	41	38	35	43	36					40
C	12 Auishiri	44	33	44	36	52	60	44	34	47	48	53		51	60	42	44	42	36	29	47	28	24	37	39	48	30	39	35	38	43				41	41
C	13 Mayoruna	44	42	42	42	56	60	44	39	41	48	44	51		58	28	34	37	26	27	23	21	17	28	34	28	25	24	31	24	24	35			33	33
C	14 Amahuaca	32	27	30	30	40	53	43	47	31	49	45	60	58		51	49	40	41	37	37	33	29	31	29	34	35	40	42	38	36	42	59	52	40	40
D	15 Nokaman	30	29	30	26	46	63	60	48	37	30	43	42	28	51		67	34	35	33	51	64	54	46	47	51	51	43	61	60	46	61				44
D	16 Kaschibo	29	29	37	37	42	43	40	42	36	32	36	44	34	49	67		39	36	42	38	37	35	39	42	46	39	60	44	49	67				40	40
E	17 Jivaro	38	32	36	33	48	48	46	38	39	46	44	42	37	40	34	39		69	67	56	45	43	42	50	60	42	41	49	43	52	46	39	45	45	45
Fd	18 Kandoshi	35	33	38	33	47	43	45	37	41	45	44	36	26	41	35	36	69		75	55	59	52	49	60	63	56	50	59	58	50	58			18	49
Fd	19 Andoa	42	45	46	40	54	46	39	42	51	47	38	34	37	33	67	75	67	75		62	62	63	67	63	64	65	61	66	72	56	79	41		53	53
Fe	20 Quijos	37	37	40	31	55	49	48	47	46	49	38	38	37	37	51	61	56	55	62		63	61	64	64	64	64	55	61	64	54	65	42	51	20	51
Fa	21 Chayahuita	30	30	34	27	44	42	57	44	49	50	37	23	33	33	51	54	63	59	62	63		81	84	80	71	60	67	60	54	61	42	51	21		51
Fa	22 Munichi	33	28	28	27	59	49	48	52	49	54	32	07	29	29	64	32	56	59	63	77	81		83	71	75	67	74	70	75	44	56	22			56
Fa	23 Jevero	28	25	28	23	44	35	57	45	43	36	28	31	46	43	52	62	63	61	84	81	89	68	71	69	74	55	65	39	51	23					51
Fa	24 Aguano	26	22	21	21	45	41	21	56	46	60	35	24	17	29	47	35	42	49	57	64	80	83	82	70	64	68	76	53	67	46	51	24			51
Fa	25 Chamicuro	29	28	33	26	50	39	45	53	51	47	46	40	37	34	51	50	59	63	68	82	71	70	67	68	62	68	55	62	45	55	25				55
Fa	26 Ssimaku	31	32	34	27	48	45	51	53	47	39	41	39	46	60	64	71	71	70	71	68	59	69	71	58	63	45	55	26					55
Fa1	27 Omurana	38	38	43	31	47	47	45	51	35	48	40	45	53	63	64	64	60	62	54	62	68	64	53	60	69	46	53	27					53
Fa2	28 Lamisto	30	31	29	29	51	39	48	46	42	46	43	38	28	42	48	50	56	67	68	68	68	60	58	62	65	71	53	51	28					51
Fb	29 Omagua	31	36	35	45	33	42	53	39	43	39	30	25	38	52	46	42	50	61	55	74	67	61	59	64	60	77	72	65	71	66	51	29			51
Fb	30 Kokama	31	30	35	29	54	37	49	42	43	41	30	36	49	41	60	56	61	66	74	76	69	52	58	77	73	68	72	47	51	30					51
Fb	31 Yameo	37	32	33	27	48	43	45	45	53	38	39	38	31	49	59	72	57	67	68	75	71	80	72	73	64	73	53	54	31					54
Fb	32 Chama	31	30	33	25	43	38	55	61	43	49	56	61	50	43	49	56	53	52	60	55	66	68	64	73	68	49	32							49
Fb	33 Panobo	29	30	30	27	48	44	53	78	65	75	65	68	63	69	71	67	68	63	69	71	72	73	73	48	55	33								55
Fb1	34 Kampa	36	39	37	35	43	40	44	33	40	36	43	59	46	49	46	46	50	42	42	39	46	45	45	46	56	47	58	48			44				44
	Mean	40	38	39	36	48	43	45	46	45	47	40	41	33	40	44	40	45	49	53	51	51	56	51	51	55	55	53	51	51	51	54	49	55	44	
		1	2	3	4	5	6	7	8	9	10	11	12	13	14	15	16	17	18	19	20	21	22	23	24	25	26	27	28	29	30	31	32	33	34	

TABLE 9

CONDENSATION OF TABLE 8 TO GROUP MEANS

Highest values for each group (read horizontally) in blackface;
unusually low ones in italics

	A	Ba	Bb	C	D	E	Fd	Fc	Fa	Fa1	Fa2	Fb	Fb1
A	85	38	39[38]	36	29	35	39	36	28	38	30	31	37
Ba	38	56	49[39]	46	44	50	47	51	46	48	45	43	43
Bb	39[38]	49[39]	49[40]	44[41]	40	40	46	45	47	46	46	44	38
C	36	46	44[41]	54	42	39	36	33	28	41	36	34	46
D	29	44	40	42	67	37	34	45	44	43	46	48	48
E	35	50	40	39	37	—[42]	68	56	47	53	50	45	46
Fd	39	47	46	36	34	68	75	59	60	64	61	59	46
Fc	36	51	45	33	45	56	59	—	63	64	53	58	42
Fa	28	46	47	28	44	47	60	63	77	63	67	66	44
Fa1	38	48	46	41	43	53	64	64	63	—	68	65	46
Fa2	30	45	46	36	46	50	61	53	67	68	—	61	53
Fb	31	43	44	34	48	45	59	58	66	65	61	70	52
Fb1	37	43	38	46	48	46	46	42	44	46	53	52	—

ings depend on this list, we give it here, as table 7.[36]

From this list we have calculated but one set of intertribal values, those for $G = c/\sqrt{ab}$, because of the labor of computing more than 500 relations anew for other measures. In the case of this Peruvian material, accordingly, we are comparing not measures among themselves, but a numerical result by a single one of our formulas against Tessmann's direct interpretations. The 561 G's are given in table 8.[37]

With so many tribes involved in comparison, it is rather expectable that some will fall on or near the borderline of such groups as eventuate, and participate in several. While some groups emerge well defined, others are clear only as to their nucleus, their limits in terms of included tribes being somewhat ambiguous.

Another difficulty is that a complete set of intertribal rankings becomes cumbersome to follow. We have indeed decided on the grouping of the tribes by this principle of ranking, as in the previous cases. But it seems unnecessary to give 34 series each of 33 rankings, as a merely more convenient rearrangement of table 8. Instead we have ordered the sequence of tribes in this table so as to depart from the geo-

graphical sequence mostly followed by Tessmann, and instead to collocate, so far as possible, tribes which show the highest G values among each other. This means that the highest ranking values should in general come along or close to the diagonal which bisects the table. In general, they do fall there, and thus evidence that our groupings are not random or arbitrary. Further to emphasize the inherent organization of the results, we have put all above-average G values in italic type, and high values in blackface. Finally, the same letter has been preposed to the name of each of the tribes seeming to compose a natural group. Thus the first four tribes are preceded by A, and form group A; the next 7 by B, and constitute subgroups a, b, and $b1$ of B; and so on.

A condensation for greater convenience is given in table 9, which contains only the means of intergroup and intra-group G values. Thus the 6 values of 87, 80, 86, 90, 86, 83 which the four A tribes show with each other in the large table, are here reduced to the single figure 85, their mean. The 12 values expressing the G relation of the same four tribes with the three of group Ba, are similarly reduced to their average of 39, and so forth.

Two groups emerge as indubitable from tables 8 and 9: four tribes on the northeastern border of the area considered (A); and about 17 (F) that are situated in all parts except the north (see map, fig. 5). About a third of the F tribes, on the lower Huallaga and Marañon, constitute a natural unit (Fa) with high G's among themselves; another third a unit (Fb) on the Ucayali; the others are somewhat doubtfully inclusible in these two (Fa1, Fa2, Fb1), or form smaller subgroups (Fc, Fd) to the northwest of the others. The strength of group F is its massiveness; of A, its distinctness. A is easily the most differentiated of all the groups; the Fa and Fb nuclei have the next highest internal G's.

An interesting group is C, consisting of three widely separated tribes, Auishiri, Mayoruna, and Amahuaca (fig. 5). Their interrelation values are low—51, 60, 52, mean 54—but those with other groups and subgroups are lower still, the means ranging from 46 to only 28. Each has a few G's above 50 with neighboring tribes; but these are scattering. In view of the geographical separation of these three tribes, even the moderate G's which they possess with each other compel the acceptance of these as significant of a genuine but probably old and partly overlaid connection between them.

The Iquitos, who adjoin the Auishiri, could be reckoned with this group, but equally with Bb. The footnotes to table 9 show the relation with C.

Another geographically broken group, D, consists of two southern tribes, the Kashibo and Nokaman.

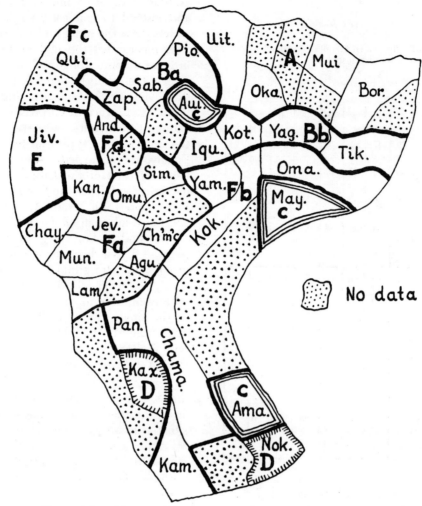

Fig. 5. Tribes of Northeastern Peru (schematic after Tessmann), showing
groups of related tribes (according to Driver and Kroeber).

Their G with each other is 67; all other values are
below 52, except for 61 between Nokamán and near-
by Chama. The means of D G's with other groups
range from 30 to 48.

The Jívaro of the western border stand well by
themselves (E). They seem really to be an assemblage of tribes with an unusually large aggregate
territory. Their relations are definitely highest with
two F tribes, Kandoshi, 69, and Andoa, 67, who constitute subgroup Fd and border on their east; next
with Quijos (Fc), Munichi (Fa), and Záparo (B)—
all 56 and none in geographical contact. With the
rest of F, E relations are only moderate. This localization of Jívaro connections probably justifies their
being kept in a separate group, which may be con-
strued as having exchanged influences with certain
of the nearer tribes of F, and in a secondary degree
of B. On the other hand, no great violence would be
done to the facts by considering the Jívaro a subgroup (Fe) of F.

The remaining seven tribes live in two areas: the
Pioché, Sabela, Záparo (Ba) on the Napo, and the
Iquitos, Koto, Yagua, Tikuna (Bb) in line along the
main Amazonas. The Napo (Ba) tribes show the
higher internal G's, mean 56, versus 49 for Bb, or
52 if Iquitos (Bb1) is excluded and reckoned in C.
Their relationship with each other (Ba-Bb) has a mean
G of 50; means with other groups range from 39
to 48.[43] The culture of both B subgroups is thus
either unusually generalized or pretty well mixed.
But they do not fit into any other groups. Their relationship is no closer to C or D than to F. The principal reason for keeping them distinct from each
other is their geographical separateness. . . .

It will be seen that three cultures, A, E, and F, can
be positively determined among the 34 tribes considered. The distinctiveness of these is in the order of
mention. Cultures A and E also seem the richest or
"highest"; F is the most widely distributed, at least
in Northeast Peru. Quantitative trait interrelations

and consideration of the nature of the traits coincide in pointing to these conclusions.

For the B, C, and D group tribes, the case is otherwise. Their trait-count interrelations suggest the three groups, though not compellingly; but consideration of specific culture traits shows such to be either wanting (B) or to consist of absences of traits found elsewhere (C, D). Groups C and D therefore may be tribes whose cultures have recently suffered losses due to ethnic misfortunes. Group B consists of a string of tribes situated like a barrier between the A and F tribes, giving no marked evidences of actual impoverishment, but possessing a definitely colorless, uncharacteristic culture. If this is in origin a blend of cultures A and F, it is a weak mixture, with few characteristic traits of either of these.

Comparison with Tessmann's Results

We are now in a position to compare our classification with Tessmann's. Although his organization of results continues along lines of the six hypothetical cultures which he assumes to begin with, it is possible to condense his numerical data in such a way as to show groupings of tribes as well. We have done this in table 10, in which his "cultures" are shown in vertical columns, while the tribal data are given

TABLE 10

TOTALS OF TESSMANN'S 212 TABULATED POSITIVE TRAITS (PRESENCES) DISTRIBUTED ACCORDING TO HIS ASSUMED CULTURES (COLUMNS) AND THE INDICATED GROUPS OF RELATED TRIBES (HORIZONTALS)

	Northern culture 35 traits	Old culture 57 traits	Sub-Andean culture 34 traits	Amazonian culture 61 traits	West Amazon subculture 16 traits	Ucayali subculture 9 traits	Total traits for tribe
(Northern Group=our A)							
Uitoto	**30**	*23*	2	2	1	–	58
Okáina	**30**	14	2	4	–	–	51
Muinane	**28**	*20*	2	5	1	1	58
Bora	**29**	*20*	2	6	2	–	59
("Old"Group=Ba, Bb, C, D)							
(Ba)							
Pioché	6	*22*	4	9	1	–	43
Sabela	–	18	2	1	–	–	21
Záparo	1	20	7	-10	2	–	40
(Bb)							
Iquitos	1	*31*	2	12	2	–	49
Koto	4	*23*	–	8	1	1	38
Yagua	5	*22*	1	6	1	–	36
Tikuna	4	14	–	*14*	4	1	37
(C)							
Auishiri	2	*40*	2	7	–	–	51
Mayoruna	1	**52**	–	3	1	–	55
Amahuaka	–	*35*	–	8	–	5	48
(D)							
Kashibo	2	24	2	14	3	4	50
Nokamán	–	24	–	14	4	7	49
(Sub-Andean Group=E)							
Jívaro	–	13	**33**	9	2	1	58
Kandoshi	–	14	11	10	4	–	41
Andoa	2	5	6	7	–	–	20
(Amazonian Group=F, Fb)							
Quijos	2	13	5	*15*	3	1	39
Munichi	–	–	–	11	3	1	15
Kokama	–	4	–	**33**	4	1	42
Yameo	2	6	2	27	4	1	42
Omagua	2	3	–	**59**	–	1	65
Lamisto	1	13	3	18	2	–	37
Pánobo	–	7	3	27	1	2	40
(West Amazon Subgroup=Fa)							
Jebero	–	4	1	**30**	**16**	1	52
Chayahuita	–	7	1	*22*	10	1	42
Chamicuro	–	9	2	19	8	–	39
Aguano	–	2	2	*22*	10	1	38
Omurana	1	16	2	13	5	2	40
Simaku	–	11	1	18	8	–	39
(Ucayali Subgroup=Fb)							
Chama	–	18	2	**27**	–	**10**	57
Kampa	4	13	4	20	1	6	49

Blackface and *italic* figures are the highest numbers in the columns representing Tessmann's putative cultures. They are not necessarily the highest numbers in the horizontal lines referring to tribes.

Tessmann's "half" traits have been included in the additions for this table, but odd halves have been dropped from the figures shown.

23

in horizontal lines with those tribes on adjacent lines whose participation in each "culture" is the greatest. This arrangement yields groups of similar tribes, to which we have affixed Tessmann's names for the "cultures" most characteristic of them, adding also our letter designations.

It is clear that the two classifications on the whole agree rather well. The greatest difference is that Tessmann unites Ba, Bb, C, and D into a single "Alt-kultur" group; although even within this our C tribes form a distinct sub-unit with the highest proportion of traits characteristic of the group.[44] Our Ba is marked off as another sub-group by higher participation in Tessmann's "Sub-Andean culture"; D, by traits characteristic of the Amazonian and Ucayali cultures.

Our one-tribe (Jívaro) group E Tessmann would probably enlarge by inclusion of the two Fd tribes (Kandoshi, Andoa); but since we admit E as possibly being Fe, the difference is greater in appearance than in fact.

Within the great F group, Tessmann's West Amazon corresponds nearly to Fa, Ucayali to the southern part of Fb, Amazon to northern Fb, Fc, and a couple of tribes of Fa.

Most of these differences are analogous to those common in taxonomy, as when a family is elevated into a new order by another student, or several families are reduced to genera of one family. That is to say, they represent legitimate differences of opinion on certain points, while the majority of phenomena are classified alike.

We admit that Tessmann did not draw up a summary like table 10 and perhaps would repudiate it. But it seems a perfectly proper procedure to convert his arbitrary "culture families" (assemblages of culture traits), substantiated chiefly by philosophical argument about their inner coherence, into groups of actually existing tribes which resemble each other in the degree in which they share in each other's culture. If his cultures are invalid, of course our table 10 tribal groupings derived from them also fall. But so far as his cultures are real, our conversion of them into their best expression in tribe-group terms is also fair. Now the fact emerges that while in our own computations and classification we have completely disregarded his assumed original "culture aggregations," we arrive at tribal culture groupings rather strikingly similar to those inferable from his trait distributions when these are viewed from the tribal angle. Our difference of opinion with Tessmann, then, is not over his implicit conclusions, which we construe as being nearly the same as ours, as soon as they are inductively formulated, but over the fact that he has refrained from drawing inductive

conclusions and instead has operated with assumptions as to culture entities which remain hypothetical We feel that he is a good ethnologist in dealing with concrete ethnological data in spite of preferring to philosophize about them. The fundamental concord of his implied tribal groupings with our own, obviously suggests that the "cultures" from which his implicit groups are derived by us also rest at least partly on reality. If the cultures were nonsensical, the tribal groupings based on them would presumably also be nonsensical in terms of our trait-count coefficient, geography, or anything else objective. We discard the Tessmann "cultures" as entities merely because we do not know how he arrived at them and do not understand the higher philosophy with which he justifies them. We believe that an inductive attempt to portray the organization of phenomena as they exist in the world today is preferable to, or certainly should precede, an intuitional leap at a reconstruction of how they were organized formerly or are organized of inherent necessity. We cast no slurs upon Tessmann's intuitional faculties, which we infer to be excellent; but his insistence on giving them precedence is scarcely good scientific method.

The upshot of this discussion is twofold. First, that the ethnologist who knows his facts and has absorbed the feel of them can come to essentially sound inferences about them without technical devices. Second, that if he publishes his facts in full and their specific occurrences in detail, the trait-count method and a simple statistical treatment will allow others to reach objectively founded general interpretations even if the facts are presented in a wrapping of assumptions or reconstructions.

Conclusions

Our findings may be summarized thus:

In culture history studies, statistical treatment by the method of presence and absence of unit traits is ancillary to the non-statistical methods in use. Statistical results can never be better than the data, whose value depends on the ethnological competence with which they are collected and analyzed.

To a large extent trait-count computations merely corroborate the ordinary ethnological findings made by students who know their field comparatively. This is true of Linton, Spier, Kroeber, and Tessmann for Polynesia, the Plains Sun dance, the Northwest Coast, and Peru.

On the other hand, statistical treatment usually expresses results more precisely and definitely. In all cases examined it also indicates greater or less corrections of the ethnological interpretations. These corrections we believe to be valid.

The several measures empirically tested by us all yield expressions of the relationship of tribal or national cultures in terms of culture traits or elements. Each tribal culture is compared with every other one; conclusions are drawn primarily by the ranking of the numerical values obtained, and then by the grouping of these rankings. All the measures used by us consist of fractions having as numerator c, the number of traits common to the two tribes in question. They differ in denominator. The simplest measure is $c/a=P$, a being the total traits known from tribe A. This of course yields two values, c/a for tribe A and c/b for tribe B, and is therefore awkward in comparisons between large series of tribes. A and G are the arithmetical and geometrical means of Pa and Pb: $A=(c/a+c/b)/2$; $G=c/\sqrt{a\cdot b}$. A fourth measure is $T=c/a+b-c)$, whose denominator is the total number of traits occurring among the two tribes in question. In application, these four measures, especially the last three, give values which differ absolutely, but which rank and group the examined tribes in very similar order.

E, the plus or minus excess of positive and negative agreements over disagreements of traits, seems to give less coherent results than A, G, and T, that is, a less consistent scheme of rankings, especially when the data do not distinguish absence of knowledge from known absence of traits. Its derivative P merely expresses the degree to which low E values are likely to be non-significant.

A, G, and T are simple formulae allowing of rapid calculation, and are logically intelligible as measures without knowledge of statistical theory. This statement does not quite hold for G, in that it substitutes the geometric for the arithmetic mean; but granted this substitution, it is equally intelligible. G is of further interest in that it has the same formula as one form of the coefficient of correlation, r.

How far negative agreements, that is, common absences of traits, should be given equal weight with positive ones, is an important theoretical question to which we give no definitive answer. It would seem that within the limits of a true natural group or field, which would ordinarily be a small one, absences should be as significant as presences; but that in proportion as the total group is not an intrinsically valid one, and this would tend to hold increasingly with increase of its size, absences may be misleading. We know, however, of no positive criterion of distinction.

For statistical purposes, nearly all ethnological data seem to be faulty, though in varying degree, in that they incline to name chiefly occurrences, leaving it to be doubtfully inferred whether unnamed traits are known to be absent or have not been considered or inquired into. But fundamentally this defect is about as serious in nonstatistical as in statistical comparative ethnology. It is merely less obtrusive.

Notes

1. To Driver are due the original concept of this essay and the calculations, to Kroeber the first draft of its formulation; other aspects of the work were performed jointly.

2. Tylor, On a Method of Investigating the Development of Institutions, RAI-J 18:245-269, 1889. Hobhouse, Wheeler, and Ginsburg, The Material Culture and Social Institutions of the Simpler Peoples: An Essay in Correlation, 1915.

3. For instance, if matrilineate and avoidance have been transmitted as an already established association or "complex" from one people to several others, this should obviously be counted as only one case of association or "adhesion," because the association in tribes b, c, d, e . . . . is derived from, and dependent upon, that in tribe a. Tylor however counted a, b, c, d, e . . . . as so many separate cases. Baptism and confession are associated in Italy, Spain, France because these countries have accepted Christianity, in which these two traits had early "adhered" or become associated. As regards the problem of inherent necessity or tendency toward association, Christianity must count as one case, not these three or more Christian nations as so many cases.

4. Within the limits of ordinary logic or common sense. Essential parts of a trait cannot of course be counted as separate traits: the stern of a canoe, the string of a bow, etc. Even the bow and arrow is a single trait until there is question of an arrow-less bow. Then we have two traits, the pellet bow and

arrow bow. Similarly, while the sinew backing of a bow cannot occur by itself, we legitimately distinguish self-bows and sinew-backed bows; and so, single-curved and recurved bows, radically and tangentially feathered arrows, canoes with blunt, round, or sharp sterns, etc.

5. Thus baptism occurs without confession in certain Christian sects or denominations.

6. The assumption seems to underlie the work of students as diverse in their methods as Boas, Ratzel, Rivers, Elliot-Smith, Wissler, Graebner, Schmidt, Lowie, Dixon, Rivet, etc.

7. A New Objective Method for Showing Special Relationships, AA 28: 585-604, 1926.

8. The Material Culture of the Marquesas Islands, B. P. Bishop Mus., Mem. 8, no. 3, 1923 (List, pp. 449-457).

9. The culture traits entering into each relationship are distributed in four "cells" containing respectively the number of traits common to the two cultures, present in the first only, present in the second only, absent from both.

10. W. D. Wallis, Probability and the Diffusion of Culture Traits, AA 30: 94-106, 1928. See especially the argument (p. 105) from a hypothetical example of New York and Hopi Indians both lacking Eskimo traits. Wallis' attitude seems to spring from a fear that once statistics are applied to culture, all

common sense will be abandoned and a juggernaut of statistical method run blindly over the field and leave it strewn only with nonsensical delusions.

11. Quantitative Method in Ethnography, AA 30: 295-310, 1928; see p. 304.

12. A slight asymmetry of data results from Linton's original study having been concerned primarily not with Polynesia as such, but with the position of the Marquesas within Polynesia. This is why there are no unreported traits for Marquesas. A large proportion of the gaps (Clements' "x" in his basic table of unit traits) are accounted for by the absence of the paper mulberry and consequently of tapa in New Zealand (11 traits reckoned as "x" when they might better have been counted "o"—which would reduce the New Zealand x's from 22 to 11); and 28 of the 41 Tongan x's due to lack of cited information (really lack of occurrence?) on details of human figure representation in art.

13. Plains Indian Tribal Correlations with Sun Dance Data, AA 33: 216-227, 1931.

14. The Sun Dance of the Plains Indians: Its Development and Diffusion, AMNH-AP 16: 451-527, 1921.

15. AA 30: 100, 104, 1928.

16. It is discussed as to its theoretical or empirical validity by T. L. Kelley, Statistical Method, 190, 1924; G. H. Thompson, Brit. Jour. Psychol., 8:275, 1916; and R. Pearl, Introduction to Medical Biometry and Statistics, 366 ff., 1930.

16a. [Kroeber wrote this section and was confused about c. $\frac{c}{\sqrt{a \cdot b}}$ is the factor formula, where c is the number of common factors, a the number in variable a, b the number in variable b, e.g.

$$\begin{array}{cc} a & b \\ \boxed{\begin{array}{ccc} 0 & 0 & 0 \end{array}}\begin{array}{cc} 0 & 0 \end{array}\begin{array}{cc} 0 & 0 \end{array} \\ 1 \ 2 \ 3 \ \ 4 \ 5 \ \ 6 \ 7 \end{array}$$

Thus if seven coins were tossed a large number of times (say 1,000), and the heads of the first five added up for a score on variable a, and the heads of coins 4, 5, 6, 7 added up for a score on variable b, the Pearsonian linear r for interval scales would be

$$\frac{c}{\sqrt{a \cdot b}} = \frac{2}{\sqrt{5 \cdot 4}} \ .]$$

17. The formula can also be given as $c/(a+b+c)$, with a and b in this case denoting not the total number of traits occurring in A and B but the number of traits peculiar to A and B, that is found respectively in A and B but lacking in B and A.

17a. [Not included in this version.]

18. As cited, Bishop Mus. Mem. 8, no. 5, 1923: "Conclusions," pp. 458-467.

19. Linton, p. 458 seq. Clements, p. 604.

20. For instance, the Marquesas-New Zealand cultural unit cuts geographically across several other Polynesian inland groups.

21. All our computations in this table are based on Clements' trait list.

22. AMNH-AP 16:451-527, 1921.

23. Clements has added several supplementary traits from page 489 and elsewhere, bringing his total up to 92, as against 82 in Spier's basic lists (in spite of a footnote reference, p. 217,

as to intactness of Spier's list, which is obviously an oversight). We have retained Spier's original 82 to avoid printing a new but only slightly different basic list of traits.

24. We computed but then omitted the various values for the Northern Cheyenne, because their ceremony is probably substantially identical with that of the Southern Cheyenne, though much less completely reported. All 17 of its known traits recur among the 47 of the southern divisions; and there is nothing to show that it lacks any considerable proportion of the other 30. The division of the Cheyenne into two "tribes" is recent—probably as late as that of the Arapaho into a northern and a southern group. We have accounts of both the Northern and Southern Arapaho Sun dances, and these, although not identical, are so nearly alike that Spier wisely listed them as one. We prefer to consider the two Cheyenne ceremonies as one until there is evidence to the contrary. The inclusion of the Northern rump complicates and tends to distort the total picture.

25. AA 33:220, 1931.

25a. [Table 3 has been excised from this version.]

26. Based on Mooney's map for 1832, BAE-R 17, pl. 57. This delimits areas, as the Wissler-Spier map does not. The Cheyenne are shown as still a unit. We have put the "Canadian" Dakota where presumably most of them came from—the Wahpeton territory.

27. BAE-R 17, pt. 1, 1898.

28. The fairly high relation between Plains Ojibwa and Canadian Dakota may be a real relation due to recent assimilation subsequent to the movement of these Dakota out of the United States; or an accident of low figures (8) on both sides.

29. Op. cit., "Historical Relations," 491-499.

30. AA 31:222, 1929.

31. Die Indianer Nordost-Perus: Grundlegende Forschungen fur eine Systematische Kulturkunde. Hamburg, 1930.

32. Pp. 656, 691, 715, 729, 751, 775; cartograms 39-42.

33. [Our figures are in error. There are 209 traits and 34 tribes. Thus there are 7,106 trait occurrences of present, absent, unknown.]

34. This renders his material unusually eligible for calculation of coefficients involving known common absences.

35. So that presence of a trait is indicated by an absence of the negative trait.

36. [Table 7 has been excised from this version.]

37. [Table 8 is retained, even though the trait list is not reproduced here.]

38. 43 Without Iquitos.

39. 50 Without Iquitos.

40. 51 Without Iquitos.

41. 42 Without Iquitos.

42. [The dashes—are 1.00 self-relationships of single tribes.]

43. For groups of several tribes. B shows mean G of 51 with Fc (Quijos only) and 50 with E (Jívaro only).

44. With Iquitos, doubtful between Bb and C, next.

3. Geographical-Historical *Versus* Psycho-Functional Explanations of Kin Avoidances*

Harold E. Driver

Since Tylor's time, ethnologists have been aware of the difficulties of giving acceptable explanations for geographical distributions and correlations of data among non-literate ethnic units with little or no documented history. Tylor ran the gamut from an extreme psycho-functional-evolutionary explanation of kin avoidances and other aspects of social organization (1889) to an extreme diffusionist explanation of resemblances in lot games between the high cultures of Asia and the Aztecs of Mexico (1879:128, 1896:66). All major schools of thought dealt with this problem in the 1st half of the 20th century without reaching agreement in theories, methods, or conclusions.

A definite advance was Murdock's *Social Structure* (1949) which gave an explicit method for testing functional hypotheses and has had more impact on cross-cultural studies of social orgnization than any other work. Whiting's and Child's *Child Training and Personality* (1935) is of comparable importance in the field of personality. Tax's (1955b) regional study of California Indian social organization set a new standard for comprehensive explanation of the area's complexities. He distinguished 3 sets of alternatives: (1) independent invention versus diffusion, (2) psychological versus sociological causation, (3) natural law versus historic accident. Driver's (1956) regional study of North American Indian social organization confirmed statistically the developmental cycles of Murdock and others with an adaptation of the Brainerd-Robinson (1951) seriation technique for determining time sequence from potsherds. Driver also discussed the role of geographical-historical in relation to functional-evolutionary factors, but offered no technique for measuring the former.

Naroll (1961, 1964) and Naroll and D'Andrade (1963) presented more specific techniques for demonstrating areal clusterings of cases, which they infer

are the result of geographical-historical factors. D'Andrade measured the relative importance of historical versus functional factors involved in producing a cross-cultural correlation. The authors concluded that both kinds of factors determine most cross-cultural correlations. They were able to demonstrate areal clustering from samples (Murdock 1957, Stephens 1962) in which many of the ethnic units were deliberately chosen for lack of geographical continuity and lack of common membership in the same language family. In short, using samples chosen to eliminate the most obvious examples of geographical-historical influence, they found nevertheless that these factors contributed a considerable share of the correlation values. Had they used large regional samples with maximum geographical continuity and paired adjacent ethnic units, the amount of geographical-historical influence on correlations would have been greater.

The present paper uses a more conventional and possibly simpler approach to the same problem and employs 277 ethnic units concentrated in North America alone. Culture area groupings and language family memberships are treated as variables for the 1st time and are correlated statistically with avoidances, in addition to forms of residence, descent, and kinship terminology.[1]

In the earliest discussion of kin avoidances worth citing, Tylor (1889) concentrated on the relation of marital residence customs to avoidances and found that where residence was matrilocal the husband avoided his wife's relatives more often than would be expected by chance. His explanation of these figures is summed up thus:

> As the husband has intruded himself among a family which is not his own, and into a house where he has no right, it seems not difficult to understand their marking the difference between him and themselves by treating him formally as a stranger (Tylor 1889:4).

He further showed that in matrilocal societies the wife avoids her husband's relatives less often than would be expected by chance and explained this by pointing out that she is not an intruder in their household and would have no reason to avoid them. His theory is supported by evidence from patrilocal societies where the wife avoids the husband's relatives more often than by chance, and the husband avoids the wife's relatives less often than by chance. Tylor arranged these figures in an evolutionary sequence, from matrilocal to matri-patrilocal to patrilocal residence. He explained the lower-than-chance frequency of the husband avoiding the wife's relatives in patrilocal societies as a survival from the earlier stage when residence was matrilocal.

*The author is indebted to Dean John W. Ashton and the Graduate School of Indiana University for a grant for library research and clerical assistance; to Gail Lerner for assisting in the library research; to Ora M. Engle and Garry Flint of the Indiana University Research Computing Center for computing correlations; and to June Helm, Edward Spicer, Evon Vogt, and Robert Weitlaner for giving guidance about negative evidence in Canada and Mexico.

Few anthropologist today would use unilinear evolution to explain such relationships, but the possible influence of residence on avoidance deserves, and has not received, adequate testing. Tylor did not list the tribes in his sample or the references from which he derived his data. Nor did he assemble all the figures he cited in 1 cross-classification table and apply a statistical test of significance to them; the correlation coefficient, mean square contingency coefficient, and chi-square were not known at that time.

Table 1 is my assemblage of Tylor's quantitative data. The figures represent the number of tribes or societies in each category; figures in parentheses are the values expected by chance. The chi-square is 17.2, and the probability of this or a higher value resulting from sampling error alone is .01, indicating a statistically significant relation between residence practices and avoidances. However, because chi-square should not be applied when the chance frequencies in any cell of a cross-classification table fall below 5, I have combined certain categories and eliminated others (Tables 2-5).

TABLE 1
TYLOR'S (1889) DATA ON AVOIDANCE AND RESIDENCE

KIN AVOIDANCE	RESIDENCE			TOTAL
	Matrilocal	Matri-Patrilocal	Patrilocal	
Husband avoids wife's kin	14 (8)	22 (19)	9 (18)	45
Both husband and wife avoid the other's kin	0 (2)	5 (3)	3 (3)	8
Wife avoids husband's kin	0 (2)	5 (5)	8 (5)	13
Neither avoids affinal kin	51 (53)	113 (118)	120 (114)	284
Total	65	145	140	350

Chi-square = 17.2   P = .01

TABLE 2
FIRST REARRANGEMENT OF TYLOR'S DATA

KIN AVOIDANCE	RESIDENCE			TOTAL
	Matrilocal	Matri-Patrilocal	Patrilocal	
Husband avoids wife's kin	14 (10)	27 (22)	12 (21)	53
Husband does *not* avoid wife's kin	51 (55)	118 (123)	128 (119)	297
Total	65	145	140	350

Chi-square = 7.9   P = .02

TABLE 3
SECOND REARRANGEMENT OF TYLOR'S DATA

KIN AVOIDANCE	RESIDENCE			TOTAL
	Matrilocal	Matri-Patrilocal	Patrilocal	
Husband avoids wife's kin	14 (10)	27 (22)	12 (21)	53
Neither avoids affinal kin	51 (55)	113 (118)	120 (111)	284
Total	65	140	132	337

Chi-square = 7.8   P = .02

TABLE 4
THIRD REARRANGEMENT OF TYLOR'S DATA

KIN AVOIDANCE	RESIDENCE		TOTAL
	Matrilocal	Patrilocal	
Husband avoids wife's kin	14 (10)	12 (21)	26
Husband does *not* avoid wife's kin	51 (55)	128 (119)	179
Total	65	140	205

Chi-square = 7.0   P = .01

TABLE 5
FOURTH REARRANGEMENT OF TYLOR'S DATA

KIN AVOIDANCE	RESIDENCE		TOTAL
	Matrilocal	Patrilocal	
Husband avoids wife's kin but wife does not avoid husband's	14 (10)	9 (13)	23
Wife avoids husband's kin but husband does not avoid wife's	0 (4)	8 (4)	8
Total	14	17	31

Chi-square = 9.0   P = .01

While Tylor's results are statistically significant, as Tables 1-5 show, they are less significant ethnologically because he failed to map or list his data. Galton (in Tylor 1889) challenged Tylor's evolutionary hypothesis on the grounds that occurrences of the phenomena must be historically independent to justify the assertion that changes in residence customs cause changes in avoidance behavior. Tylor failed to give a satisfactory answer, and not until this decade were specific techniques devised to meet this challenge (Naroll 1961, 1964; Naroll and D'Andrade 1963). Since Tylor's time there have been many mentions of avoidance behavior in anthropological literature. All of the relevant data would fill as many pages as this entire article, but the principal issues can be demonstrated with a few examples.

Frazer (1913: 77-81, 84, 95; 1911: vol. 3, 331-34) was among the 1st to explain avoidances between persons of opposite sex in terms of incest taboos. Such avoidances served to prevent incestuous relations, he said. Avoidances between persons of the same sex, he argued, were extensions of those of the opposite sex and, therefore, must have arisen at a later time. About the same time, Freud (1912: 30-33) presented essentially the same view with psychoanalytical trimmings. Neither Frazer nor Freud could explain the negative instances, the 50% or more of the world's peoples who did not practice avoidance.

Lowie (1920: 84-97, 101-7) gave by far the best discussion of avoidances up to that time. After citing positive and negative instances in all major areas of the world, he concluded that diffusion operating through intermarriage of neighboring peoples may explain multiple occurrences of avoidance in a continous area, but that independent origin must be assumed when such areas are separated by wide geographical gaps. He pointed out that the Shoshonean peoples of the Great Basin area lacked avoidances except for those in contact with the northern Plains region where avoidances were general and well developed. Although his logic was not explicit, he assumed that a single occurrence in the Shoshonean genetic language subfamily could not be a genetic heritage from some past time when proto-Shoshoneans possessed the taboo, especially when it occurred adjacent to Plains peoples. The only explanation left was diffusion by intermarriage. Lowie pointed out that the psychological explanations of Frazer and Freud failed to account for the negative instances, while Tylor's theory was able to account for some. Lowie lamented the fact that Tylor never mapped or listed his data.

Lowie was aware that most cases of avoidance were between relatives of opposite sex between whom sexual relations were forbidden. He pointed out that joking relationships prevailed between relatives, such as brothers-in-law and sisters-in-law, who were potential mates, but that all instances of avoidance and joking between relatives of the same sex need not have arisen by extension from cross-sex behavior. He postulated 2 different causal sequences resulting in convergent evolution of avoidance and joking syndromes in northeast Siberia and the Plains area of North America. Avoidances were not necessary to enforce incest taboos, he argued, because the many peoples lacking avoidances were as aware of incest taboos as those who had them. Lowie examined all 5 principal explanations of resemblances between peoples—*universality, genetic heritage, diffusion, parallel development,* and *convergent development*—rejecting the 1st as applied to avoidances,

arguing that the 2nd could not explain the Shoshoni case, and applying the others to various regions and peoples. Finally, he made a functional plea for careful study of all avoidances and joking relationships between all relatives in a single society or continuous area in order to grasp the entire context within which each functions.

Murdock (1949:272-83) assembles and discusses data on kinship behavior for the 250 societies of his sample. Information on behavior is much less complete than on kinship terminology and kinship groups: it ranges from data on 137 societies for the behavior of a man and his mother-in-law to only 10 for the behavior of a man and his wife's sister's daughter. Nevertheless, the survey embraces 17 consanguineal relatives and 13 affinal relatives, the most comprehensive collection of material on the subject. Following Eggan (1937:76), Murdock observes that patterns of kinship behavior form a continuum from complete avoidance of speech and physical contact to extreme license or obligatory joking. He divides this continuum into 5 segments: avoidance or marked restraint; respect or reserve; informality or intimacy; joking or familiarity; license or extreme joking. The frequencies of these 5 kinds of behavior among the societies in his sample are tabled for each of the 30 relatives. He finds 78 societies where a man and his wife's mother avoid each other, 35 where a man and his son's wife practice avoidance, and 30 where brothers and sisters avoid each other. Frequencies of avoidance are lower for the other 27 relatives in the list. Frequencies of license or extreme joking are much lower than of avoidance, but are highest for a man and his wife's sister (18) and for a man and his brother's wife (16).

Murdock cautions that if incest were a sufficient explanation of avoidance we should anticipate a man's avoidance of his mother and daughter as well as the relatives mentioned above. In his relatively large sample, Murdock finds only 2 societies where a man avoids his daughter and none at all where he avoids his mother. Nevertheless, he accepts incest as a partial determiner of avoidance and divides societies into 2 principal types: those in which sexual prohibitions are (1) so strongly internalized in the consciences of the members that avoidance behavior is not required to prevent incest and (2) so weakly internalized that they must be bolstered with avoidance customs to prevent incestuous unions. This internalization theory is acceptable as a psychoanalytical hypothesis, but it has at present little scientific value because the amount of internalization has not been observed independently of the behaviors it is supposed to explain. Until someone devises an independent measure of internalization, e.g., physiological response to stimuli associated with incest, its empirical relation to the presence of avoidance customs is indeterminate.

Murdock's general conclusion is that no simple hypothesis can adequately account for all the observed variation in kinship behavior, that different explanations are probable for different relatives. Few scholars today would find any fault with this restrained view.

Stephens and D' Andrade (1962) cite Murdock's 1949 discussion and mistakenly say that brother-sister avoidance is more frequent than father-in-law-daughter-in-law. The reverse is true, although the difference is small. Their findings are based on 2 samples: a world-wide sample of 85 societies and a sample of 72 California societies. For the 1st time they arrange the specific acts of avoidance between a man and his mother-in-law, a man and his daughter-in-law, and a man and his sister in a Guttman scale as follows:

1. No avoidance rules.
2. Can't talk about sex.
3. Can't talk directly.
4. Can't eat together; can't look eye-to-eye: 1 of these avoidance rules present.
5. Can't eat together; can't look eye-to-eye: both of these avoidance rules present.

This scale is their measure of severity of avoidance.

Their incest-phobia hypothesis states that avoidances are motivated by fear of sexual contact between persons observing the incest taboo, and this incest fear is triggered by incestuous wishes. The formative events for incest-phobia do not begin at puberty or marriage, when avoidances normally commence, but in the sex attraction of parent and child of opposite sex in infancy and childhood. A long post partum taboo on sexual relations of parents (coupled with a long nursing period for the son) intensifies the son-to-mother sex attraction. This encourages the development of a phobic attitude toward incest. The phobia, in turn, contributes to the severity of kin avoidances. This theory is supported by 3 positive and significant correlations based on the world-wide sample: severity of mother-in-law-son-in-law avoidance and duration of post partum sex taboo; severity of father-in-law-daughter-in-law avoidance and duration of post partum sex taboo; and severity of brother-sister avoidance and duration of post partum sex taboo.

In their discussion of these focal avoidances and extensions. Stephens and D'Andrade (1962: 137-38) offer the following generalizations:

A boy ordinarily observes no kin-avoidances until he reaches sexual maturity. At this stage, if he assumes any avoidance relationships, he will avoid his real sister (provided she is also sexually mature). He may also avoid other persons, but these will include *only* other female consanguineal kin ("blood kin") of his own generation: female cousins, usually classifactory "sisters." If he does not avoid his sister, he will avoid no one . . . When the man marries he may assume more avoidance relationships (Or assume his first avoidance relationship if he is not already avoiding his sister)—he may avoid some of his wife's kin. If he avoids any of them he will avoid his mother-in-law. The mother-in-law avoidance will be equally or more severe than the avoidance of other affines (the wife's kin) . . .

Finally, when a girl marries she may avoid some of her husband's kin. If she avoids any of them she will avoid her husband's father (the man-to-son's wife avoidance). No other affine (husband's blood kin) will be more extremely avoided than he.

Stephens and D'Andrade generalize that the cross-sex relatives avoided rarely or not at all are different generation consanguineal kin: for a man these would be mother, grandmother, aunt, daughter, niece, granddaughter; for a woman they would be the male relatives in the same categories. These findings match Murdock's (1949: 277) and are apparently partly derived from his table of frequencies. Stephens and D'Andrade further note that cross-sex avoidances are more frequent than same-sex avoidances. Of the latter, a man and his father-in-law avoid each other more often than any other combination.

Stephens and D'Andrade found further that the 3 focal avoidances (man to wife's mother, man to son's wife, and man to sister) yield positive correlations with each other and collectively show a positive correlation with licentious (sexual) joking relationships. The latter correlation is unexpected a priori.

Correlations with social structure are reported. Avoidances, especially between a man and his wife's mother, correlate positively with unilineal kin groups. The severity of a man's avoidance of his son's wife is correlated with patrilineal but not with matrilineal descent. The authors anticipate and discover a correlation of this same avoidance with patrilocal residence. This is the only significant correlation of any of the 3 focal avoidances with a residence rule, but it agrees with Tylor's findings. It is thus apparent that Stephens and D'Andrade have carried their analysis of avoidance further than anyone else to date.

Native North American Correlations

The collection of the North American avoidance data in Table 6 was begun before the Stephens and D'Andrade study was published. These data are limited to parents-in-law and children-in-law, for

TABLE 6
Tribal Distribution of Data

Society	1	2	3	4	5	6	References
Western Arctic							
Aleut	Es	B	M	BM	I	o	Human Relations Area Files (HRAF).
Eskimo: Chugach	Es	B	P	L	E	a	Birket-Smith 1953; 1959:142.
Eskimo: N. Alaskan	Es	B	B	BC	I	o	Spencer 1959.
Eskimo: Nunamiut	Es	B	B	L	E	o	Pospisil and Laughlin 1963.
Eskimo: Nunivagmiut	Es	B	P	BC	I	ab cd	Lantis 1946:235.
Eskimo: St. Lawrence Is.	Es	P	P	BC	I	o	Hughes 1958.
Central and Eastern Arctic							
Eskimo: Baffinland	Es	B	B	?	E	o	Boas 1888; 1901–07.
Eskimo: Caribou	Es	B	P	BC	E	o	Rasmussen 1930.
Eskimo: Copper	Es	B	B	BM BC	E	o	HRAF.
Eskimo: E. Greenland	Es	B	P	?	E	o	Holm 1911; Thalbitzer 1917, 1921, 1941.
Eskimo: Mackenzie	Es	B	B	L	?	o	Ostermann 1942.
Eskimo: Polar	Es	B	B	BC	E	o	Kroeber 1899; Rasmussen 1908; Steensby 1910.
Eskimo: W. Greenland	Es	B	P	?	E	o	Birket-Smith 1924:392–427; Nansen 1893.
Yukon Sub-Arctic							
Ingalik	At	B	B	L	H	o	Osgood 1958:195–200.
Kutchin, Peel River	At	M	P	BC	I	o	Osgood 1936.
Kutchin, Yukon Drainage	At	M	P	L BM BC	H	o	Osgood 1936.
Nabesna	At	M	M	BC	I	o	McKennan 1959:118–19.
Tahltan	At	M	M	BM BC	C	a	Emmons 1911:99; Teit 1956:150.
Tanaina	At	M	P	BC	I	o	Osgood 1937:151.
Tsetsant	At	M	?	?	?	a	Jenness 1932:369.
Mackenzie Sub-Arctic							
Beaver	At	B	M	L	H	ab cd	Goddard 1916:221–22.
Carrier: N.W.	At	M	A	BM	I	o	Goldman 1940:333–89; Jenness 1943: 527.
Carrier: S.E.	At	B	P	L	H	o	Ray 1942:211, 214.
Chilcotin	At	B	P	L	H	o	Ray 1942:211, 214; Morice 1893.
Chipewyan	At	B	B	L	I	o	Birket-Smith 1930; Curtis 1928: Vol. 18: 148; MacNeish 1960:287.
Dogrib	At	B	B	L	H	o	Helm and Lurie 1961.
Hare	At	B	B	BC	I	o	MacNeish 1960:287.
Kaska: West	At	M	M	BM	C	a	Honigman 1949:124, 129–30; 1954:75, 77, 158.
Sekani	At	B	P	BC	H	?	Jenness 1937:1–82.
Slave	At	B	M	BC	H	o	Honigmann 1946:71; MacNeish 1960:287; Mason 1946:32.
Eastern Sub-Arctic							
Algonkin	Ag	P	P	BC	I	o	Speck 1915a; 1915b; 1929.
Cree: Eastern	Ag	B	P	BC	I	ac	Honigmann 1953; 1956:58–64; Skinner 1911:57, 72.
Cree: Western Wood	Ag	B	P	BC	I	a	Curtis 1907–30, Vol. 18:74.
Malecite	Ag	B	P	BC	EH	o	Mechling 1958–59; Smith 1957; Wallis and Wallis 1957.
Micmac	Ag	B	P	BM BC	E	o	Wallis and Wallis 1955:226–47.
Montagnais-Naskapi: Ft. George to N.W. River	Ag	B	B	BC	H	o	Flannery 1946:268; Hind 1863; Leacock 1954:34; Lips 1947a:421, 469; Speck 1918; 1927; 1935.
Montagnais-Naskapi: Great Whale R., Ungava, Barren Ground	Ag	B	P	BC	I	o	Flannery 1946:268; Strong 1929:281; Turner 1890.
Montagnais-Naskapi: Southwestern	Ag	B	P	BC	I	o	Speck 1918; 1923; 1927; 1928.
Ojibwa: Berens R.	Ag	P	P	BC	I	ad	Dunning 1959; Hallowell 1928:537; 1937; 1938.
Ojibwa: Parry Island	Ag	B	P	BC	I	o	Jenness 1935:99.
Ojibwa: Rainy R.	Ag	B	P	BC	I	ab cd	Landes 1937:11, 19; 1938:82.
Ottawa	Ag	P	P	BC	I	o	Kinietz 1940:246–283; Perrot 1911.
Penobscot	Ag	B	B	BC	E	o	Speck 1940:206; Vetromile 1866.
Northwest Coast							
Alsea	O	B	P	L	I	o	Barnett 1937:194; Drucker 1939.
Athapaskans: Chilula, Van Duzen, Mattole	At	B	P	BC	H	o	Driver 1939:346–48.

TABLE 6 (continued)

SOCIETY	1	2	3	4	5	6	REFERENCES
Athapaskans of Oregon (not Tolowa)	At	B	P	BC	I	o	Barnett 1937:194.
Bear River: California	At	B	P	BC	H	o	Nomland 1938:101.
Bella Bella	Wa	B	P	L	I	o	Drucker 1950:220, 222.
Bella Coola	Sa	B	P	L	H	o	McIlwraith 1948:399—400.
Chinook	O	B	P	L	H	o	Ray 1938:73, 128.
Comox	Sa	B	P	L	H	o	Barnett 1939:277.
Cowichan	Sa	B	P	L	H	o	Barnett 1939:277.
Eyak	O	M	A	BC	I	a	Birket-Smith and Laguna 1938.
Gitksan	O	M	A	BM	I	a	Drucker 1950:220, 222; Durlach 1928: 129; Garfield 1939.
Haida	O	M	A	BM	C	acd	Drucker 1950:220, 222; Murdock 1934; Swanton 1909:50—51.
Haisla	Wa	M	A	BM	I	o	Olson 1940:185; Drucker 1950:220, 222.
Homalco	Sa	B	P	L	H	o	Barnett 1939:277.
Hupa	At	B	P	BC	H	o	Driver 1939:346—48; Gifford 1922:259; Goldschmidt and Driver 1940; Kroeber 1925:132.
Karok	Ho	B	P	BC	H	o	Driver 1939:346—48; Gifford 1922:259; Kroeber 1925.
Klahuse	Sa	B	P	L	H	o	Barnett 1939:277.
Klallam	Sa	B	P	L	H	o	Gunther 1927:241, 260, 303.
Kwakiutl: Vancouver Island	Wa	B	P	L	H	o	Boas 1921:303, 778; Drucker 1950:220, 222.
Lummi	Sa	B	P	L	H	o	Stern 1934; Suttles 1954.
Nanaimo	Sa	B	P	L	H	o	Barnett 1939:277.
Nooksack	Sa	B	P	L	H	o	Elmendorf 1961.
Nootka	Wa	B	P	L	H	o	Drucker 1950:220, 222; 1951.
Pentlatch	Sa	B	P	L	H	o	Barnett 1939:277.
Puyallup-Nisqually	Sa	B	P	L	H	o	Elmendorf 1961; Smith 1940:33.
Quinault	Sa	B	P	L	H	o	Elmendorf 1961; Olson 1936.
Sanetch	Sa	B	P	L	H	o	Barnett 1939:277.
Sechelt	Sa	B	P	L	H	o	Barnett 1939:277.
Slaiamum	Sa	B	P	L	H	o	Barnett 1939:277.
Squamish	Sa	B	P	L	H	o	Barnett 1939:277; Elmendorf 1961.
Tillamook	Sa	B	P	L	H	o	Barnett 1937:194; Boas 1898, 1923; Spier 1930:303.
Tlingit	O	M	A	BM / BC	C	ab / cd	Drucker 1950:220, 222; Jones 1914:145; Krause 1956; Lowie 1917:91; Swanton 1908.
Tolowa	At	P	P	BC	I	o	Barnett 1937:194; Driver 1939:347—48; Drucker 1936:246—47; Gifford 1922:259.
Tsimshian	O	A	A	BM	I	a	Boas 1916:424—25; Drucker 1950:220, 222; Durlach 1928:129; Garfield 1939.
Twana	Sa	B	P	L	H	o	Elmendorf 1946; 1960:347—71.
Wikeno Kwakiutl	Wa	B	P	L	H	o	Drucker 1950:220, 222.
Wiyot	O	B	P	BC	EH	o	Driver 1939:346—48; Gifford 1922:259.
Xaihais	Wa	B	P	BM	I	o	Drucker 1950:220—22.
Yurok	O	B	P	L	H	o	Driver 1939:346—48; Gifford 1922:259; Kroeber 1925:29.

Plateau

Coeur d'Alene	Sa	B	P	BC	H	ad	Ray 1942:211, 214; Teit 1930:172.
Columbia	Sa	B	P	BC	H	o	Elmendorf 1961; Teit 1928.
Flathead	Sa	B	P	BC	H	o	Ray 1942:211, 214; Turney-High 1937: 56, 90, 92.
Kalispel	Sa	B	B	BC	H	o	Teit 1930:382.
Klamath	O	B	P	BC	H	o	Spier 1927; 1930:48, 303; Voegelin 1942: 132, 166.
Kutenai	O	B	B	BC	H	a	Chamberlain 1892; Ray 1942:211, 214; Sapir 1918; Turney-High 1941:144.
Lillooet	Sa	B	P	L	H	o	Ray 1942:211, 214; Teit 1906.
Modoc	O	B	P	BC	H	o	Gifford 1922; Ray 1963:82—94; Voegelin 1942:132, 166.
Musqueam	Sa	B	P	L	H	o	Elmendorf 1961.
Okanagan	Sa	B	B	BC	H	o	Cline et al. 1938; Teit 1930.
Sanpoil	Sa	B	P	BC	H	o	Ray 1933:141; 1942:211.
Shuswap	Sa	B	P	L	H	o	Ray 1942:211, 214; Teit 1909.
Spokan	Sa	B	P	BC	H	o	Teit 1930:382.
Takelma	O	B	P	BC	O	o	Sapir 1907:275.
Tenino	O	B	P	BC	H	o	Murdock 1958; Ray 1942.
Thompson	Sa	B	P	L	H	o	Ray 1942:211, 214; Teit 1900:323.
Wishram	O	B	P	BC	H	o	Spier and Sapir 1930:220.

California

Achomawi	Ho	B	P	BC	H	ad	Gifford 1922:259; Spier 1930:303; Voegelin 1942:132, 166.

TABLE 6 (continued)

SOCIETY	1	2	3	4	5	6	REFERENCES
Athapaskans: Sinkyone, Kato, Lassik, Wailaki	At	B	B	BC	H	ad	Driver 1939:346–48; Essene 1942:30,–31; Gifford 1922:259; Loeb 1932:94.
Atsugewi	Ho	B	P	BC	E	ad	Garth 1944; 1953:168–69; Voegelin 1942: 132, 166.
Chimariko	Ho	B	B	BC	E	o	Dixon 1910:301; Driver 1939:346–48.
Cupeno	UA	P	P	BC	I	o	Drucker 1937:27–28; Gifford 1922:259; Strong 1929:239.
Diegueno	Ho	P	P	BC	I	o	Drucker 1937:27–28; 1941:138; Gifford 1922:259; Spier 1923:310.
Kitanemuk	UA	B	P	BM	I	o	Harrington 1942:30, 31.
Luiseno	UA	P	P	BM BC	I	o	Drucker 1937:27–28; Gifford 1922:259.
Maidu, N.	CP	B	P	BC	I	ab cd	Dixon 1905:239–40; Gifford 1922:259; Loeb 1933:177; Spier 1930:303; Voegelin 1942:132, 166.
Maidu, S.	CP	B	P	BC	H	ad	Beals 1933:371, 375; Voegelin 1942:132, 166.
Miwok, Central	CP	P	P	BC	O	ad	Aginsky 1943:430; Gifford 1916:183; 1922:259; 1926b.
Miwok, Northern	CP	P	P	BC	O	ad	Aginsky 1943:430; Gifford 1922:259; 1926b.
Miwok, Southern	CP	P	P	BM	O	ad	Aginsky 1943:430; Gifford 1916:183; 1922; 1926b.
Mono, W.	UA	B	B	BM BC	H	ab cd	Aginsky 1943:430; Driver 1937:90; Gayton 1948:235; Gifford 1922:259; 1932b: 32, 33.
Patwin	CP	P	P	BM BC	O	ad	Gifford 1922:259; Kroeber 1932:272, 292.
Pomo, Central	Ho	B	B	BC	O	a	Gifford 1928b; Gifford and Kroeber 1937; Loeb 1926:284.
Pomo, East	Ho	B	M	BC	O	ab cd	Gifford 1922; 1926a: 321, 327; 1926b; Kroeber 1917b; Loeb 1926:284.
Pomo, North	Ho	B	B	BC	D	a	Gifford 1926a; Gifford and Kroeber 1937; Loeb 1926:284; Essene 1942:30–31.
Pomo, Southeast	Ho	B	B	BC	O	a	Gifford 1926a; Gifford and Kroeber 1937.
Pomo, Southwest	Ho	B	B	BC	H	o	Gifford and Kroeber 1937.
Salinan	Ho	P	P	?	?	ad	Gifford 1922:259; Harrington 1942:31.
Shasta	Ho	B	P	BC	I	o	Dixon 1907:462; Voegelin 1942:132, 166.
Sinkyone	At	B	B	L	H	a	Nomland 1935:159.
Tubatulabal	UA	B	P	BM BC	H	o	Driver 1937:90; Gifford 1922:259; Voegelin 1938:44.
Wappo	O	B	B	BC	C	ab d	Gifford 1922:259; Driver 1936:205, 209.
Wintu	CP	B	B	BC	OI	ad	Dubois 1935:55; Gifford 1922:259; Voegelin 1942:132, 166.
Wintum, Central (Nomlaki)	CP	P	P	BC	O	ad	Gifford 1922:259; Goldschmidt 1951: 323.
Yana	Ho	B	P	BM	E	o	Sapir and Spier 1943:273.
Yokuts, N.	CP	P	P	BM	O	ab cd	Aginsky 1943:430; Driver 1937:90; Gayton 1948:30, 167, 196, 235; Gifford 1922:259; Kroeber 1925:493.
Yokuts, S.	CP	B	B	BC	H	ab cd	Driver 1937:90; Gifford 1922:259; Kroeber 1925:493.
Yuki	O	B	B	BC	H	ab cd	Essene 1942:30–31; Foster 1944:184–85; Gifford 1922:259; Kroeber 1932:371; 1925:210, 215.
Yuki, Coast	O	B	B	L	H	a	Driver 1939:346–48; Gifford 1928a, 1939.
Yuki, Huchnom	O	B	P	BC	H	ad	Foster 1944:184–85.
Great Basin							
Cahuilla	UA	P	P	BC	I	o	Drucker 1937:27–28; Gifford 1922:259; Strong 1929:46.
Chemehuevi	UA	B	B	BC	H	o	Drucker 1937:27–28.
Kawaiisu	UA	B	B	BC BM	H	o	Gifford 1922:259; Driver 1937:90, 129.
Paiute, N. (northern half)	UA	B	B	BC	H	o	Kelley 1932:166; Lowie 1924:285; Stewart 1941:405.
Paiute, N. (Owens Valley)	UA	B	B	BC	H	ab cd	Gifford 1922:259; Steward 1933:295, 302; 1941:311–12.
Paiute, N. (southern half)	UA	B	B	BC	H	o	Lowie 1924:285; Steward 1933:303; Stewart 1941:405.
Paiute, S. (Kaibab)	UA	B	B	L	E	o	Lowie 1924:285; Stewart 1942.
Paiute, S. (Kaiparowits)	UA	B	B	L	H	o	Lowie 1924:285.
Paiute, S. (Shivwits)	UA	B	B	L	H	o	Drucker 1941:138; Lowie 1924:285; Stewart 1942.

TABLE 6 (continued)

SOCIETY	1	2	3	4	5	6	REFERENCES
Serrano	UA	B	P	BM BC	I	o	Gifford 1922:259; Strong 1929:17.
Shoshoni of California	UA	B	B	BC	E	o	Driver 1937:90; Steward 1938:57, 215.
Shoshoni, Hukundika	UA	B	B	BM	H	o	Hoebel 1939; Steward 1943:279, 337–38; Stewart 1942:297.
Shoshoni, Lemhi	UA	B	P	BC	EH	a	Lowie 1909:211; Steward 1933:303; 1943: 279, 337–38.
Shoshoni of Nevada	UA	B	B	BC	E	o	Steward 1938:57, 215; 1941:252, 311–12.
Ute, Moanunts	UA	B	M	BC	H	o	Stewart 1942:297–98.
Ute, Pahvant	UA	B	M	BC	H	o	Stewart 1942:297–98.
Ute, Tompanowots	UA	B	M	BC	H	o	Stewart 1942:297–98.
Ute, Uintah	UA	B	M	BC	H	o	Steward 1933:303.
Ute, Wemenuis	UA	B	M	BC	H	o	Gifford 1940:67.
Ute, Wimonuntci	UA	B	B	BC	H	o	Opler 1940; Stewart 1942:297–98.
Washo	Ho	B	B	BC	H	o	Freed 1960; Lowie 1939:308, 310; Stewart 1941:405.
Plains							
Arapaho	Ag	B	M	BM	H	ad	Eggan 1955:55, 75–81; Hilger 1952: 209–11; Kroeber 1902:10, 12; Michelson 1934:137–39.
Assiniboin	Sx	B	P	BM	I	ac d	Denig 1930:510; Lowie 1909:41.
Blackfoot	Ag	B	P	BM	IH	a	Wissler 1911:13.
Cheyenne	Ag	B	M	BM	H	a	Eggan 1955:55, 75–81; Grinnell 1923: 145.
Comanche	UA	B	B	BM	H	o	Gladwin 1948; Hoebel 1939; 1940:12; Linton 1935; Lowie 1917:91; 1924:285; Wallace and Hoebel 1952:123, 140–41.
Cree, Plains	Ag	B	P	BC	I	ac	Mandelbaum 1940:233; Skinner 1914:72.
Crow	Sx	M	P	BM	C	ac	Lowie 1912:213; 1917:91.
Gros Ventre	Ag	B	P	BM	H	ab cd	Flannery 1953:109; Kroeber 1907:180.
Kiowa	O	B	B	BM	H	ad	Lowie 1917:91–92; Methvin 1899:163 on; Mooney 1896:233.
Kiowa Apache	At	B	M	BM	H	ad	McAllister 1955:130–33.
Lipan	At	B	M	BM BC	H	o	Gifford 1940:67.
Sarsi	At	B	P	L	H	a	Curtis 1907–30, Vol. 18:108; Jenness 1938:22, 25; Lowie 1917:91.
Shoshoni, Wind River	UA	B	M	BM	H	o	Lowie 1924:285–86; Shimkin 1947:289–325.
Teton	Sx	B	P	BM	I	ad	Dorsey 1889:157; Hassrick 1944.
Ute, Mowataviwatsiu	UA	B	B	BC	H	o	Opler 1940; Stewart 1942:297–98.
Ute, Mowatci	UA	B	B	BC	H	o	Opler 1940; Stewart 1942:297–98.
Prairies							
Arikara	Cd	B	M	G	C	o	Ewers 1950; Lowie 1917:48; Macgowan 1942.
Fox	Ag	P	B	BC	O	o	Michelson 1927; 1930; Tax 1955a:258.
Hidatsa	Sx	M	M	BM	C	ac	Lowie 1917:36, 47–48, 91.
Illinois	Ag	P	P	BM	O	?	Hennepin 1903; Kinietz 1940; Morgan 1871.
Ioway	Sx	P	P	BM	O	ad	Skinner 1915a, 1926:251–52.
Kansa	Sx	P	P	BM	O	ad	Skinner 1915b:769, 771.
Kickapoo	Ag	P	B	BM BC	O	?	Morgan 1871; Ritzenthaler and Peterson 1956; Silverberg 1957.
Mandan	Sx	M	M	BM	C	a	Bowers 1950:26–33, 54–56; Lowie 1917: 91; Will and Spinden 1906:132.
Menomini	Ag	B	P	BM	O	ac	Hoffman 1893; Skinner 1913:20, 29.
Miami	Ag	P	B	BM	O	o	Kinietz 1940; Trowbridge 1938:45.
Ojibwa, Michigan, Saugenong	Ag	P	P	BC	I	o	James 1830:146.
Ojibwa, Wisc., Minn.	Ag	P	P	BC	I	o	Densmore 1929; Kohl 1860:273 on.
Omaha	Sx	P	B	BM	O	a cd	Fletcher and La Flesche 1906:324, 334; Lowie 1917:91–92.
Osage	Sx	P	P	BM	O	?	Dorsey 1885; La Flesche 1912, 1924; Morgan 1871; Swanton 1910.
Oto	Sx	P	P	BM	O	o	Curtis 1907–30, Vol. 19:227; Withman 1937.
Pawnee	Cd	B	M	G	C	o	Dorsey and Murie 1940; Hodge 1907–10:215; Hyde 1951; James 1823:vol. 1, 262 on; Lesser 1930; Lounsbury 1956: 158–94.
Ponca	Sx	P	TP	BM	O	a	Fletcher and La Flesche 1906; Lowie 1917: 91; Morgan 1871.
Potawatomi	Ag	P	P	BC	I	a	Deale 1958; Skinner 1924–27:35, 36.

TABLE 6 (continued)

SOCIETY	1	2	3	4	5	6	REFERENCES
Santee	Sx	B	P	BM	I	ac	James 1823:vol. 1, 233–34; Neill 1872: 297; Riggs 1893:203–04; Wallis 1947:40.
Sauk	Ag	P	P	BC	O	ad	Skinner 1923–25:31–32.
Tonkawa	O	M	M	?	?	a cd	Sjoberg 1953:290.
Wichita	Cd	B	M	L	H	ab cd	Schmitt and Schmitt n.d.:49.
Winnebago	Sx	P	P	BC	O	ad	Radin 1923:135, 138.
Yankton	Sx	B	P	BM	I	a	Howard 1960; Riggs 1893:204.
Yanktonai	Sx	B	P	BM	I	a	Curtis 1907–30,vol. 3; Riggs 1893:204.
East							
Alabamu	Mu	M	M	BC BM	C	ad	Swanton 1928:451.
Caddo (Parsons)	Cd	B	M	BM	I	o	Parsons 1941.
Caddo (Spier)	Cd	B	M	BC	H	ab cd	Spier 1924.
Catawba	O	B	P	L	E	o	Speck and Schaeffer 1942:562–63; Lawson 1860; Swanton 1946.
Cherokee	O	M	M	BM	C	o	Adair 1775; Bartram 1853; Gilbert 1943: 253; 1955:302; Mooney 1932.
Chickasaw	Mu	M	M	BM BC	C	ad	Swanton 1927; 1928:451; 1946:707.
Choctaw	Mu	M	B	BM	C	ac	Swanton 1931:90, 127–29, 138; 1946: 707.
Creek	Mu	M	M	BM BC	C	o	Swanton 1928:451; 1946:707.
Delaware	Ag	M	M	L	H	o	Heckewelder 1819; Kinietz 1946:62, 108; Newcomb 1956:37; Wallace 1947.
Huron	O	M	M	BM	I	o	Brébeuf 1897; Kinietz 1940.
Iroquois	O	M	M	BM G	I	o	Human Relations Area Files.
Mahican	Ag	M	M	BM	E	o	Skinner 1925; Ruttenber 1872.
Natchez	O	M	P	BC	CE	?	Swanton 1911:97; Haas 1939.
Shawnee	Ag	P	P	BM	O	o	Wheeler-Voegelin MS.
Yuchi	O	M	P	BM BC	C	o	Speck 1909:68–99.
Oasis							
Acoma	O	M	M	BM G	C	o	Eggan 1950; White 1930.
Apache, W.	At	M	M	BC	I	a	Gifford 1940:67; Goodwin 1942:208, 251–59; Kaut 1957.
Cahita	UA	B	P	BC	H	o	Beals 1943; 1945a.
Chiricahua	At	B	M	BC	H	ac	Gifford 1940:67; Opler 1955:214–23.
Cochiti	O	M	M	G	H	o	Goldfrank 1927; Parsons 1932.
Cocopa	Ho	P	P	BC	I	o	Drucker 1941; Gifford 1933:293; Kelly 1942.
Havasupai	Ho	B	P	BC	I	o	Spier 1928:222, 227.
Hopi	UA	M	M	BM	C	o	Eggan 1950; Gifford 1940:67; Lowie 1929:384; Titiev 1944.
Huichol	UA	B	B	L	H	o	Grimes and Grimes 1962; Zingg 1938.
Isleta	O	B	B	L	H	o	Parsons 1930:231.
Jemez	O	M	B	L	E	o	Parsons 1925.
Jicarilla	At	B	M	BM BC	EI	ad	Gifford 1940:67; Opler 1936a; 1936b; 1946:56; 1947.
Kamia	Ho	P	P	BC	I	o	Gifford 1922:259; 1931.
Laguna	O	M	M	BM	C	o	Eggan 1950; Parsons 1923.
Maricopa	Ho	P	P	BC	HI	o	Drucker 1941:138; Spier 1933:222.
Mescalero	At	B	M	BM BC	H	a	Basehart 1960:114, 115; Gifford 1940:67; Opler 1936b.
Mohave	Ho	P	P	BC	H	o	Drucker 1941:138; Kroeber 1925:747, 840.
Navaho	At	M	M	BM	I	a	Aberle 1961:150–51; Gifford 1940:67; Reichard 1928:72; Stewart 1942:297–98.
Opata	UA	B	P	BC	E	o	Johnson 1950.
Papago	UA	B	P	BC	H	o	Drucker 1941:138; Gifford 1940:67; Hoover 1935; Underhill 1939.
Picuris	O	B	B	BC	E	o	Parsons 1939; Trager 1943.
Pima	UA	B	P	BC	H	o	DiPeso 1953; 1956; Drucker 1941:138; Russell 1908.
San Felipe	O	M	M	G	H	o	Parsons 1932; White 1932.
Santa Ana	O	B	B	L	H	o	Gifford 1940:67; White 1942:161–62.
Santo Domingo	O	M	M	BM	E	o	Parsons 1932; White 1935.
Taos	O	B	B	L	E	o	Parsons 1936:36; Trager 1943.
Tarahumara	UA	B	B	BC	H	o	Bennett and Zingg 1935:223; Passin 1943.
Tepecan	UA	B	P	L	?	o	Passin 1944; Vogt 1961; Weitlaner 1961.

TABLE 6 (continued)

SOCIETY	1	2	3	4	5	6	REFERENCES
Tepehuan	UA	B	P	L	?	o	Mason 1913; 1952; Passin 1944.
Tewa (San Ildefonso)	O	B	B	L	E	o	Gifford 1940:67; Parsons 1929:35.
Walapai	Ho	B	P	BC	I	o	Drucker 1941:138; Kroeber 1935.
Yavapai, N.E.	Ho	B	B	BC	C	a cd	Gifford 1936:291, 294, 296.
Yavapai, S.E.	Ho	M	M	BC	C	a cd	Gifford 1932a:189, 192, 195.
Yavapai, W.	Ho	B	M	BC	I	o	Gifford 1936:291, 294.
Yuma	Ho	P	P	BC	I	o	Drucker 1937:27—28; Forde 1931:148, 155, 201; Gifford 1922:259; Halpern 1942.
Zuni	O	M	M	BM	C	o	Bunzel 1930:478; Eggan 1950; Gifford 1940:67; Kroeber 1917a.
Baja California							
Akwa'ala	Ho	P	P	BC	I	o	Gifford and Lowie 1928:340—41; Drucker 1941:138.
Seri	Ho	B	P	BC	H	ad c	Kroeber 1931:8; Moser 1963; Spicer 1962:313.
Northeast Mexico							
Chichimeca-Jonaz	O	B	P	L	HE	o	Driver and Driver 1963:169.
Karankawa	O	B	P	BM	H	o	Gatschet 1891; Schaedel 1949.
Pame	O	B	P	L	H	o	Gibson 1954.
Meso-America							
Aztec	UA	B	P	L	H	o	Human Relations Area Files.
Cakchiquel	Ma	P	P	BM	H	o	Murdock 1957; Vogt 1961; Weitlaner 1961.
Chinantec	O	B	P	L	H	o	Merrifield 1959; Weitlaner 1951; Weitlaner and Castro Guevara 1954.
Chorti	Ma	B	B	L	H	o	Wisdom 1940.
Cora of Nayarit	UA	P	P	L	H	o	Ibarra 1943; Monzon 1945.
Huaxtec	Ma	B	P	BC BM	H	o	Guiteras Holmes 1948.
Mam of Guatemala	Ma	P	P	LG	H	o	Wagley 1941; 1949:15, 22, 23, 24, 35, 40—41.
Maya of Yucatan	Ma	P	P	BM	IH	o	Eggan 1934; Roys 1943; Tozzer 1941:101.
Mazahua	O	B	P	L BC	H	o	Mickey 1959; Rojas Gonzales 1939.
Mazatec	O	B	P	L	H	o	Cowan 1946; 1947.
Mixe	O	B	P	L	H	o	Beals 1945b.
Mixtec	O	B	P	L	H	o	Dahlgren de Jordan 1954:145—66.
Otomi	O	B	P	L BC	H	o	Carrasco 1950; Christensen 1954.
Popoluca of Vera Cruz	O	B	P	L	H	o	Foster 1942; 1949.
Quiche	Ma	P	P	BC	D	o	Bunzel 1952; Paul and Paul 1963.
Tarasc	O	B	P	L	E	o	Beals 1946; Human Relations Area Files.
Totonac	O	B	P	L	H	o	Kelly and Palerm 1952; Palerm 1952—53.
Tzeltal	Ma	P	P	BM	O	o	Guiteras Holmes 1947; Vilal Rojas 1947.
Tzotzil	Ma	P	P	BM G	O	o	Guiteras Holmes 1948; Pozas 1948; Rojas Gonzales and de La Cerda Silva 1941.
Zapotec	O	B	P	G BC	EH	o	Fuente 1949; Mendieta y Nunez 1949; Stephens 1962:134, 135, 261.
Zoque	O	B	P	L	E	o	Starr 1901—1903.
Circum Caribbean							
Choco	O	B	B	L	H	o	Faron 1961; 1962.
Cuna	O	B	M	L	H	o	Iglesias and Morgan 1939:6—7; Nordenskiöld 1938; Stout 1947; 81—82.
Jicaque	O	B	M	?	?	a	Kirchhoff 1948:225.
Miskito	O	B	M	BC	I	o	Conzemius 1932:101, 147—48.
Paya	O	B	M	?	?	a	Kirchhoff 1948:225.
Sumu	O	B	M	?	?	a	Conzemius 1932:147—48; Kirchhoff 1948: 225.

Abbreviations: 1. language family: Ag=Algonkian; At=Athapaskan; Cd=Caddoan; CP=California Penutian; Es=Eskimo-Aleut; Ho=Hokan; Ma=Mayan; Mu=Muskogean; O=other language families; Sa=Salishan; Sx=Siouan; UA=Uto-Aztecan; Wa=Wakashan.
2. descent: B=bilateral or ambilateral; M=matrilineal; P=patrilineal.
3. residence: A=avunculocal; B=bilocal, ambilocal, or neolocal; M=matrilocal; P=patrilocal.

4. kinship terminology for mother and aunts: BC=bifurcate collateral; BM=bifurcate merging; G=generation; L=lineal.
5. kinship terms for sister and cousins: C=Crow; D=distinct terms for Si, FaBrDa, FaSiDa, MoBrDa, MoSiDa (Murdock's Descriptive, Derivative and Sudanese); E=Eskimo; H=Hawaiian; I=Iroquois; O=Omaha.
6. avoidance: a=mother-in-law and son-in-law; b=mother-in-law and daughter-in-law; c=father-in-law and son-in-law; d=father-in-law and daughter-in-law; o=all absent or unreported.

which there are 4 relationships: mother-in-law and son-in-law (M-S), mother-in-law and daughter-in-law (M-D), father-in-law and son-in-law (F-S), father-in-law and daughter-in-law (F-D). The original aim was to test Tylor's marital residence hypotheses, not investigated until 1962. After seeing the work of Stephens and D'Andrade, I expanded my data to include descent. When I mapped my avoidance data and compared the geographical distribution with that of forms of descent, I anticipated lower correlations than the above authors found because descent in the Plains area, where avoidances are almost universal, is largely bilateral. Driver and Massey (1957: 417) infer that many, if not most, of the Plains tribes were once unilateral. Therefore, I added categories of kinship terminology to my data because kinship classification often lags behind descent in periods of change, thus revealing earlier forms of descent. Finally, genetic language families and culture areas (Driver 1961, maps 2 and 37) were added to emphasize geographical and historical factors in the determination of avoidances. The hop-skip-and-jump character of geographical distributions in most worldwide cross-cultural studies makes it impossible to observe geographical continuity and infer historical continuity. Only with control of genetic language classification is it possible to distinguish genetic heritage from subsequent diffusion of cultural phenomena. I will attempt to do so below.

Unlike Stephens and D'Andrade, who employ a 5-step Guttman scale of avoidance, I treat avoidance as a dichotomy of presence or absence. Steps 1 and 2 of their scale I code as absence, steps 3, 4 and 5 as presence. Step 2, "Can't talk about sex," I do not call avoidance because it would normally apply to a man's mother or daughter, neither of whom are generally avoidance relatives. It is not crucial, however, as the Stephens and D'Andrade data would yield significant dichotomous relations were the line drawn between steps 1 and 2 or 2 and 3.

The distribution of North American avoidance customs is given in Table 6 and Figure 1. Table 7 shows the frequency of avoidance for combinations, of relatives taken singly, and 2, 3 or 4 at a time. Of the 15 possibilities, only 6 actually occur. The frequencies are the number of ethnic units (tribes, societies). Thus M-S (mother-in-law-son-in-law) is reported for 84 ethnic units, F-D (father-in-law-daughter-in-law) for 47, F-S (father-in-law-son-in-law) for 15 ethnic units. When only 1 combination of relatives practices avoidance, it is always M-S. When 2 combinations avoid one another they are most often M-S and F-D (25 ethnic units), but sometimes M-S and F-S (8). When 3 combinations practice avoidance they are more often M-S, F-D, and F-S (7), but in 1 in-

stance M-S, F-D, and M-D. Thus there are only 9 exceptions among 84 ethnic units (about 10%) to a perfect cumulative scale. This agrees essentially with Stephens and D'Andrade, although I have found more exceptions.

I strongly suspect that some of these exceptions are errors in field reporting or in coding, since the failure to report any evidence is difficult to distinguish from true absence. The University of California Culture Element Survey has provided extensive reports of absences for the area west of the Continental Divide.

TABLE 7
FREQUENCY OF AVOIDANCES

M-S				29
	F-D			0
		F-S		0
			M-D	0
M-S	F-D			25
M-S		F-S		8
M-S			M-D	0
	F-D	F-S		0
	F-D		M-D	0
		F-S	M-D	0
M-S	F-D	F-S		7
M-S	F-D		M-D	1
M-S		F-S	M-D	0
	F-D	F-S	M-D	0
M-S	F-D	F-S	M-D	14
Totals 84	47	29	15	84

Abbreviations: M-S=Mother-in-law—son-in-law avoidance; F-D=Father-in-law—daughter-in-law avoidance; F-S=Father-in-law—son-in-law avoidance; F-D=Mother-in-law—daughter-in-law avoidance.

TABLE 8
INTERNAL CORRELATIONS (PHI) OF AVOIDANCES

	M-S	F-D	F-S	M-D
M-S		.68	.52	.36
F-D	.68		.50	.53
F-S	.52	.50		.65
M-D	.36	.53	.65	

See Table 7 for key to abbreviations.

Correlations (phi) among the 4 combinations of relatives practicing avoidance are all positive, as is always true of subject units forming a Guttman scale (Table 8). With 1 exception, these internal correlations are all higher than the external ones given

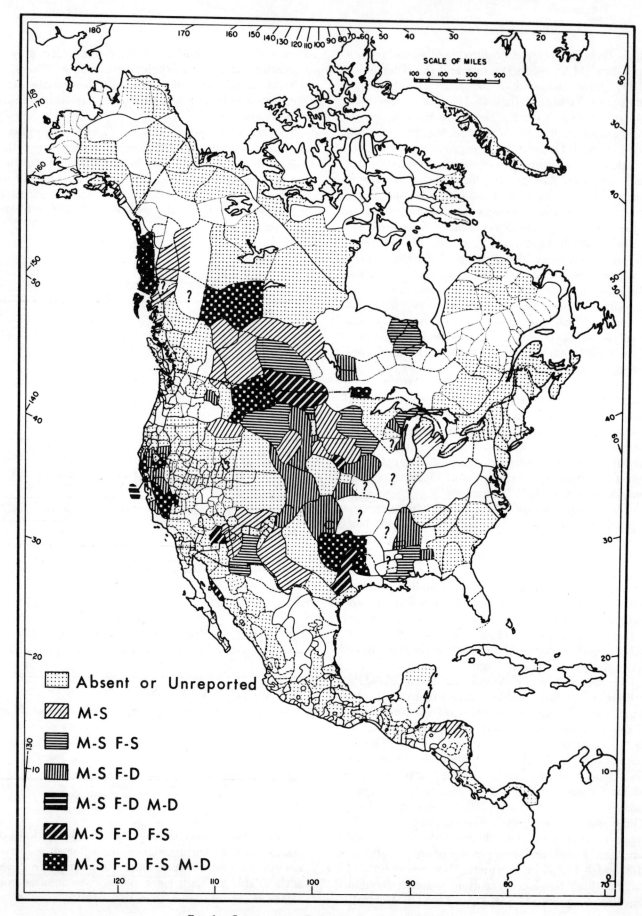

Absent or Unreported

M-S

M-S F-S

M-S F-D

M-S F-D M-D

M-S F-D F-S

M-S F-D F-S M-D

Fig. 1. Geographical Distribution of Avoidances

38

in Table 9, suggesting that avoidances between some combinations of relatives arise more often by extension from another combination than by whatever causal potency one might infer from the external correlatives. Correlations between the cross-sex combinations of avoidances (M-S and F-D) and between the same sex combinations (F-S and M-D) are higher than correlations between any pair of combinations in which one is cross-sex and the other same-sex. Because cross-sex combinations are more widespread, and same-sex combinations never occur without 1 of them (M-S), cross-sex avoidances appear to have evolutionary and historical as well as psychological priority. Same-sex avoidances apparently arise from them by extension, as Stephens and D'Andrade (1962) and others suggest.

Correlations (phi) of the 4 combinations of avoidance relatives with culture areas, language families, descent, residence, mother-aunt terminology, and sister-cousin terminology, are presented in Table 9. The highest significant correlations are with culture areas, language families, and kinship terminology. Therefore, historical factors seem to have as much or more to do with the occurrence of avoidances as do the other correlatives. The significant correlations with kinship terminology are higher than those with residence and descent. The residence correlations offer a weak confirmation of Tylor's theory: M-S avoidance correlates positively with matrilocal and avunculocal residence, and negatively with patrilocal residence; but F-D avoidance yields no significant correlations with any kind of residence. Descent does a little better: M-S correlates positively with matrilineal descent, negatively with bilateral descent; F-S correlates positively with patrilineal descent.

Bifurcate merging of mother-aunt terms produces a positive correlation, higher than those for residence and descent, with M-S, and a barely significant positive correlation with F-D. These correlations and the 3 negative correlations with lineal terminology indirectly support the Stephens and D'Andrade assertion that avoidances correlate positively with unilateral descent (matrilineal and/or patrilineal). The positive correlation between F-D and bifurcate collateral terminology tends to contradict their assertion.

Crow-type sister-cousin kinship terminology correlates positively with both M-S and F-S. This is indirect support for Tylor's findings, because most kinship specialists believe that Crow terminology is an ultra-matrilineal type. The positive correlations of M-S and F-D with Omaha terminology confuse the issues. A correlation with F-D is consistent with Tylor's ideas, but a correlation with M-S can be explained only by geographical-historical factors. On the whole, however, the positive correlations of 2

TABLE 9

CORRELATIONS OF AVOIDANCES WITH OTHER VARIABLES

	M–S	F–D	F–S	M–D
Culture Areas				
Western Arctic	.01	.00	.03	.07
Central and Eastern Arctic	−.11	−.07	−.06	−.04
Yukon Sub-Arctic	−.01	−.07	−.06	−.04
Mackenzie Sub-Arctic	−.03	−.03	.00	.05
Eastern Sub-Arctic	.00	−.01	.03	.02
Northwest Coast	−.16‡	−.13†	−.07	−.05
Plateau	−.11	−.08	−.09	−.06
California	.34*	.40*	.09	.26*
Great Basin		−.10	−.06	−.01
Plains		.13†	.12	.01
Prairies	.24*	.11	.16†	−.01
East	−.01	.03	.03	.02
Oasis	−.19‡	−.09	−.03	−.09
Baja California and Northeast Mexico	−.10	.01	.04	−.03
Meso-America	−.03	−.13†	−.10	−.07
Circum-Caribbean	.06	−.07	−.05	−.04
Language Families				
Algonquian	.09	.01	.08	.02
Athapaskan	.09	−.04	−.05	−.04
Caddoan	.03	.08	.13†	.21*
California Penutian	.29*	.43*	.12†	.21*
Eskimo-Aleut	−.08	−.06	−.02	.02
Hokan	.05	.08	.05	−.02
Mayan	−.12	−.08	−.06	−.04
Muskogean	.12	.11	.06	−.03
Other	−.06	−.07	−.06	−.01
Salishan	−.21*	−.13†	−.12†	−.08
Siouan	.31*	.16‡	.19‡	−.06
Uto-Aztecan	−.21*	−.13†	−.08	−.01
Wakashan	−.10	−.07	−.05	−.04
Descent				
Bilateral or Ambilateral	−.14†	−.11	−.01	.09
Matrilineal	.14†	−.02	.10	−.05
Patrilineal	.04	.15†	−.08	−.06
Residence				
Avunculocal	.14†	.05	.09	.06
Bilocal, Ambilocal, Neolocal	−.05	−.03	−.01	.03
Matrilocal	.15†	.05	.08	.05
Patrilocal	−.13†	−.03	−.08	−.08
Mother-Aunt Terms				
Bifurcate Collateral	.09	.16‡	.04	.11
Bifurcate Merging	.25*	.12†	.12†	−.01
Generation	−.12†	−.09	−.06	−.05
Lineal	−.30*	−.24*	−.16‡	−.08
Sister-Cousin Terms				
Crow	.19‡	.12	.21*	.04
Distinct terms for Si, FaBrDa, FaSiDa, MoBrDa, MoSiDa	.04	−.04	−.03	−.02
Eskimo	−.14†	−.11	−.13†	−.09
Hawaiian	−.21*	−.11	−.09	.02
Iroquois	.05	−.07	.01	−.02
Omaha	.29*	.31*	.06	.04
Number of Significant Correlations	22	13	8	3

* Significant at the .001 level or lower.
‡ Significant from the .01 to the .001 level.
† Significant from the .05 to the .01 level.

combinations of avoiding relatives with Crow and with Omaha terminology support the Stephens and D'Andrade assertion that avoidances tend to correlate positively with unilateral descent.

These exceptions to functional theory and the generally low magnitude of many correlations must be explained by errors in data and historical "accidents" of diffusion and migration. The 20th century researcher can do little about inadequate 19th century data, but historical inferences can be drawn from geographical position and language family affiliation.

Correlations may be raised by combining variables, as Murdock (1949:179) and Driver (1956:22) show. There are 3 ways: variable 1 *and* variable 2, meaning that a presence is recorded only when both are present; variable 1 *or* variable 2, meaning a presence is recorded when either is present, but not both; variable 1 *and/or* variable 2, meaning a presence is recorded when either or both variables are present. Murdock uses the 1st, Driver (1956) the 2nd; in this paper I use the 2nd and 3rd. Because the alloforms of culture areas, language families, residence, and descent are mutually exclusive, the *or* relationship is the only possibility; but because the alloforms of kinship terminology are not mutually exclusive, the *and* relationship also occurs; and the combination *and/or* is the most relevant.

Table 10 assembles the correlations (phi) of the 4 avoiding pairs of relatives with the combined variables. Although most of the correlations in Table 10 are higher than those in Table 9, the difference between the magnitudes in the tables is greatest for culture areas and language families, intermediate for kinship terminology, and least for residence and descent. Possibly other combinations of kinship terminology, residence, and descent would produce higher values. I will send a duplicate set of the punched cards to anyone who wants to search for such combinations. The obvious conclusion to draw from Table 10 is that geographical-historical factors are more powerful in predicting the presence or absence of avoidances than psycho-functional causes.

The fact that avoidances correlate higher with kinship terminology than with residence and descent suggests that they are conservative behaviors which generally lag behind changes in residence, descent, and even kinship terminology. Apparently they would come last in the cycles of change demonstrated by Driver (1956) and reprinted in Driver and Massey (1957:421-39). At the same time, avoidances often diffuse to peoples who lack the proper psycho-functional correlatives, as will be shown in detail.

A caution about the relationship of correlation and causality is in order. A correlation is never a sufficient proof of psycho-functional causality but is a necessary part of the proof. Phrased another way, one variable can hardly be called a psycho-functional cause of another unless a correlation can be demonstrated, but many historically determined correlations apparently have no psycho-functional causes in common. A casual inspection of the 163 maps in Driver and Massey (1957) reveals that the following subject units would show positive correlation with M-S avoidance: dog eating (map 6); hafted mauls used to grind food (map 50); both hard and soft-soled moccasins (map 115). To these one might add any subject unit of general occurrence in the Plains-Prairies area, such as the sewn-hide tipi of the 19th century, the parfleche, the travois, and even the sun dance. The plethora of such "pure" geographical-historical correlations without suggestion of psycho-functional relationship should warn against incautious assumption of psycho-functional relationship from other correlations.

Historical Inferences in Native North America

In many cases, diffusion of avoidances can be inferred from language family affiliation, presence or absence of positively correlated traits of social organization, geographical position, and documented historical contacts. I assume with Lowie (1920) that

TABLE 10

CORRELATIONS (PHI) OF AVOIDANCES WITH COMBINED VARIABLES

	M–S	F–D	F–S	M–D
California or Plains or Prairies culture area	.51*	.44*	.23*	.19‡
Caddoan or California Penutian or Muskogean or Siouan language family	.43*	.42*	.27*	.26*
Matrilineal or Patrilineal descent	.12	.05	–.01	–.09
Avunculocal or Matrilocal residence	.16‡	.07	.10	.08
Bifurcate Collateral and/or Bifurcate Merging kin terms	.30*	.24*	.16‡	.09
Generation and/or Lineal kin terms	–.34*	–.28*	–.20*	–.13†
Crow or Omaha kin terms	.29*	.24*	20*	.01
Eskimo and/or Hawaiian kin terms	–.28*	–.15†	–.16‡	–.02

* Significant at the .001 level or lower.
‡ Significant from the .01 to the .001 level.
† Significant from the .05 to the .01 level.

kin avoidances would not diffuse without intertribal marriage. I know no way to determine the frequency of intertribal marriages in or before the 19th century for all the ethnic units involved in the diffusion of avoidances, but I do not recall a single statement in any ethnography that marriages with outsiders did not exist or were tabooed. 10 years ago I started a map showing where women taken captive in war raids were raised in status from captive to wife. Although I never completed the map, I did not find a single negative instance in more than 100 ethnic units. Intertribal and interlanguage marriages were, therefore, common and probably universal, with varying frequency from one ethnic group to another.

Only 3 Uto-Aztecan ethnic units practiced kin avoidance: the Lemhi (northern) Shoshoni of Idaho, the Western Mono, and the Owens Valley Paiute of California (Fig. 1). The Lemhi Shoshoni are adjacent to the Gros Ventre and Crow Indians of the Plains, both of whom had well developed kin avoidance syndromes. The Lemhi and other northeastern Shoshoni had much contact with the northern Plains tribes after acquiring the horse about 1700. These Plains tribes obtained their first horses from the Shoshoni. The Western Mono lived adjacent to the Yokuts Indians and, by the 1920's when Ann Gayton did fieldwork among them, the 2 peoples were so mixed that several ethnic units had about equal numbers of speakers of each of the 2 unrelated languages. The Owens Valley Paiute lived east of the Sierra Nevada, but had annual trade contacts with the Western Mono on the other side, and the 2 forms of speech are dialects of 1 language.

These Uto-Aztecan instances are clear cases of acculturation and diffusion from non-Uto-Aztecan sources. Cultural heritage from proto-Uto-Aztecan is discounted because few Uto-Aztecans possess avoidances, and the 3 positive instances lie adjacent to other peoples who seem to have been donors. Independent origin appears even more far-fetched in light of geographical position and the absence of positively correlated forms of residence, descent, and kinship terminology. Thus the Lemhi have bicentered social organization except for patrilocal residence, which shows a barely significant negative correlation with M-S, their only avoidance. The Owens Valley Paiute are also completely bicentered, and the Western Mono are bicentered except that bifurcate merging terms for mother-aunts alternate with the probably older bifurcate collateral classification. When we add Shimkin's (1941) reconstruction of proto-Uto-Aztecan kin terms, all bicentered, the case for diffusion of kin avoidances to the 3 Uto-Aztecans is overwhelming.

Only 1 ethnic unit of the Salish language family, the Coeur D'Alene, practices any of the 4 avoidances

of this study. The Coeur D'Alene are located in the eastern Plateau area near the northern Plains tribes, from which they obviously acquired their M-S and F-D taboos. The argument for acculturation-diffusion parallels that for the Uto-Aztecans so closely that it need not be repeated.

Eskimo avoidances have been reported only for the Nunivak and the Chugach, in southern Alaska, who had contacts (indirect for the Nunivak) with the northern Northwest Coast where avoidances are general. Although the Nunivak are farther from possible donors, they have no traits of social organization showing significant positive correlations with avoidances except bifurcate collateral mother-aunt terms (correlated with F-D avoidance). The only explanation for the presence of all 4 avoidances seems to be diffusion.

In the Athapaskan language family, 1 or more avoidances is found in the north only among those close to northern Northwest Coast or northern Plains peoples. None of the Pacific Athapaskans in Oregon and California practiced these avoidances, but the Apacheans in the Southwest did. Documents and archaeological evidence from the early historical period and the large number of Plains culture elements in 19th-century Apachean culture (Gifford 1940) suggest that some Apacheans were in contact with Plains tribes on their southward migration and later. The absence of avoidances in the Pacific and in most of the northern area rules out cultural heritage. Although some Athapaskans in the north and in the Southwest have matrilocal residence, matrilineal descent, bifurcate merging, and Iroquoian or Crow kinship terminology, Hoijer's (1956) reconstruction of proto-Athapaskan kinship terminology suggests an originally bicentered social organization. I have postulated (Driver 1956:27-29; Driver and Massey 1957:435-36) that the matricentered social structure of the Athapaskans in the north and in the Southwest is a convergence arising from contact with matricentered peoples. I now use a similar argument for avoidances. In the north the Tlingit and Haida seem to have been donors of both matrilineal descent and avoidances, but in the Southwest the Navaho and the Western Apache seem to have derived their matrilineal descent from contact with Pueblos, and all the Apacheans their avoidances from earlier contact with Plains tribes.

Interpretation of the Algonquian language family is clouded by poorer data and gaps in knowledge represented on Figure 1 by blank spaces and question marks. Nevertheless, the apparent absence of avoidances among all Algonquians east of the longitude of James Bay and presence among most of them west of this line must again be explained by diffusion and acculturation. Traits of Algonquian social structure showing significant positive correlations with avoidances are too rare east of James Bay to postulate that they constitute a proto-Algonquian cultural heritage.

Only 2 out of 5 Caddoan ethnic units have avoidances, again suggesting acquisition by borrowing.

The Muskogeans in the Southeast are also split from east to west. Those from the Alabamu west practice avoidance behavior; those east of the Alabamu do not. However, all have features of social structure which show significant positive correlations with avoidances. It seems likely that Muskogean protoculture included avoidances and contributed them to peoples of other language families.

The case for proto-Siouan avoidance behavior and a donor role in its diffusion is even stronger. Most Siouans practice avoidance, and they lie in the center of the Plains-Prairie area. (Poor source material for the Missouri, Osage, and Quapaw has been recorded as queries rather than absences.) Matthews' (1959) reconstruction of proto-Siouan kinship terminology is of limited help because it wavers between Crow and Omaha, slightly favoring Omaha. It may be worth noting, however, that both Crow and Omaha terminology show a significant positive correlation with 2 combinations of relative avoidance. This scrambling of psycho-functional causes suggests geographical-historical factors. On the whole, the relevant elements of Siouan social structure show high correlations with avoidances.

The California cases are separated by a relatively wide gap from the Plains-Prairies-Southwest occurrences of avoidances. California had no direct and little indirect contact with those areas. These cases, therefore, have a long and independent history, if not a totally independent origin. Most traits of social organization showing significant positive correlations with avoidances are present in California suggesting that conditions were right for independent origin. Because all the California Penutians practiced avoidance, this is our best choice for the donor language family in that area. The Yukians also practiced avoidance, but their smaller numbers, isolation in the Coast Range mountains, and bicentered social structure make them a poorer candidate.

The California Hokans seem to have acquired their avoidance patterns from the Penutians, but the presence of 3 combinations of avoiding relatives among the Hokan-speaking Seri mars the simplicity of this interpretation. Does the Seri case represent an isolated survival of old Hokan customs, or did they somehow acquire their avoidance behavior later, presumably from the Apaches? The eastern Yavapai offer another dilemma. If they acquired avoidances

from the Western Apache, as they seem to have acquired matrilineal descent, why do 3 combinations of relatives avoid each other when only M-S avoidance occurs among the Western Apache? Should the Yavapai be added to the Seri to bolster an ancient association with proto-Hokan?

The isolation of 3 M-S instances in Central America suggests origin independent of all other North American cases. Possibly they share a common origin with avoidances in South America.

The northern Northwest Coast cases may also be independent of those in the rest of North America. Kroeber (1923) pointed out that Northwest Coast culture was the most foreign or un-American of any area except possibly the Arctic. Most Americanists now agree that the matrilineal social organization of the Northwest Coast arose independently of other matrilineal systems in native North America. If this is true, it would seem true also of avoidances. Because the Haida and Tlingit practice avoidances for 3 and 4 combinations of relatives, and the Tsimshian for only 1, I postulate that the Tsimshian acquired it from the Haida or Tlingit. The Eyak probably derived their taboo from the Tlingit, their neighbor to the southwest.

In the preceding historical reconstruction, I infer ancient avoidances among 12 Siouan, 3 Muskogean, 10 California Penutian, and 2 non-Athapaskan Na-Dene ethnic groups, a total of 27. The other 57 ethnic groups with avoidances appear to have derived them by diffusion or acculturation from these 4 nuclei, plus a 5th for Central America. Thus geographical-historical loom larger than psycho-functional factors.

Donor-recipient contrast is further demonstrated in Table 11 where language families are correlated with the features of descent, residence, and kinship terminology which correlate highest with avoidances in Table 9. These features of social structure are the strongest candidate for "causes" of avoidances.

From Table 11 it is apparent that the California Penutian language family shows higher positive correlations with patricentered psycho-functional "causes" of avoidances than does Hokan, as anticipated. Siouan has 2 substantial positive correlations with patricentered "causes," plus a higher positive value with bifurcate merging. Muskogean does better with 3 significant positive correlations with matricentered "causes," plus bifurcate merging. If we are to call Muskogean a donor, we must postulate a loss of avoidances for the Muskogeans east of the Alabamu. If some Siouan unknowns are actually absences, a loss must also be postulated for them.

The Algonquians show 2 significant positive correlations with patricentered "causes," both significantly lower than the highest Siouan value. The Athapas-

TABLE 11

CORRELATIONS (PHI) OF THE PSYCHO-FUNCTIONAL "CAUSES" OF AVOIDANCES WITH LANGUAGE FAMILIES

	Avunculocal Residence	Matrilocal Residence	Matrilineal Descent	Patrilineal Descent	Bifurcate Merging	Crow	Omaha
Algonquian	−.06	−.05	−.08	.22*	.07	−.11	.16
Athapaskan	.02	.16 ‡	.17 ‡	−.13†	.01	−.03	−.12
Caddoan	−.02	.29*	−.06	−.06	−.03	.15†	−.05
California Penutian	−.03	−.09	−.08	.23*	.01	−.06	.39*
Eskimo-Aleut	−.04	−.06	−.09	−.05	−.04	−.07	−.07
Hokan	−.05	−.06	−.10	.13†	−.17 ‡	−.01	.02
Mayan	−.03	−.08	−.07	.27*	.13†	−.05	.09
Muskogean	−.02	.18 ‡	.29*	−.05	.20*	.40*	−.04
Other	.20*	.09	.24*	−.23*	−.03	−.14†	−.14†
Salishan	−.06	−.16 ‡	−.14†	−.15†	−.22*	−.11	−.12
Siouan	−.04	−.03	.04	.20*	.35*	.10	.30*
Uto-Aztecan	−.07	−.01	−.14†	−.07	−.03	−.09	−.14†
Wakashan	.13†	−.07	.01	−.07	.02	−.05	−.05

* Significant at the .001 level or lower.
‡ Significant from the .01 to the .002 level.
† Significant from the .05 to the .01 level.

kans have 2 significant positive correlations with matricentered "causes," as anticipated. I did not anticipate that "other language families" would have 3 significant positive correlations with matricentered "causes," but it is understandable in that all are on the northern Northwest Coast, where the Tlingit and Haida have already been called donors. The Caddoans have 2 significant correlations with matricentered traits, although only 2 of 5 ethnic units have avoidances.

Table 11 largely supports the historical inferences based on the geographical positions of ethnic units. It also supports the view that avoidances diffuse more readily to ethnic units having "causal" traits. Thus the Algonquians west of James Bay have more "causes" than those in the east. Similarly, the Athapaskans adjacent to the northern Northwest Coast or Plains areas have more "causes" than those on the Pacific Coast or east of the Continental Divide in the far north. Because "causes" may also diffuse, it is difficult to tell whether avoidances or their "causes" arrived 1st. Perhaps sometimes they diffused together. However, correlation matrices for division of labor, land tenure, residence, descent, and kinship terminology (Driver 1956; Driver and Massey 1957: 428-434) clearly show that this material is more highly structured than avoidances, more inclined to conform to developmental cycles and, therefore, less likely to diffuse to peoples lacking the "causes." Avoidance correlations do not fit into these matrices because they often occur with both matricentered and patricentered traits of social structure.

The Plains tribes are the outstanding examples of people with the loss of many "causes" but the retention of avoidances, suggesting that the latter are com-

paratively resistant to change after they are firmly established.

Still further evidence of the importance of geographical proximity and historical contact in the determination of avoidances comes from the western Pueblos and the Iroquoians. Neither practice avoidances, yet the Pueblos possess all of the matricentered "causes," plus bifurcate merging, and the Iroquoians most of the same "causes" (lacking only Crow kinship terminology), plus bifurcate merging. The only explanation of these absences of avoidances is that the western Pueblos had no contact with people practicing avoidances until the Apacheans appeared about 500 years ago. The Iroquoians were located too far east to have had enough contact with peoples who practiced avoidance to acquire the behavior.

Since the above was written, I have computed some additional correlations between avoidances, descent, residence and kinship terminology. These are shown in Table 12. This sample includes only the "recipient" peoples. The "donor" peoples, namely, Tlingit, Haida, California Penutians, Siouians, and Muskogeans, have been eliminated. Because the highest psycho-functional correlations are found among the "donor" societies, their elimination should tend to lower correlations. A comparison of tables 9 and 12 shows that, on the whole, correlations are lower in Table 12, suggesting that avoidances diffuse to peoples who lack the psycho-functional correlatives almost as readily as to those that have them. Nevertheless, a few correlations in Table 12 are higher than the corresponding ones in Table 9; these are indicated by italics in Table 12. Although some of these differences are not statistically significant, the fact that 5 correlations involving matrilocal and pat-

TABLE 12

CORRELATIONS OF AVOIDANCES FOR RECIPIENT PEOPLES ONLY

	M–S	F–D	F–S	M–D
Descent				
Bilateral or Ambilateral	.00	.05	.09	.13†
Matrilineal	.09	–.05	–.01	–.08
Patrilineal	–.09	–.01	–.11	–.08
Residence				
Avunculocal	.13†	–.05	–.04	–.03
Bilocal, Ambilocal, Neolocal	.00	.02	–.01	.07
Matrilocal	.21*	.13†	.14†	.10
Patrilocal	–.21*	–.10	–.09	–.12
Mother-Aunt Terms				
Bifurcate Collateral	.15†	.17†	.14†	.09
Bifurcate Merging	.10	.02	–.03	–.02
Generation	–.10	–.07	–.06	–.04
Lineal	–.22*	–.18†	–.12	–.06
Sister-Cousin Terms				
Crow	.10	.10	.08	.03
Distinct terms for Si, FaBrDa, FaSiDa MoBrDa, MoSiDa	.06	–.03	–.03	–.02
Eskimo	–.09	–.06	–.11	–.09
Hawaiian	–.07	.04	–.01	.04
Iroquois	.05	–.07	.00	–.03
Omaha	.13†	.05	.09	.05
Number of significant correlations in Table 12	6	3	2	1
Number of significant correlations for the same variables in Table 9	12	5	4	0

* Significant at the .001 level or lower.
‡ Significant from the .01 to the .001 level.
† Significant from the .05 to the .02 level.
Italics=higher in table 12 than in table 9.

rilocal residence are higher in Table 12 suggests that residence is more crucial in the *diffusion* of avoidances than descent or kinship terminology. The lower correlations of residence among the donor peoples must be explained by a change in residence rules after the avoidances were established and a lag in the adaptation of avoidances to the new residence norms. The 3 higher correlations for bifurcate collateral kinship terminology seem to make no functional sense, so they are better explained as the result of geographical-historical factors.

Conclusions and Recommendations for Further Research

Probably all the psycho-functional "causes" of kin avoidances advocated by Tylor, Frazer, Freud, Lowie, Murdock, and Stephens and D'Andrade have had some influence on the origin, maintenance, and dispersal of these behaviors. Even the most extreme geographical-historical enthusiast needs a package of psycho-functional "causes" to get the avoidance behavior started. Once such behavior has become firmly extablished, however, it seems to diffuse by intertribal marriage to peoples who lack some or even most of the "causes" discovered so far. It also fails to occur among some peoples who possess most of the "causes."

This study shows that essay-style descriptions collected even in great bulk cannot produce valid generalization about so complex a phenomenon. Tabulated or mapped data also are comparatively ineffective alone and do not produce a general explanation. Cross-cultural correlations based on fewer than 100 ethnic units may shed some light on psycho-functional "causes," but reveal little of geographical-historical relationships. These methods combined, as I hope to have shown, yield a more complete explanation. In addition, historical interpretation is considerably sharpened by treating language families and culture areas as variables.

The ideal sample for this problem would be a world-wide sample of at least 1,000 ethnic units, insuring considerable geographical continuity in all but little-known areas such as South America. Cross-cultural "causes" could be more firmly established from such a sample. Following Stephens, all specific behaviors, such as not touching, not looking in the eye, not talking to, etc., should be included. All relatives, both consanguineal and affinal, and all other patterned kin behaviors, such as joking, should also be included. Because these patterned kin behaviors are sometimes practiced for a limited time and terminated in a specified manner, their duration and manner of termination should be considered. A more detailed classification of residence rules, especially the temporary initial forms, and of descent and kinship terminology might sharpen results. The more specific treatment of these subjects in Murdock's new *Ethnographic Atlas* (1962-64) gives the researcher greater help at the start.

A word of caution about overfragmentation of data: Progressive dividing of concepts like residence and descent into more and more types tends to lower correlations of individual alloforms, e.g., of residence with descent. The same is true of other aspects of social structure and culture in general. A method of offsetting this progressive lowering of correlations (Driver 1964:305-7) is to combine all alloforms of a concept, such as residence, into all combinations of 2, then 3, then 4, etc. Each of the various combinations may be correlated on an electronic computer with all the combinations of another concept, such as descent. This is an empirical way of determining significant subject units, one of the perpetual problems of comparative research.

World-wide cross-cultural studies have become numerous enough lately to attract some long-deserved attention. I hope they will soon be bolstered by more regional studies employing geographically continuous samples. The recent concentration on North America of Murdock's *Ethnographic Atlas* will greatly facilitate regional studies there. . . .

Replies to Some Comments from Critics

Harold E. Driver

[Re the point made by Douglas Chrétien] that the researcher should not interpret his data from numbers alone, I wish to remind the readers that I have mapped all of the data in this paper except avoidances in previous publications (Driver 1956: maps 3-6; Driver 1961: maps 2, 31, 32, 35, 37; Driver and Massey 1957: maps 154, 156, 160, 161).

The reason I did not emphasize more that M-S avoidance is the only one reported to occur alone, is that I had seen Jorgensen's *Addendum*, in which he shows (p. 164) that F-D avoidance occurs alone in Moslem and Hindu areas of Asia. This attribute of M-S in North America is not a worldwide phenomenon.

I agree heartily that correlation coefficients and chi-squares computed for large samples suppress or obscure a large number of relationships within non-randomly chosen parts of the sample. . . .

[Morris Freilich asked about the reliability of my coding.] A test of the reliability of avoidance coding was made possible by the recent publication of data by Murdock (1965). His coding was totally independent of that in my study and included 40 or more of the same ethnic units and 2 pairs of the same avoiding relatives. Tables 13 and 14 give the results.

The reliability of M-S avoidance coding is quite satisfactory, as the correlation is definitely higher than any of the correlations of M-S with other variables in my sample. The reliability of coding of F-D avoidance is less satisfactory, but not bad enough to require that it be excluded from the study. Both reliability coefficients are lowered by the smaller ratio of absences in Murdock's sample. He coded avoidance absent only when some other kind of behavior was reported for a pair of relatives. I, on the other hand, inferred some absences on distributional evidence alone, bolstered by the opinions of regional specialists in personal communications. Had I used Murdock's more conservative principle, my obtained correlations between F-D and other variables would probably have been lower than .59. . . .

Concerning my failure to use an explicit theory or model of avoidance, there was simply not enough known about avoidance when I began my study a few years ago to construct a model of broad application to 277 societies. As for Blalock's (1960, 1961) causal models, they manipulate only small numbers of variables and assume that no other variables have any influence whatsoever on the correlations. . . .

I would much rather try to "explain" a single variable by observing its position in a matrix of 50 or more variables than to play around with causal models involving only 4 or 5 variables. Nevertheless, Freilich's query on causal models does give me an excuse for presenting some partial correlations which I worked out later. The partial correlation technique also works with a closed system which assumes that no outside variables have any effect on any of the variables chosen to compare in this manner; but by choosing the highest correlations in the data, one can at least say that the variables not considered have less effect on the correlations than those selected. The results are given in Table 15.

The 4th variable in Table 15 does not appear in my original table of correlations of avoidances with combined variables (Table 10). I discovered later that combining 4 kinds of kinship terminology gave higher correlations than the combinations of 2 previously used. The final results are given in the last row at the bottom of the table. Thus M-S avoidance correlates highest (.34) with culture areas when language families and kinship terminology are held constant. The correlation between kinship terminology and M-S avoidance, with culture areas and language families held constant, is a poor 2nd (—.21); while the correlation between language families and M-S avoidance (.17), with culture areas and kin terms held constant, is a close 3rd.

Freilich's functional (philosophical) model is the usual tautological kind in which this school indulges. What is his measure of tension between any combination of relatives? Until he can measure tension independently of overt avoidances (perhaps physiologically), he cannot claim any correlation between the 2. . . .

Wilhelm Milke . . . asked that numerical correlations demonstrating non-functional historical relationships be computed. These are given in Table 16, and agree with my impressionistic assertion from maps alone. . . .

Milke also questioned my lumping of language families and culture areas. I agree that unless the original groupings were determined in advance, there would be a tendency to delimit culture areas and maneuver language groupings in such a manner as to yield a spuriously high correlation with avoid-

TABLE 13

RELIABILITY OF M–S AVOIDANCE CODING

		Murdock		
		Present	Absent	Total
Driver	Present	27	2	29
	Absent	2	15	17
	Total	29	17	46

Phi = .81   Chi-square = 30.2   P = *ca.* .0001

TABLE 16

NON-FUNCTIONAL CORRELATIONS WITH AVOIDANCE

	M–S	F–D	F–S	M–D
Dogs eaten	.21	.16	.20	.02
Hafted mauls used to grind food	.34	.12	.14	−.01
Both hard and soft-soled moccasins	.23	.17	.11	.00

TABLE 14

RELIABILITY OF F–D AVOIDANCE CODING

		Murdock		
		Present	Absent	Total
Driver	Present	12	5	17
	Absent	3	20	23
	Total	15	25	40

Phi = .59   Chi-square = 13.9   P = .001

TABLE 17

CORRELATIONS OF M–S AVOIDANCE AND MATRICENTERED SOCIAL ORGANIZATION

	1	2	3	4	5
1. Matrilocal Residence		.45	.38	.25	.15
2. Matrilineal Descent	.45		.60	.39	.14
3. Crow Kin Terms	.38	.60		.31	.19
4. Bifurcate Merging Kin Terms	.25	.39	.31		.25
5. M–S Avoidance	.15	.14	.19	.25	
Totals	1.23	1.58	1.48	1.20	.73

TABLE 15

PARTIAL CORRELATIONS

	1	2	3	4
1. M–S Avoidance			.51	.43	−.40
2. California or Plains or Prairies Culture Area	.51		.46	−.35
3. Caddoan or California Penutian or Muskogean or Siouan Language Family	.43	.46		−.39
4. Generation and/or Lineal and/or Eskimo and/or Hawaiian Kin Terms	−.40	−.35	−.39	

Φ 12.3 = .38 Φ 24.1 = −.19 Φ 14.2 = −.27
Φ 12.4 = .43 Φ 24.3 = −.21 Φ 14.3 = −.29
Φ 13.2 = .24 Φ 34.1 = −.26 Φ 23.1 = .31
Φ 13.4 = .32 Φ 34.2 = −.28 Φ 23.4 = .37

Φ 12.34 = .34 Φ 14.23 = −.21 Φ 13.24 = .17

ances. I was attempting to demonstrate the non-random nature of the geographical distribution of avoidances in a way which used all the ethnic units in the area rather than the arbitrarily chosen linear or curvilinear chains employed by Naroll (1961, 1964a).

I anticipated that some commentator would question the computing of correlations from culture area groupings when the areas were determined impressionistically, as is true of all continental-wide schemes. To answer this and to show the generalized nature of my method, I superimposed a political map showing states of the United States and provinces of Canada on my avoidance map. I then reasoned from the ratio of presence to absence of M-S avoidance, which is about 1/3, that any state or province in which more than 1/3 of the ethnic units possess M-S avoidance would contribute to a positive relationship between a combination of such areal units and M-S avoidance. The following list satisfied this requirement: Alabama, Alberta, Arkansas, California, Indiana, Iowa, Kansas, Louisiana, Manitoba, Michigan, Minnesota, Missouri, Montana, N. Dakota, Nebraska, Oklahoma, Saskatchewan, S. Dakota, Tennessee, Texas, Wisconsin, Wyoming. I then constructed a 2 x 2 table in which the ethnic units in these political units were opposed to all others and correlated the presence or absence of avoidances with them, with these results: M-S .50, F-D .42, F-S .26, M-D .26. All of these phi's are significant at about the .0001 level or lower; they approximate closely the magnitude of those obtained from combined culture areas and language families given in Table 10. Arbitrary sections of latitude and longitude would probably give parallel results.

It is only too true that all comparativists are in trouble over their ethnic units, as was shown by Naroll's article (1964b) and the comments on it. [Frank] Moore's example of "hierarchical classification" of ethnic units apparently refers to language classification. If we had a more accurate classification of languages with quantitative guides for such labels as dialect, language, subfamily, family, and phylum, we could accurately group all ethnic units according to their positions in such a scheme. Similarly, if we had a quantitative taxonomy of ethnic units based on thousands of culture traits, we could group them into subculture areas, culture areas, super culture areas, etc. But because neither classification at present is sufficiently refined, there is no immediate solution to the ethnic unit problem. . . .

Why not build the essential characteristics of ethnic units into every comparative correlation study? Such things as population, level of cultural attainment, language type (Naroll 1964b:287), political organization, local community structure, and ecological adjustment might yield a total of about 50 variables, some of which have already been coded by Murdock (1962-65). Then everyone making a comparative study might be required to add the variables he is concerned with, for instance avoidances, to such a matrix of ethnic unit characteristics. If the latter totalled 50 variables, then the minimum number any researcher should present would be 51, because he would have to come up with at least 1 more to add anything new. This avoidance study, with its 50 variables, would be added to the 50 on ethnic units, bringing the total to 100 variables. Then the reader could see from the larger matrix exactly how the new material was correlated with the known ethnic unit data. This would require more extensive use of electronic computers and matrix reduction technique but, as almost all universities now have this equipment and knowledge, this is no longer a problem. Therefore I believe there is some functional relationship between avoidances and residence-descent-kinship terminology, although my demonstration of it is still incomplete.

I agree with [Clyde Wilson] that what I mean by functional relationship is different from what British social anthropologists mean by that phrase. I am talk-

ing about the comparative kind of functionalism employed by Murdock (1949, especially chapters 7 and 8), Driver (1956, where bold face type in Table 1 distinguishes functional from other relationships), Naroll (1961, 1964a), and Naroll and D'Andrade (1963.) Applied to parent-in-law and child-in-law avoidances, I believe that 2 affinal relatives of opposite sex between whom sexual relations are taboo will tend to avoid each other increasingly as residence rules bring them closer and closer together. This is Tylor's view. A system of unilateral descent and exogamy which aligns kin in the same manner as the residence rule (e.g., matrilineal descent with matrilocal residence) tends to reinforce the residence rule. Kinship terminology, when it matches residence and descent (in this case Iroquoian or Crow) will also reinforce the avoidance syndrome. Such relationships I have labeled functional. . . . If residence changes from matrilocal to bilocal and eventually to patrilocal, it becomes dysfunctional because it produces an alignment of kin which is contrary to that of the matricentered variables. I would label the relation of dog-eating (Table 16) to matricentered variables and M—S avoidance as non-functional.

My "own ideas" about the lag between division of labor (and other aspects of economy), residence, descent, and kin terminology have been demonstrated by several correlation matrices (Driver 1956; Driver and Massey 1957: last chapter). Although the correlations are not as high as one might desire, and Aberle and Blalock have slightly modified the causal interpretation of part of the variables in 1 matrix (Blalock 1960), I still hold to the lag theory as the best single explanation of all the correlations. . . . Using the new and presumably more accurate data of the present study, Table 17 exhibits the kind of matrix that I have explained by the lag theory. M—S avoidance fits best in the last position, suggesting that it lags behind all the other variables. However, F—D avoidance in a patricentered matrix (Table 18) does not "scale" as well.

TABLE 18
Correlations of F—D Avoidance and
Patricentered Social Organization

	1	2	3	4	5
1. Patrilocal Residence		.31	.09	−.03	−.16
2. Patrilineal Descent	.31		.55	.15	.12
3. Omaha Kin Terms	.09	.55		.31	.23
4. F—D Avoidance	−.03	.15	.31		.12
5. Bifurcate Merging Kin Terms	−.16	.12	.23	.12	
Total (signs disregarded)	.59	1.13	1.18	.61	.63

Any change in economy, such as the introduction of horticulture or agriculture, or migration to a new environment requiring a new ecological adjustment, might start a fresh developmental cycle which would eventually alter residence, descent, kinship terminology, and possibly other related aspects of social organization. In addition to such long-range changes taking hundreds or thousands of years, there are probably many historical events which act more quickly. Intermarriages among neighbors, fortunes of war and assimilation of defeated minorities, the assimilation of prestige groups or royalty from the outside and the tendency of lower ranking persons to follow the "fashion" of the more prestigeful groups, etc. Anthropology has given far too much attention to function and far too little to dysfunction. Although functional explanations have traditionally been synchronic, the concept can be extended to include a comparative and diachronic functionalism, as several cross-cultural researchers have already done. . . .

[Roy] D'Andrade's demonstration of the positive relation of avoidances to cross distinctions in kinship terminology and their negative relation to lineal distinctions for North America makes functional sense and should be tested from a larger world sample. The correlation of -.40 (significant at about .00001) between M—S avoidance and the kinds of kinship terminology which lack the cross distinction in Table 15 tends to support his view. Since the level of significance of this correlation is lower than . . . D'Andrade's, . . . it would seem that the cross *vs.* lineal-generation distinction is the most significant dichotomy. His suggestion that avoidance affect kinship terminology, rather than the reverse, is a fresh insight into the sequence of change and must be given serious consideration. At this point I am not at all sure who is right. The lag theory still seems to me to be highly relevant for the Plains area. Perhaps we are both partly right; each of our theories may account for some instances and not others, or there may be feedback from the 2nd to the 1st variable regardless of which appears 1st in the cycle of change. . . .

In patricentered Table 18, it is apparent that F—D avoidance cycles after residence, descent, and Omaha terminology, but before bifurcate merging, which is the most recalcitrant variable in the matrix. The relation of both the matricentered (Table 17) and patricentered cycles can be seen in Table 1 in the 21 x 21 matrix in the factor analysis section by Driver and Sanday (1966). . . .

[About the rules I use to determine ethnic units,] I prefer to regard all mutually unintelligible languages as separate ethnic units. I did not employ the above-quoted rules consistently in my avoidance study,

partly because it was well launched before I formulated the rules. Had I done so, it would have reduced the number of ethnic units lacking avoidances more often than those having them and would have lowered most correlations a little. Actually, we have had too few studies of dialect and language distance to do this accurately for the entire North American continent. . . .

I endorse D'Andrade's 1st rule "that a minimum unit cannot be made of sub-units having different traits." I applied this to the Pomo, for example, and distinguished Parsons' and Spier's unlocalized and undated information on the Caddo on this basis alone.

I do not accept his 2nd rule that "2 adjacent areas which have identical sets of relevant traits will be considered as the same minimum area." Where the trait inventory is long this is satisfactory, but for limited trait samples it groups large numbers of local groups together and obscures both diffusion and heritage from a common proto-culture by making a judgment about these processes in advance. Lumping most of the Salish into 1 ethnic unit ignores the immense variation in language within this family and blocks any appraisal of the relation of language to these cultural data in this area. I agree that the cultural data considered by me are remarkably uniform for the Salish and must be explained by cultural heritage or diffusion as well as functional cohesion. My rules [Driver 1965: 328-29] place adjacent local groups in the same ethnic unit only when they speak the same language, that is, identical or mutually intelligible dialects of the same language. My ethnic units would also change with different data, but much less so than D'Andrade's.

Nevertheless, D'Andrade's reduction of ethnic units within both language families and culture areas does produce an interesting result that would have been lost had I made the same reduction in the 1st place. His discovery that functionally related sets of traits are more often shared by peoples in the same culture area and same language family, and that nonfunctional or dysfunctional assemblages more often tend to occur among peoples in such distinctive combinations that the peoples cannot be matched up in 2's, 3's or larger groupings, even though they occupy the same culture areas and belong to the same language families, is indeed an important point.

The avoidance syndrome which D'Andrade cites from Robert Textor's unpublished *Cross Cultural Survey* is an intriguing one. I would like to see the relations of these variables tested on a large world sample and the results presented in a single correlation matrix; and this followed up by some of the tests for areal and language family clustering that have been mentioned in my paper and the comments on it.

I am quite willing to concede that the relations of avoidances to other aspects of culture are more complicated than I realized before I read these comments. I hope the others who have participated in this discussion have received as much education from it as I have.

References Cited

ABERLE, DAVID F. 1961a. "Navaho," in *Matrilineal kinship*. Edited by David M. Schneider and Kathleen Gough, pp. 96—201. Berkeley and Los Angeles: University of California Press.

——. 1961b. "Matrilineal descent in cross-cultural perspective," in *Matrilineal kinship*. Edited by David M. Schneider and Kathleen Gough, pp. 655—727. Berkeley: University of California Press. [JGJ*]

ADAIR, JAMES. 1775. *The History of the American Indians*. London: E. and C. Dilly.

AGINSKY, B. W. 1943. Culture element distributions: XXIV, Central Sierra. *University of California Anthropological Records* 8:393—468.

BARNETT, HOMER G. 1937. Culture element distributions: VII, Oregon Coast, *University of California Anthropological Records* 1:155—204.

——. 1939. Culture element distributions: IX. Gulf of Georgia Salish. *University of California Anthropological Records* 1:221—95.

BARTRAM, WILLIAM. 1853. Observations on the Creek and Cherokee Indians. *Transactions of the American Ethnological Society* 3:1—81.

BASEHART, HARRY W. 1960. *Mescalero Apache subsistence patterns and sociopolitical organization*. Albuquerque: University of New Mexico Press.

BEALS, RALPH L. 1933. Ethnology of the Nisenan. *University of California Publications in American Archaeology and Ethnology* 31:335—410.

——. 1943. *The aboriginal culture of the Cahita Indians*. Ibero-Americana, no. 19.

——. 1945a. *The contemporary culture of the Cahita Indians*. Bureau of American Ethnology Bulletin 142.

——. 1945b. Ethnology of the Western Mixe. *University of California Publications in American Archaeology and Ethnology* 42:1—176.

——. 1946. *Cheran: A Sierra Tarascan village*. Smithsonian Institution, Institute of Social Anthropology, publ. no. 2. Washington, D.C.

BENNETT, WENDELL C. and ROBERT M. ZINGG. 1935. *The Tarahumara: An Indian tribe of northern Mexico*. University of Chicago Publications in Anthropology, Ethnological Series.

BIRKET-SMITH, KAJ. 1924. Ethnography of the Egesmind District. *Meddelelser om Grønland* 66:1—484. Copenhagen.

——. 1930. Contributions to Chipewyan ethnology. *Report of the Fifth Thule Expedition, Copenhagen*.

——. 1953. The Chugach Eskimo. *Nationalmuseets Skrifter Etnografisk Raekke* VI. Copenhagen.

——. 1959. *The Eskimos*. London: Methuen and Co. Ltd.

BIRKET-SMITH, KAJ, and FREDERICA DE LAGUNA. 1938. *The Eyak Indians of the Copper River Delta*. Copenhagen: Levin and Munksgaard, E. Munksgaard.

BLALOCK, HUBERT M. 1960. Correlation analysis and causal inferences. *American Anthropologist* 62:624—31. [MF•]

——. 1961. Causal inferences in nonexperimental research. Chapel Hill: University of North Carolina Press.

BOAS, FRANZ. 1888. The Central Eskimo. *Bureau of American Ethnology, Annual Report* 6:390—669.

——. 1898. Traditions of the Tillamook Indians. *Journal of American Folklore* 11:23—38, 133—50.

——. 1901—07. The Eskimo of Baffin Land and Hudson Bay. *American Museum of Natural History Bulletin* 15:1—570.

——. 1916. Tsimshian mythology. *Bureau of American Ethnology, Annual Report* 31:29—1037.

——1921. Ethnology of the Kwakiutl. *Bureau of American Ethnology, Annual Report* 35, part 1:43—794.

——. 1923. Notes of the Tillamook. *University of California Publications in American Archaeology and Ethnology* 20:3—16.

BOHANNAN, PAUL. 1963. *Social anthropology*. New York: Holt, Rinehart and Winston. [MF•]

BOWERS, ALFRED W. 1950. *Mandan social and ceremonial organization*. Chicago: University of Chicago Press.

BRAINERD, GEORGE W. 1951. The place of chronological ordering in archaeological analysis. *American Antiquity* 16:301—13.

BRÉBEUF, J. DE. 1897. "Relation of the Huron, 1636," in *The Jesuit relations and allied documents*. Edited by R. G. Thwaites, 10:124—317. Cleveland: Burroux Bros.

BUNZEL, RUTH. 1930. Introduction to Zuni ceremonialism. *Bureau of American Ethnology, Annual Report* 47:467—544.

——. 1952. *Chichicastenango: A Guatemalan village*. Publications of the American Ethnological Society, no. 22.

CARRASCO, PEDRO. 1950. *Los Otomies*. Mexico,

D.F.: Universidad Nacional Autónoma de Mexico.

CHAMBERLAIN, A. F. 1892. Report on the Kootenay Indians. *British Association for the Advancement of Science, Report* 62: 549—617.

CHRISTENSEN, B. 1954. Los Otomies del estado de Puebla. *Revista Mexicana de Estudios Históricos* 8:259—68.

CLINE, WALTER, R. S. COMMONS, M. MANDELBAUM, R. H. POST, and L. V. W. WALTERS. 1938. *The Sinkajetk or Southern Okanagon of Washington.* Edited by Leslie Spier. General Series in Anthropology, no. 6.

CONZEMIUS, EDUARD. 1932. Ethnographical survey of the Miskito and Sumu Indians of Honduras and Nicaragua. *Bureau of American Ethnology Bulletin* 106:1—191.

COWAN, F. H. 1946. Notas etnográficas sobre los Mazateco de Oaxaca. *America Indígena* 6:27—39.

——. 1947. Linguistic and ethnological aspects of Mazateco kinship. *Southwestern Journal of Anthropology* 3:247—56.

CURTIS, EDWARD S. 1907—30. *The North American Indian.* 20 vols. Seattle: E. S. Curtis; Cambridge: Harvard University Press.

DAHLGREN DE JORDAN, BARBRO. 1954. *La Mixteca.* Mexico, D.F.: Imprenta Universitaria.

DEALE, V. B. 1958. The history of the Potawotamies before 1722. *Ethnohistory* 5:305—60.

DENIG, EDWIN T. 1930. Indian tribes of the Upper Missouri. *Bureau of American Ethnology, Annual Report* 46:375—628.

DENSMORE, FRANCES. 1929. *Chippewa music.* Bureau of American Ethnology Bulletin 86.

DI PESO, CHARLES C. 1953. *The Sobaipuri Indians of the Upper San Pedro River Valley, Southeastern Arizona.* Publications of the Amerind Foundation, no. 12, Dragoon, Ariz.

——. 1956. *The Upper Pima of San Cayetano del Lumacacori.* Publications of the Amerind Foundation, no. 6. Dragoon, Ariz.

DIXON, ROLAND B. 1905. The Northern Maidu. *American Museum of Natural History Bulletin* 17:119—346.

——. 1907. The Shasta. *American Museum of Natural History Bulletin* 17:381—498.

——. 1910. The Chimariko Indians and language. *University of California Publications in American Archaeology and Ethnology* 5:295—380.

DIXON, W. J. 1964. *Biomedical computer programs.* Health Sciences Computing Facility. School of Medicine, University of California, Los Angeles.

DORSEY, GEORGE A., and J. R. MURIE. 1940. Notes on Skidi Pawnee society. *Field Museum Anthropological Series* 27:67—119.

DORSEY, J. OWEN. 1885. Osage traditions. *Bureau of American Ethnology, Annual Report* 6:373—97.

——. 1889. Teton folk-lore. *American Anthropologist* 2:143—58.

DRIVER, HAROLD E. 1936. Wappo ethnography. *University of California Publications in American Archaeology and Ethnology* 36:179—220.

——. 1937. Culture element distributions: VI, Southern Sierra Nevada. *University of California Anthropological Records* 1:53—154.

——. 1939. Culture element distributions: X, Northwest California. *University of California Anthropological Records* 1:297—433.

——. 1956. *An integration of functional, evolutionary, and historical theory by means of correlations.* Indiana University Publications in Anthropology and Linguistics, Memoir 12.

——. 1961. *Indians of North America.* Chicago: University of Chicago Press.

——. 1964. "Survey of numerical classification in anthropology," in *The use of computers in anthropology.* Edited by Dell H. Hymes. pp. 277—320. The Hague: Mouton and Co.

——. 1965. World-wide cycles of development for social organization. MS.

DRIVER, HAROLD E., and WILHELMINE DRIVER. 1963. Ethnography and acculturation of the Chichimeca-Jonaz of Northeast Mexico. Part II, *International Journal of American Linguistics* 29, no. 2; *Indiana University Research Center in Anthropology, Folklore, and Linguistics*, no. 26.

DRIVER HAROLD E., and A. L. KROEBER. 1932. Quantitative expression of cultural relationships. *University of California Publications in American Archaeology and Ethnology* 31:211—56.

DRIVER, HAROLD E. and WILLIAM C. MASSEY. 1957. Comparative studies of North American Indians. *Transactions of the American Philosophical Society* 47:165—456.

DRUCKER, PHILIP, 1936. The Tolowa and their Southwest Oregon kin. *University of California Publications in American Archaeology and Ethnology* 36:221—300.

——. 1937. Culture element distributions: V, Southern California. *University of California Anthropological Records* 1:1-52.

——. 1939. Contributions to Alsea ethnography. *University of California Publications in American Archaeology and Ethnology* 35:81—102.

——. 1941. Culture element distributions: XVII, Yuman-Piman. *University of California Anthropological Records* 6:91—230.

——. 1950. Culture element distributions: XXVI, Northwest Coast. *University of California Anthropological Records* 9:157—294.

——. 1951. *The Northern and Central Nootkan Tribes*. Bureau of American Ethnology Bulletin 144.

DuBois, Cora. 1935. Wintu ethnography. *University of California Publications in American Archaeology and Ethnology* 36:1—148.

Dunning, R. W. 1959. *Social and economic change among the northern Ojibwa*. Toronto: University of Toronto Press.

Durlach, T. M. 1928. *The relationship systems of the Tlingit, Haida, and Tsimshian*. Publications of the American Ethnological Society, no. 11.

Eggan, Fred. 1934. The Maya kinship system and cross-cousin marriage. *American Anthropologist* 36:188—202.

——. 1937. "The Cheyenne and Arapaho kinship system," in *Social anthropology of North American tribes*. Edited by Fred Eggan, pp. 35-95. Chicago: University of Chicago Press.

——. 1950. *Social organization of the western Pueblos*. Chicago: University of Chicago Press.

Ellegard, Alvar. 1959. Statistical measurement of linguistic relationship, *Language* 35:131—56.

Elmendorf, William W. 1946. Twana kinship terminology. *Southwestern Journal of Anthropology* 2:420—32.

——. 1960. *The structure of Twana culture*. Washington State University Research Studies, Monograph Supplement, no. 2.

——. 1961. System change in Salish kinship terminologies. *Southwestern Journal of Anthropology* 17:365—82.

Ember, Melvin. 1963. The relationship between economic and political development in non-industrialized societies. *Ethnology* 2:228—49. [JGJ]

Emmons, G. T. 1911. The Tahltan Indians. *University of Pennsylvania Museum Anthropological Publications* 4:1—121.

Essene, Frank. 1942. Culture element distributions: XXI, Round Valley. *University of California Anthropological Records* 8:1—97.

Ewers, John C. 1950. Edwin T. Denig's "Of the Arickaras." *Bulletin of the Missouri Historical Society* 6:198—215.

Faron, Louis C. 1961. A reinterpretation of Choco society. *Southwestern Journal of Anthropology* 17:94—102.

——. 1962. Marriage, residence, and domestic group among the Panamanian Choco. *Ethnology* 1:13—38.

Flannery, Regina. 1946. "The culture of the northeastern Indian hunters: A descriptive survey," in *Man in northeastern North America*. Edited by Frederick Johnson, pp. 263—71. Papers of the Robert S. Peabody Foundation for Archaeology, vol. 3.

——. 1953. The Gros Ventres of Montana, part I: Social life. *Catholic University of America Anthropological Series* 15:1—221.

Fletcher, Alice and Francis La Flesche. 1906. The Omaha tribe. *Bureau of American Ethnology, Annual Report* 27.

Forde, C. D. 1931. Ethnography of the Yuma Indians. *University of California Publications in American Archaeology and Ethnology* 28:83—278.

Foster, George M. 1942. *A primitive Mexican economy*. Monographs of the American Ethnological Society, no. 5.

——. 1944. A summary of Yuki culture *University of California Anthropological Records* 5:155—244.

——. 1949. Sierra Populuca kinship terminology and its wider relationships. *Southwestern Journal of Anthropology* 5:330—34.

Frazer, James G. 1913. *Psyche's task*. London: Macmillan.

——. 1911. 3rd edition. *The golden bough*. 12 vols. London: Macmillan.

Freed, S. A. 1960. Changing Washo kinship. *University of California Anthropological Records* 14:349—418.

Freilich, Morris. 1963. Toward an operational definition of community. *Rural Sociology* 28:117—27. [MF•]

——. 1964a. The natural triad in kinship and complex systems. *American Sociological Review* 29:529—40. [MF•]

——. 1964b. Toward a model for social structure. *Journal of the Royal Anthropological Institute* 94:183—200. [MF•]

Freud, Sigmund. 1912. Ueber einige Uebereinstimmungen im Seelenleben der Wilden und der Neurotiker. *Imago* 17—33; 213—27.

Fruchter, Benjamin. 1954. *Introduction to factor analysis*. New York: D. Van Nostrand.

Fuente, Julio de la. 1949. *Yalálag: Una villa Zapoteca serrana*. Serie Científica, Museo Nacional de Antropología. Mexico.

Garfield, Viola E. 1939. Tsimshian clan and society. *University of Washington Publications in Anthropology* 7:167—349.

Garth, Thomas R. 1944. Kinship terminology, marriage practices, and behavior toward kin among the Atsugewi. *American Anthropologist* 46:348—61.

——. 1953. Atsugewi ethnography. *University of California Anthropological Records* 14:123—212.

Gatschet, A. S. 1891. The Karankawa Indians. *Papers*

of the Peabody Museum of Archaeology and Ethnology, Harvard University 1:5—103.

GAYTON, ANN H. 1948. Yokuts and western Mono ethnography. *University Museum of California Anthropological Records* 10:1—301.

GIBSON, LORNA F. 1954. El sistema de parentesco Pame. *Yan* 2:77—82.

GIFFORD, EDWARD W. 1916. Miwok moieties. *University of California Publications in American Archaeology and Ethnology* 12:139—94.

———. 1922. California kinship terminologies. *University of California Publications in American Archaeology and Ethnology* 18:1-285.

———. 1926a. Clear Lake Pomo society. *University of California Publications in American Archaeology and Ethnology* 18:287-390.

———. 1926b. Miwok lineages and the political unit in aboriginal California. *American Anthropologist* 28:389—401.

———. 1928a. The cultural position of the Coast Yuki. *American Anthropologist* 30:112 on.

———. 1928b. Notes on central Pomo and northern Yana society. *American Anthropologist* 30:675—84.

———. 1931. *The Kamia of Imperial Valley.* Bureau of American Ethnology Bulletin 97.

———. 1932a. The southeastern Yavapai. *University of California Publications in American Archaeology and Ethnology* 29:177—252.

———. 1932b. The Northfork Mono. *University of California Publications in American Archaeology and Ethnology* 31:15—65.

———. 1933. The Cocopa. *University of California Publications in American Archaeology and Ethnology* 31:257—334.

———. 1936. Northeastern and western Yavapai. *University of Califronia Publications in American Archaeology and Ethnology* 34:247—354.

———. 1939. The Coast Yuki. *Anthropos* 34:292—375.

———. 1940. Culture element distributions: XII, Apache-Pueblo. *University of California Anthropological Records* 4:1—207.

GIFFORD, EDWARD W., and A. L. KROEBER. 1937. Pomo. *University of California Publications in American Archaeology and Ethnology* 27:117—254.

GIFFORD, EDWARD W., and ROBERT H. LOWIE, 1928. Notes on the Akwa'ala Indians. *University of California Publications in American Archaeology and Ethnology* 23:339—52.

GILBERT, WILLIAM H., 1943. The eastern Cherokee. *Bureau of American Ethnology Bulletin* 133:169—414.

———. 1955. "Eastern Cherokee social organization," in *Social anthropology of North American tribes.* Edited by Fred Eggan, enlarged edition, pp. 285—340. Chicago: University of Chicago Press.

GLADWIN, T. 1948. Comanche kin behavior. *American Anthropologist* 50:73—94.

GODDARD, PLINY EARL. 1916. The Beaver Indians. *American Museum of Natural History Bulletin* 10:201—93.

GOLDFRANK, ESTHER S. 1927. *The Social and ceremonial organization of Cochiti.* American Anthropological Association Memoir no. 33.

GOLDMAN, IRVING. 1940. "The Alkatcho carrier of British Columbia," in *Acculturation in seven American Indian tribes.* Edited by Ralph Linton, pp. 333—89. New York, London: D. Appleton-Century.

GOLDSCHMIDT, WALTER R. 1951. Nomlaki ethnography. *University of California Publications in American Archaeology and Ethnology* 42:303—443.

GOLDSCHMIDT, WALTER R., and HAROLD E. DRIVER. 1940. The Hupa white deerskin dance. *University of California Publications in American Archaeology and Ethnology* 35:103—42.

GOODWIN, GRENVILLE. 1942. *The social organization of the western Apache.* Chicago: University of Chicago Press.

GOODY, JACK. 1961. The classification of double descent systems. CURRENT ANTHROPOLOGY 2:3—26.   [MF●]

GRIMES, J. E., and B . F. GRIMES. 1962. Semantic distinctions in Huichol (Uto-Aztecan) kinship. *American Anthropologist* 64:104—14.

GRINNELL, G. B. 1923. *The Cheyenne Indians.* 2 vols. New Haven: Yale University Press.

GUITERAS HOLMES, C. 1947. Clanes y sistema de parentesco de Cancuc. *Acta Americana* 5:1—17.

———. 1948. Sistema de parentesco Huasteco. *Acta Americana* 7:152—72.

GUNTHER, ERNA. 1927. Klallam ethnography. *University of Washington Publications in Anthropology* 1:171—314.

HAAS, MARY. 1939. Natchez and Chitimacha clans and kinship terminology. *American Anthropologist* 41:597—610.

HALLOWELL, A. I. 1928. Was cross-cousin marriage practiced by the north-central Algonkian? *Proceedings of the 23rd International Congress of Americanists,* pp. 519—44.

———. 1937. Cross-cousin marriages in the Lake Winnipeg area. *Publications of the Philadelphia Anthropological Society* 1:95—110.

———. 1938. The incidence, character, and decline of polygyny among the Lake Winnipeg Cree and Saulteaux. *American Anthropologist* 40:235—56.

HALPERN, A. M. 1942. Yuma kinship terms. *American Anthropologist* 44:425—41.

HARMAN, HARRY H. 1960a. "Factor analysis," in

Mathematical Methods for digital computers. Edited by H. S. Wilf and A. Ralston, pp. 204—12. New York: John Wiley & Sons.

———. 1960b. *Modern factor analysis.* Chicago: University of Chicago Press.

HARRINGTON, JOHN P. 1942. Culture element distributions: XIX, central California Coast. *University of California Anthropological Records* 7:1—46.

HASSICK, R. B. 1944. Teton Dakota kinship system. *American Anthropologist* 46:338—47.

HECKEWELDER, J. G. E. 1819. An account of the history, manners, and customs of the Indian Nations, who once inhabited Pennsylvania and the neighboring states. *Transactions of the Historical and Literary Committee of the American Philosophical Society* 1:1—348.

HELM, JUNE. 1962. Personal communication.

HELM, JUNE, and NANCY O. LURIE. 1961. *The subsistence economy of the Dogrih Indians of Lac La Martre in the Mackenzie District of the Northwest Territories.* Ottawa: Department of Northern Affairs and National Resources.

HENNEPIN, LOUIS. 1903. *A new discovery of a vast country in America.* Edited by R. G. Thwaites. 2 vols. Chicago: A. C. McClurg.

HILGER, INEZ M. 1952. *Arapaho child life and its cultural background.* Bureau of American Ethnology Bulletin 148.

HIND, H. Y. 1863. *Explorations in the interior of the Labrador Peninsula.* 2 vols. London: Longman, Green, Roberts.

HODGE, FREDERICK W. 1907—10. *Handbook of American Indians north of Mexico.* Bureau of American Ethnology Bulletin 30.

HOEBEL, E. A. 1939. Comanche and Hekandika Shoshone relationship systems. *American Anthropologist* 41:440—57.

———. 1940. *The political organization and law-ways of the Comanche Indians.* American Anthropological Association Memoir no. 54.

HOFFMAN, W. J. 1893. The Menomini Indians. *Bureau of American Ethnology Annual Report* 14:11—328.

HOIJER, HARRY. 1956. Athapaskan kinship systems. *American Anthropologist* 58:309—33.

HOLM, G. 1911. Ethnological sketch of the Angmagsalik Eskimo. *Meddelelser om Grønland* 39:1—147.

HONIGMANN, JOHN J. 1946. *Ethnography and acculturation of the Fort Nelson Slave.* Yale University Publications in Anthropology, no. 33, 34.

———. 1949. *Culture and ethos of Kaska society.* Yale University Publications in Anthropology, no. 40.

———. 1953. The Attawapiskat Cree Indians. *Anthropos* 47:809—16.

———. 1954. *The Kaska Indians.* Yale University Publications in Anthropology, no. 51.

———. 1956. The Attawapiskat Swampy Cree. *University of Alaska Anthropological Papers* 5:23—82.

HOOVER, J. W. 1935. Generic descent of the Papago villages. *American Anthropologist* 37:257—64.

HOWARD, J. H. 1960. "The cultural position of the Dakota: A reassessment," in *Essays in the Science of Culture in Honor Leslie A. White.* Edited by I. E. Dole and R. L. Carneiro, pp. 249—68. New York: Crowell.

HUGHES, C. C. 1958. An Eskimo deviant from the "Eskimo" type of social organization. *American Anthropologist* 60:1140—47.

HYDE, I. E. 1951. *Pawnee Indians.* Denver: Brown.

IBARRA, ALFREDO. 1943. Entre los indios Coras de Nayarit. *Anuario de la Sociedad Folk-lórica de Mexico* 4:49—60.

IGLESIAS, MARVEL ELYA, and C. H. MORGAN. 1939. *From the cradle to the grave: The story of a typical San Blas Indian maiden.* Cristobal.

JAMES, EDWIN. 1823. *Account of an expedition . . . to the Rocky Mountains . . . in the years, 1819, 1820 . . . under the command of Major S. H. Long.* 3 vols. London: Longman, Hurst, Rees, Arme, and Brown.

———. 1830. *Narrative of the captivity and adventures of John Tanner.* London: G. and C. H. Carvill.

JENNESS, DIAMOND. 1932. *The Indians of Canada.* Ottawa: Canada Department of Mines, National Museum of Canada, Bulletin 65.

———. 1935. *The Ojibwa Indians of Parry Island.* Canada Department of Mines, National Museum of Canada, Bulletin 78.

———. 1937. *The Sekani Indians of British Columbia.* Ottawa: Canada Department of Mines, National Museum of Canada, Bulletin 84.

———. 1938. *The Sarcee Indians of Alberta.* Ottawa: Canada Department of Mines, National Museum of Canada, Bulletin 90.

———. 1943. The Carrier Indians of the Bulkley River; their social and religious life. *Bureau of American Ethnology Bulletin* 133:469—586.

JOHNSON, JEAN B. 1950. *The Opata.* University of New Mexico Publications in Anthropology, no. 6.

JONES, LIVINGSTON F. 1914. *A study of the Thlingets of Alaska.* New York: F. H. Revell Co.

JOSSELIN DE JONG, P. E. DE. 1961. Comment on: The classification of double descent systems, by Jack Goody, CURRENT ANTHROPOLOGY 2:14—15.

[MF •]

KAISER, HENRY F. 1959. Computer program for Varimax rotation in factor analysis. *Educational and Psychological Measurement* 19:413—20.

53

KAUT, C. R. 1957. *The Western Apache Clan System*. University of New Mexico Publications in Anthropology, no. 9.

KELLY, ISABEL T. 1932. Ethnography of the Surprise Valley Paiute. *University of California Publications in American Archaeology and Ethnology* 31:67—210.

KELLY, ISABEL T., and A. PALERM. 1952. *The Tajin Totonac*. Smithsonian Institution, Institute of Social Anthropology, publ. no. 13.

KELLY, WILLIAM H. 1942. Cocopa gentes. *American Anthropologist* 44:675—91.

KINIETZ, W. V. 1940. *The Indians of the western Great Lakes*. Occasional Contributions from the Museum of Anthropology of the University of Michigan, no. 10.

——. 1946. Delaware culture chronology. *Prehistoric Research Series, Indiana Historical Society* 3:1—143.

KIRCHHOFF, PAUL. 1948. The Caribbean lowland tribes: The Mosquito, Sumo, Paya, and Jicaque. *Bureau of American Ethnology Bulletin* 143, vol. 4, pp. 219—29.

KOHL, JOHANN G. 1860. *Kitchi-Gami, Wanderings round Lake Superior*. London: Chapman and Hall.

KRAUSE, AUREL. 1956. *The Tlingit Indians*. Translated by Erna Gunther. Seattle: University of Washington Press.

KROEBER, A. L. 1899. The Eskimo of Smith Sound. *American Museum of Natural History Bulletin* 12:265—327.

——. 1902. The Arapaho. *American Museum of Natural History Bulletin* 18, parts 1—2.

——. 1907. Ethnology of the Gros Ventre. *American Museum of Natural History Anthropological Papers* 1:141—281.

——. 1917a. Zuni kin and clan. *American Museum of Natural History Anthropological Papers* 18:39—204.

——. 1917b. California kinship systems. *University of California Publications in American Archaeology and Ethnology* 12:339—96.

——. 1923. American culture and the Northwest Coast. *American Anthropologist* 25:1—20.

——. 1925. *Handbook of the Indians of California*. Bureau of American Ethnology Bulletin 78.

——. 1931. The Seri. *Southwest Museum Papers*, no. 6.

——. 1932. The Patwin and their neighbors. *University of California Publications in American Archaeology and Ethnology* 29:253—423.

——. Editor. 1935. *Walapai ethnography*, American Anthropological Association Memoir no. 42.

——. 1960. Statistics, Indo-European, and taxonomy. *Language* 36:1—21.

LA FLESCHE, FRANCIS. 1912. Osage marriage customs. *American Anthropologist* 14:127—30.

——. 1924. Ethnology of Osage Indians. *Smithsonian Miscellaneous Collections* 76:104—07.

LANDES, RUTH. 1931. *Ojibwa sociology*. Columbia University Contributions to Anthropology 29.

——. 1938. *The Ojibwa woman*. Columbia University Contributions to Anthropology 31.

LANTIS, MARGARET. 1946. The social culture of the Nunivak Eskimo. *Transactions of the American Philosophical Society* 35:153—323.

LAWSON, JOHN. 1860. *The history of Carolina*. Raleigh : O. H. Perry.

LEACOCK, ELEANOR. 1954. *The Montagnais hunting territory and the fur trade*. American Anthropological Association Memoir no. 78.

LESSER, ALEXANDER. 1930. Levirate and fraternal polyandry among the Pawnee. *Man* 30:98—101.

LÉVI-STRAUSS, CLAUDE. 1964. *Totemism*. Translated by Rodney Needham. Boston: Beacon Press. [MF●]

LINTON, RALPH. 1935. The Comanche sun dance. *American Anthropologist* 37:420—28.

LIPS, JULIUS E. 1947a. Naskapi law. *Transactions of the American Philosophical Society* 37:379—492.

——. 1947b. Notes on Montagnais-Naskapi economy. *Ethnos*. 12:1—78.

LOEB, EDWIN M. 1926. Pomo folkways. *University of California Publications in American Archaeology and Ethnology* 19:149—405.

——. 1932. The western Kuksu cult. *University of California Publications in American Archaeology and Ethnology* 33:1—137.

——. 1933. The eastern Kuksu cult. *University of California Publications in American Archaeology and Ethnology* 33:139—232.

LOUNSBURY, FLOYD, G. 1956. A semantic analysis of Pawnee kinship usage. *Language* 32:158—94.

LOUNSBURY, FLOYD G. 1956. A semantic analysis of Pawnee kinship usage. *Language* 32:158—94.

——. 1964a. "The structural analysis of kinship semantics," in *Proceedings of the Ninth International Congress of Linguists*, pp. The Hague: Mouton. [RD'A●]

——. 1964b. "The formal analysis of Crow- and Omaha-type kinship terminologies," in *Explorations in cultural anthropology*. Edited by Ward Goodenough, pp. New York: McGraw-Hill. [RD'A●]

LOWIE, ROBERT H. 1909. The Assiniboine. *American Museum of Natural History Anthropological Papers* 4:1—270.

———. 1912. Social life of the Crow Indians. *American Museum of Natural History Anthropological Papers* 9:181—253.

———. 1917. Notes on the social organization and customs of the Mandan, Hidatsa, and Crow Indians. *American Museum of Natural History Anthropological Papers* 21:1—99.

———. 1920. *Primitive society.* New York: Liveright.

———. 1924. Notes on Shoshonean ethnography. *American Museum of Natural History Anthropological Papers* 20:187—324.

———. 1929. Hopi kinship. *American Museum of Natural History Anthropological Papers* 30:361—88.

———. 1939. Ethnographic notes on the Washo. *University of California Publications in American Archaeology and Ethnology* 36:301—52.

McALLISTER, J. GILBERT. 1955. "Kiowa-Apache social organization," in *Social anthropology of North American tribes.* Edited by Fred Eggan, pp. 99—172. Chicago: University of Chicago Press.

MacGOWAN, E. S. 1942. The Arikara Indians. *Minnesota Archaeologist* 8:83—122.

McEWEN, WILLIAM J. 1963. Forms and problems of validation in social anthropology. CURRENT ANTHROPOLOGY 4:155—83.   [JGJ•]

McILWRAITH, T. F. 1948. *The Bella Coola Indians.* 2 vols. Toronto: University of Toronto Press.

McKENNAN, R. A. 1959. *The Upper Tanana Indians.* Yale University Publications in Anthropology, no. 55.

MacNEISH, JUNE HELM. 1960. Kin terms of Arctic Drainage Dene: Hare, Slavey, Chipewyan. *American Anthropologist* 62:279—95.

MANDELBAUM, DAVID G. 1940. The Plains Cree. *American Museum of Natural History Anthropological Papers* 37:155—316.

MASON, J. ALDEN. 1913. The Tepehuan Indians of Azqueltán. *Proceedings of the 18th International Congress of Americanists,* pp. 344—51. London.

———. 1946. *Notes on the Indians of the Great Slave Lake area.* Yale University Publications in Anthropology, no. 34.

———. 1952. Notes and observations on the Tepehuan. *América Indígena* 12:33—53.

MATTHEWS, G. H. 1959. Proto-Siouan kinship terminology. *American Anthropologist* 61:252—78.

MECHLING, W. H. 1958—59. The Malecite Indians, with notes on the Micmacs. *Anthropologica* 7:160; 8:161—274.

MENDIETA Y NUNEZ, LUCIO. 1949. *Los Zapotecos.* Mexico, D.F.: Universidad Nacional Autónoma de México.

MERRIFIELD, W. R. 1959. Chinantec kinship in Palantia. *American Anthropologist* 61:875—81.

METHVIN, J. J. 1899. *Andele, or the Mexican-Kiowa captive.* Louisville: Pentacostal Herald Press.

MICHELSON, TRUMAN. 1927. "Fox linguistic notes," in *Festschrift Meinhof,* pp. 403—8. Hamburg.

———. 1930. Notes on the great sacred pack of the thunderbird gens of the Fox Indians. *Bureau of American Ethnology Bulletin* 95:43—183.

———. 1934. Some Arapaho kinship terms and social usages. *American Anthropologist* 36:137—39.

MICKEY, BARBARA HARRIS. 1959. The Mazahua of the Cabecera de los Indigenes. Unpublished Ph.D. thesis, Indiana University, Bloomington, Indiana.

MONZON, ARTURO. 1945. Restos de clanes exogámicos entre los Cora de Nayarit. *Publicaciones de la Escuela Nacional de Antropología* 4:12—16.

MOONEY, JAMES. 1896. Calendar history of the Kiowa. *Bureau of American Ethnology Annual Report* 17:129—445.

———. 1932. The Swimmer manuscript. Edited by F. M. Olbrechts. *Bureau of American Ethnology Bulletin* 99:1—319.

MORGAN, LEWIS H. 1871. Systems of consanguinity and affinity. *Smithsonian Institution Contributions to Knowledge* 17:291—382.

MORICE, A. G. 1893. Notes archaeological, industrial, and sociological on the western Denes. *Transactions of the (Royal) Canadian Institute* 4:1—222.

MOSER, EDWARD. 1963. Personal communication.

MURDOCK, G. P. 1934. Kinship and social behavior among the Haida. *American Anthropologist* 36:355—85.

———. 1949. *Social structure.* New York: Macmillan.

———. 1957. World ethnographic sample. *American Anthropologist* 59:664—87.

———. 1958. Social organization of the Tenino. *Miscellanea Paul Rivet* 1:299—315. Mexico.

———. 1962—65. Ethnographic atlas. *Ethnology* 1:113—33, 265—85, 387—403, 533—45; 2:109—33, 249—65, 402—5, 541—48; 3:107—15, 199—217, 329—33, 420—23; 4:114—21, 241—50.

NADEL, S. F. 1957. *A theory of social structure.* Glencoe: The Free Press.   [MF•]

NANSEN, F. 1893. *Eskimo life.* London: Longmans, Green.

NAROLL, RAOUL. 1961. Two solutions to Galton's problem. *Philosophy of Science* 28:16—39.

———. 1962. Data quality control. Glencoe: The Free Press.

———. 1964a. A fifth solution to Galton's problem. *American Anthropologist* 66:863—67.

———. 1964b. On ethnic unit classification. CURRENT ANTHROPOLOGY 5:283—312.

NAROLL, RAOUL, and ROY G. D'ANDRADE. 1963. Two further solutions to Galton's problem. *American Anthropologist* 65:1053—67.

NEILL, EDWARD. 1872. Dakota land and Dakota life. *Collections of the Minnesota Historical Society* 1: 254—94.

NERLOVE, SARA BETH, and A. KIMBALL ROMNEY, n.d. Sibling terminology and cross-sex behavior. MS.

[RD' A •]

NEWCOMB, W. W. 1956. *The culture and acculturation of the Delaware Indians.* Anthropological Papers of the Museum of Anthropology of the University of Michigan 10.

NOMLAND, GLADYS A. 1935. Sinkyone notes. *University of California Publications in American Archaeology and Ethnology* 36:149—78.

——. 1938. Bear River ethnography. *University of California Anthropological Records* 2:91—124.

NORDENSKIÖLD, ERLAN. 1938. An historical and ethnological survey of the Cuna Indians. Edited by H. Wassen. *Comparative Ethnographic Studies* 10:1—686. Göteborg.

OLSON, RONALD L. 1936. The Quinault Indians. *University of Washington Publications in Anthropology* 6:1—190.

——. 1940. Social organization of the Haisla. *University of California Anthropological Records* 2:169—200.

OPLER, MARVIN K., 1940. "The Southern Ute of Colorado," in *Acculturation in seven American Indian tribes.* Edited by Ralph Linton. pp. 119—203. New York, London: D. Appleton-Century.

OPLER, MORRIS E. 1936a. A summary of Jicarilla Apache culture. *American Anthropologist* 38: 202—23.

——. 1936b. The kinship systems of the southern Athabaskan-speaking tribes. *American Anthropologist* 38:620—33.

——. 1946. *Childhood and youth in Jicavilla Apache society.* Publications of the Frederick Webb Hodge Anniversary Publication Fund, Southwest Museum, no. 5.

——. 1947. Rule and practice in the behavior between Jicarilla Apache affinal relatives. *American Anthropologist* 49:453—63.

——. 1955. "An outline of Chiricahua Apache social organization," in *Social anthropology of North American tribes.* Edited by Fred Eggan, pp. 173—242. Chicago: University of Chicago Press.

OSGOOD, CORNELIUS. 1936. *Contributions to the ethnography of the Kutchin.* Yale University Publications in Anthropology. no. 14.

——. 1937. *The ethnography of the Tanaina.* Yale University Publications in Anthropology, no. 16.

——. 1958. *Ingalik social culture.* Yale University Publications in Anthropology, no. 52.

OSTERMANN, H., Editor. 1942. The MacKenzie Eskimos, after K. Rasmussen's posthumous notes. *Report of the Fifth Thule Expedition* 10:1—166.

PALERM, A. 1952—53. Etnografía antigua totonaca en el oriente de México. *Revista Mexicana de Estudios Históricos* 13:167—73.

PARSONS, ELSIE C. 1923. Laguna genealogies. *American Museum of Natural History Anthropological Papers* 19:133—292.

——. 1925. *The pueblo of Jemez.* New Haven: Yale University Press.

——. 1929. *The social organization of the Tewa of New Mexico.* American Anthropological Association Memoir no. 36.

——. 1930. Isleta. *Bureau of American Ethnology Annual Report* 47:193—466.

——. 1932. The kinship terminology of the Pueblo Indians. *American Anthropologist* 34:377—89.

——. 1936. *Taos Pueblo.* General Series in Anthropology, no. 2.

——. 1939. Picuris, New Mexico. *American Anthropologist* 41:206—22.

——. 1941. *Notes on the Caddo.* American Anthropological Association Memoir no. 57.

PASSIN, HERBERT. 1943. The place of kinship in Tarahumara social organization. *Acta Americana* 1:360—83, 471—95.

——. 1944. Some relationships in Northwest Mexican kinship systems. *El México Antiguo* 6:205—18.

PAUL, LOIS, and BENJAMIN D. PAUL. 1963. Changing marriage patterns in a highland Guatemalan community. *Southwestern Journal of Anthropology* 19:131—48.

PERROT, N. 1911. Memoir on the manners, customs and religion of the savages of North America. Edited by E. H. Blair. *Indian Tribes of the Upper Mississippi Valley* 1:25—272.

POSPISIL, LEOPOLD, and WILLIAM S. LAUGHLIN. 1963. Kinship terminology and kindred among the Nunamiut Eskimo. *Ethnology* 2:180—89.

POZAS A., RICARDO. 1948. Juan Pérez Jolote, autobiografía de un Tzotzil. *Acta Antropológica* 3, no. 3. Mexico.

RADIN, PAUL. 1923. *The Winnebago Tribe.* Bureau of American Ethnology Annual Report no. 37.

RASMUSSEN, KNUD. 1908. *The people of the Polar North.* London: K. Paul, Trench, Trübner.

——. 1930. Observations on the intellectual culture of the Caribou Eskimos. *Report of the Fifth Thule Expedition* 7:1—114.

RAY, VERNE F. 1933. The Sanpoil and Nespelem. *University of Washington Publications in Anthropology* 5:1—237.

——. 1938. Lower Chinook ethnographic notes. *University of Washington Publications in Anthropology* 7:29—165.

——. 1942. Culture element distributions: XXII, Plateau. *University of California Anthropological Records* 8:99—262.

____. 1963. *Primitive pragmatists: the Modoc Indians of northern California.* American Ethnological Society.

REICHARD, GLADYS. 1928. *Social life of the Navaho.* Columbia University Contributions to Anthropology 7.

RIGGS, S. R. 1893. Dakota grammar, texts and ethnography. *Contributions to North American Ethnology* 9:1—232.

RITZENTHALER, R. E., and F. A. PETERSON. 1956. The Mexican Kickapoo Indians. *Publications in Anthropology of the Public Museum of the City of Milwaukee* 2:1—91.

ROBERTS, JOHN M. 1951. *Three Navaho households: A comparative study in small group culture.* Peabody Museum of Harvard University Papers, vol. 40, no. 3.   [RD'A•]

ROBINSON, W. S. 1951. A method for chronologically ordering archaeological deposits. *American Antiquity* 16:293—301.

ROJAS GONZALES, FRANCISCO. 1939. Los Mazahuas. *Revista Mexicana de Sociología* 1:99—122.

ROJAS GONZALES, FRANCISCO, and ROBERT DE LA CERDA SILVA. 1941. Los Tzotziles. *Revista Mexicana de Sociología* 3:114—42.

ROMNEY, A. KIMBALL. n.d. "Kinship and family," in *Handbook of Middle American Indians.* Edited by R. Wauchope. Austin: University of Texas Press. In   [RD'A•]

ROYS, RALPH L. 1943. *The Indian background of colonial Yucatan.* Carnegie Institution of Washington Publication 548.

RUSSELL, F. 1908. The Pima Indians. *Bureau of American Ethnology Annual Report* 26:3—390.

RUTTENBER, E. M. 1872. *History of the Indian tribes of Hudson's River.* Albany: J. Munsell.

SAPIR, EDWARD. 1907. Notes on the Takelma Indians. *American Anthropologist* 9:251—75.

____. 1918. Kinship terms of the Kootenay Indians. *American Anthropologist* 20:414—18.

SAPIR, EDWARD, and LESLIE SPIER. 1943. Notes on the culture of the Yana. *University of California Anthropological Records* 3:239—98.

SCHAEDEL, R. P. 1949. The Karankawa of the Texas Gulf Coast. *Southwestern Journal of Anthropology* 5:117—37.

SCHMITT, KARL, and IVA OSANAI SCHMITT. n.d. *Wichita kinship.* Norman, Oklahoma: University Book Exchange.

SHIMKIN, DEMITRI B. 1941. The Uto-Aztecan system of kinship terminology. *American Anthropologist* 43:223—45.

____. 1947. Wind River Shoshone ethnography. *University of California Anthropological Records* 5:245—88.

SILVERBERG, J. 1957. The Kickapoo Indians. *Wisconsin Archaeologist* 38:61—181.

SJOBERG, ANDRÉE F. 1953. The culture of the Tonkawa, a Texas Indian tribe. *Texas Journal of Science* 5:280—304.

SKINNER, ALANSON. 1911. Notes on the eastern Cree and northern Salteaux. *American Museum of Natural History Anthropological Papers* 9:1—177.

____. 1913. Menomini social life and ceremonial bundles. *American Museum of Natural History Anthropological Papers* 13:1—165.

____. 1914. Notes on the Plains Cree. *American Anthropologist* 16:68—87.

____. 1915a. Iowa societies. *American Museum of Natural History Anthropological Papers* 11:679—740.

____. 1915b. Kansa organizations. *American Museum of Natural History Anthrological Papers* 11:741—76.

____. 1923—25. Observations on the ethnology of the Sauk Indians. *Bulletin of the Public Museum of the City of Milwaukee* 5:1—180.

____. 1924—27. *The Mascoutens or Prairie Potawatomi Indians.* Bulletin of the Public Museum of the City of Milwaukee 6:1—262.

____. 1925. Notes on Mahican ethnology. *Bulletin of the Public Museum of the City of Milwaukee* 2:87—116.

____. 1926. Ethnology of the Ioway Indians. *Bulletin of the Public Museum of the City of Milwaukee* 5:181—354.

SMITH, MARIAN W. 1940. *The Puyallup-Nisqually.* Columbia University Contributions to Anthropology 32.

SMITH, N. N. 1957. Notes on the Malecite of Woodstock, New Brunswick. *Anthropologica* 5:1—40.

SPECK, FRANK G. 1909. *Ethnology of the Yuchi Indians.* University of Pennsylvania Museum Anthropological Publications 1.

____. 1915a. The family hunting band as the basis of the Algonkian social organization. *American Anthropologist* 17:289—305.

____. 1915b. *Family hunting territories and social life of various Algonkian bands of the Ottawa Valley.* Memoirs of the Canada Department of Mines, Geological Survey, no. 70.

____. 1918. Kinship terms and the family band among the northeastern Algonkian. *American Anthropologist* 20:143—61.

____. 1923. Mistassini hunting territories. *American Anthropologist* 25:425—71.

____. 1927. Family hunting territories of the Lake St. John Montagnais. *Anthropos* 22:387—403.

____. 1928. Family hunting territories of the Waswanipi

Indians. *Indian Notes, Museum of the American Indian, Heye Foundation* 5:42—59.

——. 1929. Boundaries and hunting groups of the River Desert Algonquin. *Indian Notes, Museum of the American Indian, Heye Foundation* 6:97—120.

——. 1935. *Naskapi*. Norman: University of Oklahoma Press.

——. 1940. *Penobscot Man*. Philadelphia: University of Pennsylvania Press.

SPECK, FRANK G., and C. E. SCHAEFFER, 1942. Catawba kinship and social organization. *American Anthropologist* 44:555—75.

SPENCER, ROBERT F. 1959. *The North Alaskan Eskimo*. Bureau of American Ethnology Bulletin 171.

SPICER, EDWARD H. 1961. Personal communications.

——. 1962. *Cycles of conquest*. Tucson: University of Arizona Press.

SPIER, LESLIE. 1923. Southern Diegueño customs. *University of California Publications in American Archaeology and Ethnology* 20:297—360.

——. 1924. Wichita and Caddo relationship terms. *American Anthropologist* 26:258—63.

——. 1927. The Ghost Dance of 1870 among the Klamath. *University of Washington Publications in Anthropology* 2:43—55.

——. 1928. Havasupai ethnography. *American Museum of Natural History Anthropological Papers* 29:81—392.

——. 1930. *Klamath ethnography*. University of California Publications in American Archaeology and Ethnology, vol. 30.

——. 1933. *Yuman tribes of the Gila River*. Chicago: University of Chicago Press.

SPIER, LESLIE, and EDWARD SAPIR. 1930. Wishram ethnography. *University of Washington Publications in Anthropology* 3:151—300.

STARR, FREDERICK. 1901—3. Notes upon the ethnography of southern Mexico. *Proceedings of the Davenport Academy of Science 9*.

STEENSBY, H. P. 1910. Contributions to the ethnology and anthropogeography of the Polar Eskimos. *Meddelelser om Grønland* 34:253—405.

STEPHENS, WILLIAM N. 1962. *The Oedipus complex*. Glencoe and New York: Free Press.

STEPHENS, WILLIAM N., and Roy G. D'Andrade. 1962. "Kin-avoidance," in *The Oedipus complex* by William N. Stephens, pp. 124—50, 213—26. Glencoe and New York: Free Press.

STERN, B. J. 1934. *The Lummi Indians of Northwest Washington*. Columbia University Contributions to Anthropology 17.

STEWARD, JULIAN H. 1933. Ethnography of the Owens Valley Paiute. *University of California Publications in American Archaeology and Ethnology* 33:233—350.

——. 1938. *Basin-Plateau aboriginal sociopolitical groups*. Bureau of American Ethnology Bulletin 120.

——. 1941. Culture element distributions: XIII, Nevada Shoshone. *University of California Anthropological Records* 4:209—359.

——. 1943. Culture element distributions: XXIII, northern and Gosiute Shoshoni. *University of California Anthropological Records* 8:263—392.

STEWART, OMER C. 1941. Culture element distributions: XIV, northern Paiute, *University of California Anthropological Records* 4:361—446.

——. 1942. Culture element distributions: XVIII, Ute-southern Paiute. *University of California Anthropological Records* 6:231—360.

STOUT, DAVID B. 1947. *San Blas Cuna acculturation*. Viking Fund Publications in Anthropology, no. 9.

STRONG, W. DUNCAN. 1929. *Aboriginal society in Southern California*. University of California Publications in American Archaeology and Ethnology, vol. 26.

SUTTLES, WAYNE. 1954. Postcontact culture changes among the Lummi Indians. *British Columbia Historical Quarterly* 18:29—102.

SWANSON, GUY E. 1960. *The birth of the gods*. Ann Arbor: University of Michigan Press.　　[JGJ●]

SWANTON, JOHN R. 1908. Social condition, beliefs and linguistic relationship of the Tlingit Indians. *Bureau of American Ethnology Annual Report* 26:321—486.

——. 1909. Contributions to the ethnology of the Haida. *American Museum of Natural History Anthropological Papers* 8:1—300.

——. 1910. Osage. *Bureau of American Ethnology Bulletin 30*, vol. 2:56—58.

——. 1911. Indian tribes of the lower Mississippi Valley and adjacent coast of the Gulf of Mexico. *Bureau of American Ethnology Bulletin* 43:1—274.

——. 1927. Social and religious beliefs and usages of the Chickasaw Indians. *Bureau of American Ethnology Annual Report* 44:169—273.

——. 1928. Social organization and social usages of the Indians of the Creek Confederacy. *Bureau of American Ethnology Annual Report* 42:23—472.

——. 1931. *Source material for the social and ceremonial life of the Choctaw Indians*. Bureau of American Ethnology Bulletin 103.

——. 1946. *The Indians of the southeastern United States*. Bureau of American Ethnology Bulletin 137.

TAX, SOL. 1955a. "The social organization of the Fox Indians," in *Social anthropology of North American tribes*. Edited by Fred Eggan, pp. 243—84. Chicago: University of Chicago Press.

——. 1955b. "Some problems of social organization," in *Social anthropology of North American tribes*.

Edited by Fred Eggan, pp. 3—34. Chicago: University of Chicago Press.

TEIT, JAMES A. 1900. The Thompson Indians of British Columbia. *American Museum of Natural History Memoirs* 2:163—392.

——. 1906. The Lillooet Indians. *American Museum of Natural History Memoirs* 4:191—300.

——. 1909. The Shuswap. *American Museum of Natural History Memoirs* 4:447—758.

——. 1928. The Middle Columbia Salish. *University of Washington Publications in Anthropology* 2:83—128.

——. 1930. The Salishan tribes of the western Plateaus. *Bureau of American Ethnology Annual Report* 45:37—197.

——. 1956. Field notes on the Tahltan and Kaska Indians, 1912—15. *Anthropologica* 3:39—171.

TEXTOR, ROBERT, n.d. *Cross Cultural Survey.* New Haven: Human Relations Area Files. In press.
[RD'A•]

THALBITZER, W. 1917, 1921, 1941. The Ammassalik Eskimo. *Meddelelser om Grønland* 50:113—564, 569 —739; 53:435—81.

TITIEV, MISCHA. 1944. *Old Oraibi.* Peabody Museum of American Archaeology and Ethnology Papers, Harvard University, vol. 22.

TOZZER, ALFRED M. 1941. *Landa's relacion de las cosas de Yucatan.* Peabody Museum of American Archaeology and Ethnology Papers, Harvard University, vol. 18.

TRAGER, GEORGE L. 1943. The kinship and status terms of the Tiwa languages. *American Anthropologist* 45:557—71.

TROWBRIDGE, C. C. 1938. *Meearmeear traditions.* Edited by W. V. Kinietz. Occasional Contributions of the Museum of Anthropology of the University of Michigan, no. 7.

TURNER, L. M. 1890. Ethnology of the Ungava District. *Bureau of American Ethnology Annual Report* 11:159—84, 267—350.

TURNEY-HIGH, H. H. 1937. *The Flathead Indians of Montana.* American Anthropological Association Memoir no. 48.

——. 1941. *Ethnography of the Kutenai.* American Anthropological Association Memoir no. 56.

TYLOR, EDWARD B. 1879. On the game of patolli in ancient Mexico, and its probable Asiatic origin. *Journal of the Royal Anthropological Institute of Great Britain and Ireland* 8:116—129.

——. 1889. On a method of investigating the development of institutions; applied to laws of marriage and descent. *Journal of the Royal Anthropological Institute of Great Britain and Ireland* 18:245— 72. Reprinted in *Readings in cross-cultural Methodology.* Edited by Frank W. Moore, pp. 1—28. Human Relations Area Files, 1961.

——. 1896. On American lot games as evidence of Asiatic intercourse before the time of Columbus. *Internationaler Archiv für Ethnographie.* Vol. 9, supplement: *Ethnographische Beitrage.*

UNDERHILL, RUTH M. 1939. *Social organization of the Papago Indians.* Columbia University Contributions to Anthropology 30.

VETROMILLE, E. 1866. *The Abnakis and their history.* New York: J. B. Kirker.

VILLAS ROJAS, A. 1947. Kinship and nagualism in a Tzeltal community. *American Anthropologist* 49:578—87.

VOEGELIN, ERMINIE W. 1938. Tübatulabal ethnography. *University of California Anthropological Records* 2:1—84.

——. 1942. Culture element distributions: XX. Northeast California. *University of California Anthropological Records* 7:47—251.

VOGT, EVON Z. 1961. Personal communication.

WAGLEY, CHARLES. 1941. *Economics of a Guatemalan village.* American Anthropological Association Memoir, no. 58.

——. 1949. *The social and religious life of a Guatemalan village.* American Anthropological Association Memoir no. 71.

WALLACE, ANTHONY F. C. 1947. Woman, land, and society: three aspects of aboriginal Delaware life. *Pennsylvania Archaeologist* 17:1—35.

WALLACE, E., and E. A. HOEBEL. 1952. *The Comanches.* Norman: University of Oklahoma Press.

WALLIS, WILSON D. 1947. The Canadian Dakota. *American Museum of Natural History Anthropological Papers* 41:1—225.

WALLIS, WILSON D., and RUTH S. WALLIS. 1955. *The Micmac Indians of Eastern Canada.* Minneapolis: University of Minnesota Press.

——. 1957. *The Malecite Indians of New Brunswick.* Ottowa: Canada Department of Mines, National Museum of Canada, Bulletin 148.

WEITLANER, ROBERT J. 1951. "Notes on the social organization of Ojitlan," in *Homenaje a Don Alfonso Caso,* pp. 441—55. Mexico: Imprenta Nuevo Mundo.

——. 1961. Personal communication.

WEITLANER, ROBERT J., and C. A. CASTRO GUEVARA. 1954. *Papeles de la Chinantla.* Mexico.

WHEELER-VOEGELIN, ERMINE. n.d. Shawnee ethnography. MS.

WHITE, LESLIE A. 1930. The Acoma Indians. *Bureau of American Ethnology Annual Report* 47:17—192.

——. 1932. *The Pueblo of San Felipe.* American Anthropological Association Memoir no. 38.

——. 1935. *The Pueblo of Santo Domingo.* American Anthropological Association Memoir no. 43.

——. 1942. *The Pueblo of Santa Ana.* American Anthropological Association Memoir no. 60.

——. 1959. *The evolution of culture.* New York, Toronto, London: McGraw-Hill. [HCW●]

WHITING, JOHN W. M. 1964. "The effects of climate on certain cultural practices," in *Explorations in cultural anthropology: Essays in honor of George Peter Murdock.* Edited by Ward H. Goodenough, pp. 511—44. New York: McGraw-Hill. [RD'A, JGJ●]

WHITING, JOHN W. M., and IRVIN L. CHILD. 1953. *Child training and personality: A cross-cultural study.* New Haven: Yale University Press.

WHITING, JOHN W. M., K. KLUCKHOHN, and A. S. ANTHONY. 1959. "The function of male initiation ceremonies at puberty," in *Readings in social psychology.* Edited by N. Maccoby, W. W. Newcomb, and Hartley, pp. 359—70. New York: Holt [RD'A●]

WHITMAN, W. 1937. *The Oto.* Columbia University Contributions to Anthropology 28.

WILL, G. F., and H. J. SPINDEN. 1906. The Mandans. *Peabody Museum of Archaeology and Ethnology Papers, Harvard University* 3:81—219.

WISDOM, CHARLES. 1940. *The Chorti Indians of Guatemala.* Chicago: University of Chicago Press.

WISSLER, CLARK. 1911. Social life of the Blackfoot Indians. *American Museum of Natural History Anthropological Papers* 7:1—64.

YINGER, J. MILTON. 1960. Contraculture and subculture. *American Sociological Review* 25:625—35. [MF ●]

ZINGG, ROBERT M. 1938. *The Huichols: Primitive artists.* University of Denver Contributions to Ethnography, no. 1.

4. Diffusion and Evolution

Harold E. Driver

Marvin Harris (1968: 373) and others have called diffusion a nonprinciple and regarded it as a kind of contamination of the precious process of evolution. The study of the evidence for both diffusion and evolution from documents, unassailable inorganic evidence, and the best-known organic evidence (that on domesticated plants and animals) shows conclusively that independent invention is rare and diffusion common. Most of the building blocks for a cumulative evolution in any one locality were invented somewhere else and reached that locality by some sort of historical transmission from the outside. This is true for domesticated plants and animals, division of labor, metallurgy, writing, alphabetic writing, calendars, industrial technology, and a hundred other topics commonly mentioned by evolutionists.

Everyone agrees that when a former hunting, gathering, or fishing society, which had subsisted exclusively on wild plants and animals, changes over to domesticated plants and animals and produces most of its food in this manner, it has taken a major step upward on the evolutionary stairway. The species of domesticated plants and animals most important to man have each been first domesticated in a limited region and later have spread by diffusion and other historical processes to a large majority of the societies possessing them. If diffusion is a nonprinciple, then it makes no difference, for example, whether maize was domesticated once in southern Mexico and spread by diffusion to the hundreds of peoples cultivating it in A.D. 1492 or whether it was independently domesticated hundreds of times in each of the localities where it was found. A review of maize history is in order.

The oldest wild maize so far discovered has been found in lake beds in the Valley of Mexico. It was determined from pollen analysis of deep cores, dated at 80,000 years ago. Although this date seems too old, it has laid to rest speculation that maize may be of Old World origin. The appearance of wild maize in human habitation sites in the state of Puebla, Mexico, in 5000 B.C., and the appearance of domesticated maize in the same sites by about 4000 B.C., makes this area the most likely candidate for the origin of maize cultivation. The discovery of maize in Bat Cave, New Mexico, with a date tag of about 3000 B.C., is attributed to diffusion by human agents for the following reasons: (1) it is later than the Mexican finds; (2) the variety is close to the earlier Mexican forms; (3) no wild maize has been discovered north of the Valley of Mexico; and (4) maize cannot survive more than a few years without the care of man in any locality north of Mexico. Furthermore, it seems certain that the diffusion of maize and other southern Mexican plants to areas north of Mexico triggered horticulture in every locality in the United States and Canada where there was any farming at all. Although a handful of local endemic species were cultivated a little in both the Southwest and the Southeast, there is as yet no evidence of the cultivation of any of these local species before the introduction of maize or other Mexican endemics (Griffin 1967: 180). Therefore diffusion triggered the shift from mere food extracting to food production everywhere north of Mexico, and many Indian peoples made a step up Harris' evolutionary stairway because of diffusion.

The earliest finds of maize in South America are domesticated varieties no earlier than 1500 B.C., and these match Mexican varieties closely enough to suggest derivation from Mexico. Although the evolution from subsistence on wild plants and animals to domesticated forms was begun in South America without maize, diffusion of other plants was crucial, and diffusion of maize later sped up the process.

The histories of wheat, rice, and other staple plant foods in the Old World also exhibit the earliest domestication in a small area and subsequent diffusion to hundreds of other peoples at later dates.

It would be ideal to know exactly why each recipient society accepted one or more species of domesticated plants from the outside at the time that it did, and to know more about the hundreds of details of each society's culture that created the need and opened the doors for its satisfaction of the need. Where such knowledge is lacking, however, we may still be able to establish the fact of diffusion in the manner suggested above.

Exceptions to monogenesis for a domesticated species of plant may occur when a species is divided into two or more distinct races, each limited to its own territory. If two domesticated races, say one each in Mexico and Peru, match the wild races in those areas closely and show no evidence of hybridization, then the ethnobotanist may infer two independent domestications of the species (Heiser 1965). For every instance of this kind there are many where a single origin is indicated.

Domesticated animals are remarkable for the small number of species represented as compared with the very large number of wild forms. These few domesticated species have been diffused by man over wide areas, especially in the Old World. Nearly all seem to have been domesticated only once in a single region —such as the mountainous area around the Fertile Crescent in the Middle East—and then to have spread elsewhere, in this case over Europe, North Africa, and much of Asia. An exception to this is the pig, which stems from at least two wild species: *Sus scrofa* in the Middle East and *Sus vittatus* in southeast Asia (Dyson, 1968: 253). A West African native pig may constitute a third independent domestication. For details of animal domestication see Zeuner (1963) and Ucko and Dimbleby (1969).

My recent review of domesticated plants in the Americas in the second edition of *Indians of North America* (Driver 1969: 66-77) found no solid evidence for the pre-Columbian diffusion by man of a single species from the Old World to the New. However, the sweet potato seems to have gone the other way, from South America to Polynesia before A.D. 1492. The case for diffusion as a major process of culture change and growth is strong enough without romantic speculation about transoceanic, pre-Columbian diffusion between the hemispheres.

Everyone speculating about the first domestication of plants agrees that women were probably the first farmers. This conclusion stems from the role of women as the principal gatherers of wild plant products everywhere in the world, and also from the frequent farming of women with hand tools in many parts of the world. In North America, there are significant correlations between a female farming division of labor and matrilocal residence and matrilineal descent, leading finally to matricentered kinship terminology (Driver 1956; reprinted in Driver and Massey 1957: 421-38 and in Ford 1967: 259-89). Presumably maize and other domesticated plants diffused from women in donor societies to women in receptor societies. Thus diffusion played an important role in the determination of social structure.

Geographers have produced better generalizations about documented diffusions of innovations in the twentieth century than have anthropologists. Hägerstrand (1968) summarizes a number of such studies. He finds that, when statistical information is available, the most characteristic growth curve is an S-shaped cumulative frequency distribution. The number of adopters of the innovation is few in the beginning, then gradually increases to its maximum, and eventually tapers off to a few or none at the end. Different innovations run through this cycle at different rates of speed, and as speed of transportation and of advertising contact increases, so does the rate of diffusion.

Geographically, the spread of an innovation is often only a short distance from the point of origin in the beginning, with the distance becoming greater over time, but the spatial pattern is frequently modified by multiple centers of diffusion. Centers of innovation are also the rule and are places where an unusual number of technological or other kinds of "building blocks" are available for the construction of the new product. In spite of advertising in the mass media and salesmanship, persons (especially in rural areas) usually seek the advice of a local friend or expert before accepting the innovation. "Among farming populations in Europe and Asia the probabilities of contact decrease at a rate steeper than the square of the distance" (Hägerstrand 1968: 176).

Mathematical models of particular diffusions documented in time and space have been constructed and, with the aid of a computer, are capable of simulating a very close approximation to the actual diffusion. This work achieves a level of abstraction beyond anything done by cultural anthropologists. The principal limitation of all of these quantitative studies of diffusion is the absence of any adequate sampling method. Are the examples displaying such neat regularities representative of all documented diffusions, or have they been selected and exhibited because they are the closest approximations to the mathematical models? For a description and bibliography of a wide range of twentieth-century methods applied to twentieth-century diffusions see Clarke (1968: 463-90) and Brown (1968).

The close fit of the postdicted, unilinear evolutionary scale of Caneiro and Tobias (1963) to the documented first appearance of many of the culture traits in England is encouraging to evolutionists (Carneiro 1968). However, it must be remembered that the tribes and the traits were selected to conform to the preconceived theory and that each list was only about a 10% sample of the total number of well-known tribes and traits represented in recent large cross-cultural samples, such as that of Murdock (1967). The number of bits of data is only about 1% (10% times 10%) of the total available.

Other studies have operated on the assumption that a single scale of evolutionary development is an oversimplification and that multiple uncorrelated scales are to be anticipated. One of these is that by Gouldner and Peterson (1962), who used a small corpus of 109 culture traits in 71 societies compiled by Simmons (1945). They computed a principal axes factor analysis with varimax rotation and found two orthogonal factors, hence two dimensions of evolutionary growth. Bowden (1969), using the same data, applied Thurstone's latent-distance model, described in Torgerson (1958), and came up with three dimensions of evolution. The ten factors found by Sawyer and LeVine (1966) and the twelve factors isolated by Driver and Schuessler (1967), both from Murdock's 1957 sample, suggest as many independent lines of cultural evolution, or no evolution for some of the factors. These techniques have yet to be applied to the larger body of data in Murdock (1967). Presumably such techniques would yield still more dimensions of evolution. Recent computer programs for multiple scalogram analysis have refined methods for determining how many independent scalograms can be derived from a corpus of data.

The so-called Galton's Problem studies have all found that every correlation tested so far is influenced to some extent by diffusion. The recent study of Murdock and White (1969) concludes that, if the ethnic units in their study were spaced far enough apart to eliminate all influence of diffusion on their correlations, there would be only twenty ethnic units left in as many culture provinces around the world. This would be too few to use for any cross-cultural study. Evolutionists can no more wish away diffusion than physiologists can wish away the circulation of the blood. Their only hope is to estimate or measure the role of diffusion in culture change and culture growth.

Harris, Carneiro, and others have called attention to the capricious character of diffusion. They have chosen to ignore the equally capricious character of evolution. It should be remembered that if enough evolutionary detail were known about each of a thousand societies, no two of them would have evolved through exactly the same sequence for a thousand or so items of culture. Also, none of the cultures of the hunters and gatherers have remained changeless over the last ten thousand years or so. All that evolutionary postdictions from synchronic nonmaterial culture can show is the very broad general trend of societies as a whole. A recent study of twentieth-century cultural evolution in Mexico (Graves et al. 1969) showed that rank order correlations between two postdicted evolutionary sequences derived from Guttman scales and the actual documented sequences varied from 1.00 to -.63 among forty Mexican towns. The average was about .40 for one scale and .60 for the other, which reveals a very modest amount of conformity to the postdicted scales. I doubt if other evolutionary postdictions for as many localities would average much better, although Carneiro's (1968) study shows a higher relationship in England. The other interesting feature of the Graves study is that none of the innovations discussed originated in any of the Mexican towns, but all were introduced from the outside. Their ultimate origins were even outside of Mexico. Thus the building blocks that societies use to upgrade themselves on the stairway of evolution often reach them by diffusion from the outside.

References Cited

Bowden, Edgar
  1969   "An index of sociocultural development applicable to precivilized societies," *American Anthropologist* 71: 454-61.
Brown, Lawrence A.
  1968   *Diffusion processees and location*, Philadelphia, Regional Science Research Institute.
Carneiro, Robert L.
  1968   "Ascertaining, testing, and interpreting sequences of cultural development," *Southwestern Journal of Anthropology* 24: 354-74.
Carneiro, Robert L., and Stephen F. Tobias
  1963   "The application of scale analysis to the study of cultural evolution," *Transactions of the New York Academy of Sciences*, Series 2, 26: 196-207.
Clarke, David L.
  1968   *Analytical archaeology*, London, Methuen.

Driver, Harold E.
1956 "An integration of functional, evolutionary, and historical theory by means of correlation," *Indiana University Publications in Anthropology and Linguistics, 12*: 1-36.
1969 *Indians of North America*, 2d ed., rev., Chicago, University of Chicago Press.
Driver, Harold E., and William C. Massey
1957 "Comparative studies of North American Indians," *Transactions of the American Philosophical Society n.s. 47*: 165-456.
Driver, Harold E., and Karl F. Schuessler
1967 "Correlational analysis of Murdock's 1957 ethnographic sample," *American Anthropologist 69*: 332-52.
Dyson, Robert H., Jr.
1968 "Animal domestication," in David L. Sills, ed., *International Encyclopedia of the Social Sciences 4*: 250-54.
Ford, Clellan S., ed.
1967 *Cross-cultural approaches*, New Haven, HRAF Press.
Gouldner, Alvin W., and Richard A. Peterson
1962 *Notes on technology and the moral order*, Indianapolis, Bobbs-Merrill.
Graves, Theodore D., Nancy B. Graves, and Michael J. Kobrin
1969 "Historical inferences from Guttman scales: the return of age-area magic?" *Current Anthropology 10*: 317-38.
Griffin, James
1967 "Eastern North American archaeology: a summary," *Science 156*: 175-91.
Hägerstrand, Torsten
1968 "The diffusion of innovation," in David L. Sills, ed., *International Encyclopedia of the Social Sciences 4*: 174-78.
Harris, Marvin
1968 *The rise of anthropological theory*, New York, Crowell.
Heiser, Charles B.
1965 "Cultivated plants and cultural diffusion in Nuclear America," *American Anthropologist 67*: 930-49.
Murdock, George Peter
1967 *Ethnographic atlas: a summary*, Pittsburgh, University of Pittsburgh Press.
Murdock, George Peter, and Douglas R. White
1969 "Standard cross-cultural sample," *Ethnology 8*: 329-69.
Sawyer, Jack, and Robert A. LeVine
1966 "Cultural dimensions: a factor analysis of the *World Ethnographic Sample*," *American Anthropologist 68*: 708-31.
Simmons, Leo W.
1945 *The role of the aged in primitive society*, New Haven, Yale University Press.
Torgerson, Warren S.
1958 *Theory and methods of scaling*, New York, Wiley.
Ucko, Peter J., and G. W. Dimbleby, eds.
1969 *The domestication and exploitation of plants and animals*, Chicago, Aldine.
Zeuner, Frederick E.
1963 *A history of domesticated animals*, London, Hutchinson.

5. Historical Reconstruction and its Explanatory Role in Comparative Ethnology, a Study in Method [1]

David F. Aberle

An explanation is an intellectually satisfactory, valid answer to a "Why?" question (cf. Braithwaite 1968). Many "Why?" questions in comparative ethnology take the form: "Why is phenomenon X found in culture(s) A . . . n?" or the form: "Why do phenomena Y and Z tend to be associated in a large sample of cultures?" An answer to either question ordinarily requires reference to origins or causes or both. A genuinely historical explanation of origin or causes requires access to history—to sequential information: Where and when did phenomenon X originate? What is the regular temporal relationship of Y and Z? In comparative ethnology, however, inferences about sequences are usually made from synchronic data, because sequential data are lacking. Under these circumstances, an answer about origins takes the form of an inference that is a concluding hypothesis, subject to challenge in the light of alternative interpretations. It cannot be validated by sequential information, including controlled experiments and before-and-after observations. A hypothesis about antecedents and consequents based on synchronic comparative studies is subject to challenge by competing hypotheses, but also by means of data from other samples of cultures, which may or may not prove to exhibit the same regularities. In the absence of sequential information, rigorous inductive methods and clear criteria for choosing among competing hypotheses are crucial for selecting the best explanation for the distribution of phenomena among cultures and the association of phenomena with one another.

In a series of methodologically sophisticated essays and monographs, Harold Driver has used various inductive techniques to account for the distribution of attributes among sets of cultures and the association of attributes with one another. From earliest to latest, these studies commend themselves to his contemporaries and to future generations of anthropologists, not only for their conclusions but also for their methods, which permit other workers to deal with similar problems. In later sections, this essay will comment on certain of Driver's methods and historical reconstructions, as they appear in his "An Integration of Functional, Evolutionary, and Historical Theory by Means of Correlations." First issued by Driver in 1956, it appeared in a fuller version in "Comparative Studies of North American Indians" (Driver and Massey 1957:421-39), which is used here for citations.

The present essay argues that two types of explanations are commonly used to account for the distribution of attributes among cultures, and that these two types should be clearly distinguished. It contends that the use of reconstructive methods merits more consideration than has been given in recent decades in anthropology. It provides a method for making inferences about the social organization of a protospeech community and illustrates its use. Finally, it compares the results of applying this method with the results of certain other lines of inference. Its stress, however, is on methods rather than on the specific results presented.

Any attribute in a given culture is either (1) a retention from an antecedent stage in the history of that culture or (2) an innovation. If it is an innovation, it is either (a) a development *de novo* in that culture, or (b) borrowed from another culture. An innovation *de novo* is here called an "invention," but there is no implication that all such inventions are consciously planned. An innovation borrowed from some other culture is a "loan." Before attributes (traits, characteristics) can be classified under these headings, several decisions must be made by the analyst. First, the attribute must be treated as one of a set of attributes of a given variable. The decision that an attribute is or is not an innovation depends upon the definition of the variable and its attributes. Thus if the variable is "fire-making equipment with fuel tank," and two attributes are "propane-fueled" and "lighter-fluid fueled," the propane lighter may be viewed as a recent innovation. If the variable is "fire-making equipment," and

the attributes are "based on striking sparks," "wood-wood friction," "compressed air", etc., the propane lighter, with its sparking system, becomes part of a larger class of some antiquity. Second, the cultural unit in question must be denominated. What is a loan from one point of view is an invention from another. If the units are England, France, Germany, etc., then the steam engine is an English invention and a loan for the other cultures. If the units are Western Europe, Eastern Europe, North Africa, etc., then the steam engine is a Western European innovation. Third, the time span or stadial span in question must be stated. What is an innovation at one stage is a retention at another. Thus a lexeme might be regarded in one perspective as an innovation that followed the separation of Germanic from Proto-Indo-European, but in another as a retention from Proto-Germanic. Given a particular time span or set of stages, there is often interest in defining sequences of innovations, as well as in the differentiation of retentions and innovations.

If these decision are made and if there is historical information about the origin and spread of a set of attributes, any attribute can be classified as a retention, an invention, or a loan. In comparative ethnological research, such information is often lacking. In its absence, if the decisions described above are made, methods are available for making probabilistic choices among the alternatives, in order to classify them as retentions or innovations. If they are classified as innovations, sometimes they may also be distinguished as inventions or loans. In some cases, the methods used may result in a decision that the issue is indeterminate. Indeed, a method that indicates that no choice is possible has great value in locating points of indeterminacy.

For certain purposes, an intellectually satisfactory answer to the question: "Why is X found in culture A?" is provided by any of the following statements: (1) "Because it is retained from an earlier stage"; (2) "because it was borrowed from culture B"; or (3) "because it was invented in culture A after it became distinctive from certain related cultures." Thus if someone asks why men's coats have sleeve buttons and is told: "Because they are a retention from an earlier stage when the sleeves of a man's coat could be buttoned and unbuttoned," his curiousity may be satisfied, even though any "Why?" question can generate others until the answer becomes either: "Because that's the way it is," or "I don't know."

One type of explanation, then, is to classify attributes as retentions and innovations and to classify the type of innovation where possible. A second type of explanation is an effort to answer the question: "Why did the retention, invention, or loan occur?" Thus a retention might be explained as the result of inertia, of its continued value in the present, of a desire to maintain cultural diacriticals to define group membership, of the continuing exercise of power by those for whom the attribute has value, and so on. An invention might be explained as an adaptive effort—including efforts to increase competitive advantage with other societies—a striving toward consistency, and so on. A loan might be explained on the same bases as an invention or as a result of its utility in intercultural relations, as well as in other ways. It is possible, of course, that no explanation may come to mind, or that no rules of evidence can be thought of to choose among alternative explanations. Thus, although there is general agreement that sleeve buttons on men's coats are a retention, there is no well-accepted explanation as to why the retention has occurred.

Put simply, the first type of explanation, whereby attributes are classified as retentions, inventions, or loans, explains the distribution of attributes by reference to their origins. The second type, whereby reasons are given for retention, invention, or borrowing, explains the distribution of attributes by reference to their causes. Where historical information is inadequate, it would appear to be sound strategy to explain initially by reference to origins and only thereafter by reference to causes. There are two advantages to this strategy. First, it reduces the likelihood of explaining the reason for the recent invention of something that may have been retained for millennia, the reason for the borrowing of something that was independently invented, and so on. Second, it avoids excessive reliance on the empirical generalizations or empirical laws of ethnology, which are at present only weakly developed. Hence it is desirable to have inductive methods that provide a probabilistic basis for inferring that a given attribute in some particular time and place is best regarded as a retention, an invention, or a loan, or that it cannot be classified adequately on the basis of the methods and data available. Ideally, such methods should not depend upon propositions about why things change or remain constant, but only on the proposition that all things change in time.

Within limits, such an inductive strategy is available in the realm of lexical reconstruction. Given: (1) a subgrouping of the languages and dialects of a language family; (2) the assumption that borrowings between the languages of the family are detectable; (3) a set of meanings (variables); and (4) a group of cognate sets for each meaning (attributes), probabilistic statements can be made as to which cognate sets had particular meanings in the protolanguage

of a protospeech community. Thus our stadial interest is in the protolanguage and one or more subsequent stages. As a direct corollary of the reconstruction of a meaning of a given cognate set, any member of that cognate set that appears in that meaning in a daughter language is assigned the status of a retention in the daughter language. Any lexeme in that meaning that is not a retention is assigned the status of an innovation in the daughter language, whether in the entire language or in some of its dialects. Further analysis may make it possible to establish whether the innovation is a local invention or a loan from another language of the same family, or from some other language. Thus comparative evidence apparently establishes the Navajo word for "automobile" as a local invention, and the Navajo word for "apple" as a loan from Spanish. The decision as between retention and innovation depends upon the distribution of attributes (cognate sets) among related languages and dialects in various meanings, and not on any proposition about what kinds of changes are likely to occur. For some meanings, the distribution of cognate sets may be such that no cognate set can be assigned status as a prototerm in that meaning, and therefore, obviously, no decision can be reached as to which cognate sets are innovations. This is the state of indeterminacy to which we referred earlier.

A similar technique can be used to determine the relative ages of innovations found in the dialects of a language within the family in question. In a set of dialects, a continuously distributed innovation that interrupts the distribution of another innovation may be inferred to be more recent than the innovation whose distribution it interrupts. Sometimes a sequence of two or three more innovations can be inferred by these means. (If two dialect regions within a larger set of dialects are separated from one another but share a very large number of innovations, however, it is sometimes more appealing to infer that migration has occurred.) The reason that inductive procedures of these kinds can be employed with some rigor in lexical reconstruction is that the arbitrary bundles of sounds making up words in particular meanings are unlikely to exhibit repeated systematic correspondence in two or more related languages or dialects as a result of independent innovation. A cognate set may, however, come to hold the same meaning in two or more languages or dialects as a result of parallel transfers of meaning, but this possibility, too, can often be assessed with inductive methods. (The methods of lexical reconstruction are set forth in Dyen and Aberle [n.d.]. Aberle is indebted to Dyen for all of the material above on lexical reconstruction, but Dyen is not responsible for possible miswording or misinterpretation of his views.)

Unlike lexical items, however, many features of culture do not exhibit a sufficient number of arbitrary particularities to make it easy to apply similar inductive methods to the distribution of these features. Approximately speaking, as the number of particulars of a given attribute diminishes, indeterminacy increases as to whether its manifestations in two or more cultures have a common historical origin, either through retention or through borrowing. Attributes like descent and residence are instances in which the degree of indeterminacy is too high for comfort. When the particulars are few and the alternative attributes are also few (the principle of limited possibilities), the choice between retention, invention, and borrowing becomes especially difficult.

Hence there is a temptation to use causal explanations to decide the question of origins. The result is likely to be a mixture of explanatory principles that is logically unsatisfactory and therefore difficult to confront systematically. Thus a given attribute may be "explained" as an adaptation to local conditions, in which case the issue of whether it might be a retention of some duration may not be raised. Or it may be "explained" as a retention or a loan "because" it could not have developed *in situ*, since local conditions were not propitious. In this way, a causal analysis is used to fix on or to eliminate one or another explanation of origins. A full explanation as to origin and as to cause should include two kinds of propositions: (1) the attribute in question is a retention, invention, or loan, and (2) it was retained, invented, or borrowed because . . . . Furthermore, the two explanations should initially be kept separate. Let it be emphasized that there are many instances wherein a strong inference about origins can be made, but where inferences about causes are either weak or nonexistent. There are reasonably strong inferences about where and when various animals were domesticated, but explanations as to why they were, or why this occurred at one time rather than another, are at best plausible. It is highly likely that the commonest word for "father" in Navajo is a local innovation, but no explanation has ever been offered as to why that term developed, or why it seems to be displacing the Proto-Athapaskan term in most contexts.

In spite of the sources of indeterminacy mentioned above, it is possible to make certain probabilistic inferences about the social characteristics of a protospeech community. Sometimes it is necessary not only to to use inductive methods like those just described, which depend on the distribution of variables among a set of related cultures, but also to use inferences based on the known statistical associations of two kinds of attributes. The two lines of inference should be kept separate insofar as possible. The first step is to select a language family whose members are determinably related, one like Siouan, for instance, rather than one like Hokan-Siouan. It is necessary to recognize at the outset that just as it is usual to conceive of dialectal variation within a protospeech community (Bloomfield 1933: 42-56), so one should conceive of possible variation in social organization and other cultural features within the protospeech community. This complicates the reconstructive task. There is an additional complication. Whereas hypothetically, at least, loans between adjacent but linguistically remote languages of the same family are detectable, there is no reason to suppose that if, for example, patrilocality were a loan from one tribe to an adjacent tribe, this would be detectable on the basis of its particularities. Hence geographically interrupted distributions of social forms become at least as important as the distributions of those forms among adjacent linguistic subgroups.

A procedure for the reconstruction of features of social organization of a protospeech community will be described, with the rule of descent used as an example. (1) It is assumed that whatever rule of descent existed in the protospeech community, it is one of the rules known to us from living cultures. (2) The classification of descent rules to be used in the reconstruction is: (a) patrilineal; (b) matrilineal; (c) both (double unilineal, duolineal, or double descent); (d) neither (bilateral, ambilineal). This classification neglects certain rare forms of descent. If a different classification of rules of descent is used, the outcome of the reconstruction may be different. (3) Each of these four alternatives is considered in turn as a possible rule of descent in the protosystem. For each rule hypothesized for the protosystem, the question is: How many changes from the rule of descent in the protosystem are required to account for the distribution of descent rules in all the daughter systems for which information is available? The rule of descent that requires the fewest changes is inferred to have characterized the protosystem, on the grounds that the protosystem had at least one rule of descent, and on the grounds that the simplest inference is the best. If two rules tie for first place, the issue is indeterminate. Counting the number of changes required permits the measurement of relative simplicity. (I am especially indebted to Dyen for his development of the method for establishing the relative simplicity of a set of competing hypotheses.) Naturally, this method is applied only in the absence of data that provide information about actual sequences of changes. If kinship systems change their rule of descent relatively frequently, the likelihood that the inference is correct is lower than if they change infrequently. No estimate of frequency of change is now available. (4) Since there is no reason to assume that the protospeech community was homogeneous in its rule of descent, we ask whether any other rule of descent has a sufficiently wide or special distribution to indicate the inference that it, too, should be attributed to some regions of the protospeech community. The general procedure could be applied to a number of features of social organization, but this essay is limited to descent. The situation becomes more complex in stratified societies where different descent systems are found in the same geographical region (e.g. in a community). Here I consider only tribal societies, but with suitable modifications, the techniques proposed may prove useful even in more complex situations. As a corollary of the inference that a given rule or rules of descent should be assigned to the protosystem, other rules of descent appearing in some daughter systems are automatically classified as innovations. It may be that in some cases a rule of descent has an indeterminate status in the protosystem, and thereby the rules in some daughter systems also are indeterminate in status.

Thus when the reconstruction is completed, if there are no problems of indeterminacy, the rule of descent for every daughter system can be classified as a retention or an innovation. In the case of the innovations, further distributional analyses can assist in the task of deciding whether these innovations are inventions or loans. If the innovated descent rule (beta) in a given tribe (A) of the language family (P) whose rule of descent has been reconstructed as alpha, is adjacent only to tribes of other language families whose rule of descent differs from beta in the tribe under consideration, then the innovation is best inferred to be an invention. The situation may be made more complex by considering tribes with which tribe A may have had contact in the past, but the inferential procedure remains the same.

If the innovated descent rule beta in tribe A is the same as that in at least one adjacent tribe (B) of another language family (Q), further clarification can result from a reconstruction of the rule of descent for language family Q. If rule beta is classified as a retention in tribe B, then it is more likely that the rule of descent 'has diffused from B to A than from A to B. Nevertheless, other possibilities exist: the rule beta in tribe A may be an invention resulting from convergence under conditions like those in which tribe B has existed for some time. Hence judgmental issues arise for which no firm rule of decision exists. If tribe A and tribe B share numerous particularities in their descent systems, diffusion is more likely if they do not, but how many particularities are sufficient for such a judgment is not established. Such particularities might include clan names, clan name translations, clan name types, organizational form, activities, and symbolism such as rituals. In other words, the distributional analysis indicates that *if* diffusion has occurred, tribe B is the likely source and tribe A the likely borrower, but it does not establish *whether* diffusion has occurred.

If the innovated descent rule beta in tribe A is like that in at least one adjacent tribe (B) of another language family, and if that rule beta is inferred to be an innovation in tribe B as well as in tribe A, then it is possible that diffusion has occurred, but there is no basis for judging in which direction diffusion took place, if it occurred. Again, analysis of similar particularities found in the two systems is a guide to assessing whether diffusion occurred, and in this case may also be used to attempt to decide the direction of diffusion. Independent convergence on rule beta with borrowing of particularities in one or both directions is a possibility, as well as diffusion of the rule of descent. Thus the reconstruction of several adjacent language families affords guides to a differentiation of inventions and loans, but there are judgmental problems centering on similarities between two systems for which no clear calculus of relative probabilities can be offered. It must be kept in mind that there is some probability that two tribes that have independently invented the same rule of descent under quite different circumstances will nevertheless in the course of time come to be adjacent.

A more complicated problem arises when the inferred alpha rule in the protosystem (Proto-P) is found in daughter systems (A, B . . . n) that are adjacent to tribes (G, H . . . n) with the same rule of descent but of other language families (Q, R . . . n). The hypothesis is then available that the so-called retentions are rather to be regarded as loans from tribes Q, R, etc. This may be called the diffusion hypothesis. It should be pointed out to begin with that if the diffusion hypothesis is accepted, then a less favored inference, that the protosystem's rule of descent was beta or gamma, must be accepted, with a consequent loss of simplicity. Hence the diffusion hypothesis needs to be considered with some care. If the rules of descent for language families

Q, R, etc., have also been reconstructed, then the daughter systems of language family P may be classified as having rules like instances of innovations or of retentions in tribes of families Q, R, etc. If the inferred retentions of the alpha rule of language family P are adjacent to inferred innovations in the other language families, Q, R, etc., the likelihood is reduced that these instances of the alpha rule in language family P are loans. If, however, they are adjacent to instances in language families Q, R, etc., that are also classified as retentions, the situation is indeterminate, since the similar descent rules are possibly joint retentions, but possibly involve a loan in one direction or the other (which involves rejecting the simplest hypothesis, the alpha rule) or independent convergence (which also involves rejecting the simplest hypothesis).

Within the framework of distributional analysis of descent rules, it may be possible to move somewhat further. Thus if instances of the beta, gamma, etc., rules, inferred to be innovations in language family P, are *also* adjacent to like rules of descent in language families Q, R, etc., no advantage is to be gained by substituting the beta or gamma rule of descent. Furthermore, in any case it is clearly inadvisable to move too far down in the rank order of simplicity of competing hypotheses, since a rule of descent that is, for example, manifest in only one tribe of language family P but is not the rule of descent in any adjacent tribe will then be selected.

Nevertheless, the plausibility of the diffusion hypothesis may be sufficient to require consideration of other evidence. Where there are no reconstructions for adjacent families, the diffusion hypothesis will often appear particularly plausible. The result is the need to compare the particularities of the descent systems within language family P with each other and with those of the adjacent tribes of other language families with the same rule of descent. If the systems with rule alpha of language family P resemble each other in their particularities more than they resemble those of adjacent systems of other language families, diffusion becomes less plausible, and the alpha rule may be regarded as both the most likely and the most plausible inference for the protosystem. If the systems with rule alpha of language family P resemble each other in their particularities less than they resemble those of adjacent systems of other language families, the situation is indeterminate. It is evident that systems with different rules of descent and of different language families may nevertheless resemble each other in such particularities as clan names, name types, and name translations, which is an indication that particularities may be borrowed

while the rule of descent is not. On the other hand, there are cases of lack of shared particularities among closely related groups. Thus the Crow and Hidatsa are inferred to have been separated for a relatively short time, yet Crow and Hidatsa clan names do not resemble each other lexically nor in translation, while Hidatsa and Mandan clan names do. Mandan and Hidatsa-Crow are two subgroups of highest order within Siouan (see below). There is strong evidence that Hidatsa clan names have been relatively stable for more than a hundred years, and some evidence that Crow clan names change frequently. There is also some evidence for diffusion of clan names between Mandan and Hidatsa. There is, however, no basis for inferring that the Crow developed matrilineality independently from the Hidatsa, nor that the Hidatsa-Crow borrowed matrilineality from the Mandan, or vice versa (cf. Bowers 1965: 65-71). Hence genetically related systems retaining rule alpha may nevertheless not resemble each other as respects numerous particularities of their descent systems and may instead resemble neighboring systems of other language families in these respects.

The selection of variables for comparison of particularities and the choice of techniques for measuring similarities with respect to these particularities are thorny methodological problems. No definitive solution is proposed for dealing with the diffusion hypothesis. Distributional analysis of descent rules in several adjacent language families affords a basis under some circumstances for evaluating the relative likelihood that an innovation has been invented or borrowed, and under other circumstances for evaluating the likelihood that instances regarded as retentions are unlikely instead to be loans. Beyond this point, judgmental questions are involved, and no definitive means for converting plausibility to probability is known. Hence diffusion will not be dealt with systematically below. A few ad hoc comments will be made, particularly in connection with Driver's views. As for the inferred retained rules in Proto-Siouan, Proto-Algonquian, Proto-Eyak-Athapaskan, and Proto-Athapaskan, they occur in daughter systems that have rules like those of adjacent systems of other language families—but so do the inferred innovations. Hence, a detailed analysis of resemblances among systems of each language family and between those systems and neighboring systems of other language families would be necessary for a full discussion of the diffusion hypothesis, and that is impossible within the compass of this paper. Since substituting the beta or gamma rule in these three protosystems would raise the same question of diffusion as the alpha rule, since the alpha rule provides the simplest inference, and since further progress would require detailed work, the diffusion hypotheses will not be dealt with except in passing as respects the reconstructed rule for each language family.

Although the results of following these procedures are something of a *tour de force* unless the analysis is carried out in great detail and for several features of social organization, they will be used here as an exercise in method, as well as for the intrinsic interest of the result, and for contrast with Driver's approach in his "Integration of Functional, Evolutionary, and Historical Theory . . . ." Driver's own procedure is the reverse of that suggested here. First, he displays a series of intercorrelations, of six variables—division of labor, residence, land tenure, descent, cousin terms, and aunt terms—for three cluster: a matricentered, a patricentered, and a bicentered cluster. In an ingenious and aesthetic presentation, he shows that a matrix of correlations of the six variables ordered in the sequence just provided makes sense, given the hypothesis that the sequence is a stochastic chain: that division of labor influences residence, residence influences land tenure, and so on. If this inference is correct, we would expect division of labor to be more closely correlated with residence than with land tenure, residence to be more closely correlated with land tenure than with descent, and so on. (All based on Driver and Massey 1957: 425-35). The ordering is supported by the data. This provides Driver with a normal sequence of development, from subsistence type and division of labor to descent and cousin terms—a diachronic sequence inferred from synchronic data. Since, however, the correlations among his variables are only modest, he believes that some of the lack of integration among them is to be accounted for by the "accidents of history" (Boas's phrase), that is by the fact that tribes lacking the normal antecedents for certain social features had contact with tribes that did have these antededents, and that the social features in question were acquired by diffusion. Thus Driver is led to delimit a series of problem regions or problem tribes, which have certain characteristics even though they lack the usual antecedents of these characteristics. In many instances, the problem is one of explaining a rule of descent for a group that not only lacks the appropriate division of labor, etc., but also cannot be inferred at one time to have had it. Rather than list these and other problems that concern Driver, I will discuss some of them in the context of reconstructions to be presented below.

Lucid and logical though the stochastic argument is, there are some difficulties with it. To begin with, as Driver points out, the patricentered and bicentered clusters are not so neat as the matricentered. Balanced division of labor has a low negative correlation with the remainder of the bicentered cluster variables, and a low positive correlation with patricentered variables other than the division of labor. Patridominant division of labor has low and about equal correlations with the other variables of the patricentered cluster and the variables other than division of labor in the bicentered cluster. Hence, as respects division of labor, other stochastic chains are as plausible, and at least as probable, in accounting for the development of patricentered and bicentered systems as those posited by Driver. Furthermore, the mean correlations of the three clusters vary considerably in magnitude. The lowest correlations are for the bicentered series, the highest are found in the matricentered series, and the patricentered series is intermediate. In all three clusters, division of labor is correlated less closely with residence than is residence with land tenure or land tenure with descent. The matricentered correlation is highest, the patricentered intermediate, and the bicentered lowest and indeed random.

Driver's fundamental explanation for these low correlations is twofold: first, that systems in which one set of changes is progressing may experience a fresh change in the division of labor before the first set of changes has been completed and, second, that systems may be influenced by other systems and therefore undergo other than normal sequence shifts. (All based on Driver and Massey 1957: 430-34.) Although he mentions other possibilities, these two appeal to him most. An alternative view has two elements. First, the connection between division of labor and the remainder of the chain is weak. This is supported by the Embers' demonstration that for a world sample of cultures the expected association between the contribution of the sexes to the economy and the residential localization of the sexes does not obtain. Furthermore, and more specifically, when the contribution of women to the economy is greater than that of men, there is no association with matrilocal residence, and when the contribution of men is greater, there is no association with patrilocal residence. Nevertheless, in North America the expected positive associations obtain, as in Driver's tabulations (Ember and Ember 1971). Second, in Driver's data the correlations between adjacent variables in the chain are not strong enough to warrant heavy reliance in particular instances on the general causal explanations provided—a point on which Driver and the writer concur. This may be seen by squaring the phi values, since phi square is a measure of the percentage of the variation in the dependent variable accounted for by the independent variable.

Since this essay is concerened with descent, we will examine the phi square values for rules of descent and those variables other than kinship terminology with which they are most closely correlated. Matrilineal descent and matricentered land tenure have a phi square value of .64, so that matricentered versus other land tenure may be said to explain 64 per cent of the variance in accounting for matrilineal and other rules of descent. Patrilineal descent and patricentered land tenure have a phi square of only .08. Bilateral descent and bilocal residence, and bilateral descent and no kin-centered land tenure, have a phi square of only .08 (tied for the two variables). Under these circumstances, it would appear that the only "normal" sequence on which we should rely heavily is that between matricentered land tenure and matrilineal descent. In all other cases, the antecedents explain a sufficiently small amount of variance so that the reconstructions of descent rules that appear to violate Driver's stochastic chain sequences should not be excluded from consideration on that account. As for matricentered land tenure, there seems to be no antecedent for it that accounts for much of the variance in that variable. The point is not to deny *validity* to many of the links in Driver's chains, but to question their value for reconstructive purposes.

I shall provide a reconstruction of the rule or rules of descent in three language families, Siouan, Algonquian and Eyak-Athapaskan. In each case there is at least one lexical reconstruction of the kinship system of the entire protospeech community or a major subgroup thereof. The significance of the lexical reconstruction will be considered in each case after a distributional analysis of descent rules has been carried out. In the reconstructions that follow, descent is the variable selected. It has four attributes: patrilineality, matrilineality, double descent, and bilaterality. Retentions are rules of descent assigned to a protospeech community. Innovations are rules other than retentions appearing in ethnologically known tribes or in one instance in reconstructed protohistoric stages of such tribes. The problem of units of analysis is a difficult one. If languages or linguistic subgroups of higher order are counted as separate instances—even if they are contiguous—a contrary-minded reader may object that if two contiguous tribes, speaking related languages, share the same rule of descent, they may represent one instance of the rule, rather than two. Thus, if they constantly intermarry,

they may have adopted the rule together. On the other hand, if one portion of a dialect chain has one rule of descent and another portion another, and if one of the rules is an innovation, it could well be argued that the innovation began somewhere in the chain and not everywhere and that the innovation represents not one change but several, as the change spread from one dialect group to another. We will try to deal with this problem as it arises in each instance and will qualify our comments about the number of changes from proto-stage to daughter systems by speaking of "at least" three, four, etc., changes of descent rule. Any posited change of descent rule will be called a "shift."

Ethnographic data on descent are drawn from Driver and Massey (1957), except as noted. The consequences of utilizing different approaches are difficult to grasp if the facts considered are also different. Hence, wherever possible, the facts will be based on Driver's work.

The first language family to be considered is Siouan. I follow Matthews (1959: 253) in dividing Siouan into four linguistic subgroups of highest order. The languages listed are those with which Matthews dealt in his lexical reconstruction of Proto-Siouan kinship terminology, and so the list does not include all known Siouan languages. The subgroups are: (1) Missouri (Hidatsa, Crow); (2) Mandan; (3) Mississippi (Dakota, Chiwere, and Dhegiha); and (4) Ohio (Biloxi, Ofo and Tutelo). Within Mississippi, Dakota includes Assiniboine, Santee, and Teton; Chiwere includes Winnebago, Iowa, and Oto; Dhegiha includes Omaha, Kansa, Osage, and Quapaw. If Siouan tribes are clustered geographically, Missouri and Mandan were fully adjacent until the Crow became separated from the Hidatsa; Missouri and Mandan are separated from Mississippi and Ohio. The Mississippi group is continuously distributed and separated from Ohio. The Ohio Siouans are dispersed.

If linguistic units are utilized for reconstructive purposes, there are, then, four subgroups, three of which (Missouri, Mandan, and Ohio) are exclusively matrilineal, and the fourth of which (Mississippi) is bilateral in the north (Dakota) and patrilineal in the south (Chiwere and Dhegiha). If a patrilineal prototype is posited, at least four shifts are required to account for present distributions: (1) from patrilineal to bilateral for Dakota, and (2-4) from patrilineal to matrilineal for Missouri, Mandan, and Ohio. (According to Murdock, a direct shift from patrilineality to matrilineality without an intervening bilateral stage is regarded as highly unlikely, but we wish to reconstruct initially without considering such propositions. Cf.

70

Murdock 1949: 216-19.) A matrilineal prototype requires at least three shifts: (1) from matrilineal to bilateral for Mississippi, followed by (2-3) patrilineal shifts in Chiwere or Dhegiha; or two shifts (1) from matrilineal to patrilineal for Mississippi, followed by (2) a bilateral shift for Dakota. Since the latter sequence affords fewer shifts, it is preferred. A double descent prototype requires at least five shifts: (1-3) from double descent to matrilineal in Missouri, Mandan, and Ohio; (4) from double descent to patrilineal in Mississippi; (5) from patrilineal to bilateral in Dakota. A shift to bilaterality in Mississippi and thence to patrilineality in Chiwere and Dhegiha requires one more shift and is disregarded. A bilateral prototype requires at least five shifts: (1-3) from bilateral to matrilineal for Missouri, Mandan, and Ohio, and (4-5) from bilateral to patrilineal in Chiwere and Dhegiha.

Thus the matrilineal prototype requires only two shifts, the patrilineal four, and the bilateral and double descent five. Hence the matrilineal prototype is preferred for Proto-Siouan. At this point it should be said that if there are no double descent systems among the daughter languages, a double descent prototype will always be in last place or tied for last place in the competition for the simplest hypothesis. It has been introduced above for methodological illustration, but in all subsequent counts it will be disregarded, since none of the systems under consideration is characterized by double descent. By the same token, the failure to consider rare types of descent is of no importance, since any rare type (e.g. matrilines of females only and patrilines of males only) will compete unfavorably with other types except in contexts where at least some daughter systems are characterized by the rare type in question.

It is now possible to consider whether Proto-Siouan should be assigned two rules of descent, since the inference that matrilineality probably characterized the Proto-Siouan speech community does not eliminate the possibility that some other form of descent characterized a portion of it. With bilaterality found in only one sector of one subgroup of highest order, there seems no reason to complicate the reconstruction with a bilateral rule. If a patrilineal rule is inferred for a portion of the protospeech community, the present distribution of Siouans suggests a situation in which matrilineal rules obtained at two ends of the community, with patrilineality in the middle. This, in turn, suggests a prior matrilineal stage, with patrilineality as an innovation in the center, which returns us to the matrilineal inference for a still earlier stage in the

history of the protospeech community. Thus, if linguistic units are used for counting shifts, and if only the distribution of rules of descent is taken into account, a matrilineal rule of descent is the simplest reconstruction for Proto-Siouan. It requires two fewer shifts than its nearest competitor, which seems a reasonably good margin.

If, instead of counting linguistic units, we count contiguous clusters, there are some decisions to be made about how to cluster tribes. If Crow and Hidatsa-Mandan are treated as separate units because they are geographically separated, and if the Ohio Siouans are treated similarly for similar reasons, the inference will favor matrilineality. If for the moment Crow and Hidatsa-Mandan are treated as a single cluster because they were contiguous not too long ago, and if the Ohio Siouans are treated as a single cluster on grounds that they may once have been contiguous—if perhaps not so recently—a stiffer test can be posed for the matrilineal inference. Within Mississippi, which is a geographical as well as a linguistic unit, tribes homogeneous in rule of descent are treated as subclusters. Hence there are two subclusters: Dakota and Chiwere-Dhegiha. A patrilineal prototype requires at least three shifts: (1) a matrilineal one for Mandan-Hidatsa-Crow; (2) a matrilineal one for Ohio; and (3) a bilateral one for Dakota. A matrilineal prototype requires at least two shifts: (1) a bilateral shift for Dakota and (2) a patrilineal shift for Chiwere-Dhegiha. (Or one might posit a patrilineal shift for all the Mississippian group followed by a bilateral shift for Dakota, or a bilateral shift for all the Mississippian group followed by a patrilineal shift for Chiwere-Dhegiha, but the number of shifts remains constant.) A bilateral prototype requires at least three shifts: (1) a matrilineal one for Mandan-Hidatsa-Crow; (2) a matrilineal one for Ohio; and (3) a patrilineal one for Chiwere-Dhegiha. A matrilineal system is still favored as the prototype if geographical units, rather than linguistic ones, are used, but the margin is narrower. Treatment of Ohio Siouans as constituting more than one cluster would, however, improve the margin favoring matrilineality.

Whether one counts language units or clusters, Murdock's views on transitions from matrilineality to patrilineality would increase the advantage of the matrilineal prototype over the patrilineal, since each transition from patrilineality to matrilineality would involve an initial shift to bilaterality followed by a matrilineal shift.

The matrilineal inference, however, is not compatible with Matthews's conclusion that Pre-Siouan and Proto-Siouan had Omaha terminological features (1959). The statistical association between Omaha cousin terms and patrilineality is marked, and Dyen and Aberle (n.d.) have shown that in a world sample of kinship systems, almost all Omaha systems are patrilineal, whereas almost none are matrilineal. Hence Matthews's inferences or mine, or both, require examination. Matthews's reconstruction contains two sections. In the more extensive section, he provides a lexical reconstruction by the comparative method, which indicates the high probability that Proto-Mississippian had Omaha cousin terms. He does not in fact reconstruct Proto-Siouan cousin terms, pointing out that the Proto-Mississippian Omaha system may be either an innovation or a retention from Proto-Siouan. Such evidence as he uses to favor the inference that it is a retention from the protostage is not strong. In addition, he disregards the lexical evidence that would permit a reconstruction of Proto-Siouan Crow cousin terms for male cross cousins, a reconstruction based on the concurrence of Hidatsa and Mandan, representing two subgroups of highest order. He sets aside this evidence on grounds of Hidatsa influence on Mandan, thus reducing two instances to one. If this reduction is accepted, Proto-Siouan cross cousin terms are not reconstructed; if it is not, then Proto-Siouan probably had Crow cousin terms. Such cousin terms are strongly associated with matrilineality and double descent.

In another section, Matthews undertakes an internal reconstruction of Proto-Siouan terminology, to arrive at a Pre-Siouan stage, in which, he argues, there was a class of relatives consisting of siblings, siblings-in-law, children, siblings' children, and father's sister, divided into subclasses, and that father's sister, older parallel siblings, children, and siblings' children are relatives in this class "for which there are no specific terms, but only derived forms of the general terms . . . ," and that father's sister, older sister woman speaking, daughter, and sibling's daughter "constituted one class of relatives . . . ." It is this grouping that provides "strong evidence that Pre-Siouan had an Omaha-like kinship system . . ." (all from Matthews 1959: 275).

Thus Matthews avoids the likeliest conclusion from comparative lexical evidence, that Proto-Siouan had Crow cousin terms, selecting instead an inference based on internal reconstruction that develops an image of Omaha treatment by reference to word classes, but not clearly specifiable meanings, in Pre-Siouan. It is reasonable instead to infer either that Proto-Siouan cousin terms are not reconstructible, or that they are of Crow type, and to suspend judgment on the implications of the internal reconstruction. Hence lexical distributions

at best support, and at worst do not contradict, the inference from the distribution of descent rules that Proto-Siouan was matrilineal. If a different subgrouping of Siouan languages were to be used, it might become necessary to change both inferences about descent and inferences about kinship terminology. As things stand, the matrilineal inference seems fairly strong.

Let us now consider Driver's views of Siouan differentiation. First, he accepted Matthews's inferences and thus endows Proto-Siouan with Omaha terminology. Although he does not specifically say that the protospeech community was therefore patrilineal, given the association of Omaha cousin terms and patrilineality, this would be a normal inference. He regards the matricentered patterns of Hidatsa, Crow, and Mandan as a result of either a major horticultural dependency based on women's horticultural activities, or influences from Caddoans, or both (Driver and Massey 1957: 437-38). The Crow, having developed matrilineality, retained it even after they changed from a horticultural base to buffalo hunting (Driver and Massey 1957: 437). It is clear that Hidatsa, Crow, and Mandan matrilineality are treated as innovations, not retentions from Proto-Siouan. Driver does not specifically discuss the Ohio Siouans, but since he views southeastern matrilineality in general as locally evolved on a horticultural base, presumably he considers Ohio Siouan matriliny an innovation, whether a loan or an invention.

In order to compare the explanatory tasks resulting from two different reconstructions, it is necessary to go somewhat beyond Driver's comments and provide a sequence of differentiation for Siouan that is compatible with his remarks but includes features he did not mention. Under the hypothesis that the Proto-Siouan speech community can be inferred to have been patrilineal because of its kinship terminology, Mandan, Missouri, and Ohio matrilineality are regarded as innovations, and so is Dakota bilaterality. A causal explanation of this state of affairs would, then, attempt to account for Chiwere-Dhegiha retention of patrilineality; for the matrilineal innovations in Mandan, Missouri, and Ohio; and for the bilateral innovation in Dakota. Under the hypothesis developed here that the Proto-Siouan speech community was matrilineal, a causal explanation would attempt to account for the Mandan, Missouri, and Ohio retention of matrilineality; for the Chiwere-Dhegiha innovation of patrilineality; and for the Dakota bilateral innovation.

It seems that within Driver's frame of reference, a plausible causal explanation can be developed for either sequence. In what follows, it is asserted only that the explanations are compatible with Driver's data and inferences about stochastic chains, not that they are Driver's explanations. Given the patrilineal prototype, Chiwere-Dhegiha retention of patrilineality may be explained by continued reliance on a patridominant division of labor—in which hunting is more important than horticulture and warfare is also important—in a relatively sedentary situation, which provides a base for unilineal institutions and, given the patridominant trend, for patrilineal ones. The matrilineal sectors may be explained by an increased reliance on horticulture and perhaps by contact with Muskogeans or other Gulf peoples for the Ohio group and with Caddoans for the Missouri and Mandan groups. Given the matrilineal prototype, the matrilineal retentions may be explained by a continued reliance on horticulture. In the case of the Mandan and the Hidatsa-Crow, continued reliance on bottom-land farming throughout their movements seems characteristic and could account for the matrilineal retentions. The Proto-Mississippi Siouan patrilineal innovation may be explained by a shift from a major horticultural dependency to a greater reliance on hunting and stronger emphasis on warfare. Under either hypothesis, Dakota bilaterality may be viewed as a response to a decreasing emphasis on horticulture and a roving, rather than a semisedentary, hunting existence, oriented to the buffalo. (This is not fully adequate as an explanation for the bilaterality of the eastern Dakotas, but the inadequacy features both hypotheses.) Under either hypotheses, given the patrilineality of Dhegha, the matridominant division of labor and matrilocal residence of the Quapaw can be regarded as a result of southeastern horticulturalist influence impinging on that tribe but not on other Dhegiha tribes. Finally, under either hypothesis, Crow matrilineality on the Plains is to be viewed as a retention from a prior stage in which horticulture was dominant in the economy.

What is interesting about the two explanations is that, since either is compatible with Driver's stochastic chains, these chains do not in this instance have much power for reconstructive purposes. Hence it is reasonable to conclude that the Proto-Siouan speech community was probably matrilineal, and that the causal task is set by that reconstruction, however it is to be carried out. It is evident that the causal task changes as the reconstruction changes. It must again be stressed that this is an exercise in method, and that a different subgrouping of Siouan might yield different results.

If, however, the Proto-Siouan speech community is to be regarded as prehorticultural, the matrilineal prototype does not fit with Driver's stochastic chains (cf. Driver and Massey 1957: 435). The question then would arise: Should the reconstruction be set aside because of its implausibility, or should the putative causes of matrilineality be reconsidered? The question will arise again later in this essay.

The reconstruction of the descent rule for Proto-Algonquian rests on Hockett's (1973:302) subgrouping of Algonquian. He divides the family into four subgroups of highest order: Cheyenne, Arapaho, Blackfoot, and Central-Eastern. Central-Eastern is divided into Central and Eastern. Central includes seven subgroups: (1) Cree-Montagnais-Naskapi; (2) Ojibwa-Algonkin-Ottawa-Saulteaux; (3) Potawatomi; (4) Menomini; (5) Sauk-Fox-Kickapoo; (6) Miami-Peoria-Illinois; and (7) Shawnee. Eastern has a more hierarchial pattern of subgroups: (1) Delaware and (I assume) Mahican; (2) the remainder, subdivided into (a) Micmac, Malecite, Abenaki, Passamaquoddy, and Penobscot, and (b) other, subdivided into (i) Atlantic Coast forms and (ii) New England forms.

In terms of geographical clusters, Cheyenne and Arapaho are contiguous and separated from all Algonquian speakers. Shawnee is slightly separated from all the others but almost adjacent to Illinois. The remainder are continuously distributed, in the sense that each tribe has at least one Algonquian neighbor. The group will be treated as constituting two discrete geographical clusters: Cheyenne-Arapaho and other.

Matrilineal descent characterizes only Delaware and Mahican. The remainder of Eastern is bilateral, except for Atlantic, where the form of descent is unknown. In the remainder of the discussion, all references to Eastern must be understood to exclude Atlantic. All of Central is patrilineal except Cree-Montagnais-Naskapi, which is bilateral. Blackfoot, Cheyenne, and Arapaho are bilateral. A patrilineal prototype requires at least (1-3) three bilateral shifts in the west (Arapaho, Blackfoot, Cheyenne); (4) a bilateral shift in Eastern; followed by (5) a matrilineal shift for Delaware-Mahican; or (4) a bilateral shift for most of Eastern and (5) a matrilineal shift for Delaware-Mahican; and (6) a bilateral shift for Cree-Montagnais-Naskapi in the Central group, for a total of six. A matrilineal prototype requires at least (1-3) bilateral shifts for Arapaho, Blackfoot, and Cheyenne; (4-5) a patrilineal shift in Central Algonquian followed by a bilateral shift for Cree-Montagnais-Naskapi; (6) a bilateral shift for the remainder of Eastern, for a total of six. A bilateral prototype requires at least (1) a matrilineal shift in Delaware-Mahican and either (2-7) six patrilineal shifts in Central (by diffusion or parallel development) or (2) a patrilineal shift in Central, followed by (3) a return to bilaterality for Cree-Montagnais-Naskapi. The latter, as the simplest sequence is preferred.[2] The total is three. Hence the bilateral prototype, with three shifts, is the best inference, as compared with the patrilineal and matrilineal, tied for six shifts. Furthermore, it is the best by a fairly wide margin. If we count by clusters, a patrilineal prototype requires at least (1) a bilateral shift for Cheyenne-Arapaho, and then a series of shifts within the other, huge, Algonquian cluster. If each region that is homogeneous with respect to rule of descent is counted as a subunit within that cluster, at least two additional shifts are required: (2) a bilateral shift for a northern strip from Blackfoot to the east coast and (3) a matrilineal shift for Delaware-Mahican, for a total of three. A matrilineal prototype requires at least (1) a bilateral shift for the Cheyenne-Arapaho cluster and, within the larger cluster, at least (2) a bilateral shift for the strip from Blackfoot to the east coast and (3) a patrilineal shift for the contiguous patrilineal Central Algonquians, for a total of three. A bilateral prototype requires shifts only within the larger cluster: at least (1) a patrilineal shift for the contiguous Central Algonquians and (2) a matrilineal shift for Delaware-Mahican, for a total of two. Thus the bilateral prototype is preferred, but by a narrower margin than when linguistic units are counted. The same narrowing of the margin can be observed in the case of Siouan clusters. This results from the smaller number of units employed. Cluster counting seems to violate good sense in the Algonquian case: a single, unitary shift for the enormous bilateral northern strip, a strip that cannot be regarded as a genetic unit of smaller scale in the past, is unappealing.

This inference accords with Driver's implicit assignment of a bilateral rule of descent to Proto-Algonquian. He regards Cheyenne and Arapaho as having been matrilineal prior to their moving on to the Plains and treats this matrilineality as an innovation. The patrilineality of the bulk of the Central Algonquians is also treated as an innovation (Driver and Massey 1957: 414-15, 437). Thus bilaterality as the protoform emerges by exclusion. Driver's matrilineal stage for Cheyenne and Arapaho has implications for the reconstruction of Proto-Algonquian descent. If a reconstruction is attempted in which these two groups are treated as recently matrilineal, it can be shown that a matrilineal protosystem is the best inference, by a margin of one, with bilateral second. Thus Driver's reconstruction for Cheyenne-Arapaho is incompatible with his implicit reconstruction for Proto-Algonquian. His reconstruction for Cheyenne-Arapaho is disregarded

here, since this essay argues that reconstruction through the analysis of distributions should be undertaken initially without respect to other lines of inference, and in particular without respect to causal arguments. In any case, there are problems about the Cheyenne-Arapaho reconstruction. Driver points out that the Cheyenne and Arapaho have matrilocal residence and that, in addition, they are two of the three instances of exogamous matridemes in North America. The other is the Ute. Since both Algonquian tribes were probably horticultural before they moved on to the Plains, he infers that at that time they were matrilineal and matrilocal, and that matrilocality was retained from that period. Their matrilineal descent groups became exogamous matridemes under the impact of Plains life. This argument would be fairly strong if it could be shown or inferred that exogamous matridemes are a common result of a loss of matrilineality, and also that they are an uncommon predecessor of fully developed matrilineal descent. There are no statistical associations to support such an inference. There is only opinion, and Murdock has a contrary view. He holds that exogamous demes are a common precursor of unilineality (Murdock 1949: 75). Hence the inference for Cheyenne and Arapaho is not well supported.

Let us now examine lexical reconstruction of kinship terminology for its compatibility with one or another of the foregoing hypotheses. Hockett (1964) has reconstructed Proto-Central Algonquian kinship terms. The system appears to have Iroquois cousin terms derived from terms for siblings-in-law, rather than the reverse. This provides indications of cross-cousin marriage. Dyen and Aberle (n.d.) show that most Iroquois systems are characterized by unilineal or double unilineal descent, but that is not possible to decide between matrilineal, patrilineal, or duolineal rules on the basis of these cousin terms. The association, however, is weak, and the phi square small (.04). Since under any of the hypotheses, if linguistic units are utilized, Proto-Central Algonquian emerges with a patrilineal rule of descent, the linguistic reconstruction is compatible with the distributional analysis of descent rules. It should be said, however, that Hockett's argument that the Proto-Central Algonquians had matrilineal cross-cousin marriage and patrilocality does not seem very strong. The terminological equations he finds are not fully consistent with any one form of cross-cousin marriage, but seem most consistent with bilateral cross-cousin marriage irrespective of residence (cf. Hockett 1964: esp. 254-56).

Unfortunately, there is no reconstruction for Proto-Central-Eastern Algonquian or for Proto-

Algonquian. There are a few hints. Eggan finds some equations among Arapaho and Cheyenne kinship terms that suggest past cross-cousin marriage (Eggan 1955a: 45-46; 1955b: 531). Taken with Hockett's reconstruction, this suggests to me that Proto-Algonquian may have had Iroquois cousin terms and equations indicating cross-cousin marriage, but at this point such an interpretation cannot be put forth strongly. Since Iroquois cousin terms are more strongly associated with unilineality or double descent than with bilaterality, this highly tentative reconstruction accords better with the less favored patrilineal and matrilineal reconstructions (tied for second place) than with the bilateral one. Thus the bilateral inference is not devoid of problems. A causal interpretation of Algonquian differentiation also raises some difficulties.

It is plausible to regard the Proto-Algonquian system as having been based on hunting and gathering. Hockett posits a date of around 2,000 years ago for Proto-Central-Eastern Algonquian, and this implies an earlier date for Proto-Algonquian (Hockett 1973: 9-10). This fits with a hunting and gathering subsistence base. Nevertheless, under conditions permitting a certain stability of group membership, both patrilineal and matrilineal hunters and gatherers are known. More is said of matrilineal hunters and gatherers in the discussion of Eyak-Athapaskan. Retention of bilaterality among the Blackfoot and the northernmost Eastern Algonquians can be plausibly explained by reference to a combination of roving hunting and gathering based on fluctuating resources, changes of location in the not-too-distant past, and the impact of the fur trade. Central Algonquian patrilineality can be referred to more stable resources and sedentarization, combined with a patridominant division of labor and an emphasis on warfare, and perhaps influence from the patrilineal Siouans. Since many of the Central Algonquians were horticultural, it is necessary to argue that their horticultural activities did not provide them with a matridominant division of labor, and this accords with Driver's data, save for the Miami. With a matridominant division of labor, they are anomalous. The inferred return to bilaterality of the Cree-Montagnais-Naskapi can be referred to northward movement and the same complex of factors that accounts for bilateral retentions among the Blackfoot and the most northerly of the Eastern group. Delaware-Mahican matrilineality can be referred to the importance of horticulture in that area and perhaps to Iroquoian influence. The New England Algonquians, with a matridominant division of labor and bilaterality, are somewhat anomalous; their bilaterality could be referred to

inertial retention. Cheyenne and Arapaho matrilocality and exogamous matridemes could be explained by the adoption of both during a prior horticultural period and by inertial retention on the Plains. This sequence accords with Driver's comments, except for Cheyenne and Arapaho, but goes beyond his remarks to discuss more instances than he does. A bilateral prototype is not free from difficulties, but there is no competing reconstruction. A firm subgrouping for Algonquian, Ritwan, Muskogean, the Gulf languages, and various other language families to which Algonquian is said to be related might result in a wider reconstruction with implications for Proto-Algonquian, and a different subgrouping of Algonquian itself could affect the choice among hypotheses. The Algonquian case shows that the introduction of inferences based on internal reconstruction (Cheyenne and Arapaho) into a system of inferences based on distributions can affect the conclusions.[3]

A distributional analysis of descent rules in Eyak-Athapaskan results in a reconstruction of matrilineality in the protospeech community, and of matrilineality and perhaps some bilaterality in the Proto-Athapaskan speech community. The inference for Proto-Athapaskan fits with Kroeber's reconstruction of Proto-Athapaskan Iroquois cousin terms (1937), rather than with Hoijer's of Hawaiian cousin terms (1956). There are reasons for preferring Kroeber's reconstruction over Hoijer's. Since Dyen and Aberle (n.d.) have prepared a full account of the reconstruction of kinship terminology and rules of descent, which takes into account many alternative reconstructions by others, details are not presented here. It has often been mentioned that northern and southwestern matrilineal Athapaskans resemble their non-Athapaskan matrilineal neighbors in certain respects, but these resemblances indicate only that some descent group names have been borrowed from these neighbors; they do not prove the borrowing of the descent rule itself. Northern and southwestern matrilineal Athapaskans also resemble one another with respect to certain particularities of their descent systems, including name style and clan origin myths. No measurement of degrees of internal and external similarities has been carried out. Although it is true that northern and southwestern Athapaskan matrilineal systems are adjacent to matrilineal systems of other language families, it is also true that, broadly speaking, patrilineal and bilateral systems are also adjacent to systems with like rules of descent. Hence there is no basis for rejecting the matrilineal inference except the supposed implausibility of Proto-Eyak-Athapaskan and Proto-Athapaskan matrilineality, which, in this case and possibly in the Siouan case, cannot easily be harmonized with Driver's evolutionary processes, because there is no obvious basis for a matridominant division of labor.

Driver finds a bilateral prototype appealing for Proto-Athapaskan, basing himself partly on subsistence base and partly on Hoijer's Hawaiian reconstruction of Proto-Athapaskan kinship terminology (Driver and Massey 1957: 435). Bilaterality is the second-best hypothesis in the Dyen-Aberle treatment. Thus the competing hypotheses are matrilineal (with perhaps some bilaterality) and bilateral. Here I advert to only a few of the explanatory issues. Under the bilateral hypothesis, Driver explains Pacific Athapaskan patrilineality and northern Athapaskan and Navajo and Western Apache matrilineality as innovations, and the matrilineal instances as loans, with the borrowing resulting from the dominance and prestige of the lenders. As a result, he is led to various complex hypotheses to account for the spread of matrilocal residence, particularly among northern Athapaskans. More important, Driver finds no ecological basis for the matrilineality of the Haida, Tlingit, and Tsimshian, one or more of whom he regards as the donors of this rule of descent to the northern Athapaskans. He therefore posits influence from, or migration from, Asia to account for Northwest Coast matrilineality. Yet it is difficult to imagine a degree of extracontinental influence strong enough to be conducive to matrilineality in an area where, in his view, it could not develop *de novo*. There is no evident Asian source for borrowing, and a migration of matrilineal peoples from Asia also poses problems, since in Northeastern Asia there is no location more conducive to matrilineality than the environments of Northwestern North America. Yet in Driver's view, this matrilineality, however it reached the northern Northwest Coast, survived there while avunculocal residence developed, and was then transmitted to the Athapaskans of the area. (All based on Driver and Massey 1957: 435-36.)

A matrilineal, matrilocal Proto-Athapaskan system, on the other hand, provides for relatively simple transitions to the daughter systems, for residence as well as descent. It requires only that one admit that the bases for adopting descent rules are perhaps not yet well understood. Such an admission is suggested by the complexities that are created by the bilateral inference for Proto-Athapaskan; an ecologically based hypothesis in this case can be sustained only by inferring complicated transitions in daughter systems.

There is, then, an uncertainty as to whether the Proto-Siouan speech community, inferred to be

matrilineal, had a horticultural base, and a high likelihood that the Proto-Eyak speech community, also inferred to be matrilineal, did not have a horticultural base. Furthermore, it has been shown that Driver's normal stochastic chains can sometimes be used effectively to account for two quite different sequences of differentiation, and that they sometimes leave anomalies unexplained—a point Driver has made forcefully. The question may be raised as to whether we do understand the roots of rules of descent. A look at some other languages and language families may prove interesting. At present Haida and Tlingit must be treated as linguistic isolates, since their relationship with one another and the relationship of either with Eyak-Athapaskan has not been demonstrated. It is impossible to reconstruct a protosystem for a linguistic isolate, in the same sense that no protolanguage can be reconstructed. In the case of Haida and Tlingit, internal reconstruction suggests a matrilineal past of some depth for both, because of their avunculocality. Without a reconstruction for Penutian, the only conclusion warranted for Tsimshian is the same as for Haida and Tlingit. The result is a matrilineal past for the northern Northwest Coast and Eyak-Athapaskan, for whatever reason. The universality of matrilineality for all the Muskogeans for which Driver has information indicates a matrilineal prototype for that language family, and the same prototype seems likely for the larger unit that includes the other Gulf languages. The latter conclusion does not depend upon the subgrouping of Algonquian with respect to the Gulf languages, since even if Algonquian is a subgroup of this macrofamily, matrilineality is the most probable inference for the entire protosystem (cf. Haas 1960: 985 on the possibility that Algonquian is a member of a set of subgroups whose other members are the Muskogean family and Natchez, Tunica, Chitimacha, and Atakapa). The universality of matrilineality among Iroquoians indicates an inference of matrilineality for that protosystem. According to the Schmitts, reconstruction by means of typological similarities of kinship systems suggests that the Proto-Caddoan speech community was matrilineal (Schmitt and Schmitt n.d.). The Keresan speakers and the Zuni, as isolates, are not further reconstructible. Both groups are matrilineal. Driver believes that all of the Pueblos were matrilineal in the past. Distributional data on Tanoan require fuller examination than is possible here. Bilaterality is plausible for the prototype, but matrilineality is a possibility. No reconstruction is offered for Proto-Uto-Aztecan. Driver believes that its descent rule was either patrilineal or bilateral, and probably bilateral. Shimkin's (1941) reconstruction of Proto-Uto-Aztecan kinship terminology infers Hawaiian cousin terms, but the reconstruction is typological, and at present lexical reconstructions of cross cousin terms are not available. Driver's and Shimkin's views are concordant. More work on Proto-Uto-Aztecan-Tanoan descent rules is desirable. The southern Northwest Coast and Plateau groups seem at present to be best explained by a bilateral prototype. No reconstructions are attempted for California.

There is, then, some indication that matrilineality can be inferred for the early northern Northwest Coast, Proto-Eyak-Athapaskan, Proto-Siouan, Proto-Iroquois, Proto-Gulf, Proto-Caddoan, early Keres and Zuni, and possibly Proto-Tanoan. In terms of the historic locations of North American tribes north of Mexico, the result is a matrilineal past for a large and almost continuous area, interrupted between Athapaskan and Siouan by Algonquian, between northern and southern Iroquoians by Algonquian, and between Caddoan and Gulf on the one hand and the Puebloan Southwest on the other by various groups, most of them relatively recent arrivals. It would be interesting to remap the situation in terms of the inferred locations of protospeech communities.

Some of this matrilineality may have developed on a horticultural base. This is plausible for Caddoan, Iroquoian, Keres, Zuni, and Muskogean. It is possible for Siouan. As one moves backward from Muskogean to Gulf, a horticultural base becomes less likely. For Haida, Tlingit, and Eyak-Athapaskan, there is no support for an inference of a horticultural base. Not all of this matrilineality need have been contemporaneous, but some of it must have been. It is possible that matrilineality in many parts of this large region antedates horticulture and is based on factors not yet understood.

This broad region of reconstructions makes it possible to deal illustratively with the question of loans in the case of rules inferred to be innovations in at least one language family. Among the Algonquians, Delaware-Mahican matrilineality, as an innovation adjacent to Iroquoian, is possibly a loan from Iroquoian, whereas the reverse is unlikely. Both Central Algonquian patrilineality and Chiwere-Dhegiha patrilineality are treated as innovations. Influence from one group to the other is plausible, but there is no basis for inferring the direction of the loan. If the relative time-depth of Proto-Central Algonquian and Proto-Mississippi Siouan were known, this would provide guidance as to the direction of the loan—if a loan occurred. Dakota bilaterality, an innovation adjacent to Algonquian-retained bilaterality, might possibly involve Algonquian influence, whereas the reverse is unlikely. In the case of Athapaskan, most of the adjacent language families have not been subjected to reconstruction here; so possible loans of bilaterality and patrilineality from neighboring groups will not be discussed.

This essay has described an inductive method for inferring features of social organization of proto-speech communities and has applied it to the rule of descent in two language families: Siouan and Algonquian. It has presented without substantiating detail some results of the application of the same method to Eyak-Athapaskan. In the Siouan case, a matrilineal protosystem is the best inference; in the Algonquian case, a bilateral prototype is best; in the Eyak-Athapaskan case, matrilineality is best. Depending on the inference chosen, the daughter systems are differently classified as retentions or innovations. Within the framework of distributional analysis, there are methods for deciding under some conditions whether an attribute is likelier to be an invention or a loan and whether a retention hypothesis can plausibly be replaced by a diffusion hypothesis. Assessing the probability of a diffusional explanation by reference to similarities between putative lenders and borrowers, versus similarities among putative borrowers, is an issue not entirely resolved.

A classification of attributes as retentions and innovations, with or without a subclassification of innovations as inventions or loans, is a type of explanation, since it accounts for the distribution of descent rules in daughter systems. The task of causal explanation has been shown to depend upon the reconstruction developed by analysis of distributions. Stochastic chains do not appear to have great utility in either confirming or disproving the results of distributional analysis, partly because of the weakness of statistical associations, partly because different reconstructions are sometimes equally compatible with the chains—or equally incompatible—and partly because it is difficult to assess the results in terms of a simplicity argument. In the case of Siouan differentiation, two plausible sequences can be constructed, depending on the inference. In the case of Algonquian differentiation, the inference results in problem cases that resist causal explanation. In the case of Eyak-Athapaskan, the apparently implausible reconstruction of a matrilineal prototype creates fewer complexities in accounting for the differentiation of additional features of kinship organization (i.e. residence norms) than does a bilateral prototype. Brief attention to additional language families suggests matrilineal prototypes for several of them, and this, taken with the matrilineal reconstruction for Proto-Siouan and Proto-Eyak-Athapaskan, suggests a widespread, early, and in some cases pre- or nonhorticulturally-based matrilineality in North America. Such a possibility indicates the desirability of a rethinking of the bases for descent rules.

This essay has reversed Driver's approach to explanation. Instead of beginning with causal explanations of normal evolutionary sequences, going on to causal explanations of diffused forms of social organization, and treating retentions as a residual explanation, it has begun with the issue of retention, employing rules of simplicity in the reconstruction of the descent rules in a limited number of language families, irrespective of propositions about the causes of those rules. Beginning with explanations by reference to origins, it has generated new problems of explanations by reference to causes. The reconstructions resulting from distributional analysis are in some instances surprising, but given the weakness of empirical laws in anthropology, they are perhaps worth considering. Each inference is subject to challenge if new subgroupings are established. Each is a concluding hypothesis, open to challenge by other techniques.

The results of these particular reconstructions are, however, less important than the method of reconstruction employed. The treatment of data in this essay is open to criticism, since an empirically respectable reconstruction for each language family would require a monograph. It is likely that historical reconstruction will continue to be a necessary tool for interpretation in comparative ethnology. If so, methods that permit a precise evaluation of the relative simplicity of competing inferences in accounting for the same range of facts are critical, and this is one such method. Furthermore, it seems valuable to compare the results of distributional analysis with those derived from the stochastic chain approach employed by Driver in his "functional, evolutionary, and historical integration" of North American data. The outcome may require new explanations as to why systems change or remain constant with respect to various attributes. The essay seems suitable as a tribute to Driver, whose rigor in inductive methods has contributed much to comparative ethnology. If it owes most of all to Isidore Dyen, it owes much to Driver himself.

Notes

1. The methods used in this essay are drawn from Dyen and Aberle, *Lexical Reconstruction: The Case of the Proto-Athapaskan Kinship System* (n.d.). I am deeply grateful to Isidore Dyen for his methodological contributions to our joint work, as well as for comments on this essay. Specific indebtedness to him is noted at varied points in this essay. Thanks are due to Leland Donald, Kathleen Gough, and Joseph G. Jorgensen, for critical comments. Responsibility for errors of logic or fact is mine.

2. This sequence illustrates a difference between lexical reconstruction and reconstruction of features of social organization. In lexical reconstruction, a sequence that involves the displacement of a lexeme in a given meaning by another lexeme, and the subsequent reappearance of the first lexeme in that meaning at a later stage, is not regarded as a sound inference under most conditions. But the disappearance and reappearance of bilaterality, here inferred, is a different matter, since there need be no genetic connection between the first and second appearances of this descent rule.

3. Although Driver indicates that the rule of descent for the Atlantic tribes is unknown, there are some indications that it was matrilineal (cf. Swanton 1946; 644, 655). This, however, has no effect on the competing hypotheses. Whether we count by linguistic units or by homogeneous areas, if Atlantic is treated as matrilineal, the bilateral hypothesis is preferred, but by a margin of only one.

References Cited

Bloomfield, Leonard
1933   *Language*, New York, Henry Holt.
Bowers, Alfred W.
1965   "Hidatsa Social and Ceremonial Organization," *Bureau of American Ethnology Bulletin 194*, Washington D.C., U.S. Government Printing Office.
Braithwaite, Richard B.
1968   "Explanation," *Encyclopedia Britannica* 8: 969-73.
Driver, Harold E.
1956   "An integration of functional, evolutionary, and historical theory by means of correlations," *Indiana University Publications in Anthropology and Linguistics 12*: 1-36.
Driver, Harold E., and William C. Massey
1957   "Comparative studies of North American Indians," *Transactions of the American Philosophical Society n.s. 47*: 165-456.
Dyen, Isidore, and David F. Aberle
n.d.   Lexical reconstruction: the case of the Proto-Athapaskan kinship system, Cambridge and New York, Cambridge University Press, in press.
Eggan, Fred
1955a   "The Cheyenne and Arapaho kinship system," in his *Social Anthropology of the North American Tribes*, 2d ed., Chicago, University of Chicago Press: 35-95.
1955b   "Social anthropology: methods and results," in his *Social Anthropology of the*

North American Tribes, 2d ed., Chicago, University of Chicago Press: 485-551.

Ember, Melvin, and Carol R. Ember
1971   "The conditions favoring matrilocal versus patrilocal residence," *American Anthropologist 73*: 571-94.

Haas, Mary R.
1960   "Some genetic affiliations of Algonkian," in Stanley Diamond, ed., *Culture in History, Essays in Honor of Paul Radin*, New York, published for Brandeis University by Columbia University Press: 977-92.

Hockett, Charles F.
1964   "The Proto-Central Algonquian kinship system," in Ward H. Goodenough, ed., *Explorations in Cultural Anthropology, Essays in Honor of George Peter Murdock*, New York, McGraw-Hill: 239-57.
1973   Man's place in nature, New York, McGraw-Hill.

Hoijer, Harry
1956   "Athapaskan kinship systems," *American Anthropologist 58*: 309-33.

Kroeber, Alfred L.
1937   "Athabascan kin term systems," *American Anthropologist 39*: 602-08.

Matthews, G. H.
1959   "Proto-Siouan kinship terminology," *American Anthropologist 61*: 252-78.

Murdock, George Peter
1949   *Social structure*, New York, MacMillan

Schmitt, Karl, and Iva Osanai Schmitt
n.d.   *Wichita kinship, past and present*, Norman, Oklahoma, University Book Exchange.

Shimkin, Demitri B.
1941   "The Uto-Aztecan system of kinship terminology," *American Anthropologist 43*: 222-45.

Swanton, John R.
1946   "The Indians of the Southeastern United States," *Smithsonian Institution, Bureau of American Ethnology Bulletin 137*, Washington, D.C., U.S. Government Printing Office.

Part Three

On Methodology: Reliability, Statistics, Sampling

1. Introduction

Joseph G. Jorgensen

Harold Driver was the first anthropologist to analyze the reliability of cultural data, and as Naroll, Michik, and Naroll point out in their essay, Driver's work on the topic has never been superseded. It is, then, of considerable value to have this fine methodological essay reprinted here.

The second piece is addressed to the behavior of several statistics on the same set of data. Driver demonstrates how various statistics behave in the same contexts and why it is critical to understand the nature of the statistics with which the comparativist works in order to apply them properly. In particular our attention is directed toward the manner in which some measures of correlation and association behave when the data on which they are applied are skewed.

"The Measurement of Geographical Distribution Form" holds special interest for us because Driver formalizes Clark Wissler's age-area culture diffusion proposition and tests it empirically, using geometric distance functions. The appeal to geometric theory to test Wissler's spatial assertions was way ahead of its time. Indeed, to this day, anthropologists tend to refute propositions with assertions rather than putting those propositions to some formal, empirical test. At present, geographers, such as Waldo Tobler at the University of Michigan, and psychologists, such as James Lingoes at the University of Michigan and Louis Guttman at the Hebrew University in Tel Aviv, are using geometric theories to analyze spatial relations.

Driver's contribution to the solution of Galton's problem (with research assistance from Richard Chaney) is included here and is treated at some length, along with discussions of other solutions to the problem in the Naroll, Michik, and Naroll essay. It is important to note that Driver's solution allows one to discriminate between history and not history in samples drawn from a continuous space by using expected proportions.

Raoul Naroll, Gary Michik, and Frada Naroll have provided a thorough and up-to-date "state of the art" paper on "Hologeistic Theory Testing." The world-wide cross-cultural studies method is broken down into its many parts so that the authors can show problems within each part (e.g. sampling) and the current procedures that are used to solve the problems; but the method is also tied together into a systematic philosophical package. The reader who chooses to dig deeper into contemporary cross-cultural studies is directed toward relevant bibliography, HRAF ethnographic resources, even appropriate computer programs created to solve problems for cross-cultural researchers. The Narolls and their students have gone farther than any other group of scholars in attempting to solve the most vexing problems of worldwide cross-cultural research.

It may be relevant to point out here that Raoul Naroll is the President of the Human Relations Area Files and that Harold Driver, David Aberle, and Joseph Jorgensen have served on the HRAF Board of Directors.

2. Culture Element Distributions: VIII The Reliability of Culture Element Data

Harold E. Driver

Introduction

Previous studies in reliability of ethnographical data are almost nonexistent. Many ethnographers have made brief remarks here and there about the reliability of a certain section or statement of a report but almost none has seriously coped with the problem. Informants have been characterized by catchwords such as good, poor, reliable, unreliable, and ethnographers as good observers, prejudiced observers, and the like.

The problem of the reliability of informants' statements raises at least three questions: How consistent is the same informant in response to the same questions on two or more occasions; what is the amount of agreement between two or more informants; and how near do they come to the actual facts? Material for answers to the first two queries is readily obtainable in the field, but that for the third is limited to live cultures or those for which we have exceptionally good historical documents or previous ethnographies.

So far as I know, the best study, to date, in reliability of native informants is that made by DuBois and Demetracopoulou[1] on the mythology of the Wintu Indians of California. They recorded numerous versions of the same myths in English, in the native language, through interpreters, from the same informant on two occasions a year apart, from informants of varying ages, and so forth. Their conclusions were roughly these: (1) Longer versions of the same myth differed from shorter versions mainly in the inclusion of songs and irrelevant ethnographic detail and in repetition of the same elements. (2) "The presence of a native audience and confidence in the recorder frequently stimulate the narrator to tell longer tales." (3) Given the same careful field technique, English versions have essentially the same form and content as versions recorded in the native language. (4) "An able interpreter does not appreciably affect the content of a tale and may only slightly affect the form." (5) A lapse of time does not affect a story so much as the personality of the informant and circumstances attendant to the telling. Versions told a year apart differ no more than those told a few days apart. (6) The younger generation know far less mythology than their elders, but individual differences within a generation are greater than the differences of the norms of the two generations. (7) There were few local differences within Wintu territory.

Although these conclusions are indeed an important contribution to our knowledge of factors determining reliability of report, I believe they would have been sharpened by the use of a more definite analytical technique involving the splitting of the various versions of the same myth into elements or incidents which could then be compared numerically. Sheer length of the tale, however, is often given by some such phrase as "one-fourth longer."

The data of the present study were gathered much more rapidly and in a far less controlled manner and from fewer informants per tribe than were the Wintu myths. Nevertheless, they cover a much greater range of native culture and make possible the comparison of the reliability of various topics such as subsistence, games, shamanism, and the like. They consist mainly of responses to specific questions, whereas the Wintu myths are, of course, volunteer testimony. For these reasons, plus the difference in the nature of the material itself and the lack of general quantitative expression of the results of the Wintu study, no specific comparisons of the two will be made.

The data used in this study are mainly from culture-element lists obtained by Barnett[2] and myself.[3] Barnett worked two informants from Galice Creek in Oregon, and I two each from the Yurok, Hupa, and Karok tribes of northwestern California. Drucker filled in a column in Barnett's element list from his Tolowa data obtained previously by the usual field methods, to which was matched a list gathered by me from a single Tolowa informant. I also gleaned a few more items from Drucker's manuscript where they could be equated to elements in my list which had not appeared in Barnett's. Besides these, I read Kroeber's[4] account of the Yurok and those of Goddard[5] and Curtis[6] on the Hupa and entered the material (+ or -) into the element list used by me for the same tribes.

All the information employed in this study has been reduced to presence (+) and absence (-) form. Quite obviously this is a simplification of the true facts. In some contexts "+" means occurrence among a majority of the population, as in patrilocal residence. Matrilocal residence was practiced to some degree by all tribes in connection with "half marriage," the frequency among the Yurok being 23 per cent of 413 cases.[7] Nevertheless it was recorded "-" in the section on postnuptial residence. In other contexts "+" means present in any frequency at all, in some instances no doubt as low as one or two per cent. In still other sections, an element by its very nature would be restricted to some special group, such as sucking doctors. Unfortunately this factor of frequency has never been thoroughly discussed by any of us who have been gathering element-list material. So far no standardization has been attempted by me throughout my entire element list, but I did try to control the factor for each element individually in the field. In general, most elements present at all were recorded "+" by me. It was only, or at least mainly, where the item implied a majority, as in postnuptial residence, that the less frequent alternative was recorded "-." I do not hesitate to admit that this simplification is a short-cut device without other merit. The majority of information in monographs, however, is subject to the same limitations, which often are forced on the ethnographer by the limited knowledge of informants.

Concerning absences, few informants consistently deny the presence of elements unknown to them. They often say, "I never saw it," "I never heard of it," or "My father never told me about it." In such a situation, I usually recorded minus. Wherever I felt certain that the informant was mistaken I entered a query or wrote a note expressing my doubt. Where either the informant or myself seemed to be in doubt, I enclosed the entry in parentheses. Parenthetical entries have been included in the statistics to follow, because if they are inferior items, it is desirable to know how they behave. Not infrequently an informant would recognize my description or illustration of an element as belonging to a neighboring tribe and deny it for his own without hesitation. Other references to field technique will be made below from time to time.

While the concrete discussion to follow is limited to four tribes, the element universe extends from the Tillamook in Oregon to the Kato in California. In other words, any element present in any of the twenty-three tribes[8] in this area was included in at least some statistics below. Had a wider areal universe been chosen, it would have increased the number of common absences (--) among the four tribes and raised correlation coefficients. A narrower universe would have lowered such values.

In most of the statistical treatment to follow I have compared informants with informants. The culture elements are the units counted. Were there more duplicated bodies of data available, the problem might have been approached wholly from the other side, by determining how many pairs of informants agree in their responses to each element, and percentaging these values to arrive at a measure of the reliability of each element. This has been done for a part of the data but is inconclusive because of the small quantity of duplicated tribal inventories.

To determine the reliability of any body of source material it is necessary to use some statistical measure. It is desirable to employ the same measure to be used later on to correlate the material so that the results will have bearing on the intertribal or intertrait correlations. Thus if one expects to apply Q_6 to a number of tribal inventories to obtain groupings of tribes (culture "areas"), he should use this same formula to determine the amount of correlation or association between the responses of two informants of the same tribe. If he finds, e.g., that a number of pairs of informants show *intra*tribal

correlations of about .90, this means that *inter*tribal correlations of the same magnitude, if any, are likely to have true values of 1.00. If it can be shown that intratribal differences, which are errors on the part of at least one of the informants, are randomly distributed throughout a list of elements, then all obtained correlations will automatically be lower than their true values and can be raised to their true values by a correction device.[9]

I have chosen tetrachoric r (r_t),[10] computed graphically from Thurstone's diagrams,[11] as a measure of the correlation between the responses of pairs of informants.

Most of the fourfold distributions are nearly symmetrical[12] and any other measure would give highly parallel results. Under conditions of perfect symmetry $Q_6 = r_t$. However, where an appreciable amount of asymmetry is present, I believe Q or the r included in it are more satisfactory than r_t.

Table 3 (see at end of this study) gives the standard error of r_t. When the difference between two correlations is 2.5 times the standard error of the difference, $\sqrt{\sigma r_{t_1}{}^2 + \sigma r_{t_2}{}^2}$ the chances are approximately 99 to 1 that it is real, i.e., not owing to mere sampling error. In general, I believe it legitimate to assume that any number of elements is a sample of some very much larger totality. However, where the number of possibilities is definitely limited, as in fire-making methods or arrow releases, we cannot consider the 5 or so possibilities as being mere samples of a very large number of alternative methods. Differences in informants' testimony which occur in such universes are real if only five elements are involved. From a broader point of view, however, such elements can be considered samples of primitive technology, and ultimately as samples of the total number of kinds of human cultural behavior. Sampling concepts seem to apply to these broad categories, not to very small ones. In some of the arbitrary sections into which I have divided the data of tables 3 and 4, the elements constitute a large part of the total number of comparable variants in the area: e.g., houses or games. Other sections, such as ceremonies and shamanism, perhaps represent a smaller fraction of the total number of possible comparable details. The reality of numerical differences throughout the sections to follow will be subjectively evaluated from time to time, but in general I shall follow the usual sampling theory.

While the source material apparently offers duplicated information on five tribes, pairs of informants from two of these, Karok and Yurok, belong to different local groups. The first problem is to decide whether there is any justification for assuming that the two Karok and the two Yurok informants respectively belong to the same cultures. Certain relationships are given in the figure.

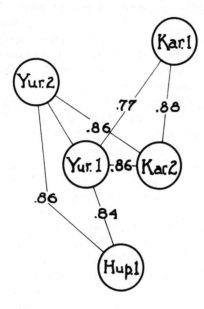

Although the two Karok groups are only slightly more disparate than the two Yurok, the external relations show a definite difference. The correlation of Karok 1 to Yurok 1 is definitely lower than that of Karok 2 to Yurok 1. This means that all the differences between Karok 1 and Karok 2 are not randomly distributed with reference to Yurok 1, as errors would be, but that some of them behave systematically. Karok 1 is more aberrant culturally as well as geographically than Karok 2. In contrast, the external relations of the two Yurok groups to Karok 2 and Hupa 1 are nearly the same. The differences between the Yurok groups are randomly distributed with reference to two neighboring localities and thus behave like errors. Because of these facts I have eliminated the Karok from the rest of the study.

Informants from the Galice and Hupa tribes are certain to belong to culturally identical local groups. The settlements of each of these tribes all fell within a 10-mile length of stream. In contrast the Yurok and Karok occupied some 40 and 50 miles of river respectively. The informants from Galice Creek are blood relatives, "cousins." Those for Hupa were unrelated but were from villages only 3 miles apart which joined together for certain ceremonies. For the Tolowa, Drucker used a number of informants, including the man who served as my only informant. Thus Drucker's material is perhaps less localized than my own, but this difference is slight because the Tolowa were a small group compared to the Yurok or Karok.

It should be remembered throughout that the three ethnographers, Drucker, Barnett, and myself, did not work under parallel field conditions. Drucker spent 70 or 80 days with a number of Tolowa informants gathering as full material as was available. Barnett began with a relatively short and generalized element list (less than 1000 elements) constructed chiefly by Kroeber for all of California, and built this up with new elements obtained from informants to about 2000. He spent a week each with his Galice informants. I began with a list of about 3000 traits, made some inquiry into all of these, added more while in the field, and spent only three or four days with each informant. Neither time nor method of inquiry were held constant by the three field investigators.

Reliability of Tribal Totalities

The totals of tables 1 and 2 summarize the chief findings. Table 1 includes all information. The values for N differ from tribe to tribe because we happened to have more duplicated information on the Yurok, e.g., than on the Tolowa. The 1366 Tolowa elements are not all included in the 2337 for the Yurok, which means that the correlations throughout this table are based on different universes for the different tribes. These universes are not strictly random samples of a larger totality, hence the correlations in this table are not strictly comparable to one another. Table 2 gives the results from the 706 elements which were positively or negatively reported for all four tribes. These correlations, made from the same universe, are wholly comparable.

The correlation coefficients (r_t) are these:

Tribes	Table 1	Table 2
Galice	.92	.92
Tolowa	.87	.90
Yourok	.91	.97
Hupa	.97	.98
Average	.92	.94

The correlations based on table 2 are higher than those of table 1, but hardly significantly so except with respect to the Yurok. I can think of no explanation whatsoever for the difference in the two Yurok values. For the phenomenon as a whole, the apparent reason is that the shorter element list (table 2) represents elements of more general knowledge. These elements are what all ethnographers (Barnett, Drucker, and myself) thought worth including in the list of queries, and at the same time what informants would readily give answers to or sometimes volunteer. Such would expectably be more reliable.

In both tables the Hupa informants show a very high reliability. The second informant was hard of hearing and slower in response than the first. I suspect I tended to equate hesitant or uncertain responses to those of the first informant. I had positive assurance that both belonged to culturally identical local groups and should agree throughout. Furthermore, they were the first two informants I worked with in the area, and my knowledge of the culture and ability to control its elements was less than for the other tribes. I do not believe their true knowledge is sufficiently superior to other informants' to account for this difference.

Barnett's Galice Creek material does not reveal this type of bias, at least in comparison with correlations of the other three tribes.

The relatively low reliability of the Tolowa is doubtless attributable to the fact that there were two ethnographers, Drucker and myself. Drucker worked without an element list, using the more usual method of inquiry where more information is volunteered. He may have erred occasionally in entering negatives, some of which were perhaps inferred from his general knowledge. However, having read his entire manuscript, I am convinced that the vast majority of differences are my errors. Furthermore, Drucker spent some 70 or 80 days with Tolowa informants, I 3 days.

Further evidences of the influence of the ethnographer on correlations are these:

Sources	+ +	+ -	- +	- -	N	r_t
Drucker's Tolowa-Galice 2	367	97	68	352	884	.84
Driver's Tolowa-Galice 2	363	119	74	328	884	.80
Drucker's Tolowa-Yurok 2	382	83	146	273	884	.70
Driver's Tolowa-Yurok 2	411	70	114	289	884	.81

Our two Tolowa lists are compared with the Galice on the north and the Yurok to the south. I had worked with a Yurok before visiting the Tolowa. Drucker had not. His information on the Tolowa and that of Barnett on the Galice are essentially independent of each other although they discussed some of the Galice material at the time Barnett was gathering it. My Tolowa information correlates .09 higher than Drucker's with the Yurok, and .04 lower with the Galice. It seems obvious to me that I projected previous knowledge, mainly Yurok, into my Tolowa data. The fact that my informant came from the southern part of the Tolowa territory nearest the Yurok, and that there were a number of admitted Yurok influences present in small frequencies, may have caused some of the foregoing differences.

Further evidence of the role of the ethnographer is given by these figures on four Hupa sources:

Sources	+ +	+ -	- +	- -	N	r_t
Goddard-Curtis	295	6	5	27	333	.97
Goddard-Driver 1	274	25	5	29	333	.90
Goddard-Driver 2	274	25	5	29	333	.90
Curtis-Driver 1	270	30	8	25	333	.85
Curtis-Driver 2	270	30	8	25	333	.85
Driver 1-Driver 2	274	4	4	51	333	.99

The values .85 and .90 are not significantly different because the standard error of the difference is about .04. The value .97 is just barely significantly higher than those of .90. Thus the significant facts are represented by the two higher correlations on the one hand and the four lower ones on the other. The very high agreement between my own informants has been interpreted above. Concerning the relationship between Goddard's and Curtis' accounts, I am convinced that Curtis drew from Goddard when he wrote his report. The following tabulation of positive elements (+) mentioned in their works proves this.

Goddard

		Not	
	Mentioned	mentioned	Totals
Curtis Mentioned	295	88	383
Not mentioned	228	478	706
Totals	523	566	1089

The total, 1089, is the number of positive entries obtained by me from the Hupa. Negatives were disregarded because of their infrequency in the published sources. The correlation of this fourfold table is r_t = .64. Had Goddard and Curtis randomly selected from 1089 positive elements, the correlation would have been r_t = .00. Perhaps some of this agreement in selection of material is due to the kind of information volunteered by informants, but I doubt if such a high agreement would have come about in this way. The actual terms and sentence structure of Curtis conform so closely to Goddard that the independence of the reports could be doubted on these grounds alone. Furthermore, Curtis' chapter on the Hupa is longer than any other chapter in his work on tribes in the general area. At the time he wrote,

Goddard's report was practically the only published literature available. Curtis does not mention names of his informants. These facts all point to one conclusion.

Within the limits of the 333 examples cited above, what superficially appeared to be four sources thus turn out to be two. The low values, .85 and .90, which represent the correlations between these two sources are of about the same magnitude as those between other more or less independent sources (totals of tables 1 and 2), and do not require any special explanation.

For fear that the 333 traits above might have been a somewhat selected rather than representative sample of the larger universe, I made another count of all elements reported by Goddard and myself. These total 613:

Sources	++	+-	-+	--	N	r_t
Goddard-Driver 1	467	56	11	79	613	.90
Goddard-Driver 2	470	53	8	82	613	.93
Driver 1-Driver 2	468	9	9	127	613	.99

They show no significant differences from the 333 discussed above.

Further relationships between element list and monographic sources are found by comparing Kroeber's (1925) account of the Yurok with the two Yurok lists obtained by me.

Sources	++	+-	-+	--	N	r_t
Kroeber-Driver 1	549	43	33	206	831	.95
Kroeber-Driver 2	536	58	29	208	831	.94
Driver 1-Driver 2	526	56	37	212	831	.93

These correlations do not differ significantly from one another. Therefore my second Yurok list was probably not directly influenced by my first. Incidentally, I interviewed the Tolowa informant between the first and second Yurok. The lapse of a few days may have contributed to the independence of results.

If more informants had been used it would have been possible to determine the influence of sex, age, native occupation (e.g., shaman), etc., on report. Had more field controls been employed, the reliability and total quantity of volunteer versus questioned testimony, time held constant, could have been determined. This is difficult to accomplish from published literature owing to the dearth of negative evidence and specific field controls.

Within the limits of the qariation among ethographers and informants in this study, the personal equation of the ethnographer seems to be as important a determinant of reliability as that of the native informant.

Reliability Within Special Topics

The topical arrangement of tables 1 and 2 is the same as that used in the field except that two or three sections have been combined occasionally to raise the total number of elements (N) to a figure large enough to minimize sampling error. Therefore the classification is not influenced by any desire to "prove" preconceived theories. Although the four reliability coefficients within a given class sometimes show appreciable differences, the following arrangement of averages in rank order provides a summary for the four tribes as a whole.

Correlation (r_t) Averages of Various Topics

Topics	Table 1	Table 2
Ceremonies	.98	
Marriage	.96	.99
Houses	.96	
Games	.95	.98
Money, tobacco, musical instruments	.94	
Weaving	.91	
Counting, astronomy	.91	
Death	.89	
Body and dress	.88	.94
Birth, menstruation	.87	.88
Navigation, technology, weapons	.86	.89
Social stratification, war	.85	
Shamanism	.85	.85
Subsistence	.80	.86

The blank spaces in the table 2 column are due to the fact that no correlations were computed when N was under 50.

While the range of this series of correlation averages is .18, there are no definite breaks within it. The variation in reliability of these 14 topics is not greater than that of the tribal totals discussed above, except for subsistence (.80). On the whole, material culture *is* no more reliable than social or religious culture. The general belief that material culture is more reliable than other sections no doubt comes from the fact that it is preserved in museums and sometimes can be photographed in the field. A novice attempting to describe living material culture is likely to accomplish more than he would with social organization. When, however, almost the entire culture is gone, and almost all information has to be salvaged from the memories of native informants, social and religious concepts can be obtained with about the same reliability as material ones.

The high reliability of ceremonies is explained partly by the fact that they are still given by some of the tribes. They are also completely exoteric except for a few magical formulae recited by a priest. Furthermore, the routine of dancing and singing is repeated in identical form for eight or ten days. In recent years these ceremonies have been biennial for the Yurok and Hupa instead of annual, but even so the average informant has seen them twenty or thirty times.

The high average reliability coefficient for marriage is attributable partly to the fact that parent-in-law child-in-law avoidances have been included in this section. These avoidances, totaling 36 traits, are entirely absent for all four tribes. Thus the common absence category of each relationship is increased by 36. This raises correlations. The elimination of avoidances would lower the average correlation to about .90.

Concerning houses, a number of Yurok and Hupa structures are still standing. I filled in some of the entries from direct observation. Where the two informants were of the same local group, as at Hupa, I eliminated my own direct observations from the statistics. Under such a condition of complete preservation, informants' descriptions would also be highly accurate.

Concerning subsistence, the relatively low reliability in table 1 can be explained by at least two factors. First, minor differences in geographical environment and ultra-localization by the informant undoubtedly introduce a number of real differences which are not errors on the part of either of two informants. This would apply mainly to the Yurok, although I eliminated from the count a few elements which obviously showed true local differences. Furthermore, I always began my inquiry with subsistence and proceeded in the order of tables 1 and 2. Many informants, anxious to please, volunteered more information in the first few hours of the interview than during the rest of it. I tended to introduce a good part of this into the element list and expanded the subsistence section to the point of diminishing returns. The significantly higher reliability from the smaller sample of table 2 corroborates this interpretation. It is obvious that the quantity of detail concerning any topic can be increased to the point where an average informant will make a high percentage of error. A small quantity of information on a given topic is also unsatisfactory because it is likely to be an insufficient sample of the informant's total knowledge and of the total number of relevant facts. The desideratum lies somewhere between. However, the relatively low correlation of two Tolowa informants is scarcely explainable on environmental grounds because the area was small, and neither does it fit very closely the over-expansion theory because the total number of subsistence elements is only 172 compared to 322 for the Yurok. The difference must therefore also have been caused by the particular knowledge of the ethnographers and informants involved.

Such interpretations could be extended to others of these topics but would become increasingly subjective and have little bearing on other areas or cultures.

Several other divisions of the total body of data have been made. One of these is material objects versus the rest of the list. Here a sharper distinction than any cited above between material objects and behavior or belief has been made. While a topic like subsistence includes many material objects, perhaps half of its elements refer to some kind of behavior or belief connected with obtaining or preparing food. It is therefore not composed entirely of material objects. The present classification attempts to include only such elements as could be photographed or observed in museum or field without any information whatsoever regarding manufacture or use. Examples: all weapons are included but whether they are used in war or hunting is ruled out; hair coiffure and tattooing are included, but the washing or greasing of hair and method of tattooing are omitted; gaming objects are included, but not the rules of play; structural features of houses are accepted but not the fact that men habitually slept in the sweat house. Tribal correlations of such elements follow. They are compared with the totals of table 1.

Pairs of informants	Material objects						Total elements
	+ +	+ -	- +	- -	N	r_t	r_t
Galice	193	28	33	217	471	.92	.92
Tolowa	257	50	35	169	511	.85	.87
Yurok	412	63	46	279	800	.91	.91
Hupa	422	20	13	280	735	.99	.97

There are no significant differences between these two sets of correlations. These facts, combined with the ranked list of topics above, are proof that material culture elements or material objects are no more reliable than other elements.

A number of illustrations were shown by me to informants in the field. This was done for both Hupa informants, both Yurok, and the one Tolowa. So far as I know, Drucker and Barnett used no illustrations. The question arises: are the responses obtained from pictures more reliable than those obtained from verbal questions alone? These are some of the relevant facts:

Informants	Illustrated elements					
	++	+-	-+	--	N	r_t
Yurok	217	18	6	54	295	.95
Hupa	225	10	4	57	296	.98

The Yurok correlation here is barely significantly larger than the Yurok figure (.91) for material objects and the total list given above. The Hupa remains the same. The fact that illustrated elements show a slightly higher correlation for the Yurok is no proof that the pictures caused this difference. A proof of the efficacy of pictures demands a control group of informants on whom no pictures were used. This control group would have to be identical in knowledge, command of language, etc., with the group shown the illustrations, so that whatever difference occurred could be attributed definitely to the pictures. These conditions are far from satisfied by these data. Nevertheless, a comparison of the reliability of the 141 illustrated elements which are reported for all four tribes with the reliability of the total body of data and material objects seems worth while.

Informants	++	+-	-+	--	N	r_t
Galice	62	5	8	66	141	.95
Tolowa	74	19	3	45	141	.91
Yurok	108	7	3	23	141	.95
Hupa	111	4	2	24	141	.98

The fact that the Galice correlations are also higher for pictured elements when no pictures were used eliminates the significance of the Yurok value. From these scraps of evidence there is no proof that illustrations improve reliability. Personally, I believe they do help. No one knows how much time either Barnett or myself spent in obtaining information on these 141 items. This would have to be held constant before the efficacy of pictures becomes determinant.

It occurred to me that more or less generic traits might show a higher reliability than more specific traits, the theory being that one forgets more details than general facts. The definition of generic versus specific is, of course, a relative one, but in order to avoid selection in favor of a preconceived theory I have almost mechanically followed indentations in my original field manuscript. For example:

Wooden chest
  Cylindrical
  Rectanguloid
  In two pieces, about equal size
  Small opening and lid
  Carved decoration
  For feathers and valuables

The indented elements all refer to the wooden chest. A generic element, then, is one which has two or more specific subvariants; a specific element, one of two or more subvariants of a generic element.

Facts concerning the total number of generic and specific elements derived from the entire list (the universes of table 1) are:

Informants	Generic elements						Total elements
	++	+-	-+	--	N	r_t	r_t
Galice	128	9	11	46	194	.93	.92
Tolowa	147	21	12	33	213	.80	.87
Yurok	209	16	10	58	293	.94	.91
Hupa	176	6	2	65	249	.99	.97
Average						.92	.92

Informants	Specific elements					
	++	+-	-+	--	N	r_t
Galice	255	31	63	367	716	.91
Tolowa	294	48	50	281	673	.90
Yurok	537	103	62	554	1256	.92
Hupa	503	51	30	517	1101	.97
Average						.93

The only statistically significant differences in these three sets of correlations are those of the Tolowa. I have no special explanation for these differences. From the facts as a whole, neither generic nor specific elements show any significant differences in reliability from the entire list.

It occurred to me further that those elements which were widely distributed in an area might be more reliable than those of limited distribution. Presumably, the more widely distributed elements would occur in higher frequencies in individual tribes and hence play a more prominent rôle in the culture. To make the contrast sharp, I chose as widely distributed elements only those which were present in 11 or more of the 15[14] tribes in the area. Elements of limited distribution are defined as those known to be absent in 11 or more of the 15 tribes but present in at least one of the four duplicate tribes. These are the findings:

Informants	++	+-	-+	--	N	Wide distribution W	r	Total elements W	r_t
Galice	188	9	23	21	241	.87	.76	.87	.92
Tolowa	263	23	5	13	304	.91	.72	.84	.87
Yurok	401	19	14	1	435	.92	.03	.86	.91
Hupa	419	12	2	4	437	.97	.65	.91	.97
Average						.92	.54	.87	.92

Informants	++	+-	-+	--	N	Limited distribution W	r_t
Galice	9	4	5	54	72	.88	.82
Tolowa	31	9	12	25	77	.73	.65
Yurok	21	28	36	64	149	.57	.10
Hupa	20	8	3	120	151	.93	.94
Average						.78	.63

Because of the highly asymmetrical nature of the fourfold distributions involved, I have computed the percentage of agreement, W, as well as the correlation coefficient.[15] Widely distributed elements show a slightly higher percentage of agreement between pairs of informants than the total list (table 1). Elements of limited distribution show a definitely lower percentage of agreement than the total list. Correlations give a very different picture. The total list is highest, next elements of limited distribution, and finally those of wide distribution. Because the type of selection automatically produces asymmetrical distributions, the meaning of the correlations becomes problematical. Therefore I am accepting the results from W as being the more meaningful. Thus widely distributed elements are more reliable than those of limited distribution.

To summarize the findings of this section: (1) While there are definite differences in the reliability of groups of elements arranged topically, the range of variation of the reliability coefficients is no greater than that of those of the four tribal totalities, and there are no definite breaks in the series. (2) Material culture or material objects show the same degree of reliability as the entire element list. (3) There is no proof that illustrations improve reliability. (4) Neither generic nor specific elements show any greater or lesser reliability than the list as a whole. (5) Widely distributed elements within a given area are apparently more reliable than narrowly distributed elements.

Reliability of Individual Elements

The reliability of an individual element can be measured in terms of the number of pairs of informants who agree in their responses to it. In the present example, when all four pairs of informants show intra-agreement the element is completely reliable. Table 4 is a compilation of the presumably least reliable elements, those for which two, threee, or four pairs of informants disagreed. The element numbers are those of my field study.[16] The universe is that of table 2, N = 706. A few additional elements have been included to give supplementary information here and there.

It is significant that only a single element shows four differences, and only nine show three differences. The distribution of these differences among the 706 elements is the following:

Element frequency	Number of pairs of informants with intradifferences				
	0	1	2	3	4
Actual frequency	477	175	44	9	1
Chance frequency	455	211	36	3	0

The chance frequencies are those which would come about if the 294 differences were randomly scattered among the 4(706) = 2824 duplicated entires.

I am indebted to Dr. J. M. Thompson for showing me the following method of deriving the chance frequencies. Let a be the probability of a difference occurring between any pair of informants for any element. Then:

a^4 = the probability that all four pairs of informants will intradiffer on the same element.

$4 a^3 (1-a)$ = the probability that exactly three pairs of informants will intradiffer on the same element.

$6 a^2 (1-a)^2$ = the probability that exactly two pairs of informants will intradiffer on the same element.

$4a(1-a)^3$ = the probability that exactly one pair of informants will intradiffer on the same element.

$(1-a)^4$ = the probability that no pair of informants will intradiffer on the same element.

Since N = 706 elements, the total number of duplicated responses is 4(706) = 2824. The total number of differences, by actual count, is 294. Therefore:

$$a^4 = .000, \text{ which, multiplied by } 706 = 0$$
$$4a^3(1-a) = .004, \text{ which, multiplied by } 706 = 3$$
$$6a^2(1-a)^2 = .052, \text{ which, multiplied by } 706 = 36$$
$$4a(1-a)^3 = .299, \text{ which, multiplied by } 706 = 211$$
$$(1-a)^4 = \underline{.645,} \text{ which, multiplied by } 706 = \underline{455}$$
$$1.000 \qquad\qquad\qquad 705$$

The frequencies of elements which show two, three, or four differences are so near chance, that we have practically no proof that they are poor elements. The accumulation of differences is therefore mainly due to unknown factors whose cumulative effect produces distributions similar to those of coins or dice. Such factors might be: error in recording on the part of the ethnographer; verbal error in response on the part of the informant; or true misunderstanding on the part of either party. The fact that the questions are never given in exactly the same words by the ethnographer on two occasions means that the stimulus is not fully controlled. Such control will probably never be achieved because the variety of cultures and languages involved is too great and the time too short to realize this ideal. A difference in the role played by an element in a culture may make an ethnographer's query meaningless to certain informants. In my experience with this type of interview I have done at least half of the talking. Each element must be described in some context before an informant will get the idea, and the ethnographer is forced to decide whether or not his description to the informant is adequate when the informant continues to respond negatively. Under such conditions of work, random error would be expectable.

On the assumption that at least some of the ten elements for which three or four intratribal differences occurred are inferior items, I shall give my impressions regarding some of the possible causes of these differences. Numbers refer to elements in table 4.

5. Informants were doubtless confused between the construction of a definite brush fence and the piling of a little brush around a natural trail or runway. This element also appears to be more typical of southern Athabascans than the Klamath and Smith River region where systematic fishing was far more profitable than small game hunting.

27-28. No doubt a secondary adaptation of a dip net, and only one of several ways to obtain woodpeckers. They were also shot and snared.

88. Individual differences within a local group are certain to have occurred. Some persons ate such animals, others did not.

423. Food was nowhere habitually sold. Within a family or small village it was communal. Without, it was bartered for other natural products or articles of value, occasionally dentalia. The caption lacks specificity.

1550. A child's toy, hence of small importance. It also seems to be more typical of central California.

1648. This was no doubt of uncommon occurrence and resorted to only when the girl's family was in desperate need of money.

1920. There seems to have been appreciable variation in the age at which children were named. There may also have been a confusion between a mere nickname and one formally bestowed.

1961. In many instances the girl was supposed to pick up a few small sticks of wood on her way home from her daily bath in the stream. She went outdoors at no other time. This was doubtless interpreted as work by some informants, but not by others.

2282. Red is only one of several colors used. Face painting was never symbolic in northwestern California, and the color used perhaps subject to local availability or individual preference.

In general, these "worst" elements appear to be unimportant or of infrequent occurrence in northwestern California culture. In order to prove that this is the cause of their unreliability one would have to determine the frequencies of "unimportant" or "infrequent" items throughout the entire list and see if intratribal differences accumulated in greater proportions in these items than in the rest of the list as a whole. This would be a difficult and subjective procedure and I shall not attempt it.

Unknown causes (chance) seem to be more potent determiners of the reliability of individual items than known causes.

Practical Recommendations

While these findings answer a few questions concerning the reliability of culture-element data, we still know relatively little about the reliability of individual items, which is the one thing we want most to know if we are going to improve our pre-field element lists. If even 25 per cent of the tribal element inventories already collected were duplicated by a second ethnographer and second informant, we would have material enough to come to definite conclusions. With fifty or so duplicated lists randomly distributed over the area of our present activity, we could empirically determine the reliability of each element with some little assurance. I see no point in undertaking intensive studies of the DuBois-Demetracopoulou type to solve the element list problem. These are expensive, good informants would drop dead around us while we were working with a single tribe, and the results would not be directly applicable to the culture-element survey.

If, from a large body of duplicated data, we still found that errors tended to be randomly distributed, we would have ample justification for correcting all obtained correlations upward to their true levels. Only local (topically as well as areally local) correlations would then differ to any important degree from their true values.

Summary and Conclusions

Compared with data of other social sciences, the reliability of culture-element material is fairly high. Reliability coefficients, r_t, of the entire body of data examined range from .87 to .97. Percentages of agreement vary from .84 to .91. The low values are likely to be nearer the true reliability because higher ones are from data collected by a single ethnographer who may have possessed a bias of some kind.

Within the limits of personal variation among the present ethnographers and informants, the personal equation of the ethnographer seems to be as important as that of the informant.

Although certain topics are definitely more reliable than others, the range of variation is little greater than that of total tribal inventories. No one major division of culture, material, social, or religious, shows any higher reliability than any other.

Material objects show the same reliability as the entire body of data.

Illustrations apparently do not increase reliability.

Generic or specific elements show no significant differences in reliability from each other or from the data as a whole.

Widely distributed elements are apparently more reliable than the unselected elements in the list; narrowly distributed elements less reliable.

Individual elements show few demonstrable differences in reliability.

There is a need for more duplicated source material if we are to learn more about the kind and cause of differences between informants and ethnographers.

TABLE 1

Intratribal Correlations from All Data

(viz., Galice Inf't 1 with Galice Inf't 2, etc.)

	Correlations (r_t)					Number of elements (N)			
	Galice	Tolowa	Yurok	Hupa	Average	Galice	Tolowa	Yurok	Hupa
Subsistence	.87	.63	.74	.95	.80	162	172	322	315
Houses	.96	.91	.98	1.00	.96	177	192	226	88
Navigation, technology, weapons	.74	.82	.89	.98	.86	126	131	240	222
Body and dress	.96	.67	.89	.99	.88	93	94	208	196
Weaving	.77		.96	1.00	.91	57	46	105	105
Money, tobacco, musical instruments	.98	.92	.88	.98	.94	73	64	84	84
Games	1.00	.96	.96	.89	.95	89	85	155	120
Counting, astronomy			.84	.98	.91	19	15	76	56
Marriage	1.00	.97	.89	.98	.96	91	94	142	138
Birth, menstruation	.84	.80	.92	.92	.87	134	121	203	166
Death	.82	.96	.83	.93	.89	79	85	142	123
Social stratification, war	.92	.56	.95	.96	.85	104	56	126	100
Shamanism	.88	.63	.96	.93*	.85	132	94	171	146
Ceremonies	.97	1.00	.96		.98	124	117	137	*
Total	.92	.87	.91	.97	.92	1460	1366	2337	1859

*I witnessed the White Deerskin Dance and obtained information about other ceremonies from only one informant.

TABLE 2
Intratribal Correlations from 706 Elements

	Correlations (r_t)					N
	Galice	Tolowa	Yurok	Hupa	Average	
Subsistence	.86	.75	.88	.94	.86	93
Houses						18
Navigation, technology, weapons	.76	.85	.93	1.00	.89	82
Body and dress	.98	.86	.92	1.00	.94	56
Weaving						35
Money, tobacco, musical instruments						49
Games	1.00	.98	1.00	.95	.98	64
Counting, astronomy						6
Marriage	1.00	1.00	.97	1.00	.99	69
Birth, menstruation	.84	.86	.97	.85	.88	71
Death						40
Social stratification, war						31
Shamanism	1.00	.44	.99	.97	.85	50
Ceremonies						42
Total	.92	.90	.97	.98	.94	706

TABLE 3

Standard Errors of Tetrachoric R

(Standard errors of r_t, or r_t, when asymmetry[*] = .00 for both variables. These increase at an increasing rate as asymmetry of either variable increases. They are increased 50 per cent when asymmetry = ± .70 for both variables, and are doubled when asymmetry = ± .82 for both variables. Compiled from Pearson, 1913.)

	Correlation Coefficient, r_t												
N	.40	.45	.50	.55	.60	.65	.70	.75	.80	.85	.90	.95	.99
50	.197	.190	.181	.172	.162	.151	.137	.124	.107	.089	.068	.042	.015
75	.160	.154	.148	.140	.132	.123	.112	.101	.088	.073	.055	.034	.011
100	.139	.134	.128	.122	.115	.107	.097	.087	.076	.063	.048	.030	.009
150	.113	.109	.105	.099	.093	.067	.079	.071	.062	.051	.039	.024	.008
200	.098	.095	.091	.086	.081	.075	.069	.062	.054	.045	.034	.021	.007
300	.081	.078	.074	.071	.066	.062	.057	.051	.044	.037	.028	.017	.005
400	.070	.067	.065	.061	.058	.054	.049	.044	.038	.032	.024	.015	.005
500	.052	.060	.057	.054	.051	.048	.043	.039	.034	.028	.021	.013	.004
700	.052	.050	.048	.046	.043	.040	.037	.033	.029	.024	.018	.011	.003
1000	.044	.043	.041	.039	.037	.034	.031	.028	.024	.020	.015	.009	.003
1500	.036	.035	.033	.032	.030	.028	.025	.023	.020	.016	.013	.008	.002
2000	.031	.030	.029	.027	.025	.024	.022	.019	.017	.014	.011	.007	.002

[*]Asymmetry is defined as $\frac{2\Sigma+}{N} - 1.00$ where plus refers to the positive responses.

TABLE 4

Distributions of Least Reliable Elements

(+, present; -, absent; Gal 1, 2, Barnett's first and second Galice informants; Tol Di, Driver's Tolowa; Tol Du, Drucker's Tolowa; Yur 1, 2, Driver's first and second Yurok informants; Hup 1, 2, Driver's first and second Hupa informants; numerals to left of columns of + and - entries = number of pairs informants who differed.)

		Gal 1	Gal 2	Tol Di	Tol Du	Yur 1	Yur 2	Hup 1	Hup 2
Subsistence									
Hunting									
1. Driving into fence with nooses in gaps		+	+	+	+	+	-	+	+
5. Rabbits	3	+	-	+	-	-	-	-	+
6. Quail	2	+	+	-	+	-	-	-	+
8. Driving with fire		-	+	-	-	-	-	+	+
11. Small game	2	-	+	-	-	-	-	-	+
13. Driving into water	2	+	+	+	+	+	-	-	+
27. Nets, bag type	3	+	-	+	-	+	+	-	+
28. Woodpeckers	3	+	-	+	-	+	+	-	+
39. Deadfalls		+	+	+	+	+	+	+	-
44. For large game	2	-	+	+	+	-	+	-	-
45. For small game	2	-	+	+	+	+	+	+	-
Animals Eaten									
88. Ursus horribilis eaten	3	+	-	+	-	-	+	+	+
89. Felis cougar eaten	2	+	+	-	-	-	+	+	-
Fishing									
175. Gill net	2	-	+	+	+	-	+	+	+
190. Crab-claw rattle on net	2	-	+	+	+	-	+	-	-
Various									
423. Food sold	4	-	+	+	-	+	-	+	-
Houses									
588. Notched plank or log ladder		-	+	+	+	+	+	+	+
589. Type b house	2	-	+	+	+	+	-	-	-
Technology									
747. Wood meat platter	2	+	-	+	+	+	+	+	-
Weapons									
879. Wooden arrow straightener			+	+		+	+	+	+
880. Perforated			+			+	+	+	+
881. Forked stick	2	-	+	+	-	+	+	+	+
895. Quiver carried at side under arm	2	-	-	+		-	+	+	+
896. Quiver carried on back				+		+	+	-	-
907-8. Slings used	2	+	+	+	-	+	-	-	-
906. For hunting, by men	2	-	+	-	-	+	-	-	-
909. For war		-	+	-	-	-	-	-	-
910. As boy's toy only		+		+	-	-	-	-	-
922. Elkhide helmet	2	-	+	+	+	+	+	-	+

TABLE 4 -- Continued

		Gal 1	Gal 2	Tol Di	Tol Du	Yur 1	Yur 2	Hup 1	Hup 2
Body and Dress									
961. Soaproot brush for hair	2	-	-	+	-	-	-	-	+
986. Cap of fur for men	2	+	+	+	-	+	-	-	-
994. Hide shirt	2	+	+	+	-	-	+	-	-
995. Buckskin	2	+	+	+	-	-	+	-	-
1001. Breechclout (between legs)	2	+	+	+	-	-	+	-	-
1002. Buckskin	2	+	+	+	-	-	+	-	-
1037. Leggings	2	+	+	+	-	-	+	+	+
1038. Buckskin	2	+	+	+	-	-	+	+	+
Weaving									
1163. Deep sifting of winnowing basket, pointed bottom	2	-	-	+	-	+	-	+	+
1241. Net mesh spacer of wood	2	+	+	-	+	+	+	+	-
1242. Net mesh spacer of bone or horn				+	+	+	+	+	+
Musical Instruments									
1311. Hide drum	2	+	+	+	-	+	-	-	-
1340-1. Bull-roarer	2	+	-	-	+	-	-	-	-
1345-6. Toy	2	+	-	-	+	-	-	-	-
Games									
Hand, Grass, Many Stick Game									
1452. Two bones or sticks per player	2	-	+	-	-	-	-	+	-
1454. Of hollow bone	2	-	+	-	-	-	-	+	-
1464. Hide in grass in hand	2	-	+	-	-	-	-	+	-
1545-6. Jacks	2	-	+	-	+	-	-	-	-
1547. With stones	2	-	+	-	+	-	-	-	-
Tops									
1550. Acorn	3	-	-	+	-	+	-	-	+
Marriage									
1647. Child betrothal before puberty		+	-	+	+	+	+	-	-
1648. With payment by groom's side	3	+	-	-	+	-	+	-	-
Birth									
1823. Birth aided by drinking vegetable concoction	2	-	-	+	-	-	+	+	+
Milk Teeth									
1911. Thrown away		+	+	+	+	-	-	+	+
1916. Over house	2	+	-	+	+	-	-	-	+
Name									
1920. Given soon after birth (up to six months)	3	+	-	+	-	+	-	-	-

TABLE 4 -- Concluded

		Gal 1	Gal 2	Tol Di	Tol Du	Yur 1	Yur 2	Hup 1	Hup 2
Girl's Puberty									
1948. Covered or veiled when going outside	5	+	+	+	-	+	+	+	+
1952. Looking at people taboo	2	+	+	+	-	-	+	+	+
1961. Work compulsory, getting wood	3	-	-	-	+	+	-	-	+
1999. Men and women dance separately	2	-	-	+	-	-	-	+	-
Death									
2083. Canoe of dead broken	2	+	-	+	+	-	+	+	+
2084. House of dead burned	2	-	+	-	+	-	-	-	-
War									
2281-2. War paint		+	+	+	+	+	+	+	+
2282. Red	3	+	-	+	-	-	+	+	+
2283. Black		-	+	+	+	+	+	+	+
2284. White	2	-	-	+	-	-	+	+	+
2293. Prisoners enslaved	2	-	-	+	-	-	-	+	-
2326. Dance of incitement: abreast	2	+	-	-	+	-	-	+	+
Shamanism									
2424. Power from human spirit or ghost	2	+	-	+	-	+	+	+	+
2431. Power from reptiles	2	+	+	+	-	-	-	+	-

Notes

1. 1932. For complete citation see References Cited.

2. See Bibliography.

3. CED:X—Northwest California, AR 1. (In press.)

4. 1925.

5. 1903.

6. 1924.

7. Waterman and Kroeber, 1934.

8. All tribes in Barnett's and my own distribution studies.

9. Cf. Spearman, 1904, 1907.

10. Pearson, 1900.

11. Chesire, Saffir, Thurstone, 1933.

12. I.e., the percentage ratio of positive to negative responses is about 50:50.

13. The raw frequencies have been included in the small tables in the text in order to give a sample of their distribution and the amount of asymmetry present.

14. The areal universe is that of table 4. The Karok and Sinkyone are counted as 2 tribes each. The rest of Barnett's material was in press, and not available to me at the time this count was made.

15. $W=(a+d)/N$ where a is the number of elements for which both informants gave positive responses, d the number for which both gave negative responses, N the total number of elements.

16. Driver, MS in press.

References Cited

Bibliographical abbreviations used

AA   American Anthropologist.

BAE-B   Bureau of American Ethnology, Bulletins.

JRAI   Journal of the Royal Anthropological Institute (Great Britain).

UC-AR   University of California, Anthropological Records.

UC-PAAE   University of California, Publications in American Archeology and Ethnology.

Barnett, H. G.
   1937   Culture Element Distributions: VII—Oregon Coast. UC-AR 1: 155-204.

Chesire, L., Saffire, M., Thurstone, L. L.
1933 Computing Diagrams for the Tetrachoric Correlation Coefficient. University of Chicago Bookstore.

Curtis, E. S.
1924 The North American Indian. Vol. 13.

Driver, H. E.
In press. Culture Element Distributions: X—Northwest California Area. UC-AR.

Drucker, Philip
1937. The Tolowa and their Southwest Oregon Kin. UC-PAAE 36:221-300.

DuBois, Cora, and Demetracopoulou, Dorothy
1932. A Study of Wintu Mythology. Journal of American Folk-lore, 45:375-500.

Goddard, Pliny Earle
1903. Life and Culture of the Hupa. UC-PAAE 1:1-88.

Kroeber, A. L.
1925. Handbook of the Indians of California. BAE-B 78.

Pearson, Karl
1900. On the Correlation of Characters Not Quantitatively Measurable. Philosophical Transactions 195A:1-47. The original derivation of r_t.

1913. On the Probable Error of a Coefficent of Correlation as Found from a Four-fold Table. Biometrika 9:22-27.

Spearman, C.
1904. The Proof and Measurement of the Association between Two Things. Amer. Jour. Psychol. 15:72-101.

1907. Demonstration of Formulae for True Measure of Correlation. Amer. Jour. Psychol. 18:161-69.

Waterman, T. T., and Kroeber, A. L.
1934. Yurok Marriages. UC-PAAE 35:1-14.

3. Culture Element Distributions: X Northwest California

Harold E. Driver

Introduction[*]

This section is concerned chiefly with theory. Its purpose is to bring my point of view, which differs

[*]In the preparation of this paper, Works Progress Administration employees were used.

in certain respects from Kroeber's and Klimek's, up to date.

Field technique.—This section attempts to dispel a number of false ideas concerning the field technique of the culture element program. Since the field program started, in 1934, there has been an increasing tendency to stay longer in each locality and to rely more and more on volunteer testimony. Gifford and Klimek worked only a single day with some and never more than two days with any of the Yana and Pomo informants. When Drucker and I surveyed Southern California and Southern Sierra Nevada areas respectively, we started on a three-day schedule and stayed longer occasionally. Some of the later field trips have averaged five or six days of actual work with each informant, a week each including traveling. The result is longer lists of traits, more supplementary notes, or both.

I would judge that almost half of the positive entries in all culture element field reports, certainly in the later ones, were filled in from essentially volunteer testimony. We have all started inquiry on a topic by asking the Indian to tell us in his own way about something. For example, "How did they play the hand game?" As he talked we filled in the element list and wrote additional information in a notebook or on the backs of list pages. Then when the informant began to slow up, which usually was after the definitive points had been given, we began to ask specific questions. Even specific questions can be put in completion form, such as, "How many sticks did you use to keep score?" It is still not necessary to suggest the answer in the question. The speed of the program is explained largely by the fact that it takes less time to record plus and minus signs than to write out a phrase the length of an average element description. The other chief time-saving factor is the mnemonic value of the list itself to the ethnographer. He has before him a large number of facts or leads, which greatly facilitates the construction of questions to the informant. Time is saved not by a rapid barrage of questions and the filling in of pluses and minuses from the Indian's grunts, but by organizing the questioning and the recording of responses.

Contrary to what most ethnographers seem to believe, element-list work is not intrinsically simpler than standard ethnography. It is definitely more difficult when done rapidly and effectively, because the ethnographer is automatically making a comparative study as he fills in each list and describes each local group.

The present report and my earlier Southern Sierra Nevada study published as CED: VI were done in thirteen months, including preparation before going into the field, field work, and writing. I believe they are less satisfactory than later work, especially when compared to Erminie Voegelin's Northeast California results (in manuscript at this time). While Mrs. Voegelin had the advantage of our previous basic work, the additional time which she was able to spend in the field and in writing up the material seems to me to show definitely in her work.

Kroeber has correctly stated that the present element list is overloaded with northern traits and underloaded with southern. The reasons for this are several: (1) I did not spend time enough preparing the prefield list; (2) Gifford's Pomo list was much briefer than later lists and offered less from which to select; (3) informants in the north were much better and volunteered more; (4) the Coast Yuki and Kato were worked last and it did not seem practical to add many items which would have only one or two positive occurrences. This is only part of the result of insufficient planning. The rest is that only about half the items in Barnett's Oregon Coast list (published as CED: VII) and the present one are comparable.[1]

Correlations computed from raw data such as these, not checked in detail against museum specimens or the previously published literature and subject to the type of sampling error shown by Kroeber, can at best give the more general groupings of tribes.

Formulas.[2]—In the past few years quantitative ethnologists have devoted considerable space to a discussion of correlation formulas. No general agreement has been reached to date because there is a confusion between the purely mathematical properties of formulas and inferences drawn from their numerical results. It is generally admitted that the absolute values of correlation coefficients have little meaning in ethnology. The argument has been chiefly over which formula gives the most satisfactory rank order of coefficients in an intercorrelation table. In the pages and diagrams to follow, it will be shown that formulas used to date give identical rank orders when the distributions compared are symmetrical, that is, when each trait or tribe has exactly 50 per cent positive and 50 per cent negative entries. Differences are brought about by different degrees and different directions of skewness.

To show the effect of skewness on various measures of relationship, I have constructed five diagrams. These are the formulae compared:

Let the fourfold table be

	+	—	
+	a	b	a+b
—	c	d	c+d
	a+c	b+d	N

$$\phi = r_{hk} = \frac{ad-bc}{\sqrt{(a+c)(b+d)(a+b)(c+d)}}$$

$$Q_2 = \frac{ad-bc}{ad+bc}$$

$$Q_6 = \mathrm{Sin}(90° \, r_{hk})$$

$$G = \frac{a}{\sqrt{(a+b)(a+c)}}$$

$$A = 1/2\left(\frac{a}{a+b}+\frac{a}{a+c}\right)$$

$$T = \frac{a}{a+b+c}$$

$$W = \frac{a+d}{N}$$

Formula for r_t :

$$\frac{\frac{d}{N}-\left(\frac{c+d}{N}\right)\left(\frac{b+d}{N}\right)}{zz'} = r_t + xx' \, r_{t^2} + \frac{}{2!}$$

$$(x^2-1)(x'^2-1) \, \frac{r_{t^3}}{3!} + (x^3-3x')(x'^3-3x') \, \frac{r_t^4}{4!} +$$

$$(x^4-6x^2+3)(x'^4-6x'^2+3) \, \frac{r_t^5}{5!} \, ...$$

where x = deviation of one variable from its mean in terms of standard deviation, x' the same for the other variable; $z=\frac{1}{\sqrt{2\pi}} e^{\frac{-x^2}{2}}$ which is the ordinate of the normal probability curve at x, z' the same for the other variable at x'.

r_t is the tetrachoric r of Pearson; r_{hk}, usually called the Boas-Yulean r but discovered earlier by Pearson; Q_2, the simple Q of Yule; Q_6, a trigonometric function of r_{hk} suggested by Pearson as an approximation to r_t which involved a great amount of labor before the appearance of Sheppard's tables to facilitate its calculation; W, used by Gifford and Kroeber. The several forms of r and Q are thoroughly discussed by Pearson, Yule, and Heron. r_t can now be computed in two or three minutes from Thurstone's diagrams and, contrary to Kroeber and Chrétien, is no longer practically forbidding.[3]

Because the greatest possible range of G, A, T, and W is 1.00 to .00 and that of forms of r and Q +1.00 to

—1.00, I have shown the short scale on the right ordinate and the long scale on the left and have plotted G, A, T, and W on the short scale and r's and Q's on the long scale. The series of fourfold tables at the bottom of each diagram are samples, chosen arbitrarily, from those used to compute formulas at about 20 ordinates.

Diagrams 1-4 hold asymmetry constant and vary correlation. The choice of r_t as the x axis on which the curves of other formulas are plotted is not meant to imply that r_t is the best formula.

Diagram 1 shows that when both variables of the fourfold table are symmetrical, all measures give parallel results. In fact the per cent in any one of the four cells would be an adequate measure of correlation because under these simple conditions the value in one cell determines those in the other cells.

Diagram 2 shows the results of a definite amount of positive asymmetry in both variables.

Diagram 3 gives the results of the same amount of negative asymmetry in both variables.

Diagram 4 shows what happens when there is positive asymmetry for one variable and negative for the other.

Because both kinds and all amounts of asymmetry frequently exist together in a single table of intercorrelation, such as in Klimek's tables,[4] it is easy to see that a given value of a certain formula (say $Q_6=0$) may be equated to a high value of another (A, G, T, or W) on one occasion and a low one on another. Anyone who doubts this can compute a sample of intertrait per cents (A, G, T, and W) from Klimek's tables and compare them with his results from Q_6.

Diagram 5 will perhaps make this point clearer. Forms of r and Q are held constant at zero, and A, G, T, and W are varied over their entire ranges simply by varying asymmetry.

There are certain situations where certain formulas produce utter nonsense. These are illustrated by hypothetical distributions

Tribes:	a	b	c	d	e	f	g	h	i	j
Trait 1	+	-	-	-	-	-	-	-	-	-
Trait 2	-	-	-	-	-	-	-	-	-	+

Comparing these two trait distributions we find: A = .00, G = .00, T = .00, W = .80, Q_2 = -1.00, r_t = -1.00, r_{hk} = -.11, Q_6 = -.17. The value of W in this situation is completely misleading. The crude summation of common presences and common absences is a hopeless procedure. It is obvious that high "relationship" between two distributions must be the result of some common presences.

In the following situation, Q_2 and r_t fail miserably.

Tribes:	a	b	c	d	e	f	g	h	i	j
Trait 3	+	+	+	+	-	-	-	-	-	-
Trait 4	+	+	+	+	+	+	+	+	-	-
Trait 5	-	-	-	-	+	+	+	+	-	-

	3:4	3:5	4:5
A	.75	.00	.75
G	.71	.00	.71
T	.40	.00	.40
W	.60	.20	.60
Q_2	1.00	-1.00	1.00
r_t	1.00	-1.00	1.00
r_{hk}	.41	- .67	.41
Q_6	.60	- .87	.60

If correlation is to mean anything at all, things which correlate positively and perfectly with the same thing must correlate positively and perfectly with each other. In other words, perfect positive correlation must indicate identical distribution. Q_2 and r_t fail to satisfy this requirement.

Q_6 and r_{hk} are functions of each other, so always give parallel results. I prefer r_{hk} merely because its calculation on a slide rule is one step less than Q_6.

A, G, and T differ from forms of r and Q in ignoring common absences. This causes the element or tribal universe and the total number of elements or tribes (N) to differ for almost every pair of elements or tribes compared. There is no tertium quid. Q_6 and r_{hk} maintain a constant universe which constitutes the tertium quid. In the long run I believe Q_6 and r_{hk} yield the most satisfactory arrangement of distributions, as in Klimek's tables, and at the same time satisfy contemporary correlation theory which demands the tertium quid.

For the sake of those who have followed Pearson and Heron[5] in favoring r_t, it should be emphasized that the assumption of normal distribution for all ethnographic traits is ridiculous. For example, in western North America the aboriginal distribution of maize in terms of bushels per annum per capita would not yield a normal curve because maize was totally absent among the vast majority of tribes. It is impossible for a normal correlation surface to have .00 in one quadrant of the fourfold table and substantial values in the other three. The fact that a large number of ethnographic fourfold tables show .00 in one cell is sufficient reason for shelving r_v.

Other numerical devices, such as a or b + c, used recently by Kroeber and Chretien, are unsatisfactory in the long run. Where distributions are nearly symmetrical they give rankings similar to other measures, providing the amount of available data is equal for all units compared. Both these conditions were satisfied by their data on Indo-European languages. But unpercentaged counts, or summations of them, are dangerous because of variation in sheer quantity of information available.

Concerning the use of rank-order comparisons, as in Gifford and Kroeber, figures 3-5,[6] I do not believe they tell us anything of importance that cannot be read from similar diagrams based on numerical intervals on the correlation scale, as in figures 1 and 2 of the same work.

Recantation Since the appearance of a paper written jointly with Kroeber[7] my views on statistical ethnology have changed considerably. Certain points of difference seem important enough to be reviewed.

Our chief aim was to establish a more objective method for reconstructing history. We imagined that there ought to be a mathematical formula, which when applied to distributional data, would yield numbers which would reflect the major historical events, contacts, or changes in an area. We therefore assembled some formulas, applied them to several sets of data, and "tested" the formulas according to the nearness of their results to the more intuitive findings of several ethnologists. It is easy to see that if statistical methods must be tested by more subjective methods they are less valid than the latter. Therefore, I fail to see that we accomplished much.

Turning to more specific criticisms, we argued (p. 212) that our method was more valid than Tylor's or Hobhouse's because we limited ourselves to a single culture area, a relatively small group of continuously distributed tribes. The real point which we touched but did not emphasize is that we considered the geographical positions of the tribes with respect to one another. This had been done previously by Boas (1895), Czekanowski (1911), and Clements (1926), but not by Tylor (1889) and Hobhouse (1915).

We confused the meaning of X^2 and P used by Clements (1926). We said that the direct measure of correlation was E, and that P merely stated the probability of E being due to chance. This is incorrect. E is a device suggested to Clements by Kroeber to simplify the situation. When we said (p. 215) that "historical relationships are referable wholly from these counted E's," we were completely ignoring X^2 and P, which in that case should never have been quoted at

all. X^2 is not a very convenient measure of correlation because it has no definite limits such as +1.00 to -1.00. When its values are converted to P, it may take 15 or 20 decimal places to express a very high correlation. The objection to this expression of correlation is merely its clumsiness. Its results will more nearly parallel those from forms of r and Q rather than W, A, G, or T.

When we said (p. 217) that Clements doubted whether r_{hk} and Q_2 were applicable to data of the Sun Dance order for reasons of statistical theory, we were misquoting him. As I remember the conversation, he merely expressed caution in applying any correlation formula to ethnological data. His doubts applied to all measures alike.

We give a table (p. 223) in which the "known Polynesian interrelationships are ranked in the order which follows logically from the way in which the cultures group themselves, in other words, from the scheme of relationships viewed as a whole." We then proceed to compare the results of several formulas with this ideal grouping. Obviously cultures do not group themselves. In this case they were grouped by inspection of the data by Kroeber. He had arranged them independently and some time before I made a parallel arrangement with the G formula, which was my favorite at the time, 1931. I have no quarrel with Kroeber's intuitive groupings of Polynesian cultures, but I believe this should have been stated in 1932.

Concerning the Plains Indian Sun Dance, we said (p. 227) that our formulas make fewer assumptions of negative evidence than forms of r and Q. This is not true. A, G, and T make exactly the same assumptions regarding any body of data as other formulas. With respect to Spier's original tabulation of traits, we have all assumed that blanks are minuses. If blanks tended to fall in the minus-minus cell more frequently than any other of the fourfold table, then A, G, and T might be more valid because they ignore minus-minuses. Since we have no evidence that this is the case, it cannot be used as an argument for these formulas.

A simple illustration will make this clear.

Tribes:	1	2	3	4	5	6	7	8	9	10
Trait a....		+	+	+	+	+	+			
Trait b....				+	+	+	+	+		
Trait c....						+	+	+	+	+	+

Suppose we make no assumptions whatsoever regarding blanks. We then get 1.00 for A, G, or T, and .00

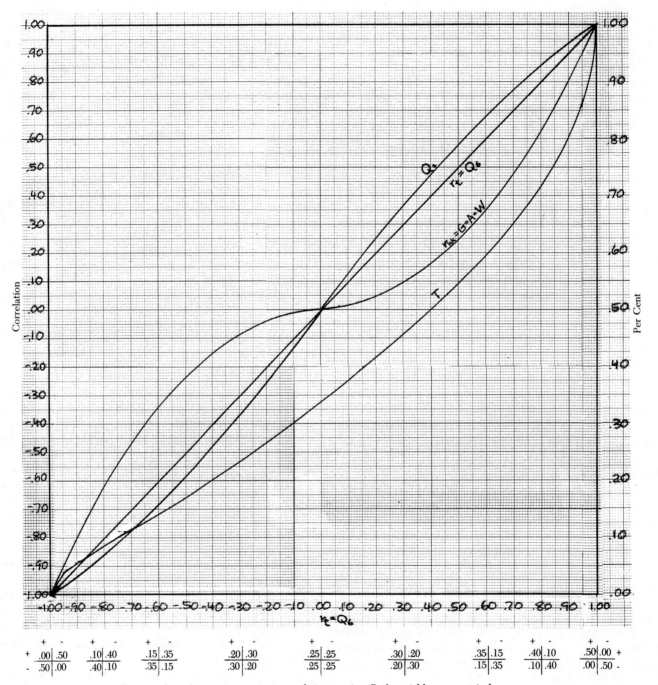

DIAGRAM 1   Asymmetry constant, correlation varying. Both variables symmetrical

	+	−	
+	a	b	.50
−	c	d	.50
	.50	.50	100

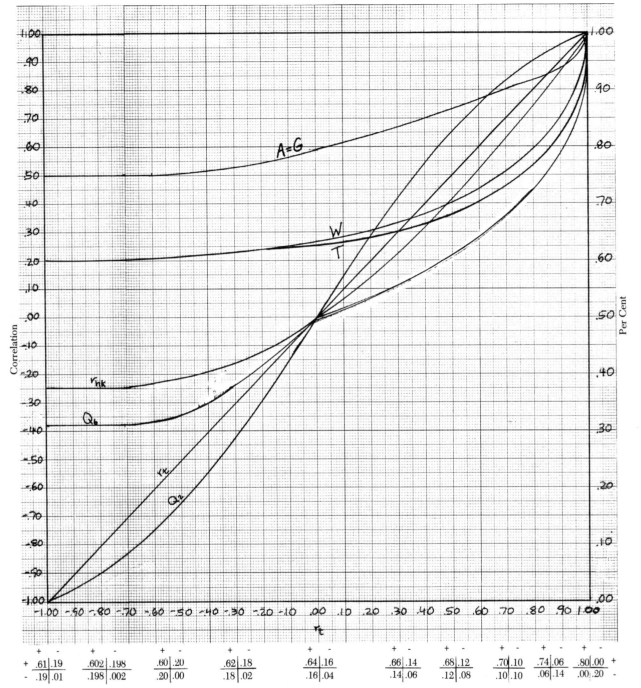

	+	-	
+	.61	.19	+
-	.19	.01	

	+	-
+	.602	.198
-	.198	.002

	+	-
+	.60	.20
-	.20	.00

	+	-
+	.62	.18
-	.18	.02

	+	-
+	.64	.16
-	.16	.04

	+	-
+	.66	.14
-	.14	.06

	+	-
+	.68	.12
-	.12	.08

	+	-
+	.70	.10
-	.10	.10

	+	-
+	.74	.06
-	.06	.14

	+	-	
+	.80	.00	+
-	.00	.20	-

DIAGRAM 2   Asymmetry constant correlation varying. Both variables asymmetrical. Asymmetry .80: .20

	+	-	
+	a	b	.80
-	c	d	.20
	.80	.20	1.00

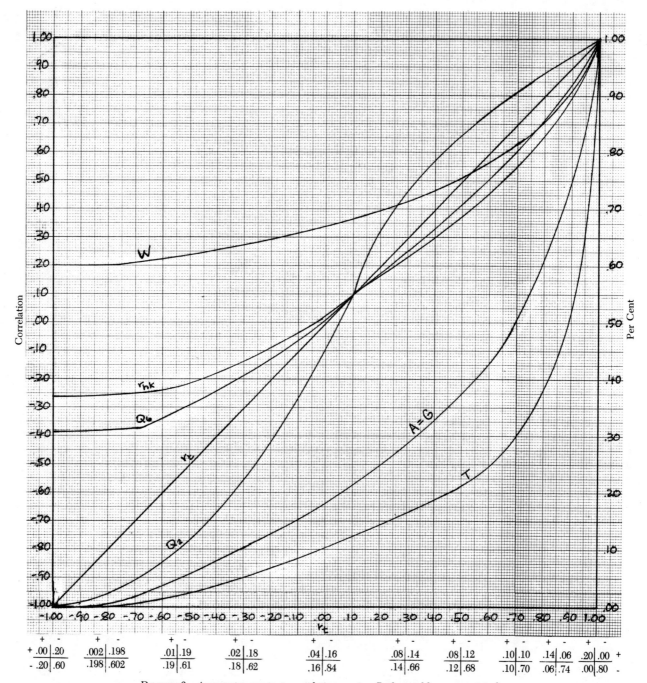

Correlation

Per Cent

r_t

	+	−		+	−		+	−		+	−		+	−		+	−		+	−		+	−		+	−		+	−
+	.00	.20		.002	.198		.01	.19		.02	.18		.04	.16		.08	.14		.08	.12		.10	.10		.14	.06		.20	.00	+
−	.20	.60		.198	.602		.19	.61		.18	.62		.16	.84		.14	.66		.12	.68		.10	.70		.06	.74		.00	.80	−

DIAGRAM 3.   Asymmetry constant, corrolation varying. Both variables asymmetrical.

Asymmetry 20:.80.

	+	−	
+	a	b	.20
−	c	d	.80
	.20	.80	1.00

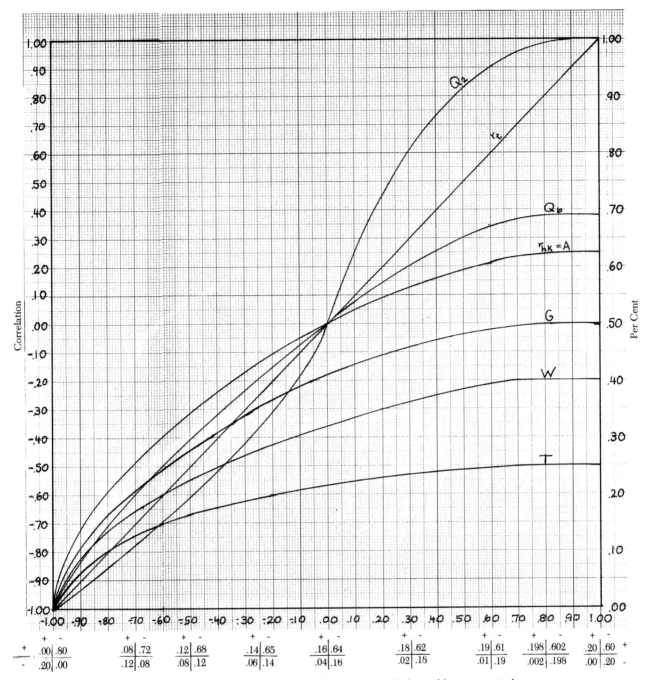

DIAGRAM 4 Asymmetry constant correlation varying. Both variables asymmetrical

Asymmetry 80:20 and 20:80

	+	−	
+	a	b	.80
−	c	d	.20
	.80	.20	1.00

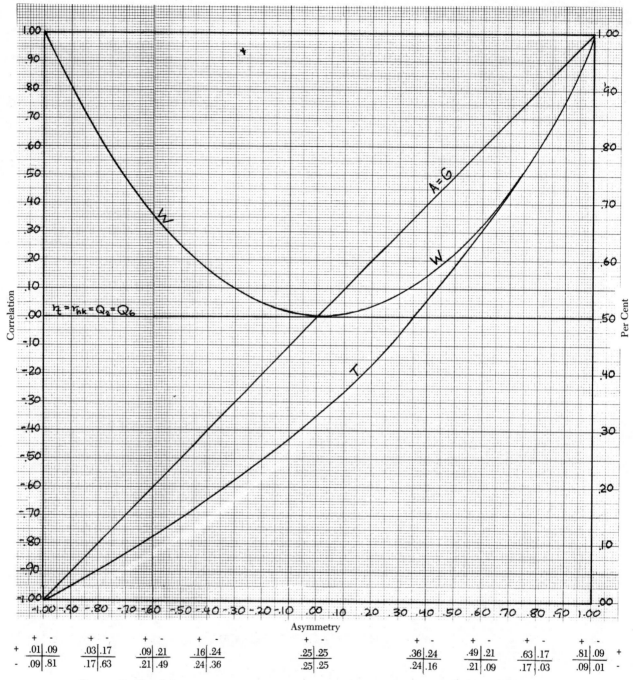

	+	−		+	−		+	−		+	−		+	−		+	−		+	−		+	−		+	−	
+	.01	.09		.03	.17		.09	.21		.16	.24		.25	.25		.36	.24		.49	.21		.63	.17		.81	.09	+
−	.09	.81		.17	.63		.21	.49		.24	.36		.25	.25		.24	.16		.21	.09		.17	.03		.09	.01	−

DIAGRAM 5.   Correlation constant at zero, asymmetry varying. Asymmetry is the same for both variables

for forms of r and Q, among all three pairs of traits, because we only have positive information and that can only show agreements. If we interpret these distributions as being other than identical we must assume that blanks are absences. This we must do regardless of formula because it is the only way to get + - and - + values. When all blanks are changed to minuses, we automatically get common absences somewhere, in this case in comparing a with b, and b with c.

Without laboring any more specific points, it can be said in summary that I now believe Kroeber and I were placing too much faith in numbers. Because for the Sun Dance our historical scheme agreed more nearly with Spier's than with Clements's, and because Spier's reconstruction was more nearly like that generally accepted for the Plains area, we thought our formulas were superior. I no longer believe one should reconstruct history so directly from numbers. Whatever superiority for this purpose our formulas seemed to have shown over others in such tests strikes me as sheer luck.

The chief purpose of statistics in ethnology, I believe, is to arrange distributed data systematically, such that the pluses and minuses fall in rows and columns. This was first done by Klimek and is an important contribution to technique. Any inference or interpretation should be derived intuitively from such a table, in preference to numbers alone. When distributions approach perfect symmetry, or when skewness is nearly uniform in amount and in the same direction for all units correlated, then correlation coefficients have more definite meaning. Under conditions of extreme variability in both amount and direction of skewness, a given correlation value can arise from a great variety of distributions, and no formula can express the ethnographical facts satisfactorily. In such a case, the percentaged values in all four cells should be given, or a table showing plus and minus entries grouped in rows and columns, or a series of maps.

Historical inference.—The best American exposition of methods used to reconstruct history is still that of Sapir.[8] Sapir mentioned a number of different criteria for inferring past history, and in a rough way ranked them according to validity. Assuming that this ranking is correct, there are still two important points omitted: (1) how much better or worse is each criterion than the others; (2) how good are any of them. Until we know these facts we cannot reconstruct history with any measurable amount of accuracy.

I do not mean to imply by this statement that all historical inferences are invalid and therefore not worth anything, but merely that their validity is not measurable.

Several persons with whom I have conversed seem to think that all statistically minded ethnologists believe that correlations express the probability of a historical inference being correct, or that all correlations in any body of data are caused by purely historical factors. Although this latter statement does seem to be true of the majority, nevertheless such "functional" factors as the compatibility of the trait with the rest of the culture may determine its acceptance in a number of cultures and its rejection in many others exposed to it. Anyone who has worked with a number of informants cannot help being impressed by the fact that almost all know of many features of foreign cultures different from their own and that every culture is exposed to many more elements than it can utilize at a given point in its history. One of the most interesting but heretofore almost untouched fields of correlation is the determination of these mutual-compatibility patterns by a combination of functional and historical theory. There may be none that are universal even for "primitive" peoples, but there are almost certain to be some which hold for large areas.

I cannot wholly accept Kroeber's[9] argument that the method of academic historians differs only in degree from that of ethnologists who work without documents, dates, or personalities. Although there is certainly much overlapping in aim and technique, the fundamentals of the two methods seem to me to be quite different.

Academic historians frequently begin with a number of events or facts reckoned by documents to have occurred in certain places at certain dates. The discussion is concerned chiefly with interpolating additional facts between the known facts, such as which earlier fact influenced a later one, or offering motives or causes for the known or interpolated sequence of events. In much of ethnology the logical process is quite different. One starts mainly with geographically distributed facts of a single time level, and extrapolates them backward into the past. Logically this process is as much like prediction of the future as the interpolation of some academic historians. The difference, however, is that ethnologists almost always have some bits of direct evidence from the past, whereas we have absolutely none for the future. To continue the analogy, extrapolation is less valid than interpolation, and less valid the farther it is extended. Ethnologists reconstruct dates in terms of centuries and millennia, historians more often in terms of years and decades.

The modern tendency to rely more and more on multiple and independently gathered evidence, such as ethnology, linguistics, anatomy, and archaeology, seems to me to be the chief way out of the dilemma.

What we need is more comparable source material, more detailed analyses of it, and briefer and less labored historical inferences. When two or more independently gathered types of evidence can be explained by a single historical inference, the probability of the inference being correct is no doubt raised. Whether such inferences contribute toward determining the "processes" of history is more doubtful. Such "processes" are usually the premises from which particular historical inferences are derived.

Nevertheless there are some historical inferences that seem so highly valid that no one but a crank would question them for a moment. For example, the fact that the Southwest Athabascans derived their language from the north. Yet this is logically an inference. But it seems highly probable because the number of linguistic elements shared by Southwestern and Northern Athabascans, which at the same time occur nowhere else in the world, is large. Because we have no evidence from documentary sources of whole languages spreading by diffusion or imitation, and much evidence that they spread by migration, the inference is drawn that some of the Northern Athabascans at some time in the past split off from the others and migrated southward. When we see that the present culture of Southwest Athabascans has been strongly influenced by the Pueblos, although the language remains distinct, cannot we say that this is a case where language was more stable than culture? Is not this inference specific enough and true enough from the world point of view to be accepted as a fact which may be used inductively to determine the "processes" of history? I believe it is, but I cannot prove it.

The difficulty in trying to determine the "processes" of history from strictly documentary evidence is that such evidence represents a very meager and highly selected fraction of the totality of human history. And even if we continue to accumulate more direct evidence of change in the form of acculturation studies, there will still be thousands of questions unanswered concerning the slower and less pretentious types of change which seem to have taken place on a more primitive level where change may have occurred in different ways.

The naïve belief, shared by some, that a first-rate mathematician can sit down and figure out the probability of two cultures independently inventing or acquiring so many similar traits is without foundation. He can only figure out probabilities for masses of data when he knows them for individual elements, and this is a matter of direct historical record, not guesswork.

Correlation technique.—Concerning the possibilities of extending correlation studies to larger areal and element universes, it is true, as Kroeber says, that we will never be able to correlate each tribe with every other tribe and each trait with every other trait. However, there are several ways to extend the range of such work; use punched cards and Hollerith electric sorting; sample large bodies of material; pool highly intercorrelated blocks of tribes and traits; correlate by inspection. A discussion of such methods will appear in the future in a study of girl's puberty rites in western North America.

Notes

1. See CED: VIII—The Reliability of Culture Element Data, UC-AR 1: 205-219, 1938.

2. This section is from my Ph.D. thesis, 1936.

3. Kroeber and Chrétien, 98.

4. Klimek, 1935, tables 2-6.

5. Pearson and Heron, 1913.

6. Gifford and Kroeber, 1937.

7. Driver and Kroeber, 1932.

8. Sapir, 1916.

9. 1935.

4. The Measurement of Geographical Distribution Form

Harold E. Driver

The stimulus for this paper is derived chiefly from the works of Wissler,[1] and criticisms of them, particularly that of Dixon.[2] While the problem perhaps belongs to the last decade, it does not seem to have been satisfactorily settled then. The present paper offers some techniques for showing how nearly a given distribution conforms to certain theoretical forms. Obviously no geographical distribution is a perfect fit to any theoretical form, and those who insist on recognizing only perfect or near perfect relationships are entertaining last century notions of correlation and causality. In social sciences where all or none relationships are practically nonexistent, the necessity for measurement of relationship is far greater than in physical sciences where very high correlations are common and recognizable at once. This point does not yet seem to be generally admitted.

The center of Wissler's theoretical right circular cone distribution form is the place of greatest frequency of a trait or complex, the geographical center of the area (the center of gravity of the flat surface), and the center of gravity of the distribution itself when every tribal location is weighted according to frequency (hereafter called center of gravity). In so far as these three independently definable and determinable points coincide, the distribution conforms to the theory. As an example, I have chosen the rather over-worked Sun Dance tabulation of Spier,[3] and have made the same assumptions regarding it as those made by Wissler and Dixon. The accompanying map gives the distribution of these data. The number of traits present in each of the 18 tribes concerned is as follows:

Arapaho	54	Ponca	24
Cheyenne	46	Arikara	23
Oglala	40	Hidatsa	21
Blackfoot	37	Assiniboin	20
Gros Ventre	36	Sarsi	19
Crow	29	Ute	13
Kiowa	28	Sisseton	11
Wind River	25	Bungi (Plains Ojibwa)	8
Plains Cree	24	Wahpeton (Plains Dakota)	5

The geographical center and the center of gravity for these data are almost identical. The tribe with the greatest frequency, the Arapaho, lies a considerable distance from these points. Thus the distribution is definitely skewed. The distance of these three points from one another can, if desired, be measured in terms of units of standard deviation about the center of gravity.

The most obvious feature of the right circular cone distribution form is the perfect inverse linear relationship between distance from the center and frequency. Figure 1 shows the relation between distance from the center of gravity and frequency. Had this relationship been perfect, all points would have fallen on the line shown, the line about which the sum of the squares of the vertical deviations of the points is least, and the correlation would have been –1.00. A simple way to demonstrate such a relation is to divide the tribes into zones according to their distances from the center and compute the average frequency of each zone. The circle on the map, whose circumference is one unit of standard deviation from the center of gravity,[4] is a convenient boundary for two

such zones which may be called simply central and marginal. Thus the nine central tribes average 30 traits, the 9 marginal 21 traits. These and other findings are summarized in Table 1.

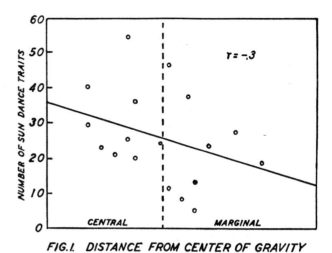

FIG. I. DISTANCE FROM CENTER OF GRAVITY

TABLE 1: SUMMARY OF SUN DANCE CALCULATIONS

Correlations (r)		Average number of elements	
	Number of elements	Central tribes	Marginal tribes
Distance from the center of gravity	–.3	30	21
Relative distance from the center of gravity	–.7	34	19
Distance from the Arapaho	–.5	31	20
Relative distance from the Arapaho	–.8	34	19

Because the Sun Dance distribution is definitely elongated, it will also be fitted to a right *elliptical* cone.[5] This requires an objective determination of the eccentricity of the ellipse and the slope of its axes. The slope of the longitudinal axis is defined as the line about which the sum of the squares of the deviations perpendicular to it is least. The y axis on the map is such a line. The x axis is, of course, perpendicular to it. The standard deviation about the x axis is 1.9 times as great as that about the y axis, hence the ratio of length to width of the ellipse becomes 1.9 to 1.

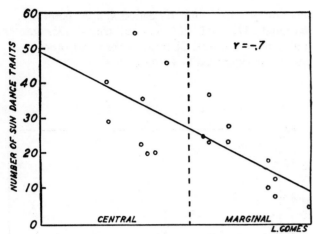

FIG. 2. RELATIVE DISTANCE FROM CENTER OF GRAVITY

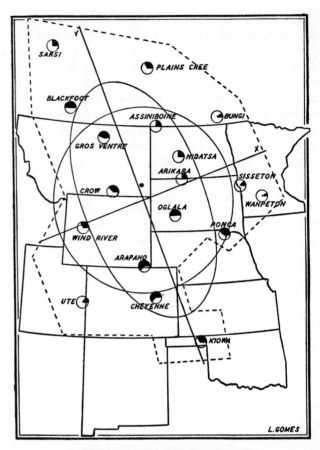

DISTRIBUTION OF THE SUN DANCE

The darkened portions of the circles indicate the per cent of Spier's 82 elements present. The intersection of the axes is the center of gravity. The dot is the geographical center. The broken line gives the approximate boundaries for the ceremony with reference to which the geographical center was determined. Tribal locations from Mooney.

Where x and y are the deviations from any two mutually perpendicular axes intersecting at the center of gravity, the distance of any tribe from the center of gravity is $\sqrt{x^2+y^2}$.[6] If the x and y values are expressed in units of standard deviation, this form results: $\sqrt{\left(\frac{x}{\sigma_x}\right)^2 + \left(\frac{y}{\sigma_y}\right)^2}$. This will be called *relative distance*. When equated to a constant it becomes the equation of an ellipse. Removing radicals, the equation of the ellipse of the map is

$$\left(\frac{x}{\sigma_x}\right)^2 + \left(\frac{y}{\sigma_y}\right)^2 = \frac{\sum\left[\left(\frac{x}{\sigma_x}\right)^2 + \left(\frac{y}{\sigma_y}\right)^2\right]}{n}$$

Figure 2 shows the relation between relative distance from the center of gravity and frequency. The correlation is definitely higher than that for actual distance. Thus the data fit a right elliptical cone more closely than a right circular cone. With reference to relative distance, marginal tribes are those without the ellipse, central tribes those within it.

As further explanation of Table 1, it should be added that relative distance from the Arapaho is calculated as if the center of the ellipse were translated

to the Arapaho. If desired, the entire computations can be made with coordinate values from an arbitrary pair of axes, but such mechanics need not be described here.

Similar calculations made from peyote data are given in Table 2. Reservation locations were obtained from a map in the annual report of the commissioner of Indian affairs,[7] the per cent "affected

TABLE 2: SUMMARY OF PEYOTE CALCULATIONS

	TIME OF INTRODUCTION			PERCENT AFFECTED BY PEYOTE		
	Correlations (r)	Averages		Correlations (r)	Averages	
		Central	Marginal		Central	Marginal
Distance from the center of gravity	.5	1894	1910	−.5	48%	15%
Distance from geographical center	−.2	1907	1898	.0	33%	33%
Distance from Cantonment	.6	1892	1909	−.5	43%	23%
Distance from Kiowa	.7	1892	1909	−.5	46%	22%

by peyote" from another government report,[8] and the dates from Wissler.[9] The actual distances of the tribes from various points of reference were used. The distribution shows only a small amount of eccentricity. It is, of course, highly skewed. These two terms are not equivalents. This study is not concerned with the ultimate origin of peyote or its entire distribution south into Mexico.

The conclusion to be drawn from these two sets of statistical facts is that both distributions conform more nearly to the verbal descriptions of Wissler than those of Dixon. While Wissler over-stated his case, he did not over-state it as much as Dixon under-stated it. The Sun Dance distribution fits an elliptical form more closely than a circular form. No doubt many kinds of distributions could not be adequately described with these techniques, e.g., a distribution following the winding course of a river. In such a case, however, some such measure as distance from the river might yield significant correlation. I agree entirely with Wissler that it is desirable to know whether or not distributions approximate certain theoretical forms.

Notes

1. Clark Wissler, *The Relation of Nature to Man in Aboriginal America*, 1926; *Man and Culture*, 1923.

2. R. B. Dixon, *The Building of Cultures*, 1928.

3. Leslie Spier, *The Sun Dance of the Plains Indians* (Anthropological Papers, American Museum of Natural History, Vol. 16, 1921), pp. 451-527.

4. The equation of this circle is $x^2 + y^2 = \dfrac{\Sigma(x^2 + y^2)}{n}$

5. I am familiar with other forms such as the normal correlation surface, but do not think it practical to fit such rough data to such a refined surface.

6. Since this line passes through the center of gravity, it is only necessary to find its slope which is
$$\tan 2\theta = \frac{2\Sigma xy}{\Sigma x^2 - \Sigma y^2}$$
where x and y are any pair of coordinates with origin at the center of gravity and θ the angle formed with the x axis. For any set of coordinates the following form makes the necessary corrections:
$$\tan 2\theta = \frac{2\left(\Sigma XY - \dfrac{\Sigma X \Sigma Y}{N}\right)}{\left(\Sigma X^2 - \dfrac{(\Sigma X)^2}{N}\right) - \left(\Sigma Y^2 - \dfrac{(\Sigma Y)^2}{N}\right)}$$
where X and Y are the deviations from the coordinates. For the proof of this formula, see G. Udny Yule, *An Introduction to the Theory of Statistics*, 1922 edition, p. 321.

7. Washington, 1912.

8. R. E. L. Newberne and C. H. Burke, *Peyote, an Abridged Compilation* (Washington, 1912).

9. *The Relation of Nature to Man in Aboriginal America*.

5. Cross-Cultural Sampling and Galton's Problem[*]

Harold E. Driver and Richard P. Chaney

Introduction

Historical factors (diffusion, acculturation, culture heritage—migration) must be considered in any comparative study, whether it includes only two or hundreds of variables, whether it is limited to two ethnic units or extended to hundreds, whether it covers a small area or the entire world, and whether it embraces a short or a long time span. The evolutionist or cross-cultural researcher who wishes to establish causal sequences among variables must commit himself with respect to the historical independence or dependence of his cases, as Tylor (1889) found out long ago when Galton challenged him. The diffusionist, aiming at establishing historical connection, must also control for independent origins, whether they be parallels or convergences.

Where ethnohistorical documents or carefully determined archaeological dates are available, the comparativist should make full use of such material and assign it priority over historical inferences derived from the analysis of essentially synchronic data. But because most of what we know about contemporary non-literate cultures has been collected within the last hundred years, time depth is shallow and deeper levels must be inferred by indirect means.

Nearly everyone today agrees that the nineteenth-century evolutionists and the early-twentieth-century diffusionists of both the Kulturkreis and Culture Area schools failed to extricate themselves from the Tylor-Galton dilemma. Nor has the neo-evolutionary school of Leslie White really come to grips with this problem, although Sahlins' distinction between specific and general evolution has begun to divide up the continuum from the most specific to the most general evolutionary trends. Carneiro and Tobias' (1963) Guttman scales are further refining the

*This research was supported by a small grant from the Office of Research and Development at Indiana University, which the authors gratefully acknowledge. Chancy chose the two sets of matched pairs of tribes, tabulated the data, and computed the observed values for the D'Andrade technique. Driver devised the new technique for determining the expected values for all 16 outcomes and expressing the magnitude of the win in terms of the variance. He also wrote the first draft. The authors wish to thank Naroll, D'Andrade, and Joseph Jorgensen for reading the manuscript and offering suggestions.

109

views of this school, but are not able to be explicit about the number of independent origins among the cultural variables scaled. Steward's multilinear evolution likewise introduces more flexibility into the concept, but he and his followers also lack an explicit inductive technique for controlling historical factors in large samples.

The cross-cultural school of evolutionists led by Murdock and Whiting has consciously played down the effect of historical factors by choosing samples in which the ethnic units are spaced so that many fall into separate culture areas (or subareas) or separate language families (or subfamilies) or both. Murdock (1966) describes a world sample of about four hundred chosen by first grouping the world's ethnic units into culture types (subculture areas) and then choosing one ethnic unit in each type to represent it. The assumption is that diffusion and acculturation within each type are obvious and that by choosing only one ethnic unit for each type one can lessen the influence of historical factors. Diffusion between types is regarded as less frequent and less serious because the representatives of each type are spaced at a minimum distance of two hundred miles from each other. Although a separation of two hundred miles in native California would insure considerable historical independence because few persons before White contact had ever traveled that far, the same distance in the Plains area in the nineteenth century would not serve as a barrier to diffusion because few persons had *not* traveled much more than two hundred miles. A glance at Mooney's (1896) *Calendar History of the Kiowa* shows that members of this tribe in the nineteenth century traveled into Canada on the north and Mexico on the south. It would require nearer one thousand miles in a north-south direction on the Plains to eliminate a sizable portion of the more recent diffusions. Although Murdock's culture types are determined without any explicit inductive technique, his world ethnographic knowledge is conceded to surpass that of any other scholar by every comparativist known to the authors, and his world typology of cultures exceeds in importance at this time the more limited culture area schemes of the past, such as Kroeber's North American culture areas of 1939. Even though his types can eliminate only the more recent historical contacts of the last few centuries, they constitute an important taxonomical advance. But for those who think of historical independence in terms of several millennia (e.g., Driver, *et al.*, 1966:144-147), two hundred miles is not enough, and greater historical depths must be inferred by other means.

Whiting (MS.), on the other hand, has recently drawn a world-wide sample of 136 ethnic units, each a member of a separate language family or subfamily. Using the rough estimates of time from glotto-chonology, Whiting's units are separated by a minimum of one thousand years of linguistic distance. Whiting is assuming that language classification matches culture classification to a high degree and that linguistic distance and cultural distance are definately related for all combinations of two ethnic units. A glance at the language family and culture area classifications and maps of almost any area in the world (e.g., North America, in Driver 1961) shows that this is far from true in every case. For instance, the Yurok, Karok, and Hupa not only belong to distinct language families but even to distinct phyla, yet their cultures are so close that repeated fieldwork has uncovered only trivial differences. In contrast, the Athapaskan languages form one of the most compact language families in North America with no more than two thousand to three thousand years of time depth, yet their cultures in the Subarctic, Pacific, and Southwest areas are so different that no one would have dreamed that they all stemmed from a single protoculture in the north without the evidence from linguistics. The correlation between linguistic distances and cultural distances among the world's ethnic units is unknown because the latter have not yet been measured but, if it is positive, it is likely to be of low or at best medium magnitude. However, if Whiting's ethnic units tend to fall into many different culture areas and are spaced as far apart geographically as is feasible, his sample of only 136 will have more historical independence within it than Murdock's larger sample of about 400, and will be useful for his purposes.

Naroll and D'Andrade Technique

Raoul Naroll (1961) was the first to offer explicit inductive techniques aimed at solving the Tylor-Galton problem. Roy D'Andrade (Naroll and D'Andrade 1963) joined him in a later paper on the same subject, and Naroll still later (1964) published another technique for this purpose, bringing the total to five. Naroll's techniques operate with strips of territory around the world and consider only the linear sequences of pairs of cultural variables along these continua. Naroll found non-random clustering of single traits and pairs of traits along his territorial strips. Clusterings between pairs of traits were labeled semi-diffusional, because they appeared to be caused both by functional adhesion and the tendency of such adhesions to diffuse together. He found that positive instances of both pairs of traits (presence-presence or absence-absence) clustered more markedly than negative pairs (presence-absence or absence-presence). His tests revealed no examples of hyper-diffusion (clusterings of non-functional or dysfunctional behaviors). He deserves the credit for the first major breakthrough in the solution of a problem which had confounded the best comparativists up to 1961.

D'Andrade's technique has the advantage that it is not limited to a linear arrangement of ethnic units along strips of territory. He compared the presence and absence of pairs of traits among pairs of ethnic units belonging to the same culture area and the same language family. He found that the results confirmed both a diffusion hypothesis and a functional hypothesis and to about the same degree for Stephen's menstrual taboo data, but that a functional hypothesis won by a wide margin for social stratification and political complexity. Both Naroll and D'Andrade used samples of discontinuous ethnic units, those of Murdock (1957) and Stephens (1959).

Driver and Chaney Test of D'Andrade's Method

We have recently tested D'Andrade's method on almost continuously distributed ethnic units in aboriginal North America. We selected two groups of paired ethnic units from a North American sample totaling 260: the first consisted of pairs of neighboring peoples located in the same culture area and speaking languages belonging to the same family; the second was made up of pairs of peoples not in the same culture area and same language family and paired randomly from a table of random numbers. Because such sampling techniques are seldom described in enough detail for the reader to replicate the experiment, we shall spell out our technique.

The 260 ethnic units in Driver's (1966) avoidance study were chosen as the test sample. We began with the first ethnic unit listed in Driver's table (1966: Table 6). With the help of the maps in Driver's book (1961:maps 2, 37) and the large tribal map by Driver *et al.* (1953), we looked for an ethnic unit adjacent or as close as possible to the first and also in the same culture area and language family. If there was more than one such ethnic unit, we assigned a face of a die to each one and rolled the die; the one to come up first was chosen and paired with the first ethnic unit. If there was a conflict between language family and culture area, we gave priority to the former. Then we proceeded to the second ethnic unit and paired it with an adjacent society other than the first on the list. The same society often appeared in two adjacent pairs but in no case were both members of two pairs identical.

Distant pairs of ethnic units are defined as those not adjacent, not in the same language family, and not in the same culture area. They were chosen by first matching each of Driver's (1966:Table 6) ethnic units with a row in a table of random numbers. For each ethnic unit we proceeded from left to right across its row and stopped with the first three-digit number from 1 to 260. If this number matched that of a nonadjacent ethnic unit of different language family and different culture area, that unit was paired with the first. Thus the Aleut was paired with the Klallam. Then the second ethnic unit on the list was paired with a distant one by proceeding across its row of random numbers. Because the same three-digit number occasionally appeared more than once in the table, or the researcher located the same number going through the table for another ethnic unit, the same ethnic unit might repeat several times as the random member of a pair; thus the Arikara appear three times as a random member of a pair and

Table 1
Sample of Paired Societies

SOCIETY	ADJACENT SOCIETY	DISTANT SOCIETY
1. Aleut	Eskimo: Chugach	Klallam
14. Ingalik	Tanaina	Shoshoni: Hukundika
25. Chipewyan	Beaver	Alabama
36. Montagnais-Naskapi	Algonkin	Cowichan
48. Bella Bella	Wikeno Kwakiutl	Mohave
59. Karok	Yurok	Kamia
69. Quinault	Twana	N. Yokuts
79. Wikeno Kwakiutl	Homalco	Otomi
89. Lillooet	Thompson	Picuris
99. Wishram	Chinook	Diegueno

Table 2
Correlation of Avoidance and Bifurcation
(Expected Probabilities in Parentheses)

		Present, A_1	Absent, A_0	Total
	Present, B	72 (.222)	120 (.517)	192 (.739)
Bifurcation	Absent, B	6 (.078)	62 (.182)	68 (.260)
	Total	78 (.300)	182 (.699)	260 (.999)

$\phi = .28$ $P < .001$

one time as an adjacent member of a pair, but none of the pairs are identical. Table 1 gives a small sample of ethnic units on the list with adjacent and distant pair-members.

Driver (1966:157, Table 15) gives a correlation (phi) of -.40 between mother-in-law son-in-law avoidance and generation and/or lineal and/or Eskimo and/or Hawaiian types of kin terms. Because all of these types of kin classification lack bifurcation and all other types recognize it, we can change the sign of the coefficient and say that there is a correlation of .40 between mother-in-law son-in-law avoidance and bifurcation, significant at less than the .001 level. The value of this same correlation (Table 2) is only .28. This difference is caused by a few languages having multiple and overlapping terms for the same relative and being coded for more than one type of kinship terminology. (See Driver *et al*. 1966, Table 6.)

We shall first test the modest correlation (phi) of .28 between mother-in-law son-in-law avoidance and bifurcation. We give the raw frequencies of this relationship in Table 2 because the considerable asymmetry of both variables in opposite directions may influence the interpretation. Table 3 shows that the diffusion hypothesis wins for adjacent

tribes by a ratio of 83:1 in the two quadrants where the contrasts occur (lower left and upper right). The bottom half of Table 3 gives an unexpected result: diffusion wins over function for distant tribes as well, where the ratio is 47:34. The implausibility of this second result suggests some flaw in the method. The clue to our more refined solution of the problem stemmed from D'Andrade's parenthetical statement:

> (This form of summarizing the results is most applicable where about 50% of the sample has each trait present. Where presence [or absence] is a rare occurrence, the table should be split by correct predictions for presence compared to correct predictions for absence.) [Naroll and D'Andrade 1963: 1064]

The expected probabilities in our Table 2 were computed as follows: $A_1B_1 = (78/260)(192/260) = .222$; $A_1B_0 = (78/260)(68/260) = .078$; $A_0B_1 = (192/260)(182/260) = .517$; $A_0B_0 = (68/260)(182/260) = .182$. These are the expected probabilities for a single tribe. Where pairs of tribes are involved, the probability of two of the above combinations occurring in both the first tribe and the second tribe is the product of the two probabilities for each of the single tribes. Table 4 gives the probabilities for all 16 outcomes for pairs of

Table 3
D'Andrade's Test for Avoidance and Bifurcation

		A. ADJACENT TRIBES DIFFUSION HYPOTHESIS		
		Wins	Losses	Total
Functional Hypothesis	Wins	98	1	99
	Losses	83	6	89
	Total	181	7	188

		B. DISTANT TRIBES DIFFUSION HYPOTHESIS		
		Wins	Losses	Total
Functional Hypothesis	Wins	33	34	67
	Losses	47	4	51
	Total	80	38	118

tribes. In row one the probability of $A_1 B_1$ for the first tribe and $A_0 B_0$ for the second tribe in the pair is $(.222)(.182) = .040$. The first two values are given in Table 2. In this manner the probabilities for all 16 outcomes were computed and are given in Table 4, eighth column from the left. In the ninth and tenth columns from the left are given the expected frequency for pairs of tribes and the observed frequency of distant pairs of tribes. From these two sets of values the variance, $(O-E)^2 / E$, is computed for each outcome, then its total which is chi-square and, in the last column, the proportion of total variance for each outcome.

Table 4

Correlation of Avoidance and Bifurcation Among Distant Pairs of Tribes (Table 2). A_1, Trait A Present; A_0, Trait A Absent; B_1, Trait B Present; B_0, Trait B Absent.

Position as in Table 3, and draws.	Pairs of tribes		Functional-causal hypothesis		Historical-diffusion hypothesis		Prob-ability of occur-rence	E. Ex-pected fre-quency of pairs	O. Ob-served fre-quency of distant pairs	$(O-E)^2$/E	Propor-tion of total variance
	1st	2nd	Wins	Losses	Wins	Losses					
1. Upper right	$A_1 B_1$	$A_0 B_0$	2	0	2	2	.040	10.5	20.0	8.59	.147
2. Upper right	$A_0 B_0$	$A_1 B_1$	2	0	0	2	.040	10.5	14.0	1.16	.020
3. Upper left	$A_1 B_1$	$A_1 B_1$	2	0	2	0	.049	12.8	21.0	5.25	.090
4. Upper left	$A_0 B_0$	$A_0 B_0$	2	0	2	0	.033	8.6	11.0	.67	.011
5. Lower right	$A_1 B_0$	$A_0 B_1$	0	2	0	2	.041	10.5	3.0	5.36	.092
6. Lower right	$A_0 B_1$	$A_1 B_0$	0	2	0	2	.041	10.5	1.0	8.59	.147
7. Lower left	$A_0 B_1$	$A_0 B_1$	0	2	2	0	.267	69.5	46.0	7.94	.136
8. Lower left	$A_1 B_0$	$A_1 B_0$	0	2	2	0	.006	1.6	1.0	.22	.004
9. Positive	$A_1 B_1$	$A_0 B_1$	1	1	1	1	.115	29.9	32.0	.15	.003
10.	$A_1 B_1$	$A_1 B_0$	1	1	1	1	.017	4.5	0.0	4.50	.077
11. draws	$A_0 B_1$	$A_1 B_1$	1	1	1	1	.115	29.9	41.0	4.12	.070
12.	$A_1 B_0$	$A_1 B_1$	1	1	1	1	.017	4.5	2.0	1.39	.024
13. Negative	$A_0 B_0$	$A_1 B_0$	1	1	1	1	.014	3.7	2.0	.78	.013
14.	$A_0 B_0$	$A_0 B_1$	1	1	1	1	.094	24.5	34.0	3.68	.063
15. draws	$A_0 B_1$	$A_0 B_0$	1	1	1	1	.094	24.5	32.0	2.30	.039
16.	$A_1 B_0$	$A_0 B_0$	1	1	1	1	.014	3.7	0.0	3.70	.063
Totals							.997	259.7	260.0	$\chi^2 = 58.40$	.999

P<.001

Table 5

Correlation of Avoidances and Bifurcation Among Adjacent Pairs of Tribes

	E. EXPECTED FREQUENCY OF PAIRS	O. OBSERVED FREQUENCY OF ADJACENT PAIRS	$\frac{(O-E)^2}{E}$	PROPORTION OF TOTAL VARIANCE
1.	10.5	0	10.50	.030
2.	10.5	1	8.60	.025
3.	12.8	50	108.11	.311
4.	8.6	48	180.51	.519
5.	10.5	2	6.88	.020
6.	10.5	4	4.02	.012
7.	69.5	82	2.25	.006
8.	1.6	1	.22	.001
9.	29.9	20	3.28	.009
10.	4.5	2	1.39	.004
11.	29.9	16	6.46	.019
12.	4.5	3	.50	.001
13.	3.7	0	3.70	.011
14.	24.5	12	6.38	.018
15.	24.5	19	1.24	.004
16.	3.7	0	3.70	.011
	259.7	260	x^2 =347.74	1.001

P < .001

The probability of obtaining a chi-square of 58.40 or higher from sampling variability is much less than .001, thus indicating a highly significant difference between the observed and expected values. If we single out the rows where diffusion and functional hypotheses show a contrast, rows one and two versus seven and eight, corresponding to the upper right and lower left quadrants of Table 3B, it is clear that the apparent victory of diffusion over function is reversed. The 47 wins for diffusion are definitely below the expected 71 while, in contrast, the 34 wins for function are above the expected 21. If we add the variance in rows 1, 2, 7, and 8, we may say that the functional hypothesis wins over diffusion by a variance of 17.9, which is .307 of the total variance.

Table 5 gives parallel figures for adjacent pairs of tribes and the same correlation, that between kin avoidance and bifurcation. The apparent landslide victory of diffusion over function in Table 3A is reduced to a variance of 21.6 or .062 of the total variance. The enormous chi-square (347.7) is probably significant at less than one in a billion.

Table 6 introduces another correlation, that between kin avoidances and bifurcation only in sibling and cousin terms. Table 7 gives the results for pairs of adjacent tribes. Comparison of expected and observed frequencies in rows 1 and 2 shows that the observed values for the functional hypothesis are lower than the expected, while in rows 7 and 8 the observed values for the diffusion hypothesis are higher than the expected. A summation of the amount of variance in rows 1, 2, 7, and 8 shows that diffusion wins over function by 21.2 or .060 of the total variance.

Table 6

Correlation of Avoidance and Bifurcation Only In Sibling and Cousin Terms. (Expected Probabilities In Parentheses)

		AVOIDANCE		
		Present, A_1	Absent, A_0	Total
BIFURCATION FOR SIBLINGS AND COUSINS	Present, B_1	53 (·130)	57 (.293)	110 (.423)
	Absent, B_0	27 (.178)	123 (.399)	150 (.577)
	Total	80 (.308)	180 (.692)	260 (1.000)

ϕ =.32   P < .001

Table 8 gives the results from the same correlation (Table 6) when distant pairs of tribes are tested. Function wins over diffusion by a variance of 31.6 or .551 of the total variance.

Table 9 introduces still another correlation, that between bifurcation in terms for parents, uncles, aunts, with bifurcation in terms for siblings and cousins. Table 10 shows that for adjacent pairs of tribes diffusion wins over function by a variance of 7.0 or .016 of the total variance.

Table 11 reveals that for distant pairs of tribes function wins over diffusion by a variance of 64.5 or .474 of the total variance.

Table 12 summarizes the results for the matched pairs tests. Diffusion wins for all sets of adjacent pairs and function wins for all sets of distant pairs. It is impossible to generalize from such a small sample of tests, but there is a suggestion that diffusion is more likely to occur among adjacent pairs than distant pairs of tribes, a conclusion that Tylor would have endorsed nearly one hundred years ago. The contrast between diffusion and function can be sharpened by isolating the total variance (chi-square) of rows 1, 2, 7, 8, as given in Table 12, and testing it for significance with three degrees of freedom apart from the other 12 rows. All of the values in Table 12 are significant at less than .001 except that for the third correlation and adjacent pairs, which is significant at less than .10.

A comparison of Tables 4, 5, 7, 8, 10, 11 shows that chi-square values are much higher for adjacent pairs of tribes than for distant pairs. This is probably due to a combination of ecological and historical factors. Also, as correlations increase in positive magnitude, the frequencies of outcomes 3 and 4 will increase. The fact that these frequencies are higher for adjacent pairs suggests that functionally related traits tend to diffuse together, thus supporting the semi-diffusional nature of these data or of other variables which "cause" them.

Table 7

Correlation of Avoidance and Bifurcation
Only In Sibling and Cousin Terms for
Adjacent Pairs of Tribes

	PROBABILITY OF OCCURRENCE	E EXPECTED FREQUENCY OF PAIRS	O. OBSERVED FREQUENCY OF ADJACENT PAIRS	$\dfrac{(O-E)^2}{E}$	PROPORTION OF TOTAL VARIANCE
1.	.052	13.5	3	8.17	.023
2.	.052	13.5	3	8.17	.023
3.	.017	4.4	34	199.18	.569
4.	.159	41.3	99	80.61	.230
5.	.052	13.5	1	11.57	.033
6.	.052	13.5	6	4.17	.012
7.	.086	23.4	34	4.80	.014
8.	.032	8.3	9	.06	.000
9.	.038	9.9	8	.36	.001
10.	.023	6.0	6	.00	.000
11.	.038	9.9	7	.85	.002
12.	.023	6.0	7	.17	.000
13.	.071	18.5	5	9.85	.028
14.	.117	30.4	17	5.91	.017
15.	.117	30.4	11	12.38	.035
16.	.071	18.5	10	3.90	.011
	1.000	261.0	260	X^2 =350.10	.998

Table 8
Correlation of Avoidance and Bifurcation only in Sibling and Cousin Terms for Distant Pairs of Tribes

	E. EXPECTED FREQUENCY OF PAIRS	O. OBSERVED FREQUENCY OF DISTANT PAIRS	$\dfrac{(O-E)^2}{E}$	PROPORTION OF TOTAL VARIANCE
1.	13.5	25	9.80	.171
2.	13.5	26	11.57	.202
3.	4.4	9	4.81	.084
4.	41.3	54	3.90	.068
5.	13.5	6	4.17	.073
6.	13.5	7	3.13	.055
7.	23.4	14	3.78	.066
8.	8.3	1	6.42	.112
9.	9.9	11	.12	.002
10.	6.0	6	.00	.000
11.	9.9	14	1.70	.030
12.	6.0	8	.67	.012
13.	18.5	12	2.28	.040
14.	30.4	33	.22	.004
15.	30.4	22	2.32	.041
16.	18.5	12	2.28	.040
TOTALS	261.0	260	$x^2 = 57.17$	1.000

P<.001

In Tables 4 and 5, five of the expected values for the number of pairs of tribes fall below 5. If row 7 is combined with 8, 13 with 14, and 15 with 16 to eliminate the three lowest expected frequencies, the chi-square of Table 4 is reduced to 50.62, but with the degrees of freedom reduced from 15 to 12, it is still significant at much less than .001. Collapsing the same categories of Table 5 reduces its chi-square to 344.54, a difference of only about 1 per cent. Therefore the chi-squares in Tables 4 and 5 are essentially correct in spite of some low expected frequencies.

D'Andrade (personal communication) suggests that more light could be thrown on the relation of language and culture by comparing the following four sets of matched pairs:

1) geographically adjacent, same language family;
2) not geographically adjacent, same language family;
3) geographically adjacent, different language family;
4) not geographically adjacent, different language family.

The not geographically adjacent pairs could be chosen randomly. This is a good suggestion and will be followed at some time in the future.

An adequate solution to the Tylor-Galton problem by the matched pair method would also require a world-wide sample and a wide spectrum of culture inventory, such as that of Murdock (1967:109-236). Murdock's sample is the largest and best so far, but its cultural inventory is largely lacking in so-called material culture, which is probably more diffusible than most of the categories he uses. Some of the categories in Driver and Massey's (1957) work would round out Murdock's trait coverage. If one chose to compare adjacent tribes, he would have to do a lot of additional coding, because Murdock's sample never includes two adjacent tribes. Nevertheless, it would be possible to match the nearest pairs obtainable from Murdock's (1967) sample and test them for a large number of correlations, perhaps a random sample of all possible dichotomous relationships. Needless to say, this would require a computer program.

Diffusion of Traits

It further seems untenable to postulate that bifurcation can diffuse as a unit, or that any component of kinship semantics can diffuse as a unit. According to the lag theory, which is the one most generally

Table 9
Correlation of Bifurcation in Terms for Parents Uncles, Aunts with Bifurcation in Terms for Siblings and Cousins. (Expected Probabilities in Parentheses)

BIFURCATION FOR PARENTS, UNCLES, AUNTS

		Present, A		
BIFURCATION FOR SIBLINGS AND COUSINS	Present, B	103 (.299)	5 (.117)	108 (.416)
	Absent, B	84 (.420)	68 (.164)	152 (.584)
	Total	187 (.719)	73 (.281)	260 (1.000)
		$\Phi = .44$	P<.001	

116

Table 10
Correlation of Bifurcation in Avuncular with Bifurcation in Sibling and Cousin Terms for Adjacent Pairs of Tribes

	PROBABILITY OF OCCURRENCE	E. EXPECTED FREQUENCY of pairs	OBSERVED FREQUENCY OF ADJACENT PAIRS	$\dfrac{(O-E)^2}{E}$	VARIANCE
1.	.049	12.7	11	.23	.001
2.	.049	12.7	8	1.74	.004
3.	.089	23.1	78	130.48	.287
4.	.027	7.0	49	252.00	.554
5.	.049	12.7	1	10.78	.024
6.	.049	12.7	0	12.70	.028
7.	.014	3.6	0	3.60	.008
8.	.176	45.8	54	1.47	.003
9.	.035	9.1	2	5.54	.012
10.	.126	32.8	12	13.19	.029
11.	.035	9.1	2	5.54	.012
12.	.126	32.8	20	5.00	.011
13.	.069	17.9	11	2.66	.006
14.	.019	4.9	0	4.90	.011
15.	.019	4.9	3	.74	.002
16.	.069	17.9	9	4.42	.010
Totals	1.000	259.7	260	$x =454.99$	1.002

Table 11
Correlation of Bifurcation in Avuncular with Bifurcation in Sibling and Cousin Terms for Distant Pairs of Tribes

	E. EXPECTED FREQUENCY OF PAIRS	DISTANT PAIRS	$\dfrac{(O-E)^2}{E}$	VARIANCE
1.	12.7	30	18.05	.133
2.	12.7	33	32.45	.239
3.	23.1	46	22.70	.167
4.	7.0	14	7.00	.051
5.	12.7	2	9.02	.066
6.	12.7	2	9.02	.066
7.	3.6	0	3.60	.026
8.	45.8	24	10.38	.076
9.	9.1	1	7.21	.053
10.	32.8	26	1.41	.010
11.	9.1	2	5.54	.041
12.	32.8	38	.82	.006
13.	17.9	20	.25	.002
14.	4.9	0	4.90	.036
15.	4.9	1	3.10	.023
16.	17.9	21	.54	.004
Totals	259.7	260	$x =135.99$	.999

$P<.001$

Table 12

Summary of Results of Matched Pairs Tests in Total Amount of Variance in Rows 1, 2, 7, 8 (Chi-Square), and Proportion of Total Variance (In Parentheses)

	ADJACENT PAIRS OF TRIBES	DISTANT PAIRS OF TRIBES
First correlation	Diffusion wins by 21.6 (.062)	Function wins by 17.9 (.307)
Second correlation	Diffusion wins by 21.2 (.060)	Function wins by 31.6 (.551)
Third correlation	Diffusion wins by 7.0 (.016)	Function wins by 64.5 (.474)

accepted for kinship terminologies, economy or ecology would tend to change first, followed by residence, family organization, descent, and then kinship terminology. There is abundant evidence that tools, weapons, domesticated animals and plants, and knowledge of how to make use of geographical environment can and do diffuse. Residence and descent are certainly less diffusible, yet there is some evidence that they can diffuse without the ecological adjustment having been made (Driver 1956). But until someone can find a few morphemes shared by languages belonging to different families and a corresponding sharing of meanings not explainable in terms of residence, descent, or other aspects of social organization, the case for diffusion of semantic distinctions in kin terms apart from the features of social organization which seem to generate them is nonexistent. Our technique, therefore, hardly seems to be ferreting out diffusion. It seems to be measuring continuity of geographical distribution, which is often, but not always, caused by diffusion. (See Driver and Massey 1957, maps 160, 161, for continuity of distribution of types of kinship terminology, and Driver 1966:142 for continuity of kin avoidances.)

In Driver's paper on kin avoidances he has correlated all the material with culture areas and language families and his general conclusion (1966:157, Table 15) is that diffusion accounts for the greatest amount of mother-in-law son-in-law avoidance variance, bifurcation in kinship terminology the second greatest amount, and language family membership (as an indicator of culture heritage) the third greatest amount. With the change from .40 to .28 in the correlation mentioned above, bifurcation would take third place. Forms of residence and descent appear to have less causal potency, although as determiners of kinship terminology their roles may be greater than their correlations show. This last paper is too long and

technical to review here in detail. Suffice it to say that we think he has given a general method applicable to all large-sample comparative studies where ethnic units are continuously distributed.

In simplified and brief form, this method begins with the correlation over the entire area of all the variables thought to be related to the variable the study seeks to explain. Those variables which show significant positive correlations with the phenomenon to be explained and lend themselves to functional interpretation are called the functional correlatives. The next step is to ferret out the negative instances where the phenomenon is present but where all or most of the functional correlatives are absent. If these negative instances occur among language families where the phenomenon is rare and not likely to represent a culture heritage from the protoculture associated with the protolanguage, then the case for diffusion is strengthened. If at the same time these negative instances are geographically close to positive instances in other language families with well-developed functional syndromes, then the case for diffusion-acculturation becomes overwhelming. It is thus possible to establish diffusions of a phenomenon off the top so to speak, without the recipient society possessing any or many of the variables thought to generate or cause the phenomenon. There were many such negative instances for kin avoidances in North America. There were also many negative instances where the known functional correlatives were present and avoidances absent.

Diffusion may occur almost anywhere in some evolutionary sequences, as an inspection of the Guttman scale of Carneiro and Tobias (1963) suggests. For instance, diffusions for domesticated plants and animals have been worked out in greater detail than those of most cultural manifestations. Calendar systems, the arch, and papermaking, appearing higher up on the scale, exhibit much evidence of diffusion in areas of continental size, although the first and last seem to have been independently invented in the Old and New Worlds.

Numbers of Origins of traits

Those who argue that all we want to know is the general evolutionary sequence and that the number of origins of a phenomenon does not matter, because it will diffuse only to areas possessing functional correlatives capable of generating it independently anyway, are taking a much too cavalier attitude toward culture history. It surely makes a difference whether a widespread cultural behavior has a single, a dozen, or a hundred historically independent origins. Historical independence is also a matter of degree: every ethnic unit possesses some cultural behaviors which are unique to it and therefore historically independent of all other such unique behaviors among other ethnic units; every ethnic unit likewise shares some historically determined resemblances with its cultural or linguistic near neighbors, and still others with a larger number of ethnic units. An ethnic unit may be historically linked to others for some of its cultural inventory and be independent with respect to other aspects of culture. We can seldom determine the exact number of origins of the similarities we distribute in space and time in comparative studies, but we can choose between few and many, and between hundreds and thousands of years of independence.

Importance of Continuity of Distribution

Continuity of geographical distribution is still one of the important clues to diffusion and numbers of origins. Comparative studies which deliberately separate the ethnic units in geographical, cultural, and linguistic space to lessen mutual historical influence are eliminating the connecting links needed to establish the amount of historicity involved and are thereby creating a biased sample. No one would think of taking a 10 per cent random sample of a single community to generalize about the kinship relations of that community, because the 90 per cent eliminated would remove the connecting links between the 10 per cent drawn in this manner for analysis. The same principle holds for comparative studies. Any sample which eliminates most of the geographical and historical connecting links is a biased sample and will be insufficient for assessing the importance of historical factors. The researcher needs the entire parameter or most of it to do this and no sample of any kind is as adequate for this purpose. Nevertheless, a sample can yield valid functional correlations, which are a necessary part of a program for ferreting out diffusions off the top, as Driver has applied it to kin avoidances.

Part of the difference between those who stress independent origin and innovation and those who emphasize diffusion is semantic. Even when a material object diffuses it must be preceded by a felt need and some lessons in its use and operation. If it is to be manufactured in the new area, the details of this process must be passed on also. If the materials available for manufacture in the new area are different from those in the donor area, this calls for innovation on the part of the maker. If the two cultures differ enough, the meaning, use, or function of the object may be changed by the recipient people. Diffusion is always accompanied by some innovation. A sufficient explanation of most cultural behaviors in most localities requires mention of the outside contact with the donor group which triggers the spread of the culture behavior, the inside innovations of the recipient groups which adapt it to their needs, and why it was needed at the particular time when it diffused instead of earlier or later.

Rates of Diffusion

Different rates of diffusion are generally assumed to exist not only in different times and places, but also among differing aspects of culture in the same or adjacent sections of time and space. When documentary and accurately dated archaeological materials are lacking, rates are difficult to determine. Barnett (1964) suggests that material objects are generally most diffusible, social organization least diffusible, with organized religions taking an intermediate position. Although this generalization is arrived at by citing authoritative opinions rather than by assembling a large sample of datable diffusions, it may well be correct.

The maps on North American Indian culture assembled by Driver and Massey (1957) and Driver (1961) all show non-random areal clustering of all of the data. Although the multiple number of some of the clusters suggests multiple origins of these phenomena, the geographical continuity within clusters suggests diffusion within each cluster. Although significant positive correlations among functional correlatives have been established by many researchers in the field of social organization (e.g., Murdock 1949 and Driver 1956), some such correlations are based on as few as 60 per cent positive instances and as many as 40 per cent negative instances. The middle to low range of many of the correlations suggests that diffusion of one variable without the other is contributing to the number of negative instances.

Social Organization and Kinship Terminology

The diffusion or acculturation of social organization would certainly require intimate and prolonged contact of the donor and recipient peoples. Intertribal marriages seem to have been not only common but universal in native North America (except for the Polar Eskimo who were isolated for centuries from all neighbors), and the assimilation of sizable parts of tribes decimated by war and disease by their conquerors or by friendly tribes was probably more common than the record shows. Ceremonies of adoption for foreign individuals were common, e.g., in the United States east of the Mississippi. We do not need to look far to find the ways and means for the diffusion of aspects of social organization.

Fifty years ago Lowie (1916) wrote a well-balanced paper on "historical and sociological interpretations of kinship terminologies." He pointed out certain features of kinship terminology which could be adequately explained by known variables of social organization and language family classification. At the same time he called attention to other components of kinship terminology which cross-cut language classification yet formed continuous areal clusters. Those which could not be explained by associated features of social organization or by correlations with language families were attributed to diffusion. Probably some of the features he attributed to diffusion could now be shown to correlate with some other social variable, but I suspect that no matter how exhaustive the analysis there are likely to be some details of kinship terminology that form areal clusters and cross-cut not only language family classification but also kinship typologies.

Although it has been said by a number of persons that social structure is comparable to language in its structural integration and resistance to change from without its system, linguists (e.g., Emeneau 1956 and Taylor 1963) have given examples not only of words and phones but also of morphological features diffusing across genetic family boundaries. Kinship and social structure specialists might also find comparable diffusions in their fields if they searched for them.

The brief discussion by Köbben (1967) of the role of diffusion in creating exceptions to the general rules established by correlations and tests of significance is an excellent treatment of the subject and wholly in accord with the view expressed here. In addition he gives the most complete inventory so far of the many other ways in which negative instances may arise. Every cross-cultural researcher should examine his own data with these points in mind to see which ones may be applied to the interpretation of his exceptional cases.

Although the methods we have mentioned in this brief statement are complicated and subject to debate on many points, we believe that comparativists should debate them, refine them, and apply them, and not just relax and admit that they have made little progress in these matters since Tylor's and Galton's time.

Bibliography

BARNETT, HOMER G.
   1964 Diffusion rates. In Robert A. Manners, ed., *Process and pattern in culture*. Chicago, Aldine.
CARNEIRO, ROBERT L., and STEPHEN G. TOBIAS
   1963 The application of scale analysis to the study of cultural evolution. *Transactions of the New York Academy of Sciences*, Ser. II, Vol. 26, No. 2:196-207.
DRIVER, HAROLD E.
   1956 *An integration of functional, evolutionary, and historical theory by means of correlations*. Indiana University Publications in Anthropology and Linguistics, Memoir 12.
DRIVER, HAROLD E., et al.
   1966 Geographical-historical versus psychofunctional explanations of kin avoidances. *Current Anthropology* 7:131-182.
DRIVER, HAROLD E., JOHN M. COOPER, PAUL KIRCHOFF, WM. C. MASSEY, DOROTHY RAINIER LIBBY, and LESLIE SPIER
   1953 *Indian tribes of North America*. Indiana University Publications in Anthropology and Linguistics, Memoir 9.
DRIVER, HAROLD E., and WM. C. MASSEY
   1957 Comparative studies of North American Indians. *Transactions of the American Philosophical Society* 47:165-456.
EMENEAU, MURRAY B.
   1956 India as a linguistic area. *Language* 32: 3-16.
KÖBBEN, A.J.F.
   1967 Why exceptions? The logic of cross-cultural analysis. *Current Anthropology* 8:3-34
LOWIE, ROBERT H.
   1916 Historical and sociological interpretations of kinship terminologies. In *Holmes anniversary volume: anthropological essays presented to William Henry Holmes . . .* December 1, 1916 by his friends and Colaborers. Washington, D.C.

MOONEY, JAMES
1896 Calendar history of the Kiowa Indians. *Bureau of American Ethnology, Annual Report*, No. 17, Pt. 1.

MURDOCK, GEORGE P.
1957 World ethnographic sample. *American Anthropologist* 59:664-687.
1966 Cross-cultural sampling. *Ethnology* 5:97-114.
1967 Ethnographic atlas: a summary. *Ethnology* 6:109-236.

NAROLL, RAOUL
1961 Two solutions to Galton's problem. *Philosophy of Science* 28:15-39. Also in Frank W. Moore, ed., *Readings in cross-cultural methodology*. New Haven, Human Relations Area Files.
1964 A fifth solution to Galton's problem. *American Anthropologist* 66:863-867.

NAROLL, RAOUL, and ROY G. D'ANDRADE
1963 Two further solutions to Galton's problem. *American Anthropologist* 65:1053-1067.

STEPHENS, WM. N.
1959 *Menstrual taboos and castration anxiety.* Ph.D. dissertation, Graduate School of Education. Cambridge, Harvard University.

TAYLOR, DOUGLAS
1963 The origin of West Indian Creole languages: evidence from grammatical categories. *American Anthropologist* 65:800-814.

TYLOR, EDWARD B.
1889 On a method of investigating the development of institutions; applied to laws of marriage and descent. *Journal of the Royal Anthropological Institute of Great Britain and Ireland* 18:245-272.

WHITING, JOHN W. M.
1968 Methods and problems in cross-cultural research. In Lindzey and Aronson, eds., *Handbook of social psychology*, 2nd ed. Reading, Mass., Addison-Wesley.

6. Hologeistic Theory Testing

Raoul Naroll, Gary L. Michik, and Frada Naroll

Introduction: The Need for Hologeistic Studies

This paper is a general review of problems of comparative method—especially of hologeistic method. As such, it complements an earlier general review of hologeistic theory (Naroll 1970b; Naroll and Naroll 1973). Readers familiar with that earlier review may wish to skip this "Introduction"—taken almost verbatim from the former—and begin directly with the discussion of significance tests on page.

The hologeistic method of research is a method for the empirical testing of theories which attempt to explain some general characteristics of human existence. The method measures theoretical variables in a large, worldwide sample of human cultures and examines statistical correlations among those variables to determine whether the intervariable relationships are as predicted by the theory. Nearly all of the necessary computations can be performed with the computer programs in the Human Relations Area Files' hologeistic computer program package (HRAF 1974). Within the last twenty-five years, the social sciences have produced a large body of hologeistic literature (see Moore 1966, Ford 1967, Naroll 1970b, Gillespie and Nesvold 1971). While some of this literature is concerned with *developing* theories, the major contribution of hologeistic method to the social sciences has been in *testing* theories. We will, therefore, deal primarily with the use of hologeistic methodology to test theories. Since we will discuss the detailed aspects of hologeistic methodology concisely and technically, the reader will find a background of elementary statistics (e.g. Freund 1967 or Dixon and Massey 1969) helpful in following our discussion. (We hope to produce a less technical manual for users of the Human Relations Area Files.)

To many social scientists, hologeistic studies seem crude, clumsy, blunt, and awkward tools for the understanding of human affairs. And so do they seem to us (Naroll and Naroll 1973). It is regrettable that until now hologeists have not made clear the distinction between the strategy of scientific discovery and the strategy of scientific proof. This confusion seems also to have been present in the mind of one of the keenest of twentieth-century epistemologists, Karl Popper (1959). His great work was originally titled

Die Logik der Forschung, that is to say "The Logic of Research"; but the English translation, presumably with Popper's full knowledge and consent, was entitled "The Logic of Scientific Discovery." Actually, Popper's book is not about scientific *discovery* at all; it is about scientific *proof*.

Although original discoveries have been made through the use of hologeistic method, we do not know of any important or striking original insights which thus came about. It appears that the original insights, original discoveries, great illuminations about social and cultural affairs usually come from minds meditating long about particular cases deeply studied—rarely from statistical studies of necessarily much simplified data like hologeistic studies (Naroll and Naroll 1973).

From such studies of particular cases, we have Marx's insights into the role of economics in politics; we have Freud's insights into the role of the unconscious in everyday behavior and in the neuroses; we have Toynbee's penetrating insight that the key distinction between higher civilizations and primitive societies lay in the division of labor; we have the archeologists' perception of the prime importance of the growth of cities to the process of cultural evolution.

But from such studies in just the same way, we have many other penetrating insights that are inconsistent with some of these—insights most social scientists today believe to be entirely mistaken. We have Herodotus's perception that higher civilizations arise in the countries which have the most favorable natural environments. We have Houston Stewart Chamberlain's insight that higher civilizations are a product of the "superior" genetic material of a "superior Aryan" race. We have Lewis Henry Morgan's theory that cultural evolution explains the variation in kinship structure around the world: from a hypothesized prehistoric period of complete promiscuity, through group marriage, to matrilineal households, to patrilineal households, to bilateral households. Scientific research consists of two related processes. There are insightful "discoveries," which may be right or may be wrong. Then come the rigorous empirical tests, which sift the right ones from the wrong ones.

Therefore, we do not claim for hologeistic studies any special value as instruments of new discovery. At times they may be helpful. (But a hologeistic study whose correlations suggest new hypotheses must be considered only a pilot study, not a test of those same hypotheses. These new hypotheses need to be tested again on a new sample.) So far hologeistic studies have played only a small part here. Therefore, we will not deal extensively with the generation of new insights from hologeistic studies.

We do claim that the hologeistic method is the second-best method known to science for testing to see whether insights are right or wrong. The best method for that purpose, of course, is controlled experiment. However, controlled experiments about propositions concerning human social and cultural affairs are not very widely used and are even less widely cited as important tests of hypotheses. The reasons are obvious. Controlled experiments on whole societies or cultures, or large groups within them, often would take too long—key changes may need hundreds of years to take effect. Such experiments seldom can be done without the experimental subjects knowing what is going on; but if the subjects know they are being experimented on, that fact changes the conditions, breaks the control. (Medical experiments with new drugs require that no one, neither the patient nor his doctor, know whether the patient is getting the experimental drug or, instead, the sugar-pill placebo.) Such experiments often would violate the law or the ethical standards of both experimenters and subject; we could try an experiment to *decrease* the suicide rate, for example, but we could not try one to *increase* it. More important, such experiments usually deal with the people of one society or culture as subjects; if so, they are collectively but a single case.

The need for cross-cultural comparisons, comparisons of many cases, has become widely realized by behavioral scientists in the last twenty years. The need is often not apparent to physical scientists or biologists. Only one set of laws governs physics and chemistry. All the plants and animals we know on earth follow a fundamental set of common rules, governed by a single genetic code. In the double helix there is only one genetic "language," with only four "phonemes."

In contrast, there are some four thousand human languages spoken today. The speakers of each constitute a distinct culture, with their own underlying laws of behavior, their own images of reality. (Nor do speakers of a common language necessarily or even usually share a homogeneous culture; usually there are many local variants.) The degree of variation imposed by culture on human behavior—even on matters of physiology and perception—has been realized by psychologists only in the last twenty years. (See the reviews of this literature by Triandis 1964 and Dawson 1971.)

The limitation of individual case studies as tools for generalizing widely about society and culture has been set forth by Köbben (1970), to whom the following inventory of conflicts is partly due. From his study of the Siriono of Bolivia, Holmberg (1950) concluded that hunting and gathering tribes tended to be underfed and obsessed by food. From his celebrated study of Western European nations during the 1880s and 1890s, Durkheim (1951) concluded that in general social isolation tends to drive a person to suicide. Hauser's study (1959) of the Thai led him to believe that in general the more atomistic a society, the more it would resist modernization. Raulin (1959), studying the people of Gagnia and Daloa, concluded that in general uprooted peoples would be more interested in modernization than those still at home in the land of their ancestry.

But, Needham (1954), studying the Punan of Borneo, concluded that hunting and gathering tribes were usually well fed and unobsessed by food. Asuni (1962), studying the people of western Nigeria, concluded that social isolation had nothing to do with suicide. Adair and Vogt (1949), studying the Zuni, concluded that the less atomistic a society, the more it would resist modernization. Waal Malefijt (1963), studying the Javanese, concluded that uprooted peoples would be less interested in modernization than would stay-at-homes.

Concomitant variation studies are similarly restricted in their scope by the cultural context of the region in which they are set (see Clignet 1970). For example Redfield (1941: 338ff.), in his justly celebrated study, listed eleven traits with respect to which more highly developed communities tended to differ from less highly developed ones in Yucatan. Of these eleven, the worldwide general applicability of three has been definitely confirmed by hologeistic studies (heterogeneity, division of labor, money economy); that of two others has been definitely discredited (kinship institutions, black magic); that of three others has not been formally tested cross-culturally, but seems plausible (isolation, impersonality, freedom of action); and that of the remaining three, also untested, seems questionable (secularity of specialists, general religiosity, explanations of illness).

Another urgent need for comparative studies lies in the difficulty of untangling the relevant factors in a given cultural situation from the irrelevant factors also found there.

When we look at a single society, or at a few closely related societies, there is no real possibility of testing supposed functional linkages. There are so many common features, any of which may explain the relationship we are interested in. It is only when we examine a large variety of societies, which differ widely from each other in most respects, that we can expect the *irrelevant* attributes to vary. Thus when we compare the Netsilik Eskimos of 1900 with the English of that same day, we find almost nothing alike in their cultures. The Netsilik live at the most

primitive known level of social complexity; with incredible skill, they use a highly specialized technology based on bone, stone, and sinew to forage a precarious living from winter sealing and summer hunting and fishing. The English at the same time are a highly industrialized state, ruling a worldwide empire from a great city. In material culture, in religion, in moral attitudes, in modes of thought, these two cultures have almost nothing in common. And yet, as it happens, they do agree with respect to their basic kinship system, their family structure. In this respect, the English of 1900 happen to resemble the Netsilik Eskimos far more closely than they do the Ancient Romans, for example, or the Chinese or the Hindus—not to speak of the Crow or Omaha or Iroquois Indians.

So if we compare the English family system in 1900 with that of the French or German of the same day, we find (from the anthropological view) no difference of consequence; but we cannot draw conclusions about the associations of constituent elements in that family system from looking at all three peoples, since they share so many other traits in common. They have a common religion, a common moral system, a common economic system, to a considerable extent a common fund of literature, and so on. But when we compare the English kinship system with that of the Netsilik Eskimos, we find that several crucial elements of their kinship system are shared, despite all the other differences in their societies and cultures. The so-called Eskimo kinship system, which the English likewise have, is but one of six major types of kinship system, each of which has subtypes or variants. The hologeistic study surveys many examples of each of these types and subtypes, looking for correlation, for covariation. The universe studied is the universe of all known human cultures. The ultimate goal is to elicit cause-effect relationships among the constituent traits.

However, merely to compare the English and Eskimo kinship systems is not enough. The comparison of only two natural instances may prove a fruitful *source* of insight. (Most anthropological "case studies" of single primitive tribes are really comparisons between the culture of the tribe studied and the culture of the ethnographer.) But such a comparison is an inadequate *test* of that same insight. Consider the comparison of the Oedipus complex in Freud's Vienna and Malinowski's Trobriands. As Donald T. Campbell has said:

Between Trobriand and Vienna there are many dimensions of differences which could constitute potential rival explanations and which we have no means of ruling out. For comparisons of this pair, the *ceteris paribus* requirement (that other things be equal) becomes untenable [Campbell and Naroll 1972: 449].

Hologeistic studies are studies of large worldwide samples. Culture presumably varies within the sample as much as it ever does at all. *So other things are presumed equal. Irrelevant factors are presumed to vary randomly.* That is the great strength of the hologeistic study. It is a quasi experiment—not as good as a true controlled experiment, but the next best thing.

A final advantage to hologeistic studies over most case studies is their relative objectivity. In most case studies the investigator tends deliberately or unconsciously to select the data to fit his insight. Two case studies of the same society by two different investigators can lead to diametrically opposite conclusions about fundamental points. (For a discussion of such studies of Tepoztlan and of the Arapesh, see Naroll 1970a: 928-29.) Hologeistic studies are designed to weed out and count such inconsistent, discrediting evidence as fully as consistent, supporting evidence.

Hologeistic Method in General

For the usual routine of carrying out a hologeistic study, see Otterbein (1969). Hologeistic study method has been widely criticized (Köbben 1952, 1967; Schapera 1953; Lewis 1956; Barnes 1971); the classic defense is Whiting (1954, 1968). Köbben's critiques are especially careful, responsible, and measured. See also McEwen (1963); Cohen (1968); Pelto (1970); Holt and Turner (1970); Rokkan (1970); Naroll (1970b); Przeworski and Teune (1970); Chaney (1971); Gillespie (1971); Campbell and Naroll (1972); Sipes (1972).

Statistical Significance

The widely used concept of "statistical significance" can best be understood in terms of its rarely used opposite or antonym—statistical insignificance. A relationship or measurement is statistically insignificant if we might plausibly expect to get such a relationship merely by random sampling error—in other words, by chance. To say some quantity is statistically insignificant is to say that it is no more than we would expect to get by chance through sampling error from a universe where the quantity in question did not exist—i.e. was zero. The measurement of statistical significance is the subject matter of statistical inference—statistical inference in turn is the main concern of the science of mathematical statistics. The elements of the mathematical reasoning underlying statistical inferences are set forth in such introductory texts as Kenney and Keeping (1951) and Mood (1950). The general application of these techniques to the social sciences is outlined

(without the underlying mathematical logic) in such texts as Freund (1967) and Blalock (1972).

There are two main types of statistical inference— inference about differences and inference about associations. In hologeistic studies, we deal chiefly with the second of these. The present discussion assumes at least an elementary acquaintanceship with the statistics of inference about associations. We speak here only about the two aspects of statistical inference that bear with special force on hologeistic studies: (1) the problem of applying inferential statistics to data which may not meet the necessary mathematical assumptions and (2) the problem of arbitrarily dichotomizing probabilistic statements into those which support a hypothesis and those which do not. Hologeistic studies examine the relationships among variables in large, worldwide samples in the universe of all known cultures which the sample represents; they test theoretical predictions about the nature of those relationships. The relationships are described by measures of association (or correlation), and the probability of their existence in the sampling universe is assessed by tests of statistical significance (for discussions of these statistical operations see Freund 1967: 355-77; Blalock 1972: 361-464; Naroll 1974).

The significance tests measure the probability that the observed association would have occurred by chance in a sample representing a universe in which no associations actually existed under the following assumptions: (1) that each of the units in the universe had an equal probability of inclusion in the sample; (2) that each of the units was defined in the same manner; and (3) that each of the units in the sample was independent of all other units in the sample. Violation of these assumptions may produce errors in the determination of an association's probability of chance occurrence. However, a study of all the units in a universe—a 100 percent sample—may still be thought of as a study of a sample representing a hypothetically infinite macrouniverse with the characteristics of the actual universe studied. Here, too, significance tests can still be useful. The investigator often wants to know whether the relationship he finds in his actual universe is nothing more than one he might well have expected by chance if his actual universe had in fact been a random sample from that hypothetical macrouniverse.

The data of most hologeistic studies do not meet the assumptions required for parametric measures.[1] Consequently, although parametric statistics (e.g. Pearson's r) are more accurate than nonparametric statistics (e.g. gamma, phi, tau-b)—and should be used whenever possible because they are more sensitive (see Siegel 1956; Dixon and Massey 1969; Pierce 1970; Blalock 1972)—the discussion here will refer to nonparametric statistics unless otherwise stated. The logic of the manipulations involved is, of course, equally applicable to parametric statistics. Computer programs ORDMAT (for nonparametric data) PROMO (for parametric data) and RPB (for combinations of parametric and nonparametric data) can compute the associations and significance levels for hologeistic studies (HRAF 1974).

Generally speaking, investigators choose an arbitrary probability value and decide that associations having a probability of chance occurrence less than or equal to that value are not attributable to chance, while those associations having a probability of chance occurrence greater than that value are attributable to chance. According to this decision rule, associations which are not attributable to chance are considered to be "statistically significant" at the probability level used to make the decision (0.05, 0.10, and 0.01 are common probability values used for this purpose). Thus, when an investigator reports that his results are statistically significant (at some probability level) and asserts that the relationships he observed actually exist in the universe being studied, he may be wrong; some probability remains that his associations could have occurred by chance (see Winch and Campbell 1969; Naroll 1971b).

Rarely, if ever, are all of the assumptions underlying the use of statistical significance tests met in hologeistic studies. Nevertheless, significance tests can still be useful in evaluating the probability that an observed association may be reasonably explained as a chance occurrence. Errors in determining the probability of chance occurrence produced by violating the assumptions underlying significance tests can be divided into two categories: random error and systematic error (or bias). It is important to note that these two kinds of error have different effects on the magnitude of the association observed in the sample and on their probability of chance occurrence as determined by significance tests. Random errors, by definition, tend to cancel each other out. These errors always tend to lower associations and, thus, tend to increase the probability of chance occurrence indicated by significance tests. Therefore, an association which *is* found significant, despite circumstances suggesting considerable random error, may paradoxically be presumed to exist in the universe being studied with *even greater confidence* than the significance level suggests. Accordingly, we need not be overly concerned with random errors.

Systematic errors, however, may well produce spurious inflation of observed association, and thereby decrease the probability of chance occurrence indicated by significance tests. Therefore, if all systematic errors are measured and their influences on the magnitudes of the observed associations are statistically controlled, the results of significance tests can be interpreted as the upper limit of the probability of chance occurrence (i.e. if a significance test indicates that $p = 0.05$ then in fact $p \leq 0.05$). Although this application of significance tests does not produce accurate measurement of the probability of chance occurrence, the error is conservative; it favors acceptance of the hypothesis that the observed association does not exist in the universe studied.

In order for a systematic error to have an effect on the magnitude of an association, it must be significantly associated with *both* of the theoretical variables. The question of whether the associations observed in a hologeistic study have been influenced by systematic error is answered empirically by: (1) measuring the hypothetical systematic error and (2) testing the significance of its associations with the theoretical variables in each association (which, hypothetically, have been influenced by it). If some systematic error factor reveals an influence on an association between two theoretical variables in this manner, then the magnitude which that association would have manifested if it had not been influenced by the systematic error factor may be estimated as the partial association between the two theoretical variables with respect to the systematic error factor (see Blalock 1972: 433-42 for discussion and explanation of the concept of partial association). Computer program PARTAU (HRAF 1974) can compute the partial associations between the theoretical variables with respect to each error factor.

To use partial association in this way, we must first assume that the error factor is measured accurately and that any other factors associated with it are also associated with the theoretical variables (Brewer, Campbell, and Crano 1970). If these assumptions are not tenable, the partial association may be spuriously inflated. However, if the influence of the biasing error factor is such that the resulting partial association between the theoretical variables is no longer significant (when subjected to standard significance tests), the conclusion that the original association was determined to be significant because it had been spuriously inflated by systematic error is tenable. It is tenable regardless of the characteristics of the measure of systematic error. If the assumptions about the measure of systematic error are not tenable and the resulting partial association between the theoretical variables is still significant, factor analysis is necessary to determine the nature of the influence of the biasing error factor on the theoretical association (Brewer, Campbell, and Crano 1970).

It is well to remember that all measures of association are valid descriptions of a relationship only when that relationship is monotonic: when the value of one variable is changed in a specific direction, the direction in which the other variable changes will remain constant (Blalock 1972: 415-16). An easy way to examine the relationship between two variables is first to plot each case on a coordinate axis representing the two variables and then to determine, by inspection, whether the line approximating the average value of the relationship changes direction with respect to either of the variable axes. If it does change, the relationship is nonmonotonic.

Group Significance

If a large number of associations are computed from the same data, a certain percentage of them can be expected to be "statistically significant" purely by chance. That chance significance is the concern of group significance tests. Leo Simmons (1945) presents no fewer than 1,145 coefficients of association. Most of these are not statistically significant. Are so few individually significant coefficients well within the number that might be expected by chance even if our data were taken from a table of random numbers or other meaningless garbage? A hologeistic study designed to test a theory—or to select which one from a number of theories is most tenable—must determine whether the number of associations found to be significant is greater than the number of associations that would be expected to be found significant if none of the associations actually existed in the universe being studied. Murdock (1949) computed hundreds of coefficients of association to test his theory of kinship. It is the group of tests as a whole, not any one test, that constitutes his basic argument. Yet most of his tests were not statistically significant. If the number of significant correlations is too small, the results of the study as a whole may plausibly be explainable as chance occurrences. The necessary comparison, then, is between the number of observed significant associations and the number of significant associations we would expect by chance.

With parametric data, the number of significant associations that might be expected by chance can be determined by multiplying the number of associations computed by the probability level used to determine significance. However, this procedure often will not work if the data are nonparametric, because the distribution of the coefficients of association (and their probability levels) is not continuous.

Figure I.

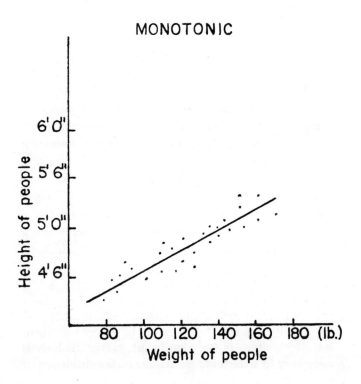

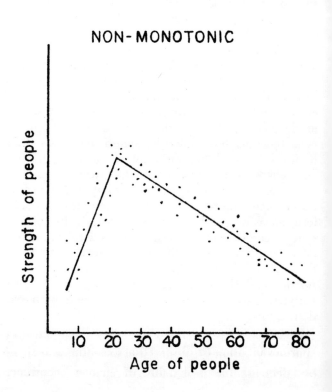

Thus Textor (1967: 56) computed 2,500 coefficients of association from four-fold contingency tables derived from random numbers—his so-called "Whiskers Variables." Theoretically, we would expect 250 of these to be "significant" at the 10 percent level; in fact, only 126 were. Naroll (1969) ran a similar series of tests on his War, Stress, and Culture sample, with similar results. With nonparametric data the best way to estimate the number of significant associations expected by chance is the "Whiskers Variable" method of Banks and Textor (1963). (See also Textor 1967: 54-59; Tatje, Naroll, and Textor 1970: 649-52.) A Whiskers Variable is a nonsense variable coded from a table of random numbers or from the random numbers generator of a computer. A set of Whiskers Variables is generated for each substantive variable, each of these random variables having the same frequency distribution as the substantive variable for which it was generated (see Naroll, Bullough, and Naroll 1973). Computer program MONTE (HRAF 1974) can generate as many Whiskers Variables for each variable as are desired. The associations between each of these Whiskers Variables and the substantive variables are then computed, to estimate the distribution of the coefficients of association (and their probability levels) expected by chance. In this manner can be estimated the percentage of associations that could be expected to be "significant" if none of them actually existed in the universe being studied.

Galton's Problem

Most cultural characteristics tend to spread readily by borrowing or migration—by cultural diffusion. Galton's problem examines the independence of cultures in a hologeistic study. It is concerned with whether the units of study in a hologeistic survey are independent of each other, or whether they have been affected by diffusion. Thus, if cultures are interdependent with respect to the characteristics being studied, the actual number of independent observations may be less than the number of cultures the investigator examined. The effect of interdependence on the significance tests of a study might be similar to that of systematic error. The spuriously high number of cases involved in the computation of statistical significance would tend to decrease the probability of chance occurrence indicated by those tests. This probability of chance decreases because the standard errors of measures of association are all inverse functions of the number of cases. In addition, the inclusion of interdependent cases can produce spuriously inflated (or deflated) coefficients of association (Loftin 1972; Erickson 1972); for a review

of this problem in hologeistic research, see Naroll (1970a: 974-89).

The hologeistic method is a way of testing empirically those theories which attempt to explain characteristics of human existence. For such theories to be valid they must apply in all human cultures or in a defined set of such cultures. Hologeistic studies examine a sample of cultures, each of which is considered an example of how people live. These studies use inferential statistics to estimate the validity of the presumption that the observed characteristics reflect the characteristics of human existence in general. Strictly speaking, the use of a sample of cultures for this purpose is questionable unless each of the cultures observed can be considered an independent example of the way people live.

The basic question is whether diffusion is influencing the results of a hologeistic study. At present we are aware of seven operational approaches to this problem, all of which rely on geographical propinquity to measure interdependence (i.e. the smaller the distance between two cultures, the greater the probability that similarities between them are due to diffusion). These are: (1) the bimodal sift method (Naroll 1961: 31-34); (2) the interval sift method (Naroll and D'Andrade 1963: 1058-62); (3) the cluster method (Naroll 1961: 34-38); (4) the matched pair method (Naroll and D'Andrade 1963: 1062-66); (5) the linked pair method (Naroll 1964a and Loftin and Hill n.d.); (6) a modified version of the matched pair method (Driver and Chaney 1970); and (7) a version of the linked pair method with some characteristics of the interval sift method (Murdock and White 1969). Driver and Chaney's method uses linguistic criteria as well as geographical propinquity to measure diffusion; Murdock and White's method, as interpreted by Loftin and Hill, uses a large number of cultural characteristics.

The bimodal sift and interval sift methods attempt to eliminate the influence of diffusion with specialized sampling procedures, and then test statistically to determine whether they succeed. The matched pair method, as well as Driver and Chaney's method, test the hypothesis that diffusion is an adequate explanation of the observed relationships. The cluster test operates on the assumption that if two cultural characteristics tend to diffuse together more often than separately, then the relationship between those variables can be considered relevant to an explanation of human existence in general. It should be noted that the cluster test is not articulated with testing theories by computing associations and measuring their probability of chance occurrence; it constitutes instead a method of theory testing in itself.

Each of these five solutions to Galton's problem depends on imposing further restrictions of sample selection beyond the bibliographic restrictions (see the section on sampling, below). However, these additional restrictions do not require further departures from probability sampling procedures, except possibly in the case of the interval sift method. In the interval sift method we hope to so stratify the sampling universe that each stratum is not influenced by diffusion from any other stratum, and one culture is selected from each stratum. Since the number of cultures varies from stratum to stratum, the probability of a culture being included in the sample is dependent on the number of cultures in the stratum in which it falls.

This problem of the number of cultures per stratum may be solved by (1) testing the hypothesis that the number of cultures per stratum is significantly related to the characteristics of the cultures being studied and (2) if necessary, controlling for the influence of this factor on the results of the study in the manner described in the section on statistical significance. (See Naroll 1970a: 899-902; Greenbaum 1970; Schaefer et al. 1971.) The linked pair test is a measure of spatial auto-correlation; thus it measures the extent to which diffusion can be considered responsible for similarities between neighboring units. Murdock and White's method selects a stratified sample to reduce the influence of diffusion and measures the remaining diffusional effect by the linked pair method.

Each of the associations computed in a hologeistic study should be examined by one of these methods (excluding the cluster test) to determine whether the hypothesis that it has been influenced by diffusion is tenable. *This hypothesis is tenable only if both of the variables have been influenced by diffusion among the cultures in the sample.* If any one of these methods indicates that diffusion has not affected an association, the investigator can conclude that Galton's problem is not a problem for that association in that study.

If the matched pair (or modified matched pair), linked pair (or modified linked pair), or interval sift method provides evidence in favor of the hypothesis that diffusion has affected the results, the linked pair test furnishes a way of estimating the extent to which diffusion can be considered to have affected the results. The linked pair test yields coefficients of association between propinquity and each of the variables; these coefficients make it possible to compute the partial association between the variables with respect to the measure of diffusion as an estimate of what the magnitude of the association would have been if it had not been influenced by diffusion.

These partial associations tend to overestimate the influence of diffusion; the association between propinquity and Variable A will have been produced by a different configuration of data than the association between Variable B and propinquity unless the two variables are perfectly associated. For example the worldwide association between propinquity and Variable A may be entirely due to the operation of diffusion in North America and South America, while that between Variable B and propinquity may be entirely due to the operation of diffusion in Africa and Asia. In such a case diffusion could not be considered to have had a systematic effect on the association between the two variables. These partial associations do not deal with the influence on the results of the significance tests produced by the reduction in the number of independent observations which the inclusion of interdependent units in the sample implies.

Computer programs ORDMAT, PROMO, and RPB (HRAF 1974) can compute the associations (and their significance levels) between propinquity and the variables for the linked pair test. Computer program PARTAU (HRAF 1974) can compute the partial associations between the theoretical variables with respect to the linked pair measure of diffusion, and applies a standard significance test to them.

Of all the solutions to Galton's problem, we have found that the one most generally useful is the linked pair test. This is the way we think the linked pair test should be used: First compute the linked pair association to see whether diffusion has had a significant effect on the results of the study, as discussed above. If there is no significant association, nothing further is needed. But if interdependence is found to be a potential problem, its influence on the association can be partialed out and the significance of the difference between the partial association and the original association can be tested (see Blalock 1972: 405-07, 420-21). If the difference between the two coefficients is not significant, Galton's problem may be considered of no consequence for that relationship. If the difference is significant, the value of the partial association is a better estimate of the actual relationship in the universe being studied than the original association.

However, if the investigator uses the number of cultures (usually symbolized N) which he studied to compute the significance of such partial associations (as program PARTAU does), the probabilities of chance occurrence indicated by these tests will be higher than they should be. We do not know of any statistical method to control for inflated N. Subjectively, the investigator may reduce the number of cases used to compute the significance tests, or instead he may assume that errors increasing significance are offset by other errors reducing significance: (1) by the conservative nature of the linked pair correction for interdependence (which assumes that the auto-correlations were computed from equal configurations of data and does not allow for the tendency of functionally related traits to diffuse together, as does the cluster test); (2) by random errors in data generation and sample selection.

The partialing out of the apparent effect of diffusion may or may not leave a partial coefficient showing an apparently significant main effect. If so, it may be concluded that the original correlation was not an artifact produced by diffusion. If not, then the investigator is wise to use the cluster test. That test measures the tendency of "hits" (cases supporting the theoretical hypothesis) to cluster more than "misses" (cases tending to discredit that hypothesis). If the cluster test shows no greater tendency for hits to cluster than for misses to cluster, then in fact that main effect correlation is indeed a mere artifact of diffusion. This battery of tests then rejects the hypothesis of a functional relationship between the substantive variables in question. But if the cluster test shows that hits do tend to cluster significantly more frequently than misses, then this tendency is direct evidence that the hits do tend to diffuse together, and is direct evidence of functional relationship. And because the cluster test is a test of the diffusion process itself, the problem of defining a diffusion-free unit does not arise. The cluster test assumes that all units are affected by diffusion; it asks only if those manifesting hits are affected more than those manifesting misses. The only unit definition problem—or unit counting problem—relevant to the cluster test is the problem of defining units the same way, consistently, both for hits and for misses.

Sample Selection

Sample selection discusses how to obtain a sample of cultures with the same characteristics as the universe of interest. Has each unit of study in the sampling universe an equal probability of being included in the sample? That is the assumption underlying the use of significance tests to evaluate the probability that an association observed in the sample exists in the sampling universe. However, because most of the units in the universe of all known cultures are not described well enough to be studied, it is not possible to use such strictly probabilistic methods in hologeistic studies.

The salience of this departure from the assumptions underlying significance tests has been demonstrated by a number of studies of systematic sampling bias in hologeistic studies. In a restudy using a dif-
ferent sample, Murdock (1957) has reported that the relationships examined in the earlier study (Murdock 1949), were influenced by systematic sampling error. Chaney (1966) has demonstrated that the sample used by Spiro (1965) was systematically biased; Spiro (1966) has conceded that his sample was biased and that it caused him to conclude falsely that one of his propositions was supported by the data in his earlier study. Further evidence of variation in relationships between variables as a function of the sample examined is provided by Köbben (1952: 140); Chaney and Ruiz Revilla (1969); Tatje, Naroll, and Textor (1970: 657-75); Naroll (1970c); Rohner and Pelto (1970); Chaney (1970); Buckley and Goody (n.d.).

The solution proposed here to this problem of systematic sampling bias is two-fold. First, limit sampling bias to a few well-defined restrictions and otherwise use probability sampling. Second, measure the biases involved in these restrictions and control for their influence on the relationships being examined. Ideally, the sampling universe for hologeistic studies should be all known cultures, primitive and civilized, ancient and modern. Murdock's *Outline of World Cultures* (1972) represents an attempt to list this universe; even here, because of the difficulty of the task rather than any departure from principle, the areas of Australia and New Guinea are incomplete. Murdock's list, combined with Capell's linguistic survey (1962) and Greenway's Australian bibliography (1963), yield a sampling universe that is not significantly different from the universe of all primitive cultures. The greatest bias inherent in the selection of samples from this universe is a bibliographic bias. The variables under study must be described well enough to be examined in each unit. By accepting this bias, we are able to produce a bibliographically defined universe from which probability samples can be selected. It is well to remember that the more stringent the bibliographic restrictions, the smaller the bibliographic universe, and the greater the probability of its being systematically different from the universe of all known cultures.

The bibliographic restrictions may produce differences between the relationships observable in the sample and the actual relationships in the universe of all known cultures. Since some of the units in the sample can be expected to fulfill the bibliographic selection requirements to a greater degree than others, measurements of this variation can be considered estimates of bibliographic error. The hypothesis that bibliographic error has an influence on the results of the study can be tested, and, if necessary, that influence can be controlled in the manner described in the section on statistical significance.

The validity of this procedure for controlling bibliographic sampling error depends on the following assumption: The observed influences of bibliographic quality in the sample must reflect the actual influences of sampling selection bias on the association in question. In other words, bibliographic controls must estimate the degree to which the relationships in the universe of all known cultures have been misrepresented in the sample because of systematic sampling errors produced by the bibliographic restrictions on sampling. The validity of this assumption is doubtful if (1) the relationships between selection bias and the variables are not monotonic or (2) if examination of a different sample (drawn with the same bibliographic restrictions) yields results significantly different from those of the original sample. Demonstrating that the bibliographic restrictions on sample selection produce systematic errors in representation of some specified culture types or culture areas would also cast doubt on this assumption. If by one or more of the strategies described above, the investigator attempts to demonstrate that he is not able to rely on his control procedures for bibliographic error, and if he fails to do so, then he has produced an empirical basis for presuming that his bibliographic bias has been controlled. A conclusive test would require examination of a sample selected without bibliographic restrictions: with such a sample, the bibliographic restrictions would not have been imposed in the first place. For further discussion of bibliographic error and how it may be controlled, see Naroll (1970a: 911ff.).

Additional restrictions on sample selection may be imposed (1) to apply the interval sift solution to Galton's problem; or (2) to satisfy the requirement that all units in the sample are defined in the same manner. These additional restrictions may cause the investigator to deviate from probability sampling procedures in selecting his sample from the bibliographically defined universe. In some cases the errors introduced can be measured and, if necessary, controlled in the manner described in the section on statistical significance. However, in other cases these errors by definition are unmeasurable and require qualification of the definition of the universe being studied—the universe of all known nonindustrialized cultures. (For a more complete discussion of hologeistic sampling methods, see Naroll 1970a: 889-926).

Unit Definition

A unit definition is a statement of the boundaries of the tribal or societal unit of study in a hologeistic survey. What is the "skin" of a society or culture?

Consider the people of the Gyem area of the Gabor district of Gabon. This area is in effect the boundary between the Fang people and the Ntumu people. Both Fang and Ntumu are names of languages. Fang and Ntumu are along a single language chain (linguistic continuum). The Ntumu of Bitam call the Gyem people Fang. The Fang of Mitzik call them Ntumu. The Gyem people themselves say that they do not know whether they are Fang or Ntumu (Fernandez 1963: 8). We have indicated above that Murdock's *Outline of World Cultures* (1972), together with Capell (1962) and Greenway (1963) constitute a satisfactory definition of the universe of all known cultures. The problem with using these lists is that the definition of the cultures in them is not always consistent or explicit.

How may the culture-bearing units that form the basis for hologeistic surveys be defined? There has been no agreement among anthropologists. (See Naroll 1964b; Helm 1968; Barth 1969; Jorgensen 1969; Murdock and White 1969; Naroll 1970a: 721-65; Naroll 1971a.) The definition of the culture-bearing units in a hologeistic study depends on the nature of the theoretical variables being studied. If differences in state organization are of interest, for example, it may be appropriate to use states as units of study; in such a case the universe of all known states rather than that of all known cultures is being studied. A state is here defined as a group of several territorially distinct subgroups, whose leaders assert and wield the exclusive right to declare and conduct warfare.

For such variables as, for example, child-rearing practices, kinship organization, and descent rules, it may be possible to forego exact delineation of cultural boundaries and use as the data point for that culture a particular local community falling within one of the "cultures" listed in Murdock (1972), Capell (1962), or Greenway (1963). One solution to such a unit definition problem relies on language to isolate the parameters of the culture-bearing unit (Naroll 1971a). The most recent and perhaps the most useful summary of the difficulties in using language to define culture-bearing units is that by Hymes (1968). Hymes provides a clear discussion of the two major objections: (1) that speech communities often have fuzzy, vague, indistinct boundaries, which are in practice sometimes impossible to delineate; and (2) that speech communities are often culturally heterogeneous and do not have one homogeneous culture. The difficulty in delineating speech communities may be solved by separating each community from all other communities being studied by a double language boundary: instead of attempting to locate one vague boundary between two speech communities, require that each of the units has at least two such boundaries between it and all other units in the sample studied. If more than one language appears to be spoken in a community, a specific language or dialect should be specified as the speech community being studied—ordinarily the one spoken by the fieldworker's principal informants. For further discussion of this approach to unit definition see Naroll (1971a).

The problem of cultural heterogeneity within speech communities is concerned with the extent to which the description of a single community represents the speech community to which it belongs. It is generally accepted that cultural characteristics usually change from local group to local group—indeed from subculture to subculture and even from household to household (see Murdock 1953: 477-79; Whiting 1954: 526). The major justification for the use of communities as units of study is that nearly all the ethnographic descriptions of cultures are primarily based on information gathered in such units. However, that justification provides no logical basis for presuming that such data are representative of the entire culture. Presumably, the selection bias introduced in this way is measured indirectly by the measures of bibliographic sampling error discussed in the preceding section of this paper.

The most elaborate and precisely-tested attempt at a general theory of ethnic unit definition is Naroll's cultunit concept. Naroll distinguishes four types of ethnic units: a *Hopi* type—a stateless society defined solely by language and community contact; a *Flathead* type—a linguistically homogeneous state; an *Aymara* type—a linguistically defined subordinate, politically subject people in a linguistically heterogeneous state; and an *Inca* type—a linguistically homogeneous group of imperial rulers in a linguistically heterogeneous state (Naroll 1970a: 731-65).

Culture varies temporally as well as spatially. Since the investigator often finds more than one bibliographic source for some of his units, and since these sources may be describing the same unit at different times, it is necessary to choose a specific temporal focus for each unit. Normally this selection will be based on the relative quality of the descriptions of the variables being studied. However, if the theory does not predict that the relationships among the variables will be observable if the cultures are examined at only one point in time, then, in order to test the theory, it will be necessary to select at least two separate time focuses for each unit of study.

The general approach to the problem of unit definition advocated here may be described as follows: Ordinarily, the language may be used as a sampling unit. For each sampling unit, a focal community is to be chosen (together with one or more focal points in time). The double language boundary method may then be used to ensure that no two focal communities in the sample speak mutually intelligible dialects—deciding all doubts and questions in favor of the hypothesis of intelligibility. If the natural unit of study is wider than a community—for example a state or a language group—that unit should be defined from the point of view of the focal community. If the wider unit is an entire language group, the double boundary method will have to be used to make sure that no two such groups in the sample overlap. This method permits the language groups to have fuzzy, vague, and indeterminate boundaries.

Data Accuracy

Data accuracy is concerned with errors which may be introduced into hologeistic studies by informants, reporters, and comparativists. The data in hologeistic surveys may be defined as the results of the measures of the variables which are used to compute the associations. These measurements are based on reports of observations of the units being studied. There are, then, three general sources which may produce inaccuracies in hologeistic data: (1) Informant error—the people from whom the information was gained may not have known their own culture accurately. (2) Reporter error—the person writing the report on the culture may be inaccurate in his interpretations of what the informants told him about the culture; he may not have gathered enough of the available information for an accurate report; and he may not report all the relevant information that he *has* gathered. Or, most important of all, his informants may have deliberately deceived him. (If they deliberately deceived him, *they* were making no mistake; his mistake was to believe them, to fail to check them and thus detect the error and the practice of deception.) (3) Comparativist error—hologeistic investigators may be inaccurate in interpreting the observers' reports and may indicate that the reports show presence of the variables of interest when those variables are in fact absent.

The accuracy of hologeistic data has been seriously questioned on the basis of errors arising from all three of these sources (Webb et al. 1966; Haas 1968: 71n; Naroll 1970a: 928-30; Rummel 1970; Janda 1970; Haekel 1970; Burrowes 1973). It has been demonstrated that the results of some hologeistic studies are at least partially explainable as artifacts caused by inaccurate data (compare Gilbert 1971; Denton and Oksanen 1972); in some cases, data inaccuracy itself constitutes a sufficient and plausible explanation for some of the associations (Naroll 1962: 146-51; Rohner, Dewalt, and Ness n.d.).

To guard against the real possibility that inaccuracy of data is influencing the results of a hologeistic study, the control factor method of data quality control can be used. This method rests on the assumption that there is variation in the degree of accuracy of hologeistic data, and that this very variation is related to characteristics of the process by which the data are generated. A control factor can be any characteristic of the data generation process which is thought to be related to the accuracy of the data. Did the reporter participate in the activities he describes? How many informants provided information on the subject? How were they selected? Did the reporter obtain his information directly from people who had observed the phenomena, or did he obtain it through intermediaries? Control factors should be measured for each of the variables in each of the units of study and should deal with possible errors from all three of the major categories of sources which may produce data inaccuracy. The hypothesis that the data on a variable are inaccurate may be examined by computing associations between that variable and the control factors suspected of being related to its accuracy. If the associations are not significantly different from zero, a presumption is created that the data on that variable are not systematically distorted by errors in data generation; and that therefore associations between that variable and other variables are not artifacts of data inaccuracy. Computer programs ORDMAT, PROMO, and RPB (HRAF 1974) can perform these computations. Computing associations will not measure random errors in data generation, but since random errors tend to lower associations, we need not be overly concerned about them. It may be argued that if this residual random error is associated with another variable (or the error in its measurement) the association between the two substantive variables may be spuriously inflated. However, spurious inflation could occur only in the presence of some undetected systematic error; in such a case the error would not actually be random.

The fact that control factors are associated with the data does not necessarily imply that those data are inaccurate. For example, an association between witchcraft attribution and length of time the fieldworker spent collecting data may indicate: (1) that fieldworkers who spend more time collecting data tend to be more accurate in learning about witchcraft; or (2) that fieldworkers who spend more time collecting data tend to exaggerate the importance of craft attribution are more interesting, and therefore

witchcraft; or (3) that cultures with much witch-encourage fieldworkers to study them longer. The association, like any other, needs to be explained. If the investigator is able to rule out plausible alternative explanations of the associations between the control factors and the variables—if he can provide evidence that people in cultures high in witchcraft attribution are reluctant to talk about witchcraft with fieldworkers they do not know well, and that therefore such cultures are unattractive to fieldworkers—and if he can assume that at least *some* of his data are really accurate, then he can treat those associations as measures of systematic error and, if necessary, control for influences on his results in the manner described in the section on statistical significance. Causal analysis of the associations between theoretical variables and control factors may also be helpful in explaining them (see the section on causal analysis, below).

Five control factors are now known to be especially useful, to be especially sensitive to systematic error. (Data on all five of these are to be found in the new HRAF Probability Sample Files; see the section on the HRAF Probability Sample, below.) These five factors are given by the answers to the following five questions: (1) How long did our ethnographer live among the people he describes? (2) How well does he claim to know their native language—the language they speak among themselves at home? (3) Does our ethnographer describe the life of the people as it was lived while he was there with them, or does he instead describe life as it was previously lived some years or decades earlier, from the memory of elderly informants? (4) What sorts of systematic checks on native statements did our ethnographer use? Did he systematically ask a number of informants the same questions to see if their answers agree? Did he use psychological tests? Did he take a formal census or a household sample survey? (5) How many earlier publications by earlier ethnographers describing these same people did our ethnographer use and cite?

The extent to which the control factor method solves the problem of data accuracy in a hologeistic study is directly related to the extent to which all plausible sources of systematic error have been examined by it. Additional strategies for detecting and controlling comparativist error will be discussed in the section on conceptualization, classification, and coding below. For further discussion of data accuracy in hologeistic studies and the control factor method see Naroll (1962, 1970a: 927-45); Rummel (1970).

Regional Variation

Regional variation is concerned with variation among major geographical regions. The worldwide associations produced by a hologeistic study do not reflect possible variations in the magnitude of these associations among the major geographical regions; they therefore may not be representative of the actual relationships in each of those regions. Several measures of association have varied widely when computed by region. In failing to examine this possibility, some hologeistic investigators have erroneously interpreted their results as reflecting worldwide tendencies (Sawyer and LeVine 1966: 719-27; Driver and Schuessler 1967: 336-47; Bourguignon and Greenbaum 1968; Chaney and Ruiz Re-villa 1969: 618-25).

To see if the correlation is truly worldwide, the investigator should recompute associations separately for each geographical region and determine if any of them manifests significant variation among the regions. Computer program PARTAU (HRAF 1974) can perform the regional recomputations of the associations and their significance levels. The significance of variations in the magnitude of an association among the regions may be determined by testing the significance of the difference between the largest and smallest regional associations. If that difference is not significant, the association based on all the units in the sample may be considered to reflect a worldwide tendency. Such a worldwide tendency would seem especially clear if all the associations in every region not only have the same sign but also range upward in absolute value from .20 (ø, tau b, or r) or .30 (gamma, Yule's Q).

Significant regional variation may indicate that the theory in question omits some relevant factors. However, it is possible that the regional variations could reasonably be explained in terms of the methodological variables involved in the hologeistic study (see the section on deviant cases, below). This explanation can be examined independently in each region by considering each region as a separate sample and testing and, if necessary, controlling for sampling bias, errors in data generation and Galton's problem. As far as we know, this has as yet never been done in any hologeistic study.

Conceptualization, Classification, and Coding

This section is concerned with the comparability of phenomena among cultures—with the translation of written reports on the units of study into statistics. Defining the theoretical concepts in such a way that they will be useful in explaining characteristics of human existence in all cultures is a basic problem in hologeistic research. The approach advocated here distinguishes between *emic, etic,* and *theoric* concepts; it is derived from linguistics (Goodenough 1970: chap. 4; Naroll 1971c).

As Goodenough (1956: 37) has pointed out, the definition of a variable may differ, depending on whether it is to be used in explaining the characteristics of one particular culture or in explaining some characteristics of human existence in all cultures. In an explanation of Norwegian culture, the concept "cannibalism" could be defined as eating human flesh and approving of the pratice. It involves two distinctions: eating or not eating human flesh and approving or not approving of the practice; these distinctions are sufficient to describe cannibalism as it relates to the rest of Norwegian culture, and would be an *emic* definition of cannibalism. However, when a large number of cultures are considered, additional distinctions must be examined if the concept is to be helpful in explaining the relationships between cannibalism and the rest of the culture for *all* of the cultures being studied. For example in Fiji (ca. 1850), it was important to distinguish whom you ate (it being a great triumph to eat your enemies). In other cultures, human flesh may be eaten to gain some quality of the victim: eat a brave man's heart to gain courage; eat a baby to gain youth. Although we do not know for sure, we suppose that in the Mbau language of Fiji, there is a word that means "eating the flesh of one's enemy"; we likewise suppose that in some languages there is a word that means specifically "eating a brave man's heart to gain courage"; again, we suppose that in other languages there is a word that means "to eat a baby to gain youth". If in fact such distinctions are made in any human language, then each of them is an *etic* concept. (At this writing, color terms and kinship terms are the only domains of meaning known to us where thorough etic analysis has been worldwide.) Etic concepts are abstractions generated by social scientists from the analysis of emic definitions.

In order to define an emic concept adequately, it is necessary to be aware of all its relevant etic components. The set of all the distinctions that are made in any culture concerning the significance of eating human flesh is equivalent to the universe of etic concepts relevant to the definition of all emic concepts of cannibalism. Each of these etic concepts describes a distinction which is relevant to explaining the relationships between consuming human flesh and other aspects of existence in at least one culture. Surprisingly enough, the etic universe needed to define all emic concepts of a specific aspect of existence may be rather small. Only eight etic distinctions describe all emic definitions of kinships terms, for example (Goodenough 1970: chap. 4).

This discussion of emic and etic concepts has been aimed at developing comparability among diverse systems of classifications of phenomena in different cultures. The great danger in making such comparisons is in attempting to use the emic concepts of one culture to explain characteristics of existence in another. For example early investigators were distressed to learn that Hawaiians did not know their own parents; they called all their uncles *father* and all their aunts *mother*. By applying etic analysis to Hawaiian kin terms, we see that in one sense this is true, but that in another sense it is absurd. The Hawaiians distinguish relatives by sex of alter (the relative being referred to) and by generation, but not by collaterality. Hawaiian has no words for father, mother, uncle, or aunt as such. Their kin term system is functional in their extended bilateral households. The English kin term system is functional in our nuclear family households. Each system teaches young children in the prevalent household system to classify relatives according to their social roles in the life of the child.

When anthropologists perceived how kin term systems operated, they predicted that these kin systems would be related to social structure: to rules of descent and residence. In order to test this prediction of the relationship between kin terms and social structure, kin term systems were classified according to one crucial diagnostic feature: the term a male used to refer to his female cross-cousins (see Murdock 1949). This term was compared with the terms used to refer to sisters, aunts, nieces, and female parallel cousins. We have, for example, the Eskimo type, in which female cross-cousins are referred to by the same term as female parallel cousins, but not by the same terms as sisters, aunts and nieces;[2] we have the Hawaiian type, in which female cross-cousins are referred to by the same term as sisters and parallel cousins, but not by the same terms as aunts and nieces; we have the Iroquois type, in which female cross-cousins are referred to by different terms from all other female relatives, and so on.

Each of these types is a *theoric* concept (or theoretical variable) and is defined in terms of a specific set of etic concepts. The *usefulness* of a theoric concept is established by demonstrating that it is related to other variables in explaining some universal characteristics of human existence.

These theoric kin term concepts have demonstrated their usefulness as variables in the explana-

tion of cross-cultural variation in kinship terminology (see Naroll 1970b: 1238-40).

The anthropologists who developed these theoric concepts began their theoric work with a clear grasp of both the emics and the etics of kinship terminology. They understood the native kin categories from the native viewpoint for scores of kin term systems. They analyzed each in terms of etic kinship concepts and generated useful variables (theoric concepts).

In summary, emic concepts are those used in a specific culture by the natives thereof to classify a given semantic domain. Etic concepts are those used by social scientists to analyze the conceptual distinctions made by emic systems. There are hundreds of different kinds of kin terms, but all can be defined in terms of the eight etic concepts listed by Goodenough (1970). Theoric concepts are those used by social scientists to explain variations in human cultures.

Among the variations to be explained are variations in emic systems. If we assume that a science of human behavior is possible, we must assume that much variation in emic systems is related as cause or effect to variation in other aspects of human existence. Consequently, if we do not understand the range of variation of emic systems, we have not defined our theoretical problems adequately. Development of an etic universe is the most parsimonious way of defining and describing the range of variation of emic systems. But that development is not enough. There is no reason to suppose that the etic concepts are likely to be powerful otherwise in constructing theories. The development of useful theoric concepts is a necessary step in generating sufficient explanations of characteristics of human existence. Much light on this development has been shed by papers on conceptualization in hologeistic studies (see Ford 1967; Moore 1969; Cohen and Naroll 1970; Tatje 1970; Ember 1970; LeBar 1970).

A theory which seeks to explain some characteristics of human existence may be viewed as a set of variables (theoric concepts), combined with statements of the nature of the relationships among those variables. Each of the variables may be considered as a category which encompasses some specified set of phenomena. In a hologeistic survey, the universe of phenomena studied is defined by the written reports on all the cultures in the sample—what reporters say about the cultures—rather than by the cultures themselves. (The problem of inconsistencies between what the reporters say and the actual characteristics of the cultures is dealt with in the section on data accuracy, above.)

The variables in a hologeistic study, then, must be defined so that they can be measured by examining the reports on the units of study. Such definitions are descriptions of indicators (or coding rules), which provide information about the variables. If the reports contain quantified data (e.g. average rainfall, census reports) on the variables of interest, the coding rules are easy to design. However, hologeistic investigators are often forced to deal with more impressionistic statements about their variables of interest.

Where the data are not quantified in the reports, we suggest that the investigator develop a set of coding rules to yield a ranking of the units of study on the variables of interest. A set of coding rules developed for the War, Stress, and Culture study (Naroll 1969) to measure frequency of witchcraft attribution provides an illustrative example: One reporter says that among the Kapauku, witchcraft is the most common form of revenge against an enemy of another political unit; another reports that some bands among the Hottentot practice witchcraft openly, others secretly. A comparison of these two statements fails to provide convincing evidence that the true frequency of witchcraft attribution among the Kapauku is actually greater than that among the Hottentot. However, there is a frequency statement made about the Kapauku, namely that certain kinds of witchcraft are more "common"; but none about the Hottentot. It is, then, possible that among the Hottentot all sorts of witchcraft are rare; it is not possible among the Kapauku—according to the reports at hand. For this variable, the task was to rank the reports in terms of degree of commitment of the reporter about the relative frequency of witchcraft attribution.

The investigator first ranked the reports intuitively and then analyzed that intuitive ranking to identify the elements of the reports that had influenced the rank decisions. The following set of coding rules resulted:

Group I: All deaths and illnesses are believed by the natives to be results of witchcraft.

Group II: All deaths are believed by the natives to be the results of witchcraft.

Group III: All illnesses are believed by the natives to be the results of witchcraft. (Illness attributions ranked after death attributions because presumably the latter is more infuriating to survivors. On the other hand, one might have argued for the reverse order, on the grounds that illnesses are presumably more frequent than deaths.)

Group IV: All deaths except those due to old age are believed to be the result of witchcraft.

Group V: All deaths except those due to warfare are believed to be the results of witchcraft.

Group VI: All deaths except those due to old age and warfare are believed to be the results of witchcraft.

Group VII: Words are used by the reporter implying that in general witchcraft attributions are "common" or "not infrequent" (might be broken down into two groups).

Group VIII: Words are used implying that in certain specified circumstances witchcraft attributions are "common" or "not infrequent" (might be broken down into two groups).

Group IX: Witchcraft is alluded to, without any commitment by the reporter about its frequency or rarity. N.B. Where words are used implying that witchcraft attribution is rare, except in specified circumstances, such language implies that in the specified circumstances the attribution is not infrequent (i.e. Group VIII).

Group X: Witchcraft attribution is stated to be uncommon, or words to that effect (adjective unmodified by intensive adverb).

Group XI: Witchcraft attribution is stated to be extremely uncommon (adjective modified by intensive adverb).

Group XII: Witchcraft attribution is denied by the reporter.

The coding rules and the reports for each unit of study were then given to coders who had no knowledge of the theory being tested. By examining the reporters' statements, the coders (1) determined which group each unit of study was to be considered a member of and (2) placed each unit in the lowest numbered group for which the reporter had made the necessary statements. This process produced an ordinal measure of the frequency of witchcraft attribution for the units in the sample.

The operational definitions of the variables, then, are the coding rules *as interpreted by the coders*. The immediate question concerns the reliability of the measurement process. Can we assume that if different coders applied the same coding rules to the same reports, they would generate the same data? If not, it must be concluded that the data reflect, at least in part, the characteristics of the coders rather than simply the theoretical variables. Explicit coding rules reduce coding error—the coders are less likely to be able to exercise their own judgment in measuring the variables. However, it must be remembered that the coding rules constitute, in effect, the bibliographic restrictions on sample selection. If they are too restrictive, it may not be possible to obtain an adequate sample of cultures, one for which the available information is sufficient to allow for measurement of the variables.

The solution advocated here for the problem of coding reliability is (1) to make the coding rules as explicit as possible, given the nature of the data base and (2) to measure the reliability of the coding process and assess the extent to which the coding rules are responsible for the data generated. The reliability of the coding process can be estimated by having two or more coders measure the same variables from the same materials, according to the same coding rules. At least one of the coders should be completely naive—by naive here is meant entirely ignorant of the purposes of the study, of the theory being tested. The coders must not discuss the codings with each other at all until a third person has compared their work; nor must either coder know the codings of the other. Intercoder reliability may be determined by measuring the extent to which the coders produce equivalent data with an appropriate measure of association: for example Kendall's coefficient of concordance (Siegel 1956: 229-38). These intercoder reliability coefficients may be interpreted as the maximum extent to which the coding rules may be considered to constitute the operational definitions of the variables. Since hologeistic studies do not seek to measure the characteristics of the coders in order to test theories, the reliability coefficients should be high, so that it is plausible to assume that the data are relatively free of coder bias. We feel that if the reliability coefficients are less than 0.80, the coding rules are unsatisfactory and should be refined. The effectiveness of intercoder reliability coefficients for measuring coder error in the data is directly related to the number of independent coders used in the study and the extent to which they form a heterogeneous population.

We also need to be concerned about the validity of the data generated. Do those data actually reflect the characteristics of the theoretical variables in the units of study? If the measures of association support the relationships predicted by the theory, there is reason to have some confidence in the validity of the data. A stronger presumption of validity may be created by comparing the data produced by different groups of coders, using different coding rules to measure the variables (see Campbell and Fiske 1959). The strongest possible presumption in favor of the validity of the data is created when different researchers examine the same theoretical variables in different samples, using different coding rules, and find similar relationships among the variables. While reliability *does not* imply validity, validity *does* imply reliability—reliability is a necessary, but not sufficient, condition for validity.

It should be stressed that the variables examined in a hologeistic study are operationally defined according to the phenomena by which they were measured; an assertion that those variables represent anything else must be evaluated on the basis of the strength of the presumption that the data are valid

measures of the variables. A problem occurs when some, but not all, of the phenomena that define the variables can be measured from the reports on the units of study. For example: anxiety is *defined* by suicide frequency and frequency of mental illness, *but operationally defined only by suicide frequency*; and stress is *defined* by population density and difficulty in obtaining food, *but operationally defined only by population density*. In a hologeistic study, then, it is questionable whether the assertion that a significant association between those two variables, *as they were operationally defined*, is interpretable as indicating that there is a significant association between mental illness frequency and difficulty in obtaining food. For further discussion of strategies for dealing with the problems of reliability and validity see Cronbach and Meehl (1955); Campbell and Fiske (1959); Baggaley (1964: 60-90).

For further discussion of the problems involved in conceptualization, classification, and coding in various contexts, see Bendix (1963); Ford (1967); Moore (1969); Berry (1969); Cohen and Naroll (1970); Tatje (1970); Ember (1970); LeBar (1970); Long (1970); Osgood (1971); Chaney (1971); Durbin (1972); Hermann (1972); Otterbein (1972); and Thomas and Weigert (1972).

Data Paucity

The problem of data paucity arises when reports on the units of study do not contain adequate direct information on the variables of interest. Hologeistic tests of theory depend on these reports to yield the data necessary for measuring the theoretical variables. When topical coverage of these reports is uneven, it is not possible to test explanations of some characteristics of human existence in enough cultures to form an adequate sample.

Where a variable cannot be measured directly, it must be measured indirectly (Webb et al. 1966; Cohen and Naroll 1970). An indirect measure (or proxy) may be defined as a measurement of some variable which is associated with the variable of interest. While it may not be possible to measure the variable of interest directly, the characteristics of that variable may be inferred from measurements of the proxy, on the basis of its association with the variable of interest.

It is necessary to establish that the proxy is, in fact, associated with the variable of interest—that the proxy is valid as a measure of the variable of interest. A presumption in favor of the validity of the proxy may be established by providing evidence that it is significantly associated with the variable of interest in some specified manner; better still, by providing evidence that the association between the proxy and the variable of interest can be reasonably estimated as being of some specific magnitude and direction.

Naroll (1969) shows how he dealt with a presumption that a proxy was associated in some specified manner with a variable of interest—suicide frequency. Nearly all the units in Naroll's study lacked adequate data on suicide rates. The proxy was the amount of attention given to suicide by the reporter, as measured by the percentage of words about suicide in the report. Naroll found that the proxy was highly associated with divorce rules, marriage negotiation rules, drunken brawling, warfare, homicide frequency, and wifebeating. The most reasonable and parsimonious explanation of this pattern of association was that more attention was given to suicide where there was more suicide to attract attention. Thus, in the absence of plausible alternative explanations of the associations, it is reasonable to assume that the proxy has a significant positive association with the variable of interest.

Hologeistic studies yield coefficients of association between variables. These associations are estimates of the reliability of measuring one variable indirectly through measurement of the other variable. Bacon, Barry, and Child (1965) found an association between instrumental dependence in adulthood and frequency of drunkenness. Thus, frequency of drunkenness, for example, may be used as a proxy of instrumental dependence.

The validity of this procedure relies on the assumption that Bacon, Barry, and Child's association reflects an actual association in the universe of cultures studied and may be evaluated by examining their methods. The ingenuity of researchers in developing and validating proxies is a significant determinant of what variables can or cannot be measured with the available information. Developing and validating proxies has the effect of increasing the applicability of hologeistic method and reducing the bibliographic restrictions on sample selection.

The ideal solution to the problem of data paucity in the literature would be to collect whatever data are lacking in the field. There have been some efforts in this direction (Whiting et al. 1963; Minturn and Lambert 1964; Campbell and LeVine 1970). While these efforts have been difficult to carry out and have been limited to very small numbers of cases, we can look to improvements in methodology from them. Although such efforts help, they cannot be expected to solve the problem; most of the culture areas in the universe of all known culture areas no longer exist and, therefore, cannot be re-examined.

Causal Analysis

This section is concerned with whether the results of a hologeistic study reflect specific causal relationships among the variables involved. Theoretical explanations of characteristics of human existence often predict that a particular pattern of association will occur among the variables because these variables are causally related in some specified manner. In such a prediction, variable A is defined as a cause of variable B if, and only if, producing a change in the value of variable A (assuming that such a change can be produced at will) thereby produces a change in the value of variable B. (For further discussion of this concept of causality, see Köbben 1970: 89-98.) If the predicted pattern of relationships among the variables is not found in a hologeistic study, it may be concluded that the hypothesized causal relationships do not exist. If the predicted pattern of relationships is found, a presumption in favor of the existence of the hypothesized causal relationships is created.

There will still be, of course, plausible alternatives to the hypothesized causal explanation of the pattern of relationships. For example a significant association between variable A and variable B may occur because: A causes B; B causes A; or both variables have been influenced by some other variable or variables. The salience of these alternative explanations is demonstrated by the fact that the causal explanations of the association yielded by some hologeistic studies have been demonstrated to be false. Young (1962), for example, showed that the associations on which Whiting, Kluckhohn, and Anthony (1958) based their explanations of initiation rites were attributable to the influence of another variable. While it is never possible to rule out *all* possible alternatives to a hypothesized causal explanation empirically, there are statistical techniques by which *some* of those alternatives can be demonstrated to be less plausible than the explanation posited by the theory. Our reasoning is: the more rival explanations that become less plausible than the main theory, the stronger the presumption that the hypothesized causal relationships do, in fact, exist.

These statistical techniques discriminate between groups of mathematically possible causal explanations of the relationships among the variables on the basis of their relative plausibility; they analyze the relationships among the association coefficients between all possible pairs of variables (see Rozelle and Campbell 1969; Griffiths n.d.). If the hypothesized causal explanation falls within the group that has been determined to be most plausible, a strong presumption is created in favor of its validity. If some or all of the other possible explanations can be ruled out on logical grounds, an even stronger pre-

137

sumption is created for the validity of the theoretical explanation—for example if agricultural techniques are associated with average rainfall, it is reasonable to reject the hypothesis that agricultural techniques are a cause of average rainfall. If the hypothesized explanation does not fall in the most plausible group of explanations and it is impossible to rule out *all* the explanations in the more plausible groups, then the hypothesized explanation is untenable. Examination of the explanations demonstrated to be more plausible than the hypothesized explanation may be very useful in correcting the theory, but such an altered theory cannot be considered to have been tested by the hologeistic study that prompted its generation; the probability of obtaining some specific pattern of relationships in a hologeistic study, after the relationships have been obtained from it, is equal to one. The new theory must be tested with different data, preferably from a different sample. Statistical methods of causal analysis can deal only with one-way causality; if A is a cause of B and B is a cause of A, the algebraic sum of the two relationships will be dealt with.

Statistical techniques of causal analysis can usefully be divided into two categories: synchronic, if they require data from one point in time, or diachronic, if they require data from two or more points in time. Synchronic techniques can be applied in any situation where there are at least three variables involved. Boudon (1970) has provided us with a powerful method of synchronic causal analysis which may be applied when parametric measures of association have been used (see also Land 1969; Tanter 1970). Techniques of synchronic causal analysis, whether for parametric or nonparametric measures of association, are discussed in Blalock (1964); Boudon, Degenne, and Isambert (1967); Naroll (1970a: 108-10); Griffiths (n.d.).

A convenient tool for synchronic causal analysis is HRAFLIB Program TRIAD (HRAF 1974), the work of Donald Griffiths. The program deals with the causal relationships among three variables—no more, no less. There are twelve logically possible patterns of causal analysis among three variables. By studying the pattern of intercorrelations, the program reduces these possible patterns considerably. In some circumstances, it can pinpoint a single one of the twelve possibilities as the one most consistent with the correlation pattern. In other circumstances, it may report that none of the twelve possibilities are plausible; such a report implies that some fourth variable needs to be considered. Most commonly, the program singles out a group of three of the twelve possibilities; each of these three is reported as equally consistent with the correlation pattern; but the other nine logi-

cal possibilities are dismissed as less consistent with the correlation pattern. Program TRIAD also states the confidence with which it reaches its conclusions. All of its conclusions, however, depend upon the assumption that any fourth (outside) variable creates results completely unrelated to that created by any inside variable (Blalock 1964: 46). They depend further upon the assumption that any outside variable is not simultaneously affecting more than one inside variable (Blalock 1964: 48). Given these restrictions, Program TRIAD is useful in narrowing down the possible causal relationships among three variables.

Diachronic techniques of causal analysis are more powerful than synchronic techniques and may be applied whenever there are two or more variables. Their main disadvantage is that they require data on the units of study for at least two points in time, restricting the sample selection bibliographically. Their main advantage is clear enough. Suppose variable A is not merely *correlated* with variable B but usually precedes it (changes first). Clearly such a state of affairs supports the hypothesis that A is cause and B is effect more strongly than mere correlation would. True, as economists have long known, lagged correlations may simply reflect stages in a single underlying process (see Croxton and Cowden 1955: 579-85, for example). But there are far fewer underlying processes in this world than there are raw variables. A rival hypothesis of an unknown (lurking), underlying process is inherently far less plausible than a rival hypothesis of an unknown, underlying, simple variable. In other words, the verification of sequence alongside of correlation reduces the lurking variable problem to the lurking process problem. Such a reduction is substantial. It is worth considerable trouble and expense. In practice, for most social science hypotheses, it constitutes the strongest test open to an investigator.

The potential power of diachronic analysis may be illustrated from some doctoral dissertation research at the State University of New York at Buffalo. In a preliminary, prize-winning paper, Divale (1974) set forth a theory of the origin of matrilocal residence. That theory saw patrilocal residence as the normal type among primitive peoples. It postulated matrilocal residence as a special adjustment to migration: matrilocal residence breaks up fraternal interest groups and thus discourages internal warfare (feuding). Peoples who have recently migrated into new territories commonly have serious external war problems with the earlier inhabitants. Matrilocal residence thus is seen as adaptive; it enables the new migrants to concentrate their military attention on their external enemies. Divale (1974) tested this theory with simple correlations.

Now, in current work on his yet unfinished doctoral thesis, Divale has done ethnohistorical studies seeking to date the entry into their present territory of each society in his holocultural sample. Divale's theory involves a whole chain or sequence of changes —a process. His theory sees migration by a patrilocal, patrilineal people leading to a cycle of changes in their kinship systems: (1) first to uxorilocal-patrilineal; (2) next to uxorilocal-bilateral; (3) then to matrilocal-matrilineal; (4) then to avunculocal-matrilineal, and (5) finally, back to patrilineal-patrilocal. His theory predicts that on the average, patrilocal-patrilineal peoples would be longest in their present homes, next avunculocal-matrilineal, and so on. His preliminary results seem to confirm these expectations. These techniques of diachronic analysis are discussed in Pelz and Andrews (1964) and in Rozelle and Campbell (1969); while the authors discuss diachronic techniques only in terms of parametric data, these thechniques can also be used with nonparametric data, even though less efficiently.

The techniques of causal analysis discussed above cannot deal with the possibility that some unconsidered, unmeasured variable has influenced the pattern of associations. It must be assumed that the factors not included in the causal analysis—random errors, for example—are not producing changes in the pattern of the coefficients of association. The danger of this assumption has been demonstrated by Barrett and Franke (1970); they showed that a previous causal explanation of rates of aggressive and inhibitive deaths, which was supported by diachronic causal analysis, was wrong; not all of the relevant variables had been examined. Causal analysis can never demonstrate causality. It can only create a basis for presuming that some causal relationships exist; that presumption is always subject to disproof on the basis of further evidence.

Deviant Cases

A deviant case is a unit of study which does not conform to the theoretically predicted relationships among the variables. This section is concerned with how such deviant cases may be explained. For a theory to constitute a sufficient explanation of some characteristics of human existence, it must explain the variations in value of its variables among the units of study. Theoretical explanations of these variations are generally in the form of statements such as: variable B, slavery, manifests a specific pattern of variation because variable A, availability of resources, manifests a specific pattern of variation. The variation in some of the variables is explained by varia-

tion in other variables. In a hologeistic study, the extent to which a theory explains the variations of its variables is measured by computing tau coefficients of association; these describe the relationships among the variables. Squaring each of these coefficients of association roughly estimates the percentage of variation of one variable that may reasonably be explained by variation of the other variable. When a number of variables are involved, factor analysis can determine the extent to which the variables change as a result of their interrelationships (Baggaley 1964: 91-168).

If a hologeistic study yields results which indicate that the theory does not explain all of the variation of the variables, there must have been some cultures which did not manifest the predicted theoretical relationships. By printing out the name of each culture in the appropriate cell, computer program ORDMAT (HRAF 1974) can reproduce the ordinal matrix from which each coefficient of association was computed, making it easy to determine which cases deviate from the predicted relationships. If a sufficient explanation is desired, these deviant cases must be accounted for. Köbben (1967) discusses how deviant cases can occur in hologeistic studies.

Can deviant cases be explained in terms of the methodological variables —sampling error, errors in data generation, cultural diffusion, and random error? If an investigator wishes to explain deviant cases arising from a test of Niebor's (1910) hypothesis, "Where slavery, there open resources," the absolute value of the difference of each unit's ratings may be computed. The hypothesis predicts that the ratings on the two variables will be equal for each unit. Thus the computations are a measure of the extent to which each unit is responsible for the failure of the theory to explain the variation of the variables. This measure can be labeled "deviance," and if its variation can be reasonably explained by variation in the methodological variables, we can conclude that the hypothesis provides an adequate explanation of the variation of its variables—that the deviant cases could be reasonably explained as artifacts produced by the method of study. In evaluating whether the deviance is accounted for, multivariate analysis of the relationships among the methodological variables and deviance would be helpful.

If the deviant cases cannot be reasonably explained in terms of the methodological variables, the theory does not deal with *all* of the factors which are relevant to a *sufficient* explanation of the characteristics of human existence which it purports to explain. The investigator then selects particular deviant cases for further study—particular societies where slavery is present, but open resources are absent, or, contrariwise, particular societies where slavery is absent but open resources are present. The ethnographic literature on each deviant case is studied thoroughly, seeking for any one of the six following possible explanations for the discrepancy:

(1) The investigator seeks for indications of multicausality (the Boolean conjunction). Do open resources make for slavery only if there is also some other condition present?

(2) He seeks for indications of parallel causality (the Boolean disjunction). Can slavery alternatively be brought about by some other condition unrelated to open resources?

(3) He seeks for functional equivalents of slavery. Is there some other mechanism which supplies an alternate response to open resources?

(4) He seeks for an intervening variable. Do open resources lead to slavery only by way of some third intervening variable (for example, warfare) which would prevent the expected result when interfered with?

(5) He seeks for signs of cultural lag. Have open resources been so recently introduced that they have not yet had time to produce slavery as their effect? Perhaps several generations are required.

(6) He seeks for some unusual individual leader. Has some charismatic person, who opposes slavery for personal emotional reasons, interfered with the normal or usual cause-effect relationship in the situation?

Any one of these questions, positively answered, supplies in effect a revised theory. However, the revised theory cannot be considered to have been tested by the study that prompted its generation. It must be tested by a new, independent hologeistic study.

The HRAF Probability Sample Files (PSF)

The Human Relations Area Files Probability Sample Files program is an attempt to make the task of the hologeistic theory tester much easier. It offers a solution to most of the problems of hologeistic method that we have discussed here.

The PSF sample itself is a probability sample with a clearly defined bibliographic bias; see Naroll (1967) for details. Each unit in the PSF has been focused in time and space; much of the focusing data are given in Schaefer (1973), and the remainder are scheduled to be published by HRAF in its forthcoming manual on the use of the PSF.

To apply the linked pair test for interdependence as a solution to Galton's problem interdependence alignments have been published by Schaefer (1969) and Loftin and Hill (n.d.).

Data quality control factor information on the sources used in the Probability Sample Files are given in the special blue-sheet HABS analyses of sources, filed in Rubric No. 111 of each set of the Probability Sample Files.

The HRAFLIB (HRAF 1974) computer program library (including programs ORDMAT, MONTE, PARTAU, PROMO, RPB, and TRIAD) computes four standard measures of association, tests their individual significance, tests their group significance, performs the linked pair test for interdependence, uses control factor codings to test for systematic error, and measures partial correlations to allow for the biases detected by the control tests. Intercorrelation matrices of three variables are examined by the computer and plausible causal hypotheses are distinguished from implausible ones.

HRAF is exploring the possibility of making its computer program library widely available. Three options of use are planned: (1) User sends coding sheets to HRAF, and HRAF punches IBM cards and processes them through its program library; (2) user furnishes prepunched IBM cards for processing; or (3) user or his computing center acquires copies of HRAF programs and adapts them to the local computer. For information on the current status of these plans, write HRAF, P.O. Box 2054, Y.S., New Haven, CT 06520. HRAF is also compiling a computer archive of standard cross-cultural codings, to use with this program library. To make use of the HRAF Probability Sample Files, visit a set of the paper files at any one of the following institutions:

City University of New York
Cornell University (Ithaca)
École Pratique des Hautes Études (Paris)
Federal City College (Washington, D.C.)
Indiana University (Bloomington)
Kyoto University
Princeton University
Southern Illinois University (Carbondale)
State University of New York at Buffalo
University of Chicago
University of Colorado (Boulder)
University of Illinois (Urbana)
University of Iowa (Iowa City)
University of Massachusetts (Boston)
University of Michigan (Ann Arbor)
University of North Carolina (Chapel Hill)
University of Pennsylvania (Philadelphia)
University of Pittsburgh
University of So. California (Los Angeles)
University of Texas (Austin)
University of Utah (Salt Lake City)
University of Washington (Seattle)
Yale University (New Haven)

The Contribution of Harold E. Driver to Hologeistic Method

Driver has generally confined his attention to the statistical analysis of the culture of North American Indians. His only important hologeistic study was the factor analysis of the World Ethnographic Sample, which he did with Schuessler (Driver and Schuessler 1967). Nevertheless, the impact of his work on hologeistic studies has been profound. He has made contributions of striking importance to four major problems of hologeistic method: data quality control, measurement of association, Galton's problem, and cultural unit definition.

Data Quality Control

Driver's pioneer work on the reliability of ethnographic data was ignored for an entire generation. His Ph.D. thesis, "The Reliability of Culture Element Data," at the University of California at Berkeley, was done under the nominal supervision of A. L. Kroeber and R. H. Lowie; but these eminent and influential ethnologists seem to have failed to grasp the importance of the work. A brief summary of it was published—or should we say buried—in Volume 1 of the *Anthropological Records* series (1938, pp. 205-19) and was for a long time completely forgotten. Naroll's *Data Quality Control* (1962) ignores it; but his 1970 chapter on Data Quality Control in the *Handbook of Method in Cultural Anthropology* gives it more than two full columns of attention (1970a: 930-31). After thirty years, Driver's work on the reliability of ethnographic data remains the standard—and classic—treatment of its subject; nothing that has been done since is nearly as comprehensive, thorough, or useful. For that reason, it is reprinted in this volume.

Driver's method compared the reports of six ethnographers on four tribes of the central Pacific Coast of North America: the Tolowa of Oregon and the Yurok, Hupa, and Karok of northern California. Driver found percentages of agreement among these independent observers to range from 84 percent to 91 percent. He found no one major division of culture (material culture, social culture, or religious culture) to be significantly more reliable than any other. This work of Driver's urgently needs replication. It can no longer be done in North America: the informants are all dead. But it could still be replicated in Highland New Guinea, for example.

Coefficients of Association

Driver's work on quality control was done as part of Kroeber's Culture Element Distribution project. Another task he performed as part of that project was the review and analysis of coefficients of associa-

tion. This review was one of the most thorough of its type and for its day (Driver and Kroeber 1932; Driver 1939, 1953). Driver's achievement was the more remarkable because he has never been trained as a mathematical statistician, but has always operated as a cultural anthropologist.

Galton's Problem

Driver's studies of quality control and of measurement of association were, as we have said, part of his work on Kroeber's Culture Element Distribution project. (For a general review of that project, and of the larger body of literature related to it, see Driver's chapter in the 1970 *Handbook of Method in Cultural Anthropology*, pp. 625-30.) These statistical studies of diffusion naturally led him to a consideration of Galton's problem. His specific stimulus seems to have been Murdock's *Social Structure* (1949), for Driver's first major treatment of Galton's problem came in another gem of statistical analysis buried in another obscure monograph series, his 1956 paper, in Memoir 21 of the *University of Indiana Publications in Anthropology and Linguistics*. That paper tackled the Main Sequence kinship theory of Murdock, using an exhaustive survey of all of the North American Indian tribes on which Driver could find data. His trait distribution maps clearly showed that Murdock's correlations were reflecting historical (diffusional) as well as functional factors. Naroll's later work on Galton's problem was much influenced by this study; Naroll gave careful attention to Driver's maps and cited them in most of his later writings on Galton's problem. There is still no better place to get a vivid picture of the "diffusion patch" than these same maps; however, it is now more convenient to consult the later versions of them in Driver's *Indians of North America* (1961), where they are supplemented by many other like maps of other traits.

Another seminal work of Driver's on Galton's problem was his 1966 paper in *Current Anthropology*, "Geographical-Historical Versus Psycho-Functional Explanations of Kin Avoidances." In this paper, he takes up the specific theoretical problem treated by Tylor in the first hologeistic study—the topic of kin avoidance. Pursuing the notion that statistical independence in one sense can best be determined by establishing independent invention, Driver traces the diffusion patterns of kin avoidance practices throughout North America and concludes that there were only five independent nuclei of kin avoidance practices in North (and Central) America. Using statistical comparisons, he shows that diffusional factors are stronger than functional ones in North America as a whole.

Statistical Classification of Culture Units

In his 1956 paper, Driver used the language as his basic ethnic unit. Since his study covered all native North American societies, he was able to modify that definition: where territorial groups speaking a single language differed with respect to the traits studied, he classed each differing group as a separate ethnic unit. The essential sturdiness of his approach—despite the many problems involved, which Hymes (1968) reviewed—was brilliantly demonstrated by Driver's student, Joseph Jorgensen; Jorgensen (1969) showed a high correlation between language variation and variation in other culture traits among the Salish-speaking peoples.

Driver's most important contribution to cultural unit classification, however, was made by his work in the statistical definition of culture areas. This interest began, of course, in his work with Kroeber's Culture Element Distribution project (Driver and Kroeber 1932; Driver 1939; Driver and Schuessler 1957). But its major achievement is his statistical analysis of North American Indian tribes (Driver, Kenny, Hudson, and Engle 1972). Here he and his collaborators classify North American societies into ten coarse, or thirty-four fine, geographical groupings. His work along these lines continues, in collaboration with Jorgensen. We are promised further correlations of language difference and culture difference in other language families of North America, to replicate Jorgensen's work with the Salish.

Notes

1. Parametric statistics may be applied whenever the variables have been measured by an interval or a ratio scale and the variation of those data can be assumed to approximate a normal distribution (see Freund 1967: 172-88; Blalock 1972; 15-20). If a normal distribution cannot be assumed, computer program FITTER (HRAF 1974) may be able to provide the necessary algebraic transformation to produce an adequate approximation of normality.

2. First cousins are classed as either parallel cousins or cross-cousins, depending on the sex of the two linking relatives. Parallel cousins are linked by relatives of the same sex; cross-cousins are linked by relatives of the opposite sex. In many kinship systems, these differences are crucially important. For example often a man's female parallel cousins are sexually taboo, like sisters, while at the same time his female cross-cousins are considered desirable brides for him.

References Cited

Adair, John, and Evon Z. Vogt
  1949 "Navaho and Zuni veterans: a study of contrasting modes of culture change," *American Anthropologist n.s. 51:* 547-61.

Asuni, T.
  1962 "Suicide in Western Nigeria," *British Medical Journal 22* (reprinted in *International Journal of Psychiatry 1:* 52-61, 1965).

Bacon, Margaret K., Herbert Barry III, and Irvin L. Child
  1965 "A cross-cultural study of drinking: II. relations to other features of the culture," *Quarterly Journal of Studies on Alcohol, Supplement 3:* 29-48.

Baggaley, Andrew R.
  1964 *Intermediate correlational methods,* New York, Wiley.

Banks, Arthur S., and Robert B. Textor
  1963 *A cross-polity survey,* Cambridge, M.I.T. Press.

Barnes, John A.
  1971 *Three styles in the study of kinship,* Berkeley and Los Angeles, University of California Press.

Barrett, Gerald V., and Richard H. Franke
  1970 "'Psychogenic' death: a reappraisal," *Science 167:* 304-06.

Barth, Fredrik, ed.
  1969 *Ethnic groups and boundaries: the social organization of culture difference,* London, George Allen and Unwin.

Bassoul, René
  1967 "L'analyse mathématique des faits sociaux de Raymond Boudon," *Revue française de sociologie 8:* 367-68.

Bendix, Reinhard
  1963 "Concepts and generalizations in comparative sociological studies," *American Sociological Review 28:* 532-39.

Berry, John W.
  1969 "On cross-cultural comparability," *International Journal of Psychology 4:* 119-28.

Blalock, Hubert M., Jr.
  1964 *Causal inferences in nonexperimental research,* Chapel Hill, University of North Carolina Press.
  1972 *Social statistics,* 2d ed., New York, McGraw-Hill.

Boudon, Raymond
  1967 "Les relations causales: problèmes de définition et de verification," *Revue française de sociologie 8:* 389-402.
  1970 "A method of linear causal analysis—dependence analysis," in Raoul Naroll and Rondald Cohen, eds., *A Handbook of Method in Cultural Anthropology,* Garden City, Natural History Press: 99-108.

Bourguignon, Erika, and Lenora Greenbaum
1968 "Diversity and homogeneity: a comparative analysis of societal characteristics based on data from the Ethnographic Atlas," *Ohio State University, Department of Anthropology, Occasional Papers in Anthropology 1*, (revised edition, *Diversity and homogeneity in world societies*, published in 1973 by HRAF Press, New Haven).

Brewer, Marilynn B., Donald T. Campbell, and William D. Crano
1970 "Testing a single-factor model as an alternative to the misuse of partial correlations in hypothesis-testing research," *Sociometry 33*: 1-11.

Buckley, Joan, and Jack Goody
n.d. *Problems involved in sample selection*, unpublished manuscript.

Burrowes, Robert
1973 "Mirror, mirror, on the wall . . . : a comparison of sources of external event data," in James Rosenau, ed., *Comparing Foreign Policy: Theories, Findings and Methods*, Beverly Hills, Sage Publications.

Campbell, Donald T., and Donald W. Fiske
1959 "Convergent and discriminant validation by the multitrait-mutimethod matrix," *Psychological Bulletin 56*: 81-105.

Campbell, Donald T., and Robert A. LeVine
1970 "Field-manual anthropology," in Raoul Naroll and Ronald Cohen, eds., *A Handbook of Method in Cultural Anthropology*, Garden City, Natural History Press: 366-87

Campbell, Donald T., and Raoul Naroll
1972 "The mutual methodological relevance of anthropology and psychology," in Francis L. K. Hsu, ed., *Psychological Anthropology*, rev. ed., Cambridge, Schenkman: 435-63.

Capell, Arthur
1962 *A linguistic survey of the South-western Pacific*, new and rev. ed., Nouméa, South Pacific Commission.

Chaney, Richard Paul
1966 "Typology and patterning: Spiro's sample re-examined," *American Anthropologist 68*: 1965-70.
1970 "Conceptual contention: a reply," *American Anthropologist 72*: 1956-61.
1971 *On the intertwined problems of sampling, data patterning and conceptual organization in cross-cultural research*, unpub-

lished doctoral dissertation, Bloomington, Indiana University, Department of Anthropology.

Chaney, Richard Paul, and Rogelio Ruiz Revilla
1969 "Sampling methods and interpretation of correlation: a comparative analysis of seven cross-cultural samples," *American Anthropologist 71*: 597-633.

Clignet, Remi
1970 "A critical evaluation of concomitant variation studies," in Raoul Naroll and Ronald Cohen, eds., *A Handbook of Method in Cultural Anthropology*, Garden City, Natural History Press: 597-619.

Cohen, Ronald, and Raoul Naroll
1970 "Method in cultural anthropology," in Raoul Naroll and Ronald Cohen, eds., *A Handbook of Method in Cultural Anthropology*, Garden City, Natural History Press: 3-24.

Cohen, Yehudi A.
1968 "Macroethnology: large-scale comparative studies," in James A. Clifton, ed., *Introduction to Cultural Anthropology: Essays in the Scope and Methods of the Science of Man*, Boston, Houghton Mifflin: 402-49.

Cronbach, Lee J., and Paul E. Meehl
1955 "Construct validity in psychological tests," *Pyschological Bulletin 52*: 281-302.

Croxton, Frederick E., and Dudley J. Cowden
1955 *Applied general statistics*, 2d ed., New York, Prentice Hall.

Dawson, John L. M.
1971 "Theory and research in cross-cultural psychology," *Bulletin of the British Psychological Society 24*: 291-306.

Degenne, Alain
1967 "Problèmes d'identification et d'interpretaion," *Revue française de sociologie 8*: 385-88.

Denton, Frank T., and Ernest H. Oksanen
1972 "A multi-country analysis of the effects of data revisions on an econometric model," *Journal of the American Statistical Association 67*: 286-91.

Divale, William Tulio
   1974 *Migration, external warfare and matrilo-·cal residence: an explantion for matrilo-cal residence systems* (in press).

Dixon, Wilfrid J., and Frank J. Massey, Jr.
   1969 *Introduction to statistical analysis*, 3d ed., New York, McGraw-Hill.

Driver, Harold E.
   1938 "Culture element distributions: VIII the reliability of culture element date," *University of California Anthropological Records 1*: 205-20 (reprinted in this volume).
   1939 "Culture element distributions: X Northwest California," *University of California Anthropological Records 1*: 297-433.
   1953 "Statistics in anthropology," *American Anthropologist 55*: 42-59.
   1956 "An integration of functional, evolutionary, and historical theory by means of correlations," *Indiana University Publications in Anthropology and Linguistics 12*: 1-35.
   1961 *Indians of North America*, Chicago, University of Chicago Press (2d rev. ed., 1969).
   1966 "Geographical-historical versus psycho-functional explanations of kin avoidances," *Current Anthropology 7*: 131-82. (reprinted in this volume).
   1970 "Statistical studies of continuous geographical distributions," in Raoul Naroll and Ronald Cohen, eds., *A Handbook of Method in Cultural Anthropology*, Garden City, Natural History Press: 620-39.

Driver, Harold E., and Richard P. Chaney
   1970 "Cross-cultural sampling and Galton's problem," in Raoul Naroll and Ronald Cohen, eds., *A Handbook of Method in Cultural Anthropology*, Garden City, Natural History Press: 990-1003 (reprinted in this volume).

Driver, Harold E., James A. Kenny, Herschel C. Hudson, and Ora May Engle
   1972 "Statistical classification of North American Indian ethnic units," *Ethnology 11*: 311-39 (reprinted in this volume).

Driver, Harold E., and Alfred L. Kroeber
   1932 "Quantitative expression of cultural relationships," *University of California Publications in American Archaeology and Ethnology 31*: 211-56.

Driver, Harold E., and Karl F. Schuessler
   1957 "Factor analysis of ethnographic data," *American Anthropologust 59*: 665-63.

Driver and Schuessler
   1967 "Correlational analysis of Murdock's 1957 ethnographic sample," *American Anthropologist 69*: 332-52 (reprinted in this volume).

Durbin, Marshall
   1972 "Basic terms—off color?" *Semiotica 6*: 257-78.

Durkheim, Emile
   1951 *Suicide: a study in sociology*, John A. Spaulding and George Simpson, trans., Glencoe, Free Press (first publication: *Le suicide*, Paris, F. Alcan 1897).

Ember, Melvin
   1970 "Taxonomy in comparative studies," in Raoul Naroll and Ronald Cohen, eds., *A Handbook of Method in Cultural Anthropology*, Garden City, Natural History Press: 697-706.

Erickson, Edwin E.
   1972 *Galton's worst: a note on Ember's reflection*, paper presented at the American Anthropological Association Meeting, Toronto.

Fernandez, James W.
   1963 *Redistribution and ritual reintegration in Fang culture*, doctoral dissertation, Evanston, Northwestern University, Department of Anthropology.

Ford, Clellan S., ed.
   1967 *Cross-cultural approaches: readings in comparative research*, New Haven, HRAF Press.

Freund, John E.
   1967 *Modern elementary statistics*, 3d ed., Englewood Cliffs, N.J., Prentice Hall.

Gilbert, Claire W.
   1971 "Communities, power structures & research bias," *Polity 4*: 218-35.

Gillespie, J. V.
   1971 "An introduction to macro-cross-cultural research," in John V. Gillespie and Betty

A. Nesvold, eds., *Macro-Quantitative Analysis*, Beverly Hills, Sage Publications: 13-27.

Gillespie, John V., and Betty A. Nesvold, eds.
1971 *Macro-quantitative analysis: conflict development and democratization*, Beverly Hills, Sage Publications.

Goodenough, Ward
1956 "Residence rules," *Southwestern Journal of Anthropology* 12: 22-37.
1970 *Description and comparison in cultural anthropology*, Chicago, Aldine.

Greenbaum, Lenora
1970 "Evaluation of a stratified versus an unstratified universe of cultures in comparative research," *Behavior Science Notes* 5: 251-89.

Greenway, John
1963 *Bibliography of the Australian aborigines and the native people of Torres Strait to 1959*, Sydney, Angus and Robertson.

Griffiths, Donald
n.d. *Causal analysis in the three-variable case*, State University of New York at Buffalo, Department of Anthropology (in preparation).

Haekel, Josef
1970 "Source criticism in anthropology," Terrence A. Tatje and Emile M. Schepers, trans., in Raoul Naroll and Ronald Cohen, eds., *A Handbook of Method in Cultural Anthropology*, Garden City, Natural History Press: 147-64.

Hauser, Phillip M.
1959 "Cultural and personal obstacles to economic influence in the less developed areas," *Human Organization* 18: 78-80.

Helm, June, ed.
1968 *Essays on the problem of tribe*, Seattle, American Ethnological Society.

Hermann, Charles F.
1972 "Policy classification," in James N. Rosenau, Vincent Davis, and Maurice A. East, eds., *The Analysis of International Politics*, New York, Free Press.

Holmberg, Allan R.
1950 "Nomads of the long bow: the Siriono of eastern Bolivia," *Smithsonian Institution, Institute of Social Anthropology, Publication 10*, Washington D.C., Government Printing Office.

Holt, Robert T., and John E. Turner, eds.
1970 *The methodology of comparative research*, New York, Free Press.

Human Relations Area Files (HRAF)
1974 *Hologeistic Computer Program Package*, State University of New York at Buffalo, Department of Anthropology (in preparation).

Hymes, Dell
1968 "Linguistic problems in defining the problem of 'tribe'" in June Helm, ed., *Essays on the Problem of Tribe*, Seattle, American Ethnological Society: 23-48.

Isambert, François
1967 "Traduction mathématique et verification de quelques systèmes de relations causales," *Revue française de sociologie* 8: 369-84.

Janda Kenneth
1970 "Data quality control and library research on political parties," in Raoul Naroll and Ronald Cohen, eds., *A Handbook of Method in Cultural Anthropology*, Garden City, Natural History Press: 962-73.

Jorgensen, Joseph G.
1969 "Salish language and culture; a statistical analysis of internal relationships, history, and evolution," *Indiana University Publications, Language Science Monographs* 3.

Kenney, John F.
1947-51 *Mathematics of statistics*, 2d ed. (2 vols.), Princeton, Van Nostrand (3d ed., with E. S. Keeping, 1964-65, New York, Van Nostrand).

Köbben, André J. F.
1952 "New ways of presenting an old idea: the statistical method in social anthropology," *Royal Anthropological Institute of Great Britain and Ireland, Journal* 82: 129-46 (reprinted in Moore 1966: 166-92).
1967 "Why exceptions? The logic of cross-cultural analysis," *Current Anthropology* 8: 3-19.

1970a "Cause and intention," in Raoul Naroll and Ronald Cohen, eds., *A Handbook of Method in Cultural Anthropology*, Garden City, Natural History Press: 89-98.

1970b "Comparativists and non-comparativists," in Raoul Naroll and Ronald Cohen, eds., *A Handbook of Method in Cultural Anthropology*, Garden City, Natural History Press: 581-96.

Land, Kenneth C.
1969 "Principles of path analysis," *Sociological Methodology 1*: 3-37.

LeBar, Frank M.
1970 "Coding ethnographic materials," in Raoul Naroll and Ronald Cohen, eds., *A Handbook of Method in Cultural Anthropology*, Garden City, Natural History Press: 707-20.

Lewis, Oscar
1956 "Comparisons in cultural anthropology," in William L. Thomas, ed., *Current Anthropology: A Supplement to Anthropology Today*, Chicago, University of Chicago Press: 259-92.

Loftin, Colin
1972 "Galton's problem as spatial autocorrelation: comments on Ember's empirical test," *Ethnology 11*: 425-35.

Loftin, Colin, and Robert Hill
n.d. *A comparison of alignment procedures for tests of Galton's problem*, unpublished manuscript.

Long, Norton E.
1970 "Indicators of change in political institutions," *Annals of the American Academy of Political and Social Science 388*: 35-45.

Malefijt, A. De Waal
1963 *The Javanese of Surinam*, Assen, Van Gorcum.

McEwen, William
1963 "Forms and problems of validation in social anthorpology," *Current Anthropology 64*: 165-83.

Minturn, Leigh, and William W. Lambert
1964 *Mothers of six cultures: antecedents of child rearing*, New York, John Wiley.

Mood, Alexander
1950 *Introduction to the theory of statistics*, New York, McGraw-Hill.

Moore, Frank W., ed.
1966 *Readings in cross-cultural methodology*, reset ed., New Haven, HRAF Press.

1969 "Codes and coding," *Behavior Science Notes 4*: 247-66.

Murdock, George Peter
1949 *Social structure*, New York, Macmillan.
1953 "The processing of anthropological materials," in Alfred L. Kroeber, ed., *Anthropology Today; An Encyclopedic Inventory*, Chicago, University of Chicago Press: 476-87.
1957 "World ethnographic sample," *American Anthropologist 59*: 644-87.
1972 *Outline of world cultures*, 4th ed., revised, New Haven, HRAF Press.

Murdock, George Peter, and Douglas R. White
1969 "Standard cross-cultural sample," *Ethnology 8*: 329-69.

Naroll, Raoul
1961 "Two solutions to Galton's problem," *Philosophy of Science 18*: 15-39.
1962 *Data quality control—a new research technique: prolegomena to a cross-cultural study of culture stress*, New York, Free Press.
1964a "A fifth solution to Galton's problem," *American Anthropologist 66*: 863-67.

1964b "On ethnic unit classification," *Current Anthropology 5*: 283-312.
1967 "The proposed HRAF Probability Sample," *Behavior Science Notes 2*: 70-80.
1969 "Cultural determinants and the concept of the sick society," in Robert F. Edgerton and Stanley C. Plog, eds., *Changing Perspectives in Mental Illness*, New York, Holt, Rinehart and Winston: 128-55.
1970a "Influence analysis—an appendix," "The culture-bearing unit in cross-cultural surveys," "Cross-cultural sampling," "Data quality control in cross-cultural surveys," and "Galton's problem," in Raoul Naroll and Ronald Cohen, eds., *A Handbook of Method in Cultural Anthropology*, Garden City, Natural History Press: 108-10, 721-65, 889-926, 927-45, 974-89.

1970b "What have we learned from cross-cultural surveys?" *American Anthropologist 72*: 1227-88.
1970c "Chaney and Ruiz Revilla: sampling methods," *American Anthropologist 72*: 1451-52.
1971a "The double language boundary in cross-cultural surveys," *Behavior Science Notes 6*: 95-102.

1971b *Review of*: "The significance test controversy," Denton E. Morrison and Ramon E. Henkel, eds., *American Anthropologist* 73: 1437-39.

1971c *"Conceptualizing the problem" as seen by an anthropologist*, paper presented at the 1971 Meeting of the American Political Science Association, Chicago.

1974 "An exact test of significance for Goodman and Kruskal's gamma," *Behavior Science Notes* (in press).

Naroll, Raoul, Vern R. Bullough, and Frada Naroll
1973 *Military deterrence in history*, Albany, State University of New York Press.

Naroll, Raoul, and Ronald Cohen, eds.
1970 *A Handbook of method in cultural anthropology*, Garden City, Natural History Press (reissued in 1973 by Columbia University Press, New York).

Naroll, Raoul, and Roy D'Andrade
1963 "Two further solutions to Galton's problem," *American Anthropologist* 65: 1053-62.

Naroll, Raoul, and Frada Naroll, eds.
1973 *Main currents in cultural anthropology*, New York, Appleton-Century-Crofts.

Needham, Rodney
1954 "Siriono and Penan: a test of some hypotheses," *Southwestern Journal of Anthropology* 10: 228-32.

Nieboer, Herman Jeremias
1910 *Slavery as an industrial system: ethnological researches*, 2d rev. ed., The Hague, Martinus Nijhoff.

Osgood, Charles E.
1971 "Exploration in semantic space: a personal diary," *Journal of Social Issues* 27, no. 4: 5-64.

Otterbein, Keith F.
1969 "Basic steps in conducting a cross-cultural survey," *Behavior Science Notes* 4: 221-36.

1972 *Comparative cultural analysis: an introduction to anthropology*, New York, Holt, Rinehart and Winston.

Pelto, Pertti J.
1970 *Anthropological research: the structure of inquiry*, New York, Harper and Row.

Pelz, Donald C., and Frank M. Andrews
1964 "Causal priorities in panel study data," *American Sociological Review* 29: 836-47.

Pierce, Albert
1970 Fundamentals of nonparametric statistics, Belmont, Cal., Dickenson.

Popper, Karl R.
1959 *The logic of scientific discovery*, New York, Basic Books.

Przeworski, Adan, and Henry Teune
1970 *The logic of comparative social inquiry*, New York, Wiley-Interscience.

Raulin, H.
1959 *Problèmes fonciers dans les régions de Gagnoa et Daloa*, Paris, Office de la Recherche Scientifique et Technique Outre-Mer.

Redfield, Robert
1941 *The folk cultur of Yucatan*, Chicago, University of Chicago Press.

Rohner, Ronald P., B. R. Dewalt, and R. C. Ness.
n.d. *Ethnographer bias in cross-cultural research: an empirical study*, unpublished manuscript.

Rohner, Ronald P. and Pertti J. Pelto
1970 "Sampling methods: Chaney and Ruiz Revilla, comment 2," *American Anthropologist* 72: 1452-56.

Rokkan, Stein
1970 "Cross-cultural, cross-societal and cross-national research," in *Main Trends in the Social and Human Sciences. Part One: Social Sciences*, UNESCO, Paris, The Hague, Mouton/UNESCO.

Rozelle, Richard M., and Donald T. Campbell
1969 "More plausible rival hypotheses in the cross-lagged panel correlation technique," *Psychological Bulletin* 71: 74-80.

Rummel, Rudolph J.
1970 "Dimensions of error in cross-national data," in Raoul Naroll and Ronald Cohen, eds., *A Handbook of Method in Cultural Anthropology*, Garden City, Natural History Press: 946-61.

Sawyer, Jack, and Robert A. LeVine
1966 "Cultural dimensions: a factor analysis of the *World Ethnographic Sample*," *American Anthropologist* 68: 708-31.

Schaefer, James M.
1969 "Linked pair alignments for the HRAF quality control sample universe," *Behavior Science Notes* 4: 299-320.

1973 *A hologeistic study of family structure and sentiment, supernatural beliefs, and drunkenness*, doctoral dissertation, State

University of New York at Buffalo, Department of Anthropology.

Schaefer, James M., et al.
1971 "Sampling methods, functional associations, and Galton's problem: a replicative assessment," *Behavior Science Notes* 6: 229-74.

Schapera, Isaac
1953 "Some comments on comparative method in social anthropology," *American Anthropologist* 55: 353-61.

Siegel, Sidney
1956 *Nonparametric statistics for the behavioral sciences*, New York, McGraw-Hill.

Simmons, Leo W.
1945 *The role of the aged in primitive society*, New Haven, Yale University Press.

Sipes, Richard G.
1972 "Rating hologeistic method," *Behavior Science Notes* 7: 157-98.

Spiro, Melford E.
1965 "A typology of social structure and the patterning of social institutions: a cross-cultural study," *American Anthropologist* 67: 1097-1119.

1966 "A reply to Chaney," *American Anthropologist* 68: 1471-74.

Tanter, Raymond
1970 "Toward a theory of political development," in Raoul Naroll and Ronald Cohen, eds., *A Handbook of Method in Cultural Anthropology*, Garden City, Natural History Press: 111-27.

Tatje, Terrence A.
1970 "Problems of concept definition for comparative studies," in Raoul Naroll and Ronald Cohen, eds., *A Handbook of Method in Cultural Anthropology*, Garden City, Natural History Press; 689-96.

Tatje, Terrence A., Raoul Naroll, and Robert B. Textor
1970 "The methodological findings of the *Cross-Cultural Summary*," in Raoul Naroll and Ronald Cohen, eds., *A Handbook of Method in Cultural Anthropology*, Garden City, Natural History Press: 649-75.

Textor, Robert B.
1967 *A cross-cultural summary*, New Haven, HRAF Press.

Thomas, Darwin L., and Andrew J. Weigert
1972 "Determining nonequivalent measurement in cross-cultural family research," *Journal of Marriage and the Family* 34: 166-77.

Triandis, Harry
1964 "Cultural influences upon cognitive processes," *Advances in Experimental Social Psychology* 1: 1-48.

Webb, Eugene J., Donald T. Campbell, Richard D. Schwartz, and Lee Sechrest
1966 *Unobtrusive measures: nonreactive in the social sciences*, Chicago, Rand McNally.

Whiting, Beatrice B., Irvin L. Child, William W. Lambert, and John W. M. Whiting
1963 *Six cultures: studies of child rearing*, New York, John Wiley.

Whiting, John W. M.
1954 "The cross-cultural method," in Gardner Lindzey, ed., *Handbook of Social Psychology* 1, Reading, Mass., Addison-Wesley: 523-31.

1968 "Method and problems in cross-cultural research," in Gardner Lindzey and Elliot Aronson, eds., *Handbook of Social Psychology*, 2nd ed., Reading, Mass., Addison-Wesley: 693-728.

Whiting, John W. M., Richard Kluckhohn, and Albert S. Anthony
1958 "The function of male initiation ceremonies at puberty," in Eleanor E. Maccoby, Theodore M. Newcomb, and Eugene L. Hartley, eds., *Readings in Social Psychology*, 3d ed., New York, Holt, Rinehart and Winston: 359-70.

Winch, Robert F., and Donald T. Campbell
1969 "Proof? No. Evidence? Yes. The significance of tests of significance," *American Sociologist* 4: 140-43.

Young, Frank W.
1962 "The function of male initiation ceremonies: a cross-cultural test of an alternative hypothesis," *American Journal of Sociology* 67: 379-96.

Part Four

Worldwide and Continuous Area Comparisons

1. Introduction

Joseph G. Jorgensen

Harold Driver has conducted worldwide and continuous area cross-cultural studies; yet his methodologies and interpretations, whether for worldwide or continuous area samples, depart markedly from the methodologies and interpretations normally associated with these two modes of inquiry. Driver was trained in the continuous area approach by Kroeber, although as a maturing graduate student he began to disagree with some of the goals and some of the assumptions of Kroeber's approach. Most specifically, Driver was skeptical of the goal to postdict historical relationships to the exclusion of other relationships, and he was skeptical of the underlying assumption that similarity among variables from several tribes in the same continuous area meant that the similar variables had a common or homologous origin. Driver argued that parallel origins could, and probably did, occur, yet he also argued that all similar variables among tribes were not necessarily independently created.

In the following studies, one a continuous area piece, "Girls' Puberty Rites in Western North America,"[*] and the other a worldwide piece, "Correlational Analysis of Murdock's Ethnographic Sample," we see how Driver goes beyond history to account for the similarities and differences among puberty rites, and beyond parallel and independent origins of kinship and social organization relationships to account for similarities in the worldwide sample.

My own essay probes the two modes of inquiry: their histories, methodologies, and assumptions.

---

[*]"Girls' Puberty Rites in Western North America" has been abridged for inclusion in this volume. The "psychological" section, among others, has been deleted.

2. Culture Element Distributions: XVI Girls' Puberty Rites in Western North America

Harold E. Driver

Introduction

The present comparative study deals with girls' puberty rites among nearly all the tribes for which culture-element data have been recently collected (see Kroeber, 1939).[1] Besides, all previously published ethnographical literature available was used. Part I is written for ethnologists in general, Part II for specialists in statistics or their application to ethnology. The author has been more interested in methodology and in evaluating the culture-element-survey data than in girls' puberty rites per se. In fact Professor Kroeber was the one who suggested girls' puberty rites for a possible topic of investigation.

One legitimate question often asked is: How much has the culture-element survey increased the amount of comparative data in western North America? In order to answer this for the subject under discussion each source was kept separate in the original distribution tables (tables 13, 14). When these tables finally were as complete as the source material permitted, a count was made of the entries from essay-type sources, including unpublished essay-type manuscripts, and then, for comparison a count was made of the total entries. The following was the result:

	Essay-type sources	Total sources
Positive evidence (+)	3538	8707
Negative evidence (-)	4295	18488
Total evidence	7833	27195

The total evidence now available is about three and one-half times as great as the evidence from essay sources alone. (It is important to remember that this figure is computed from only about three-fourths of the culture-element material. All field work had not been completed when this count was made. Probably all data available at the time this paper goes to press would yield a ratio of at least four to one.) The culture-element data overlap the essay data to a great extent so that the total amount of the former is nearer the grand total than the difference between it and essay sources. The greater difference is in negative evidence.

Much more space has been given to pure description than in most previous statistically conscious studies. The purpose is twofold: to give a detailed idea of the main types of areal differentiation, and to present each individual trait in a context so that anyone can understand clearly the meaning of the captions in the distribution tables.

At the suggestion of Kroeber I spent about a month working only with culture-element data. The purpose was to see whether these data could be used satisfactorily without reference to essay sources. It proved not possible. The culture-element data on this topic were too uneven. For example, those from the Pomo area were so abbreviated and consisted so largely of widespread traits, such as the meat taboo and the scratching stick, that comparisons with other areas showed only very high correlations. The lack of sufficient negative evidence made it impossible to demonstrate any marked differences with other areas. To a lesser extent such inadequacies were apparent from other areas where the element data on girls' puberty were scant, the Southern Sierra Nevada area worked by me. I finally set up criteria for inferring absences (given in Part II) and applied them to essay and element-list sources alike. The real issue here is not whether element-list sources are better or worse than essay sources for a single topic or generally, but whether or not one wishes to neglect part of the primary source material.

Because the present author has had at his disposal several times as many data as anyone who has previously written on girls' puberty in western North America, it would seem pedantic to criticize these earlier works in detail. Therefore only brief discussion of them, in chronological order, will be attempted.

Kroeber[2] in three early publications of his tabulated trait distributions for girls' puberty in California, and constructed maps and chronological schemes for this and related religious ceremonies. Later[3] he reviewed the Kuksu Cult system and its relation to male initiations in other parts of North America. In his three early works, girls' adolescence rites are attributed to the earliest cultural stratum in western North America and boys' rites to later periods; in his later work, boys' rites in Central California, Southern California, Lower California, and the Pueblo Southwest are thought to have a common origin presumably at an early date because of the great amount of specific differentiation in historic times. In discussing girls' puberty rites, Kroeber did not draw a sharp distinction between private observances and highly publicized ones. I therefore agree with him to the extent that a number of girls' puberty traits seem to be very old, but disagree to the extent of believing that public recognition is late in most areas. We concur on the fundamentals of boys' rites, although my placing them in the second earliest period and my postulating from them the development of certain girls' rites is new.

Lowie[4] has pointed out that the Great Basin shares with California a considerable stress on girls' puberty observances in contrast to the Plains and Eastern Woodland where such customs are fewer and less important in the native mind. He also points out that Northern California has more in common with Basin Shoshoneans than Southern California in spite of the linguistic affinity of the two latter areas. This fact is partly substantiated by the present data, but the emphasis I have given the public aspect makes the major line of cleavage run north and south. The Basin and Plateau become a unit in contrast to either the North Pacific Coast or Northern California. Lowie suggests historic unity as an explanation of continuous distributions of a few traits, but he does not present an inclusive historical scheme. In a recent paper,[5] he explains that the wide distribution of the head scratcher is due to its probable association with an "extremely early layer of American culture." This is completely in accord with my opinion.

Loeb,[6] who was primarily concerned with boys' rites, believes that certain features of both boys' and girls' rites are very old and that public group initiations of girls are in some instances derived from boys' initiations. These beliefs agree with my general ideas. I do not follow him in detail, however.

Spier[7] has cited distributions over most of North America, especially west of the Rockies, from extant published literature. He was the first to show that tribes east of the Rockies do not have a public ceremony for a pubescent girl. Public rites west of the Rockies he divided into four types, which correspond rather closely to those of the present paper: 1, Northwest Coast; 2, Northern California and Oregon; 3, Central and Southern California; 4, Non-Pueblo Southwest. The chief difference is that he groups Central California with Southern California whereas I have grouped it with Northern California. As is characteristic of him, Spier was reticent about drawing historical inferences, but he does admit diffusion within restricted areas such as the four mentioned above. His one interareal clue to diffusion concerned the dance routines of the White Mountain Apache and Pima, which are "suspiciously like those of Northern California and Oregon." This hunch has been amply borne out by the present fuller data.

Cora Du Bois,[8] in an unpublished Ph.D. thesis in the University of California Library, did a more thorough job both extensively and intensively than any of her predecessors. She confirmed Spier's statement that tribes east of the Rockies have no definite publicization of girls' puberty. She followed Spier in grouping public rites of the west into four types, but joined Central California with Northern California instead of with Southern. She cited a number of distributions over all of North America but mostly for widespread traits with Old World analogues. For this reason her areal types cannot be derived empirically from her distributed evidence. They are intuitive, as with others previously offered. Du Bois was extremely chary about drawing historical inferences; she expressed doubt about there being any demonstrable historical relation between boys' and girls' rites. Similarly, in a chapter on physiological and psychological considerations, she concludes that there are no proven innate reactions by either males or females toward menstruation. In spite of the dearth of conclusions in her paper, I found it the most helpful single source and I developed the habit of checking my work against it for ideas as well as for bibliography.

Although I believe that the more rigid method I have used has contributed to the more definite results I have achieved, I admit that the additional material available to me was the chief factor. In other words, if I had to choose between new and old method versus old data and new method I would choose the former for this puberty study. . . .

PART I. ETHNOGRAPHY

Girls' Puberty Patterns

This section consists of a series of sketches of girls' puberty rites in the areas shown in map 2. Four sketches are divided into two parts each: description and discussion; the rest consist only of discussion.

The purpose of the descriptions is to provide the reader with a convenient yet detailed picture of several patterns in order to preserve some of the integration of the elements as they occur in native cultures and also to give some idea of the enormous content of these rites. A trait list cannot do this. Because no two puberty rites are exactly alike, these descriptions are composite pictures to which no single tribe actually conforms. The other alternative would be to choose a typical tribe from each area and describe it in full exactly as in the primary source material. I have selected the composite sketch because the available information on single tribes is usually inadequate, probably in some instances not containing information on half the actual variants present. Unless otherwise stated, all features occurring in or reported for a single locality are localized in footnotes.

The part labeled discussion points out the distinctive features of each pattern, its typological relation to others in western North America, its relation to other rituals in the same area, and the social prominence of the puberty rite in the culture as a whole.

Tables 13 and 14 should be consulted for specific distributions. . . .[9]

Girls' Puberty Trait - Complexes

There are a number of groups of traits whose distributions are internally similar and externally dissimilar from those of other groups of traits. Such a group of highly intercorrelated traits is here labeled a trait-complex.[10] The more compact of these complexes are set off by Roman numerals in table 13, but broader and looser ones may also be distinguished. Although it is possible to define such complexes quantitatively, according to the amount of correlation among the constituent elements, I do not believe such rigid definition has much value ethnographically. For a mechanical operation such as the pooling of traits to facilitate the grouping in table 13, specific definition *is* necessary and has been given under "Statistical Methods."

There are a number of broad complexes easily distinguishable. In the lower middle section of table 13 there are some dozen tratis which are universal or nearly so. Immediately above there is a group of traits virtually universal among those tribes having public recognition (complex X). Above this there is another group of traits that is associated with public recognition, but which occurs in Northern California and to the south, and is absent on the North Pacific Coast (complexes XIII and XIV). Next there is a rather loose cluster of traits occurring mainly in Northern California; then a group shared mainly by the Plateau, Northern California, and the Great Basin (complex XVI); then still another group of traits that is North Pacific Coast, Plateau, Northern California, and doubtfully Great Basin (complexes II, III); and

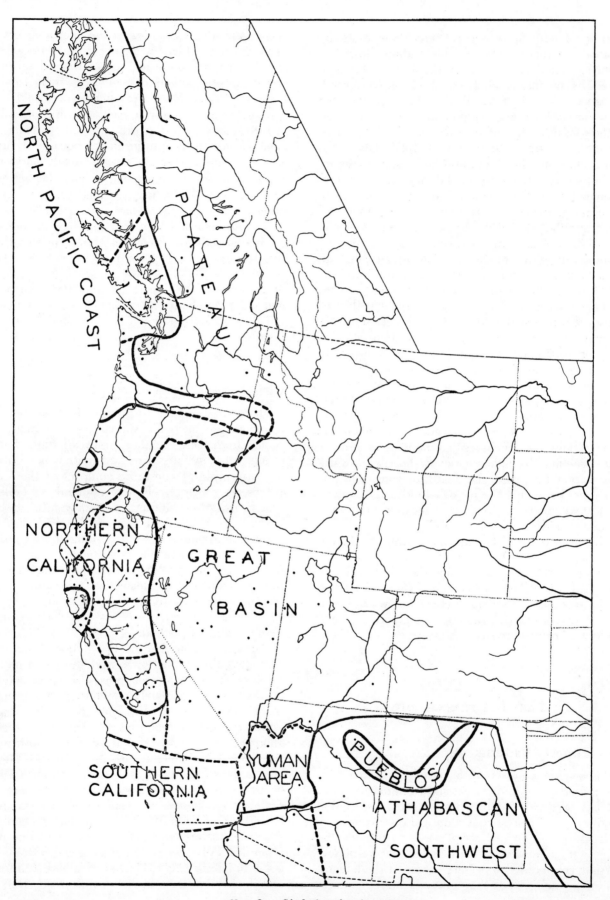

Map 2. Girls' puberty areas.

finally a group of exclusively North Pacific Coast traits. Below the universals there comes first a somewhat vague group mainly Plateau, Northern California, and Great Basin (complex XII); then a rather well-defined nexus occurring in Southern California and the Southwest (complex V); then a rather vague group, mainly Southern and Central Californian (complex IV); then a definite cluster present only in Southern California (complex I); and finally a few traits confined to the Athabascan Southwest (complex IX).

The great majority of high correlations are of the "accidental" variety, the only explanation for which is an historical one. An example is the correlation of the sand painting and the turtle-shell rattle in Southern California. These two items are not a unit in native ideology, they both occur in other cultural contexts, they are not made of the same materials or with the same techniques, and their roles in girls' puberty rites are very different. However, there are a number of trait associations which can be explained by factors other than historical "accident." Relatively high correlations, such as for those traits set off by Roman numerals in table 13, will be discussed from this point of view first.

Complex VII.

The carved wooden comb used as a scratcher, the carved hollow-wood rattle, and the carved wooden masks worn by male dancers are all examples of North Pacific Coast wood-carving technique. Although the mere presence of a wood-carving technique is not sufficient to explain the use of these three articles in a puberty ceremony, its absence would limit the distribution of the objects, partly determining their correlation in that manner.

Complexes II and III.

There are four traits here which are concerned with light or with seeing or being seen: the taboo on gazing at the sun, moon, or sky, or of the sun or moon shining on the girl; the avoidance of fire, including often the taboo on looking at fire; the taboo on gazing at people; and the seclusion of the girl in a screened-off portion or separate compartment of the dwelling house. Avoidance of the sun or moon and fire are close in native conceptualization because both are most frequently explained by the same rationalization, namely, that weak eyes or blindness would result. The other two traits, however, do not seem to be functionally related to this concept or to any other idea.

Complex XII.

Compulsory running and wood gathering are logical correlatives because both are relatively strenuous outdoor activities.

Complex I.

Moiety paint patterns, the girls in the group ceremony being of the same "clan" or moiety, and the direction of the ceremony being in the hands of a leader of a reciprocal "clan" or moiety all reflect the social organization of Southern California.

There are two other trait-complexes, each of which is loosely intracorrelated in space but which reflects a single dominating idea. These I term the work complex and the rest complex.

The work complex.

The most obtrusive elements of this complex are: the sitting or squatting posture in seclusion; the taboo on hot food; running at time of menstruation; working at time of menstruation, especially outdoors; and bathing outdoors at time of menstruation. Somewhat more doubtful members of this complex are: the complete fast for a few days; seclusion in a separate hut; the vision quest; perhaps the scrubbing with boughs at bathing; and scarification or bleeding of the girl. These traits refer to strenuous physical activity and severe bodily deprivation. They occur mainly on the Plateau, in the Great Basin, and on the middle section of the North Pacific Coast from Vancouver Island to northern California. Other crisis rites and the seeking of supernatural power in this area seem to follow the same fundamental pattern.

The rest complex.

This includes: lying in seclusion on a hot bed; no physical exertion of any kind during menstruation; and the taboo on drinking or bathing in cold water. Seclusion was in the dwelling or in a special structure or enclosure where the total inactivity of the girl could be enforced. These traits occur to some extent in the Great Basin and in the Southwest, but are most characteristic of California. They seem closer to the treatment of the mother at birth than to any other phase of culture there.

While the distributions of these two complexes are far from mutually exclusive, they are sufficiently distinct to be significant. Conceptually the two ideas are direct opposites. However, in areas where the girl's inactivity is strictly enforced she often does initiatory work immediately after menstruation. Nevertheless I believe the rest and work complexes represent two fundamentally different kinds of religious behavior and belief which are shared by other departments of culture in the same areas.

Universals.

There are a number of traits which are virtually universal in western North America. Briefly these are: seclusion; attendant; restrictions on food and drink; scratching taboo; work at time of menstruation or after; bathing and changing clothes at the end of seclusion or menstruation; instruction; and probably avoidance of hunters, fishermen, gamblers, or men generally. The majority of these traits, and probably all, occur in South America and the Old World as well. All are widespread over the whole of North America. Therefore they represent no unifying complex which distinguishes western North America from other areas. The only material object included in this group is the scratching stick; all other items refer to behavior or beliefs. Thus material objects show more areal variation than do beliefs of behavior.

To these universals should be added several generic beliefs which were considered too obvious and broad to be included in the trait list. These are the following: (1) that the girl is unclean and may harm other people or nature; (2) that she is especially susceptible to harm if she does not strictly observe the various taboos; (3) that her actions at first menstruation predetermine her behavior throughout life. Every individual observance of the girl in every area fits one or more of these explanations. To the native, the puberty rite represents a logical procedure because he relates specific observances to such integrating concepts.

This raises an interesting theoretical point. How much of the form and content of girls' puberty rites is consistent with the concept of functional wholes, and how much with the idea that culture is a randomly associated conglomerate? From the viewpoint of a single tribe at a single point in its history, no doubt every element of its puberty rite is believed or felt to be an integral part of a unified whole. Any good informant, if pressed hard, would probably construct enough rationalizations to make any ceremony appear to have functional unity. In the girls' puberty rite, the obscene songs sung by the crowd might be explained as a part of the spirit of merriment and rejoicing over the maturity of the girl. To cite an actual example: in Northern California the most widespread native reason for public recognition is to keep the girl awake. As pointed out previously, however, a few women would be sufficient to keep the girl awake. Furthermore, this explanation fails to account for particular dance forms or regalia. My own opinion in regard to Northern California is that the first menstruation of a girl was little more than a catalytic agent which initiated a social good time.

The broader the comparative universe in either space or time, the looser the integration of single parts of single cultures at a single point in history will appear to be. The reason is that the elements which constitute a small spatial and temporal unit of culture are almost invariably found to have wider distributions and different associations in a broader spatial and temporal frame. Natives have less comparative knowledge than ethnologists and consequently they would be expected to believe or feel the presence of a relatively small number of integrating impulses in their cultures which to them produce or maintain the harmonious whole. An ethnologist cannot really believe or feel such unity unless he suddenly develops a state of mind in which he eliminates his comparative knowledge. The description of relationships within single folk cultures as seen by native participants is an important task for ethnology, but it will never be complete description or a substitute for the broader relationships that are revealed by comparative studies.

Correlations with Geographical Environment

In any large group of culture elements, certain ones are bound to correlate with elements of geographical environment. By distributing various geographical elements among tribal territories one could determine numerical correlations between geography and culture. In the present study, exact distributions of geographical features have not been determined and no numerical correlations have been computed. The purpose of this section is to cite the obvious rather than to exhaust the problem.

Only those correlations with geography that are readily explained in terms of geography will be discussed here. There are, of course, many correlations between culture and geography that are fortuitous from the point of view of geography: for example, the correlation between the presence of salmon and sitting or squatting in seclusion.

Drumming on a plank (element 209) at girls' puberty is found on the North Pacific Coast. It has a high correlation with heavy rainfall and a certain species of cedar from which almost all North Pacific Coast planks are split. Planks cannot be conveniently split from other kinds of wood with native tools. Thus the limit of the climate and the correlated flora determine the limit of drumming on a plank.

The gourd rattle (element 206) is limited to Southern California and the Southwest because gourds grow only in these areas. I believe the three occurrences of gourd rattles in the San Joaquin Valley, California, are errors, or at best, importations of the manufactured article in Spanish times. Nevertheless the general southern provenience holds.

The absence of suitable cocoons for cocoon rattles (element 205) on the North Pacific Coast may have served as a limiting factor for that area. I do not know the distribution of cocoons in the Great Basin and the Southwest.

The taboo on fresh meat only, or the allowance of dried meat or fish in the menstruant's diet (element 50) occurs only in the North Pacific Coast (including Northern California) and in the Plateau. These are the areas where meat and fish constituted the staple diet. In areas to the south, vegetable foods constituted a greater part of the diet than meats. The reason for permitting menstruants to eat dried-meat products in the north seems to be one of expediency, there being little else to eat much of the time. In the south vegetable foods were an ever-ready substitute.

The seclusion of the girl outdoors or in a roofless enclosure (elements 20, 21) would only be practical in a warm dry climate. Except in association with vision seeking in the southern Plateau and in Northeastern California, these elements are of extreme southern provenience. Some tribes in the north specify that vision seeking outdoors was confined to the summer season. This confirms the suggested interpretation.

Similarly, the holding of the public recognition ceremony outdoors (element 169) or in a roofless enclosure (element 168) occur in the southern half of the area, where there is less rainfall. In the North Pacific Coast the use of the plank house for large gatherings was a social necessity. Although individuals would have survived the rain physically, the degree of comfort necessary for social intercourse would have been lacking.

The use of bone in the north and wood or plant products in the south for scratching sticks and drinking tubes may somehow be determined by geographical environment. As already mentioned, subsistence in the north was more dependent on animals; presumably then the presence of a greater quantity and variety of bones around habitation sites encouraged the greater use of bones for implements.

The distribution of public recognition seems to have been limited by geography. With the exception of the Southwest, public recognition occurs in the areas of greatest population, of most sedentary population, and of most favorable environment from a subsistence outlook. Inland on the Plateau and in the Great Basin it was much more difficult to get sufficient food, and the poplulation wandered about in small bands over large stretches of territory. Under such conditions it would have been difficult if not impossible to assemble and feed a large group every time a girl menstruated for the first time. Assuming that the idea of publicly celebrating first menstruation originated on the Pacific Coast, these less favorable environments would check its diffusion eastward. The Southwest does not fit this simple interpretation because there it is the economically lowest tribes which celebrate girls' puberty publicly. For ceremonialism as a whole in the Southwest, however, the economically most advanced peoples—the Pueblo—far surpass their poorer neighbors. We may therefore say that there is a definite correlation in western North America between economic well-being and elaboration of ritual. Where girls' puberty rites follow the general trend (North Pacific Coast, Plateau, California, Great Basin) this generalization holds for them. Where they do not follow the general trend of ritual (Southwest), it does not hold. The difference between the Southwest and the rest of western North America with respect to puberty can be explained only in terms of historical factors, which will be discussed under "Historical Speculations."

There is some tendency for the girls' puberty areas of map 2[11] to fit geographical areas. Because these areas are determined mainly by the presence or absence of public recognition, the economic interpretation offered above would apply to puberty material as a whole. The Southwest is again anomalous.

In spite of the general conformity between puberty and geographical areas, only about ten per cent of the specific traits seem to be determined by specific geographical factors.

Correlations with Language

In any large group of culture elements, some are almost certain to have a high correlation with some linguistic unit. This is not equivalent to saying that culture in general has a high correlation with language or that one can be inferred from the other. Such is certainly not so.

The method of this section differs from that of Klimek[12] in one important respect. Klimek correlated only the broadest linguistic units with culture: Athabascan, Hokan, Penutian, Shoshonean, and the like. I have used in addition subdivisions when those subdivisions were represented by sufficient tribes to make the result significant. Thus in addition to Hokan, I add Northern Hokan and Yuman. It may be suspected that in the long run the highest correlations between language and culture will be among compact and relatively recent linguistic groups, such as the Southwest Athabascan, rather than among broad, loose, and old groups, such as the Na-Dene.

The linguistic classification used is that of Sapir,[13] with more detailed subdivisions in California from Dixon and Kroeber.[14] Linguistic classes represented by less than three local groups are omitted. Table 2 gives the facts. Correlations are based on the universe of table 11.[15] All correlations were not computed because of limitations of time. A group of presumably high correlations were selected by inspection, computations made, and those above 0.3 entered in the table. The value 0.3 is an arbitrary choice but it is about the middle of the range of inter-trait correlations (tables 9 and 11).

With the exception of Hokan and Hokan-Siouan, all correlations above 0.3 between puberty and language involve linguistic units of continuous or nearly continuous geographical distribution. The Southwest Athabascans and the Southern California Shoshoneans form two generally recognized types of culture. North Pacific Coast culture as a whole does not fit the entire Algonkin-Wakashan group, nor even Wakashan, very neatly. Of the 118 traits given in table 13, only 26 (or 22 per cent) correlate above 0.3 with language. Therefore, language itself, or the historical relationships inferred from language, determine or partly determine only a small percentage of puberty distributions. As with geography, language explains only a small part of the facts. Historical implications are discussed in more detail under "Historical Speculations."

TABLE 2
Correlations $\phi(r_{hk})$ of Puberty with Language
(Blanks are values of 0.3 or less)

Language	Girls' puberty elements							
	VII	III	147	131	202	IV	I	IX
I. Algonkin-Wakashan	0.7	0.6	0.5	0.5				
A. Wakashan								
B. Salish	0.5							
II. Penutian								
A. California Penutian								
B. Oregon Penutian								
C. Plateau Penutian								
III. Hokan-Siouan						0.4		
A. Hokan						0.4		
1. Northern Hokan								
2. Yuman								
IV. Athabascan								
A. Pacific Coast Athabascan . . , ...					0.4			
B. Southern Athabascan								0.7
V. Shoshonean								
A. Basin Shoshonean								
1. Mono-Bannock (N Paiute)								
2. Shoshoni-Comanche (Shoshoni).								
3. Ute-Chemehuevi (S Paiute)							0.7	
B. Southern California Shoshonean							0.7	

*Roman and Arabic numbers heading columns are those of table 13.

Native Explanations of Observances

Native explanations of observances are catalogued by tribe in Part II, and correlated with each other and with various elements of behavior in table 3 below.[16] This table makes no attempt to distinguish areal differences because this cannot be done reliably from so small a sample. The elongated appearance of the table is an exaggeration of the true facts because the thirteen elements are telescoped summaries of behavior, whereas the detailed list of rationalizations is much closer to the original source material. The frequencies within a single section, such as the section headed "Sickness," often do not add up to the figure that is entered for the head for two reasons: the same tribe may have two or more specific variants; the source material may only give the information in generic form, in which instance it can be entered only for the heading.

Several generalizations obtrude. First, the sanction of the taboos and prescribed acts is mainly fear. Almost always the native explanation is in terms of what will happen to the girl if she does not obey the rules. This is, of course, partly a matter of expression: thus living a long life and not experiencing premature old

156

age or death are the same thing. But the consistent negative form of the statement of the rationalization reflects, I believe, a fundamental characteristic of primitive religion, at least of beliefs concerning menstruation. Furthermore, it is certain that in most instances the harm that may come to the girl is concrete bodily harm, which is easily comprehended by anyone under taboo. Even soul loss, which at first blush strikes one as a sophisticated abstraction, expresses itself overtly in sickness or even in death for the unfortunate person whose soul has been stolen.

Perhaps the next most striking result of table 3 is the scattered appearance of the frequencies. No element of behavior is explained by a single belief, and only the most specific and least frequently reported beliefs are confined to a single element of behavior. If fairly complete distributions of native explanations were obtainable, it would be possible to determine whether behavior or beliefs were distributed more widely or more continuously and perhaps to throw some light on the relative stability of these two kinds of culture. This cannot be done from the meager evidence at hand.

The great bulk of explanations are, of course, fictions of native mentality; but a few possess grains of efficacy, and still others reflect more general types of native belief. The efficacy, or lack of it, of the various observances is discussed in detail under "Physiological and Psychological Aspects."

The meat taboo is rationalized in two chief ways: that the girl will be harmed; that the luck of hunters will be spoiled. These explanations do not seem to be confined to separate areas. The latter reason is a specific variant of the generic belief that menstruation, and probably everything to do with sex, is unclean. Should the girl eat meat, animal spirits would be offended and would not permit their bodies to be killed.

Rationalizations for the scratching taboo consistently center around afflictions of the hair and skin. Although the hands, and especially the nails, might easily infect the body in scratching, it is difficult to see that a stick used for the purpose would be more sterile, unless it was changed often, which does not seem to have been done. In Northern California, at least, many women wore the scratching stick all the time on a cord around the neck, and used it when their hands were soiled from preparing food or were otherwise unfit for scratching.

The fundamental reasons for covering the head or eyes, and probably for seclusion itself, are to prevent the girl's seeing people or being seen by them, and to prevent her from seeing the sun, moon, or fire. Seeing people or being seen by them may harm both the girl and the people. Seeing the sun, moon, and fire is most frequently thought to cause blindness. There may be a germ of truth in the last belief, because too much exposure to the smoke and heat of a fire could cause eye troubles.

The chief explanation of the restriction on sleep is to prevent the girl from dreaming of the dead and having her soul stolen by a ghost. This is reported only for Northern California but I suspect it occurs in the North Pacific Coast, the Plateau, and the Athabascan and Yuman Southwest. Thus, for the Maricopa tribe, Spier reports that everyone regularly arose at dawn to avoid bad dreams and the resulting sickness, and that children were told stories to keep them awake late at night.

Under the taboo on talking or laughing, garrulousness refers to talking, wrinkles to laughing.

Physical exertion or work is prescribed more often for the good of the girl's character than to strengthen her body, although both are common reasons. There is good reason to believe that the instruction and practice in women's tasks at this time actually does help to make the girl a more accomplished woman. This is the nearest approach to formal education among many tribes.

The statement from Northern California that public singing and dancing is held to keep the girl awake and prevent her from dreaming of the dead is a nice instance of the assignment of a noble motive to a pleasurable task.

Summary.

Although a few native reasons seem to be based on fact, most are scientific fictions. . . .

Historical Facts

The following are direct statements of ethnographers or informants and refer to changes within the last fifty or sixty years unless otherwise stated. They are so few that a listing by tribe is practical. Prodigious combing of old sources would no doubt reveal a much larger array of this kind of evidence, but the return per unit of effort would still be small. Puberty rites are practically nonexistent in most of western North America at the present time. It is unfortunate that ethnographers have recorded so little concerning this process of cultural decay or of substitution of new beliefs and materials for old.

Tahltan.

Formerly the girl was secluded alone in a separate hut. Recently she has been screened off in a corner

157

of the dwelling. This may be an imitation of coast practice, or a diminishing of the severity of observances, or both.

Alberni Nootka.

A one-headed drum or tambourine has recently replaced the hollow-wood rattle. According to Philip Drucker, the tambourine has probably arrived late to the Middle North Pacific Coast, where it is most often connected with the hand-game. The source is more northern. Sapir is impressed with the fact that the Nootka "still cling tenaciously to the observances of girl's puberty ceremonies," although the individual restrictions are shorter and less severe than formerly. This is also true of the Apache.

Eastern Navaho

Sugar is now taboo during menstruation, apparently in imitation of the salt taboo.

Mescalero Apache.

At present, puberty rites at or near the time of first menstruation are mere family affairs. But annually, from the first to the fifth of July, a group rite is held for all girls who have menstruated for the first time within the past year. This development is certainly independent of Southern California or any other locality where a rite for a group of girls is held. Reasons or causes of this change seem to be several. First, the individual girl's puberty rite was the most important single ceremony of the Mescalero. It probably tended to be given more often in summer than in winter because of the available food supply and clement weather. In imitation of Americans, most Indians make a holiday out of the fourth of July anyway, so what could be simpler than to give the girls' puberty ceremony then? Because there is only one fourth of July and several girls to make their débuts, a group rite was the logical solution. Perhaps also the sharing of the expense by several families provided an added incentive.

San Carlos Apache.

In recent times the girl grinds wheat instead of corn for initiatory work. This is an instance of substitution of a product of similar use.

Yuma.

The Yuma were visited in 1775 by Eixarch,[17] in 1889 by Trippel, in 1931 by Forde, and in 1936 by Halpern. The following differences are noted. Eixarch: (a) The hotbed consisted only of warmed sand under and over the girl, no mention of arrowweed or other plants. (b) The girl was tossed in the air three times and let fall the last time, apparently to insure future good health. Forde: (a) On the hotbed the girl lies on arrowweed, over sand and stones. (b) She is not tossed in the air, but a man of fine physique steps on her back to make her "grow straight." Halpern: A woman walks on the girl's back.

Whether the use of plants or sand for the hotbed represents a local or family variation that might occur at any period in history, or a true temporal difference, is difficult to say. But the substitution of the back-stepping for the tossing of the girl does seem to be a true historical change. Forde apparently inquired concerning the tossing, but obtained only denials of it. Since the tossing is not reported for any other tribe, it is difficult to construct reasons for the change.

Diegueño.

Formerly two shell scratchers were used, recently two sticks. This seems to be an instance of degeneration. The shell material and the manufacturer may not have been available in recent times. The sticks are a substitute.

Luiseño.

"In very ancient times" scratchers consisted of oblong pieces of stone or of haliotis, perforated at one end and fastened with a string to the wrist. Recently two sticks have been used. This is a parallel to the stick substitution among the Diegueño.

Walapai.

Recently sugar has been tabooed during menstruation. It is thought to cause loss of teeth. This seems to be an extension of the salt taboo, and it is a parallel to the sugar taboo among the Eastern Navaho and to the substitution of wheat for maize among the San Carlos Apache.

Historical Speculations

The paucity of historical facts in the preceding section explains in part why most ethnologists indulge in historical speculations. In the present study we have seen that the distributions of the bulk of girls' puberty facts cannot be satisfactorily explained in terms of native ideology or function, feminine physiology, geography, or language. The present section offers some historical inferences which are thought to explain further the distributional facts. Although the author believes these inferences are more likely to be correct than not, he knows no way of determining their correctness. Past history is not automatically resurrected by correlation techniques, as

TABLE 4
Historical Speculations
(Reading from the bottom up)

North Pacific Coast	Northern California	Southern California	Plateau	Great Basin	Southwest
					Individual public puberty cere-mony of the non-Pueblo
	Individual public puberty ceremony				
Individual public puberty ceremony					
Work complex	Work complex				Work complex
				Work complex	
			Work complex		
	Female initiations	Female initiations			Female initiations
	Male initiations	Male initiations			Male initiations
Rest complex	Rest complex	Rest complex		Rest complex	Rest complex
Universals					

Klimek seems to argue.[18] However, correlations do facilitate an organization of data, which is a desirable prelude to historical speculations. Table 4 gives an outline of the speculations in this section.

The oldest traits are believed to be those which are universal, or nearly so, in western North America. The sporadically worldwide distribution of these traits is probably a better indication of their great age than universality in a single area. Another indication of great antiquity is the fact that certain traits, at least food and drink restrictions, scratching taboo, and seclusion, are prominent in many departments of single cultures.[19] The universal traits, already listed in the section on "Girls' Puberty Trait-Complexes" under the side heading "Universals," are: the beliefs that the girl is unclean, that she is especially susceptible to harm, that her actions at puberty predetermine her behavior throughout life; seclusion; attendant; food and drink restrictions; scratching taboo; initiatory work; bathing and changing clothes at end of menstruation or seclusion; instruction; avoidance of men. Because these traits are sporadically worldwide in distribution they do not indicate any migra-tion or diffusion within western North America. They could have been brought to this area by several different waves of immigrants, or have been diffused at various times from Asia, or from more easterly North America. In general, however, I believe they were brought to North America by the first immigrants. There is no evidence of these concepts spreading rapidly over a large area as did the 1890 Ghost Dance in North America.

The next oldest group of traits are thought to be those whose nucleus is the rest complex: lying on a hot bed usually in a pit; no physical exertion of any kind during actual menstruation; and the taboo on drinking or bathing in cold water. To this list may be added the salt taboo, ceremonial numbers 3 and 6, and possibly the covering of the girl's head with a utilitarian basket. The distributional evidence for the unity of this list is not very satisfactory. However these items occur mainly in the southern half of the area, especially California.

Male initiations of Central California, Southern California, Lower California,[20] and among the Pueblo are believed, along with Kroeber, to have a

159

common origin in a very early period. These have been included in the historical scheme because I believe female initiations in California and among the Pueblo were derived from them. Some evidence (the similarity in ritual content) has already been given in the discussions of puberty patterns for the respective areas. The astounding ritual parallels in Tierra del Fuego and even the Old World compel me to be sympathetic toward the view that these rituals were brought into America by immigrants at a very early time, that they have been supplanted in most areas by later ceremonies and beliefs, and now survive only in marginal areas. The increasing evidence for Australoid or Oceanoid physical types in the Americas seems to lend support to this view.

At a later period another type of puberty rite arrived from Asia or developed in the northern interior of North America. The nucleus of this is the work complex: the sitting or squatting in seclusion; the hot-food taboo; running, working, and bathing outdoors during first menstruation; and perhaps the complete food fast, seclusion in a separate hut, the vision quest, and scarification and bleeding of the girl.[21]

The work complex presumably moved southward from the northern Plateau, spreading westward to the Pacific coast from Vancouver Island to Northern California, and southward through the Great Basin into the Southwest. The mechanism of spread must have been chiefly migration, although diffusion no doubt also played a part. The direction was mainly north to south although some traits may have traveled in other directions.[22]

Public recognition of the pubescence of a single girl at the time it occurred probably originated on the North Pacific Coast whence it spread south into Northern California and into the Athabascan Southwest. The total trait distributions (tables 13, 14), the intertribal correlations (tables 10, 12),[23] and the inferred linguistic history of the Southwest Athabascans lend themselves to this interpretation.[24] The great emphasis on publicization of individual crises or changes of social status on the North Pacific Coast, as exemplified specifically in the potlatch, seems to me to be further presumptive evidence of the northern origin of these girls' puberty rites. Other relevant evidence has already been given in the discussions of puberty patterns; and the section, "Residual Distributions," gives a few items highly suggestive of north to south contact. Traits shared by the Athabascan Southwest with both Northern California and the North Pacific Coast are thought to be the oldest stage of this development, those common only to Southwest Athabascans and Northern Californians a later stage, and finally those exclusively Southwest Athabascan or shared

with neighboring southern tribes the latest. These have already been cited in the discussions of individual areas and plotted in distribution tables and need not be repeated here.

There are a few Southern California features which seem to me to have been derived from the north via the Great Basin. These are: the race at the conclusion of the rite; the wearing of bands around arms and legs; rock painting; and the delousing ceremony of the Cupeño. Kroeber long ago pointed out certain parallels between northern and southern California which were lacking in central California: for example, the basket hat and the basket mortar. From the results of the culture-element survey, we now know these distributions to be nearly continuous through the western edge of the Great Basin. Therefore, the girls' puberty items cited above seem to be only a small part of an important block of traits indicative of north to south contact via the Great Basin. Predominantly northern elements found in the Yuman area and the Pueblo Southwest have been given in the discussions of these areas. These items strengthen the thesis of this paragraph.

Without laboring through the entire remaining list of items, I believe that continuous distributions most often represent historical contact, whether diffusion or migration. Diffusion within the major areas shown on map 2 is too obvious to need more than bare mention.

Conclusion.

Broadly speaking, we seem to have here an example of convergence. The Southern California public rite seems to have developed independently of those of other areas.[25] It seems at present to be a sort of survival of a very old and formerly more widespread type of rite. The predominant type of public puberty ceremony originated on the Northwest Coast and spread southward mainly by migration, perhaps entirely in the custody of Athabascans. Subsequent diffusion took place in both Northern California and the Southwest. Although the intruders seemed to have been rather successful in imposing their new ideas on the earlier occupants of these areas, they also seem to have absorbed a great deal from the latter. The unfavorable environment of the Great Basin, and to a lesser extent of the Plateau, seems to have checked the diffusion of public recognition eastward.

Summary

Table 13 and map 2 constitute a summary of the distributional facts. The traits are not randomly distributed with respect to each other but fall into two kinds of groupings: tribe and trait. Mostly the boundaries of these groups are not sharp but shade into

160

one another. Statistics were used to construct table 13. Although possibly it could be done intuitively, statistics greatly facilitate the linear arrangements of tribes and traits which show the best classification of the material.

Only about ten per cent of the traits listed in table 13 correlate with geographical environment and actually seem to have been determined (at least partly) by geography.

About twenty per cent of the traits in the same table show significant correlations with language. In most instances the correlative linguistic units are of continuous or near continuous geographical distribution.

From a compilation of native explanations of observances it was found that no element of behavior is explained by a single element of belief and conversely that few beliefs are confined to a single element of behavior. The sanction of taboos and prescribed acts is chiefly fear. Most native explanations are rationalizations from the point of view of modern science.

Not more than ten per cent of the entire list of traits have any innate basis. At least ninety per cent are purely cultural in contrast to biological.

Historical facts are too few to yield any important generalization.

Historical speculations are summarized in table 4 and under "Conclusion" of the preceding section.

PART II. STATISTICS

Statistical Methods

The statistical methods used here are mainly those of Klimek.[26] Klimek correlated (using Q_6) tribes with tribes, traits with traits, and trait-complexes with tribes. All tribes were intercorrelated, but because there were some 425 elements, it was practically impossible to correlate each of these with every other one. For this reason Klimek broke up the total number of elements into five sections. Interelement correlations were determined within each of these five sections and the "strata" in each defined and shown graphically in tables.[27] In the discussion of the results he intuitively equated certain "strata" in one table with those of another.

The present technique differs in certain respects. Instead of Q_6, I have used r_{hk} as a measure of correlation.

$$\emptyset = r_{hk} = \frac{ad\text{-}bc}{\sqrt{(a\text{+}c)\,(b\text{+}d)\,(a\text{+}b)\,(c\text{+}d)}}, \text{ where "a"}$$

is the number of cases in which both phenomena compared are present, "b" the number of cases in which the first is present and the second absent, "c" the number of cases in which the second is present and the first absent, "d" the number of cases in which both are absent. Q_6 and r_{hk} are true mathematical functions and will always give parallel results. I prefer r_{hk} merely because it can be computed on a slide rule with one step less than Q_6.[28] The time required is less than one minute.

Because the statistics in the present study are based on 159 tribes and 118 traits, it was impractical to compute all the intercorrelations between either type of unit. Dual divisions of both the tribes and traits would have resulted in four different statistical universes. The intuitive equating of certain trait-complexes or tribal-complexes in each of the four universes would have been difficult and unconvincing. Therefore I have used a method of pooling similarly distributed groups of traits and similarly distributed tribal inventories into larger units, of constructing a single composite distribution to represent the group, and of intercorrelating each group with every other group. The correlations within both trait and tribe pools are given in tables 5 and 6.[29] The final result is shown in tables 11-13 (at end). This method eliminates one intuitive step from Klimek's routine. I have not computed correlations between traits or trait-complexes and individual tribes or tribal pools. These relationships seem obvious enough from inspection of table 13.

Because the pooling technique has not been used before in ethnology, it will be described in detail. The first step is to tabulate the data on two sets of data sheets, each of which is a cross-file of the other. The first data sheet is headed with a culture element and the presence or absence among tribes of each element is entered. The second sheet is headed with a tribe and the presence or absence of each trait is entered. One of each type of data sheet is illustrated in the samples on page 67.

It does not matter whether tribes or traits are intercorrelated first. Therefore let us arbitrarily begin by correlating tribes.

(1) Choose any tribe from the second type of data sheets and compare its trait inventory with that of every other tribe. (2) Select all those tribes with which you think it will correlate above some arbitrary level, such as 0.50, and make a list of those

TABLE 6
Correlations within Tribal Pools*

A

	BlCl	BlBl	Kwak	CNoo	ANoo
BlCl		7	8	8	6
BlBl	7		9	6	6
Kwak	8	9		8	7
CNoo	8	6	8		7
ANoo	6	6	7	7	

B

	Pent	Cmx	Klah	Sesh	Squa	Sane	Cow	Nan	Lum	Mak	Klal
Pent		10	9	7	8	9	7	8	7	6	6
Cmx	10		9	7	9	9	7	8	7	7	6
Klah	9	9		7	9	8	8	8	7	8	7
Sesh	7	7	7		7	7	6	6	6	4	7
Squa	8	9	9	7		9	8	8	7	7	7
Sane	9	9	8	7	9		9	10	8	7	7
Cow	7	7	8	6	8	9		9	7	7	7
Nan	8	8	8	6	8	10	9		7	7	7
Lum	7	7	7	6	7	8	7	7		7	8
Mak	6	7	8	4	7	7	7	7	7		7
Klal	6	6	7	7	7	7	7	7	8	7	

C

	Coos	Gal	Chet	Tol
Coos		7	7	7
Gal	7		8	8
Chet	7	8		7
Tol	7	8	7	

D

	Kar	Hupa	Chil
Kar		7	6
Hupa	7		8
Chil	6	8	

E

	VanD	Matt	Sin
VanD		7	7
Matt	7		8
Sin	7	8	

F

	Kato	Wail	CYHu	Yuki	NPo	CoMi	HWin
Kato		7	6	8	8	8	7
Wail	7		8	8	8	7	7
CYHu	6	8		7	7	6	7
Yuki	8	8	7		8	8	8
NPo	8	8	7	8		8	7
CoMi	8	7	6	8	8		7
HWin	7	7	7	8	7	7	

G

	Klam	Mod	ESha	WSha
Klam		7	6	7
Mod	7		7	6
ESha	6	7		8
WSha	7	6	8	

H

	Atsu	Yana	WAch	EAch
Atsu		8	8	7
Yana	8		7	7
WAch	8	7		8
EAch	7	7	8	

I

	TWin	MWin	SWin
TWin		7	8
MWin	7		7
SWin	8	7	

J

	MMai	FMai	MNis
MMai		7	7
FMai	7		6
MNis	7	6	

K

	NMi	CeMi	SMi	KiYo
NMi		6	8	7
CeMi	6		7	5
SMi	8	7		8
KiYo	7	5	8	

L

	ENav	WNav	JicA	LipA	MesA	WSA	HuA	TonA	CiA	WMA	SCA
ENav		8	6	7	4	5	5	8	8	7	6
WNav	8		5	7	5	6	6	9	8	7	7
JicA	6	5		7	7	6	6	6	6	8	7
LipA	7	7	7		8	7	7	6	6	6	6
MesA	4	5	7	8		9	9	4	5	7	7
WSA	5	6	6	7	9		10	6	6	8	8
HuA	5	6	6	7	9	10		5	6	8	8
TonA	8	9	6	6	4	6	5		8	7	7
CiA	8	8	6	6	5	6	6	8		8	7
WMA	7	7	8	6	7	8	8	7	8		9
SCA	6	7	7	6	7	8	8	7	7	9	

M

	DDie	WDie	MDie	Luis	SSer	Cup	MCah	PCah	DCah
DDie		8	7	7	6	6	6	5	6
WDie	8		9	8	5	8	8	6	6
MDie	7	9		8	5	8	8	6	6
Luis	7	8	8		6	9	8	7	6
SSer	6	5	5	6		6	7	6	7
Cup	6	8	8	9	6		8	7	6
MCah	6	8	8	8	7	8		8	6
PCah	5	6	6	7	6	7	8		7
DCah	6	6	6	6	7	6	6	7	

*Underlined figures are those computed from distributions skewed more than 0.80:0.20 or 0.20:0.80.

TABLE 6 (Continued)

N

	Shus	Lill	Thom
Shus		10	9
Lill	10		9
Thom	9	9	

O

	Sanp	Kali	Pcwa	Wen
Sanp		7	7	7
Kali	7		6	6
Pcwa	7	6		10
Wen	7	6	10	

P

	Als	Sius	SixR	Yur	Wiy
Als		9	9	7	8
Sius	9		9	7	8
SixR	9	9		7	8
Yur	7	7	7		8
Wiy	8	8	8	8	

Q

	CCpa	LkPo	Wap	LkNi
CCpa		9	8	9
LkPo	9		9	10
Wap	8	9		10
LkNi	9	9	10	

R

	Kit	Tub	Kaw
Kit		8	8
Tub	8		7
Kaw	8	7	

S

	Pana	Owen	FLK	Ash	Bty	Lida	GSmV	SmCr	RsRi	Hmlt	Ely	SprV	Elko	Egan	RubV	BtlM	NPMC
Pana		8	7	8	9	9	8	8	6	8	6	8	7	6	6	6	6
Owen	8		7	8	9	8	8	8	8	8	8	7	7	7	5	7	5
FLK	7	7		10	8	8	8	6	8	8	7	6	7	7	7	6	4
Ash	8	8	10		9	8	8	6	8	8	7	6	7	7	7	6	7
Bty	9	8	8	9		9	9	6	7	8	8	8	8	7	7	6	6
Lida	9	8	8	8	9		9	6	7	8	8	8	8	7	7	7	6
GSmV	8	8	8	8	9	9		6	8	9	9	8	8	8	7	7	6
SmCr	8	8	6	6	6	6	6		7	9	9	7	7	6	6	6	5
RsRi	6	8	8	8	7	7	8	7		9	9	8	7	8	7	7	5
Hmlt	8	8	8	8	8	7	9	9	9		9	8	8	8	7	7	6
Ely	6	8	7	7	8	8	9	9	9	9		8	9	9	8	8	7
SprV	8	7	6	6	8	8	8	7	8	8	8		10	8	7	7	7
Elko	7	7	7	7	8	8	8	7	7	8	9	10		8	7	7	7
Egan	6	7	7	7	8	7	7	6	8	8	9	8	8		8	6	4
RubV	6	5	7	7	7	7	8	6	8	8	8	7	7	8		6	4
BtlM	6	5	7	7	7	7	7	6	7	7	8	7	8	6	6		7
NPMC	6	5	4	7	6	6	6	5	6	7	7	7	7	4	4	7	

U

	SnRi	LeSh	BoSh	Ban	GCSh	PrSh	Skul	DeCr
SnRi		8	8	8	6	9	8	7
LeSh	8		9	8	7	7	8	8
BoSh	8	9		7	7	7	8	8
Ban	8	8	7		6	8	8	8
GCSh	6	7	7	6		8	10	9
PrSh	9	7	7	8	8		9	9
Skul	8	9	8	8	10	9		9
DeCr	7	8	6	8	9	9	9	

V

	Tasi	Kuyu	Kupa	Toe	Tov	Pak	Atsa	Sawa	Tago	Wada
Tasi		8	7	8	8	7	8	7	8	7
Kuyu	8		6	7	7	6	7	7	8	6
Kupa	7	6		7	7	7	8	7	8	6
Toe	8	7	7		9	9	8	8	8	7
Tov	8	7	7	9		8	8	9	8	6
Pak	7	6	7	9	8		6	6	6	6
Atsa	8	7	8	8	8	6		9	10	6
Sawa	7	7	7	8	9	6	9		9	8
Tago	8	8	8	8	8	6	10	9		9
Wada	7	6	9	7	7	6	6	8	9	

W

	Mes 2	Mes 1
Mes 2		9
Mes 1	9	

X

	Moha	Hava	Wala	WYa	Coco
Moha		7	9	7	8
Hava	7		7	8	7
Wala	9	7		8	9
WYa	7	8	8		8
Coco	8	7	9	8	

tribes. (3) Then choose a second tribe and likewise compare it by inspection with every other tribe, listing other probable high correlatives. (4) Continue this process until all presumably high correlations have been abstracted from the total number. In practice this is not as mechanical as it may seem because geographically neighboring tribes most often show highest correlations. (5) Compute all correlations thus selected. If the selection is made cautiously and conservatively there should be a fair number of coefficients that fall ten or twenty points below the arbitrary dead line. In this situation there should be some values in the 0.40's and 0.30's. This is necessary in order to make sure that none above 0.50 have been overlooked. If some values within the desired range *are* overlooked, it is not serious. It simply means that certain tribes will not be grouped into pools but will remain separate variables. Ultimately their correlations with other tribes or pools of tribes will be determined and the overlooked values will automatically appear in the final intercorrelation table. Incomplete pooling merely increases the amount of mechanical labor. Nothing of importance is lost. (6) Group together in a pool all tribes whose correlations with each other average higher than the arbitrary level set.

There is no rule for determining the arbitrary lower limit of average correlation within a pool. This is purely a practical matter. The point is to boil down the total number of variables to be ultimately intercorrelated to some convenient number such as 50, certainly not more than 80 because Hollerith type punched cards have only 80 columns. In the present study, I chose 0.65 for the tribal pools, and 0.50 for the trait pools. This yielded 50 tribal variables (table 12) and 62 trait variables (table 11). A certain amount of trial and error is necessary in making the preliminary selection of presumably high correlations. The results of the application of this technique to the present data will be described below.

Now construct a composite tribal inventory for each pool of tribes. This could be done by simply recording plus for each trait present among the majority of tribes and minus for those present among a minority or no tribes. However, a more refined technique is the the following:[30] (a) count the total number of presences for all tribes in the pool; (b) divide this figure by the total number of entries, both presences and absences, for all tribes in the pool. This decimal represents the relative frequency of presences in the pool, or the mean ratio of presences in all tribes. When a trait is more frequent in the pool than this mean, record it present; when less frequent, record it absent. Thus the mean ratio of presences in a certain pool of ten tribes might be 0.35. In this

case, when a trait is present for four or more of the ten tribes, record it present for the pool, because 0.40 is greater than 0.35. When present for less than four tribes, record it absent. Repeat this for every trait. The result is a composite tribal inventory for the pool. Such composite tribal inventories may be ultimately correlated with each other or with individual tribal inventories (table 12). The pooling of traits is exactly the same in principle. The final result of both is table 13.

The justification for the use of the mean ratio of presences instead of the simpler majority-minority principles need not be gone into in detail here; suffice it to say that the mean concept is mathematically more correct and can be used in many ways, such as in Milke's variability formula. Actually what happened is this. In constructing tribal pools for the Great Basin, the mean ratio of presences was 0.20. A trait occurring in barely more than one-fifth of the tribes in such a pool is recorded present for the pool. For other areas this ratio ran as high as 0.50. For these a trait had to be present for more than half the tribes before it was marked present for the pool.

The following facts concerning the application of pooling techniques to the present data give some idea of the actual amount of labor saved. The 159 tribes yield 12,561 interrelationships.[31] In the construction of the tribal pools, 1703 correlations were computed; and in computing table 12, 1225 more; total 2928. This last figure is 23 per cent of the first; the saving is 77 per cent. For the trait pools the facts are similar: 6903 interrelationships among the original 118 traits; 429 correlations computed in constructing trait pools; 1891 for table 11; total 2320, which is 34 per cent of the first; saving 66 per cent. Combining these two sets of figures, we get the following results:

Total number of interrelationships		19,464
Number of correlations computed in constructing pools	2,132	
Number of correlations computed after pooling	3,116	
Total number of correlations computed		5,248
Saving, number of correlations		14,216

In per cent the saving is 73. However, additional time is consumed in inspecting slips, constructing composite distributions, and other tasks. Probably the present job was done in about one-third the time required to have computed every intercorrelation.

For most bodies of data I do not believe it is practical to compute two sets of correlations as done here.

A briefer compromise method will be described. Let us assume that we have 500 traits distributed among 50 tribes. First intercorrelate the 50 tribes to determine the most ideal linear order of tribes. Then tabulate the distribution of each trait on a thin strip of paper with the tribes in this predetermined order. Finally, sort these strips by inspection into groups with similar distributions and construct a table such as table 13 or a condensed equivalent. In the present study, the arrangement of traits in table 14 was done in this manner in two days. These distributions in table 14 are too imperfectly known to establish the validity of such an inspection method; however, the technique is far more rapid than the most efficient brand of numerical computation. Without the previous determination of the order of tribes by intercorrelating them, the grouping of traits by inspection would be an extremely difficult task. Where the data are such that the number of traits is less than the number of tribes, it is obviously more practical to compute intercorrelations for traits, then to group tribes by inspection.

The Hollerith type electric punched card sorter is the only practical way to make the counts from which correlation coefficients are computed.[32] When tribes are to be compared with tribes, use a card for each trait. Assign each tribe to a column of the card and punch presence or absence[33] in each of the columns according to the distribution of the trait. To compare tribes 1 and 2, set the sorter on column one. It automatically sorts the cards into two piles, presence and absence for tribe 1, and counts the frequency of each. Then take the pile of presences for tribe 1 and sort them for tribe 2 in column two. Again two piles appear. Because all the cards in both of these latter piles were present for tribe 1, they represent the number of traits present for both tribes (a), and the number present for tribe 1 and absent for tribe 2 (b). This gives half the fourfold table. Continue sorting the traits present in tribe 1 for presence and absence in all the other tribes, recording frequencies on a data sheet. After this, take the pile of absences for tribe 1, and sort them in the same manner for presence and absence in all the other tribes. This gives the other two cells (c and d) of all the fourfold tables in which tribe 1 is compared. Then split tribe 2, and sort each of its divisions in turn for presence and absence among tribes 3, 4, and so on to the end. Continue in this manner until each tribe has been compared with all other tribes.

When traits are to be compared with traits, use a card for each tribe. Sort as described above. When more than 80 phenomena are to be compared, the method becomes clumsy because there are only 80 columns on a card. For most purposes, however, 80

variables are plenty. If more than 80 occur, select by inspection those variables likely to be highly correlated and punch them on the same set of cards. Group them into pools so that there are no more than 80 variables left for the final intercorrelation.

All correlations in this paper are carried to only one decimal place. The reasons are: the standard errors (table 7) average about one unit in the first decimal place; the observational errors are large (see "Reliability and Validity of Data," below); the incomparability of some of the data produces more errors (see "Comparability of Data" p. 169; the intercorrelation tables are large and confusing as it is, and two places would make them more difficult to read.

Reliability and Validity of Data

This section is concerned with errors of observation as distinguished from sampling errors. The latter are mentioned under "Statistical Methods" and, with reference to the formula r_{hk}, are given in table 7.

Following the distinction made by psychologists, reliability refers to the consistency of response, that is, the amount of agreement of a single informant on two occasions or of two informants of the same local group; validity refers to the truth of the testimony in either instance. Most of the material in this section is concerned with reliability. The paragraph labeled "Validity" is an attempt to get at the truth or falsity of responses. If errors of two informants of the same tribe are equal in number but uncorrelated, it can be shown that the validity of the testimony of either is higher than the reliability coefficient obtained by comparing the testimony of the two. Under the same conditions, elimination of the elements on which the two informants disagree raises the validity figure much higher than the reliability figure. However, at present we know too little about reliability and validity to utilize such corrections.

The problem of reliability and validity has recently been discussed by Kroeber[34] and the author.[35] Kroeber's findings are based on relatively indirect evidence. Nowhere does he use the report of more than one informant for each local group. His results are inferred from several kinds of evidence: occurrence of unique elements; ratio of positive to negative responses; total number of responses; dialectic affiliations; cultural positions with respect to neighboring tribes. Although the cumulative effect of all these criteria, handled with caution, does give results of some significance, the method is too subjective to be recommended as a general procedure. Furthermore,

TABLE 7
Standard Error of r_{hk} for Symmetrical Distributions*

N	r_{hk}									
	0.00	0.10	0.20	0.30	0.40	0.50	0.60	0.70	0.80	0.90
20	0.22	0.22	0.22	0.21	0.21	0.19	0.18	0.16	0.13	0.10
40	0.16	0.16	0.15	0.15	0.14	0.14	0.13	0.11	0.09	0.07
60	0.13	0.13	0.13	0.12	0.12	0.11	0.10	0.09	0.08	0.06
80	0.11	0.11	0.11	0.11	0.10	0.10	0.09	0.08	0.07	0.05
100	0.10	0.10	0.10	0.10	0.09	0.09	0.08	0.07	0.06	0.04
120	0.09	00.09	0.09	0.09	0.08	0.08	0.07	0.07	0.05	0.04
140	0.08	0.08	0.08	0.08	0.08	0.07	0.07	0.06	0.05	0.04
160	0.08	0.08	0.08	0.08	0.07	0.07	0.06	0.06	0.05	0.03

*These errors increase at an increasing rate as skewness increases. When skewness is 90:10 for both variables, these values are approximately doubled. Computed from formula given by Yule, p. 604.

the method makes certain a priori generalizations regarding primitive cultures which are the very ones ethnology should be trying to prove a posteriori: for example, that geographically neighboring tribes are more similar in culture than geographically separated tribes. If exceptions to this rule are eliminated because the data are thought to be invalid, the chain of reasoning becomes entirely circular and sterile. In this instance, however, Kroeber has not pushed the method that far. Nevertheless, I disagree with him that "The ultimate test of reliability [validity] of any list of course is its degree of fit into the totality of the picture." I believe the only satisfactory test of reliability and validity is the testimony of two or more informants from each local group in which there are that many fairly well-informed survivors left. What the majority or at least what all agree on can then be accepted as true regardless of its "degree of fit" to any intuitive scheme.

Although reliability coefficients give the total amount of error, they do not tell which of two contradictory entries is true. In areas in which informants are too few to make it possible to check all information, such as that of the Pomo, the criteria used by Kroeber to determine the correctness of individual elements and total lists are of value.

Because reliability and validity are always relative to the size of the area, the particular topic, and the broadness or fineness of the trait analysis, they should always be determined anew for each numerical study. This is the procedure long employed by other sciences.

Tables 8 and 9 summarize the relevant facts for the present study.[36] The counts were all made from the universe of table 13. Reliability coefficients (r_{hk}) were computed only for those tribes or traits for which there were 50 or more duplications. When

three or more entries were available for a single trait of a single tribe, I usually chose the two which were from the two fullest sources. Exceptions to this rule were made only when the two fullest sources were the work of a single ethnographer. In that event it seemed more desirable to choose the work of a second ethnographer, providing the total amount of his information was nearly as great as that of the first. Most of the pairs of entries used to determine reliability are from two ethnographers. Correlations are carried only to one place because the statistical universes average only about sixty cases.

Only rarely are the sources compared truly independent. Most later essay-type sources seem to have taken considerable information from earlier sources without giving specific references to them. Only where a point is doubtful are we sure to find reference to the earlier source. Also, the ethnographer seldom separates the testimony of his various informants. Presumably, completely independent sources would yield lower reliability correlations.

Reliability of Elements.

The reliabilities of elements are spread rather evenly over the range from 1.0 to 0.0. Correlations involving the least reliable traits are presumably worthless.[37] The average reliability coefficient is 0.6. This may be interpreted as meaning that most values above this figure are very high or perfect correlations. In general, differences in true distributions can be assumed to exist only when the correlation is less than this figure. If reliability coefficients for all elements could be determined, they could be used to correct obtained values upward to their true levels. They would also have important bearing on the construction of pools discussed in the section on "Statistical Methods."

Element reliabilities have been examined further by making three pairs of divisions, as indicated in table 8. The only significant difference in averages is between definitely skewed and not definitely skewed elements. It is interesting to note that, according to our correlation coefficient, observational errors as well as sampling errors are greater for skewed distributions.

Reliability of Tribal Inventories.

Reliabilities of tribal inventories range from 1.0 to 0.1, averaging 0.7. Here also skewed distributions appear to be less reliable than more symmetrical ones. The fact that these figures are higher than those for element-with-element correlations is a nice illustration of the relativity of correlation coefficients. It may also be noted in comparing tables 11 and 12 that tribal correlations are higher than those for elements. The two lowest tribal reliabilities, 0.2 and 0.1, are due to disagreement with respect to the presence or absence of public recognition of girls' puberty. A disagreement on this generic concept automatically introduces differences for all elements referring to group dancing, feasting, singing, and such. Both tribes are on the borderline between areas which have definite public recognition and those which do not. Map 15 gives the geographical location of reliability coefficients and the boundaries of girls' puberty areas of map 2. In general it cannot be said that there is any definite tendency for low reliabilities to fall near major boundaries. In fact there are several high reliabilities near such boundaries.

TABLE 9
Reliability Coefficients (r_{hk}) of Tribal Inventories[*]

BlBl	0.8	LkPo	0.8	KiMo	0.7	WSA	0.9
Kwak	0.9	Klam	0.8	KiYo	0.1	HuA	0.9
Cow	0.7	WSha	0.7	LkYo	0.5	TonA	0.7
Lill	1.0	EAch	0.7	BaPa	1.0	Pap	0.5
Tol	0.6	MWin	0.7	Tub	0.6	Moha	0.8
Gal	0.9	MMai	0.7	Pana	0.9	DDie	0.9
Kar	0.6	FMai	0.6	Owen	0.8	WDie	0.7
Yur	0.9	VMai	0.6	Kuyu	0.9	MDie	0.8
Hupa	0.8	FNis	0.6	Kidu	0.7	Luis	0.8
Matt	0.8	NMi	1.0	ENav	0.8	Cup	0.8
Sin	0.6	SMi	0.4	Jic	0.4	MCah	0.7
Kato	0.6	SJYo	0.8	Mes	1.0	DCah	0.7
CYHu	0.2						

Average 0.7
Average of skewed distributions 0.6
Average of distributions not skewed 0.8

*Correlations based on skewed distributions (as defined in table 8) are underlined.

As they stand, most of the correlations in tables 11 and 12 are scarcely correct to one place. Two places is certainly sufficient for any ethnological purpose.[38] The use of three places, by Kroeber and me,[39] and by Kroeber alone,[40] is a waste of space, and any rank ordering or other manipulation based on the third place is worthless.

It should be remembered that r_{hk} = 0.6 is equivalent to Q_6 = 0.8. For symmetrical distributions, tetrachoric r would be the same as Q_6 and Q_2 would be 0.9. Therefore, this is not a hopeless reliability. There is merely no point in stressing minor numerical differences between correlations.

Validity.

Table 10 represents an attempt to compare the validity of element lists with other sources. Such a comparison is of limited value because other sources give so little definite negative evidence. I have applied the same criteria for inferring absences to both kinds of data, and have chosen only those traits for which all sources on a given tribe listed in table 10 provide data. For each tribe, there is at least one element-list source and one other source. An aberrance, in this context, is defined as an entry that is different from the majority of others for a single trait and single tribe. Thus, for the Alberni Nootka (ANoo) there are thirty-eight traits for which all three sources commit themselves. Of these thirty-eight traits, all three sources agree on thirty-five. For the remaining three, Sapir and Drucker give plus, Curtis minus. Curtis is therefore aberrant on the minus side in three instances. Where four sources occurred, three out of four is of course a majority, and for the seven sources of the Luiseño, four out of six, or four out of seven, was chosen as a majority.

The per cents and averages at the end of table 10 summarize the results. The correlations are determined by constructing a "true" inventory for each tribe by choosing the majority opinion on each element, and then correlating each source in turn with the "truth."

On the whole, element lists are no more aberrant than other sources, but their aberrances are mostly negative. If the majority of aberrances are errors, which I believe is more true of negatives, then element lists contain an erroneously large ratio of minuses. This result may be due entirely to selection, since essay-type sources offer so little negative evidence. However, this is what one would expect from recent field work done among progressively perishing cultures. Practically, I believe this situation is inevitable, at least ultimately, because informants will be less and less well informed about native cultures as time goes on. At the present time I believe

167

TABLE 10
Validity of Tribal Inventories

Totals	Aberrances			Number of traits (n)			•Validity (r_{hk})
	+	−	Total	+	−	Total	
Total	44	76	120	317	272	589	
Total for element lists	11	49	60				
Total for other sources	33	27	60				
Per cent for total	14	28	20				
Per cent for element lists	3	18	10				
Per cent for other sources	10	10	10				
Average correlation for total							0.9
Average correlation for element lists							0.9
Average correlation for other sources							0.9

it is better for the field worker to try to come to a decision in each instance, if necessary, by using a second or third informant, than to leave a great many blanks which produce a distortion of their own (see "Comparabilty of Data," p. 169). To date, most of us have left too many blanks in our element-list reports.

How much error is assignable to informants, how much to field workers, and how much to the compiler of distributions from several field reports is impossible to determine without more carefully controlled field conditions.

O. Stewart's Entries

Tribe	New entries		Ratio of + to to-
	+	−	tal information*
Tasi	1	41	0.13
Kuyu	1	13	0.17
Küpa	1	13	0.16
Toe	2	13	0.13
Töv	2	14	0.17
Pak	0	12	0.11
Wash	4	21	0.29
Atsa	2	13	0.18
Sawa	2	13	0.16
Tagö	2	13	0.18
Wada	1	13	0.16
Kidü	2	18	0.26
Totals	20	172	

*Included for comparison with ratio of + for new entries. Total information includes the additional entries herein. In general the ratio of + for new entries is close to that for the total.

The fact that validity correlations are higher than reliability correlations probably expresses the truth, but it should be remembered that the statistical universes vary considerably and the samples are small.

Corrections of author's distributions by Barnett and O. Stewart.

When I had completed the first draft of the distributions, Barnett, Stewart, and Gifford previewed them. Barnett and Stewart made some new entries. Counts of these, compiled only from the 118 traits of table 13, are given in the following.

Barnett's Entries

Tribe	New entries		+ + Barnett Driver	+ l Barnett Driver	l + Barnett Driver	l l Barnett Driver	Correlation of original with corrected distributions (r_{hk})
	+	−					
Pent...	9	10	35	4	0	74	0.9
Cmx ...	4	5	38	5	0	80	0.9
Klah...	4	6	47	1	1	70	1.0
Sesh...	6	8	25	12	0	79	0.8
Squa...	3	5	39	12	0	74	0.8
Sane...	3	7	47	2	2	72	0.9
Cow....	4	7	47	4	2	69	0.9
Nan....	5	9	43	1	2	73	1.0
Totals.	38	57	321	41	7	591	

Barnett had revisited his Salish tribes the summer following his element-list survey. Therefore his corrections of my entries represent additional knowledge as well as my misinterpretation of his element-list report. On the assumption that the entries as they now stand are correct, those which contradict my own show the amount of error made by an element-list field worker and a compiler of distributions combined. Except for the Seshelt and Squamish, this is small. For these two tribes, the original data deny public recognition of girls' puberty. Later field work affirmed this. It is significant to note that more inquiry and better acquaintance with native cultures alters previous results by increasing the ratio of pluses. More superficial work contains too many minuses. The new entries by Barnett illustrate, roughly, the amount of additional information on 118 traits which twice as long an acquaintance with native cultures supplies. Except for the Seshelt and Squamish, Barnett's corrections would not significantly alter intertribal correlation coefficients.

None of O. Stewart's entries contradict my own. They consist mostly of minuses. He did no additional field work. His additions would not affect correlations significantly.

Validity of Klimek's girls' puberty distributions.

I plotted my own data in Klimek's distribution tables to obtain the comparisons shown in the tabulation below.

It was difficult to equate some of Klimek's elements with my own. Klimek's element 399 seems to be equivalent to the roasting pit, although Gifford's original data on the Miwok did not mention heat. I have constructed an additional distribution, x, which seems to be the concept to which Klimek's element 332 refers; but I have also retained comparison with my 28. At any rate, Klimek's distributions contain far too many negative entries. Most of these were inferred merely from lack of mention of the elements in essay-type sources. The excess of minuses in Klimek's data is greater than the apparent excess of minuses in culture-element data (see "Validity," p. 167, and "Corrections of Author's Distributions," p. 168. Nevertheless, his results may be no wilder than those derived from distributions full of blanks (see "Comparability of Data," below). This illustrates the condition of California's ethnology before the culture-element survey. Other ethnologists who have worked in the area have no doubt erred as much as Klimek, but, because they often made no attempt to give specific distributions including absences, they have not laid themselves open to such direct criticism.

Element	+ + Driver Klimek	+ − Driver Klimek	− + Driver Klimek	− − Driver Klimek	r_{hk}
28. (Girl must lie in seclusion on heated spot) In definite pit: Klimek's 332, Girls' rite with pit-roasting ceremonial...	7	11	0	18	0.5
x. Girl roasted in pit with public participation: Klimek's 332..	7	2	0	30	0.9
30. Hot stone on belly: Klimek's 347, Crescentic stone in girls' rite..........	1	2	0	8	0.5
144. Girl eats or drinks tobacco: Klimek's 234, Girls' rite with drinking tobacco.	6	0	0	49	1.0
149. Girl looks into haliotis: Klimek's 406, Haliotis looked into in girls' puberty..	1	1	0	58	0.7
152. East significant: Klimek's 420, East significant in girls' rite.................	5	5	0	1	0.3
187. Girl dances at public rite: Klimek's 404, Girl dances in puberty rite	11	16	3	29	0.4
Totals	38	37	3	193	4.3
Average					0.6

Comparability of Data

It is possible for data to be perfectly reliable yet very imperfectly comparable. If each fact in each field report on each tribe could be equated to a similar fact in all other reports on all other tribes in an area, then all the data would be perfectly comparable. It is obvious to anyone who has ever made a comparative study over a continuous area of any size that the comparability of most sources is very low. The majority of facts have no comparative value because they cannot be matched with similar facts from other tribes. The result is nothing or a series of wild inferences regarding absences. This is a sad state of affairs scientifically. How comparable are the present data?

The 214 puberty traits listed in Appendix 1 do not exhaust the culture-element reports, yet of these, only about 118 were complete enough to be used in the statistics: about 75 per cent. The line was not drawn

169

exactly at that figure because certain traits seemed to have more significance than others, and the blanks for some were more nearly randomly distributed than for others. In a few instances traits were eliminated because of low reliability, which, usually, was combined with limited positive occurrence or apparent unimportance in native culture; for example, ceremonial number 6. Even though two distributions are 75 per cent complete, mutual exclusiveness of the blanks may leave only 50 per cent for the correlation.

Unless blanks are randomly distributed, which is seldom the case, they introduce errors in correlations. Thus:

	Tribes											
	a	b	c	d	e	f	g	h	i	j	k	l
Trait 1	x	x	x	x	x	x	x	x	-	-	-	-
Trait 2	x	x	x	x	-	-	-	-	x	x	-	-
Trait 3	x	x	x	x							-	-

For these hypothetical distributions, trait 3 correlates 1.00 with both 1 and 2, but 1 and 2 correlate 0.00 with each other.[41] This logically impossible result is caused by the use of different universes in computing the three correlations. Error of this type exists in some quantity in almost all correlations in this study, because few distributions contain no blanks at all. It is impossible to measure it because there is no way to determine complete distributions for all traits. There is perhaps some justification for filling in blanks, when they do not run over say 25 per cent, according to one's impressions of what ought to be there. This I have not done except as indicated in the section "Inferred Absences," which offers suggestions as to how negative evidence may be increased. However, the only real remedy is more carefully constructed lists, and more careful field work including the use of a second informant at least for those items unknown or uncertain to the first. None of us were sufficiently aware of these difficulties when in the field.

For broad comparisons of the culture-area type, 50 per cent comparability is sufficient. The entire list must be cut down anyway because of the terrific amount of computatory labor. A sample of 1000 traits would yield intertribal correlations as valid as 2000 or 4000. Thus I found that there were no significant differences between reliability coefficients based on 706 traits and on about 2000 traits, even though the universes in the latter data varied.[42] But for specific studies such as the present one, every fact counts. Although comparability will never be perfect, I believe it could be raised without much increase in time or expense.

Inferred Absences

Every comparative ethnologist in the past has inferred most of his negative evidence. Those who have been conscious of this have seldom bothered to make their methods explicit. I have been fortunate in having at my disposal a considerable quantity of negative evidence, mainly from the culture-element survey. Nevertheless, unevenness of these reports, discussed under "Comparability of Data," makes it necessary to infer a large number of absences.

1. Whenever a trait was stated to be absent in the entire culture of a tribe, I recorded it absent for girls' puberty of that tribe. For example, if tattooing was not practiced, it could not have been done at puberty. This sounds simple. In practice it means searching through many sections of monographs for an occasional negative statement, and checking over many sections of culture-element lists. Similarly, traits derived from or dependent on other traits were assumed to be absent when the latter were absent. For example, if boats were not used in a culture, paddles, sails, ferriage customs, and such obviously are absent.

2. Elements which were logically contradictory, conceptually mutually exclusive, or nearly exclusive in known distribution were assumed to be mutually exclusive in the remaining distribution. Two such are 23, girl must sit or squat in seclusion, and 24, girl must lie in seclusion. Logically these would seem mutually exclusive because a girl cannot sit and lie at the same time. It is possible, however, that the girl sits part of the time and lies the rest of the time, or that certain families prescribe sitting and others lying. An empirical comparison of the two distributions compiled only from specified negative evidence showed that, with very few exceptions, the two were actually mutually exclusive, and that sitting or squatting was mainly northern, lying mainly southern. Because this sample included more than half the total, it should be representative. Therefore, whenever one of the traits was marked plus and the other left blank, a minus was substituted for the blank. Thus a high negative correlation was assumed to be a perfect negative correlation for remaining data and the original data thus extrapolated to yield more data. Under such circumstances I prefer this procedure to the leaving of many blanks, which in most instances would distort the correlations more than the extrapolation (see "Comparability of Data"). Many cases are not as clear as the above, and because this procedure is partly gratuitous, the elements to which it has been applied are listed.

When one member of the following groups of traits is reported present, the rest of the group are assumed to be absent; nothing to the contrary: 2, 3, 5, 6, 7, 9, 10; 14, 15, 16; 17, 19, 20, 21, 22; 23, 24; 58, 59; 98, 99, 100; 101, 102; 136, 137; 139, 140; 156, 157; 159, 160; 165, 166, 167, 168, 169; 192, 193; 195, 196; 198, 202, 205, 206, 207, 208.

When two members of the following groups of traits are reported present, the rest of the group are assumed to be absent, nothing to the contrary: 78, 79, 80, 81, 82, 83; 126, 127, 128, 129, 131, 132, 133. For these groups, two alternatives were frequently reported present for single tribes, rarely three. Therefore, it seemed safe to infer that when two were present the remaining ones were absent.

A partial proof of the legitimacy of the procedure may be found in Barnett's corrections of my entries in the Georgian Gulf area, described under "Reliability and Validity of Data," p. 165. Although Barnett reversed forty-eight of my entries, not a single one of the alterations affected absences inferred in this manner.

3. Occasionally I inferred absences on what might be called simply distributional grounds. Thus element 31 (girl lies prone, massaged) was only reported for Southern California and the adjacent Southwest. It seemed an obvious enough part of a puberty rite to have been reported by someone in the north if it occurred there. Furthermore, it is often associated with pit roasting, which apparently has a wider distribution but which is still confined to the southern half of western North America. Other elements for which at least some absences were thus inferred are: 53, 57, 66, 106, 107, 148, 158, 210. As above, none of Barnett's alterations affected absences inferred for these elements. . . .

Notes

1. The University of California project of the Works Progress Administration Official Project No. 665-08-3-30, Unit A-15 has contributed heavily to the computing, graph drafting, and typewriting of this study.

2. 1922, 311-314; 1923, 300-301; 1925, 861-865.

3. 1932, 391-420.

4. 1923, 145-147.

5. 1936, 314-315.

6. 1929, 285; 1931, 517.

7. 1930, 314-325.

8. 1932.

9. Driver's areal descriptions have been deleted, as has table 14.

10. This is the same as Klimek's stratum, but I am avoiding the term stratum here because it implies history.

11. All of the other trait distribution maps have been deleted. Driver originally published trait distribution maps for every complex.

12. Klimek, 1935.

13. Sapir, 1929.

14. Dixon and Kroeber, 1919.

15. Table 11 has been deleted from this version.

16. Table 3 has been deleted from this version.

17. See Bolton.

18. Klimek, 1935, p. 61.

19. See table 1.

20. Cited by Kroeber, 1932:414-415.

21. These items may have been brought southward by Penutians or Aztec-Tanoans. The physical type of these peoples is thought to have been definitely Mongoloid.

22. It is worth stating perhaps that such inferences are not based on puberty material alone, but on all of the modest knowledge I have of aboriginal America. All the evidence from linguistics, ethnology, physical anthropology, and archaeology seems to me to indicate many movements of peoples, most of them from north to south, because the bulk of Indians, if not all, certainly came from Asia via Alaska. Although certain traits, such as maize agriculture, obviously originated in Middle America and diffused outward in both directions, I believe this theory of diffusion has been overdone. For North America we have relied too much on diffusion from the south and too little on migration from the north. For the two Americas, Nordenskiöld has shown that the most striking similarities are found between western North America, especially California, and South America from the Chaco to Tierra del Fuego. These traits seem best explained as marginal survivals of an Urkultur. The higher cultural developments of Middle America, and migrations from north to south over the eastern parts of the two continents, plus probable diffusions in other directions, seem to have obliterated most if not all of the connecting links.

23. Table 10 has been reduced to totals and averages in this version.

24. If much of the material had been explainable in terms of innate physiology it would have been advisable to eliminate such traits from the group used to infer history, because independent origin would have to be taken into account. To a lesser extent this would apply to geographical correlatives.

25. Excepting the limited occurrences of girls' "schools" in Northern California, which, I assume, have a derivation from boys' initiations as do Southern California girls' rites.

26. Klimek, 1935.

27. Ibid., tables 2-6.

28. The steps in the computation are these: (1) Compute the numerator in the most convenient way, with tables, calculating machine, or slide rule; and write it down. (2) Take the slide rule and multiply the four values in the denominator on the A and B scales of a Keuffel and Esser rule. The square root of their product automatically appears on the D scale. (3) Put the numerator on the C scale and divide it by the value on the D scale. (4) Read r_{hk} from the C scale.

29. Table 5, correlations within trait pools, or the R-mode correlations in modern usage, has been deleted.

30. I am indebted to W. Milke for this point. It is one step in his formula for measuring variability of distribution within a pool. Information from a personal communication from Milke to A. L. Kroeber.

31. The formula for combinations of n things taken 2 at a time is: $nC_2 = \frac{n(n-1)}{2}$. Substituting the 159 tribes for n, $\frac{159 \times 158}{2} = 12,561$.

32. The Works Progress Administration employees are a temporary solution, and they have been of great assistance in this paper. Small jobs of course can be done by hand. But we already have here at the University of California sufficient data on western North America to keep about five hand-sorters going ten years. If ever the area is expanded, more efficient methods will become an absolute necessity.

33. In each column there are ten spaces to punch. Arbitrarily assign one space to presence and another to absence.

34. Gifford and Kroeber.

35. Driver, 1938.

36. Table 8 has been deleted from this version.

37. For skewed distributions with a small percentage of pluses, say 10 per cent, two distributions of the same element may correlate zero yet show substantial agreement in most correlations with other elements. Reason: most correlations with other elements will be negative, and those other elements which have no common positive occurrences with the two distributions of the original element will yield negative correlations of similar magnitude.

38. Correct to two places does not mean absolute accuracy in the second place. It means that the second place is not more than one unit off from the true value.

39. Driver and Kroeber.

40. Gifford and Kroeber.

41. These values would be the same for all forms of r and Q.

42. Driver, 1938.

Appendix 4: Bibliography by Authors

Abbreviations:

AA	American Anthropologist.
AAA-M	American Anthropological Association, Memoir.
AFLS-M	American Folk-Lore Society, Memoir.
AMNH-AP	American Museum of Natural History, Anthropological Papers.
-B	Bulletin
-HS	Handbook Series.
-M	Memoir.
BAAS-R	British Association for the Advancement of Science, Report.
BAE-B	Bureau of American Ethnology, Bulletin.
-R	Report.
CNAE	Contributions to American Ethnology.
CU-CA	Columbia University, Contributions to Anthropology.
JRAI	Journal of the Royal Anthropological Institute.
RCI-P	Royal Canadian Institute, Proceedings.
-Tr	Transactions.
UC-AR	University of California, Anthropological Records.
-PAAE	Publications in American Archaeology and Ethnology.
UPM-AP	University of Pennsylvania Museum, Anthropological Publications.
UW-PA	University of Washington Publications in Anthropology.
YU-AP	Yale University Publications in Anthropology.

Aginsky, Bernard W.
MS.   Culture Element Distributions: XXIV—Central Sierra. UC-AR (in press, 1941).

Barnett, Homer
1937.   Culture Element Distributions: VII—Oregon Coast. UC-AR 1: 155-204 (180-181).
1939.   Culture Element Distributions: IX—Gulf of Georgia Salish. UC-AR 1: 221-295 (256-258).

Beaglehole, Ernest
1937.   Notes on Hopi Economic Life. YU-AP No. 15: 1-88 (74).

Beaglehole, Ernest and Pearl
1935.   Hopi of the Second Mesa. AAA-M 44: 5-65 (45-46).

Benedict, Ruth F.
1924.   A Brief Sketch of Serrano Culture. AA 26: 366-392 (380-381).

Birket-Smith, Kaj
1929.   Caribou Eskimos: Material and So-
             cial Life and Their Cultural
             Position. 5th Thule Exped., Rept.
             5, pt. 2 (Analytical): 1-416.
Boas, Franz
1890.   First General Report on the Indians
             of British Columbia. BAAS-R 59:
             801-893 (836-842).
1891.   Second General Report on the In-
             dians of British Columbia. BAAS-
             R 60: 562-715 (574, 592-594,
             641-642).
1892.   Third Report on the Indians of
             British Columbia. BAAS-R 61: 408-
             449 (418).
1894.   Chinook Texts. BAE-B 20: 1-278
             (246-247).
1895.   Indianische Sagen von der Nord-
             Pacifischen Küste Amerikas. Ber-
             lin: A. Asher & Co., pp. 1-363.
1916.   Tsimshian Mythology. BAE-R 31: 1-
             1037 (531).
1921.   Ethnology of the Kwakiutl. BAE-R
             35: 43-1473 (699-702).
1923.   Notes on the Tillamook. UC-PAAE
             20: 1-16 (6-7).
1935.   Kwakiutl Culture as Reflected in
             Mythology. AFLS-M 28: 1-190
             (33).
Boas, Franz, and Hunt, George
1905.   Kwakiutl Tests. AMNH-M 5: 1-532
             (87).
Bolton, H. E.
1931.   Anza's California Expeditions, 5: 1-
             426 (335-337). University of Cali-
             fornia Press.
Chadwick, M.
1932.   The Psychological Effects of Men-
             struation. Nerv. and Ment. Dis.
             Publ. Co., No. 56: 1-70.
Curtis, E. S.
1907-30.   The North American Indians. Vols.
             1, 2, 7-16. (See indexes for puberty
             references.)
Densmore, Frances
1929.   Papago Music. BAE-B 90: 1-229
             (164).
Devereux, George
MS.   Mohave notes.
Dixon, R. B.
1905.   The Northern Maidu. AMNH-B 17:
             119-346 (232-238).
1907.   The Shasta. AMNH-B 17: 381-498
             (457-461).

1910.   The Chimariko Indians and Lan-
             guage. UC-PAAE 5: 293-380 (301).
Dixon, R. B. and Kroeber, A. L.
1919.   Linguistic Families of California.
             UC-PAAE 16: 47-118.
Driver, H. E.
1936.   Wappo Ethnography. UC-PAAE
             36: 179-220 (198-199).
1937.   Culture Element Distributions: VI—
             Southern Sierra Nevada. UC-AR
             1: 53-154 (135-136).
1938.   Culture Element Distributions: VIII
             —The Reliability of Culture Ele-
             ment Data. UC-AR 1: 205-219.
1939.   Culture Element Distributions: X—
             Northwest California. UC-AR 1:
             297-433 (351-353).
MS.   Kitanemuk notes.
Driver, H. E., and Kroeber, A. L.
1932.   Quantitative Expression of Cultural
             Relationships. UC-PAAE 31: 211-
             256.
Drucker, Philip
1937a.   The Tolowa and Their Southwest
             Oregon Kin. UC-PAAE 36: 221-
             300 (254).
1937b.   Culture Element Distributions: V—
             Southern California. UC-AR 1: 1-
             52 (32-33).
MS.   Culture Element Distributions—
             Northwest Coast.
DuBois, Constance G.
1908.   Religion of the Luiseño. UC-PAAE
             8: 69-186 (93-96).
Du Bois, Cora
1932a.   Tolowa Notes. AA 34: 248-262 (248-
             251).
1932b.   Girls' Adolescence Observances in
             North America. Unpublished
             Ph.D. Thesis. Univ. of Calif. Li-
             brary.
1935.   Wintu Ethnography. UC-PAAE 36:
             1-148 (52-54).
Emmons, G. T.
1911.   The Tahltan Indians. UPM-AP 4:
             1-120 (104-105).
Essene, Frank
MS.a.   Notes on the Wailaki.
MS.b.   Notes on the Central Wintun.
Forde, C. D.
1931.   Ethnography of the Yuma Indians.
             UC-PAAE 28: 83-278 (152-154).

Frachtenberg, Leo J.
  MS.   Quileute (Puberty data abstracted by Drucker from unpublished manuscript).

Gifford, E. W.
  1931.   The Kamia of Imperial Valley. BAE-B 97: 1-94 (53).
  1932.   The Southeastern Yavapai. UC-PAAE 29: 177-252 (198-199).
  1933.   The Cocopa. UC-PAAE 31: 257-334 (289-290).
  1936.   Northeastern and Western Yavapai. UC-PAAE 34: 247-354 (301-302).
  1940.   Culture Element Distributions: XII—Apache-Pueblo. UC-AR 4: 1-207.
  MS.a.   Miwok notes.

Gifford, E. W., and Klimek, Stanislaw
  1936.   Culture Element Distributions: II—Yana. UC-PAAE 37: 71-100 (83-84, 87, 93, 98).

Gifford, E. W., and Kroeber, A. L.
  1937.   Culture Element Distributions: IV—Pomo. UC-PAAE 37: 117-254 (151).

Goddard, P. E.
  1903.   Life and Culture of the Hupa. UC-PAAE 1: 1-88 (53-54).
  1913.   Indians of the Southwest. AMNH-HS 2: 1-191 (166-168).

Goldfrank, Esther S.
  1927.   The Social Ceremonial Organization of Cochiti. AAA-M No. 33: 1-129 (83).

Goldschmidt, Walter
  MS.   Central Wintun (Nomlaki) notes.

Gunther, Erna
  1927.   Klallam Ethnography. UW-PA 1: 171-314 (239-241).
  MS.   Culture Element Distributions—Puget Sound.

Haeberlin, Hermann, and Gunther, Erna
  1930.   The Indians of Puget Sound. UW-PA 4: 1-84 (45-46).

Halpern, A. M.
  MS.a.   Notes on the Yuma.
  MS.b.   Notes on the Patwin.

Harrington, John P.
  MS.   Culture Element Distributions: XIX— Central California Coast. UC-AR (in press, 1941).

Hill-Tout, Charles
  1904a.   Report on the Ethnology of the Siciatl (Seshelt). JRAI 34: 20-91 (32-33).
  1904b.   Ethnological Report on the Stsee'lis. . . . JRAI 34: 311-376 (319-320).
  1905.   Report on the Ethnology of the Stlatlumh (Lillooet) of British Columbia. JRAI 35: 126-218 (136-137).

Hooper, Lucille
  1920.   The Cahuilla Indians. UC-PAAE 16: 315-380 (347-348).

Hopkins, S. W.
  1883.   Life Among the Paiutes, 1-268 (48). Boston: Cupples Upham & Co.

Jacobs, Melville
  MS.   Culture Element Distributions—Kalapuya.

Kelly, Isabel T.
  1932.   Ethnography of the Surprise Valley Paiute. UC-PAAE 31: 67-210 (162-163).
  MS.   Southern Paiute Ethnography. I, Eastern Bands (Kaibab).

Krause, Aurel
  1885.   Die Tlinkit-Indianer, 1-420 (218). Jena: H. Costenoble.

Kroeber, A. L.
  1922.   Elements of Culture in Native California. UC-PAAE 13: 259-328.
  1923.   Anthropology. New York: Harcourt Brace.
  1925.   Handbook of the Indians of California. BAE-B 78. (See index for puberty references.)
  1932.   The Patwin and Their Neighbors. UC-PAAE 29: 253-423 (271, 291).
  1939.   Culture Element Distributions: XI—Tribes Surveyed. UC-AR 1: 435-440.

Kroeber, A. L. (ed.)
  1935.   Walapai Ethnography. AAA-M 42: 1-293 (136-139).

Loeb, E. M.
  1926.   Pomo Folkways. UC-PAAE 19: 149-405 (270-274).
  1932.   The Western Kuksu Cult. UC-PAAE 33: 1-138. (See Contents for puberty references.)
  1933.   The Eastern Kuksu Cult. UC-PAAE 33: 139-232. (See Contents for puberty references.)

Lowie, R. H.
  1920.   Primitive Society. New York: Boni and Liveright.

1923. The Cultural Connection of California and Plateau Shoshonean Tribes. UC-PAAE 20: 143-156.

1924. Notes on Shoshonean Ethnography. AMNH-AP 20: 185-314 (272-274).

1936. Cultural Anthropology: a Science. Amer. Jour. of Sociol. 42: 301-320.

McCance, R. A., Luff, M. C., and Widdowson, E. E.
1937. Physical and Emotional Periodicity in Women. Jour. of Hygiene, 37: 571-611.

Morice, A. G.
1890. The Western Denes. RCI-P, ser. 3, v. 7: 109-174 (162-164).

1895. Notes on the Western Denes. RCI-Tr 4: 5-222 (82).

Nash, Philleo
MS. Klamath and Modoc notes.

Nomland, Gladys A.
1935. Sinkyone Notes. UC-PAAE 36: 149-178 (161-162).

1938. Bear River Ethnography. UC-AR 2: 91-124.

Olson, R. L.
1936. The Quinault Indians. UW-PA 6: 1-190 (104-106).

MS. Haisla and Bella Bella notes.

Opler, M. E.
MS. a. The Girls' Puberty Rite at Mescalero.

MS. b. The Girls' Puberty Rite of the Chiricahua Apache.

Parsons, E. C.
1929. Social Organization of the Tewa of New Mexico. AAA-M 36: 1-309.

1932. Isleta, New Mexico. BAE-R 47: 193-466.

Powers, Stephen
1877. Tribes of California. CNAE 3: 1-635 (85).

Ray, Verne F.
1932. The Sanpoil and Nespelem. UW-PA 5: 1-237 (133-135).

MS. Culture Element Distributions: XXII—Plateau. UC-AR (in press, 1941).

Reichard, Gladys A.
1928. Social Life of the Navaho Indians. CU-CA 7: 1-239 (135-139).

Russell, Frank
1908. The Pima Indians. BAE-R 26: 3-390 (182-183).

Sapir, E.
1907. Notes on the Takelma Indians of Southwestern Oregon. AA 9: 251-275 (273-274).

1913. A Girl's Puberty Ceremony among the Nootka Indians. Roy. Soc. Can. Proc. Trans., 3d ser., v. 7, sec. 2, pp. 67-80.

1929. Central and North American Languages. Encyclopedia Britannica, 14th ed., pp. 138-140.

Seward, Georgene H.
1934. The Female Sex Rhythm. Psych. Bull. 31: 153-192.

Sparkman, P. S.
1908. Culture of the Luiseño Indians. UC-PAAE 8: 187-234 (224-226).

Spier, Leslie
1928. Havasupai Ethnography. AMNH-AP 29: 81-392 (325-326).

1930. Klamath Ethnography. UC-PAAE 330: 1-338 (68-71, 314-325).

1933. Yuman Tribes of Gila River, pp. 1-433 (324-327). Univ. of Chicago Press.

Spier, Leslie, and Sapir, Edward
1930. Wishram Ethnography. UW-PA 3: 151-300 (262).

Spinden, H. J.
1908. The Nez Percé Indians. AAA-M 2: 165-274.

Sproat, G. M.
1868. Scenes of Studies of Savage Life, pp. 1-317 (93-94). London: Smith Elder & Co.

Stephen, A. M.
1936. Hopi Journal. CU-CA 23: 1-1417 (139-143).

Stern, Bernhard J.
1934. The Lummi Indians of Northwest Washington, CU-CA 17: 1-127 (24-26).

Stevenson, M. C.
1904. The Zuñi Indians. BAE-R 23: 1-608 (303).

Steward, Julian
1933. Ethnography of the Owens Valley Paiute. UC-PAAE 33: 233-350 (293).

MS. a. Culture Element Distributions: XIII—Nevada Shoshoni. UC-AR (in press, 1941).

MS. b. Culture Element Distributions: XXIII—Northern and Gosiute Shoshoni.

Stewart, Omer
    MS.   Culture Element Distributions: XIV—Northern Paiute. UC-AR (in press, 1941).

Strong, W. D.
    1929.   Aboriginal Society in Southern California. UC-PAAE 26: 1-358. (See Contents for puberty references.)

Swanton, John R.
    1905.   Contributions to the Ethnology of the Haida. AMNH-M 8: 1-300 (48-50).
    1908.   Social Conditions, Beliefs, and Linguistic Relationship of the Tlingit Indians. BAE-R 26: 391-485 (428).

Teit, James
    1900.   The Thompson Indians of British Columbia. AMNH-M 2: 163-392 (311-317).
    1906.   The Lillooet Indians. AMNH-M 4: 193-300 (263-265).
    1909.   The Shuswap. AMNH-M 4: 443-789 (587-590).
    1930.   The Salishan Tribes of the Western Plateaus. BAE-R 45: 23-396 (168-169, 282-283).

Trippel, E. J.
    1889.   The Yuma Indians. Overland Monthly, 2d ser., 13: 561-584; 14: 1-11.

Underhill, Ruth
    1936.   The Autobiography of a Papago Woman. AAA-M 46: 1-64 (31-36).

Van Waters, Miriam
    1913.   Adolescent Girl Among Primitive Peoples. Jour. Relig. Psych. 6: 375-429; 7: 75-120.

Voegelin, Erminie
    1938.   Tübatulabal Ethnography. UC-AR 2: 1-84.
    MS.   Culture Element Distributions: XX—Northeast California. UC-AR (in press, 1941).

Waterman, T. T.
    1910.   The Religious Practices of the Diegueño Indians. UC-PAAE 8: 271-358 (285-293).

White, Leslie
    1932a.   The Acoma Indians. BAE-R 47: 17-192.
    1932b.   The Pueblo of San Felipe. AAA-M 38: 1-69.
    1935.   Santo Domingo. AAA-M 43: 1-210.

Yule, G. Udny
    1912.   On the Methods of Measuring Association between Two Attributes. Jour Royal Stat. Soc. 75: 579-652.

3. Correlational Analysis of Murdock's 1957 Ethnographic Sample[*]

Harold E. Driver
Karl F. Schuessler

This paper parallels that of Sawyer and LeVine (1966) in some respects: it reduces Murdock's 210 categories to 30 variables, and intercorrelates and factor-analyzes the variables for the six world subdivisions as well as for the entire world. Differences from Sawyer's and LeVine's treatment include the use of Cramér's coefficient to compare all categories, the opposition of the modal category to the others to produce the 30 dichotomous variables, use of the phi coefficient, the testing of the correlations within each of the six areas for significant differences between areas, a different technique for measuring the amount of similarity between areas, a section on factor analysis as a method, and a section contrasting and interpreting correlations in the two areas that differed the most, North America and the Circum-Mediterranean.

With the recent appearance of Coult's and Habenstein's (1965) volume of correlations of all the data in Murdock's (1957) world ethnographic sample and Robert Textor's (1967) massive compilation of cross-cultural correlations from a greater variety of sources, it is clear to every anthropologist that there is a need for reducing this plethora of detail to some more succinct form of expression. Techniques for reducing correlation matrices have long been used in psychology, where they date from the pioneer work of Charles Spearman, culminating in his 1927 book. From this beginning Thurstone (1938, 1947) did the basic work on multiple factor analysis, the most widely used reduction technique in the field of psychology, where such papers are numbered in the hundreds. A recent compilation by Schuessler (MS) of studies employing factor analysis in the four leading sociological journals in the United States yields 63 articles from 1951 to 1963. In the field of political science there has been a recent explosion of factor analyses, starting with Schubert (1962), Rummel (1963), and Alker (1964).

In anthropology the clustering of coefficients in matrices by inspection goes back to Boas (1894), Barrett (1908), and Czekanowski (1911), but was not done with a numerical technique until the paper of Clements (1954). Factor analysis in anthropology begins with the work of the psychologist Waldron (1940), who applied it to anthropometric variables, but the first anthropologist to so use it was Howells

[*] We should like to express our thanks to Charles Starnes and Gerald Slatin, who assisted creatively in the statistical analysis upon which this article is based.

(1951). Tugby (1958) was the first archaeologist to use factor analysis, and he employed it in the classification of artifacts into types. It was not employed in cultural anthropology until Schuessler and Driver (1956) used a Q-technique to arrive at an areal classification. This was followed by Gouldner's and Peterson's (1962) analysis of Simmons' cross-cultural data and Hickman's (1962) quest for the number of factors involved in the folk-urban continuum.

A little later Romney and D'Andrade (1964) ran two factor analyses on English kinship data; Charles Osgood (1964) ran a number on cross-language-culture semantic comparisons; Bacon, Barry, and Child (1965) applied the technique to alcohol drinking and related variables; Driver and Sanday (1966) made two such analyses on kin avoidances and related variables, and Sawyer and LeVine (1966) did a completely independent but closely similar study to the one of this paper, using Murdock's 1957 world ethnographic sample. Factor analysis and other multivariate techniques are mentioned or used in Driver (1965), Ihm (1965), Milke (1965), and Needham (1965). D'Andrade has two additional factor analyses in typescript, one on beliefs about illnesses and another on character terminology.

The study reported herein may be regarded as a continuation of the aforementioned efforts to apply correlational methods to ethnographic data. Its major purposes are as follows: (1) to measure the correlations between cultural traits of the societies in Murdock's sample and to analyze the pattern of these correlations; (2) to determine whether these intercorrelations could be due to a small number of factors that might be given a plausible socioanthropological interpretation; (3) to establish possible differences among Murdock's regions in respect to the pattern of intercorrelations; and (4) to consider in the light of (3) the tenability of the broad hypothesis that correlations are the product of functional necessity, against the alternative hypothesis that they are the product of more specific ecological and historical circumstances.

The data of this study then are taken entirely from Murdock's (1957) World Ethnographic Sample. These data are tabled in 15 numbered columns, each consisting of a set of mutually exclusive categories designated by capital letters and another such set represented by lower case letters, bringing the total to 30 sets of categories. Altogether there are 210 categories in these 30 classifications, for an average of seven per set. We have used these categories, unchanged.

Our first step was to cross-classify every trait (set) by every other trait in order to determine the degree to which traits taken two at a time are associated with one another. To measure the degree of association between traits, we had recourse to Cramér's (1946) coefficient of dependence, which is a function of chi-square and therefore a gauge of statistical independence as well as dependence between traits. This measure may reach its upper limit of 1.00 regardless of the dimensions of the contingency table, and in that respect is less restricted than either Pearson's C or Tschuprow's T. Although it has the usual shortcomings of measures of association between attributes (Goodman and Kruskal 1954, 1959, 1963), it is still a useful device for comparing two or more contingency tables, particularly when there are many (435) of them as in this study.

In Table 1, we have arranged the Cramér coefficients in conventional manner; from this triangular display the reader may roughly judge which traits tend to cluster together. In addition, we have given the mean value of Cramér's coefficient for each trait; from these values it is possible to rank traits by tendency (of each) to associate with all the others. Also, we have encircled those values that are significant at the 5 percent level, under the null hypothesis of statistical independence between traits.

As may be seen from this table, the results more often support the hypothesis of independence between traits rather than the alterntive of dependence. Few of the coefficients reach the 5 percent level of significance, and of these, most are only moderately large in magnitude. No one single variable is consistently correlated with all the rest, or even with a small subset of them. Except to hint at possible clusters of traits, these results serve only to demonstrate that categories would have to be combined into broader groupings if relations among traits are to be detected.

Accordingly, we proceeded to combine categories in order possibly to obtain higher correlations, and from these correlations to clarify the system of interrelationships among traits and the principal components of that system. Our general procedure, given in greater detail in a later section, was to reduce each variable to a dichotomy and to manipulate variables in that simplified form. Because each set of categories may be dichotomized in $k/2$ ways, where k is the number of categories, it was necessary to select a single uniform procedure for performing this operation on each set. The technique we adopted was to oppose the category with the largest frequency to all the others. These modal categories are listed in Table 2. As "variables," they are somewhat awkward: five of them refer to absences of the phenomenon, and one, *animal husbandry absent or unimportant*, recurs in three variables. *Patrilocal residence* appears in two "variables" (15 and 16), as the dominant form of residence in the first and leading alternative form in the second. When there was no form alternate to dominant patrilocal, it was recorded twice by Murdock, and the positive correlation between dominant and alternate patrilocal confirms this.

Although the procedure of putting the modal category against the others is arbitrary and conceals information about the less frequent categories, it did permit us to set up a matrix of point intercorrelations (phi coefficients) that could be factor-analyzed. Further, by applying this technique separately to each of the six areas into which Murdock has divided the world, it was possible to draw comparisons among these areas on the pattern of their intercorrelations. Such modal dichotomies have a minor statistical advantage to the extent that they produce marginals that are approximately 50%:50% for both variables, the division required for phi to attain a value of 1.00. Half of Murdock's 210 categories have a frequency of less than 10 percent; the extreme asymmetries produced by such low frequencies in 2x2 tables lower the maximum values that phi may attain and accordingly the magnitude of the factor loadings.

Statistical Analysis of Dichotomies

The matrix of phi coefficients for the entire world sample of 565 ethnic units is shown in Table 3, and the frequency distribution of these same coefficients is given in Table 4. The loadings satisfying the varimax criterion on the first 12 factors are given in Table 5, where values of .40 or higher are set off in boldface type. The most general conclusion to be drawn from this table is that relatively many factors are required to reproduce the intercorrelations with some degree of accuracy, and the meaning of each is difficult to reconstruct because of the necessarily limited number of variables loading it. It would be possible to attach names to all 12 of them; however, for reasons given later, we restrict our interpretation to those factors having at least three loadings in excess of .40. Of this group of six, little significance should be attached to the first listed in Table 5, since it is the result principally of having included the same variable three times as Nos. 2, 5, and 6. When this factor is eliminated, we are left with five factors, which we have tentatively characterized as follows:

TABLE 1. CRAMÉR COEFFICIENTS OF WORLD SAMPLE

		1	2	3	4	5	6	7	8	9	10	11
1	Cultivated plants											
2	Domesticated animals	.110										
3	Agriculture	.218	.052									
4	Division of labor	.184	.080	.235								
5	Animal husbandry	.150	.350	.195	.096							
6	Division of labor	.086	.291	.052	.080	.278						
7	Fishing, etc.	.077	.061	.092	.051	.055	.045					
8	Division of labor	.054	.058	.018	.039	.048	.090	.235				
9	Hunting & gathering	.114	.090	.100	.112	.064	.074	.095	.028			
10	Division of labor	.069	.054	.046	.048	.047	.035	.016	.022	.250		
11	Settlement pattern	.122	.052	.132	.092	.072	.038	.019	.015	.094	.028	
12	Community organization	.032	.040	.024	.049	.025	.028	.019	.016	.032	.024	.039
13	Family	.017	.012	.017	.026	.012	.018	.038	.020	.015	.016	.026
14	Household	.035	.056	.034	.037	.040	.033	.029	.020	.042	.017	.030
15	Marital residence (modal)	.031	.076	.029	.040	.058	.058	.034	.054	.046	.024	.026
16	Marital residence (alternative)	.030	.074	.030	.040	.056	.040	.032	.028	.052	.029	.037
17	Marriage	.023	.044	.022	.044	.026	.045	.026	.050	.044	.023	.026
18	Consideration	.033	.088	.015	.028	.076	.056	.038	.029	.044	.024	.021
19	Patrilineal kin groups	.041	.072	.030	.038	.088	.052	.028	.026	.032	.020	.030
20	Exogamy	.020	.056	.020	.032	.039	.040	.021	.013	.030	.022	.028
21	Matrilineal kin groups	.015	.018	.014	.017	.014	.014	.022	.015	.013	.012	.012
22	Exogamy	.014	.032	.011	.017	.026	.023	.019	.018	.017	.017	.026
23	Bilateral & bilineal kin groups	.046	.062	.028	.028	.050	.042	.034	.058	.046	.025	.033
24	Cousin marriage	.030	.044	.022	.030	.032	.030	.040	.024	.032	.029	.028
25	Kin terms, cousin	.033	.048	.018	.030	.048	.047	.024	.058	.034	.032	.025
26	Kin terms, avuncular	.047	.028	.036	.048	.026	.025	.024	.045	.030	.028	.028
27	Social stratification	.045	.063	.026	.050	.066	.051	.021	.026	.054	.049	.032
28	Slavery	.024	.033	.010	.026	.026	.038	.010	.023	.032	.028	.011
29	Political integration	.052	.077	.038	.039	.070	.052	.028	.024	.060	.038	.026
30	Succession	.027	.046	.026	.034	.034	.026	.028	.034	.038	.029	.029

		1	2	3	4	5	6	7	8	9	10	11
Total, each variable (C)		1.779	2.167	1.590	1.670	2.167	1.787	1.261	1.203	1.714	1.101	1.177
Average, each variable (C̄)		.061	.074	.054	.057	.074	.061	.043	.041	.059	.037	.040

Total of averages   1.507
Average of averages   .050

Factor II: Typical patricentered organization. All of the variables heavily loaded by this factor include patrilineal descent or patrilocal residence except brideprice, which has long been known to be correlated with the others. This is the most important and areally ubiquitous factor.

Factor III: Agriculture. All variables refer to agriculture except "compact villages and towns," which has long been known to correlate with agriculture and the sedentary way of life it requires. This is the second most important and areally ubiquitous factor.

Factor IV: Matrilineal descent. The absence of this trait is combined with the "forbidding of marriage of a man to his MoSiDa" and a low loading (.44) of "Hawaiian kin classification."

Factor V: Deviant patricentered organization. This odd combination of "patrilineal descent and kindreds unreported," "patrilineal succession other than

brother or son, or where preference is unspecified," and "hunting and gathering important but not dominant" is totally unanticipated on ethnographic grounds, and its standing is even more provisional than the others.

Factor VI: Social stratification. Its absence and the absence of slavery are associated with "autonomous communities under 1,500 persons."

Summarizing: the 30 cultural traits for all 565 societies in Murdock's sample may be said to express at least five major social and ecological circumstances, which we have provisionally named: typical patricentered organization, agriculture, matrilineal descent, deviant patricentered organization, and social stratification. If we had analyzed a different set of cultural traits, we would probably have isolated a different set of general factors. But for the variables in hand, the above-named factors seem to be the principal source of variation within classifications and of the covariation between them.

TABLE 1—(*Cont.*)

12	13	14	15	16	17	18	19	20	21	22	23	24	25	26	27	28	29	30
.014																		
.036	(428)																	
.062	.048	.048																
.058	.042	.038	(241)															
.029	.026	(111)	.058	.048														
.042	.024	.054	.080	.064	.050													
.065	.020	.036	.068	.049	.034	.059												
(100)	.016	.038	.060	.058	.032	.042	(173)											
.018	.005	.014	.064	.088	.009	.020	.032	.020										
.030	.014	.022	.061	.069	.020	.021	.027	(246)	(160)									
.069	.020	.039	(137)	(121)	.036	.094	(250)	(134)	(246)	(146)								
.040	.025	.024	.037	.048	.036	.031	.036	(226)	.039	(242)	.054							
.062	.032	.035	.038	.035	.050	.048	.062	.074	.052	.082	.098	.056						
.038	.022	.041	.051	.042	.030	.036	.039	.044	.026	.052	.060	.045	(206)					
.024	.024	.045	.054	.051	.032	.052	.026	.029	.012	.024	.016	.038	.051	.034				
.021	.015	.052	.033	.034	.052	.044	.030	.023	.010	.016	.021	.020	.036	.030	.081			
.022	.022	.030	.036	.034	.028	.038	.024	.022	.012	.021	.029	.030	.046	.030	(170)	.059		
.046	.032	.038	.074	.060	.046	.034	.046	.056	.086	.076	.092	.032	.042	.046	.083	.056	(175)	
1.104	1.046	1.502	1.726	1.628	1.100	1.285	1.533	1.719	1.089	1.549	2.114	1.400	1.502	1.237	1.329	.894	1.332	1.471
.039	.036	.051	.059	.056	.037	.044	.052	.059	.037	.053	.072	.048	.051	.042	.045	.030	.045	.050

TABLE 2. MODAL CATEGORIES

*	**	
C	1	Cereal grains dominant or codominant
o	2	Animal husbandry absent or unimportant
D	3	Agriculture dominant
b	4	Agriculture sex division of labor about equal
O	5	Animal husbandry absent
o	6	Animal husbandry absent or unimportant
I	7	Fishing important but not dominant
m	8	Fishing sex division of labor: male dominance
I	9	Hunting and gathering important but not dominant
m	10	Hunting and gathering sex division of labor: male dominance
V	11	Compact villages or towns
a	12	Agamous communities
I	13	Independent family, nuclear or polygamous
n	14	Nuclear family households
P	15	Patrilocal residence (modal)
p	16	Patrilocal residence (alternative)
L	17	Limited polygyny, under 20%
b	18	Brideprice
O	19	Patrilineal descent absent
f	20	Marriage to FaBrDa forbidden and patrilineal exogamy absent
O	21	Matrilineal descent absent
f	22	Marriage to MoSiDa forbidden and matrilineal exogamy absent
p	23	Patrilineal descent, kindreds unreported
f	24	Cross-cousin marriage forbidden symmetrically
H	25	Hawaiian kin terms
m	26	Bifurcate merging: FaBr=Fa, MoBr= separate term
O	27	Social stratification absent
o	28	Slavery absent
A	29	Autonomous communities under 1,500 persons
p	30	Patrilineal succession other than Br or So or where preference is unspecified

* Murdock
** Driver-Schuessler

Regional Comparison

Most cross-cultural researchers to date have been content with a single set of correlations computed from all ethnic units in the sample. Only a few have devoted attention to the significance of areal differences.

Murdock took a critical attitude toward areal differences when he wrote in 1940:

> A valid cross-cultural hypothesis should hold true in any area. If, however, some areas are discovered to yield negative coefficients, it must be concluded that the apparent statistical confirmation of the hypothesis is fictitious and accidental, and the hypothesis must either be rejected entirely or modified and tested again [1940: 369].

This principle must be modified because many small areas that run contrary to the general world trend can be found in any sample. Areas to be tested for such differences should be relatively large, they should be continuous and conform to major geographical barriers, and they should contain somewhere near 100 societies each in order to minimize sampling error. Murdock's six areas fit these standards fairly well except for the less completely reported traits, which may be known for as few as about 50 peoples. For instance, there are only 52 societies in South America where matrilineal descent in one form or another is known to be present or absent (Coult and Habenstein 1965: 22).

Kimball Romney has made the following remarks on areal differences:

> Since diffusion occurs mainly within continental areas, one would expect functional correlations to hold up within a continental area, if valid; but if areal clustering seriously affects such correlations, one would expect them not to do so. One of Romney's students had done a thesis on the correlations in Murdock's *Social Structure* (1949), making a significance test within each continental area and showing that none of the correlations held if so run [Hymes 1965: 393].

The ambiguity of the last sentence was cleared up in a personal communication from Romney, who said that all of the correlations held in some of the areas but that none of them held for all continental areas. Driver (1956) and Driver and Sanday (1966) have confirmed some of Murdock's correlations for North America with a sample of almost 300 ethnic units. However, Driver (MS) found that South American data from Murdock's *Outline of South American Cultures* produced lower correlations between the same variables, some of them not significantly different from zero. The poor quality of most South American sources may be part of the explanation, because randomly distributed errors in any corpus of data tend to lower all correlations.

In analyzing areal differences, our first step was to set up phi correlation matrices for the same variables in each of Murdock's six areas. The means and standard deviations of the phi coefficients for these areas show remarkably little variation from each other (Table 6). All of the frequency distributions are approximately normal around zero, so that about two-thirds of the coefficients in each area lie between −.20 and +.20, and approximately 95 percent between −.40 and +.40. The means and standard deviations of all areas but the Circum-Mediterranean are inflated by the perfect correlations between variables 2, 5, and 6, which all read *animal husbandry absent or unimportant*. Because all peoples in the Circum-Mediterranean area possessed domesticated animals, the lack of negative instances made it impossible to obtain correlations other than zero between these "constant variables" and the others.

If each of the correlations were of about the same magnitude in each of the six areas, each matrix would closely match the other five. To determine the degree of that matching, we compared the areas two at a time by means of both a conventional scatter diagram and the corresponding correlation coefficient. These correlation coefficients are given in Table 7. Africa, East Eurasia, and Insular Pacific form a fairly compact cluster, with East Eurasia showing the highest total *r* with all other areas. South America shows slightly higher relations, on the whole, with the central core and all five other areas than does North America. The Circum-Mediterranean area is by far the most deviant of the six. (The low correlations between Circum-Mediterranean and the other areas are due in part to the zero correlations produced by variables 2, 5, and 6.)

To investigate in stricter manner the differences among the *r*'s in all six areas, we set up the statistical hypothesis that the true correlation for each pair of traits was the same in all areas, and tested that hypothesis by standard methods (Hays 1963). In symbols:

$$H_0 : r_1 = r_2 = \ldots = r_6$$

This analysis was performed in response to the possibility that differences among areas were no larger than would be expected if societies had been randomly assigned to the six areas. We ran 435 such tests corresponding to the $n(n-1)/2$ intercorrelations among the 30 variables. Of these 435 comparisons, 69 (16 percent) were significant at the 5 percent level. Since that many significant comparisons in 435 trials would occur infrequently by chance (p<.01), we inferred that there are other than random factors operating to produce differences among the correlations for the areas. (When the number of ethnic units, *n*, for a given correlation between the same two variables differed by areas, as it usually did, we assumed that all *n*'s were equal to the smallest. This made the computer program much simpler. Had we retained the different *n*'s in every such comparison, the results would have shown more areal differences significant at the 5 percent level.)

The 69 significant comparisons are identified on the lower-left side of the principal diagonal in Table 8, whose rows and columns represent the 30 cultural variables. The number of times each variable was involved in a significant comparison is given in the margin at the right of that table. For example, No. 3

was involved in 11 significant comparisons, No. 30 in only two. The conclusion is that the 30 variables differ in the similarity of their correlations from one area to another.

Although it is logical to start with the general hypothesis that all areas have the same correlation, the results of its testing are limited in that they conceal those differences that led to its rejection in specific instances. To identify those differences, we set up all possible comparisons between areas two at a time for each of the 69 six-fold comparisons that had been accepted as significant. This analysis was a response to the general question: given the finding that the six areas differ among themselves, on which of the differences between areas two at a time does that finding depend?

A summary of the results of this analysis is given on the upper-right side of the principal diagonal in Table 8, each entry being the number of paired comparisons out of 15 that were significant at the 5 percent level. From these figures, it is clear that in some cases practically every paired comparison was significant, while in others as few as 2 in 15 were significant. (In these comparisons, we assumed that both *n*'s were equal to the smallest.)

Of greater interest is the number of times the difference between specific pairs of area was significant, since those results answer to the question: which areas are most different, which are most alike? A list of the number of times in 69 each pair of areas was significant is given in Table 9, together with the rank order of these frequencies and the rank order of the correlations coefficients between areas (Table 7). As anticipated, the pairs of areas showing the lowest correlations tend to have the largest number of significant differences and the pairs showing the highest correlations tend to have the smallest number of differences.

We next obtained the principal factors for each regional matrix of intercorrelations and drew comparisons among these results. These are given in Table 10, where the variables have been grouped by inspection to match the factor loadings. Although as many as a dozen factors were needed to account for as much as 90 percent of the common factor variance in some areas, we have retained in Table 10 only those factors with three or more loadings in excess of .40 after rotation. The redundant *animal husbandry absent or unimportant*, which constitutes variables 2, 5, and 6, has been reduced by retaining variable 2 and eliminating 5 and 6. We have attempted to match up the factors in the six areas with those of the entire world and with each other by the roman numerals at the tops of columns. As none of the factors are identical from area to area, this is a rough

TABLE 3. PHI COEFFICIENTS OF WORLD SAMPLE

	2	5	6	18	15	16	19	20	23	1	3	4	11	21
2														
5	1.00													
6	1.00	1.00												
18	−.43	−.43	−.50											
15	−.32	−.32	−.36	−.42										
16	−.22	−.22	−.22	.27	.46									
19	.33	.33	.35	−.41	−.57	−.40								
20	.33	.33	.37	−.30	−.41	−.29	.73							
23	−.33	−.33	−.36	.39	.51	.39	−.87	−.67						
1	−.36	−.36	−.36	.17	.12	.11	−.14	−.18	.19					
3	−.29	−.29	−.20	.03	.07	.06	−.06	−.09	.11	.47				
4	−.29	−.29	−.28	.06	.07	.08	−.14	−.16	.14	.29	.35			
11	−.07	−.07	.03	−.04	.06	.09	−.01	−.06	.03	.16	.41	.15		
21	−.07	−.07	−.14	.11	.24	.17	−.22	−.26	.42	.06	−.03	.00	−.07	
22	.11	.11	.08	.01	.14	.10	−.08	.20	.17	−.05	−.03	.00	−.08	.56
25	.14	.14	.20	−.05	−.07	−.05	.22	.21	−.19	−.04	.04	−.01	.01	.14
9	.21	.21	.25	−.06	−.13	−.11	.05	.08	−.05	.02	.11	−.07	.06	−.07
30	−.09	−.09	−.07	.15	.24	.15	−.33	−.20	.27	.01	−.04	−.04	−.04	.14
27	.35	.35	.41	−.28	−.20	−.09	.11	.15	−.12	−.23	−.16	−.10	−.14	−.08
28	.23	.23	.22	−.29	−.16	−.08	.14	.12	−.16	−.19	−.10	−.02	−.06	−.02
29	.39	.39	.42	−.15	−.18	−.06	.10	.16	−.16	−.29	−.26	−.09	−.09	−.12
13	.06	.06	.07	−.04	−.11	−.04	.13	.07	−.15	−.09	−.05	−.03	−.15	−.04
14	.04	.04	.09	−.18	−.15	−.07	.21	.12	−.20	.00	.00	−.06	−.06	.05
7	.12	.12	.17	−.13	−.11	−.10	.12	.08	−.11	−.14	.20	.07	.12	−.09
8	.14	.14	.14	−.12	−.11	−.06	.13	.01	−.09	−.03	−.02	−.07	.11	.05
26	−.07	−.07	−.03	.04	.01	.01	−.12	−.02	.01	−.08	.06	.03	.02	−.30
10	−.14	−.14	−.09	.13	.06	.09	−.12	−.13	.15	.16	.17	.05	.11	.02
12	.07	.07	.05	−.19	−.13	−.10	.20	.12	−.18	.03	−.02	−.03	.04	.09
17	.08	.08	.07	−.01	−.04	.04	.06	.05	−.01	.00	.04	.08	.11	.03
24	−.07	−.07	−.07	−.02	.12	.04	−.03	.14	.00	−.04	.04	.02	.00	.02
Av.*	.25	.25	.26	.19	.20	.14	.23	.21	.23	.15	.13	.10	.08	.13

* Signs disregarded

procedure to call attention to similarities rather than identities.

Table 10 reveals considerable areal differences in factor loadings, as might have been anticipated from Table 7. The most dominant factor, in terms of both the number of variables and the number of areas where they are found, is number II, *typical patri-centered organization*. It includes variables 15, 16, 18, 20, and 23, all with the prefix *patri-* somewhere in their captions except for brideprice (18), which has long been known to correlate with the other members of the set; at least three members of this set are loaded on the same factor in all areas. The second most obtrusive factor is number III: at least two members of this set stay together on some factor in each of the areas. The functional relations of the variables heavily loaded on each of these factors are too obvious to require more than bare mention. Other sets of mutually exclusive variables are less ubiquitous.

Table 10 has been reduced in Table 11, which distinguishes a larger number of overlapping sets of variables and gives the number of areas in which each set is found in its entirety without any drop-outs. Thus no set of three or more variables is found in all six areas, only one such set in five areas, three other sets in three areas each, and four other sets in two areas each. The set with the largest number of vari-

ables (5) occurs in the smallest number of areas (2). The East Eurasian area has by far the largest number of these sets (8), while North and South America each have the smallest number (3). The other Old World areas—Africa, Insular Pacific, and the Circum-Mediterranean—each have four sets that they share with East Eurasia, while the two American areas share a set not found anywhere in the Old World. In spite of East Eurasia's inclusion of all the sets in all other Old World areas, the Circum-Mediterranean shares only two sets with Africa and only one with Insular Pacific. The Circum-Mediterranean shares only one set with North America and none at all with South America.

Tables 10 and 11 provide an amount of detail that is intermediate between the very succinct correlations of Table 7 and the overwhelming detail in the six intercorrelation matrices of the six areas. Factors are therefore useful in establishing gross differences and similarities among culture areas. But the general picture that emerges is far from simple. Areas display as much diversity as uniformity in their factorial pattern, and such diversity strongly suggests that differences in geography, ecology, and history affect the specific character of "functional relations" within each area and limit their mode of operation. This same point has been previously made by Driver.

TABLE 3.—(Cont.)

22	25	9	30	27	28	29	13	14	7	8	26	10	12	17	24
.19															
.04	−.02														
.13	.00	.02													
.07	.01	.11	.01												
.06	−.07	−.06	−.16	.33											
.06	.03	.15	−.03	.38	.17										
.02	−.11	−.04	−.10	.18	.17	.08									
−.02	.02	−.09	−.07	.08	.14	−.03	.36								
−.03	−.03	.01	−.08	.04	.06	−.03	.06	.03							
−.04	−.04	.13	.04	−.03	.07	.06	−.03	.07	.27						
−.04	−.04	−.01	.00	.13	.07	.04	.08	−.09	.08	−.13					
−.06	.04	.08	.05	−.06	−.15	−.08	−.08	−.02	−.01	−.01	.06				
.05	.05	−.01	−.08	−.07	.07	−.01	.05	.18	.07	.04	−.11	−.10			
.01	.13	−.02	.04	.01	.05	.03	−.06	.08	.04	.03	−.06	−.02	.07		
.29	.07	−.04	.05	.08	.05	−.02	.02	.05	.02	−.04	.07	.03	−.08	−.03	
.10	.08	.08	.09	.15	.13	.14	.09	.09	.09	.08	.06	.08	.08	.05	.06

Interpretations of Areal Differences

The magnitudes of the areal differences (Tables 7, 8, 9, 10, 11) are such that many of the correlations in the matrices of the more dissimilar pairs of areas, such as the Circum-Mediterranean and North or South America, would show statistically significant differences from area to area. A frequency distribution of the differences between all 435 correlations (phi's) in the Circum-Mediterranean and North American areas shows the following: average .21, range from .01 to 1.04, and standard deviation of .17. Some of the more striking differences will be discussed individually to illustrate the role of geographical and historical differences between areas.

(A) The correlation between *agriculture dominant* (3) and *hunting and gathering important but not dominant* (9) is .46 in North America and −.32 in the Circum-Mediterranean area (the difference is significant at the .01 level). The world correlation is .11. Where such sharp differences occur, the explanation is likely to be found in ecological and historical circumstances. In North America the dominance of agriculture, where it occurred, was less complete than around the Mediterranean, which includes Europe. There was still opportunity for considerable hunting and gathering throughout the Prairies and East cul-

ture areas because agriculture never became so dominant or population so heavy that wild plant foods and game became seriously depleted. Kroeber (1939: 219-220) has estimated that these Indians farmed only a fraction of 1 percent of the land that was suitable for farming, and thus created little disturbance of wild animals and plants, which were still important in their diet at White contact and even later.

In the Southwest, farming dominated hunting and wild plant gathering by a wide margin only among the Pueblos and a few peoples on the west coast of Mexico. Although the earliest farming in the Southwest appears about 3600 B.C. (Manglesdorf *et al.* 1964), corn and other plants did not reach the eastern

TABLE 4. FREQUENCY DISTRIBUTION OF PHI COEFFICIENTS OF WORLD SAMPLE

−.89 to −.80	1	.11 to .20	63
−.79 to −.70	0	.21 to .30	16
−.69 to −.60	1	.31 to .40	16
−.59 to −.50	2	.41 to .50	7
−.49 to −.40	5	.51 to .60	2
−.39 to −.30	12	.61 to .70	0
−.29 to −.20	20	.71 to .80	1
−.19 to −.10	48	.81 to .90	0
−.09 to .00	121	.91 to 1.00	3
.01 to .10	117		
		Total	435

TABLE 5. ROTATED FACTORS OF WORLD SAMPLE

	1	2	3	4	5	6	7	8	9	10	11	12
2	−.93	−.19	−.14	.05	−.06	−.12	−.00	−.05	.03	−.04	.02	−.06
5	−.93	−.19	−.14	.05	−.06	−.12	−.00	−.05	.03	−.04	.02	−.06
6	−.95	−.23	−.05	.01	−.08	−.12	.02	−.08	−.02	.01	.05	−.03
18	.41	.40	−.13	−.03	−.07	.30	−.09	.14	−.07	.16	.05	.05
15	.16	.69	.03	.06	.10	.22	−.07	.09	−.00	−.03	.00	.28
16	.00	.63	.13	−.08	.14	.10	.06	.18	.09	−.01	.14	.31
19	−.19	−.87	−.00	−.09	.09	.04	.12	−.02	.14	−.08	.05	.09
20	−.22	−.75	−.05	.03	−.01	.04	.03	.08	−.03	−.11	.05	.37
23	.19	.83	.06	.25	−.64	−.03	−.12	−.00	−.00	.11	−.06	−.13
1	.35	.07	.59	.05	−.16	.09	.04	.23	.17	.07	−.04	−.14
3	.19	.01	.81	.04	−.07	.06	.02	−.12	−.12	.11	−.01	.02
4	.36	.04	.49	.11	.09	−.34	−.15	−.00	−.11	.02	.17	−.14
11	−.14	.11	.67	−.23	.04	.15	−.12	−.16	.07	−.06	.13	.19
21	.05	.32	−.05	.77	.05	.10	.05	−.03	.34	−.03	−.01	−.06
22	−.11	.08	−.02	.78	−.10	−.07	−.02	.04	−.01	−.08	−.03	.11
25	−.18	−.30	.03	.44	.16	.24	−.10	.12	−.11	.23	.39	.05
9	−.23	−.10	.20	−.02	−.75	−.00	−.07	.02	.04	.05	−.15	−.02
30	.11	.34	−.24	.14	−.48	.17	−.01	−.11	−.10	−.01	.32	.08
27	−.32	−.07	−.15	.03	−.19	−.60	.15	.06	−.20	.11	.05	.07
28	−.17	−.07	−.02	.00	.23	−.67	.15	−.09	.05	−.15	−.02	.08
29	−.38	−.06	−.23	−.11	−.27	−.41	−.06	.13	−.05	−.01	.17	.05
13	−.02	−.00	−.09	−.03	−.00	−.17	.75	.01	−.17	−.04	−.14	.01
14	−.01	−.15	.01	.02	.08	−.02	.81	−.04	.16	.01	.14	.02
7	−.12	−.09	.15	.02	.12	.01	.03	−.79	−.25	−.03	−.05	−.02
8	−.06	−.05	−.03	−.10	−.22	−.04	.01	−.68	.45	.03	.06	.06
26	.03	.06	.01	−.16	−.02	−.07	.01	−.06	−.81	.04	−.05	.09
10	.03	.08	.20	.03	−.07	.19	.12	−.01	−.03	.75	.01	−.06
12	−.07	−.17	.14	.18	−.03	.20	.27	−.03	.03	−.62	.09	−.23
17	−.04	−.00	.09	−.02	.03	−.08	.01	−.03	.07	−.06	.84	−.04
24	.12	−.00	.02	.20	−.01	−.11	.03	−.04	−.10	.08	−.05	.76
% TV	12	12	7	6	5	5	5	4	4	4	4	4 72

half of what is now the United States until the first millennium B.C. (Jennings and Norbeck 1964: 237, 261-262), and farming did not dominate other sources of subsistence until the Christian era.

TABLE 6. MEANS AND STANDARD DEVIATIONS OF PHI'S OF SIX AREAS AND WORLD

AREAS	MEAN	STANDARD DEVIATION
2 Circum-Mediterranean	.03	.21
1 Africa	.01	.21
3 East Eurasia	.02	.24
4 Insular Pacific	.01	.20
6 South America	.01	.19
5 North America	.02	.20
World	.02	.21

Around the Mediterranean, in contrast, the domestication of animals and plants goes back to about 8500 B.C. (Flannery 1965). Forest and other natural vegetation became depleted as farming and herding became more intensive, and the rate of regrowth was much less rapid in the savannas, semideserts, and deserts of North Africa and the Middle East than in the woodlands of the eastern United States. The increase of human population following the domestication of animals and plants hastened the alteration of the landscape and the depletion of wild animal and plant food resources, such that the latter in the 19th and 20th centuries has contributed only a trivial portion of the diet.

(B) *Independent family, nuclear or polygynous* (13), and *patrilocal residence* (15) correlate −.11 for the world, −.01 in North America, and −.51 around

TABLE 7. INTERCORRELATIONS (r) OF THE SIX AREAS

	2	1	3	4	6	5
2 Circum-Mediterranean		.24	.41	.21	.17	.16
1 Africa	.24		.57	.55	.40	.46
3 East Eurasia	.41	.57		.56	.48	.38
4 Insular Pacific	.21	.55	.56		.48	.46
6 South America	.17	.40	.48	.48		.48
5 North America	.16	.46	.38	.46	.48	
Totals	1.19	2.22	2.40	2.26	2.01	1.94

TABLE 8. SIGNIFICANT COMPARISONS OF VARIABLES

	1	2	3	4	5	6	7	8	9	10	11	12	13	14	15	16	17	18	19	20	21	22	23	24	25	26	27	28	29	30	TOTAL COMPARISONS
1		8												8				4								3	3	4			6
2			7		5	5								5		5										5	5				7
3	X	X					7	5			7	4						3					3			4	3		5		11
4																												4			1
5		X	X			5								5		5										5	5				7
6		X	X		X									5		8	3									5	5				8
7																			4			5									2
8																		5	4				4								3
9		X																			2							2			3
10		X																													1
11	X	X			X	X																									4
12																			4					4							2
13															3				4			5									3
14		X			X	X									4		3														5
15					X								X	X						9			5								5
16																				5	3										2
17														X				4													2
18	X		X					X				X				X	X		9				6								8
19									X	X				X		X	X	X		6		2	11								9
20																			X		9	5	5	3							5
21																						11	5					3			3
22							7												X	X	X		7	6	5	4					8
23		X						X	X					X		X		X	X	X	X	X									10
24																						X		X							2
25																						X		X		5					3
26	X	X			X	X									X								X		X						7
27	X	X	X		X	X																									5
28	X		X																			X									3
29											X																				1
30		X	X																												2

the Mediterranean (the difference between the latter two is significant at the .01 level). These traits are uncorrelated in North America but show a substantial relationship in the Mediterranean area. In North America patrilocal residence is the most frequent form for the continent as a whole and is common in all areas except the Arctic, Great Basin, and East. Bilocal residence is dominant in the Arctic and Great Basin, matrilocal residence in the East. The independent family is obtrusive in the Arctic, Mackenzie Sub-Arctic, Plateau, Great Basin, and Northeast Mexico. It would show a positive correlation with bilocal or neolocal residence, not with patrilocal.

Around the Mediterranean, patrilocal residence dominates all other forms to a greater extent than in North America, but it tends to be associated with lineal, stem, and extended families. The well-defined property concepts around the Mediterranean go back, no doubt, almost to the first domestication of animals and plants, and have tended to encourage strict rules of inheritance and unilineal organization for thousands of years. The progressive desiccation of the Middle East, brought about as much by overfarming and overgrazing as by diminution of rainfall, increased the competition between human social groups for natural resources and encouraged the development of extended families, lineages, and clans, for an individual or his nuclear or polygynous family could survive better as a member of a larger kin or local group. Nowhere in the Circum-Mediterranean area do we find independent nuclear and polygynous families roaming the landscape alone in search exclusively of wild foods, as was done in the Artic, Mackenzie Sub-Arctic, Great Basin, and Northeast Mexican areas of North America. This sharp contrast in ecology and history in the two areas contributes to an explanation of the differences in the magnitude of correlations between residence rules and family structure.

TABLE 9. FREQUENCY OF AREAL DIFFERENCES

PAIRS OF AREAS	FREQUENCY	RANK ORDER	RANK ORDER r_{ij}
1 2	29	4.5	4.0
1 3	18	10.0	15.0
1 4	14	12.0	13.0
1 5	30	3.0	8.5
1 6	12	14.5	6.0
2 3	19	9.0	7.0
2 4	29	4.5	3.0
2 5	37	1.5	1.0
2 6	24	8.0	2.0
3 4	12	14.5	14.0
3 5	37	1.5	5.0
3 6	26	7.0	11.0
4 5	27	6.0	8.5
4 6	13	13.0	11.0
5 6	18	10.5	11.0

(C) *Agamous communities* (12) and *brideprice* (18) correlate -.19 for the entire world, -.58 around the Mediterranean, and -.06 in North America (the difference between the latter two is significant at the .01 level). As in the preceding example, we have an absence of correlation in North America and a substantial relation in the Mediterranean area. In the Circum-Mediterranean brideprice is most frequent in North Africa and agamous communities in Europe. Brideprice is associated with the more primitive peoples living in smaller communities on a land that can only support a sparse population and that is adjacent to the rest of Africa, where brideprice is more frequent than in any other of the six areas. Diffusion has certainly played a part here. Communities in North Africa are more frequently exogamous because they more often consist of single kinship groups. In Europe, in contrast, communities more often include several or many distinct kinship groups and hence permit agamy, and dowry or no substantial economic exchange at marriage is the rule. In North America brideprice and agamy fail to align in any meaningful way; hence their correlation is approximately zero. There is no contrast in marriage practices as great as that between North Africa and Europe.

(D) *Brideprice* (18) and *patrilineal descent* (19) yield a world-wide correlation of .41, but in North America it is only .03, while around the Mediterranean it is .60 (the difference between the latter two is significant at the .01 level). (These correlations all have negative signs in the tables because the variable reads "patrilineal descent absent." Discussion is facilitated by dropping the word "absent" in the caption and dropping the minus signs of the coefficients.) North America contrasts not only with the Circum-Mediterranean but with the world as a whole. The correlation of -.12 in South America shows that the preponderance of positive instances that produce the world-wide correlation of .41 are from the Old World. The contrast is, therefore, between the two hemispheres.

TABLE 10. FACTORS OF WORLD SAMPLE AND THE SIX AREAS

	World					East Eurasia					Africa			
	2	3	4	5	6	2	3	13	14	15	2	3	16	17
12									.49					
14									.78					
13									.75				-.78	
7														
8														
10								-.44					.62	
9			-.75					-.87						
11	.67					.70					.57			.44
3	.81					.87					.60			
1	.59					.80								
4	.49					.82								
28				-.67							-.64			
27				-.60										
29				-.41				-.57						.50
2														
18	.40					-.57								
16	.63					-.57								.71
15	.69					-.82					.61			
19	-.87					.93					-.75			
23	.83		-.64			-.88					.88			
20	-.75					.58			.41		-.70			
30			-.48								.66			
17														
21			.77			-.53					.85			
22			.78					.80			.78			
24								.85			.41			
25			.44										.43	
26														
CFV	.12	.07	.06	.05	.05	.14	.10	.06	.06	.06	.15	.06	.04	.06

* Heavily influenced by variables 5 and 6, which are not on this table.

Murdock (1949: 20-21) gives two cross-classification tables from which one may derive a significant positive correlation between brideprice and patrilocal residence and between the former and "removal of the bride from her local community." The correlation between brideprice and patrilocal residence is significantly positive (.42) in his (1957) world ethnographic sample and in each of the six world areas except the Insular Pacific, where it is only .08. Why patrilineal descent does not also correlate with brideprice in the Americas is difficult to explain. In light of the development cycle for residence and descent postulated by Murdock (1949: 184-259) and empirically demonstrated for North America by Driver (1956), we must assume that in the New World patrilineal descent lagged behind changes in residence, which were more closely related to brideprice. In the Old World no such lag took place, or patricentered social organization had more time to become stable. The correlation between patrilocal residence and patrilineal descent is much higher in the Old World areas, ranging from .47 to .83; in North America it is .11 and in South America .17 in Murdock's (1957) sample. Driver's (1966) sample gives a correlation of .31 for North America, but this is still lower than those in the Old World. This confirms our suspicion that patricentered organization is less developed in the Americas because it originated later and is associated with a less integrated ecology.

Because archeologists cannot dig up examples of residence and descent with a shovel and date them by the radiocarbon method, any statement about their antiquity is somewhat speculative. Nevertheless, there is good reason to postulate that unilineal descent systems are much older in the Old World than in the New. We agree with Murdock (1955: 2) that the early immigrants to the New World were most probably bilateral in descent, bilocal in residence, and Hawaiian in cousin terminlogy, and that all unicentered systems developed independently in the New World, most of them within the last few thousand years. In the Old World, in contrast, we find an intricately

TABLE 10—(Cont.)

Insular Pacific					South America					North America					Circum-Mediterranean					
2	3	4	6	8	2a	19	2b	3	6	3	20	2a	4	21	2	13	3	15	22	8
															.59					
										−.50				.42				.73		
										−.72								.86		
														−.84	.70					
														−.44	.71					
						.77				−.51										
								−.74		−.53		.40								
.42								−.56		−.50							.84			
	.46							−.66			−.90						.75			
		.75				.59					−.88						.76			
			.74																	
						−.72		−.43		−.67										
						−.44		−.84		−.76					−.45			−.44		
	−.40							−.60										−.57		
	−.97																			
							.45			.44					−.58					
.64							.76												−.49	
	.79						.90								−.50		−.57			
		−.92			.93							−.97			.74					
			.73		−.92							.96			−.74					
				−.74	.73							−.95				.85				
			−.46																−.62	
			−.64																−.66	
	−.85												−.87					.86		
	−.83												−.87			.91				
								−.65								.86				
−.42												−.64								
	.60																			
.12	.13*	.08	.06	.05	.09	.06	.06	.06	.07	.10	.08	.13	.09	.05	.12	.09	.06	.07	.06	.06

187

developed unilineal (double) descent system among most Australians, whose material culture remained at an Upper Paleolithic stage in many respects, which suggests an age of at least 10,000 years for the descent system. Unilineal descent may, therefore, have an antiquity of 10,000 years or more in the Old World.

Aberle's (1961) list of factors that tend to eliminate matrilineal descent and encourage patrilineal descent are relevant here: increased importance of male labor; increased importance of male-owned property, such as domesticated animals; increased male control of tools of production, such as the plow and potter's wheel; nonkinship control of political organization; large political units; segmentary descent groups; advanced technology and high level of productivity. The patrilineal systems of the Old World possessed these features in greater frequency than those of the New World, and some (the plow and potter's wheel, and one might add the transportation wheel) were absent everywhere in the New World. The first appearance of most of these factors and their increase in frequency sufficient to influence social organization occurred much earlier in the Old World.

Matricentered systems, however, do not show the same contrast between the Old and New Worlds. Matrilineal kin groups and matrilocal residence in Murdock's (1957) world sample show a correlation of .30 (Coult and Habenstein 1965: 381); North America alone, from Driver's (1966) sample of 277 ethnic units, yields a value of .45; South America alone, from Driver's (MS) sample, based largely on Murdock (1951), shows a value of .32. Aberle's positive correlations between matrilineal descent, hoe farming, and savanna or lightly forested areas fit both hemispheres equally well. Africa and Melanesia possess the first two features in many localities; and the eastern United States, the Circum-Caribbean, and the Tropical Forest culture area in South America conform in many localities if we substitute the more generalized concept of hand tools for the more specific hoe.

For the world as a whole, it is apparent that descent has shifted from matrilineal to patrilineal (sometimes with a bilateral stage in between) more often than it has changed in the opposite direction. The 19th-century evolutionists were partly right about the major sequence of change, but their reasons for the change were the wrong ones. It is the evolution of technology and government that favors patrilineal over matrilineal descent, not the recognition of biological fatherhood and the abandonment of promiscuity or "group marriage." However, after societies have attained an advanced level of technology and political organization, unilineal descent groups of all kinds tend to disappear, as they have done in most of Europe and its derivative cultures.

(E) The worldwide correlation between *matrilineal descent absent* (21) and *marriage to MoSiDa forbidden and matrilineal exogamy absent* (22) is .56; but the correlation between the same two variables in the Circum-Mediterranean area is —.14, and in North America it is .90 (the difference between the latter two is significant at the .01 level). All but a few North American ethnic units forbid marriage of this parallel cousin, and matrilineal descent is absent among these as well as among a large majority of other ethnic units.

Around the Mediterranean this parallel-cousin marriage is allowed by a substantial minority of ethnic units, but only one (the Tuareg) has matrilineal exogamy. There are only two other ethnic units with matrilineal exogamy, and these forbid parallel-cousin marriage. The small frequencies in some of the cells of the 2x2 tables involved in these correlations probably contribute to the sharp difference between areas. The Circum-Mediterranean has the greatest frequency of parallel-cousin marriage of any area of its size in the world. Although there is far from complete agreement on the causes of this practice, it is generally coupled with a desire to keep property in land and domesticated animals within the lineage by marrying one's father's brother's daughter or mother's sister's daughter. In the Middle East, which has progressively mined the resources necessary for the survival of man and his animals for thousands of years, the pressure to keep dwindling resources within a kinship group has been enormous. It seems likely that the earliest form of lineage in the Middle East was exogamous and that subsequent ecological pressures were more powerful than the incest taboo, which was relaxed for parallel cousins, to make the lineage endogamous. Because all but three Circum-Mediterranean societies allowing marriage of the mother's sister's daughter also allow or prefer marriage of the father's brother's daughter, the preference for the latter parallel cousin suggests historical priority and later extension to the former. The reasons for a fair amount of parallel-cousin marriage in Europe are not as clear, but may also be concerned in part with keeping property and prestige within the kinship group.

(F) The worldwide correlation between *bifurcate merging kin terms* (Fa=FaBr≠MoBr, 26) and *Hawaiian* (generation) *kin terms* (25) for siblings and cousins is —.04, but in North America it is —.25 and in the Circum-Mediterranean area .57 (the difference between the latter two is significant at the .01 level). As has been shown many times (e.g., Murdock 1949, Driver 1956), bifurcate merging terminology theoretically matches unicentered kinship structure, while the generation principle should go with bicentered

188

TABLE 11. SETS OF VARIABLES IN THE SIX AREAS

	19 20 23	15 19 23	1 3 11	15 19 20 23	20 22 24	15 16 18	3 9 11	15 16 19 20 23	15 18 19 23	Total Sets
East Eurasia	×	×	×	×	×	×		×	×	8
Africa	×	×		×	×					4
Insular Pacific	×	×		×		×				4
Circum-Mediterranean		×	×		×				×	4
North American	×		×				×			3
South America	×						×	×		3
Total Areas	5	4	3	3	3	2	2	2	2	26

organization. The negative correlation in North America is, therefore, the expectable relationship. The relatively high positive correlation in the Circum-Mediterranean is the result of a single positive instance of the two kinship features occurring together, 53 instances where both are absent, 2 instances where Hawaiian terminology is present without bifurcate merging, and no instances of the latter without the former. This highly skewed 2x2 table gives a relatively high correlation, with only a single case where both traits are present; such a relationship is nearly meaningless ethnologically, is in part an accident of the arbitrary delineation of the Circum-Mediterranean area, and is statistically unreliable.

Some of the areal differences in correlations could be eliminated by choosing a larger number of more specific trait categories and narrowing the range of meaning. For example, if the trait *agriculture dominant* (3) were divided into three subdivisions (agriculture provides 25-50 percent of the diet, 51-75 percent, and 76-100 percent), most North American instances would fall in the lower two, but most Circum-Mediterranean would be coded in the highest subdivision. The sharp differences between the correlation of *agriculture dominant* (3) and *hunting and gathering important but not dominant* (9) in North America and around the Mediterranean (given in section A above) would be eliminated. But there will always remain some significant areal differences that can be accounted for by differences in history and ecology. Experience has shown that in the long run the splitting of data into more and more categories of lower and lower frequency tends to depress correlations to the point where many of them fail to meet a test of significance, because the error variance increases relative to the total variance.

If such sharp areal differences in correlations appear between areas not selected to produce such differences, what would happen if the researcher deliberately delimited areas so as to give the maximum differences obtainable in the correlations among a group of variables? No one can say for sure until it is done, but we will venture a guess that the world could be divided into six continuous areas of about the same size as Murdock's (1957) that would show greater differences than those shown in this paper. To put it more specifically, it might be possible to find two areas, comparable in size to Murdock's, whose matrices of correlations for the same variables would correlate zero with each other, instead of the low of .16 between his Circum-Mediterranean and North American areas. This is a complicated problem and we know of no technique for solving it, but it is something to think about. It certainly casts a shadow on the meaning of correlations computed from world samples without any regional subdivisions. When such correlations are based on fewer than 100 cases not chosen by any explicit sampling technique, they are doubly suspect and should be regarded as only tentative hypotheses to be further tested for areal differences with larger samples.

Methodological Note

Construction of Variables

It is often necessary to reconstruct variables in order that each pair of them may be represented by Pearson's *r*, the quantity from which factors are derived and which the factors in turn are required to reproduce. In our case, such manipulation was required since the variables for the most part consisted of several or more unordered categories that could not in our judgment be presumed to lie on a well-defined continuum. For pairs of such sets of un-ordered categories, the product-moment point r is equivocal in meaning since its magnitude will vary according to the arrangement of categories, with this exception: for a 2x2 table its value is unaffected by order in which categories are placed, hence, by arranging several or more categories in a two-fold classification, it is possible to obtain product-moment r's for cross-classifications that will be independent of the order of categories. Given our decision not to create rank orders, our problem thus was to select that two-fold grouping of categories for each set which would be best for the purposes of this study.

Since our purpose was to investigate the interrelations among cultural classifications, it seemed to us that classifications should be formed on the basis of relevant anthropological criteria, hence we first attempted to obtain the best dichotomies by inspection of content. But this procedure was abandoned after some trials since, at least in some cases, there appeared to be no basis for choosing among equally plausible arrangements. We then sought a mechanical procedure for constructing dichotomies.

From a statistical standpoint, it would seem best to group categories so as to maximize the quantity Σr^2_{ij} ($i{\neq}j$), or the total amount of association subject to linear measurement. However, at the time this analysis was undertaken, no machine program for maximizing this quantity was available (although one might have been composed); consequently, we turned to a procedure that might be readily performed by the machine, although probably not best in the sense of maximizing covariation. To construct two-fold classifications, we set up in each case the category with the largest frequency as one class, and the remaining categories as the other class; thus, for six categories, the residual class would be composed of five categories. The crudities of this procedure should be mentioned: it gives no assurance that marginal frequencies will be uniform, as would be desirable in analysis of phi coefficients; furthermore, the residual class will consist of categories that differ considerably in sociocultural content. In fact, as noted, our residual class in some instances consisted of categories representing very different, if not incompatible, cultural practices. Nevertheless, the procedure in application was not without advantages: it produced marginal distributions that were not severely skewed; also it could be executed on the machine with no special program.

The variables of Sawyer and LeVine (1966: Table 1) differ from ours in that only ten are dichotomies,

while the other 20 are scales of three or four steps. Their ten dichotomies match seven of ours (our Table 2: 1, 2, 14, 18, 19, 21, 28) exactly, except that we list the absence of the phenomenon instead of its presence for four of the dichotomies (2, 19, 21, 28). In four of our dichotomies (5, 13, 25, 27) one member matches one of the terminal categories of their scales; consequently these variables differ only in that we have cut the continuum at one point, whereas they have cut it at two or three points. For ten of our dichotomies (3, 6, 8, 10, 11, 12, 15, 23, 29, 30) one of our members is joined in one of their terminal categories by at least one other of Murdock's original traits. For eight of our dichotomies (4, 7, 9, 17, 20, 22, 24, 26) we oppose one of their middle categories to both ends of their scale and the remaining category.

The average correlation of each variable with every other variable (signs disregarded) gives an indication of the effect of the choice of variables on the magnitude of correlations. Our seven dichotomies that match those of Sawyer and LeVine average .02 lower than theirs. Our 14 dichotomies where one side matches or is found in one of the terminal steps in their scales average .04 lower; while our eight dichotomies that oppose a middle category of their scales to both ends average .07 lower. These differences are reflected in the total amount of variance extracted by the 10 factors in each analysis: Sawyer and LeVine (1966: Table 3) .74; this study (Table 5) .64. The general conclusion from these comparisons is that the variables of Sawyer and LeVine are, on the whole, more efficient than ours in terms of the magnitude of the correlations and the factor loadings.

This generalization does not apply to every variable, however, or even to all of the eight variables where we oppose a middle category to both ends of Sawyer's and LeVine's scales. In the latter group, our *marriage to FaBrDa forbidden and patrilineal exogamy absent* (Table 2: 20) has an average correlation (signs disregarded) of .21 with all others, while Sawyer's and LeVine's corresponding *patrilineal exogamy* (Table 2: 6B) averages only .17 with all other variables.

Köbben (1967: 13-14) correlates *bilateral kinship* with an evolutionary economic scale of three steps: *hunters and collectors, non-Western farmers and herders, modern Western society.* He finds that when *hunters and collectors* is combined with *modern Western society* and opposed to *non-Western farmers and herders*, the correlation with bilateral kinship is higher than with either end of the scale taken singly and opposed to the remainder. Therefore no a priori rule about the shape of relationship applies to all data.

Driver (1965: 330-331) has suggested that the best combination of categories within a single variable, such as *patrilineal descent*, be empirically determined by testing every combination of 2, 3, 4, etc., categories until the combination that gives the maximum correlation with another variable, such as *residence*, is found. Every combination of residence categories would also have to be tested for correlation with every combination of descent. This method could be extended to the 30 variables of Murdock's (1957) sample and would yield a single combination for dichotomizing each variable that would produce the maximum correlation with the "best" combinations within each of the other 29 variables. This idea has not yet been implemented with a computer program, but it suggests an empirical operation to solve a problem that is not likely to be settled with theoretical argument. The application of this trial-and-error method to categories arranged in scales of three or four steps would be more difficult but probably not impossible.

Driver and Sanday (1966: 170) deliberately opposed each category to every other one in its group, thus repeating the same category in more than one variable. The purpose was to display each category in the list of captions, so that none would be lost in combinations as they are in this study and that of Sawyer and LeVine. Coult and Habenstein (1965) have likewise repeated the same categories in more than one variable.

Estimating the Communalities

If the principal object of the investigation is to analyze the common factors, it is necessary to estimate communalities (i.e., the proportion of variance due to common factors) from the range of possible values. Ideally, and expressed informally, we choose communalities that, together with the intercorrelations, will yield the smallest possible number of common factors. But in practice we usually begin with a set of provisional values that may be successively adjusted if such refinement is required. Our procedure was to assign a value of 1.00 to each communality according to the principle that factorial results are not seriously disturbed by this maximum value when the number of variables is relatively large (Thurstone 1947). However, the insertion of 1.00 as an arbitrary communality has its drawbacks: (a) it carries the possibly misleading suggestion that all variance is common-factor variance; (b) additionally, it carries the implication that interest lies in the variables themselves rather than in their intercorrelationships; and (c), where interest is in the common-factor variance, it will require that the factor analysis

be repeated, using communalities that will have been derived from the initial analysis. But however the problem of communalities is resolved, it is desirable that estimated communalities be reported so that related findings on different samples of peoples and their traits may be reliably compared.

Method of Factoring

With the correlation matrix set up, it becomes necessary to adopt a factoring method from among those that are available to the research worker. Other things being equal, we use the method of principal components, which satisfies the criterion of least squares and which by that criterion provides the best fit of factors to the given data. However, it is practically impossible to perform this analysis by hand, owing to the great bulk and intricacies of the computations; in consequence, unless computer facilities are available, it will be necessary to use the centroid method of factoring or one of its adaptations. Thus, in an earlier analysis of 16 Indian tribes (Driver and Schuessler 1957), we used the centroid method, while in this study we used the method of principal components. We mention this to illustrate, and perhaps clarify, a circumstance that may have puzzled some readers: the almost exclusive reliance on the centroid method before roughly 1955 and its replacement by the method of principal components since that date.

Elimination of Factors

From empirical correlations, it is always possible to extract as many factors as there are variables (Kendall 1957); however, they will not be of equal statistical importance in terms of their contribution to the common-factor variance. Hence, it becomes necessary to eliminate those of little or no statistical consequence. Over a dozen criteria have been proposed to distinguish between important and trivial factors. A simple procedure with a sound theoretical base (Kaiser 1960), and that followed in this study, is to eliminate factors contributing less than $1/n$ to the aggregate variance, where n is the number of variables. But this criterion, like all others, is somewhat arbitrary, and will eliminate factors on the borderline that will be virtually indistinguishable from some that will be retained. A sensible working rule is to retain too many rather than too few factors; for trivial factors may later be ignored, but discarded factors of consequence will be practically difficult to recover.

Transformation of Loadings

With the loadings provided by the factoring in hand, the next issue confronting the analyst has to do with their conversion into values that will be most subject to meaningful and useful interpretation. There are infinitely many ways of writing a set of factor loadings, given the intercorrelations among the factors themselves. However, these intercorrelations among factors are not given by the data and, like the assumptions of any statistical model, must be fixed by the analyst. The usual practice, exemplified by our analysis, is to treat the intercorrelations among factors as identically zero and to transform the loadings as initially obtained under this restrictive but simplest assumption. If, as in this study, the primary purpose is to identify the primary common factors and their relative strength, there will be little need to depart from this rule and adopt a more complex but less restrictive set of assumptions. But whether factors are taken to be mutually uncorrelated (orthogonal) or intercorrelated (oblique), it is still necessary to select a criterion of rotation, which may be either analytic or judgmental. Since the method due to Kaiser (1959), which maximizes the variance of the loadings, also tends to produce loadings that have a simple structure, as defined by Thurstone, we adopted that analytic criterion.

Interpretation of Factors

Our next problem had to do with the identification (not validation) of factors whose effects are presumably measured by the loadings. Of course we may forego interpretation, treating the results as a convenient condensation of an unwieldy distribution. But usually interpretation is regarded as an integral part of the process of factor analysis. In this process it would be possible to interpret every factor having at least one substantial loading. However, such interpretations would obviously be less reliable than those based on factors having several or more substantial loadings. Our somewhat unorthodox procedure was to interpret only factors having three or more relatively large loadings ($a_{ij} > .40$), since an ambiguity produced by two variables might be resolved by a third. An even more conservative procedure would be to require at least four large loadings, again possibly to break a deadlock resulting from three nominally different variables. But however this matter is resolved, and there will be differences of opinion on this, little significance should be attached to factors that account for only a small portion of the total variance and correspondingly contribute only negligibly to the set of variables.

Consideration of the Results

With names attached, the factor analysis may be regarded as completed, but additional issues are sure to arise concerning the generality and validity of the terminal results. Some of these we put in the form of questions and tentative answers.

(a) Is the sample of 565 societies representative of all societies in the population being investigated? The population being investigated has never been adequately defined and delimited by anthropologists. The article by Naroll (1964) on ethnic unit classification, and the comments on it, succeed in raising the principal issues involved but do not offer solutions acceptable to all or even a majority of anthropologists. Nevertheless, Murdock's 1957 sample is the best up to that date and is only being superseded by his own sample (1962-66) in his Ethnographic Atlas.

(b) Would the results and corresponding conclusions be identical or similar if more refined measures were available? We postulate that they would be similar but not identical. Sawyer's and LeVine's (1966) scales of two, three, or four steps yield similar but not identical results.

(c) Would the results be similar if different variables or traits had been measured and intercorrelated? Not necessarily; some results would be similar and others would differ. For instance, our table omits the correlations of matrilocal residence, matrilineal descent, and Crow kin classification, which Aberle (1961) gives in his assemblage from the same sample of those variables correlating with matrilineal descent. Matrilocal residence becomes lumped in our treatment with all other forms of residence in opposition to patrilocal, which is the model variant. Similarly, Crow kin classification becomes lumped with all other kinds except Hawaiian, the modal category to which all the others are opposed. Furthermore, Driver and Sanday (1966), using only North American data, found two distinct matricentered factors that do not appear in either the world sample or the North American sample of this paper.

(d) Do the data permit a test of the hypothesis that some interrelationships are universal owing to the functional necessities of social existence? While not providing a strict test, they shed light on this possibility. The two most obtrusive and ubiquitous factors of Table 10 both reveal functional relationships among their constituent variables. This is true also of other factors. The geographical distributions of the factors, which we have mapped but not figured in this paper, exhibit multiple clusterings of the positive occurrences of the member variables, with each clustering separated by a distinct geographical gap from the other clusterings. In light of the culture history inferable from genetic language classification, genetic biological classification, archeology, and comparative ethnology, we must postulate multiple independent origins of all or most of the geographical clusters and factors of this study. This is not to deny the spread of the behaviors within each of the geographical clusters by means of migration and diffusion.

(e) Do the data permit a test of the hypothesis that traits appear at different stages of cultural development? The data and techniques of this paper do not demonstrate such an evolution, but Murdock (1949) has asserted a sequence from sexual division of labor, to postnuptial residence, to descent of membership in kin groups, to classification of relatives in kinship terminology. Driver (1956) has statistically confirmed the broad outlines of this cycling, as it is better labeled, for North America. Aberle (1961) offers a series of technological changes that tend to eliminate matrilineal descent and replace it with patrilineal or bilateral descent. These are given above in the section "Interpretations of Areal Differences," under D. Aberle's suggestions are definitely evolutionary and incline one to believe that matrilineal descent was much more common in Paleolithic or Neolithic times and that it has been often replaced in later periods by patrilineal or bilateral descent. This agrees with the sequence postulated in the 19th century, but for different reasons. The positive correlation of bilateral descent with *hunters and collectors* and *modern Western society* makes the point that a variable common in an early stage may be largely rejected in an intermediate stage, only to reappear in a later stage of social evolution.

The best evidence of cultural evolution is, of course, archeological; it is uncontestable in its broad outlines. Where nonmaterial variables show substantial synchronic correlations with material variables datable by archeological methods, there is reason to suppose that the correlation is also diachronic. For instance, the synchronic correlation between farming with hand tools by women and matrilineal descent is probably also a diachronic one. It cannot be overemphasized that diachronic correlations should be determined from all available evidence, including archeological, and not from the limited evidence of this or any other synchronic correlation study.

References Cited

ABERLE, DAVID F., 1961, Matrilineal descent in cross-cultural perspective. *In* Matrilineal kinship. David M. Schneider and Kathleen Gough, eds. Berkeley and Los Angeles, University of California Press. Pp. 655-727.

ALKER, HAYWARD R., JR., 1964, Dimensions of conflict in the general assembly. American Political Science Review 58: 642-657.

BACON, MARGARET K., HERBERT BARRY III, AND IRVIN L. CHILD, 1965, A cross-cultural study of drinking: II. Relations to other features of culture. Quarterly Journal of Studies on Alcohol 26, Supplement No. 3: 29-48.

BARRETT, SAMUEL A., 1908, The ethnogeography of the Pomo and neighboring Indians. University of California Publications in American Archaeology and Ethnology 6: 1-322.

BOAS, FRANZ, 1894, Indianische Sagen von der Nord-Pacifischen Küste Amerikas. Berlin, A. Asher and Co.

CLEMENTS, FORREST E., 1954, Use of cluster analysis with anthropological data. American Anthropologist 56: 180-199.

COULT, ALLAN D., AND ROBERT W. HABENSTEIN, 1965, Cross tabulations of Murdock's world ethnographic sample. Columbia, University of Missouri Press.

CRAMÉR, HARALD, 1946, Mathematical methods of statistics. Princeton, Princeton University Press.

CZEKANOWSKI, JAN, 1911, Objective Kriterien in der Ethnologie. Korrespondenz-Blatt der Deutschen Gesellschaft für Anthropologie, Ethnologie und Urgeschichte 42: 1-5.

DRIVER, HAROLD E., 1956, An integration of functional, evolutionary, and historical theory by means of correlations. Indiana University Publications in Anthropology and Linguistics, Memoir 12.

1965, Survey of numerical classification in anthropology. *In* The use of computers in anthropology. Dell Hymes, ed. The Hague, Mouton. Pp. 301-344.

1966, Geographical-historical versus psycho-functional explanations of kin avoidances. Current Anthropology 7: 131-182.

MS, Correlations of economy and social organization in South America.

DRIVER, HAROLD E., AND PEGGY R. SANDAY, 1966, Factors and clusters of kin avoidances and related variables. Current Anthropology 7: 169-176.

DRIVER, HAROLD E., AND KARL F. SCHUESSLER, 1957, Factor analysis of ethnographic data. American Anthropologist 59: 655-663.

FLANNERY, K. V., 1965, The ecology of early food production in Mesopotamia. Science 147, 3663: 1247-1256.

GOODMAN, LEO A., AND WILLIAM H. KRUSKAL, 1954, Measures of association for cross classifications. Journal of the American Statistical Association 49: 732-764.

1959, Measures of association for cross classifications. II: Further discussion and references. Journal of the American Statistical Association 54: 123-163.

1963, Measures of association for cross classifications. III: Approximate sampling theory. Journal of the American Statistical Association 58: 310-364.

GOULDNER, ALVIN W., AND RICHARD A. PETERSON, 1962, Technology and the moral order. Indianapolis, Bobbs-Merrill.

HAYS, WILLIAM L., 1963, Statistics for psychologists. New York, Holt, Rinehart, and Winston.

HICKMAN, JOHN M., 1962, Dimensions of a complex concept: method exemplified. Human Organization 21: 214-218.

HOWELLS, W. W., 1951, Factors of human physique. American Journal of Physical Anthropology 9: 159-191.

HYMES, DELL, ED., 1965, The use of computers in anthropology. The Hague, Mouton.

IHM, PETER, 1965, Automatic classification in anthropology. In The use of computers in anthropology. Dell Hymes, ed. The Hague Mouton. Pp. 357-378.

JENNINGS, JESSE D., AND EDWARD NORBECK, EDS., 1964, Prehistoric man in the New World. Chicago, University of Chicago Press.

KAISER, HENRY F., 1959, Computer program for varimax rotation in factor analysis. Educational and Psychological Measurement 19: 413-420.

1960, The application of electronic computers to factor analysis. Educational and Psychological Measurement 20: 141-151.

KENDALL, M. G., 1957, A course in multivariate analysis. London, Charles Griffin and Co.

KÖBBEN, A. J. F., 1967, Why exceptions? the logic of cross cultural analysis. Current Anthropology 8: 3-34.

KROEBER, A. L., 1939, Cultural and natural areas of native North America. University of California Publications in American Archaeology and Ethnology 38.

MANGELSDORF, PAUL C., RICHARD S. MACNEISH, AND WALTON C. GALINAT, 1964, Domestication of corn. Science 143: 538-545.

MILKE, WILHELM, 1965, Statistical processing. In The use of computers in anthropology. Dell Hymes, ed. The Hague, Mouton. Pp. 189-204.

MURDOCK, GEORGE PETER, 1940, The cross-cultural survey. American Sociological Review 5: 361-370. Reprinted in Readings in cross-cultural methodology. Frank W. Moore, ed. New Haven, Human Relations Area Files, 1961. Pp. 45-54.

1949, Social structure. New York, Macmillan.

1951, Outline of South American cultures. New Haven, Human Relations Area Files.

1955, North American social organization. Davidson Journal of Anthropology 1, 11: 1-11.

1957, World ethnographic sample. American Anthropologist 59: 664-687.

NAROLL, RAOUL, 1964, On ethnic unit classification. Current Anthropology 5: 283-312.

NEEDHAM, R.M., 1965, Computer methods for classification and grouping. In The use of computers in anthropology. Dell Hymes, ed. The Hague: Mouton. Pp. 345-356.

OSGOOD, CHARLES E., 1964, Semantic differential technique in the comparative study of cultures. American Anthropologist 66, no. 3, pt. 2: 171-200.

ROMNEY, A. KIMBALL, AND ROY G. D'ANDRADE, 1964, Cognitive aspects of English kin terms. American Anthropologist 66, no. 3, pt. 2: 146-170.

RUMMEL, R.J., 1963, Dimensions of conflict behavior within and between nations. In A. R. Rapport and L. von Bertalanffy (eds.), General Systems: Yearbook for the Society for General Systems Research, VIII. Ann Arbor: Mental Health Research Institute.

SAWYER, JACK, AND ROBERT A. LeVINE, 1966, Cultural dimensions: a factor analysis of the world ethnographic sample. American Anthropologist 68: 708-731.

SCHUBERT, GLENDON, 1962, The 1960 term of the Supreme Court: a psychological analysis. American Political Science Review 56:90-107.

SCHUESSLER, KARL F., MS. Bibliography of factor analyses in sociology.

SCHUESSLER, KARL F., AND HAROLD E. DRIVER, 1956, A factor analysis of 16 primitive societies. American Sociological Review 21: 493-499.

SPEARMAN, CHARLES, 1927, The abilities of man, their nature and measurement. New York, Macmillan.

TEXTOR, ROBERT B., 1967, A cross-cultural summary. New York, Taplinger.

THURSTONE, L. L., 1938, Primary mental abilities. Chicago, University of Chicago Press.

1947, Multiple factor analysis. Chicago, University of Chicago Press.

TUGBY, DONALD J., 1958, A typological analysis of axes and choppers from southeast Australia. American Antiquity 24: 24-33.

WALDRON, R. S., 1940, A factorial study of the components of body-build. Psychological Bulletin 37: 578 (abstract).

4. On Continuous Area and Worldwide Studies in Formal Comparative Ethnology

Joseph G. Jorgensen

Introduction

Harold Driver was perhaps the first methodologist in cross-cultural inquiry to comprehend fully the important, yet unresolvable, problem raised by Sir Francis Galton when he asked E. B. Tylor (1889) about the independence of each unit or tribe in his worldwide sample of 350 tribes. Whereas Tylor had used simple tests of empirical probabilities to determine whether relations among social institutions were attributable to chance or to lawful processes, he had failed to distinguish which of the institutional similarities possessed by groups of tribes in his sample had been inherited from a protoculture or had been acquired through borrowing, and which of the institutional similarities among tribes had been independently invented. The probability statistic that Tylor used, and all probability statistics used by cross-cultural methodologists since Tylor's time, assumed independence of sampling units, or tribes, yet the tribes in question have not

been independent. Hence, the probability statistics employed have been violated by the data. Driver recognized the complex interdependencies that obtain among tribes and worked to ferret out these interdependencies.

Driver was trained by Kroeber to postdict historical relationships among tribes by comparing intertribal relationships statistically. In statistical parlance, such studies of tribes with tribes based on agreement of trait inventories are known as Q-mode. Driver's joint essay with Kroeber—the first contribution from Driver in this volume—lays out the methodology and the goals of this type of analysis. Driver saw that this mode of inquiry was a bit reckless because it assumed near total dependencies of adjacent tribes which shared similar traits. It left no room for assessment of functions, independencies, and interdependencies.

As a graduate student, Driver attended Robert Lowie's classes and was lectured about the interplay between diffusion and independent invention. Lowie had great knowledge of world ethnography, but little understanding of inductive inquiry; yet he was aware of the question of complex interdependencies among tribes, either through borrowing or inheritance of traits, or both (see Lowie 1920). Indeed, Lowie's classic work, *Primitive Society* (1920), is a dialectic with Lewis Henry Morgan's emphasis on extreme diffusion (e.g. the origin and distribution of matriliny) and ubiquitous independent inventions (e.g. the origins of types of political integration) in Morgan's *Ancient Society* (1877). Lowie was concerned with the origin, function, and distribution of the traits of social organization —such as postnuptial residence, descent, kinship terminologies, and kin avoidances—as well as with the similarities and differences of the tribes that possessed the traits. The conclusions Lowie drew were provocative, but needed formal testing, in Driver's view.

So of Driver's teachers, Kroeber's methodology did not provide for statistical tests of traits with traits (or intervariable tests, known as R-mode relations in statistical parlance), and Lowie's R-mode type of hypotheses were not subjected to intervariable tests. Driver read Tylor (1889), Leo Simmons (1937), and George Peter Murdock (1937) and was influenced both by their methods to test hypotheses between pairs of variables with inferential statistics (chi-square was used by Murdock) and by their functional-evolutionary hypotheses, which posited independent development of sets of variables in various contexts. Driver himself was using probability parameter estimates to determine significances of differences among pairs of tribes. Tylor, and later Murdock and Simmons, unlike Kroeber, used worldwide samples to test their hypotheses. Whereas there were important benefits to be gained from worldwide studies, there were also serious shortcomings in the method. Specifically, Murdock and others from this school sought to solve the problem raised by Galton about interdependencies among tribes by selecting sample units that they had reasons to believe were not closely related through a common history of inheritance or borrowing. Here the focus was on independence of sample units, and the interpretations of correlations and tests of significance assumed that the units were, indeed, independent. Driver saw the folly in this approach as (1) providing no real controls for interdependence and (2) obscuring the question of independence, because interdependences had been so obscured. Yet he was much influenced by this approach, because it did not assume that all similarities were historical and also because it provided a more explicit propositional nature to ethnology.

Stanislaw Klimek, a student of Jan Czekanowski's, visited Kroeber at the University of California in order to become more conversant with Kroeber's methodology while integrating it with the methodology currently in use among the formalists in Germany and elsewhere in Eastern Europe. Whereas Kroeber primarily used tribe-tribe comparisons (Q-mode), the Europeans were using trait-trait comparisons in geographic space (R-mode). The Europeans' use of R-mode differed from Murdock's use, in that the samples were continuous and the correlations were displayed in large correlation matrices similar to Q-mode matrices. Klimek (1935) did both R-mode and Q-mode intercorrelational analyses of California Indian tribes and variables, and went one step further by placing tribes and traits along two dimensions of a single matrix, thus generating large scalograms that grouped tribes together on the basis of shared traits and grouped traits together on the basis of the tribes that shared them.

Klimek's interpretations of the results of his California Indian study were incautious, because trait origins were pinned to particular groups of societies at particular points in prehistory, the migrations of these societies, and the subsequent diffusion of the traits in clusters. Driver felt that Klimek had made considerable contributions to method by controlling for the propinquity of societies and the trait resemblances that made them similar or dissimilar, but that Klimek's interpretations did not properly account for parallelism, convergence, or the possi-

bility that ecological factors influenced similarities and differences among societies.

In a number of monographs Driver worked at integrating evolutionary, historical, and functional hypotheses to account for correlations among societies and traits. Thus, he rejected some of Kroeber's historical emphasis and some of Murdock's evolutionary-functional emphasis; yet he attempted to test hypotheses on continuous area samples. Rather than obscuring history and propinquity, Driver tried to control for the influence of borrowing and inheritance on correlations while also attempting to show that nomothetic relations (lawlike, postdictive regularities) obtained in the data.

We can put both the continuous area and the worldwide cross-cultural studies in better perspective by examining them separately. Driver has made contributions to both types of inquiry, as the preceding essays demonstrate.

Continuous Area Studies*

It is of more than passing interest to note that Franz Boas (1894) conducted the first formal comparative study on a continuous area sample in North America. Boas's study, in fact, is fascinating because it demonstrates considerable methodological sophistication as well as naiveté, and profound thought about ethnological questions as well as very loose conceptualization—at least in an operational sense—of ways to answer those questions.

Boas analyzed a corpus of folktale elements from several adjacent Northwest Coast and Plateau tribes, a tribe in eastern Canada, and a tribe on the Plains. He calculated the similarities and differences, and summarized and ordered the results in matrices. The more similar each pair of tribes, the closer they were placed to each other in the square matrix. Thus, as early as 1894, Boas had developed a method in which similarities and differences among many tribes could be assessed at a glance, and his was the first example of cluster analysis by inspection in ethnology. Boas did not use a test for the significance of difference between the folklore inventories of pairs of tribes.

Boas demonstrated that the Northwest Coast and Plateau groups showed much more internal similarity than they demonstrated with the eastern

---

*See Harold E. Driver, 1970, "Statistical Studies of Geographical Distributions" (listed in Driver's bibliography) for a detailed review of this topic.

Canadian and Plains tribes. This was ample evidence that the Northwest Coast tribes and the adjacent Plateau tribes shared many folktale elements in common, and that borrowing of tale elements from other tribes, as well as inheritance of tale elements from protocultures, were operating to cause this similarity. Yet neither the similarities nor the differences were explained by Boas's analysis. He wanted to know why Northwest Coast tribes shared a common pattern, or a family of resemblances, as did the Plateau groups, and why the two were formed into a still larger family of resemblances, yet also why the resemblances were only resemblances and not identicalities.

Boas was interested that the same tale elements were often combined in different ways by different societies. Moreover, some societies apparently accepted some elements and rejected others that they had learned through borrowing or inheritance. Thus Boas saw the incompleteness of his own study and raised more questions than he answered when it was finished.

It is probable that Boas's philosophical predilections caused him to abandon further quantitative and matrix analyses of ethnological materials. In subsequent years he did not attempt to analyze, in a formal fashion, cultural materials that are generally assumed to be less volatile than folklore, such as social and kinship organization materials. Had he done so, Boas might have been more optimistic about the potentialities of inductive inquiry in ethnology. It is critical to note that Boas's intention in conducting the folklore study was not to create a culture area taxonomy, but to put loose boundaries around a family of folklore resemblances in order to better understand, or *verstehen*, the folklore of each society. He argued that no society's folklore—a part of culture—could be understood without analyzing that folklore in the wider context of, say, Northwest Coast folklore.

Furthermore, neither the folklore of the society in question nor the folklore throughout the Northwest Coast could be understood without knowledge of other aspects of culture—such as the potlatch and secret societies on the Northwest Coast—aspects of the environment, and general features of human perception.

Alfred Kroeber, formerly a student of Boas's, began using Q-mode matrices to organize interlanguage and intertribal relations, as well as relations among and within archeological sites in the early twentieth century. (See Driver 1965 for a detailed history of Kroeber's activities.) By the late 1920s, Kroeber had stimulated several students to follow

him in using proximity coefficients organized in matrices to determine the clustering of ethnic units in continuous geographical areas. The related goals in all of these studies were (1) classifying the relationships among the ethnic units or aspects of the cultures of these units, such as the Sun Dance, and (2) reconstructing the history of the units or cultural items in question. Indeed, the "history" was inferred from the relationships among the ethnic units or cultural features as determined by the proximity coefficients. The generalizations drawn from the analyses were always after the fact rather than before the fact, and on the whole the studies were not undertaken to test propositions. Kroeber and some of his students merely assumed that inductive inquiry into the similarities and differences among ethnic units, when summarized by proximity coefficients in square matrices, allowed for the reconstruction of history. Thus, the results were at best cultural taxonomies and concluding hypotheses about how the various groups might be related historically. Driver's own skepticism of the assumptions made by Kroeber are clearly spelled out in several essays (see pp. 95-104).

In the early 1930s, Stanislaw Klimek obtained a grant from the Rockefeller Foundation and joined Kroeber at California. Klimek took Kroeber's California Indian data, representing about 800 culture traits distributed among sixty tribes, and began to intercorrelate tribes and traits, using Pearson's Q6 statistic. Klimek soon learned that information on all 800 traits was not available for every tribe, so he reduced the number of traits to 411, heavily stressing material culture items, for which there was information in most tribes.

Not only did Klimek intercorrelate tribes with tribes and traits with traits but he also produced scalograms that demonstrated the traits possessed by the tribes. Thus Klimek integrated the Q-mode technique used by Kroeber with the R-mode technique being used by the Europeans. In an attempt to go even further, Klimek made gross comparisons between language dialect groups and culture areas and showed that dialect groups and clusters of cultures were very similar. He made these comparisons, and even some cruder analyses of racial types, in order to assess the relations of race, language, and culture, and thereby reconstruct California Indian history.

This remarkable and provocative study (1935) is seldom cited in the ethnological literature, but it should be both cited and read. Certainly Klimek's analysis had its shortcomings. For instance, he called the generalizations that he drew from the distributions of traits among tribes as demonstrated in the scalograms "historical facts." In Klimek's view, these "historical facts" from synchronic data were not inferences, or even concluding hypotheses: they were *facts*.

Kroeber said that the traits Klimek used were reliable; the methodology he employed was sound; and that the clustering of tribes, traits, and tribes with traits was probably valid; but Kroeber strenuously objected to Klimek's reconstruction of the historical sequences of California Indians through the "strata" Klimek created. His "strata" were synchronic resemblances among societies interpreted as diachronic levels. Klimek stressed the role of various migrations into California of language groups and the subsequent developments of those groups in his scheme. Kroeber wrote a separate introduction to Klimek's work, in order to challenge some of the interpretations provided therein.

Harold Driver went still further with the continuous area method and in several papers, but especially "Girls' Puberty Rites in Western North America," published in 1941, he attempted to balance his interpretations of the meanings of correlations obtained by integrating historical, psychological, and other explanations. This paper represented a major break from the historical and ecological interpretations employed by Kroeber and the historical interpretations made by Klimek, yet it also incorporated the Q-mode, R-mode, and scalogram type of analysis employed by Klimek. Indeed, whereas Driver might not admit it, his "Girls' Puberty" study was much in line with what Boas wanted to do, but was unable to do, in his study of folklore elements.

It was at about this same time that Harold Driver incorporated hypothesis testing in continuous area studies. He tested Clark Wissler's hypothesis about diffusion with a geometric analysis of the spatial distribution of Sun dance traits. (See pp. 106-08 of this volume).

Later, Wilhelm Milke (1955) created several mathematical models to simulate cultural growth among continuously distributed tribes, and Driver (1956; Driver and Massey 1957) modified the economic-kinship organization hypotheses of Tylor (1889), Lowie (1920), and Murdock (1949)—to mention some of the contributors to these hypotheses —and tested them on a sample of about 280 North American Indian societies. Using the phi correlation coefficient to measure the relationship between each pair of variables in the study, Driver, by inspection, ordered the phis into matrices and tested for the evolution and functional integration of these variables. The functional hypotheses asserted

that division of labor, residence, tenure, descent, and terminological variables were integrated. Driver modified the hypothesis by controlling for lag. That is to say, at any point in time a society need not be fully integrated, but need only be integrating, or straining toward functional integration. Thus, if there was a change in one variable in the posited set of functionally related variables, soon the other variables of that set would change in a predicted pattern. Driver's synchronic tests for lag resulted in a set of stochastic processes, or partial-ordering laws, wherein he demonstrated that if all things were equal and an indefinite amount of time was assumed, the most probable direction of postdicted change for the variables in question was from division of labor to postnuptial residence pattern to land tenure practices to descent principle to cousin terminologies to mother-aunt terminologies. In general, Driver's research confirmed many parts of the hypotheses advanced by Lowie and Murdock, and he did so by exercising controls for contiguity never used by Murdock and formal tests of correlation and significance never used by Lowie. Driver inferred the roles of inheritance and borrowing in the correlations obtained by assessing the spatial distributions of the variables among the tribes and assessing the known histories of these tribes. In this fashion, he posited at least three basically independent developments for matricentered societies in North America (the Southwest, the Prairies and the East, and the Northwest Coast), and three basically independent developments of patricentered societies (the Prairies, California, and Mexico), but he did not speculate about the number of origins of bicentered societies. It is probable that there was substantially more than one origin of bicentered organization in North America; indeed the differences among Northwest Coast forms, Great Basin forms, and Northeastern forms are surely distinct.

Thus, Harold Driver applied the evolutionary and functional postulates (lawlike regularities) of the "scientific" school of comparative ethnology, and the historical assumptions of the so-called "historical" school of comparative ethnology, in an attempt to resolve the question about the interplay between evolution and history (borrowing and inheritance) in comparative explanations.

Driver's emphasis on parallel regularities in culture change demonstrates that continuous area studies have had propositional or hypothesis-testing dimensions. But the empirical generalizations obtained from these tests have applied only to the universe in question, and never to the world, and the tests have always inferred processes (regular changes among phenomena) from synchronic data.

Another approach to continuous area studies was advanced by Eggan (1954). He asserted that the cross-cultural methodologist should study small groups of adjacent societies in areas where the ethnologist understood the local ecology as well as the local cultures. After similarities and differences were accounted for in one area, the ethnologist should move on to another area, and so forth. Eggan offers no explicit method to apply in these inquiries, even though he calls it the "method of controlled comparisons."

Recently I analyzed the relations between language and culture among thirty-two Salish tribes of the Northwest Coast and Plateau regions of North America through nonmetric, Q-mode analyses (Jorgensen 1969). First I demonstrated relations among languages while controlling for environmental and language barriers. I did the same for cultural relations, then tested the hypotheses for lexicon and cultural variables that technology correlated more closely with environment than did social organization or religion. The hypotheses were confirmed, as were many others. The importance of the study is that language and culture interdependencies among tribes were obvious, but that the strength of these interdependencies diminished as spatial distances increased among the tribes. Furthermore, the lag hypothesis vis-à-vis evolutionary regularities in the relations among environment, technology, religion, and social organization were also confirmed. Thus credibility for the spirit of Driver's synchronic comparative method was enhanced. My methods and hypotheses vary somewhat from Driver's, however.

At present, Harold Driver and I are completing a massive study of 430 variables (2,000 attributes) and 172 societies in western North America. Our ecological, evolutionary, functional, and historical inquiry is proving to be the largest and most detailed postulational and "discovery" (interpretations after the fact) study ever conducted—continuous area or worldwide.

Worldwide Cross-Cultural Studies

The history of worldwide cross-cultural studies has been laid out in several places by several authors.[*] I will not duplicate these other works here, but will focus on the assumptions and goals of worldwide cross-cultural studies. In brief, cross-cultural research received its major push in the modern era from George Peter Murdock at Yale

University and from his student, John Whiting, who later established himself at Harvard University. These two men sought to validate generalizations for all of the world's societies in time and space from samples thought to be representative of the whole.

Murdock's classic work, *Social Structure* (1949), and Whiting's best known piece (with Irvin Child), *Child Training and Personality* (1953), explicated the methodology and stated the assumptions that have been basic to this mode of inquiry for twenty years. On the whole, cross-cultural researchers have correlated variables with variables (e.g. postnuptial residence with cousin terminologies), following Tylor's lead. And, surprisingly, except for the work with worldwide samples done by me (Jorgensen 1966), by Driver and Schuessler (1967), and by Chaney and Ruiz-Revilla (1969), the practitioners of this art have seldom used cluster analysis, factor analysis, or even partial correlation analysis to analyze more than a pair of variables at a time. Correlations and tests of significance of those correlations are usually treated one at a time, yet they are also treated as if strings of these correlations are built into causal sequences.

It is the assumption of causal sequences, of course, that makes worldwide studies interesting, but this same assumption, given the nature of the data and the methodology employed, also makes worldwide studies most suspect.

Hypotheses, or sets of statements about relations among variables, are postulated by cross-cultural researchers before inquiry is begun. Because many of these hypotheses have had long histories, especially Freudian assertions about personality and evolutionary and functional assertions about social organization, the researchers have had only to operationalize variables through clear definitions into mutually exclusive and mutually inclusive sets, draw samples, rate the coded variables for the sample societies, and test for the relationships among the variables through descriptive and inferential statistics. Needless to say, large problems have surfaced at each step in the inquiry, and practitioners have worked hard and intelligently to solve these problems.

A brief assessment of Murdock's monumental work, *Social Structure* (1949), with focus on subsequent attempts to resolve the tricky issues that

[*]For general reviews of this topic see Harold E. Driver, 1973, "Cross-Cultural Studies" (cited in Driver's bibliography section of this volume) and Raoul Naroll (1970b) "What Have We Learned from Cross-cultural Surveys?"

emerged upon analysis of that work will serve our purposes here. Murdock was aware of Galton's problem and of the need to test propositions on worldwide samples in order to explain the evolution and functions of social structure. Drawing from the hypotheses of Morgan, Tylor, his own work in kinship, and the contributions of others, Murdock postulated that the dominant sexual division of labor caused an adjustment in postnuptial residence to complement it, and that postnuptial residence forms caused forms of descent to adjust and complement residence. Next, he postulated that the semantics of kinship terminologies—cousin and avuncular—adjusted to the descent form. This postulate was functional, as well as diachronic. That is to say, Murdock postdicted that sets of economic and social structural variables became integrated and harmonious, but he also postdicted that integration of sets of variables took time and that some changes precede other changes and, in fact, stimulate those changes.

For instance, Murdock postulated that matridominant food production caused matrilocal residence, caused matrilineal descent, caused bifurcate merging avuncular terms, caused Crow-type cousin terms. So long as other changes to the division of labor did not interrupt the sequence (all things being equal), matridominant division of labor would trigger adjustments in the rest of the chain so that they became functionally integrated (given an indefinite amount of time).

The functional integration hypothesis was linked to an evolutionary hypothesis, better understood as a cyclical development hypothesis, that postulated cycles of change from patricentered forms of social structure to bilateral forms to matricentered forms, or from any other point in the cycle to other forms. That is to say, social structures not only became functionally integrated but also transformed from one integrated set to another dependent upon changes to the division of labor.

In order to test his hypotheses, Murdock collected a sample of 250 societies from around the world, representing several points in time. Murdock was aware that historical relatedness among societies could influence correlations. Because he had no inventories of all the world's societies, past and present, and because he assumed that the entire range of cultural complexity was available in the ethnographic literature, he used his own judgment about which societies were most representative of the world's societies, and which were the least related. Thus, Murdock's sample was judgmental and based on his own knowledge of the range of the world's societies. The sample, then, was biased toward all of those things in the world's ethnographic literature that Murdock knew about, and toward all of those things that Murdock did not think about. Criticism of the size and scope of his 1949 sample prompted Murdock to create larger samples, first of 565 (1957) and later of over 1,000 societies (Murdock 1967; Murdock et al. 1962-), and to develop a useful, yet judgmental, way to draw samples from the largest sample (Murdock and White 1969). Scores of researchers have sampled Murdock's samples, sometimes judgmentally and sometimes following randomizing procedures. Recently Raoul Naroll, in some methodological essays (1967, 1970a), has attempted to solve the sampling problem by deriving a probability sample from over two hundred societies in the sixty culture-geographic clusters originally defined by Murdock. The result is a part-probability and part-judgmental sample of societies, presumably unrelated for the most part.

The various samples have been drawn to exercise controls for historical relatedness, or to give each unit an equiprobable chance to be included in the study, or both. As I pointed out a few years ago (Jorgensen 1966), drawing samples from a judgmental sample that "controls" for time and space by disregarding both is still a judgmental sample of societies with unknown interdependencies.

Much of the work to achieve samples of societies very little influenced by interdependencies among those societies is a result of Galton's challenge to Tylor, on the one hand, and common sense, on the other. If researchers are attempting to demonstrate causal regularities in cultural evolution, or functions, it behooves these researchers to separate parallel developments from shared history. Furthermore, the inferential statistics employed by cross-cultural researchers since 1888 have *assumed* (1) independence of sample units and (2) independence of sampling traits. Karl Pearson's venerable test of significance for goodness-of-fit, chi-square (X^2), for instance, has been used by the vast majority of cross-cultural researchers because it is appropriate for nominal data in NxN tables, provided the data meet the assumptions of the statistic. Murdock himself used X^2 along with Yules Q, a test for inclusion or one-way strength of association, in *Social Structure* (1949).

Chi-square assumes that the sampling traits are independent of one another and infinitely samplable. Thus, if the X^2 value for matrilocality and matrilineality yields a probability value of less than one in one thousand, one can appeal to real theory—the axioms of probability theory—to interpret the results. That is to say, one does not have to appeal to prejudice, or to authority, or to one or two positive examples, or to impression, or to polemic to demonstrate the merit of the hypothesis and its validation. One can appeal to a theory, pure theory, that logically integrates wholly axiomatic principles and that asserts that "these relationships are this way because this is the way the world is." Thus, if the data are independent, as are the sample units, the high sum of X^2 tells you that the relationship very seldom occurs by chance.

One problem here is that by drawing random samples from some list one does not ipso facto create independence of sampling traits. Indeed, it is clear that sample units are not fully independent, nor are they fully dependent. Rather, and using a vast patch of continuously distributed societies in southern and western North America for an example, some cultural phenomena, such as bows and arrows, maize, beans, and squash, spread to the vast majority of these societies. So these societies, or units, are related through sharing homologous traits. On the other hand, perhaps some of these same societies have masked dancing ceremonies, and some do not; furthermore, some practice matrilineal descent and some of these also have Crow-type terminologies; yet all of the societies that possess matrilineal organization do not practice masked dancing, and so forth. The ways in which the societies in this huge patch of southern and western North America are interrelated are undoubtedly very complex, and if several tribes from this area, which measures over 2,000 miles east to west and 500 miles north to south, are placed on a judgmental list from which a probability sample is to be drawn, the very information that might help ferret out some of the interdependencies is obscured. To compound the problem, when the sampling traits are correlated and tested, the assumptions of X^2—or any other statistic, such as the "nonparametric" Fisher's Exact and Kolmogorov-Smirnov tests, that requires a probability sample of independent sampling units—are violated, and the probability values cannot be interpreted in accordance with the sampling theory on which the values are based.

Attempts to solve the problems of statistical inference have not been successful. Conditional probabilities based on probability rates for known interdependencies for N-samples are required in order to solve this problem; yet no one, including myself, has even tried to create a conditionally-based inductive theory applicable for worldwide and continuous area studies. Another tack that has been taken is to treat probability values as "plausibility estimates" (Jorgensen 1966). Better still, the strong and significant correlations should be treated as plausible relations to be integrated in some

concluding hypotheses and investigated further. Common sense and knowledge of the theories of induction do not allow us to conclude otherwise; nevertheless, this cautious position is usually disregarded, and probability values are interpreted as if the requirements of the statistical theory are satisfied.

The last statement leads us to the relationships among hypotheses, the tests of these hypotheses, and the meanings of the results. In *Social Structure* (1949), Murdock interpreted the many tests of relationships as if (1) they were validating hypotheses that integrated many relationships and (2) these relationships were temporal and causal in connection. Thus, significant positive association between patrilocal residence and patrilineal descent was verbally linked to positive and significant association between patrilineal descent and bifurcate merging avuncular terms. Moreover, Murdock showed that the relations between residence and avuncular terms were not so positive nor so significant as between residence and descent or descent and avuncular terms. So his verbalization posited a stochastic process about the direction of change through time and accounted for variance by positing lag in the sequence.

Murdock did not use multivariate analysis, even simple cluster analysis, to test for the sequences he posited; but his analysis clearly anticipated more complex statistical tests. In recent years, Driver's matrix seriation analysis (Driver 1956; Driver and Massey 1957), Blalock's elaboration of partial correlation analysis (1960), Driver's uses of factor analysis (in several studies beginning in 1956, including pp. 176-94), and my own uses of least-space analysis —initially in Q-mode (Jorgensen 1969), but now in R-mode, multidimensional scales, and conjoint measures—have provided ways to test for interrelations among many variables and to display the relations in a single matrix or N-dimensional space. These methods, when used in large computers, allow for the testing of all the relations that obtain in the sample, and not only those that the researcher thinks are significant beforehand.

Yet even when many correlations are analyzed in a cluster analysis, or path analysis, or factor analysis, the basic problem remains about how to interpret the results. Murdock and most other practitioners built chains of causal sequences by correlating two variables at a time. They have never worked with many variables (seldom more than ten), and they have not tested for the actual interrelations among them, so the sequences are non sequiturs. But even when clustering methods are used to test, say, Murdock's sequences, as I did when demonstrating that the lag hypothesis for the integration of residence, descent, and cousin and avuncular terms held for a random sample of a judgmental synchronic sample, the tests do not *validate* diachronic hypotheses. Indeed, no matter what particular multivariate statistics are employed, multivariate analysis of autocorrelations—timeless state correlations—yield best fits among timeless variables. They allow the researcher to describe "what is," not the developmental sequence of "how things came to be," and certainly not the developmental sequence of "what had to be" in the inevitable sense.

Ultimately synchronic samples, even if all units are independent, can only yield descriptive information about how variables are related, the strength of those relationships, and the probability of their co-occurrences. Evolutionary, or causal, analysis is diachronic; as is functional, or causal-effect analysis. Causal-effects are effect relations that become self-persisting. To validate either kind of proposition, diachronic data are required, and these data must represent prior conditions or states, transitional conditions or states, and result conditions or states. So the comparisons must be temporal. No large, inductive, comparative ethnological study—worldwide or continuous area in scope—has been diachronic.

Nevertheless, it is not a coincidence that Driver (1956), Aberle (1961), and Jorgensen (1966), to mention a few researchers, confirmed most of Murdock's (1949) generalizations using areal samples (Driver), the 565-unit "World Ethnographic Sample" (Aberle), and a random sample drawn from the "World Ethnographic Sample" (Jorgensen). It suggests to me that the generalizations validated by autocorrelations probably hold for dynamic correlations as well, and that the lag hypothesis is a powerful concluding hypothesis that should be tested through comparative, inductive, historical research on a sample of the world's societies, as well as on continuous area samples.

A final issue of importance in cross-cultural analysis is the problem of areal differences. This issue is, of course, related to Galton's problem, sampling theory, statistical theory, and hypothesis formulation. In 1940, Murdock (p. 369) argued that a valid cross-cultural hypothesis should hold true in any area of the world. My own (Jorgensen 1966) worldwide study of in-law avoidances shows that geographic propinquity is the strongest postdictor of in-law avoidances. Indeed, tribes in some geographic areas where avoidances were nearly absent possessed the variables hypothesized to "cause" in-law avoidances, but did not practice avoidances; in other geographic areas where practice of avoidances were common, societies with few or none of the hypoth-

esized causal variables practiced avoidances nevertheless. The general results suggested that the hypotheses to account for in-law avoidances hold in part, yet will have to be modified. Most important, the cross-cultural researcher will have to come to grips with areal correlation. Coming to grips with areal correlation will require larger, continuously distributed samples, and not smaller ones, and control of many more environmental and historical variables than have ever been used.

In the preceding study by Driver and Schuessler, we see how many significant differences obtain among the six major regions of Murdock's 1957 sample. In a loose way, these differences are accounted for as being due to different ecological and historical circumstances in the various areas. Furthermore, some similarities are accounted for by positing parallel or convergent evolution, even among societies in adjacent areas. What remains to be done is to create measurable variables in order to test historical relatedness and the effects of similar and different environments. Driver and Schuessler have provided some concluding hypotheses toward that end. Jorgensen and Driver are engaged in a massive study in which we will contribute to operationalizing and testing many hypotheses about the relations among history, environment, and evolution.

References

Aberle, David F.
    1961 "Matrilineal descent in cross-cultural perspective," in David M. Schneider and Kathleen Gough, eds., *Matrilineal Descent*, Berkeley, University of California Press: 655-727.

Blalock, Hubert M., Jr:
    1960 "Correlational analysis and causal inferences," *American Anthropologist* 62: 624-32.

Boas, Franz
    1894 *Indianische Sagen von der Nord-Pacifischen Küste Amerikas*, Berlin, Asher.

Chaney, Richard Paul, and Rogelio Ruiz-Revilla
    1969 "Sampling methods and interpretations of correlation: a comparative analysis of seven cross-cultural samples," *American Anthropologist* 71: 597-633.

Driver, Harold E.
  1956 "An integration of functional, evolutionary, and historical theory by means of correlations," *Indiana University Publications in Anthropology and Linguistics 12*: 1-36.
  1965 "Survey of numerical classification in anthropology," in Dell Hymes, ed., *The Use of Computers in Anthropology*, The Hague, Mouton: 301-44.
  1970 "Statistical studies of continuous geographical distributions," in Raoul Naroll and Ronald Cohen, eds., *A Handbook of Method in Cultural Anthropology*, Garden City, Natural History Press: 620-39.

Driver, Harold E., and William C. Massey
  1957 "Comparative studies of North American Indians," *Transactions of the American Philosophical Society n.s. 47*: 165-460.

Driver, Harold E., and Karl F. Schuessler
  1967 "Correlational analysis of Murdock's 1957 ethnographic sample," *American Anthropologist 69*: 332-52.

Eggan, Fred
  1954 "Social anthropology and the method of controlled comparison," *American Anthropologist 56*: 743-63.

Jorgensen, Joseph G.
  1966 "Geographical clusterings and functional explanations of in-law avoidances: an analysis of comparative method," *Current Anthropology 7*: 161-69.
  1969 "Salish language and culture: a statistical analysis of internal relationships, history, and evolution," *Indiana University Language Science Monographs 3*.

Klimek, Stanislaw
  1935 "Culture element distributions: I: the structure of California Indian culture," *University of California Publications in American Archaeology and Ethnology 37*: 1-70.

Lowie, Robert H.
  1920 *Primitive society*, New York, Liveright.

Milke, Wilhelm
  1955 *Theorie der Kulturellen Ähnlichkeit*, Geseke, Westfalen.

Morgan, Lewis Henry
  1877 *Ancient society*, New York, Henry Holt.

Murdock, George Peter
  1937 "Correlations of matrilineal and patrilineal institutions," in George Peter Murdock, ed., *Studies in the Science of Society*, New Haven, Yale University Press: 445-70.
  1940 "The Cross-Cultural Survey," *American Sociological Review 5*: 361-70.
  1949 *Social Structure*, New York, MacMillan.
  1957 "World ethnographic sample," *American Anthropologist 59*: 66-87.
  1967 *Ethnographic atlas: a summary*, Pittsburgh, University of Pittsburgh Press.

Murdock, George Peter, and Douglas R. White
  1969 "Standard cross-cultural sample," *Ethnology 8*: 329-69.

Murdock, George Peter, et al.
  1962 "Ethnographic atlas," *Ethnology 1* to date.

Naroll, Raoul
  1967 "The proposed HRAF Probability Sample," *Behavior Science Notes 2*: 70-80.
  1970a "Cross-cultural sampling," in Raoul Naroll and Ronald Cohen, eds., *A Handbook of Method in Cultural Anthropology*, Garden City, Natural History Press: 889-926.
  1970b "What have we learned from cross-cultural surveys?" *American Anthropologist 72*: 1227-88.

Simmons, Leo W.
  1937 "Statistical correlations in the science of society," in George Peter Murdock, ed., *Studies in the Science of Society*, New Haven, Yale University Press: 495-571.

Tylor, Edward B.
  1889 "On a method of investigating the development of institutions: applied to laws of marriage and descent," Royal Anthropological Institute of Great Britain and Ireland, *Journal 18*: 245-72.

Whiting, John W.M., and Irvin L. Child
  1953 *Child training and personality: a cross-cultural study*, New Haven, Yale University Press.

Part Five

Culture Areas and Language and Culture

Introduction

Joseph G. Jorgensen

In this section we see three of Harold Driver's most recent contributions to culture analysis and language-culture relations. In several places during his career, Harold Driver voiced criticisms of culture area schemes, because (1) most have been intuitively (impressionistically) derived, and (2) "genetic" inferences about relations among members of the same culture areas were unwarranted. On the other hand, Harold Driver always argued that culture area schemes, even if intuitively derived, had pedagogical value.

The two papers on North American culture areas printed here attempt to go beyond intuition and pedagogy as Driver and his students inductively analyze (1) the North American tribes and variable ratings from George P. Murdock's 1957 "Ethnographic Atlas," and (2) the North American tribes and variable ratings from Harold E. Driver and William C. Massey's *Comparative Studies of North American Indians* (1957). Murdock's sample stressed social organization variables, and, when analyzed, yielded culture area schemes that had little relation to the major intuitive schemes proposed by Wissler, Kroeber, Murdock, Driver, and others. Indeed, the clusters of cultures better resembled "culture types" rather than "culture areas." Upon investigation of the results obtained from the "Ethnographic Atlas" sample, Driver concluded that the culture clusters did not provide a useful set of strata for organizing North American tribes. One of his intentions for doing the study in the first place was to classify North America into several areal strata so that further comparative studies could draw objective, continentwide, stratified samples. He reasoned that a cluster analysis that yielded strata for a sampling universe had more than pedagogical value.

The second paper corrects for the overemphasis on so-called "functional" variables in the "Ethnographic Atlas." In this study, Driver runs a Q-mode analysis on his own sample of North American cultures and derives areas which fit rather well with the major intuitive culture area schemes for North America. Driver's comments about culture area classifications and the variables on which they are based are useful for modern sampling techniques and problems.

Driver's paper on language and culture relations among several North American Indian language families is the largest study of its kind. He shows that language-culture relations can be measured by operationalizing features of both, and that language-culture relations vary for the several language families in the study. Nevertheless, Driver also shows that language and culture are not independent of one another for the variables analyzed.

Richard Chaney, in discussing culture area and language-culture relations, focuses on problems of conceptualizing comparative social inquiry so that it is meaningful.

2. Statistical Classification of North American Indian Ethnic Units[1]

Harold E. Driver
James A. Kenny
Herschel C. Hudson
Ora May Engle

The culture area concept has been around since Mason (1896) postulated eighteen cultural and environmental areas in the Americas. This was followed by Holmes' (1903) scheme of nineteen geo-ethnic areas for North America; and a year later by Farrand's (1904) sevenfold classification of North America and Kroeber's (1904) fourfold grouping of California Indian cultures (ethnic units). Although Wissler first mentioned culture areas in 1906, his material culture areas of 1914 and his general culture areas in the first edition of *The American Indian* in 1917 attracted more attention than any of the earlier schemes. Kroeber's (1939) *Cultural and Natural Areas of Native North America* discussed and interpreted a three-level classification with seven major areas and subdivisions of these into about 80 smaller units. These and other systems have been cited and reviewed in the last decade by Ehrich and Henderson (1968) and Driver (1962). All continentwide culture area classifications to date have been made with no more explicit method than intuition.

From 1926 to 1941 at the University of California at Berkeley a number of regional classifications of ethnic units were made with statistical techniques comparing each ethnic unit with every other in terms of the proportion of culture traits shared. These studies have been reviewed recently by Driver (1970b). The largest culture classification in this group was that of Klimek (1935), who grouped 60 California Indian ethnic units into culture areas on the basis of 400 culture traits drawn from a fairly wide spectrum of culture inventory.

The present paper is the first to determine culture groups for an entire continent with an explicit statistical technique. The data used are the North American part of Murdock's (1967) *Ethnographic Atlas*. Although Murdock did not have this in mind when he coded the data, the authors thought that for their purpose his atlas was the best sample so far coded.

A culture area classification can be put to many uses. One use is to treat the groups of ethnic units as "strata" from which to choose stratified probability samples for conventional cross-cultural correlations where culture traits are correlated with culture traits. Using Murdock's intuitively generated culture areas in his 1967 Atlas as the "strata," Naroll drew a stratified probability sample of 60 societies for the Human Relations Area Files. This was done first by rating all the societies on a quality scale of A for best and B for next best, and then drawing a random sample from the A group, or from the B group also, if not enough A ratings occurred. This has come to be called the HRAF Quality Control Sample (Naroll 1970: 910). Driver (1970a) criticized this and other such samples because neither the number of culture areas nor the number and allocation of the societies (ethnic units) within each was objectively determined. He suggested that a numerical classification based on Murdock's (1967) coded data would produce a more objective set of culture areas from which a more objective and meaningful stratified sample could be drawn.

Methodology

As measures of correlation in this study, we computed two coefficients, the well known phi coefficient and the less known G coefficient of Driver, first used by Driver and Kroeber (1932: 219). In the symbols for the 2x2 table of Karl Pearson, the G coefficient does not take into account the common absences in the d cell, while phi uses frequencies in all four cells. The relation of G to phi has recently been shown by Driver (1970b: 624). Jorgensen (1969) used both G and phi and obtained identical groupings from each. With our larger number of tribes we obtained almost identical groupings; our ordered matrix of 37,128 phi's produced Pearson's curvilinear eta coefficient of .975 and a linear r coefficient of .974 with our ordered matrix of the corresponding G's. This difference is so slight that we have used only the phi values because phi is better known and can also be factor analyzed.

The close relation of G to phi for Murdock's data was anticipated from Driver's (1939: 301) diagram 3, which shows the relation of these and other coefficients when the skewness of the 2x2 table is 20 per cent present to 80 per cent absent for both variables. The cultural and social inventories of Murdock's North American sample approximate this ratio of presence to absence. Driver's diagrams showed the effect of skewness (asymmetry) in the marginal totals of the 2x2 table on eight different coefficients: four conventional ones, phi, Karl Pearson's tetrachoric r and Q_6, and Yule's Q; and four unconventional measures, defined in the above reference and labeled A, G, T, and W. When the proportion of marginal totals in both variables was .50 to .50, all measures gave closely parallel results. When skewness was varied in a number of ways (both variables positively skewed, both negatively skewed, and one positively and the other negatively skewed) the various combinations of pairs of measures gave both parallel and very disparate results.

In addition to the North American data given in Murdock (1967), we have obtained data on additional ethnic units from Murdock on punched cards and corrected all of them from all the issues of *Ethnology* through January, 1971. This constitutes the sample of our study.

There were 85 variables coded by Murdock (1967). Of these, 57 were primary items (column headings with capital letters) and 28 were secondary or alternate modes (coded in small letters). Not all of these variables were used in our study. There were several reasons for omission. If over 90 per cent of the tribes were coded "insufficient information" for the variable, it was eliminated. All of the secondary variables were omitted for this reason, as was one of the primary variables ("male genital mutilations") which was universally absent in native North America. A second reason for omission was repetition. If the data were repeated in another summary category, then one of the items was eliminated to avoid duplication. For example, Murdock summarizes hunting, gathering, fishing, etc. in a single column called "subsistence economy." This column (EA I col. 54) is not listed in the *Ethnographic Atlas* but occurs on the computer cards. As a result, the five separate subsistence items in columns 7-11 were omitted from consideration in our study. The codification of "linguistic affiliation" was not considered, because it is best kept separate from nonverbal culture.

Where the data formed an ordinal scale under the variable, it was frequently compressed into from two to four divisions or "attributes." The decision to combine and split at particular points was based on both logical and distributional criteria. Driver had the final say on the point of divisions because of his greater familiarity with the data. Thus the scales under "Type and Intensity of Agriculture" (col. 28), "High Gods" (col. 34), "Post-partum Sex Taboos (col. 36), and "Segregation of Adolescent Boys" (col. 38) were dichotomized. The scales under "Settlement Pattern" (col. 30) and "Mean Size of Local Communities" (col 31) were compressed to form three categories. And the following scales on the division of labor between the sexes were compressed into four categories: "Metalworking" (col. 42), "Weaving" (col. 44), "Leather Working" (col. 46), "Pottery" (col. 48), "Boat Building" (col. 50), "House Construction" (col. 52), "Gathering (col. 54), "Hunting" (col. 56), "Fishing" (col. 58), "Animal Husbandry" (col. 60), and "Agriculture" (col. 62). As a result, of the original 85 variables, we decided to use only 49. In sum, we used all the major columns in the *Ethnographic Atlas* except columns 7-11 (subsistence items) and column 37 (male genital mutilations). Their column numbers are: 12, 14, 14.1, 16, 19, 20, 22, 24, 25, 27, 28, 28.1, 30, 31, 32, 32.1, 34, 35, 36, 38, 39, 39.1, 42, 44, 46, 48, 50, 52, 54, 56, 58, 60, 62, 67, 69, 71, 73, 74, 74.1, 76, 76.1, 78, 80, 81, 82, 83, 84. These, plus the two "new summary code" items, complete the 49 variables used in this study.

Murdock's data are mostly in the form of nominal and ordinal scales. In order to engineer a fit with Jorgensen's programs, described briefly below, we had to convert these scales into a series of dichotomies. Thus, each "variable" (e.g. "Mode of Marriage.") had a number of traits or "attributes" (e.g., "bride-price," "bride-service," "exchange," "dowry"). These "attributes" were each treated separately and scored zero (0) for attribute absent, one (1) for attribute present, and two (2) for insufficient information. In other words, instead of "Mode of Marriage," we used "bride-price" (for example) as the attribute to be correlated on a present-absent basis. Proceeding in the manner described above, the 49 variables were expanded into 279 "attributes" or traits. Simply, then, our task was to compare 273 North American ethnic units in terms of the proportion of 279 cultural traits shared.

Jorgensen's (1969) computer programs employ both an ordered (sorted) correlation matrix and tree diagrams derived from it. Ordered correlation matrices have been common since the publications of the California comparative school from 1926 to 1941 and will not be described here. Tree diagrams are newer in anthropology and deserve a little comment. They were used at least a century ago to illustrate intuitively determined phylogenetic relationship between biological taxa, including man. Since about 1950, tree diagrams showing the relations of biological taxa have been generated with explicit statistical techniques and computers (Sokal and Sneath 1963). Because most of the observations biologists make on the small organisms most often classified in this manner are phenotypic, the tree diagram showing their relationships is best labeled phenetic, rathern than phylogenetic.

In comparisons of languages and cultures, resemblances may be grouped into four kinds: (1) universals; (2) parallels or convergences that are historically independent; (3) diffusions that spread from one language or society to another and are, therefore, historically dependent; and (4) common heritages from a protolanguage or protoculture that have been retained, often over long periods of time. In biological taxonomy the fourth group is much the most common because convergences are very rare and most operational taxonomic units cannot cross-breed to produce gene flow, analogous to cultural diffusion. With cultural data all four kinds of resemblances may occur. The first may easily be eliminated by deleting all universals from the sample on the grounds that they are constants, not variables. The second, third, and fourth kinds of similarities may occur in any large corpus of coded cultural data and can only be separated with detailed analysis of archeological, ethnohistorical, linguistic, and human biological data to support the mixed package of more or less synchronic cultural data. This will not be attempted in this paper.

If the reader looks at Table 1 and Figure 2, he will see 35 groups of societies with two or more members each when the average correlations of each society with the other members of its set is phi = .68 or higher. There are 35 vertical lines in Figure 2 at this point on the phi scale, corresponding to the 35 taxa. When the average internal correlation within the groups is reduced to .67, groups 19 and 20 become combined, thus reducing the number of groups to 34. When the correlation level is reduced to .66, groups 16 and 17 are combined, and also groups 25 and 26, thus reducing the total number of groups to 32. If this process is continued, the original 34 groups are reduced to a single group at the level of phi = .28.

We originally ran Jorgensen's (1969) tree diagram computer program for all 273 ethnic units. The number of groups ranged from 272 (because there was one perfect correlation between one pair of tribes) to 271, 270, 269, etc., down to one. In this paper we have used 55 groups to match the Voegelins' (1966) 55 language families, 35 groups to match Murdock's (1967) 35 culture provinces, ten groups to match the ten culture areas of Murdock (1967) and others, nine groups to match the Voegelins' (1966) nine language phyla, and seven groups to match Kroeber's (1939) seven major culture areas and seven levels of cultural intensity. The magic of the tree diagram program is that it produces any number of groups desired to match the number in any previous scheme of classification.

Our 35 Principal Statistical Groups

We have arbitrarily chosen to begin our presentation with our 35 principal statistical groups because this number matches the number of Murdock's (1968) sampling provinces in North America. These groups are given in Table 1, Figures 1 and 2, and Map 1. Because all but one of Murdock's 35 North American sampling provinces contain more than one ethnic unit, we decided to eliminate our statistical "groups" with only a single member each. To do this we looked for the place in our tree diagram printout where 35 groups would remain after the singletons were eliminated. This was at a bridge of a phi of .68, where the total number of "groups" was 75, the singletons 40, and the groups with two or more members 35. These groups have been assigned names which appear in Table 1, Figure 2, and Map 1.

In Figure 1 we have arbitrarily chosen a solid black square to represent phi's from .80 to 1.00, and a slanting line to represent phi's from .68 to .79. The cut-off point of .68 matches the bridge where our 35 principal statistical groups (plus 40 singletons) occurred. This type of figure was first used in cultural anthro-

pology by Czekanowski (1911), but his pupil, Klimek (1935), used it much more extensively and the numerical taxonomists in biology also employ it (Sokal and Sneath 1963).

Figure 2 shows the same groups in a tree diagram. This can be divided into as many levels as one wishes to use for a hierarchy of classes within classes. The ten groups occurring at phi = .52 do not exactly match the ten principal groups of Table 3 and Map 2 because the 40 singletons eliminated from the 35 principal groups get combined and recombined with each other into multiple-member groups that appear in the smaller numbers of groups. The seven groups at phi = .48 in the tree diagram are a closer fit, but again not exact. Figure 2 may be labeled a phenetic scheme. Although it may contain some resemblances resulting from culture heritages from common proto-cultures, and to this extent be phylogenetic, it also contains far more resemblances brought about by diffusion (gene flow in biology) than do the tree diagrams of biologists, and also far more similarities caused by independent origin (parallels and convergences) than do similar biological diagrams. All cultures that come in contact can and do exchange some culture while, in contrast, most of the operational taxonomic units compared by biologists cannot interbreed. The occurrence of most of Murdock's culture categories in all major areas of the world among totally unrelated linguistic phyla and very remotely related human biological types is overwhelming evidence of the independent origin of many resemblances. This has been a dominant assumption of R-type cross-cultural correlation studies for the last 35 years. The authors believe that they know enough to sort out these three distinct kinds of resemblances, but forego doing so at monograph length because they all have other commitments that have temporal priority.

Map 1 gives the geographical locations of the same 35 groups, with the largest fourteen arbitrarily represented by patterns and the remaining 21 only by numbers. It is apparent that almost all of these larger groups form continuous or near-continuous geographical distributions. Some exceptions can be spotted by noting the hyphenated names of the patterns. It seems obvious that the similarities shared by the groups with continuous or near-continuous distributions are determined in part by geographical and historical factors. On the other hand, such farflung groups as 20, 17, and 2 do not lend themselves to this explanation. For them independent parallel development of some of their shared cultural and social inventory plays a larger role. Other groups whose members are a thousand miles or more apart are 22, 19, and 15. It is thus apparent that the broad spectrum of many of Murdock's trait categories, chosen to demonstrate functional and dysfunctional relationships and position on an evolutionary scale of a half dozen or fewer steps, leave plenty of room for historically independent parallel or convergent developments to occur. The early intuitive culture-area schemes of Ratzel, Wissler, Kroeber, and Graebner were based principally on museum specimens and other aspects of material culture and technology related to them. Such traits were heavily determined by geographical environment and historical contacts. This is much less true of Murdock's sample.

Table 2 gives the cross-classification of Murdock's 34 sampling provinces and our 35 principal statistical groups. The frequencies represent numbers of ethnic units. If the correlation of the two classifications were perfect, there would be only one frequency entry in each row and column. This is far from the case. The elimination of our 40 singletons reduces five of Murdock's provinces to singletons, and eliminates his one singleton entirely, thus reducing his provinces to 34. We think our procedure is a more meaningful comparison than one in which all singletons were retained. As it is, our group 20 contains 64 ethnic units. If we had chosen 35 groups with singletons included, the number of ethnic units in the largest of our groups would have been 107, and the second and third largest groups would also have been substantially larger. This would have produced a poorer fit to Murdock's provinces.

In Table 2 only two groups in both classifications match exactly: Murdock's Northern Northwest Coast matches our group number 30 exactly; and his Pueblo-Navaho fits perfectly with our number one. If we opposed the column and row of each frequency with the remaining columns and rows to produce a series of 2x2 tables, some of these would produce significant relationships. For instance, twelve out of fifteen ethnic units in Murdock's Southern California province fall in our group 14, and twelve out of fourteen ethnic units in our group 14 fall in Murdock's Southern California province. With only five exceptions in the total of 230 ethnic units, the phi-square value is .667, the chi-square 153, and the probability of it occurring by an accident of sampling so low that it would not appear in conventional tables and probably would be less than one in a billion. Other high relationships may be spotted by inspection. We have decided not to ramify each cross-classification table into the maximum number of dichotomies but have done so for one table below in the section on comparisons with linguistic groups.

The overall relationship of the two groupings in Table 2 is not high. We can measure the strength of the overall relationship by means of Cramèr's coefficient (1946: 441-445):

$$f^2 = \frac{\chi^2}{N(Q-1)}$$

where χ^2 is chi-square, N the total number of cases, and Q the number of rows or columns, whichever is fewer, in this case 34. The value of Cramèr's coefficient for Table 2 is 0.488 on a scale of 0.000 to 1.000 but, because the expected frequencies are much too low, the chi-square sampling distribution cannot be used to obtain the probability of this value arising by an accident of sampling and the computation of Fisher's exact probability for such a large table is impractical. The significance of this and other relationships will be discussed below.

Comparisons of Smaller Numbers of Statistical Groups with Culture Areas

Because no one has ever presented a culture area with only a single member, we have eliminated singletons in our statistical groups for these comparisons. At a bridge of phi = .48 our program gives fifteen groups, five of which are singletons, leaving ten groups with two or more members (Table 3, Table 4, Map 2).

An inspection of Map 2 reveals an ecological correlation which has been incorporated in the names of the groups. Almost all members of group 1 subsisted primarily on the products of hunting and gathering, and they form a nearly continuous geographical distribution. Most members of group 2 were primarily fishers and lived on or near the Northwest Coast, with a few outliers in the Arctic and eastern Sub-Arctic. Groups 3-10 were all farmers. Six of these groups of farmers fall in continuous or nearly continuous geographical areas but the other two (5 and 10) are widely split.

A cross-classification of Murdock's (1967: 102-118) culture areas, represented by letters a to j in his atlas, with our ten groups is given in Table 4. Again the frequencies represent numbers of ethnic units. There are no perfect correlations between any of his intuitive groups, and our statistical groups. However, there are a number of high correlations, for instance, between his group g and our group 6, Eastern Farmers. Here the phi-square is .812, the chi-square is 220, and the probability of these values happening by an accident of sampling is probably less than one in a billion. Although other relationships of pairs of groups are not as high as the above, many would pass a significance test at a probability of .01 or even .001. A single overall conclusion about the relation of the two groupings is given by a chi-square of 899 and a

Cramèr's coefficient of .373, but the expected frequencies are still too low to make an accurate probabilistic statement about level of significance.

We have also computed Cramèr's coefficient for our ten principal statistical groups and a tenfold reduction of Driver's (1969: Map 2) culture areas. Driver's seventeen areas were reduced to ten by combining the two Arctic areas, the three Sub-Arctic areas, the Plateau and Great Basin, and eliminating Baja California, Northeast Mexico, and the Circum-Caribbean areas. This relationship yielded a chi-square of 830 and a Cramèr's coefficient of .349.

A similar comparison with a reduction of Spencer's and Jennings' (1965: inside front cover, 120, 154, 170, 215, 230, 274, 289, 339, 385, 397, 406, 437) twelve areas to ten was made by combining their two Sub-Arctic areas and their two Ultra-Mississippi areas. This yielded a chi-square of 645 and a Cramèr's coefficient of .267.

We also ran off cross-classification tables for all combinations of the intuitive culture area schemes of Driver, Murdock, Spencer and Jennings, and Kroeber (1939: Map 6). The Cramèr coefficients for these relationships are given in the larger triangle in Table 10. These values are substantially higher than those for the relations of our ten principal statistical groups with the three tenfold, intuitive culture area schemes given in the rectangle in Table 7. Whether this is caused by the later culture area intuitors following the earlier, or by all of them using a genuinely different cultural and social inventory than that of Murdock's (1967) Ethnographic Atlas sample is not obvious. However, we favor the latter interpretation because Murdock's intuitive scheme matches the other intuitive schemes closer than it does the statistical grouping derived from his 1967 (and later) sample. This suggests that his 1967 sample, or our selection from it, is a biased sample giving social structure, in the broad meaning of that phrase, more attention than other major aspects of culture.

Sampling Social and Cultural Inventory

Although we have had a number of recent discussions of the ethnic unit and how to draw samples of ethnic units (Naroll 1964; Naroll and Cohen 1970; Helm 1968; Murdock and White 1969), there has been no comparable discussion of how to define and sample cultural and social inventory for a Q-type (ethnic unit by ethnic unit) comparison. We suggest that the best sampling design so far for this kind of comparison is the *Outline of Cultural Materials* (Murdock *et al.* 1961). This is the subject index of the Human Relations Area Files. A relatively good sample of the entire range of this inventory could be obtained by drawing an equal number of cultural and social variables, or of the more detailed traits (attributes) within such variables, from each of the two-digit categories, except for numbers 10, 11, 12, 13, 14, 18, and 19, which do not contain conventional culture content.

A better sample would result from the weighting of each two-digit category according to the number of lines of print present in it in the entire world sample. If more than twenty years' experience with the subject indexing of ethnographies in many languages and all major areas of the world shows that one two-digit category contains ten times as many lines as another, it should get ten times as much weight in the sample. Just as an ethnic unit sample must be drawn pragmatically from the known extant ethnographies, so must a cultural variable sample be drawn from the known extant range of cultural and social inventory.

Our allocation of the 49 variables used in this study reveals that they are contained within the following 23 two-digit categories: 16, 22, 23, 24, 28, 32, 34, 36, 39, 42, 52, 56, 58, 59, 60, 61, 62, 63, 64, 77, 83, 84, 88. The total number of two-digit categories in the OCM is 72, when the seven categories given two paragraphs above are eliminated. Therefore, the categories we used from Murdock (1967) represent 32 per cent of the total number and contain no information of any kind from the remaining 49 categories. Therefore they are not representative of the entire range of social and cultural inventory given in the OCM.

Thanks to Frank Moore, who supplied the data, we list below in Table 5 the number of lines of printed information in the two-digit categories. If we add up the proportions of lines in the 23 two-digit categories into which Murdock's data fall, the total is .378. This is higher than the 32 per cent mentioned above and is a better measure of the breadth of coverage of his sample. We suspect that if this procedure were done for three-digit categories, the percent of categories and the proportion of lines would be much smaller because often only one or two three-digit categories within a two-digit category were sampled. However, it seems obvious that a stratified sample of social and cultural inventory weighted according to the proportions of lines in Table 5 would be superior to any such sample used so far.

Comparisons with Kroeber's Cultural Intensity

Kroeber (1939: Map 28, facing page 22) classified North American Indian ethnic units on a scale of seven levels of cultural intensity. This corresponds fairly closely to what would be called evolutionary levels today. It is unexpected to see in our Table 10 that Kroeber's seven levels of cultural intensity match the tenfold intuitive culture area classifications of Driver, Murdock, and Spencer and Jennings more closely than they do the seven principal statistical groups or Kroeber's sevenfold system of culture areas. Relationships between all three combinations of sevenfold groupings, given in the smaller triangle in Table 10, average lower than any other comparable group of coefficients.

Comparisons with Linguistic Groups

Comparisons with the Voegelins' (1966) nine language phyla, Table 6 and Table 10 (second lowest row), show a higher relation (.61) between these language groups and Kroeber's seven major culture areas than with any other grouping in Table 10. This relatively high relationship is unexpected; it is hard to believe that it is caused primarily by culture heritage of the members of each phylum from the proto-culture associated with the phylum, even if one optimistically accepts the phyla as genetic groups. These proto-cultures would have to have been retained over time spans of up to 10,000 years to produce an overall correlation between language and culture as high as .61.

In Table 7 we have computed a phi value for each language phylum with each culture area. There is one perfect relationship, that between the Arctic Coast Area and the Arctic-Paleosiberian phylum. Without repeating all the figures in the table, it is clear that each language phylum has at least one medium to high relation with an area, and each area has at least one such substantial relation to a phylum. Table 8 gives a frequency distribution of the phi values in Table 7. It is clear that only a few high and medium values are enough to produce a fairly high Cramèr's coefficient for the cross-classification (Table 6) as a whole.

It should be remembered that none of the groupings of cultures or languages compared in Table 10 are geographically random. All show a tendency to form nonrandom geographical clumps or clusters. Any information that tends to form areal clusters would be likely to correlate significantly in a cross-classification table with any other such information. This applies to the inorganic rocks and soils of geology and geography, to the organic fauna and flora of biology, as well as to human language and culture. It even applies to modern political boundaries, as Driver (1966: 158) has shown. For this reason, almost any cross-classification of two sets of geographically clustered data will yield a chi-square high enough to pass a conventional significance test, as we show in the next section below.

A comparison of the 55 language families of the Voegelins (1966) with our 55 statistical cultural groups (Table 9) was also made. For this comparison we retained singletons because about half of the language families had single members, called language isolates by the Voegelins. The cross-classification table is too large to print conveniently, but it contains three perfect matches, all of singletons in both schemes. The overall relation of the 55 language families and the 55 cultural groups may be again expressed by a Cramèr's coefficient of .29, a low value. Thus language phyla correlate higher with culture than do language families when singletons are included in the families. This seems to be an artifact of the size of the groups and their tendency to form continuous geographical distributions. The relatively large numbers of singletons in the 55x55 comparison fragment the data and scatter them around on the map. The much smaller number of language phyla compresses the data into a much smaller number of continuously or near-continuously distributed groups. The most scattered phyla are Na-Dene, Penutian, and Hokan, but because our sample does not include the Mayan family within the Penutian phylum, the Penutians we retain are mostly in California and Oregon, where their distribution is almost continuous.

Statistical Significance of Relationships

The lowest Cramèr's coefficient in Table 10 is that between Kroeber's seven culture areas and our seven principal statistical groups. It is only .24. We exhibit the entire cross-classification table as Table 11. In Table 12 we have combined categories as indicated to raise expected values high enough to approximate the sampling distribution of chi-square. The chi-square value of Table 12 is 277 and Cramèr's coefficient .343. With twelve degrees of freedom, the probability of this chi-square value occurring by an accident of sampling is too low to appear in conventional tables but is probably about one in a billion. If our lowest relationship passes this significance test by so wide a margin, we can postulate that if all other cross-classification tables were collapsed they too would pass a significance test. Therefore, all the coefficients shown in Table 10 are probably statistically significant and not mere accidents of sampling.

However, the Cramèr's coefficients show that strength of relationship varies widely. At exactly what level of magnitude this coefficient becomes anthropologically significant is indeterminate. However, one reason why our cultural groups determined statistically from Murdock's data correlate lower, on the whole, with intuitive groupings than the latter do among each other is the geographically split distributions of some of the Murdock-derived groups.

In this respect these split distributions resemble some language families and phyla.

We are also inclined to doubt the classificatory validity of the large numbers of singletons that appear at nearly all levels in our tree diagram printout, parts of which we give in our Tables 1, 3, and 9. Although we have made no attempt to recode any of Murdock's data from field sources, we suspect that the many errors in the field reports and their low level of comparability with each other, added to whatever errors were made in coding, have produced too much idiosyncrasy in the coded data. We believe that more accurate data would produce fewer singletons.

Discussion and Conclusions

Our principal conclusion is that Driver (1970a) was wrong when he argued that groups of tribes ("strata") derived statistically from Murdock's (1967 and later) sample would make better "strata" for a "stratified" probability sample than the intuitively derived groups of Murdock or others. We think that Murdock's intuitive sampling provinces or his ten culture areas are better for this purpose than our statistically obtained groups of tribes. This is because the latter are derived from a subject sample largely made up of social organizations, deficient in the quantity of material culture and technology, which reflect geographical and historical relationships more strongly. The stronger agreement of all intuitive culture area schemes tested among each other than with our statistically determined groups of tribes supports this conclusion.

Relations between language and culture have been given by treating language groups and culture groups as nominal categories and comparing the two classifications in terms of the number of ethnic or language units shared by each pair of groups in cross-classification tables. We make the point that all such relationships are invariably significant, and that those derived from small numbers of groups of language and culture are higher than those derived from large (55) numbers of such groups. Where lexicostatistics or some other quantitative measure of linguistic relationship is available, the correlation between linguistic similarity and culture similarity can be computed, as Jorgensen (1969) has done for the Salish group. This will be done in the future, with newly coded cultural data, by Jorgensen and Driver for a number of language families.

The relationships between language and culture given in Table 10 should not be interpreted as proof that the phonology, morphology, syntax, or basic lexicon of any language group causes a certain assemblage of culture. Conversely, it should not be argued that the culture of any group causes a number

of linguistic features. When multiple language-bearing groups and multiple culture-bearing groups exist in the same geographical space, is is inevitable that the overall relationship will be significant, as we have found it to be. This may reflect some degree of common linguistic and cultural heritages from common proto-languages and protocultures for at least some of the groups positively related, but not a direct causal relationship.

An R-type of correlation analysis, maps, and utilization of archeological and biological data would at least partly unscramble the culture heritages, the diffusions, and the parallel and convergent developments in Murdock's data. Some of the Galton-problem tests could also be applied to further demonstrate the nonrandom areal clustering in the data. Because of other commitments, this will be left to the future.

TABLE 1
Our 35 Principal Statistical Groups
(Note: Bridge occurred at .68 giving 75 groups. When singletons were omitted, 35 groups remained. Total ethnic units = 273)

1. *West Pueblos*: Hano, Hopi, Zuni, Laguna, Acoma, Jemez, Sia, Cochiti, Santa Ana.
2. *Tanoan-Catawba*: Catawba, Isleta, Tewa, Taos, Picuris.
3. *Meso-America*: Mixe, Popoluca, Zapotec, Totonac.
4. *Great Lakes*: Winnebago, Shawnee, Ottawa, Potawatomi, Menomini, Miami.
5. *Siouans*: Iowa, Oto, Ponca.
6. *River Yumans*: Maricopa, Yuma, Cocopa, Kamia, Mohave.
7. *Village Tribes*: Arikara, Hidatsa, Mandan.
8. *East*: Creek, Cherokee, Delaware, Huron, Iroquois.
9. *Yuchi-Choctaw*: Yuchi, Choctaw.
10. *W. Southwest*: Walapai, Yaqui, Pima, Papago.
11. *Hasinai-Caddo*: Hasinai, Caddo.
12. *Apacheans*: Jicarilla, Mescalero, Chiricahua.
13. *Eastern Sub-Arctic*: Eastern Cree, Naskapi, Rainy River Ojibwa, Northern Saulteaux, Nipigon, Katiketgon.
14. *California*: Chumash, Salinan, Lake Yokuts, Yokuts, Wukchumni, Monachi, Miwok, Gabrielino, Nomlaki, Cahuila, Serrano, Cupeno, Luiseno, Diegueno.
15. *Kilawa-E. Ojibwa*: Kiliwa, Eastern Ojibwa.
16. N. California: Maidu, Yana, Huchnom, Achomawi, Northern Pomo, Sinkyone, Chimariko.
17. *Arctic-California*: Eastern Pomo, Wappo, Lake Miwok, Southern Pomo, Eastern Mono (Owens Valley N. Paiute), Seri, Labrador Eskimo, Netsilik, Iglulik.
18. *Sanpoil-Sinkaietk*: Sinkaietk, Sanpoil.
19. *Micmac-Karankawa*: Micmac, Karankawa.
20. *Great Basin-Sub-Arctic*: Plains Cree, Uncompahgre Ute, Southern Ute, Bannock, Pahvant Ute, Uintah Ute, Moanunts Ute, Taviwatsiu Ute, Moache Ute, Beaver, Bohogue Shoshoni, Slave, Sekani, Kidutokado (Surprise Valley N. Paiute), Agaiduka (Lemhi River Shoshoni), Tukudika Shoshoni, Chipewyan, Satudene, Dogrib, Taqamiut, Antarianunts S. Paiute, Gosiute Shoshoni, Tubaduka Shoshoni, Atsakudokwa N. Paiute, Sawakudokwa N. Paiute, Wadadokado (Harney Valley N. Paiute), Toedokado·N. Paiute, Kuyuidokado (Pyramid

Table 1 (continued)

Lake N. Paiute), Tagotoka N. Paiute, Washo, Wadaduka Shoshoni, Panguitch S. Paiute, Wiyambituka Shoshoni, Mazateco, Tunava N. Paiute, Beatty Shoshoni, Lida Shoshoni, Panamint Shoshoni, White Knife Shoshoni, Yahanduka Shoshoni, Wadatkuht N. Paiute, Elko Shoshoni, Chichimec, Coast Yuki, Lassik, Wenatchi, Klikitat, Wintu, Yuki, Nisenan, Ely Shoshoni, Mahaguaduka Shoshoni, Hamilton Shoshoni, Spring Valley Shoshoni, Shivwits S. Paiute, Las Vegas S. Paiute, Kaibab S. Paiute, Moapa S. Paiute, Koso Shoshoni, Chemehuevi S. Paiute, Yavapai, Tolkepaya (Western Yavapai), Kawaiisu S. Paiute, Tubatulabal.
21. *Baffinland-Copper*: Baffinland, Copper Eskimo.
22. *Mistassini-Polar*: Mistassini, Polar Eskimo.
23. *East Plateau*: Coeur D'Alene, Kalispel, Flathead, Nez Perce, Umatilla, Kutenai.
24. *Plains*: Wind River Shoshoni, Lipan, Comanche, Kiowa-Apache, Arapaho, Blackfoot, Kiowa, Sarsi, Blood, Piegan, Gros Ventre (Atsina), Assiniboin, Teton.
25. *Northwest Coast* Shasta, Wiyot, Karok, Hupa, Chinook, Coos, Alsea, Siuslaw, Yurok, Quileute, Tillamook, Quinault, Klallam, Kwakiutl, Nootka, Makah, Twana, Lummi, Comox, Klahuse, Squamish, Cowichan, Puyallup,

26. *Bella-Bellacoola*: Bellabella, Bellacoola.
27. *West Plateau*: Tenino, Lillooet, Modoc, Thompson, Shuswap, Klamath, Stalo, Wishram, Alkatcho Carrier.
28. *Atsugewi-Chilcotin*: Atsugewi, Chilcotin.
29. *Tolowa-Tututni*: Tututni, Tolowa.
30. *N. Northwest Coast*: Tsimshian, Haida, Tlingit, Haisla.
31. *Eyak-Tahltan*: Eyak, Tahltan.
32. *Nunivak-Ingalik*: Ingalik, Nunivak.
33. *Greenland Eskimo*: Greenlanders, Angmagsalik.
34. *Quebec Cree*: Montagnais, Attawapiskat Cree.
35. *Ojibwa*: Ojibwa, Pekangekum.
Singletons and their positions among the 35 numbered groups:
Aztec, Tarasco, Tlaxcalans, 1, 2, Chinantec, Huave, 3, Huichol, Tarahumara, Fox, 4, 5, Omaha, 6, Natchez, Pawnee, 7, Timucua, 8, 9, Seminole, Western Apache, Navaho, Keweyipaya, Havasupai, 10, 11, Wichita, Cheyenne, 12, San Juan, Chippewa, 13, Bungi, 14, 15, Patwin, 16, 17, Caribou Eskimo, 18, Hukundika Shoshoni, 19, 20, 21, 22, 23, 24, Santee, Crow, Nabesna, Kutchin, Nunamiut, Kaska, Takelma, Mattole, 25, 26, 27, 28, 29, Aleut, Tanaina, Carrier, 30, 31, Tareumiut, 32, 33, Penobscot, 34, Chugach Eskimo, 35, Sivokakmeiut Eskimo.

TABLE 2
Cross-classification of Murdock's 34 Sampling Provinces and Our 35 Principal Statistical Groups.

Murdock's 34 Sampling Provinces	Our 35 Principal Statistical Groups														
	1	2	3	4	5	6	7	8	9	10	11	12	13	14	15
W. Esk. 132	0	0	0	0	0	0	0	0	0	0	0	0	0	0	0
C. & E. Esk. 133	0	0	0	0	0	0	0	0	0	0	0	0	0	0	0
N. E. Atha. 134	0	0	0	0	0	0	0	0	0	0	0	0	0	0	0
Yukon 135	0	0	0	0	0	0	0	0	0	0	0	0	0	0	0
S. C. Alaska 136	0	0	0	0	0	0	0	0	0	0	0	0	0	0	0
N. N. W. Coast 137	0	0	0	0	0	0	0	0	0	0	0	0	0	0	0
Car.-Nah. 138	0	0	0	0	0	0	0	0	0	0	0	0	0	0	0
Wak.-Bell. 139	0	0	0	0	0	0	0	0	0	0	0	0	0	0	0
Cst. Salish 140	0	0	0	0	0	0	0	0	0	0	0	0	0	0	0
C. Pac. Cst. 141	0	0	0	0	0	0	0	0	0	0	0	0	0	0	0
N. E. Calif. 142	0	0	0	0	0	0	0	0	0	0	0	0	0	0	0
C. Calif. 143	0	0	0	0	0	0	0	0	0	0	0	0	0	1	0
S. Calif. 144	0	0	0	0	0	0	0	0	0	0	0	0	0	12	0
Yuma 145	0	0	0	0	0	5	0	0	0	1	0	0	0	1	1
W. Gr. Bas. 146	0	0	0	0	0	0	0	0	0	0	0	0	0	0	0
E. Gr. Bas. 147	0	0	0	0	0	0	0	0	0	0	0	0	0	0	0
Sah.-Chinook 148	0	0	0	0	0	0	0	0	0	0	0	0	0	0	0
N. Plateau 149	0	0	0	0	0	0	0	0	0	0	0	0	0	0	0
N. Plains 150	0	0	0	0	0	0	0	0	0	0	0	0	0	0	0
Cree-Mont. 151	0	0	0	0	0	0	0	0	0	0	0	0	2	0	0
Mar. Algonk. 152	0	0	0	0	0	0	0	0	0	0	0	0	0	0	0
Ojibwa 153	0	0	0	1	0	0	0	0	0	0	0	0	4	0	1
Upper Mo. 154	0	0	0	0	0	0	2	0	0	0	0	0	0	0	0
Prairie 155	0	0	0	5	3	0	0	0	0	0	0	0	0	0	0
N. E. Wood. 156	0	0	0	0	0	0	0	3	0	0	0	0	0	0	0
Cher.-Yuchi 157	0	0	0	0	0	0	0	1	1	0	0	0	0	0	0
Muskogee 158	0	0	0	0	0	0	0	1	1	0	0	0	0	0	0
Caddo-Nat. 159	0	0	0	0	0	0	1	0	0	0	2	0	0	0	0
S. Plains 160	0	0	0	0	0	0	0	0	0	0	0	0	0	0	0
Apache-Tan. 161	0	4	0	0	0	0	0	0	0	0	0	3	0	0	0
Pueb.-Nav. 162	9	0	0	0	0	0	0	0	0	0	0	0	0	0	0
N. W. Mex. 163	0	0	0	0	0	0	0	0	0	3	0	0	0	0	0
C. Mex. 165	0	0	1	0	0	0	0	0	0	0	0	0	0	0	0
Tehuantepec 166	0	0	3	0	0	0	0	0	0	0	0	0	0	0	0
Total	9	4	4	6	3	5	3	5	2	4	2	3	6	14	2

Chi-Square = 3813
Cramèr's Coefficient = .488

Table 2 (continued)

16	17	18	19	20	21	22	23	24	25	26	27	28	29	30	31	32	33	34	35	Total
0	0	0	0	0	0	0	0	0	0	0	0	0	0	0	0	0	1	0	0	1
0	3	0	0	1	2	1	0	0	0	0	0	0	0	0	0	0	0	2	0	9
0	0	0	0	6	0	0	0	0	0	0	0	0	0	0	0	0	0	0	0	6
0	0	0	0	0	0	0	0	0	0	0	0	0	0	0	0	0	1	0	0	1
0	0	0	0	0	0	0	0	0	0	0	0	0	0	0	0	1	0	0	0	1
0	0	0	0	0	0	0	0	0	0	0	0	0	0	4	0	0	0	0	0	4
0	0	0	0	0	0	0	0	0	0	0	0	0	0	0	1	0	0	0	0	1
0	0	0	0	0	0	0	0	0	4	2	1	0	0	0	0	0	0	0	0	7
0	0	0	0	0	0	0	0	0	9	0	1	0	0	0	0	0	0	0	0	10
1	0	0	0	1	0	0	0	0	7	0	0	0	2	0	0	0	0	0	0	11
3	0	0	0	1	0	0	0	0	1	0	2	1	0	0	0	0	0	0	0	8
3	3	0	0	4	0	0	0	0	0	0	0	0	0	0	0	0	0	0	0	11
0	1	0	0	2	0	0	0	0	0	0	0	0	0	0	0	0	0	0	0	15
0	0	0	0	2	0	0	0	0	0	0	0	0	0	0	0	0	0	0	0	10
0	1	0	0	34	0	0	0	0	0	0	0	0	0	0	0	0	0	0	0	35
0	0	0	0	8	0	0	0	1	0	0	0	0	0	0	0	0	0	0	0	9
0	0	0	0	1	0	0	2	0	2	0	2	0	0	0	0	0	0	0	0	7
0	0	2	0	1	0	0	4	0	0	0	3	1	0	0	0	0	0	0	0	11
0	0	0	0	1	0	0	0	7	0	0	0	0	0	0	0	0	0	0	0	8
0	0	0	0	0	0	0	0	0	0	0	0	0	0	0	0	0	0	2	0	4
0	0	0	1	0	0	0	0	0	0	0	0	0	0	0	0	0	0	0	0	1
0	0	0	0	0	0	0	0	0	0	0	0	0	0	0	0	0	0	0	2	8
0	0	0	0	0	0	0	0	0	0	0	0	0	0	0	0	0	0	0	0	2
0	0	0	0	0	0	0	0	0	0	0	0	0	0	0	0	0	0	0	0	8
0	0	0	0	0	0	0	0	0	0	0	0	0	0	0	0	0	0	0	0	3
0	0	0	0	0	0	0	0	0	0	0	0	0	0	0	0	0	0	0	0	2
0	0	0	0	0	0	0	0	0	0	0	0	0	0	0	0	0	0	0	0	2
0	0	0	0	0	0	0	0	0	0	0	0	0	0	0	0	0	0	0	0	3
0	0	0	1	0	0	0	0	4	0	0	0	0	0	0	0	0	0	0	0	5
0	0	0	0	0	0	0	0	1	0	0	0	0	0	0	0	0	0	0	0	8
0	0	0	0	0	0	0	0	0	0	0	0	0	0	0	0	0	0	0	0	9
0	1	0	0	0	0	0	0	0	0	0	0	0	0	0	0	0	0	0	0	4
0	0	0	0	1	0	0	0	0	0	0	0	0	0	0	0	0	0	0	0	2
0	0	0	0	1	0	0	0	0	0	0	0	0	0	0	0	0	0	0	0	4
7	9	2	2	64	2	1	6	13	23	2	9	2	2	4	2	2	2	2	2	230

TABLE 3
Our 10, 9, and 7 Principal Statistical Groups.

10 Groups
(Note: Bridge occurred at .48 giving 15 groups. When singletons were omitted, 10 groups remained.)

1. *Hunters-Gatherers*: Chippewa, Katikitegon, Nipigon, Northern Salteaux, Rainy River Ojibwa, Naskapi, Eastern Cree, Bungi, Chumash, Salinan, Lake Yokuts, Yokuts, Wukchumni, Monachi, Miwok, Gabrielino, Nomlaki, Cahuilla, Serrano, Cupeno, Luiseno, Diegueno, Kiliwa, Eastern Ojibwa, Patwin, Chimariko, Sinkyone, Northern Pomo, Achomawi, Huchnom, Yana, Maidu, Eastern Pomo, Wappo, Lake Miwok, Southern Pomo, Eastern Mono (Owens Valley Paiute), Seri, Labrador Eskimo, Netsilik, Iglulik, Caribou Eskimo, Sanpoil, Sinkaietk, Hukundika Shoshoni, Karankawa, Micmac, Plains Cree, Uncompahgre Ute, Southern Ute, Bannock, Pahvant Ute, Uintah Ute, Moanunts Ute, Taviwatsu Ute, Moache Ute, Beaver, Bohogue Shoshoni, Slave, Sekani, Kidutokado (Surprise Valley N. Paiute), Agaiduka (Lemhi River Shoshoni), Tukudika Shoshoni, Chipewyan, Satudene, Dogrib, Taqagmiut, Antarianunts S. Paiute, Gosiute Shoshoni, Tubaduka Shoshoni, Atsakudokw N. Paiute, Sawakudokw N. Paiute, Wadadokado (Harney Valley N. Paiute), Toedokado N. Paiute, Kuyuidokado (Pyramid Lake N. Paiute), Tagototoka N. Paiute, Washo, Wadaduka Shoshoni, Panguitch S. Paiute, Wiyambituka Shoshoni, Mazateco, Tunava N. Paiute, Beatty Shoshoni, Lida Shoshoni, Panamint Shoshoni, White Knife Shoshoni, Yahanduka Shoshoni, Wadatkuht N. Paiute, Elko Shoshoni, Chichimec, Coast Yuki, Lassik Wenathci, Klikitat, Wintu, Yuki, Nisenan, Ely Shoshoni, Mahaguaduka Shoshoni, Hamilton Shoshoni, Spring Valley Shoshoni, Shivwits S. Paiute, Las Vegas S. Paiute, Kaibab S. Paiute, Moapa S. Paiute, Koso Shoshoni, Chemehuevi S. Paiute, Yavapai, Tolkepaya (W. Yavapai), Kawaiisu S. Paiute, Tubatulabal, Baffinland, Copper Eskimo, Mistassini, Polar Eskimo, Kutenai, Umatilla, Nez Perce, Flathead, Kalispel, Coeur D'Alene, Wind River Shoshoni, Lipan, Comanche, Kiowa-Apache, Arapaho, Blackfoot, Kiowa, Sarsi, Blood, Piegan, Gros Ventre (Atsina), Assiniboin, Teton, Santee, Crow, Nabesna, Kutchin, Nunamiut, Kaska.
2. *Fishers*: Pekangekum, Ojibwa, Chugach Eskimo, Attawapiskat Cree, Montagnais, Penobscot, Greenlanders, Angmagsalik, Ingalik, Nunivak, Tareumiut, Tahltan, Eyak, Tsimshian, Haida, Tlingit, Haisla, Carrier, Tanaina, Aleut, Tututni, Tolowa, Atsugewi, Chilcotin, Chilcotin, Tenino, Lillooet, Modoc, Thompson, Shuswap, Klamath, Stalo, Wishram, Alkatcho Carrier, Bellabella, Bellacoola, Puyallup, Cowichan, Squamish, Klahuse, Comox, Lummi,

Table 3 (continued)

Twana, Makah, Nootka, Kwakiutl, Klallam, Quinault, Tillamook, Quileute, Yurok, Suislaw, Alsea, Coos, Chinook, Hupa, Karok, Wiyot, Shasta, Mattole, Takelma,

3. *S. W. Farmers*: Western Apache, Navaho.

4. *Meso-American Farmers*: Aztec, Tarasco.

5. *Midwest-S. W. Farmers*: Winnebago, Shawnee, Ottawa, Potawatomi, Menomini, Miami, Ponca, Oto, Iowa, Omaha, Maricopa, Yuma, Cocopa, Kamia, Mohave.

6. *Eastern Farmers*: Seminole, Yuchi, Choctaw, Creek, Cherokee, Delaware, Huron, Iroquois, Timucua.

7. *Mexican Farmers*: Tarahumara, Huichol, Mixe, Populuca, Zapotec, Totonac, Huave, Chinantec.

8. *Missouri River Farmers*: Pawnee, Arikara, Hidatsa, Mandan.

9. *Peripheral S. W. Farmers*: San Juan Paiute, Jicarilla, Mescalero, Chiricahua, Cheyenne, Wichita, Hasinai, Caddo, Papago, Pima, Yaqui, Walapai, Havasupai.

10. *Pueblo-Catawba Farmers*: Hano, Hopi, Zuni, Laguna, Acoma, Jemez, Sia, Cochiti, Santa Ana, Picuris, Taos, Tewa, Isleta, Catawba.

Singletons: Tlaxcalans, Fox, Keweyipaya (S. E. Yavapai), Natchez, Sivokakmeiut.
Total: 273 tribes.

9 Groups
(Note: Bridge occurred at .48 giving 14 groups. When singletons were omitted, 9 groups remained.)
See our 10 groups. The tribes in group nine are added to the tribes in group one, with group nine being dropped as a class.

7 Groups
(Note: Bridge occurred at .45 giving 11 groups. When singletons were omitted, 7 groups remained.)
See our 10 groups. Groups eight, nine, and ten are eliminated as classes. Group one gains the tribes in group nine. Group seven gains the tribes in group ten. Group six gains the tribes in group eight. Group five gains the singleton Fox.

TABLE 4
Cross-Classification of Murdock's Culture Areas with our 10 Principal Statistical Groups.

		1	2	3	4	5	6	7	8	9	10	Total
	a	28	14	0	0	2	0	0	0	0	0	44
	b	3	36	0	0	0	0	0	0	0	0	39
	c	31	3	0	0	0	0	0	0	0	0	34
	d	58	6	0	0	0	0	0	0	3	0	67
Murdock's 10 Culture Areas	e	16	1	0	0	0	0	0	3	1	0	21
	f	0	0	0	0	8	0	0	1	3	0	12
	g	0	1	0	0	0	9	0	0	0	1	11
	h	1	0	2	0	5	0	0	0	3	13	24
	i	2	0	0	0	0	0	3	0	3	0	8
	j	1	0	0	2	0	0	5	0	0	0	8
	Total	140	61	2	2	15	9	8	4	13	14	268

Column header (spanning): 10 Principal Statistical Groups

Chi-square = 899
Cramèr's coefficient = .373

TABLE 5
Frequency and Proportion of Lines of Copy in the HRAF 2-Digit Categories.

HRAF Category	Number of Lines	Proportion of Lines	HRAF Category	Number of Lines	Proportion of Lines
15	2578	.011	54	861	.004
16	5590	.024	55	4366	.019
17	9797	.042	56	4900	.021
20	1810	.008	57	5207	.022
21	1416	.006	58	6138	.026
22	3779	.016	59	4354	.019
23	3006	.013	60	3657	.016
24	4189	.018	61	2586	.011
25	2071	.009	62	5134	.022

Table 5 (continued)

26	3519	.015	63	2076	.009
27	3109	.013	64	4885	.021
28	2806	.012	65	3302	.014
29	3282	.014	66	2137	.009
30	3210	.014	67	1525	.007
31	3387	.015	68	3404	.015
32	2163	.009	69	2097	.009
33	511	.002	70	1112	.005
34	3807	.016	71	1010	.004
35	2455	.011	72	2959	.013
36	3306	.014	73	1648	.007
37	1173	.005	74	894	.004
38	960	.004	75	5554	.024
39	405	.002	76	5121	.022
40	419	.002	77	8134	.035
41	3354	.014	78	6686	.029
42	4790	.021	79	5139	.022
43	6456	.028	80	1514	.007
44	1056	.005	81	564	.002
45	1217	.005	82	5488	.024
46	4572	.020	83	3353	.014
47	1806	.008	84	3829	.016
48	3113	.013	85	3318	.014
49	2265	.010	86	2052	.009
50	1835	.008	87	2099	.009
51	3659	.016	88	2228	.010
52	3027	.013			
53	7199	.031	Total	232388	1.010

TABLE 6
Cross-Classification of Kroeber's 7 Culture Areas and the Voegelins' 9 Language Phyla.

	Arctic-Paleosiberian I	Na-Dene II	Macro-Algonquian III	Macro-Siouan IV	Hokan V	Penutian VI	Aztec-Tanoan VII	Undetermined, Other VIII	Oto-Manguean IX	Total
A Arctic Coast	16	0	0	0	0	0	0	0	0	16
NW Northwest Coast	0	6	2	0	1	7	0	18	0	34
SW Southwest	0	6	0	0	13	1	16	5	0	41
I Intermediate	0	5	0	0	10	16	46	14	0	91
E Eastern	0	1	21	21	1	0	5	2	0	51
N Northern	0	15	13	0	0	0	0	0	0	28
M Mexican	0	0	0	0	0	4	3	1	4	12
Total	16	33	36	21	25	28	70	40	4	273

Chi-square = 1001. Cramer's f^2 = .611

TABLE 7
Phi Coefficients Between Kroeber's 7 Culture Areas and the Voegelins' 9 Language Phyla.

	Arctic-Paleosiberian I	Na-Dene II	Macro-Algonquian III	Macro-Siouan IV	Hokan V	Penutian VI	Aztec-Tanoan VII	Undetermined, Other VIII	Oto-Manguean IX
A Arctic Coast	+1.00	−.09	−.10	−.04	−.04	−.08	−.15	−.10	−.03
NW Northwest Coast	−.09	+.06	−.08	−.09	−.08	+.13	−.22	+.41	+.05
SW Southwest	−.11	+.03	−.16	−.12	+.33	−.11	+.13	−.03	−.05
I Intermediate'	−.16	−.21	−.27	−.20	+.04	+.17	+.40	+.01	−.09
E Eastern	−.12	−.15	+.41	+.60	−.12	−.16	−.17	−.15	−.06
N Northern	−.08	+.43	+.33	−.10	−.11	−.11	−.20	−.14	−.04
M Mexican	−.05	−.06	−.08	−.06	−.07	+.16	.00	−.04	+.57

TABLE 8
Frequency Distribution of Correlations (Phis)
Among Kroeber's 7 Culture Areas
and the Voegelins' 9 Language Phyla.

+.91	to	1.00	1
+.81	to	.90	0
+.71	to	.80	0
+.61	to	.70	1
+.51	to	.60	1
+.41	to	.50	3
+.31	to	.40	3
+.21	to	.30	0
+.11	to	.20	4
+.01	to	.10	4
00	to	-.09	23
-.10	to	-.19	18
-.20	to	-.29	5
Total (N)			63

TABLE 9
Our 55 Statistical Groups

(*Note*: Bridge occurred at .63, giving 55 groups. Singletons were included.)
1. Nabesna.
2. Ingalik, Nunivak, Tareumiut.
3. *Great Basin, California, Plateau, Sub-Arctic, Arctic:* Caribou Eskimo, Sanpoil, Sinkaietk, Hukundika Shoshoni, Karankawa, Micmac, Plains Cree, Uncompahgre Ute, Southern Ute, Bannock, Pahvant Ute, Uintah Ute, Moanunts Ute, Taviwatsiu Ute, Moache Ute, Beaver, Bohogue Shoshoni, Slave, Sekani, Kidutokado (Surprise Valley Paiute), Agaiduka (Lemhi River Shoshoni), Tukudika Shoshoni, Chipewyan, Satudene, Dogrib, Taqagmiut, Antarianunts S. Paiute, Gosiute Shoshoni, Tubaduka Shoshoni, Atsakudokw N. Paiute, Sawakudokwa N. Paiute, Wadadokado (Harney Valley N. Paiute), Toedokado N. Paiute, Kuyuidokado (Pyramid Lake N. Paiute), Tagotoka N. Paiute, Washo, Wadaduka Shoshoni, Panguitch S. Paiute, Wiyambituka Shoshoni, Mazateco, Tunava N. Paiute, Beatty Shoshoni, Lida Shoshoni, Panamint Shoshoni, White Knife Shoshoni, Wadatkuht N. Paiute, Elko Shoshoni, Chichimec, Coast Yuki, Lassik, Wenatchi, Klikitat,Wintu, Yuki, Nisenan, Ely Shoshoni, Mahaguaduka Shoshoni, Hamilton Shoshoni, Spring Valley Shoshoni, Shivwits S. Paiute, Kaibab S. Paiute, Koso Shoshoni, Chemehuevi S. Paiute, Yavapai, Tolkepaya (Western Yavapai), Kawaiisu, Tubatulabal, Baffinland, Copper Eskimo, Mistassini, Polar Eskimo, Yahanduka Shoshoni, Las Vegas S. Paiute, Moapa S. Paiute.
4. Kaska.
5. *Sub-Arctic:* Bungi, Eastern Cree, Naskapi, Rainy River Ojibwa, Northern Saulteaux, Nipigon, Katkitegon.
6. Crow.
7. Montagnais, Attawapiskat Cree.
8. Tarahumara.
9. Tanaina, Aleut.
10. Chugach Eskimo.
11. Sivokakmeiut.
12. Nunamiut.
13. Mixe, Popoluca, Zapotec, Totonac.
14. *Tanoan-Catawba:* Catawba, Isleta, Tewa, Taos, Picuris.
15. Tlaxcalans.
16. *Apachean, Plains:* Jicarilla, Mescalero, Chiricahua, Cheyenne, Wichita.
17. *Southwest:* Havasupai, Walapai, Yaqui, Pima, Papago.
18. *Plateau:* Atsugewi, Chilcotin, Chilcotin, Tenino, Lillooet, Modoc, Thompson, Shuswap, Klamath, Stalo, Wishram, Alkatcho Carrier.
19. Carrier.
20. Kutchin.
21. *River Yumans:* Maricopa, Yuma, Cocopa, Kamia, Mohave.
22. *California-Arctic:* Iglulik, Netsilik, Labrador Eskimo, Seri, Eastern Mono (Owens Valley N. Paiute), Southern Pomo, Lake Miwok, Wappo, Eastern Pomo, Maidu, Yana, Huchnom, Achomawi, Northern Pomo, Sinkyone, Chimariko, Patwin.
23. *Plains:* Wind River Shoshoni, Lipan, Comanche, Kiowa-Apache, Arapaho, Blackfoot, Kiowa, Sarsi, Blood, Piegan, Gros Ventre (Atsina), Assiniboin, Teton.
24. Greenlanders, Angmagsalik.
25. Western Apache.
26. Aztec.
27. Eyak, Tahltan.
28. Fox.
29. *Village Tribes:* Pawnee, Arikara, Hidatsa, Mandan.
30. Hasinai, Caddo.
31. *California:* Chumash, Salinan, Lake Yokuts, Yokuts, Monachi, Miwok, Gabrielino, Nomlaki, Cahuilla, Serrano, Cupeno, Luiseno, Diegueno, Wukchumni.
32. Navaho.
33. Santee.
34. Ojibwa, Pekangekum.
35. *Pueblos:* Hano, Hopi, Zuni, Laguna, Acoma, Jemez, Sia, Cochiti, Santa Ana.
36. Chippewa.
37. Natchez.
38. Penobscot.
39. Kiliwa, Eastern Ojibwa.
40. *Great Lakes:* Winnebago, Shawnee, Ottawa, Potawatomi, Menomini, Miami.
41. Seminole.
42. Tarasco.
43. Yuchi, Choctaw.
44. Huichol.
45. *E. Plateau:* Coeur D'Alene, Kalispel, Flathead, Nez Perce, Umatilla, Kutenai.
46. *N. N. W. Coast:* Tsimshian, Haida, Tlingit, Haisla.
47. *N. W. Coast:* Mattole, Shasta, Wiyot, Karok, Hupa, Chinook, Coos, Alsea, Siuslaw, Yurok, Quileute, Tillamook, Quinault, Klallam, Kwakiutl, Nootka, Makah, Twana, Lummi, Comox, Klahuse, Squamish, Cowichan, Puyallup, Bellacoola, Bellabella.
48. Kewyipaya (S. E. Yavapai).
49. Timucua.
50. Huave, Chinantec.
51. Tutuni, Tolowa.
52. San Juan S. Paiute.
53. *Siouans:* Omaha, Iowa, Oto, Ponca.
54. Takelma.
55. *East:* Creek, Cherokee, Delaware, Huron, Iroquois.
TOTAL: 273 tribes.

TABLE 10
Cramèr's Coefficients (f^2) for All Relationships Discussed.

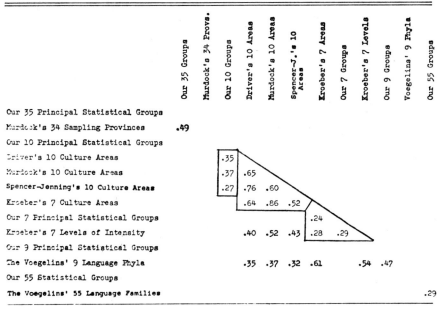

	Our 35 Groups	Murdock's 34 Provs.	Our 10 Groups	Driver's 10 Areas	Murdock's 10 Areas	Spencer-J.'s 10 Areas	Kroeber's 7 Areas	Our 7 Groups	Kroeber's 7 Levels	Our 9 Groups	Voegelins' 9 Phyla	Our 55 Groups
Our 35 Principal Statistical Groups												
Murdock's 34 Sampling Provinces	.49											
Our 10 Principal Statistical Groups												
Driver's 10 Culture Areas			.35									
Murdock's 10 Culture Areas			.37	.65								
Spencer-Jenning's 10 Culture Areas			.27	.76	.60							
Kroeber's 7 Culture Areas				.64	.86	.52						
Our 7 Principal Statistical Groups							.24					
Kroeber's 7 Levels of Intensity				.40	.52	.43	.28	.29				
Our 9 Principal Statistical Groups												
The Voegelins' 9 Language Phyla				.35	.37	.32	.61		.54	.47		
Our 55 Statistical Groups												
The Voegelins' 55 Language Families												.29

TABLE 11
Cross-classification of Kroeber's 7 Culture Areas with our 7 Principal Statistical groups.

		Our 7 Principal Statistical Groups							
		1	2	3	4	5	6	7	Total
	A Arctic Coast	9	6	0	0	0	0	0	15
	NW Northwest Coast	0	34	0	0	0	0	0	34
Kroeber's 7 Culture Areas	SW Southwest	19	0	2	0	5	0	14	40
	I Intermediate	80	11	0	0	0	0	0	91
	E Eastern	25	1	0	0	10	13	1	50
	N Northern	18	9	0	0	1	0	0	28
	N Mexico	2	0	0	2	0	0	7	11
	Total	153	61	2	2	16	13	22	269

Chi-Square = 394.

Cramèr's Coefficient = .244

219

TABLE 12
Reduction of Table 8 for significance test.

| | | | Our 7 Principal Statistical Groups | | | |
		1	2	3-5-6	4-7	Total
Kroeber's Culture Areas	A-NW	9	40	0	0	49
	SW-M	21	0	7	23	51
	I	80	11	0	0	91
	E	25	1	23	1	50
	N	18	9	1	0	28
Total		153	61	31	24	269

Chi-square = 277

Cramer's coefficient = .343

Figure 1. Schematic ordered intercorrelation matrix of all 273 ethnic units, with the 35 principal groups numbered on the margins. A solid black square indicates a phi coefficient from .80 to 1.00 inclusive; a slanting line indicates a phi from .68 to .79 inclusive; a blank space indicates a phi of —.04 to .67 inclusive.

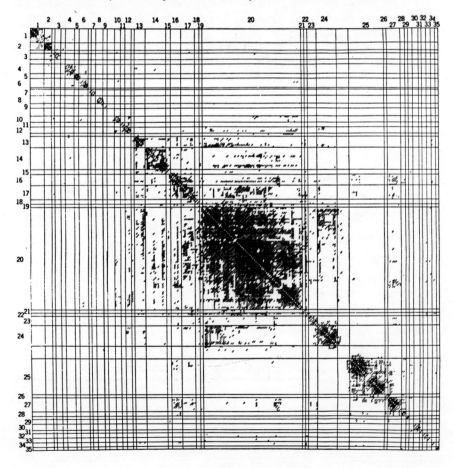

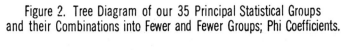

Figure 2. Tree Diagram of our 35 Principal Statistical Groups
and their Combinations into Fewer and Fewer Groups; Phi Coefficients.

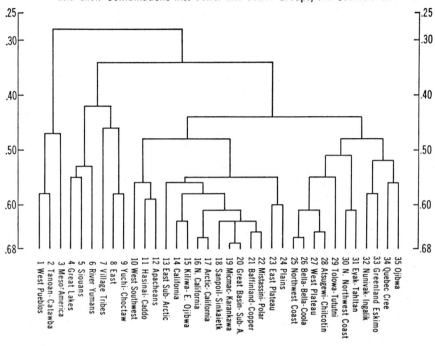

MAP 1   Our 35 Principal Statistical Groups

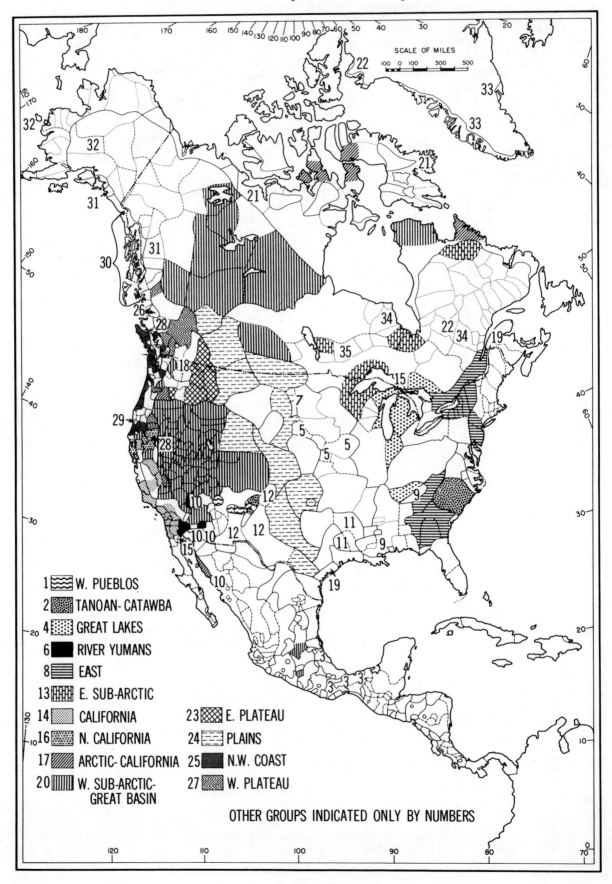

SCALE OF MILES
100   0   100   300   500

1 ⩥⩥ W. PUEBLOS
2 ▒ TANOAN- CATAWBA
4 ▦ GREAT LAKES
6 ■ RIVER YUMANS
8 ▤ EAST
13 ▦ E. SUB-ARCTIC
14 ▒ CALIFORNIA   23 ▨ E. PLATEAU
16 ▨ N. CALIFORNIA   24 ▤ PLAINS
17 ▨ ARCTIC-CALIFORNIA   25 ■ N.W. COAST
20 ▥ W. SUB-ARCTIC-   27 ▧ W. PLATEAU
       GREAT BASIN

OTHER GROUPS INDICATED ONLY BY NUMBERS

MAP 2 Our 10 Principal Statistical Groups

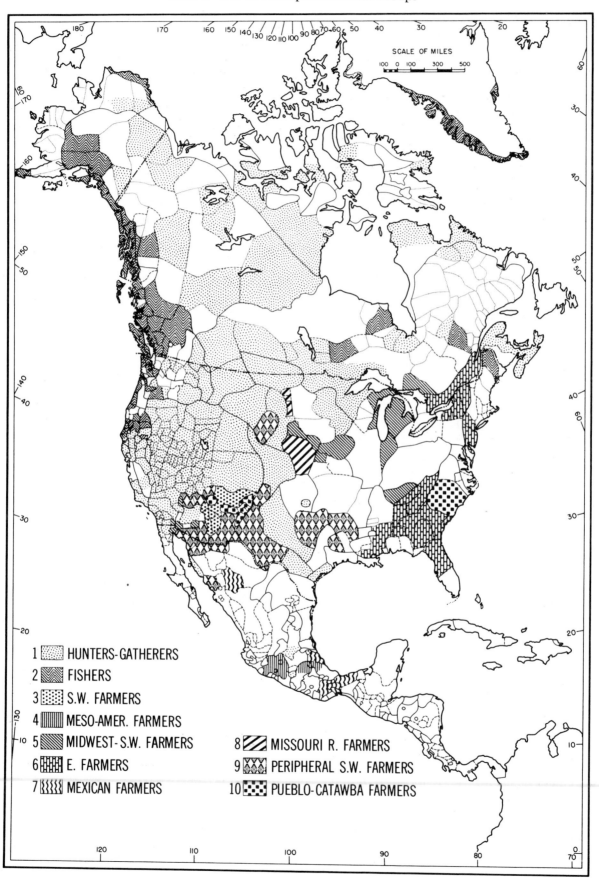

SCALE OF MILES
100 0 100   300   500

1 HUNTERS-GATHERERS
2 FISHERS
3 S.W. FARMERS
4 MESO-AMER. FARMERS
5 MIDWEST-S.W. FARMERS   8 MISSOURI R. FARMERS
6 E. FARMERS   9 PERIPHERAL S.W. FARMERS
7 MEXICAN FARMERS   10 PUEBLO-CATAWBA FARMERS

Note

1. This paper is related to a National Science Foundation Grant, GS-2951, awarded to Jorgensen and Driver, although it was not mentioned in the proposal to NSF nor funded by the grant. Kenny and Hudson received graduate credit for their work, and Engle, employed full time by the Indiana University Research Computing Center, wrote a program to repunch the cards and adapt them to Jorgensen's computer programs. The authors wish to thank G. P. Murdock for kindly sending us his worldwide data on over 1,200 societies on punch cards, from which the 273 North American societies were taken, and Joseph Jorgensen for his computer programs, without which we would not have begun this study. We also are grateful to Joseph Kenny, son of James A. Kenny, for coding data for the cross-classification tables and helping to draft Figure 1, and to Frank Moore of the Human Relations Area Files for sending us the number of lines of copy in each subject category of the files that we give in table 5.

Bibliography

Cramèr, H. 1946. Mathematical Methods of Statistics. Princeton.

Czekanowski, J. 1911. Objektive Kriterien in der Ethnologie. Korrespondenz-Blatt der Deutschen Gesellschaft für Anthropologie, Ethnologie und Urgeschichte 42: August-December, 1-5.

Driver, H. E. 1939. Culture Element Distributions: X Northwest California. University of California Anthropological Records 1: 297-433.

_____ 1962. The Contribution of A. L. Kroeber to Culture Area Theory and Practice. Indiana University Publications in Anthropology and Linguistics, Memoir 18.

_____ 1966. Geographical-Historical versus Psycho-Functional Explanations of Kin Avoidances. Current Anthropology 7: 131-160.

_____ 1969. Indians of North America, 2nd ed., rev. Chicago.

_____ 1970a. A Comment on "Evaluation of a Stratified versus an Unstratified Universe of Cultures in Comparative Research," by Lenora Greenbaum. Behavior Science Notes: 4: 284-287.

_____ 1970b. Statistical Studies of Continuous Geographical Distributions. A Handbook of Method in Cultural Anthropology, ed. R. Naroll and R. Cohen, pp. 620-639. New York.

Driver, H. E., and A. L. Kroeber. 1932. Quantitative Expression of Cultural Relationships. University of California Publications in American Archaeology and Ethnology 31: 211-256.

Ehrich, R. W., and G. M. Henderson. 1968. Culture Area. International Encyclopedia of the Social Sciences 3: 563-566.

Farrand, L. 1904. The Basis of American History. New York.

Helm, J., ed. 1968. Essays on the Problem of Tribe. Seattle.

Holmes, W. H. 1903. Classification and Arrangement of the Exhibits of an Anthropological Museum. Annual Report of the Smithsonian Institution for the year ending June 30, 1901, pp. 253-278.

Jorgensen, J. 1969. Salish Language and Culture. Indiana University Language Science Monographs 3.

Klimek, S. 1935. The Structure of California Indian Culture. University of California Publications in American Archaeology and Ethnology 37: 1-70.

Kroeber, A. L. 1904. Types of Indian Culture in California. University of California Publications in American Archaeology and Ethnology 2: 81-103.

_____ 1939. Cultural and Natural Areas of Native North America. University of California Publications in American Archaeology and Ethnology 38: 1-242, 28 maps.

Mason, O. T. 1896. Influence of Environment upon Human Industries or Arts. Annual Report of the Smithsonian Institution for 1895, pp. 639-665.

Murdock, G. P. 1967 (and later). Ethnographic Atlas. Pittsburgh: (The phrase "and later" refers to additional data and corrections published in _Ethnology_ through January, 1971).

_____ 1968. World Sampling Provinces. Ethnology 7: 305-326.

Murdock, G. P., and D. R. White. 1969. Standard Cross-cultural Sample. Ethnology 8: 329-369.

Murdock, G. P. _et al._ 1961. Outline of Cultural Materials. New Haven.

Naroll, R. 1964. On Ethnic Unit Classification. Current Anthropology 5: 283-312.

_____ 1970. Cross-Cultural Sampling. A Handbook of Method in Cultural Anthropology, ed. R. Naroll and R. Cohen, pp. 889-926. New York.

Naroll, R., and R. Cohen, eds. 1970. A Handbook of Method in Cultural Anthropology. New York.

Sokal, R. R. and P. H. A. Sneath. 1963. Principles of Numerical Taxonomy. San Francisco.

Spencer, R. F., and J. D. Jennings. 1965. The Native Americans. New York.

Voegelin, C. F., and F. M. Voegelin. 1966. Map of North American Indian Languages. Seattle: American Ethnological Society.

Wissler, C. 1906. Ethnic Types and Isolation. Science 23: 147-149.

_____ 1914. Material Cultures of the North American Indians. American Anthropologist 16: 447-505.

_____ 1917. The American Indian. New York.

3. Statistical Classification of North American Indian Ethnic Units from the Driver-Massey Sample

Harold E. Driver
and James L. Coffin

The paper above by Driver et al. (1972) was the first to classify the ethnic units of an entire continent with a numerical technique. The results, from Murdock's (1967; Murdock et al. 1962-) data, were so different from all intuitive culture area schemes that one of the goals of the study, to provide a better set of areas to be used for a stratified probability sample for intertrait correlations, was not achieved. At this writing Coffin and Driver are working on a similar type of statistical analysis of monograph length, based on the Driver and Massey 1957) sample. This short paper is a summary of the results so far.

The Driver-Massey data are about three-fourths material culture and technology and about one-fourth social organization or other nonmaterial culture. They were published on 163 maps, without any tables of the coded data. Our first step was to code a selection of 392 culture traits directly from the original copies of the maps, which were 11 by 17 inches in size and much easier to read than the smaller ones that had been published. We then proceeded to update the data by reading more recent sources and a few older ones that were missed in the original mapping.

We next reduced the number of ethnic units from the 273 used in the paper above to 245, largely by eliminating many of the Great Basin bands, which were as much alike as peas in a pod and would have been given too much weight for the intertrait correlations being run for the monograph in preparation. We also added a half dozen Mayan ethnic units, which Murdock had allocated to South America. This increased Murdock's sampling provinces from 34 or 35 to 36, and the Voegelins' language families from 55 to 56. These differences are so trivial that we have ignored them and exhibited Cramèr's coefficients based on these slight differences in numbers of ethnic units or language families in the same tables. Each of the 245 tribes in the present sample are coded by Murdock (1967; Murdock et al. 1962-), so that the two samples of cultural data may be combined if anyone chooses to do so.

The number of singletons in the tree diagram printout from the Driver-Massey sample were far fewer than those from the Murdock sample. For this reason we did not eliminate singletons in any of the groups derived from the Driver-Massey sample.

A glance at Maps 1 and 2 and at the tree diagram is sufficient to show that the statistical groups of tribes from the Driver-Massey sample are much nearer previous intuitive groupings than the statistical groups from the Murdock sample. Map 2 gives a nine-fold classification, but, because there are only two ethnic units (Seri and Karankawa) in one taxon, it is essentially an eight-fold scheme. The reason for choosing nine groups, instead of ten or any other number, is that this number of groups remains unchanged for a greater distance on the correlation scale of the tree diagram (from phi = .350 to .287) than any other number of groups.

These nine groups differ from recent intuitive culture area schemes by combining Northwest Coast with Plateau, California with the Great Basin, and the Northeast with the Southeast United States. However, at a bridge of phi = .350, the Northeast and Southeast split up, producing a ten-fold scheme, or nine without the Seri and Karankawa. The California-Basin combination does not begin to split up until a bridge of phi = .425 is reached, and the total number of groups is seventeen; and Central California does not separate from the Basin until a bridge of phi = .474 is reached and the total number of groups is twenty-three. Thus the California-Basin combination is internally more closely related than the Northeast-Southeast combination. The Northwest Coast-Plateau union does not subdivide until a bridge of phi = .455 is reached and the total number of groups is twenty. Thus the cohesion within this combination of areas is comparable with that for California and the Basin, and greater than that between Northeast and Southeast.

The Tarahumara in northwestern Mexico obviously does not belong in Meso-America. Driver and Massey relied almost exclusively on the twentieth-century field report of Bennett and Zingg, which apparently reflected considerable diffusion from Meso-America in the historic period.

In Table 1, the relations between the two statistical classifications, one from Murdock's sample and the other from the Driver-Massey sample, are given, and each is compared to a number of intuitive culture area schemes by means of Cramèr's coefficient. The relations among all intuitive groups are enclosed in the triangle. The obvious conclusion is that the Driver-Massey sample yields a much more conventional set of culture areas than does Murdock's sample. Thus a sample heavily loaded with material culture and technology produces a more conventional scheme of culture areas than one loaded heavily with nonmaterial culture. This is not surprising, because the early culture area classifiers were largely employed in museums, and so-called material culture is better reported in most field studies with a nineteenth-century or earlier time level than is nonmaterial culture. Material culture also diffuses more readily than nonmaterial culture and is more closely determined by geographical environment. Therefore, the Driver-Massey sample reflects geographical and historical factors more strongly than Murdock's sample, and its areas make a better set of "strata" from which to draw a stratified sample for intertrait cross-cultural correlations.

Comparisons of culture area schemes with the Voegelins' nine-language phyla and Georg N. Neumann's thirteen physical varieties of Indians are also given in Table 1. (Neumann's map gives fifteen physical varieties, but only thirteen occur among the tribes in the samples used in this paper.) The language phyla match the ten statistical areas derived from Murdock's sample more closely than the nine statistical areas derived from the Driver-Massey sample. The converse is true for physical types. However, when all seven of the Cramèr's coefficients between language phyla and the various culture area schemes are averaged, the result is .41. When the same is done for physical types, the average is .42. Furthermore, the Cramèr's coefficient between the language phyla and physical types is .41. Because Neumann never gave the data from which his classification of physical types was derived, and it is suspected that he was influenced to some extent by both cultural and linguistic classifications, we can say that he was influenced to an equal degree by both and was not heavily influenced by either. Cramèr's coefficients of .41 and .42 apparently show little more concordance than one would anticipate from the artifactual superimposition of two schemes of continuous or near-continuous areas on each other.

Table 2 gives Cramèr's coefficients for the relationships among large groups of thirty-five or thirty-six units and of fifty-five or fifty-six units. Comparisons among the thirty-five or thirty-six units are higher than anticipated, and Murdock's intuitive culture provinces match the two statistically determined sets equally well. Coefficients among the fifty-five- or fifty-six-unit groups are lower, as might be anticipated.

Bibliography

Driver, Harold E., James A. Kenny, Herschel C. Hudson, and Ora May Engle, 1972, "Statistical classification of North American Indian ethnic units, *Ethnology 11*: 311-39 (reprinted in this volume).

Driver, Harold E., and William C. Massey, 1957, "Comparative studies of North American Indians," *Transactions of the American Philosophical Society 47*: 165-460.

Murdock, George Peter, 1967, *Ethnographic Atlas: a summary*, Pittsburgh, University of Pittsburgh Press.

Murdock, George Peter, et al. 1962-, "Ethnographic atlas," *Ethnology 1* to date.

Neumann, Georg, n.d., *Varieties of American Indians* (fifteen physical varieties mapped from the Arctic to Panama on the base map of Driver et al. used in this article.

Table 1. Cramèr's Coefficients among Small Groups

	10 Statistical Areas, Murdock's Sample	9 Statistical Areas, Dr.-Mas. Sample	Driver's 10 Intuitive Areas	Murdock's 10 or 11 Intuitive Areas	Spen.-Jen.'s 10 Intuitive Areas	Kroeber's 7 Intuitive Areas	N.A. Hdbk. 11 Intuitive Areas	Voegelins' 9 Language Phyla	Neumann's 13 Physical Varieties
10 Statistical Areas, Murdock's Sample									
9 Statistical Areas, Dr.-Mas. Sample	.29								
Driver's 10 Intuitive Areas	.35	.69							
Murdock's 10 or 11 Intuitive Areas	.37	.53	.65						
Spen.-Jen.'s 10 Intuitive Areas	.27	.69	.76	.60					
Kroeber's 7 Intuitive Areas	.24[1]	.71	.64	.86	.52				
N.A. Hdbk. 11 Intuitive Areas	.28	.70	.79	.56	.88	.84			
Voegelins' 9 Language Phyla	.47[2]	.32	.35	.37	.32	.61	.40		
Neumann's 13 Physical Varieties	.27	.43	.45	.37	.45	.51	.47	.41	
Kroeber's 7 Intuitive Levels of Intensity	.29[1]	.29	.40	.52	.43	.28	.43	.54	.34

[1]Derived from 7 statistical groups from Murdock's sample.
[2]Derived from 9 statistical groups from Murdock's sample.

Table 2. Cramèr's Coefficients among Large Groups

	Murdock's 34 or 36 Intuitive Sampling Provinces	35 or 36 Statistical Groups, Murdock's Sample	55 or 56 Statistical Groups, Murdock's Sample	55 or 56 Statistical Groups, Driver-Massey Sample
Murdock's 34 or 36 Intuitive Sampling Provinces				
35 or 36 Statistical Groups, Murdock's Sample	.49			
35 or 36 Statistical Groups, Driver-Massey Sample	.50	.38		
55 or 56 Statistical Groups, Driver-Massey Sample			.43	
Voegelins' 55 or 56 Language Families			.29	.33

Figure 1   Diagram of 36 Statistical Groups; Phi Coefficients.

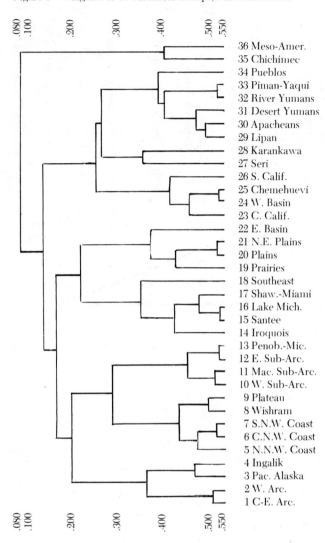

more volatile, and often blend so rapidly that, without the help of linguistic and other evidence, it would be impossible to reconstruct the earlier cultures that became blended.

Fortunately, in native North America, language units and ethnic units correspond fairly closely, because field workers have tended to equate them. Therefore most distinct ethnic units are also distinct language units. The most glaring exceptions to this somewhat oversimplified statement occur in the Arctic, Sub-Arctic, and Great Basin areas. In the Arctic, the Central-Greenlandic Eskimo language extends in a chain of mutual intelligibility all the way from about the mouth of the Yukon River in Alaska to eastern Greenland. In the Sub-Arctic area, the Cree-Montagnais-Naskapi language is spread from Alberta to Labrador. In the Great Basin area, the Shoshoni language extends from California to Wyoming to Texas (Comanche). Where single languages cover such wide territories, ethnographers invariably find significant differences in the cultures in the parts of these territories and assign separate labels to them.

Although genetic language classification is controversial to the specialists engaged in refining it, it is more objective than present classifications of cultures into areas, provinces, or clusters. So far no one has published a continentalwide scheme of culture groups determined in any objective manner, although Driver, Kenny, Hudson, Engle (ms. [1971]) have such a study in typescript.[*] The largest published statistical study at this writing is still that of Klimek (1935), who employed sixty ethnic units and 400 culture traits. Jorgensen (1969) grouped twenty-eight Salish "tribes" from 285 culture traits, covering almost as wide a range of culture and social inventory as did Klimek.

4. Culture Groups and Language Groups in Native North America[1]

Harold E. Driver

Any discussion of the relation of linguistic groups to culture groups must be concerned with the nature of the language bearing unit and the culture bearing unit. In most cases, language units are easier to define and distinguish, because, when two or more languages come in contact, speakers almost always use one or the other rather than a blend of two or more. This is not true of culture bearing units, which we shall call ethnic units, because their cultures are less structured than their languages, are

Nominal Categories of Language and Culture

This paper will begin by treating language groupings and culture groupings as nominal categories and matching them in cross-classification tables in which the frequencies are the number of languages, dialects, and/or ethnic units shared by each combination of a language group and a culture group. Table 1 is such a table. The nine principal statistical groups of cultures were determined by a Q-type correlational analysis of Murdock's (1967 and later) sample. Forty-nine of Murdock's variables (columns) and the 279 culture traits in them constitute the sample of cultural and social inventory.

---

[*][Since published (1971) in *Ethnology 11:* 311-39.]

Table 1. Cross-Classification of the Voegelins' Nine Language Phyla and the
Driver et al. (Ms. [1971] Nine Principal Statistical Groups of Cultures

	Hunters-Gatherers	Fishers	S.W. Farmers	Meso-American Farmers	Midwest-S.W. Farmers	East Farmers	Mexican Farmers	Missouri River Farmers	Pueblo-Catawba Farmers	Total
	1	2	3	4	5	6	7	8	9	
I Arctic-Paleosiberian	9	6	0	0	0	0	0	0	0	15
II Na-Dene	17	14	2	0	0	0	0	0	0	33
III Macro-Algonquian	18	7	0	0	5	4	0	0	0	34
IV Macro-Siouan	7	0	0	0	5	4	0	4	1	21
V Hokan	16	3	0	0	5	0	0	0	0	24
VI Penutian	13	10	0	0	0	0	4	0	1	28
VII Aztec-Tanoan	59	0	0	1	0	0	2	0	7	69
VIII Undetermined or Other	12	21	0	1	0	1	0	0	5	40
IX Oto-Manguean	2	0	0	0	0	0	2	0	0	4
Total	153	61	2	2	15	9	8	4	14	268

Chi-square = 1013.   Cramèr's f² = .472

Each of 273 ethnic units was compared with every other one by determining the percentage of culture traits shared. Following Jorgensen (1969) we used both the phi and G coefficients. The latter was first used by Driver in Driver and Kroeber (1932), and has been rediscovered several times since, most notably by Ellegard (1959). The correlation of phi and G for the 37,128 combinations of 273 "tribes" taken two at a time was .974 for Karl Pearson's r, and .975 for his eta. Such a high relationship shows that there is no significant difference between cultural groups determined by the two coefficients. This plethora of coefficients was reduced to the nine principal cultural groups of Table 1 by Jorgensen's (1969) tree diagram computer program. The huge number of Aztec-Tanoans is caused by Murdock's having included every Great Basin band in his cultural sample. Most of these band differences in language were at the dialect level.

The overall strength of the relationship in any cross-classification table can be measured by Cramèr's (1946: 441-45) coefficient:

$$f^2 = \frac{\chi^2}{N(Q-1)}$$

where χ^2 is chi-square, N the total number of cases, and Q the number of rows or columns, whichever is fewer, in this case nine. For a 2 x 2 table, this coefficient equals phi-square. The value of .472 given in Table 1 is easily significant, although an exact probabilistic statement cannot be derived from the chi-square, because too many of the expected frequencies fall below five. By combining categories, however, their number can be reduced and the expected frequencies raised high enough for a significant test. This will be done below.

The Voegelins' (1966) nine language phyla were also compared with a number of other classifications of culture with the following Cramèr's coefficients resulting:

Kroeber's (1939: map 6) seven culture areas	.61
Kroeber's (1939: map 28) seven levels of cultural intensity	.54
Spencer's and Jennings' (1965) culture areas, reduced to ten units	.32
Murdock's (1967) ten culture areas	.37
Driver's (1969: map 2) culture areas, reduced to ten units	.35

Because the first is the highest value in the list, we give the entire cross-classification table in Table 2. The frequencies in this table are numbers of languages, dialects, and/or ethnic units and the sample is that of Murdock (1967 and later).

In Table 3, the column of each cell in Table 2 has been opposed to all the other columns, and the row of each cell to all the other rows to form sixty-three 2 x 2 tables, and a phi coefficient computed for each. In Table 4 is given a simple frequency distribution of the phis in Table 3. There is only one perfect relationship, that between the Arctic culture area and the Arctic-Paleosiberian language phylum.

Table 2. Cross-Classification of Kroeber's Seven Culture Areas
and the Voegelins' Nine Language Phyla

	Arctic-Paleosiberian	Na-Dene	Macro-Algonquian	Macro-Siouan	Hokan	Penutian	Aztec-Tanoan	Undetermined, Other	Oto-Manguean	Total
	I	II	III	IV	V	VI	VII	VIII	IX	
A Arctic Coast	16	0	0	0	0	0	0	0	0	16
NW Northwest Coast	0	6	2	0	1	7	0	18	0	34
SW Southwest	0	6	0	0	13	1	16	5	0	41
I Intermediate	0	5	0	0	10	16	46	14	0	91
E Eastern	0	1	21	21	1	0	5	2	0	51
N Northern	0	15	13	0	0	0	0	0	0	28
M Mexican	0	0	0	0	0	4	3	1	4	12
Total	16	33	36	21	25	28	70	40	4	273

Chi-square = 1001. Cramèr's f^2 = .611

However, the modest number of high and medium positive values is enough to produce the relatively high Cramèr's coefficient of .611. Where no languages or ethnic units are shared by a phylum and an area, the phi value is not a perfect negative (-1.00) but a low negative (00 to -.29). These low negatives make up 73 percent of the phis, because most phyla and areas share no common languages or ethnic units.

Driver et al. (Ms. [1971]) found a Cramèr's coefficient of only .24 between their seven principal sta-tistical groups and Kroeber's seven culture areas. Because this was the lowest value in their study, they combined a few categories and reduced this 7 x 7 table to a 4 x 5 table. This raised the expected frequencies to an acceptable level for a chi-square test, and this value was 277. The probability of obtaining such a high chi-square by an accident of sampling is too low to appear in any table of chi-square probabilities, and is probably about only one in a billion. If such a low (.24) Cramèr's coefficient is so highly significant, it seems obvious that all the

Table 3. Phi Coefficients Between Kroeber's Seven Culture Areas and the Voegelins' Nine Language Phyla

	Arctic-Paleosiberian	Na-Dene	Macro-Algonquian	Macro-Siouan	Hokan	Penutian	Aztec-Tanoan	Undetermined, Other	Oto-Manguean
A Arctic Coast	+1.00	-.09	-.10	-.04	-.04	-.08	-.15	-.10	-.03
NW Northwest Coast	-.09	+.06	-.08	-.09	-.08	+.13	-.22	+.41	+.05
SW Southwest	-.11	+.03	-.16	-.12	+.33	-.11	+.13	-.03	-.05
I Intermediate	-.16	-.21	-.27	-.20	+04	+.17	+.40	+.01	-.09
E Eastern	-.12	-.15	+.41	+.60	-.12	-.16	-.17	-.15	-.06
N Northern	-.08	+.43	+.33	-.10	-.11	-.11	-.20	-.14	-.04
M Mexican	-.05	-.06	-.08	-.06	-.07	+.16	.00	-.04	+.57

cross-classification tables in this study and that of Driver et al. (Ms. [1971]) would pass this significance test.

Does the above test prove the relationships in these cross-classification tables are linguistically and culturally significant? The answer is an unequivocal no. Driver (1966: 158) combined some states in the United States and provinces in Canada and obtained a statistically significant correlation between Indian kin avoidances and these modern political units. It should be remembered that none of the groupings of languages or cultures compared in this paper are geographically random to begin with. All such groups tend to cluster in continuous or near-continuous patches. When two sets of such nonrandom clusters are compared, it is inevitable that the overall relationship will be statistically significant. This is as true for the inanimate rocks and soils of geologists and geographers and for the animate fauna and flora of biologists as it is for language and human culture. Therefore there need be no causal relationship between a language group and a culture group for the two to be coterminous or to show a significant overlap in geographical distribution. Such a relationship is a matter of history, either a common social inheritance of a modern language and culture from an ancient protolanguage and protoculture or common migration to a new region and parallel change in culture and perhaps some diffusion of language as well as culture among members of the

Table 4. Frequency Distribution of Correlations (Phis) Among Kroeber's Seven Culture Areas and the Voeglins' Nine Language Phyla

+.91	to	1.00	1
+.81	to	.90	0
+.71	to	.80	0
+.61	to	.70	1
+.51	to	.60	1
+.41	to	.50	3
+.31	to	.40	3
+.21	to	.30	0
+.11	to	.20	4
+.01	to	.10	4
.00	to	-.09	23
-.10	to	-.19	18
-.20	to	-.29	5
	Total (N)		63

same family or phylum. An indefinite amount of historical speculation could be written about the relations of language and culture groups, but it is sufficient to refer the reader to Taylor (1961), where archeological groups are compared with linguistic groups.

Table 5. Correlations (Phis) Among Driver's (1961) Culture areas and Selected
Language Families (Driver and Sanday 1966: 172-73)

	Plateau	Great Basin	W. Arctic	Central and E. Arctic	Southwest	E. Sub-Arctic	Northwest Coast	Yukon Sub-Arctic	Mackenzie Sub-A.	East	Plains	Prairies	California	Meso-America
Salish	+.45	-.10	-.05	-.06	-.13	-.08	+.47	-.06	-.07	-.08	-.08	-.11	-.13	-.10
Uto-Aztecan	-.11	+.66	-.06	-.07	+.12	-.09	-.17	-.07	-.08	-.10	+.07	-.13	+.01	-.04
Eskimo-Aleut	-.06	-.06	+.67	+.73	-.09	-.05	-.09	-.04	-.04	-.05	-.05	-.07	-.08	-.06
Algonkian	-.09	-.10	-.05	-.06	-.13	+.64	-.14	-.06	-.07	+.07	+.16	+.26	-.13	-.10
Caddoan	-.03	-.04	-.02	-.02	-.05	-.03	-.05	-.02	-.03	+.21	-.03	+.24	-.05	-.04
Wakashan	-.04	-.04	-.02	-.02	-.06	-.03	+.37	-.02	-.03	-.04	-.04	-.05	-.05	-.04
Athapaskan	-.09	-.10	-.05	-.06	+.03	-.08	+.02	+.45	+.54	-.09	+.06	-.11	-.06	-.10
Muskogean	-.03	-.03	-.02	-.02	-.05	-.03	-.05	-.02	-.02	+.51	-.03	-.04	-.04	-.03
Siouan	-.06	-.07	-.04	-.04	-.09	-.05	-.10	-.04	-.05	-.06	+.15	+.59	-.09	-.07
Mayan	-.04	-.05	-.03	-.03	-.07	-.04	-.07	-.03	-.03	-.04	-.04	-.05	-.06	+.60

Driver and Sanday (1966: 172-73) gave a 50 x 50 table of phi coefficients between certain aspects of social structure, kin avoidances, language families, and culture areas. Those between language families and culture areas are presented again in Table 5. They are based on 277 language and/or culture units, a minority of which do not appear in Murdock's sample of 273 units. About three-fourths of the ethnic units in each sample are shared with the other, but the Driver-Sanday sample includes only a few Great Basin bands. These phis in Table 5 based on language families are comparable to those of Table 3 based on language phyla. Most culture areas show at least one substantial, positive relationship to a language family and some two or three. Similarly, all language families have one or more substantial, positive relationships to culture areas. The frequency distribution of these relationships in Table 6 shows that most phi values are in the low negative range, because most combinations of language families and culture areas share no languages or "tribes" at all. This parallels the results from comparing language phyla and culture groups.

Driver et al. (Ms. [1971]) also compared all of the Voegelins' (1966) language families present in Murdock's (1967 and later) sample with the same number of statistically determined culture groups from

Table 6. Frequency Distribution of Correlations (Phis) Among Driver's (1961) Culture Areas and Selected Language Families (Driver and Sanday 1966: 172-73)

+.71	to	.80	1
+.61	to	.70	3
+.51	to	.60	4
+.41	to	.50	3
+.31	to	.40	1
+.21	to	.30	3
+.11	to	.20	3
+.01	to	.10	6
.00	to	-.09	98
-.10	to	-.19	18
	Total (N)		140

the same sample. There were fifty-five language families, including singletons (language isolates), and these were compared with fifty-five culture "groups," about half of which were singletons. The Cramèr's coefficient for this 55 x 55 table was only .29, a relatively low value. The explanation seems to be that as groups become more numerous and

232

contain fewer and fewer members each, in this case about half singletons, they do not match each other as well. They are more nearly random than larger geographical groups. This would also seem to apply to any geographical clusters as well as to those of language and culture.

Similarity Coefficients in Language-Culture Comparison

Jorgensen (1969) was the first to use both the percentages of "culture free" cognate words shared and the percentages of culture traits shared to show the relation of language and culture in a scatter diagram and to reduce it to two values of a single coefficient, Karl Pearson's eta. He found that the overall relation between Salish language and culture given by the two eta-squares was .508 and .390 (Jorgensen 1969: 107). The square roots of these values of eta are .713 and .624, unexpectedly high curvilinear relationships. Here I apply the same method to the Athapaskan, Salish, Uto-Aztecan, and Yuman languages and cultures, using the G coefficient for culture similarity computed from Murdock's (1967 and later) data.

Eta values between these measures of linguistic and cultural similarity within four language families are presented, along with their scatter diagrams and regression lines: Athapaskan, Figure 1; Salish, Figure 2; Uto-Aztecan, Figure 3; and Yuman, Figure 4. The following sources were used for the lexicostatistical

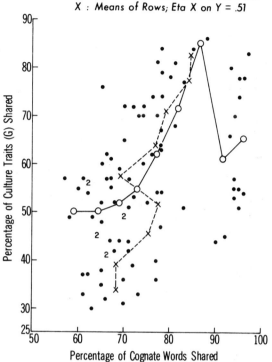

Figure 1. Athapaskan Language and Culture
O : Means of Columns; Eta Y on X = .55
X : Means of Rows; Eta X on Y = .51

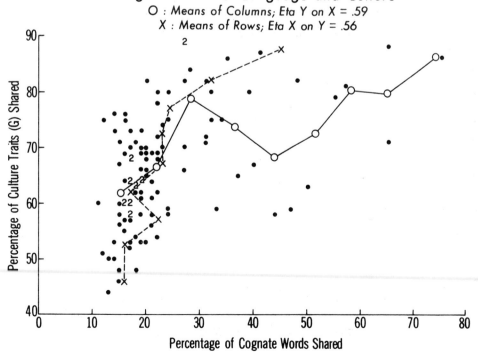

Figure 2. Salish Language and Culture
O : Means of Columns; Eta Y on X = .59
X : Means of Rows; Eta X on Y = .56

233

Figure 3. Uto-Aztecan Language and Culture
O : Means of Columns; Eta Y on X = .71
X : Means of Rows; Eta X on Y = .74

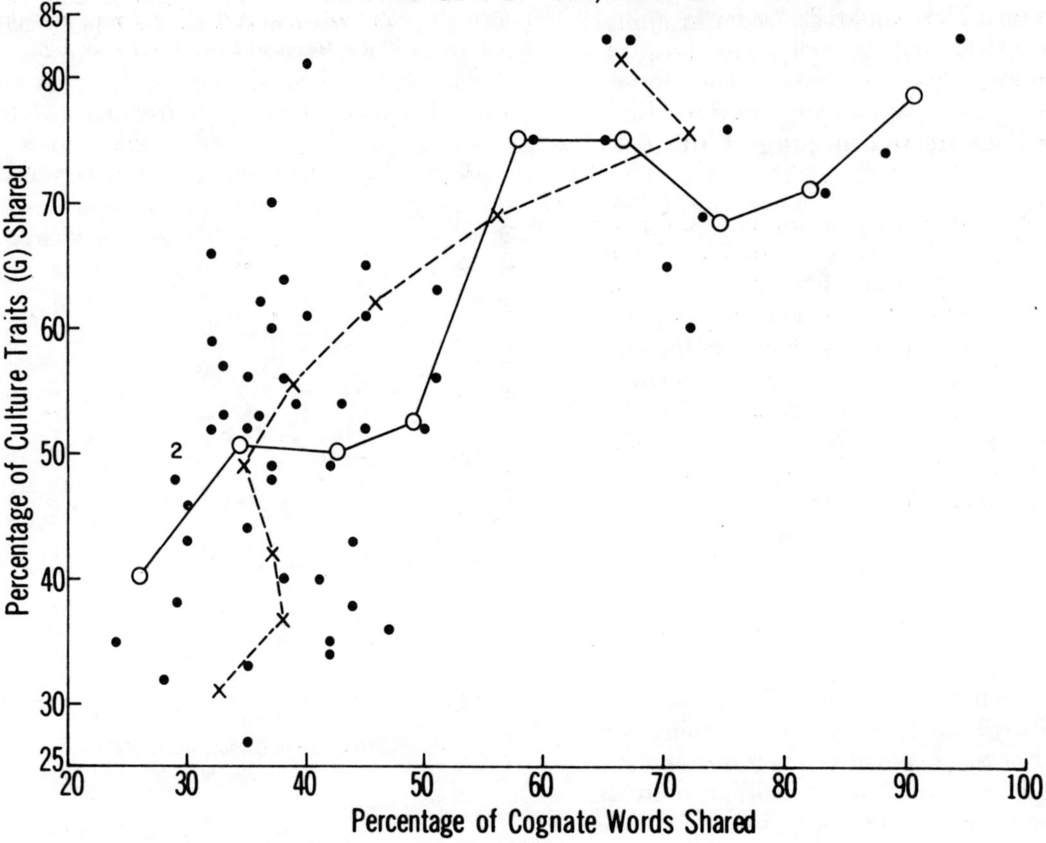

Figure 4. Yuman Language and Culture
O : Means of Columns; Eta Y on X = .60
X : Means of Rows; Eta X on Y = .85

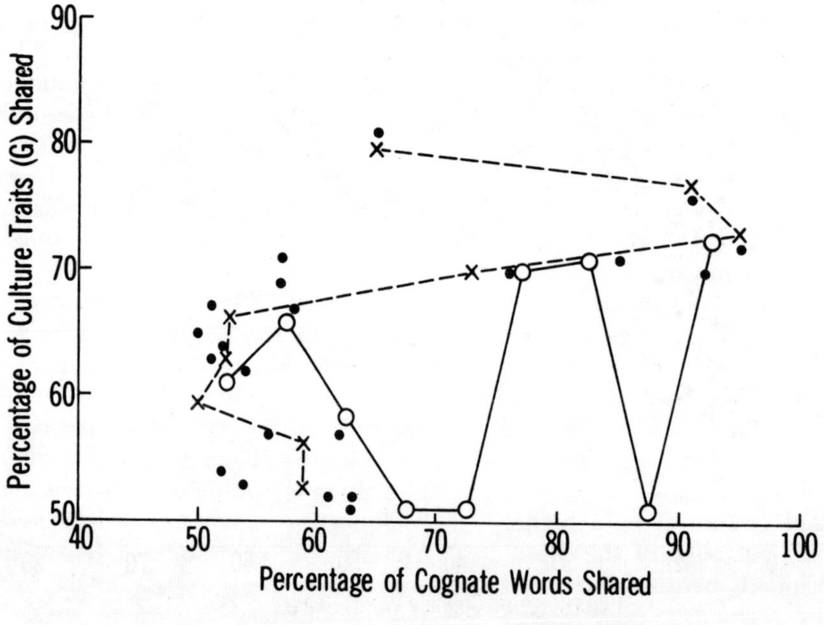

data: Athapaskan (Hoijer 1956, 1962; Kroeber 1959); Salish (Jorgensen 1969); Uto-Aztecan (Hale 1958); Yuman (Winter 1957). All relationships are positive and curvilinear, and the eta values range from .51 to .85.

My Salish relationships are lower than those found by Jorgensen (1969), apparently because Murdock's culture trait categories are broader and less specific on the whole than those of Jorgensen. The latter's trait list includes more material culture, technology, and religion, and less social organization than does Murdock's list.

with the sixteenth-century cultures. Had a sizeable number of sixteenth-century Uto-Aztecans in Meso-America been included, the enormous differences in culture between them and the others would surely have lowered the relationship.

Athapaskan and Salish present an interesting contrast: Athapaskan shows a short range (57 to 97) in percentage of cognate words shared, and a longer range (30 to 86) in percentage of culture traits shared; Salish shows just the opposite, a long range (11 to 75) in percentage of cognate words shared, and a shorter range (44 to 89) in percentage of culture

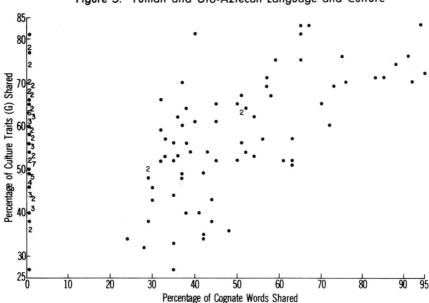

Figure 5. Yuman and Uto-Aztecan Language and Culture

The relations between Athapaskan languages and cultures are expectedly the lowest, because the relatively recent and rapid dispersal of these peoples has brought about less change in languages than in culture. The acculturation of the Oregon and California Athapaskans to the earlier cultures in those areas was virtually complete, while the acculturation of the Apacheans in the Southwest to Pueblo cultures was at best half achieved by the Navaho, with the others shading off to a much lower figure, and the Kiowa-Apache remaining wholly Plains.

The Yuman language and culture relationships are relatively high, with the River versus Desert Yumans showing relatively high relationships in both language and culture within each group and considerably lower relationships between the two groups.

Uto-Aztecan language and culture gives a higher relationship than anticipated, but none of the Meso-American groups were included, because the word lists from modern villages seemed a poor match

traits shared. We have already mentioned the relatively recent, rapid, and geographically extensive migrations of the Athapaskans. The Salish, in contrast, all are located in a continuous geographical area, except for the Bella Coola and Tillamook, and their cultures have had less reason to change over the millenia because they are located in only two ecological areas, Northwest Coast and Plateau, which differ less from each other than the Sub-Arctic, Northwest Coast, and Southwest of the Athapaskans. The glottochronological estimate of time depth for language change is about twice as great for Salish as for Athapaskan.

In Figure 5, the Yuman and Uto-Aztecan relations between language and culture are combined in a single scatter diagram. Because these language families are in separate phyla as well, the percentages of "culture free" cognate words shared between every Yuman and every Uto-Aztecan language will be zero. These zeros appear in the vertical column on the zero ordinate (extreme left). The cross-family and cross-phylum relations of the cultures, in contrast, range from 27 to 81. Because this split frequency distribution with a mode of zero for the language data lacks continuity, I have not computed etas for the relationship. However, it is obvious that combining two language families from two distinct phyla lowers the relation between language and culture. If I had combined all four language families in this manner, the proportion of zero cognate words shared would have been much higher and the relation of language and culture much lower. The more phyla compared in this manner, the lower the relation of language and culture.

Note

[1]This paper is related to a National Science Foundation Grant, GS-2951, awarded to Joseph Jorgensen and the author, although it was not mentioned in the proposal to NSF and was not funded by the grant. The computer programs used are those of Jorgensen (1969: Appendix A), who generously sent them to me on punch cards. I also wish to thank G. P. Murdock for sending me his worldwide data on more than 1,200 societies on punch cards, from which the 273 North American societies used in this paper are taken. I am further grateful to James A. Kenny, Herschel C. Hudson, and Ora May Engle for updating and repunching the cards and otherwise adapting the data to the hardware in Indiana University's Research Computer Center and running the programs. I also owe a debt to James A. Kenny for writing the cross-classification program for Cramèr's coefficient, and to Martha Kendall for assembling the lexicostatistical data.

References

Cramèr, Harald, 1946, *Mathematical methods of statistics*, Princeton, Princeton University Press.

Driver, Harold E., 1961, *Indians of North America*, Chicago, University of Chicago Press.

1966, "Geographical-historical versus psycho-functional explanations of kin avoidances," *Current Anthropology* 7: 131-60 [reprinted in this volume].

1969, *Indians of North America*, 2d rev. ed., Chicago, University of Chicago Press.

Driver, Harold E., James A. Kenny, Herschel C. Hudson, and Ora M. Engle
Ms. [1971], *Statistical classification of North American Indian ethnic units*. [Since published (1971) in *Ethnology 11*: 311-39, and reprinted in this volume].

Driver, Harold E., and Alfred L. Kroeber, 1932, "Quantitative expression of cultural relationships," *University of California Publications in American Archaeology and Ethnology 31*: 211-56 [reprinted in this volume].

Driver, Harold E., and Peggy R. Sanday, 1966, "Factors and clusters of kin avoidances and related variables," *Current Anthropology 6*: 139-76.

Ellegard, Alvar, 1959, "Statistical measurement of linguistic relationship," *Language 35*: 131-57.

Hale, Kenneth, 1958, "Internal diversity in Uto-Aztecan: I," *International Journal of American Linguistics 24*: 101-07.

Hoijer, Harry, 1956, "The chronology of the Athapaskan languages," *International Journal of American Linguistics 22*: 219-32.

1962, "Linguistic subgrouping by glottochronology and by the comparative method," *Lingua 11*: 192-98.

Jorgensen, Joseph G., 1969, "Salish language and culture: a statistical analysis of internal relationships, history and evolution," *Indiana University Language Science Monographs 3*.

Klimek, Stanislaw, 1935, "Culture element distributions: I: the structure of California Indian Culture," *University of California Publications in American Archaeology and Ethnology 37*: 1-70.

Kroeber, Alfred L., 1939, "Cultural and natural areas of native North America," *University of California Publications in American Archaeology and Ethnology 38*: 1-242, 28 maps.

1959, "Reflections on Athapaskan glottochronology," *University of California Publications in American Archaeology and Ethnology 47*: 241-58.

Murdock, George Peter, 1967, *Ethnographic atlas: a summary*, University of Pittsburgh Press. (The phrase "and later" associated with this reference refers to subsequent issues of *Ethnology* through January 1970, where additional data are published.)

Spencer, Robert F., and Jesse D. Jennings, eds., 1965, *The native Americans*, New York, Harper and Row.

Taylor, Walter W., 1961, "Archaeology and language in Western North America," *American Antiquity 27*: 71-81.

Voegelin, C. F., and F. M. Voegelin, 1966, *Map of North American Indian languages*, Seattle, University of Washington Press (American Ethnological Society).

Winter, Werner. 1957, Yuman language I: first impressions," *International Journal of American Linguistics 23*: 18-23.

5. On the Concepts of "Culture Area" and "Language Culture"

Richard Paul Chaney

Well, I am very pleased except that I stand in the way of younger men [Galton's private comment upon receiving the Darwin medal, quoted in Pearson 1914-30, 3A:237].

I

From a present vantage point, a fundamental anthropological perplexity has been to what extent there are regularities in psychohistorical phenomena. Essentially, some have stressed some form of invariant relationship; whereas others have gestured at some degree and kind of spatial-temporal clustering of psychohistorical phenomena. The one sought similarities; the other stressed differences. An interrelated fundamental perplexity has been the nature of these "universal categories of culture" (Kluckhohn 1953). A number of writers (Bidney 1953, 1967; Kroeber and Kluckhohn 1952; Kluckhohn 1953; Wallace 1961, 1970; Leach 1968; Singer 1968; Stocking 1968; Barnes 1971) have emphasized rather profound conceptual differences in the patterning of "understanding" for the details of human explanation, emotion, and action in the "discipline" of anthropology.

In retrospect, the work of Harold E. Driver can be appreciated as an extended attempt to help sort out some discussions in the history of anthropology through explicit, comparative, statistical studies, with special attention to the details of North American Indian ethnology. Driver's task has not been to utter merely some prose-laden principle first, but rather to evaluate two major abstract explanatory frames in the history of anthropology,—historical-diffusional and functional-causal—in terms of their coordination with empirical data.

The conceptual plots in the history of the numerical classification that Driver's work on the concept of "culture area" fits into are quite complex and poorly understood at present. An initial problem is the lack of a community of awareness as to how there are a number of somewhat diverse discussions going on among even comparative-statistical researchers. In general, comparative-statistical studies have employed various samples of ethnic units sprinkled around the world and expressed deviations from nonpredictability as indicating some form of functional and/or causal relations between variables. Much of the contemporary comparative-statistical work has its conceptual roots in the first worldwide statistical analysis by Edward B. Tylor: "On a method of investigating the development of institutions applied to the laws of marriage and descent" (1889).

Sir Francis Galton (in Tylor 1889: 270), who helped to construct much of the foundation of statistical inference as we know it today, criticized Tylor's evolutionary interpretation of the "adhesions" (or "associations") in terms of the cases not being historically independent. The conceptual thrust of Galton was at the meaning of the deviations from nonpredictability. From a statistical point of view, the cases (ethnic units) of seemingly joint occurrence of sociocultural phenomena would have a different meaning (a) if they were all historically independent of each other versus (b) if they were historically interconnected to some degree. Further, following his own lead in plotting wind and pressure maps which led to the concept of "anticyclone" in *Meteorographica: Or, Methods of Mapping the Weather* (1863), Galton suggested that insight into the nature of the relationships discussed by Tylor might be derived through mapping their distribution.

The underlying conceptual framework, in much of the discussion by few individuals who have realized that there are perplexities, has been that there is one basic deviation from nonpredictability and that Galton's problem is merely one of inflation (or deflation) of cell frequencies that are statistically summarized. At the present time, the concepts of "frequency distribution" and "probability distribution" are intimately intertwined. Although the early statistical work of the 1880s by Francis Galton and Karl Pearson indicated that distributions of living material were often skewed or asymmetrical, no one has come to grips with the masking effects of coefficients of association for data summaries of psychohistorical phenomena which are heterogeneous not only with respect to single variables but also in terms of sometimes diverse configurations.

Driver's work has more of its historical roots in Boas' 1894 study of 214 elements (motifs, incidents, and tale types) of North American Indian tales and myths among twelve ethnic units. Driver (1970: 620-21), in the only comprehensive account of statistical studies of continuous geographical distributions of sociocultural phenomena, summarized Boas' principal conclusions of his 1894 and 1916 studies of folklore motifs as follows:

1. Neighboring peoples share more folklore inventory than distant peoples. The ethnic units in the continuous areas on the Northwest Coast and Plateau share more with each other than with the Ponca, Micmac,

interior Athapaskan group. Therefore very strong diffusions among neighboring peoples have taken place. 2. Tribes speaking languages of the same family show significantly greater internal similarity with each other. Thus Boas distinguishes the culture heritage-migration explanation of resemblances from the diffusion one which must be postulated for elements spilling over language family fences. 3. Most resemblances do not arise independently from "elementary ideas" shared by all peoples on the earth, but are determined by contacts of peoples. . . . 4. The elements (motifs) of a particular tale type or tale cycle tend to diffuse independently of each other as well as independently of the larger tale unit, which never diffuses as a whole. 5. The elements assembled in a tale type of a single society, however, are reinterpreted and integrated into each local literary style. 6. There is no way to tell which version of a tale type is prior historically and by this means to arrange them in an historical or evolutionary sequence. These and the earlier conclusions of 1894 gave rise to the theory of culture which Lowie (1920: 441) phrased as "that planless hodgepodge, that thing of shreds and patches called civilization. . . ." [Driver 1970 620-21].

In retrospect, one might say that Boas was providing an explicit empirical demonstration of what Galton had presented as a conceptual problem. Unfortunately, almost to a person, recent comparative statistical attempts of the worldwide variety have completely ignored the implication of the "continuously distributed ethnic units" approach. Driver has been almost alone until recently in stressing the value of examining continuously distributed ethnic units (see Chaney 1971, n.d.).

II

"Comparative studies of North American Indians" by Driver and Massey (1957) was essentially a "series of broad generalizations about North American Indian cultures together with the data on which they are based. Most of the data are given on a series of schematic maps on which territories of individual 'tribes' are differentiated by means of boundary lines" (Driver and Massey 1957: 165). These new mapped data were held to represent a further step toward integrating knowledge of North American Indian ethnic units in the tradition of Wissler (1917) and Kroeber (1939).

> The generalizations offered are of two major kinds, which may be called descriptive and relational. The descriptive generalizations are concerned primarily with the geographical distributions of single traits or small clusters of variants on a single topic. The

relational generalizations are concerned with the correlations between the traits of one topic with those of another topic, which is often described in another chapter. We have attempted to indicate only the most obvious correlations except in the last chapter. [Driver and Massey 1957: 165].

This last chapter was based mainly on Driver's (1956) paper, "An integration of functional, evolutionary, and historical theory by means of correlations." The lead in transition to this paper as the last chapter expresses an essential view of Driver.

> Up to this point the authors have been content with an essentially empirical presentation of facts distributed in space and, less frequently, in time. This has been done as simply as possible with the minimum of controversial interpretation of the distributed data. We believe that classification and distribution of data in space and time can be accomplished without recourse to fine-spun and tenuous theories of interpretation. At the same time we have no objection to speculative elaboration as long as it is not confused with a straightforward presentation of the data on which it is based. Other social scientists have criticized anthropology for its plethora of unproven theoretical notions, its paucity of objective methods to demonstrate theory, its common confusion of fact with inference and of typological classification with spatial and temporal position. Rouse (1955) has recently untangled some of the confusion in archaeology. We hope to do the same for certain aspects of ethnology.
>
> The history of ethnological theory bristles with the conflicts among evolutionists, culture historians, and functionalists, each of whom has often explained or accounted for geographical distributions of ethnographic data in a manner not at all acceptable to the other two groups. Although at the present time a more eclectic attitude is taken for granted, and recent histories of ethnological theory manage to find something of value in each of these approaches, an adequate integration of the three has seldom been attempted [Driver and Massey 1957: 421-22].

Driver evaluated this paper as the first statistical attempt at integrating the culture area-diffusion approach of Wissler and Kroeber with the cross-cultural-evolutionary method of Murdock and Whiting. In this paper, Driver examined the relationship between division of labor in subsistence pursuits, residence, land tenure, descent, and kinship terminology in a sample of 280 North American Indian ethnic units. In 1956, the paper was thought to confirm for the most part the developmental cycle from division of labor to residence to descent to kinship terminology which had been postulated by Murdock in his 1949 book, *Social Structure*. Essentially, the relationships that are discussed are interpreted with functional theory, and negative instances are viewed as the result of historical-diffusional factors.

In 1961, Driver presented an expansion of "Comparative studies of North American Indians" under the title *Indians of North America*. This volume is topically arranged, but discusses each topic in terms of areas of continuously distributed traits and impressionistic culture areas. In the preface, Driver enunciates his basic view of "culture areas" as an organizing device for phenomena expressing diverse areas of historical spread when viewed individually:

> The variation in language and way of life of the Indians of North America was much greater than that in Europe at the time America was discovered by Europeans. There were literally thousands of Indian societies, each with its separate territory, language, or culture. In a broad work of this kind it is impossible even to mention each of these distinct ethnic units, but by grouping them into culture areas, one can study the essentials of their ways of life without getting lost in a plethora of detail [Driver 1961: v-vi].

> The time level varies from the sixteenth century for the Aztecs and their neighbors in Mexico to the nineteenth for the Indians of about half the United States and most of Canada. Some peoples became extinct, at least as independent cultures and languages, before others were discovered, making it impossible to limit the time span of a work of continental scope even to a single century. To have salted in the proper century or decade to which each section or paragraph referred would have turned the book into a technical monograph unsuitable as an introduction to its subject. Someday, a competent ethnohistorian will write such a monograph, but so far every major synthesis on the Indians of North America has telescoped the time scale in favor of geographical differentiation and the culture area concept. I have attempted to describe Indian cultures as they were before serious disturbance by Whites, but, because no written records of any consequence were left by Indians before White contact, reliance almost exclusively on the writings of Europeans makes it impossible to rule out European influence altogether [Driver 1961: vi-vii].

> Diffusion as a process of culture change has been given considerable attention because it has been neglected for at least a decade . . . [Driver 1961: vi].

At about the same time, Driver (1962) published a succinct acknowledgment of "The contributions of A. L. Kroeber to culture area theory and practice." This is the best overall summary of the development and use of the concept of "culture area" with North American Indian data.

In 1966, Driver re-examined Tylor's original study of kin avoidance, in which Tylor had found relationships between marital residence and kin avoidances. Central to Driver's re-examination was a "new method of measuring the potency of geograph-ical-historical versus psycho-functional explanations of comparative data" (Driver 1966: 147). Language families and culture areas were employed as variables and correlated with residence, descent, kinship terminology, and avoidance. Unlike other cross-cultural researchers, who assume that they control for the Tylor-Galton problem by using samples of societies geographically sprinkled around the world, Driver incorporated the Tylor-Galton problem into his research. Rather than reading the answer off from correlation coefficients, he examined the extent of the diffusion across language families and culture areas with a sample of 277 nearly continuously distributed ethnic units of North American Indians.

As Driver (1966: 134, 141) has emphasized: "The hop-skip-and-jump character of geographical distributions in most world-wide cross-cultural studies makes it impossible to observe geographical continuity and infer historical continuity. Only with control of genetic language classification is it possible to distinguish genetic heritage from subsequent diffusion of cultural phenomena." Further, unlike many cross-cultural researchers, Driver used his comparative knowledge of North American Indian literature in his interpretations. In contrast, the majority of cross-culture researchers lack the comparative ethnological knowledge that would hold in check some of the speculatory systems that are being built up from a few coefficients of association.

Driver's main conclusion was that for North American Indian data historical-diffusional factors provide a better "explanation" for the presence of kin avoidances than the association with functional and/or causal factors.

A main motif in all of Driver's work has been that one has to address himself to the distribution of phenomena in space-time in order to derive the nature of the joint occurrences of sociocultural phenomena. In this, he has followed Kroeber and Lowie (see Driver 1962, 1968).

> The broader the comparative universe in either space or time, the looser the integration of single parts of single cultures at a single point in history will appear to be. The reason is that the elements which constitute a small spatial and temporal unit of culture are almost invariably found to have wider distributions and different associations in a broader spatial and temporal frame. Natives have less comparative knowledge than ethnologists and consequently they would be expected to believe or feel the presence of a relatively small number of integrating impulses in their cultures which to them produce or maintain the harmonious whole. An ethnologist cannot really believe or feel such unity unless he suddenly develops a state of mind in which he eliminates his comparative knowledge. The description

of relationships within single folk cultures as seen by native participants is an important task for ethnology, but it will never be complete description or a substitute for the broader relationships that are revealed by comparative studies [Driver 1941: 51].

It is when one moves to these "broader relationships" that one's attention is shifted to problems of degree of regularity and to problems concerning the nature of the regularity. To reiterate, there have been two major abstract theoretical frames with respect to the patterning of psychohistorical phenomena, irrespective of the multitude of "explanations," "notions," etc. that have overlaid these frames. However, this has not always been clear. Thus, we find Driver in 1962 stating:

Steward's discussion of the relationships of cross-cultural units of classification to the classic culture area (1955: 88-92) is enlightening. He suggests that the phrase *culture area type* be used to designate a sociocultural system which is logically and relativistically distinctive and that *cross-cultural type* be used to designate one that is found in several historically unrelated areas or traditions. Second, it is proposed that the term *uniformities* be understood to refer to the similarities of form and content which characterize a single area or co-tradition and that *regularities* be understood to mean similarities which recur cross-culturally in historically separate areas or traditions (1955: 88).

A major difference between *culture area type* and *cross-cultural type* is that the former should be used on the total culture or a representative sample of it, while the latter is always based on a single subject or a few subjects such as kinship, social structure, or government, as Steward points out on the same page. Therefore, Steward's *culture area type* is equivalent to Kroeber's culture area, while his cross-cultural type is exemplified by Murdock's (1949) types of social organization or Steward's examples of ecological adaptation (1955: 122-50) [Driver 1962: 22-23].

The papers in this section are a continuation of Driver's work in numerical classification of coded ethnological data. "Statistical Classification of North American Indian Ethnic Units" is the first explicit, numerical classification of ethnic units for an entire continent. Characteristically, Driver does not just present a "new" classification but compares it with the main "culture area" and "language area" schemes for North American Indian ethnic units. Central to this explicit reanalysis was Jorgensen's (1969) tree diagram computer program, which produced a branching tree of degrees of relatedness for the 273 ethnic units.

From the present interpretive perspective, a very interesting aspect of the data patterning in this Q-type of analysis (Ethnic Unit clustering in terms of shared cultural inventory) is the rather high $\emptyset$ of .68 at which one finds the "35 Principle Statistical Groups" with 40 singletons. Further, all of the 273 Ethnic Units are associated at a $\emptyset$ of .28. Although much of this association is based on traits counted up in the common absence cell, the data patterning is still interesting. An R-type of analysis of this same data would never cluster the traits to such a degree. In other words, historical, diffusional factors are patterning much of this data to a greater extent than functional, causal factors. This kind of interpretation dovetails with Driver's (1966) discussion of historical-diffusional factors providing a better "explanation" for the presence of kin avoidances than the association with functional and/or causal factors and the worldwide mapping of nonrandom configurations of this same kind of data (Chaney 1971, 1972).

Norwood Russell Hanson (1969: 404-05) in a discussion of "probability and probable reasoning in science" has stressed that:

It should be remembered that none of the groupings of languages or cultures compared in this paper are geographically random to begin with. All such groups tend to cluster in continuous or near-continuous patches. When two sets of such nonrandom clusters are compared, it is inevitable that the overall relationship will be positive and statistically significant.

The paper "Culture Groups and Language Groups in Native North America" is a further discussion of the distribution of "sociocultural traits" and "linguistic affiliation." An important stress is:

A still further snare is encountered when high correlations are obtained just by mixing together two sets of data in each of which no correlation whatever was discovered before mixing. If the ages of husbands and wives are uncorrelated in each of two communities, *some* correlation will be found when the records of the two communities are mingled. This fact has been demonstrated with maximum mathematical rigor. The correlation will arise from the purely formal (i.e., mathematical) properties of the two sets of data, and cannot on any reckoning be taken as evidence of an invariable connection between the ages of husbands and those of their wives.

It is in some such way as this that Mr. Spencer Brown of Oxford University has challenged the alleged discoveries of modern statistical investigations of psychical phenomena and the extra-sensory powers of mediums and mystics. Spencer Brown has achieved correlations equally as good as those of psychical researchers like Dr. J. B. Rhine simply by mingling and then correlating Sir Ronald Fisher's random number tables, tables which are relied upon by geneticists to be paradigms of unrelated and unconnected clusters of numbers [Hanson 1969: 404-05].

III

The majority of recent comparative-statistical studies have been of the *cross-cultural type* (see Naroll 1970). The conceptual thrust of Galton and the empirical enumeration of Boas are gesturing at what has been called "culture areas" or areal configurations. The "solutions" or discussions of the Tylor-Galton problem by Naroll (1961, 1964) and by Naroll and D'Andrade (1963) have all used propinquity and culture inventory similarity as indicating historical-diffusional factors. The essential idea has been one of controlling for *culture area type*, so that one could proceed to a discussion of some form of nomothetic cross-cultural type. Murdock has presented a number of worldwide judgmental samples in which he has attempted to control for "obvious" recent historical influences through structuring a universe of cultures into "provinces," "culture clusters," etc.

Recent papers (Chaney 1970; Chaney, Morton, and Moore, 1972) have underscored problematic features in both of these two approaches, which presently preclude their status as "solutions" for the nature of a joint occurrence or a sequence of psychohistorical phenomena.

The paper by Murdock and White (1969) is of special interest, in that it represents both a continuation of Murdock to derive a more representative sample and a somewhat different attempt to deal with problems of sampling. Essentially, Murdock was joining Driver in stressing the problematic feature of historical, diffusional relations. However, their "solution" consisted of using a modified linked pair method with their sample of 186 societies linked in "a continuous geo-cultural series."

> Our alignment of the sample of societies in a continuous geo-cultural series from 1 to 186 makes possible the application of four of the solutions to Galton's problem proposed by Naroll (1961, 1964; Naroll and D'Andrade 1963) the Linked Pair, Cluster, and Bimodal Sift Methods, which depend upon alignment, and the Matched Pair method, which may utilize but does not require an alignment [Murdock and White 1969: 348].
>
> The method formulated by the authors might be called the Successive Pairs test to determine the size of patches of historical relatedness, or a sixth solution to Galton's problem [Murdock and White 1969: 351].

The basic problem as they saw it was to select a sample of societies that would take into consideration the "size of patches of historical relatedness." From an illustration of this analysis they (1969: 351) state that the "true functional correlation" between agriculture and supracommunity sovereignty "probably lies between [a $\emptyset$ of] .32 and .36, still statistically sig-

nificant after a reduction from the original correlation by about 30 percent, the portion of the correlation due to historical influences in the sample."

Unfortunately, the "discussion of the results in terms of a worldwide coefficient of association masks the degree and kinds of regional data patterning" (Chaney 1970: 1460). The problem was exposed by presenting the actual cell frequencies for a three-by-three comparison of the variables of jurisdictional hierarchy beyond the local community and subsistence type with a sample of 863 ethnic units (Murdock 1967), which diversely inflated ethnic units of various "patches of historical relatedness."

> Thus, whereas the use of the linked-pair method with worldwide correlations yields data patterns that might lead one to conceptualize a "true functional correlation" of .32 –.36 as merely a weak or strong relationship, an examination of the actual cell frequencies in a regional comparison approach yields data patterns that lend themselves to a conceptualization that deals with the nature of regional differences. An explication of regional differences leads to a discussion of boundaries to communication, native categories, and the texture of knowledge.
>
> The problem of observation and conceptualization are intimately intertwined [Chaney 1970: 1460].

In this case a *cross-culture type* coefficient of association was being evaluated with respect to the six main geographical areas of the world (a crude form of culture area type).

Further, I wish to underscore that a $\emptyset$ of .32 –.36 is not much of a deviation from nonpredictability. What insight does this give us other than there is not much of a relationship? For Pearson's r, one multiplies the coefficient by itself to determine the percent of variation in one variable attributable to another variable. Although $\emptyset$ was originally invented to approximate Pearson's r, it does not do so. However, if one were to follow this line of thinking, the explained variance in the above would be interpreted as .10 –.13. This much deviation could easily be the result of mixing two kinds of nonrandomly distributed data. Further, none of this kind of thinking will ever discuss the diverse qualities of interaction and decision-making at the "same" level of administrative hierarchy.

Recently, the worldwide mapping of *configurations* of phenomena has been presented. Any phenomena (artifacts, agrofacts, mentifacts, languafacts, etc.) that can be localized in terms of latitude-longitude can be plotted in terms of coded configurations of up to six variables with any number of category breakdowns. This visual presentation indicates the masking effects of worldwide and regional coefficients of association. Further, it makes no assumption of independence of units in space-time. It merely plots the same crude data that others are using with other kinds of comparative, statistical data pattern analysis (see Chaney 1971, 1972). These initial maps expose nonrandom clustering of diverse data patterning. Reflection on this fact shifts the conceptual problem from one of a basic pattern with exceptions to one of treating all of the data as parts of the data patterning—an overall frame with multiple local distortions.

IV

In the open field of history and philosophy of scientific inquiry, one encouters a recent emerging shift of interest to perplexities in explanatory shifts in the pattern appreciation of observational distributions. Whereas many popular discussions of scientific inquiry gesture at Kepler's three laws as paradigms of explanation and prediction, Norwood Russell Hanson (1958: 90) has indicated that Kepler's search was rather "conclusions in search of a premise." Kepler had Tycho Brahe's observational data on Mars. Further, he was historically presented the pattern appreciation of circles being the most perfect form for planetary movement. Hanson lays out a rather complex conceptual plot of Kepler first returning again and again to recalculation of the observational distributions. It was only much later that Kepler employed the new keystone idea of an orbital ellipse with equal area being swept in equal time. Hanson further indicates that this "retroductive" procedure of thinking back from data details to pattern statements is fundamental to theoretical physics. In *The Concept of the Positron* (1963) Hanson outlines the perplexities in the emergence of this idea of an antiparticle, which shifted what was thought to be in need of explanation in theoretical physics. Reflections on things such as this has suggested to Hanson that "seeing is a 'theory-laden' undertaking" (1958: 19). A. R. Hall has discussed the tension between authority and investigation in the emergence of scientific inquiry (1954, 1963). Thomas Kuhn has presented a discussion of *The Structure of Scientific Revolutions* (1962, 1970), in which he stresses the idea of paradigm as a community of discussion organized to various degrees around a keystone idea, which structures what is thought to be in need of explanation. He also stresses communicational problems between "language communities" sharing diverse explanatory paradigms. Although there has been much criticism of the concept of paradigm and abrupt shifts, there has been a shifting emerging awareness of the importance of conceptual shifts in the history of scientific inquiry (see Lakatos and Musgrave 1970).

Stephen Toulmin has recently discussed "Conceptual Revolutions in Science" (1967) as indicating that genetic studies are necessary to an understanding of knowledge and scientific understanding. Toulmin underscores the importance of R. G. Collingwood's contention that a study of conceptual *history* is an essential task of conceptual *analysis*. This is also at the heart of Hanson's contention that detective work in the so-called "context of discovery" yields a reconceptualization of the so-called "context of justification" as being "methods of representation" in a frame of potential retroductive reasoning from anomalies in existing appreciations of observational distributions to more meaningful patternings. For Collingwood, the crucial changes in science or society have been changes in the basic "constellations of presuppositions." These entail the "abandonment of his most firmly established habits and standards of thought and action." Further reflection by Toulmin on conceptual variation in the history of scientific inquiry and in the morality and ethics of the various peoples on which we have information has led to Toulmin's presentation of *Human Understanding: The Collective Use and Evolution of Concepts* (1972). This is essentially stressing that what is in need of explanation is conceptual variation.

At the present time, while some social scientists are still rummaging around occasionally in philosophy of science for a methodological directive that will allow them to grind out "laws," "invariant relationships," "causal arrows," etc. between the "parts" or "events" of psychohistorical phenomena, a new wave of historians and philosophers of scientific inquiry is stressing that there have been profound conceptual shifts in our appreciation of detail statements for the nature of physical phenomena. To reiterate, a salient characteristic of scientific inquiry is that it attempts to be "self-corrective."

A major lesson for the human sciences from the history of the physical sciences is not a methodological directive on how to grind out the truth but rather the elusive awareness that "what requires explanation cannot itself figure in the explanation" (Hanson 1963: 42). Another major lesson is that an explanation not only allows one to perceive phenomena in meaningful packets but is at once an obstacle to reconceptualization.

A transilient step to contemporary discussions of the concept of "evolution" in sociocultural anthropology by individuals such as Service (1968) and Harris (1968) exposes problematic features in much of the employment of "evolution" for sociocultural phenomena. Both Service and Harris are searching for invariant relationships between the parts. The rather curious thing about the employment of the concept of "evolution" for psychohistorical phenomena by anthropologists on the whole is that they have attempted to derive universals merely in terms of phenomena and/or drawn "causal arrows" from one thing to another thing. I wish to stress that these actuarial attempts are at most mere data summaries, not understanding in terms of scientific inquiry. These universals in terms of data patterning would be analogous to "understanding" beveled mirrors expressing a spectrum in the sunlight by saying that all beveled mirrors do this. The "problem" rather is: What would the nature of sunlight have to be in its interaction with a medium of diverse densities? This leads to an understanding in terms of diverse refractibility of light. Further, the idea of "evolution" of life phenomena is organized at present around the keystone idea of the "double helix." This is, if you like, a "concept by postulation" invented by human beings to pattern our understanding of both regularity and variation in living phenomena in space-time. Phenotypes or observables are not explained in terms of themselves, rather an understanding is derived in postulating the nature of genotype. Our task in understanding psychohistorical phenomena in human beings is analogously one of searching for the characteristics of a "potential circuit breaker" to explicate both regularity and variability in human explanation, emotion, and action. An appreciation of this fact shifts the attention from the prose-laden imposing of the concepts of "natural selection," etc. on psychohistorical phenomena to the imposing task of coordinating and merging the findings on the growth, transmission, and spatial-temporal distribution of diverse concepts and what they lead to for the people involved as found in ethnographic, historical, psychological, philosophical, and scientific studies.

As we shift to an overview of the histories and logics of explanatory networks (and the histories and logics of these), we also shift to an overall target universe of discussion: a space-time-mode-meaning-significance continuum of human experience expressing multiple local-distortions.

This conceptual vista also exposes an additional relationship between "language and culture" in terms of *explanatory networks*, which can exist within the same "language family" and/or cross-cut language families. Chomsky has spoken of a creative aspect of language use in terms of the "ability to produce and interpret new sentences in independence from 'stimulus control'—i.e., external stimuli or independently identifiable internal states" (1967: 83). The present discussion, however, is not addressing itself to variations within a syntactic structure but rather to the *additional* aspect of variation in semantic net-

works that are exposed in an examination of recorded culture histories of meanings that have existed at various space-time coordinates of human existence for which we have information.

This reflection further leads past the typological frames of culture-society, culture areas, civilizations, generations, periods, etc. to a more fluid concept of transient *metaggregates* (people not necessarily living at the same time or in the same district, city, etc or under the same local laws; people linked by kinds of intentions) emerging through the formation of communities of discussion within which any understanding, felt not to be coordinating with some set of data and/or experience can be called into question.

Note

[1]This paper was conceived and written while on a Post-Doctoral Fellowship at Indiana University from the National Endowment for the Humanities (1972-73).

For general introductions to the concepts, see Ehrich and Henderson (1968) for "culture area," Bright (1968) for "language and culture," and Sherzer and Bauman (1972) for "language as a key to historical study of culture contact." For a careful, detailed analysis of some relationships between language and culture within one language family, see Jorgensen's (1969) *Salish language and culture*. The present discussion attempts to call attention to (1) related explanatory problems in the history of comparative-statistical analysis in psychosociocultural anthropology and (2) emerging redefinition of the conceptual foundations of knowledge in the field of history and philosophy of scientific inquiry. Some structural interconnections of various sections of understanding are suggested. This transilient procedure, it is hoped, will better position the shift in focus to some form of genetic study (historico-distributional).

References

Barnes, J. A., 1971, *Three styles in the study of kinship*, London, Tavistock Publications.

Bidney, David, 1953, *Theoretical anthropology*, New York, Columbia University Press.

1967, *Theoretical anthropology*, 2d ed., New York, Columbia University Press.

Boas, Franz, 1894, *Indianishe Sagen von der Nord-Pacifischen Kuste Amerikas*, Berlin, Ashar.

1916, "Tsimshian mythology," *Bureau of American Ethnology Annual Report 31*: 27-1037.

Bright, William, 1968, "Language and culture," *International Encyclopedia of the Social Sciences 9*: 18-22.

Chaney, Richard Paul, 1970, "Conceptual contention: a reply," *American Anthropologist* 72: 1456-61.

1971, *On the intertwined problems of sampling, data patterning and conceptual organization in cross-cultural research*, Ph.D. dissertation, Bloomington, Indiana University.

1972, "Scientific inquiry and models of socio-cultural data patterning: an epilogue," in David Clarke, ed., *Models in Archaeology*, London, Methuen.

n.d., "Comparative analysis and retroductive reasoning or conclusions in search of a premise," *American Anthropologist* 75: (in press).

Chaney, Richard Paul, Keith Morton, and Turrell Moore, 1972, "On the entangled problems of selection and conceptual organization," *American Anthropologist* 74: 221-30.

Chomsky, Noam, 1967, "Recent contributions to the theory of innate ideas," in Robert S. Cohen and Marx W. Wartofsky, eds., *Boston Studies in the Philosophy of Science, Vol. 3.*, Dordrecht, Holland: D. Reidel.

Driver, Harold E., 1941, "Culture element distributions: XVI: girls' puberty rites in western North America," *University of California Anthropological Records* 6: 21-90 (reprinted in this volume).

1956, An integration of functional, evolutionary, and historical theory by means of correlations," *Indiana University Publications in Anthropology and Linguistics* 12: 1-36, with 8 maps.

1961, *Indians of North America*, Chicago, University of Chicago Press.

1962, "The contribution of A. L. Kroeber to culture area theory and practice," *Indiana University Publications in Anthropology and Linguistics* 18: 1-28.

1966, Geographical-historical *versus* psycho-functional explanations of kin avoidances," *Current Anthropology* 7: 131-82 (reprinted in this volume).

1968, "Robert H. Lowie," *International Encyclopedia of the Social Sciences* 9: 480-83.

1970, "Statistical studies of continuous geographical distributions," in Raoul Naroll and Ronald Cohen, eds., *A Handbook of Method in Cultural Anthropology*. Garden City, Natural History Press: 620-39.

Driver, Harold E., and William C. Massey, 1957, "Comparative studies of North American Indians," *Transactions of the American Philosophical Society* 47: 165-456.

Ehrich, Robert W., and Gerald M. Henderson, 1968, "Culture area," *International Encyclopedia of the Social Sciences* 3: 563-68.

Galton, Francis, 1863, *Meteorgraphica: or, methods of mapping the weather*, London, Macmillan.

Hall, A. R., 1954, *Scientific revolution 1500-1800*, London, Longmans, Green (2d ed., 1962).

1963, *From Galileo to Newton 1630-1720*, New York and Evanston, Harper & Row.

Hanson, Norwood Russell, 1958, *Patterns of discovery*, Cambridge, at the University Press.

1963, *The concept of the positron*, Cambridge, at the University Press.

1969, *Perception and discovery*, San Francisco, Freeman, Cooper.

Harris, Marvin, 1968, *The rise of anthropological theory*, New York, Thomas Y. Crowell.

Jorgensen, Joseph G., 1969, "Salish language and culture: a statistical analysis of internal relationships, history, and evolution," *Language Science Monographs* 3.

Kluckhohn, Clyde, 1953, "Universal categories of culture," in A. L. Kroeber et al, eds., *Anthropology Today*, Chicago, University of Chicago Press.

Kroeber, Alfred L., 1939, "Cultural and natural areas of Native North America," *University of California Publications in American Archaeology and Ethnology* 38: 1-242, 28 maps.

Kroeber, Alfred, and Clyde Kluckhohn, 1952, "Culture: a critical review of concepts and definitions," *Papers of the Peabody Museum of American Archaeology and Ethnology* 47.

Kuhn, Thomas S., 1962, *The structure of scientific revolutions*, Chicago, University of Chicago Press.

1970, *The structure of scientific revolutions*, 2d ed., Chicago, University of Chicago Press.

Lakatos, Imre, and Alan Musgrave, 1970, *Criticism and the growth of knowledge*, Cambridge, at the University Press.

Leach, Edmund, 1968, "The comparative method in anthropology," *International Encyclopedia of the Social Sciences* 1: 339-45.

Murdock, George Peter, 1949, *Social structure*, New York, Macmillan.

1967, *Ethnographic atlas: a summary, Ethnology* 6: 109-236.

Murdock, George Peter, and Douglas R. White, 1969, "Standard cross-cultural sample," *Ethnology* 8: 329-69.

Naroll, Raoul, 1961, "Two solutions to Galton's problem," *Philosophy of Science 28*: 16-39.

1964, "A fifth solution to Galton's problem," *American Anthropologist 66*: 863-67.

1970, "What have we learned from cross-cultural surveys?" *American Anthropologist 72*: 1227-88.

Naroll, Raoul and Roy G. D'Andrade, 1963, "Two further solutions to Galton's problem," *American Anthropologist 63*: 1053-67.

Pearson, Karl, 1914-30, *The life, letters and labours of Francis Galton*, 3 vols. Cambridge, at the University Press.

Rouse, Irving, 1955, "On the correlation of phases of culture," *American Anthropologist 57*: 713-22.

Service, Elman R., 1968, "Cultural evolution," *International Encyclopedia of the Social Sciences 5*: 221-28.

Sherzer, Joel, and Richard Bauman, 1972, "Areal studies and culture history: language as a key to the historical study of culture contact," *Southwestern Journal of Anthropology 28*: 131-52.

Singer, Milton, 1968, "The concept of culture," *International Encyclopedia of the Social Sciences 3*: 527-43.

Steward, Julian H., 1955, *Theory and culture change*, Urbana, University of Illinois Press.

Stocking, George W., 1968, *Race, culture, and language*, New York, Free Press.

Toulmin, Stephen, 1967, Conceptual revolutions in science, in Robert S. Cohen and Marx W. Wartofsky, eds., *Boston Studies in the Philosophy of Science*. Dordrecht, Holland, D. Reidel.

1972, *Human understanding: the collective use and evolution of concepts*, Princeton, Princeton University Press.

Tylor, Edward, 1889, "On a method of investigating the development of institutions applied to the laws of marriage and descent," *Journal of the Royal Anthropological Institute 18*: 245-72.

Wallace, Anthony F. C., 1961, *Culture and personality*, New York, Random House.

1970, *Culture and personality*, 2d ed. New York, Random House.

Wissler, Clark, 1917, *The American Indian*, New York, Douglas C. McMurtrie.